Economics for Business and Management

Visit the *Economics for Business and Management* Companion Website at **www.pearsoned.co.uk/griffithswall** to find valuable **student** learning material including:

- Learning objectives for each chapter
- Multiple choice questions to help test your learning
- Annotated links to relevant sites on the web

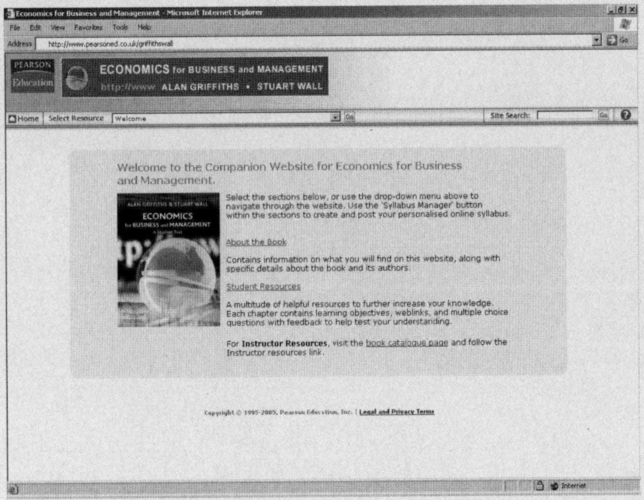

Economics for Business and Management

A Student Text

Alan Griffiths
Stuart Wall (eds.)

FT Prentice Hall
FINANCIAL TIMES

An imprint of Pearson Education
Harlow, England • London • New York • Boston • San Francisco • Toronto • Sydney • Singapore • Hong Kong
Tokyo • Seoul • Taipei • New Delhi • Cape Town • Madrid • Mexico City • Amsterdam • Munich • Paris • Milan

Pearson Education Limited
Edinburgh Gate
Harlow
Essex CM20 2JE
England

and Associated Companies throughout the world

Visit us on the World Wide Web at:
www.pearsoned.co.uk

First published 2005

ISBN 0 273 68549 X

British Library Cataloguing-in-Publication Data
A catalogue record for this book is available from the British Library

10 9 8 7 6 5 4 3 2 1
09 08 07 06 05

Typeset in 10/12.5pt Sabon by 25
Printed by Ashford Colour Press Ltd., Gosport

The publisher's policy is to use paper manufactured from sustainable forests.

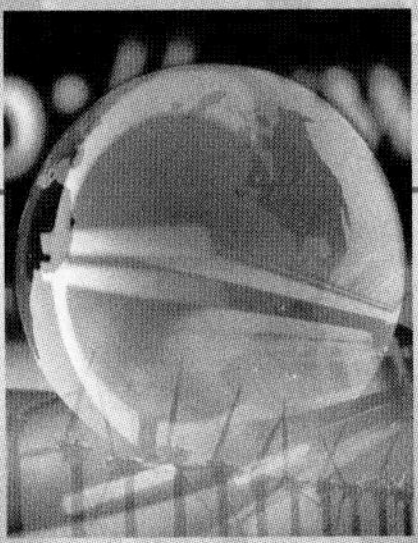

Brief contents

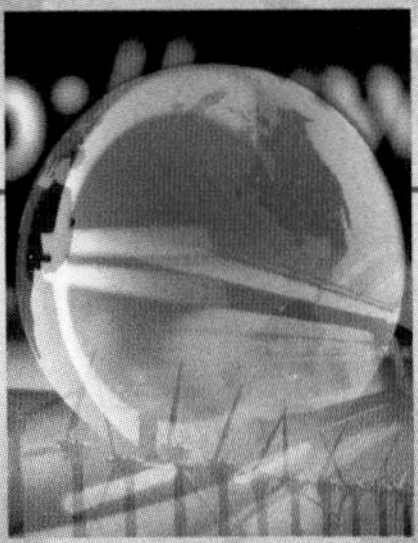

Contents

Supporting resources

Visit **www.pearsoned.co.uk/griffithswall** to find valuable online resources

Companion Website for students

- Learning objectives for each chapter
- Multiple choice questions to help test your learning
- Annotated links to relevant sites on the web

For instructors

- Complete, downloadable Instructor's Manual including mini-cases
- PowerPoint slides that can be downloaded and used as OHTs

Also: The Companion Website provides the following features:

- Search tool to help locate specific items of content
- E-mail results and profile tools to send results of quizzes to instructors
- Online help and support to assist with website usage and troubleshooting

For more information please contact your local Pearson Education sales representative or visit **www.pearsoned.co.uk/griffithswall**

OneKey: All you and your students need to succeed

OneKey
OneKey is all you need
Convenience, Simplicity, Success

OneKey is an exclusive new resource for instructors and students, giving you access to the best online teaching and learning tools 24 hours a day, 7 days a week.

OneKey means all your resources are in one place for maximum convenience, simplicity and success.

A OneKey product is available for *Economics for Business* for use with Blackboard™, WebCT and CourseCompass. It contains:

- An interactive study guide
- Introductory quizzes for each section
- Further assignments and further reading sections
- Quick tests throughout each topic

For more information about the OneKey product please contact your local Pearson Education sales representative or visit **www.pearsoned.co.uk/onekey**

Guided Tour

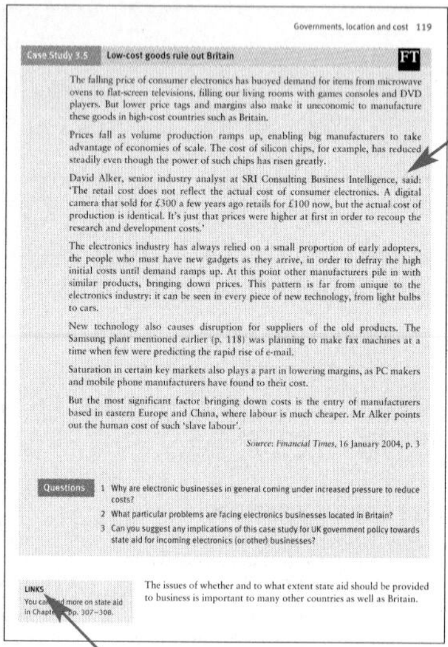

Governments, location and cost 119

Case Study 3.5 **Low-cost goods rule out Britain**

The falling price of consumer electronics has buoyed demand for items from microwave ovens to flat-screen televisions, filling our living rooms with games consoles and DVD players. But lower price tags and margins also make it uneconomic to manufacture these goods in high-cost countries such as Britain.

Prices fall as volume production ramps up, enabling big manufacturers to take advantage of economies of scale. The cost of silicon chips, for example, has reduced steadily even though the power of such chips has risen greatly.

David Alker, senior industry analyst at SRI Consulting Business Intelligence, said: 'The retail cost does not reflect the actual cost of consumer electronics. A digital camera that sold for £300 a few years ago retails for £100 now, but the actual cost of production is identical. It's just that prices were higher at first in order to recoup the research and development costs.'

The electronics industry has always relied on a small proportion of early adopters, the people who must have new gadgets as they arrive, in order to defray the high initial costs until demand ramps up. At this point other manufacturers pile in with similar products, bringing down prices. This pattern is far from unique to the electronics industry: it can be seen in every piece of new technology, from light bulbs to cars.

New technology also causes disruption for suppliers of the old products. The Samsung plant mentioned earlier (p. 118) was planning to make fax machines at a time when few were predicting the rapid rise of e-mail.

Saturation in certain key markets also plays a part in lowering margins, as PC makers and mobile phone manufacturers have found to their cost.

But the most significant factor bringing down costs is the entry of manufacturers based in eastern Europe and China, where labour is much cheaper. Mr Alker points out the human cost of such 'slave labour'.

Source: Financial Times, 16 January 2004, p. 3

Questions
1 Why are electronic businesses in general coming under increased pressure to reduce costs?
2 What particular problems are facing electronics businesses located in Britain?
3 Can you suggest any implications of this case study for UK government policy towards state aid for incoming electronics (or other) businesses?

LINKS
You can find more on state aid in Chapter 8, pp. 307–308.

The issues of whether and to what extent state aid should be provided to business is important to many other countries as well as Britain.

Case Studies: four or more real cases for each chapter, covering a wide range of contemporary business, economic and management issues. Ideal to illustrate concepts in practice, with questions to guide thinking. Solutions and extra case studies are available to Instructors.

Links signpost other parts of the book with more information on a particular topic.

Check the Net boxes identify useful relevant websites.

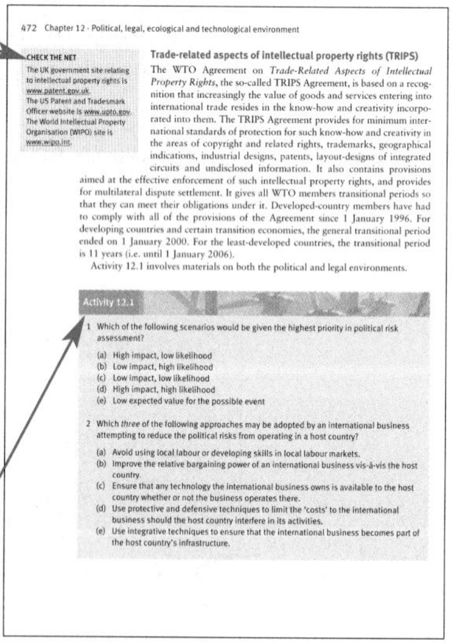

472 Chapter 12 · Political, legal, ecological and technological environment

CHECK THE NET
The UK government site relating to intellectual property rights is www.patent.gov.uk.
The US Patent and Trademark Office website is www.uspto.gov.
The World Intellectual Property Organisation (WIPO) site is www.wipo.int.

Trade-related aspects of intellectual property rights (TRIPS)

The WTO Agreement on *Trade-Related Aspects of Intellectual Property Rights*, the so-called TRIPS Agreement, is based on a recognition that increasingly the value of goods and services entering into international trade resides in the know-how and creativity incorporated into them. The TRIPS Agreement provides for minimum international standards of protection for such know-how and creativity in the areas of copyright and related rights, trademarks, geographical indications, industrial designs, patents, layout-designs of integrated circuits and undisclosed information. It also contains provisions aimed at the effective enforcement of such intellectual property rights, and provides for multilateral dispute settlement. It gives all WTO members transitional periods so that they can meet their obligations under it. Developed-country members have had to comply with all of the provisions of the Agreement since 1 January 1996. For developing countries and certain transition economies, the general transitional period ended on 1 January 2000. For the least-developed countries, the transitional period is 11 years (i.e. until 1 January 2006).

Activity 12.1 involves materials on both the political and legal environments.

Activity 12.1

1 Which of the following scenarios would be given the highest priority in political risk assessment?
(a) High impact, low likelihood
(b) Low impact, high likelihood
(c) Low impact, low likelihood
(d) High impact, high likelihood
(e) Low expected value for the possible event

2 Which *three* of the following approaches may be adopted by an international business attempting to reduce the political risks from operating in a host country?
(a) Avoid using local labour or developing skills in local labour markets.
(b) Improve the relative bargaining power of an international business vis-à-vis the host country.
(c) Ensure that any technology the international business owns is available to the host country whether or not the business operates there.
(d) Use protective and defensive techniques to limit the 'costs' to the international business should the host country interfere in its activities.
(e) Use integrative techniques to ensure that the international business becomes part of the host country's infrastructure.

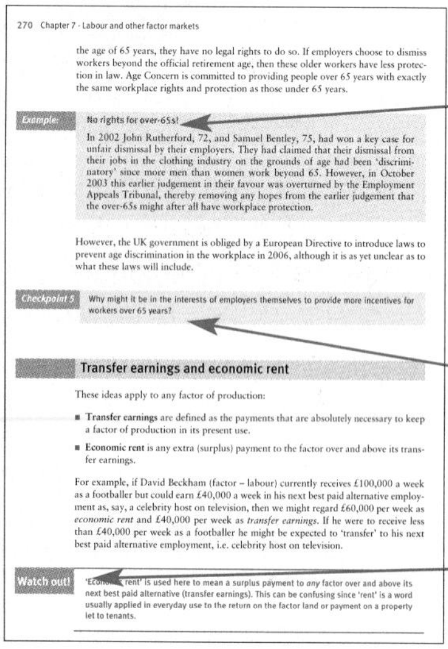

270 Chapter 7 · Labour and other factor markets

the age of 65 years, they have no legal rights to do so. If employers choose to dismiss workers beyond the official retirement age, then these older workers have less protection in law. Age Concern is committed to providing people over 65 years with exactly the same workplace rights and protection as those under 65 years.

Example: **No rights for over-65s!**

In 2002 John Rutherford, 72, and Samuel Bentley, 75, had won a key case for unfair dismissal by their employers. They had claimed that their dismissal from their jobs in the clothing industry on the grounds of age had been 'discriminatory' since more men than women work beyond 65. However, in October 2003 this earlier judgement in their favour was overturned by the Employment Appeals Tribunal, thereby removing any hopes from the earlier judgement that the over-65s might after all have workplace protection.

However, the UK government is obliged by a European Directive to introduce laws to prevent age discrimination in the workplace in 2006, although it is as yet unclear as to what these laws will include.

Checkpoint 5 Why might it be in the interests of employers themselves to provide more incentives for workers over 65 years?

Transfer earnings and economic rent

These ideas apply to any factor of production:

- **Transfer earnings** are defined as the payments that are absolutely necessary to keep a factor of production in its present use.
- **Economic rent** is any extra (surplus) payment to the factor over and above its transfer earnings.

For example, if David Beckham (factor – labour) currently receives £100,000 a week as a footballer but could earn £40,000 a week in his next best paid alternative employment as, say, a celebrity host on television, then we might regard £60,000 per week as *economic rent* and £40,000 per week as *transfer earnings*. If he were to receive less than £40,000 per week as a footballer he might be expected to 'transfer' to his next best paid alternative employment, i.e. celebrity host on television.

Watch out! 'Economic rent' is used here to mean a surplus payment to any factor over and above its next best paid alternative (transfer earnings). This can be confusing since 'rent' is a word usually applied in everyday use to the return on the factor land or payment on a property let to tenants.

Examples from the real world show you why a concept is important.

Checkpoints and Activities are found throughout each chapter to help you check your understanding as you work through the book. Answers can be found at the end of the book.

Watch Out! tips highlight common pitfalls to ensure you understand core concepts.

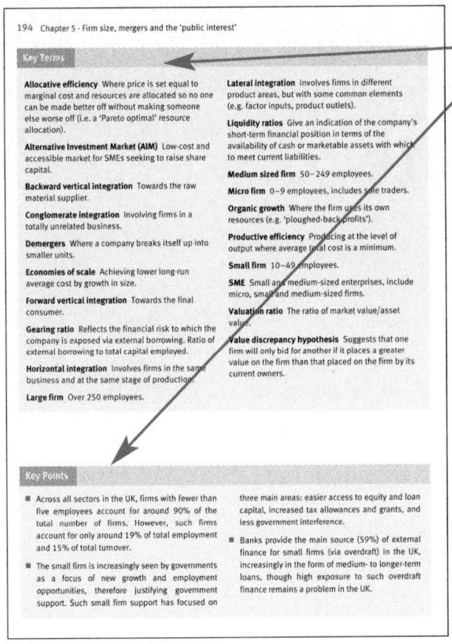

194 Chapter 5 · Firm size, mergers and the 'public interest'

Key Terms

Allocative efficiency Where price is set equal to marginal cost and resources are allocated so no one can be made better off without making someone else worse off (i.e. a 'Pareto optimal' resource allocation).

Alternative Investment Market (AIM) Low-cost and accessible market for SMEs seeking to raise share capital.

Backward vertical integration Towards the raw material supplier.

Conglomerate integration Involving firms in a totally unrelated business.

Demergers Where a company breaks itself up into smaller units.

Economies of scale Achieving lower long-run average cost by growth in size.

Forward vertical integration Towards the final consumer.

Gearing ratio Reflects the financial risk to which the company is exposed via external borrowing. Ratio of external borrowing to total capital employed.

Horizontal integration Involves firms in the same business and at the same stage of production.

Large firm Over 250 employees.

Lateral integration Involves firms in different product areas, but with some common elements (e.g. factor inputs, product outlets).

Liquidity ratios Give an indication of the company's short-term financial position in terms of the availability of cash or marketable assets with which to meet current liabilities.

Medium sized firm 50–249 employees.

Micro firm 0–9 employees, includes sole traders.

Organic growth Where the firm uses its own resources (e.g. 'ploughed-back profits').

Productive efficiency Producing at the level of output where average total cost is a minimum.

Small firm 10–49 employees.

SME Small and medium-sized enterprises, include micro, small and medium-sized firms.

Valuation ratio The ratio of market value/asset value.

Value discrepancy hypothesis Suggests that one firm will only bid for another if it places a greater value on the firm than that placed on the firm by its current owners.

Key Points

- Across all sectors in the UK, firms with fewer than five employees account for around 90% of the total number of firms. However, such firms account for only around 19% of total employment and 15% of total turnover.
- The small firm is increasingly seen by governments as a focus of new growth and employment opportunities, therefore justifying government support. Such small firm support has focused on three main areas: easier access to equity and loan capital, increased tax allowances and grants, and less government interference.
- Banks provide the main source (59%) of external finance for small firms (via overdraft) in the UK, increasingly in the form of medium- to longer-term loans, though high exposure to such overdraft finance remains a problem in the UK.

Definitions of **Key Terms** are provided at the end of each chapter along with a brief summary of **Key Points** covered in the chapter.

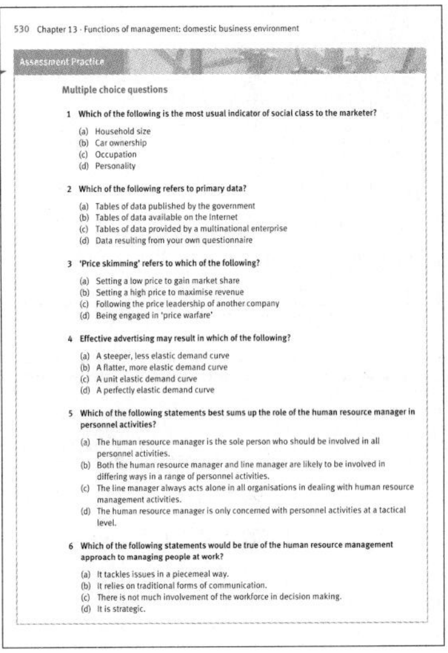

530 Chapter 13 · Functions of management: domestic business environment

Assessment Practice

Multiple choice questions

1 **Which of the following is the most usual indicator of social class to the marketer?**

(a) Household size
(b) Car ownership
(c) Occupation
(d) Personality

2 **Which of the following refers to primary data?**

(a) Tables of data published by the government
(b) Tables of data available on the Internet
(c) Tables of data provided by a multinational enterprise
(d) Data resulting from your own questionnaire

3 **'Price skimming' refers to which of the following?**

(a) Setting a low price to gain market share
(b) Setting a high price to maximise revenue
(c) Following the price leadership of another company
(d) Being engaged in 'price warfare'

4 **Effective advertising may result in which of the following?**

(a) A steeper, less elastic demand curve
(b) A flatter, more elastic demand curve
(c) A unit elastic demand curve
(d) A perfectly elastic demand curve

5 **Which of the following statements best sums up the role of the human resource manager in personnel activities?**

(a) The human resource manager is the sole person who should be involved in all personnel activities.
(b) Both the human resource manager and line manager are likely to be involved in differing ways in a range of personnel activities.
(c) The line manager always acts alone in all organisations in dealing with human resource management activities.
(d) The human resource manager is only concerned with personnel activities at a tactical level.

6 **Which of the following statements would be true of the human resource management approach to managing people at work?**

(a) It tackles issues in a piecemeal way.
(b) It relies on traditional forms of communication.
(c) There is not much involvement of the workforce in decision making.
(d) It is strategic.

Assessment Practice Questions can be found at the end of each chapter. A range of multiple choice, data response, matching pair, true/false and essay questions are provided. Solutions are available to Instructors.

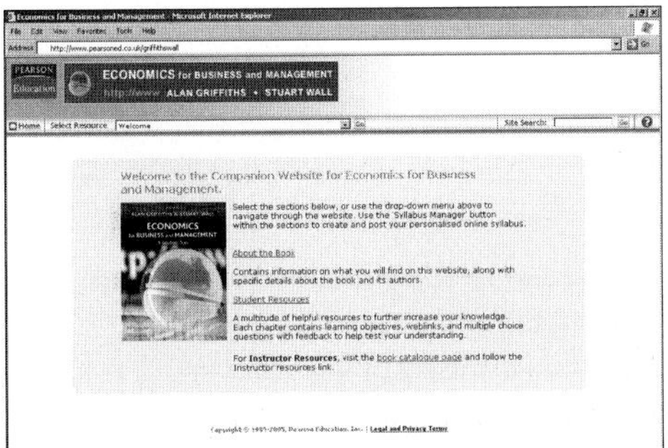

Companion Website to accompany this book can be found at www.booksites.net/griffithswall. Students will find extra questions and answers plus links to relevant websites. Instructors resources include an Instructors's Manual with answers and extra case material, and PowerPoint lecture slides.

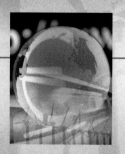

Guided Tour of the Website

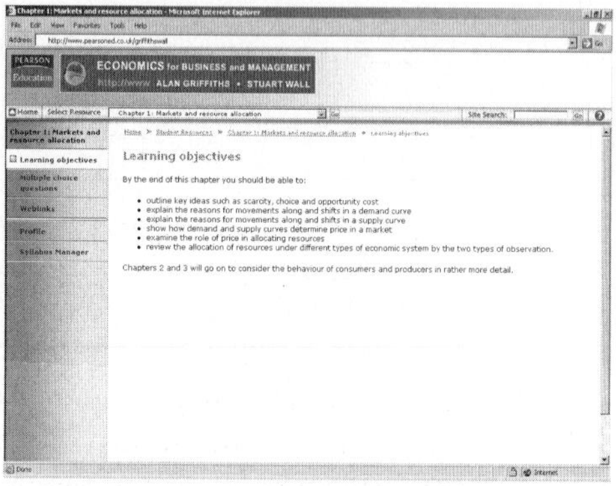

Learning objectives

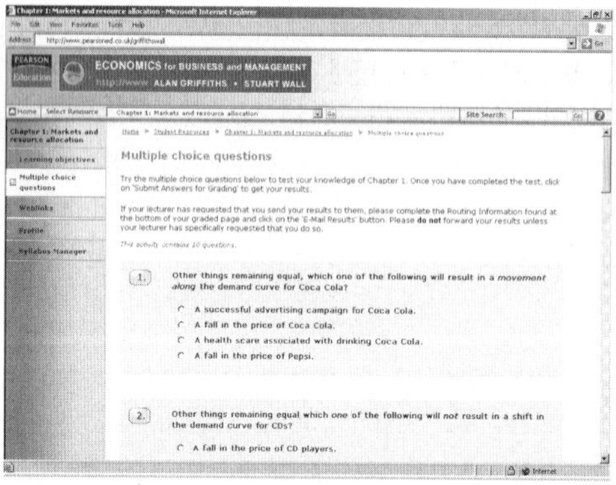

Multiple choice questions

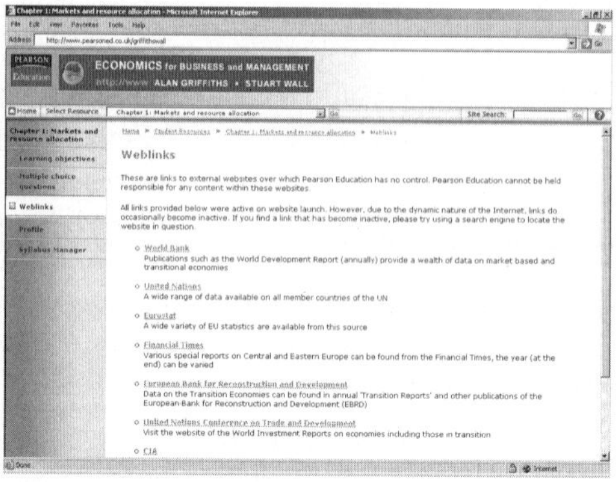

Weblinks

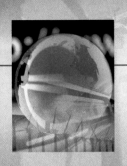

Preface: Using this book

This book is written for students beginning undergraduate or equivalent courses with an economics, business or management focus. It adopts a highly interactive approach throughout, seeking to engage students in a broad range of case study and self-check exercises and activities, rather than present unbroken stretches of text more suited to passive reading. The book will be relevant to a wide range of modules which emphasise the economic perspectives needed to understand the various functional and strategic areas of business and management. The key principles of microeconomics and macroeconomics are presented and applied to a wide variety of situations encountered by decision makers. Detailed consideration is also given to the political, legal, demographic, socio-cultural, ethical and environmental dimensions which characterise the business environment in which decision makers must operate.

A wide variety of up-to-date case study materials, drawn from many business sectors, are presented and discussed in all chapters of the text. Although the UK provides the setting for many of the applied materials, the EU and global contexts of business activity are extensively discussed, together with the regulatory and institutional environment facing national and international businesses.

Whilst students can find answers and responses to all the activities, exercises and checkpoints encountered in the text itself, to support the teaching process some answers and responses are restricted to lecturers in the accompanying Instructor's Manual (IM). For example, since the case studies in each chapter might be used for discussion purposes in seminars/tutorials, detailed responses to the questions at the end of each case study are available in the IM only. Similarly, since 'Assessment Practice' questions at the end of each chapter might be given to students to attempt prior to seminars/tutorials and discussed with lecturers on those occasions, downloadable answers are again available in the IM only. Where core modules have large numbers of students and where many lecturers are involved in seminars/tutorials, a structured programme can be readily devised from these case study and assessment practice materials to assist overstretched teaching resources.

Although the distinction between micro and macro business environments is somewhat artificial, with the effective analysis of many issues requiring both micro and macro perspectives, Part I of the book contains eight chapters with a broadly micro business orientation and Part II a further eight chapters with a broadly macro business orientation.

Each chapter concentrates on a particular topic area and begins with a set of learning objectives, which provide a useful guide to the chapter content, and concludes with a summary of the key points raised in the chapter and definitions of the key terms used. Other features within each chapter include the following.

- **Activities, exercises and checkpoints.** At different points in each chapter students will encounter a variety of questions, exercises and checkpoints to self-check their understanding of the materials presented. Answers and responses to all these are found at the end of the book.
- **Case study materials.** Four or five carefully selected and up-to-date case studies are presented in most chapters, putting into practice many of the ideas encountered. Questions are set at the end of each case study to guide students' thinking, and outline answers and responses are provided in the Instructor's Manual accompanying the text.
- **Assessment practice.** At the end of the each chapter there is a structured set of multiple choice questions, data response and stimulus-based questions, matching pair and true/false questions, as well as essay-based questions. These will check student understanding of the materials presented throughout the chapter and give them valuable practice in preparing for examinations and assignments. Outline answers and responses are provided to all these questions in the Instructor's Manual accompanying the text.
- **Companion student website.** Students can find extra questions and activities (with answers) on the companion student website, together with annotated weblinks and further up-to-date reading lists.
- **Companion lecturer website.** On this secure, password protected website can be found an electronic downloadable version of the Instructor's Manual (IM) containing additional teaching materials, extra case studies for download, PowerPoint slides for use in lectures together with full solutions and responses to all Case Study and Assessment Practice questions in the text.

Acknowledgements

Alan Griffiths and Stuart Wall are indebted to the colleagues who have contributed chapters to this title, namely George Carrol (Chapter 6), Margaret O'Quigley (Chapters 9 and 10), Rita Carrol (Chapter 11), Jonathan Wilson (Chapter 14) and David McCaskey (Chapter 16). Further details on these contributors can be found at the end of the book. All other chapters have been written by ourselves.

We would also like to acknowledge the major contribution to this title made by Eleanor Wall of the Ashcroft International Business School who has played a key role in developing our wide range of up-to-date case and website materials. 'We would also like to thank Hermione Macintosh and Paul Weeks for helpful materials and comments.

Publisher's Acknowledgements

We are grateful to the Financial Times Limited for permission to reprint the following material:

Case Study 3.5 Low-cost goods rule out Britain, © *Financial Times*, 16th January 2004; Case Study 7.2 Concerns over the new NMW (Minimum wage is tangled problem for hairdressers), © *Financial Times*, 3 October 2003; Case Study 8.4 Merger rulings set for more challenges, © *Financial Times*, 4 December 2003; Case Study 9.3 China's $29 test, © *Financial Times*, 21 January 2004; Case Study 11.1 Carry on working, © *Financial Times*, 16 January 2004; Case Study 12.5 Environmental sustainability sells, © *Financial Times*, 5 December 2003; Case Study 12.6 The picture gets brighter, © *Financial Times*, 26 November 2003; 'Multi-tasking' machines to feed demand for all shapes and sizes in quick time, © *Financial Times*, 21 November 2003; Case Study 13.1 The 'no brow' consumer (The low-down on the no-brow consumer, © *Financial Times*, 27 November 2003; Case Study 13.3 Why accounting standards matter, © *Financial Times*, 10 March 2003; Case Study 15.2 IKEA and growth strategies, © *Financial Times*, 24 November 2003; Case Study 15.3 Outsourcing: opportunity or threat!, © *Financial Times*, 3 December 2003; Case Study 15.4 Coca Cola and Nestle combine, © *Financial Times*, 11 December 2003; Safeway and Coca-Cola dream up a merchandising cocktail, © *Financial Times*, 13 November 2003; From milk churn to washing machine: a history of innovation, © *Financial Times*, 14

November 2003; Steps to keep Beaconsfield Footwear marching on, © *Financial Times*, 25 November 2003; Hardy casts around for a route to recovery, © *Financial Times*, 2 December 2003; Case Study 16.2 Rock and Rollers just keep on rocking, © *Financial Times*, 27 November 2003; Case Study 16.4 Basketball and shoes, © *Financial Times*, 10 November 2003.

We are grateful to the following for permission to use copyright material:

Case Study 11.6 Neighbourhood takes over from occupation, from *The Financial Times Limited*, 8 October 2003, © Richard Webber; Case Study 12.1 Freight companies pay for security threat, from *The Financial Times Limited*, 13 January 2004, © Sarah Murray; Case Study 14.4 Bilateral trade treaties are a sham, from *The Financial Times Limited*, 14 July 2003, © Jagdish Bhagwati and Arvind Panagariya; Case Study 16.1 GDS and airlines, from *The Financial Times Limited*, 21 January 2004, © Roger Bray; Figure 15.5 reprinted with the permission of The Free Press, a Division of Simon & Schuster Adult Publishing Group, from COMPETITIVE ADVANTAGE: Creating and Sustaining Superior Performance, by Michael E. Porter. Copyright @ 1985, 1998 by Michael E. Porter. All rights reserved. Figure 16.2 reprinted from *Creative Arts Marketing*, Hill, E., O.Sullivan, C, O'Sullivan, T., pp 106–107, Butterworth Heinemann, Oxford 1995, with permission from Elsevier.

In some instances we have been unable to trace the owners of copyright material, and we would appreciate any information that would enable us to do so.

Part I

Micro Business Environment

Chapter 1

Markets and resource allocation

Introduction

Why did sales of CDs reach an all-time high in 2003, with over 228 million albums sold in the UK, despite the relentless advance of CD burners and MP3 downloaders? To understand how the market for CDs (or any other market) operates you must study the contents of this chapter which looks at the role of demand and supply in determining prices and outputs. Prices give vital signals to both buyers and sellers and play a key role in the allocation of resources, including factor inputs such as land, labour and capital required in production.

Learning objectives:

By the end of this chapter you should be able to:

- outline key ideas such as scarcity, choice and opportunity cost
- explain the reasons for movements along and shifts in a demand curve
- explain the reasons for movements along and shifts in a supply curve
- show how demand and supply curves determine price in a market
- examine the role of price in allocating resources
- review the allocation of resources under different types of economic system.

Chapters 2 and 3 will go on to consider the behaviour of consumers and producers in rather more detail.

Wants, limited resources and choice

A problem facing all consumers is that whilst our wants (desires) may be unlimited, our means (resources) to satisfy those wants are limited, with the result that we must choose between the various alternatives. For example, this year we might want to buy a second-hand ('starter') car and have a holiday overseas but our limited income may force us to choose between these two alternatives. If we choose the car, then we forgo the holiday, or vice versa. The 'next best alternative forgone' is referred to as the **opportunity cost** of our choice.

This central problem of **scarcity**, which then results in choice, is not confined to consumers. Producers must also choose how to allocate their scarce resources of raw materials, labour, capital equipment and land between the different outputs that these resources can produce.

Production possibility curve

Figure 1.1 usefully illustrates this situation with a small recording studio having the capacity to produce a certain number of *albums* per year (OA) if all its resources are fully used. However, if it used all its capacity for *singles* instead, then rather more can be produced per year (OS). Of course, it might choose to produce both albums and singles, the various possibilities being shown by the curve AS. We call AS the **production possibility curve** (or frontier) and consider its precise shape in Chapter 3 (p. 92). If the recording studio chooses to be at point R on the curve, then it is seeking to produce OA_1 albums and OS_1 singles per year.

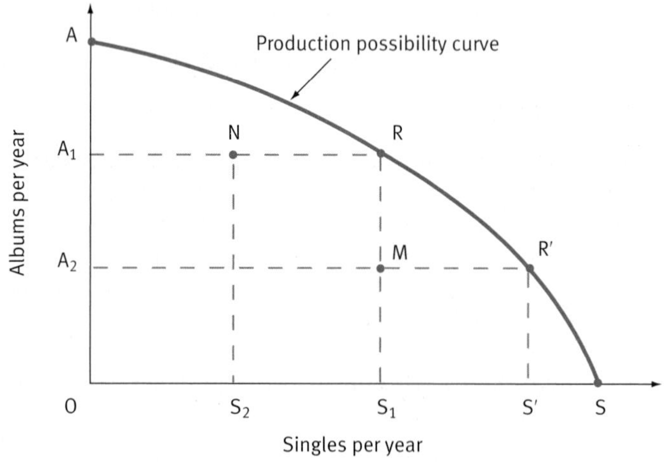

Fig 1.1 The production possibility curve

Activity 1.1

Look again at Figure 1.1.

(a) What are the production possibilities for the recording studio if it chooses to operate at point R′?
(b) In moving from point R to R′, what is the opportunity cost to the studio in terms of albums forgone? Explain what is happening.
(c) If the studio starts at point N and moves to R, what is the opportunity cost in terms of albums forgone? Explain what is happening.
(d) Suppose the studio starts at point M, what possibilities are available in the segment MRR′?

Answers to Checkpoints and Activities can be found on pp. 705–35.

Demand curves and functions

NOTE
From this point onwards, whenever we use the term 'demand' we shall mean 'effective demand'.

Demand is the amount of a product (good or service) consumers are willing and able to purchase at a given price. Demand is a *flow* concept, relating quantity to time (e.g. CDs per month). The term 'effective demand' indicates that there is not just a desire to purchase, but desire supported by the means of purchase. For example, I might desire to purchase a private aeroplane, but unless I have the income to support that potential purchase it is not an 'effective demand', just wishful thinking.

Demand curve

The **demand curve** in Figure 1.2(a) is a visual representation of how much of the product consumers are willing and able to purchase at different prices. The demand curve (D) slopes downwards from left to right, suggesting that when the price of X falls, more of product X is demanded, but when the price of X rises, less of product X is demanded. Of course, we are assuming that only the price of the product changes, sometimes called the *ceteris paribus* (other things equal) assumption. In this case changes in the price of the product will result in *movements along* the demand curve, either an *expansion* (movement down and to the right) or a *contraction* (movement up and to the left).

For example, suppose in Figure 1.2(a) product X is CDs. If the price of CDs falls from P_1 to P_2, the demand for CDs will *expand* from Q_1 to Q_2 (other things equal) because CDs will now be cheaper than other substitutes in consumption (e.g. cassettes, mini disks, vinyl records etc.). We can expect some individuals to switch towards CDs and away from these now relatively more expensive substitutes in consumption. Even if the alternative to purchasing the CD is downloading 'free' music from the Internet,

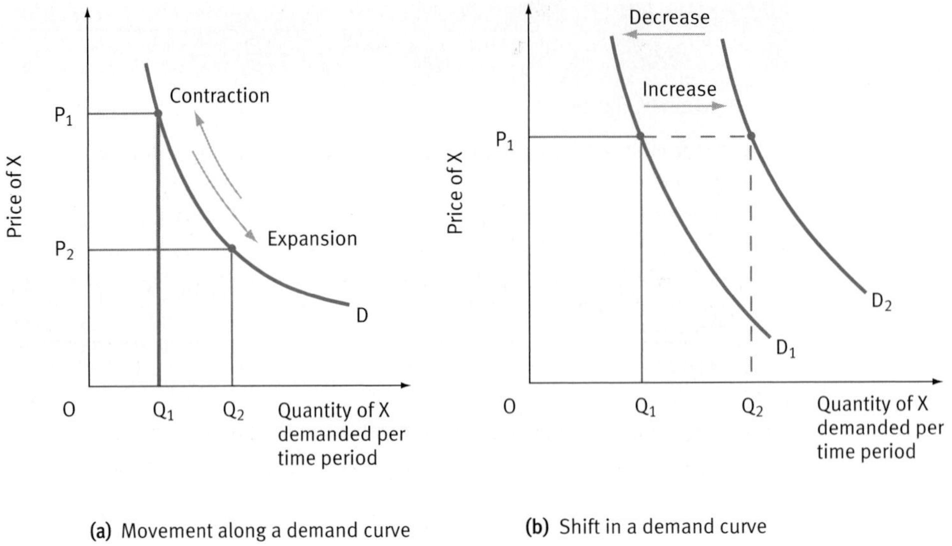

Fig 1.2 Movements along and shifts in a demand curve

> **CHECK THE NET**
> You can find more information on the music industry at websites such as:
> www.emigroup.com
> www.virginrecords.com
> www.bip.co.uk

rather than one of these other substitutes in consumption, the time and effort required to download various tracks can now be set against a cheaper CD, and some consumers may choose to purchase the now lower-priced CD.

If the price of CDs rises from P_2 to P_1 then, for the opposite reasons, we can expect the demand for CDs to *contract* from Q_2 to Q_1 (other things equal).

Conditions of demand

Of course, other things may not remain equal! This brings us to the **conditions of demand** which refer to the factors that cause the demand curve for product X to *shift* either to the right or to the left.

In Figure 1.2(b):

- A shift to the right from D_1 to D_2 (*increase*) means more of product X is demanded at any given price. For example, at price P_1 demand increases from Q_1 to Q_2.
- A shift to the left from D_2 to D_1 (*decrease*) means less of product X is demanded at any given price. For example, at price P_1 demand decreases from Q_2 to Q_1.

> **Watch out!**
> It is really important that you try to use the correct terms to distinguish between *movements along* a demand curve (expansion/contraction) and *shifts in* a demand curve (increase/decrease). Otherwise it is easy to confuse the two.

Variables within the 'conditions of demand' include the price of other products (P_o), the real income of households (Y), the tastes of households (T), advertising expenditure on product X and so on.

To understand more about these 'conditions of demand' it will help if you are familiar with a number of terms.

Useful terminology in demand analysis

- *Substitutes in consumption.* Used when two (or more) products are seen by consumers as alternatives, possessing broadly similar characteristics, e.g. different brands of washing powder.
- *Complements in consumption.* Used when two (or more) products are seen by consumers as fitting together, in the sense that purchasing one product will usually involve purchasing the other(s). Personal computers and printers are obvious examples of complements in consumption, as are tennis rackets and tennis balls.

Examples:

Substitutes and complements in beverage consumption

- 'Mecca Cola' was launched in late 2002 with the slogan 'Think Muslim, drink Muslim' as a substitute for Coca-Cola and Pepsi Cola. It sold over 2 million bottles in France alone within two months of its launch.
- In Britain we drink 165 million cups of tea every day and 98% of people take milk (complement to tea) in their tea.

- *Real income* refers to the actual purchasing power of the consumers. If money income doubles but average prices also double, then the consumer will only be able to purchase the same as before, so that real income will be unchanged. However, if money income rises by a larger percentage than average prices, then the consumer can actually purchase more than before, so real income has risen.
- *Normal products* refer to goods or services for which demand tends to consistently increase (shift to the right) as the real income of the consumer rises, and decrease (shift to the left) as the real income of the consumer falls. Most products come under this heading, with some products tending to be more responsive to changes in real income than others. For example, as real incomes increase, the demand for education, for health services, for travel and for tourism all tend to increase quite sharply.

LINKS

This brings into play the idea of *income elasticity of demand* – see Chapter 2, p. 64.

- *Inferior products* refer to goods or services which are cheaper but poorer quality substitutes for other goods or services. As a result, consumer demand for the inferior product may at first increase as real income rises, as this is all that can be afforded, but as real income continues to rise then the more expensive but better quality substitute may eventually come within the purchasing power of the consumer. The consumer may now switch away from the inferior product with further rises in real income, so that demand for the inferior product decreases (shifts to the left). Cheaper but poorer quality butter, margarine and coffee products are possible examples of inferior products.

Box 1.1 gives you some practice in applying these various 'conditions of demand' to a situation involving an *increase* in demand.

Box 1.1 **Variables causing an increase in demand**

Here we consider briefly the major variables that might cause an *increase in demand* for a good or service. For simplicity we consider an increase in the demand for oranges, but we could apply the same reasoning to any other good or service.

- *A rise in the price of a substitute in consumption*. Substitutes for oranges might be apples, bananas or pears. If any of these substitutes rise in price, then oranges become more attractive to the household. At any given price the household can be expected to buy more oranges and less of the substitutes, so that the whole demand curve for oranges shifts bodily to the right, from D_1 to D_2 in Figure 1.2(b).
- *A fall in the price of a complement in consumption*. Suppose our household buys oranges mainly for making (sweetened) orange squash or marmalade, so that it buys sugar whenever it buys oranges. We would then say that oranges and sugar are complements in consumption for this household, i.e. products that are bought together. A fall in the price of sugar, the complement, might encourage our household to buy more oranges at any given price, since both orange squash and marmalade would now be cheaper to make. Again the whole demand curve for oranges would shift bodily to the right, from D_1 to D_2 in Figure 1.2(b).
- *A rise in income*. Most products are what economists refer to as normal goods, i.e. more is bought when income rises. It is quite likely that oranges would come into this category. A rise in income would cause the demand curve for oranges to shift bodily to the right, from D_1 to D_2 in Figure 1.2(b).
- *A change in tastes of the household in favour of oranges*. If the tastes of the household altered so that it now preferred oranges to other types of fruit, this would shift the demand curve for oranges from D_1 to D_2 in Figure 1.2(b), with more oranges bought at any given price.
- *A rise in advertising expenditure on oranges*. Suppose the 'orange growers' federation' or a major orange grower (e.g. Outspan oranges) undertakes an advertising campaign stressing the health and other benefits of eating oranges. The extra advertising may influence consumer perceptions and tastes in favour of oranges, shifting the demand curve for oranges to the right from D_1 to D_2 in Figure 1.2(b).

Checkpoint 1 Now write down the variables that might cause a *decrease in demand* for oranges, i.e. a *leftward* shift in the demand curve.

Demand function

It will be useful at this stage to introduce *all* the variables that might be involved in movements along the demand curve or in shifting the demand curve to the right or left. This is what the **demand function** does by expressing the relationship between the quantity of product X demanded per unit of time (Q_x) and a number of possible variables. These include the own price of product X(P_x), and a number of other variables known collectively as the 'conditions of demand'.

The demand function is often shown as a shorthand expression:

$$Q_x = F(P_x, P_o, Y, T, A_x \ldots)$$

This can be read as meaning that the quantity demanded of product X (Q_x) *depends upon* its own price (P_x), the price of other products (P_o), real household income (Y), household tastes (T), advertising expenditure on product X (A_x) and so on.

Remember

- **Any change in the product's own price P_x (other things equal) will result in a *movement along* a demand curve.**
- **Any change in a variable within the 'conditions of demand' will cause a *shift* in a demand curve.**

Case Study 1.1 will help you to apply the ideas of movement along and shifts in a demand curve to an actual market situation involving CDs.

Case Study 1.1 Death of the CD!

In August 2003, EMI announced the agreement of the Rolling Stones to offer all the band's post-1971 recordings through digital downloads for the first time. EMI had already announced a deal in April 2003 to offer most of its back catalogue through 10 online music retailers in Europe, though the Rolling Stones had at that time been one of the few groups (together with the Beatles) to refuse that approach. Many see this move by EMI as part of a strategy by music companies to combat the growing threat of illegal music downloads, with EMI claiming that the (legal) downloads it is now offering take up only half the disc space of a typical MP3 file and are of better quality.

To some observers, all this is further proof of the end of the CD. Yet new figures in August 2003 from the British Phonographic Industry (BPI), the UK music trade body, showed that CD album sales had exceeded 228 million units over the past 12 months, a 3% rise on the previous year. Much of this increase in album sales has been linked to heavy and sustained discounting of prices, with the average price of an album in the UK falling to £9.79 in 2003, the cheapest ever. Extensive mark-down in prices of albums by supermarkets have forced music shops to hold almost permanent sales and to keep extending their 'limited offers'. Further evidence of price reductions being the driving force behind album sales is contained in the fact that over the past 12 months revenue from album sales actually fell by 2% despite the volume rising by 3%.

Another factor driving album sales would seem to have been a more attractive set of new releases. The BPI noted that 'cheap retail prices combined with strong new titles are sustaining the UK album market at a high level'. Even piracy is seen by some

Case Study 1.1 continued

commentators as increasing album sales, with many people illegally copying certain tracks as 'samplers' but then going on to buy albums containing those tracks. Record companies also point to the higher disposable income of the twenty- and thirty-'somethings' who are the main purchasers of albums.

On the downside, the BPI points to continuing problems for the singles CD market, which slumped by 26% in both volume and value in the year to August 2003. In fact demand for singles has halved over the past five years and singles now make up only 6.5% of the total sales value of the music industry. One of the problems is the now relatively high average price of singles (£4) compared to albums (£9.79). Also more piracy is taking place amongst teenagers, the main buyers of singles, who then download the single without subsequently purchasing it.

Questions

1. In the market for albums, what evidence is there for a 'movement along' the demand curve?
2. Can you find any evidence for a 'shift' in the demand curve for albums? Identify the variables in the 'conditions of demand' that might be involved here.
3. What is happening to the demand curve for singles?
4. Do you agree with the suggestion that the CD has 'no future'? Explain your reasoning.

Our demand function may contain a number of variables which are often omitted from standard textbook presentations. Here we consider three such variables, technology, advertising and credit.

Technology (T_n)

Although, as we shall see, *new technology* is more often associated with shifts in supply, it can also bring about shifts in demand.

Example: **Technology and shifts in demand**

The year 2003 became known in Hollywood as the year of the failed block-buster, and the industry is blaming texting by movie-goers. Teenagers are instantly messaging their friends with their verdict on new films – even as they are watching them, often contradicting expensive promotional claims for the blockbusters. Whereas, five years ago, the average audience drop-off between a film's opening weekend and its second weekend was 40%, in 2003 that drop-off was over 51%, with the movie moguls blaming the technology of hand-held text message devices.

Advertising (A_x, A_s, A_c)

Advertising expenditure on product X itself (A_x), on a substitute in consumption for X (A_s) and/or a complement in consumption for X (A_c) may all contribute to a shift in the demand curve for product X. As we see in Chapter 6, advertising expenditure is particularly important in oligopoly markets dominated by a few large firms, each seeking to differentiate its product offerings from those of its rivals.

Example:

Advertising and shifts in demand

Prunella Scales, who played Sybil in *Fawlty Towers*, has emerged as the most successful celebrity to appear in a British advertising campaign. Hamish Pringle, director general of the *Institute of Practitioners in Advertising*, claimed in his 2004 book *Celebrity Sells* that the advertising campaign of Prunella Scales for Tesco helped boost sales by an estimated £2.2bn between 1998 and 2003. Jamie Oliver was second best, boosting Sainsbury's sales by £1.12bn over only 18 months.

LINKS

We consider the idea of advertising elasticity of demand in Chapter 2, p. 66).

Of course, if those producing *substitutes* for your product spend more on their advertising (A_S), then the demand curve for X may shift bodily to the left (decrease). However, if those producing *complements* for your product X spend more on their advertising (A_c), then the demand curve for X may shift bodily to the right (increase).

Credit availability (C_A) and price (C_P)

Two important but often neglected variables can exert an important influence on the demand for a product, namely the availability of credit (C_A) and price of credit (C_P). This is especially important in countries such as the UK, where there is a substantial 'debt overhang'.

Example:

Cheap and easy credit!

In 2004 the Bank of England expressed concern that the easy availability of low-cost credit in the UK had resulted in the average indebted household owing £3,516 in *unsecured debt*, over 40% of which involved credit cards. When we take into account *secured debt*, the 'debt overhang' is even more serious and was estimated to exceed £1 trillion in late 2004. It has been estimated that if interest rates rise to 5%, then those with mortgages of £100,000 with interest rates at the then 3.5% in late 2003 will have to pay an extra £125 per month.

When the extra unsecured (e.g. credit card) debt repayments are added to these extra mortgage payments we can clearly expect a reduction in credit availability (as risks of default increase) to accompany the higher price of credit. The result will be a leftward shift (decrease) in the demand curves for a whole range of products, and especially those with high income elasticities of demand (see Chapter 2, p. 64).

Activity 1.2 will help to check your understanding of movements along and shifts in a demand curve.

Activity 1.2

1 Look carefully at Figure 1.3:

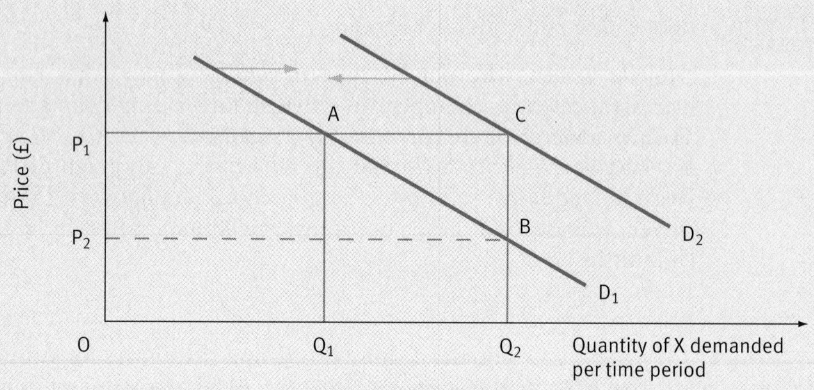

Fig 1.3

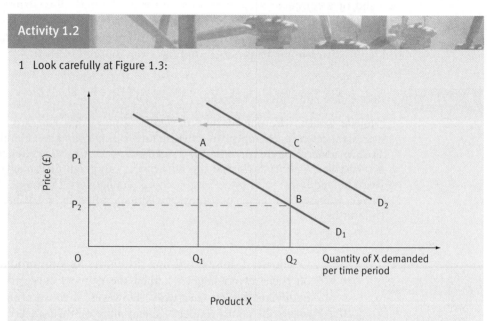

We start at price P_1 with quantity Q_1 of product X demanded on demand curve D_1. Select 'True' or 'False' for each of the following statements.

(a)	A move from point A to B represents an expansion of demand.	True/False
(b)	A move from point A to C represents an increase of demand.	True/False
(c)	A move from point C to A represents an increase of demand.	True/False
(d)	A move from point B to A represents a decrease of demand.	True/False

2 This question checks your understanding of the variables in the 'conditions of demand' which can shift the demand curve to the right (increase) or to the left (decrease).
For an *increase in demand*, insert letter I.
For a *decrease in demand*, insert letter D.

Changes in variable	Letter (I or D)
Rise in real income (for a normal good)	
Fall in price of a substitute in consumption	
Fall in price of a complement in consumption	
Change of tastes in favour of the product	
Fall in real income (for a normal good)	
Rise in price of a substitute in consumption	
Rise in price of a complement in consumption	
Change of tastes against the product	

3 This question checks your understanding of *normal goods* and *inferior goods* and of *substitutes in consumption* and *complements in consumption*, all of which often appear in discussions about demand.

(a) The demand for a normal good will always increase as real incomes rise and decrease as real incomes fall. True/False
(b) An inferior good is often a cheap but poor quality substitute for some other good. True/False
(c) A complement in consumption refers to a product that is a rival to another product. True/False
(d) The demand for an inferior good may increase at first as real incomes rise but may decrease as real incomes rise beyond a certain level. True/False
(e) A substitute in consumption refers to a product that is consumed jointly with another product. True/False

Answers to Checkpoints and Activities can be found on p. 705–35.

Supply curves and functions

The **supply curve** in Figure 1.4(a) is a visual representation of how much of the product sellers are willing and able to supply at different prices. The supply curve slopes upwards from left to right, suggesting that at a higher price more will be supplied, and at a lower price less will be supplied.

For example, suppose product X is CDs, if the price of CDs rises from P_1 to P_2, the supply of CDs will *expand* from Q_1 to Q_2 (other things equal) because producers of CDs will now be making higher profits and so will have both the incentive and the ability to buy in the extra resources to raise output.

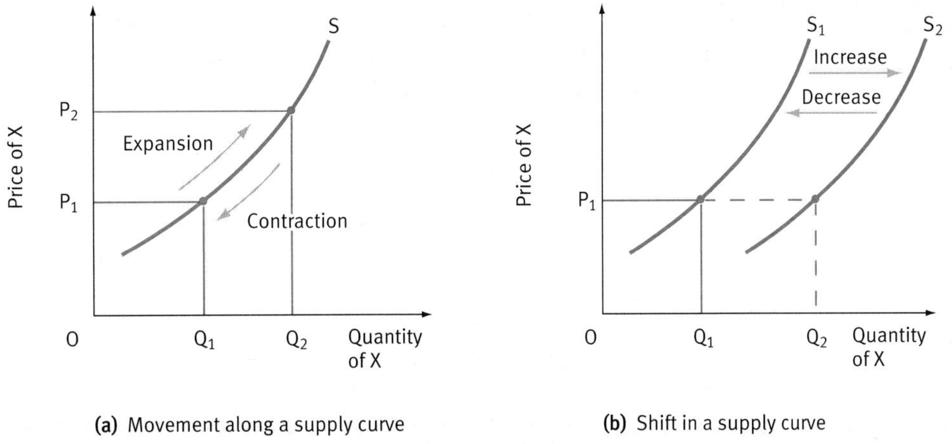

Fig 1.4 Movements along and shifts in a supply curve.

If the price of CDs falls from P_2 to P_1 then, for the opposite reasons, we can expect the supply of CDs to *contract* from Q_2 to Q_1 (other things equal).

Changes in the price of the product will (other things equal) result in *movements along* the supply curve, either an *expansion* (movement up and to the right) or a *contraction* (movement down and to the left).

Conditions of supply

Of course, other things may not remain equal! This brings us to the **conditions of supply** which refer to the factors that cause the supply curve for product X to *shift* either to the right or to the left.

In Figure 1.4(b):

- A shift to the right from S_1 to S_2 (*increase*) means more of product X is supplied at any given price. For example, at price P_1 supply *increases* from Q_1 to Q_2.
- A shift to the left from S_2 to S_1 (*decrease*) means less of product X is supplied at any given price. For example, at price P_1 supply *decreases* from Q_2 to Q_1.

Variables within the 'conditions of supply' include the price of other products (P_o), the costs of production (C), tax rates (T_x), tastes of producers (T_p) and so on.

To understand more about these 'conditions of supply' it will help if you are familiar with a number of terms.

Useful terminology in supply analysis

- *Substitutes in production*. Used when another product (O) could have been produced with the *same resources* (land, labour, capital, raw materials, etc.) as those used for product X. Suppose product X is wheat, then barley, rye and rape seed are other agricultural products that need similar types of soil, climate and other factor inputs and so can be regarded as substitutes in production for wheat.
- *Complements in production*. Used when the process of production for X yields a by-product. In producing mutton or lamb (X) the fleece of the sheep also yields wool (O), which can be regarded as a by-product for X. These complements in production are also known as *jointly supplied products*.

Examples:

Substitutes and complements in sports-wear production

- Nike faced a crucial decision in 1987, namely whether to continue allocating its finance, factory and warehousing space, labour, raw materials and sales resources across a wide range of athletic and non-athletic shoes (*substitutes in production*) or whether to focus all its limited resources on the then newly developed air-technology sports trainer. It chose the latter and its *Air Max* sports shoes catapulted Nike into market leadership of the sports trainer industry.
- Some of the moulds used by Reebok in producing more tennis shoes can also be used for producing more generalised leisure footwear (*complements in production*).

- *Lump-sum tax* is a tax of a constant absolute amount per unit, e.g. £1 a unit.
- *Ad valorem tax* is a tax which varies in absolute amount at different prices. A percentage tax such as VAT is an ad valorem tax as 17.5% of a higher price will give a greater absolute amount in tax revenue.

Box 1.2 gives you some practice in applying these various 'conditions of supply' to a situation involving an *increase* in supply.

Box 1.2 Variables causing an increase in supply

Let us consider briefly what might cause an *increase in supply* of product X, i.e. a shift in the supply curve for X from S_1 to S_2 in Figure 1.4(b) on page 13. Here we take product X to be wheat, though the idea can be applied to any good or service.

- *A fall in the price of a substitute in production.* If barley, rye or rape seed (O) falls in price, then wheat (X) becomes relatively more attractive, and the farmer may choose to grow wheat on land previously used to grow these other products, so that more wheat is supplied at the given price, P_1.
- *A rise in the price of a complement in production.* When wheat (X) is harvested the grain is separated from the dried stalks, which are known as straw (O). The combine harvester threshes and bags the grain as it is cut, leaving the straw behind in the field. Straw is clearly a by-product (complement) of wheat production, and has many uses. It can be used as bedding or fodder for animals, and manure (fertiliser). If straw (O) rises in price, so that the farmer can sell it for more profit, then this might even encourage him to grow more wheat (X). In other words, a rise in the price of the complement in production (straw) may lead to an increase in the supply of wheat (X), more wheat being supplied at each and every price.
- *A fall in the costs of production.* A fall in the costs of production of wheat could lead to an increase in the supply of wheat. You can think of this in either of two ways: at *any given price* the farmer will now be able to supply more wheat (A to B in Figure 1.5, p. 18), or *any given quantity* of wheat can now be supplied at a lower price (A to C in Figure 1.5, p. 18). In other words, a *rightward* shift of the supply curve is the same as a *downward* shift of the supply curve. In both cases supply increases.
- *Changes in the tastes of producers in favour of X.* The farmer may now *prefer* to produce wheat rather than to engage in other types of farming. We call this a change of the producer's tastes in favour of wheat.
- *Tax reductions.* Taxes have an effect on supply. When the government removes or reduces a tax on a good, this has exactly the same effect as a fall in the costs of production. A tax cut on products therefore increases supply, i.e. shifts the supply curve from S_1 to S_2 in Figure 1.5, p. 18.
- *Subsidies.* A subsidy has exactly the same effect as a tax cut. It will tend to increase supply, i.e. shift the supply curve from S_1 to S_2 in Figure 1.5, p. 18. This is because a subsidy of, say, 5% has the same effect as a 5% reduction in costs of production.
- *Favourable weather conditions.* For most agricultural commodities the weather might have a major influence on supply. Favourable weather conditions will produce a bumper harvest and will tend to increase the supply of wheat.

Checkpoint 2

Now write down the factors that might cause a *decrease* in supply of wheat, i.e. a *leftward* shift in the supply curve.

Supply function

It will be useful at this stage to introduce *all* the variables that might be involved in movements along the supply curve or in shifting the supply curve to the right or left. This is what the **supply function** does by expressing the relationship between the quantity of product X supplied per unit of time (Q_x) and a number of possible variables. These include the own price of product X (P_x), and a number of other variables known collectively as the 'conditions of supply'.

The supply function is often shown as a shorthand expression:

$$Q_x = F(P_x, P_o, C, T_n, T_x, T_p \ldots)$$

This can be read as meaning that the quantity supplied of product X (Q_x) *depends upon* its own price (P_x), the price of other products (P_o), costs of production (C), technology (T_n), tax rates (T_x), tastes of producers (T_p) and so on.

Remember

- **Any change in the product's own price P_x (other things equal) will result in a *movement along* a supply curve.**
- **Any change in a variable within the 'conditions of supply' will cause a *shift* in a supply curve.**

Case Study 1.2 uses an actual example involving Dyson, the well-known producer of vacuum cleaners, to consider further some of these supply-related issues.

Case Study 1.2 Dyson relocates production to South East Asia

In August 2003 Dyson announced that it was moving production of its washing machines from the UK to Malaysia, which followed its earlier decision in 2002 to shift production of its revolutionary dual cyclone bagless vacuum cleaner to Malaysia with the loss of over 800 jobs at the Dyson factory in Malmesbury, Wiltshire, which had produced some 8,000 vacuum cleaners per day.

Dyson is keen to point out that since the day the first Dyson dual cyclone vacuum cleaner went on sale in 1993, the company has been operating in a price-cutting market in which its competitors have been able to pass on to their customers the lower costs from manufacturing outside the UK. In contrast, Dyson has faced the further problems of rises in UK labour costs, land prices, taxation and other overhead costs whilst still trying to substantially increase its investment in new technology. For example, direct labour costs in Britain had doubled over the past ten years, partly because of the need to pay high wages in an area around Swindon with almost zero unemployment.

Case Study 1.2 continued

Dyson claims that the sums no longer add up and it faces going out of business if it continues manufacturing its products in the UK. As of September 2002 all vacuum cleaner production was shifted to Malaysia. The company argues that its production costs will benefit from the much lower wages in Malaysia, equivalent to £1.50 per hour as compared to the minimum wage in 2003 of £4.50 per hour in the UK. Indeed the company estimates that lower wages will reduce its unit production costs by around 30%. Further cost savings will also come from now having most of its component suppliers nearby (South East Asian component suppliers having progressively replaced those from the UK) and from now being much closer to emerging new markets in Japan, Australia and the Far East. In addition, the Malaysian government has offered various 'subsidies' in the form of grants for setting up the Dyson factories there, lower taxes and other benefits.

Whilst lamenting the loss of UK jobs, the consolation to Dyson in moving his vacuum cleaner manufacturing to Malaysia is that it will now generate enough cash to maintain the company's commitment to reinvesting up to 20% of turnover in research and development (R&D). Dyson believes that it is the technological advantages secured by R&D that will keep the company alive and ensure that 1,150 other jobs in Malmesbury are safe, more than 300 of which involve engineers, scientists, designers and testers – the brains that ensure Dyson products remain a step ahead of the rest. Dyson claims to have exported the brawn, keeping the higher-level value-added parts at home, since Dyson's comparative advantage lies in researching and designing new products to ensure the company stays two steps ahead of its rivals, most of whom manufacture in the Far East. Indeed he claims that to have followed the rest of British industry, which invests an average of only 2% of turnover, would have been to neglect Dyson's engineering and technological heritage and to follow in the footsteps of Britain's car, television and other domestic appliances.

Early indications of the profitability to Dyson of switching its vacuum cleaner manufacturing to Malaysia have been encouraging. It has reported profits for 2003 of £40m on vacuum cleaners, compared to £18m in 2002, with sales revenue of £275m in 2003 compared to £235m in 2002. Overseas sales had grown dramatically to 40% of turnover, with Dyson now selling to the US direct from Malaysia. R&D spending in 2003 was £18m, an increase of 50% on 2002.

Questions

1 In the market for vacuum cleaners, how will moving to Malaysia help to shift Dyson's supply curve to the right (*increase*)?

2 If Dyson had not moved to Malaysia, why does it believe that staying in the UK would have meant that its supply curve would have shifted to the left (*decrease*)?

3 What is the basis for Dyson's argument that shifting production to Malaysia is in the best interests of British workers?

Activity 1.3 will help you check your understanding of movements along and shifts in a supply curve.

Activity 1.3

Look carefully at Figure 1.5.

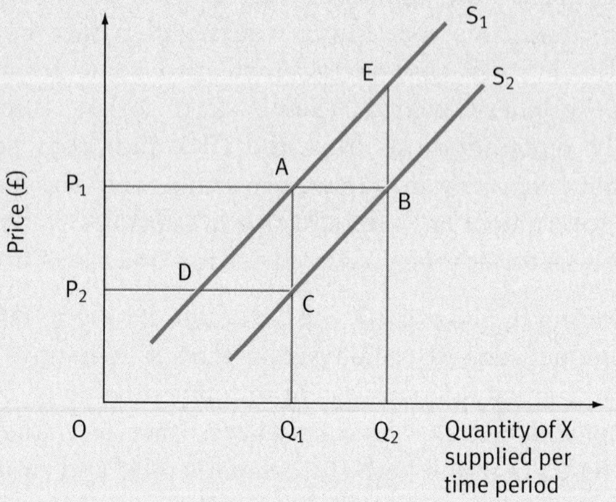

Fig 1.5

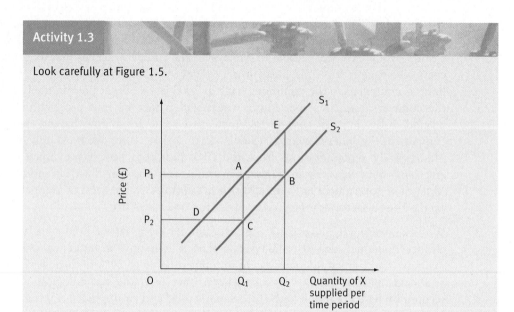

1 Match the *number* of each term on the left with the correct *letter* for its movement in Figure 1.5 on the right.

Terminology	**Movement**
(i) Expansion in supply of X	(a) A to B
(ii) Contraction in supply of X	(b) C to D
(iii) Increase in supply of X	(c) A to E
(iv) Decrease in supply of X	(d) A to D

2 If product X in Figure 1.5 is *petrol* then the move from A to B could be caused by which *two* of the following:

(i) Existing oil fields running dry
(ii) New oil fields being discovered
(iii) An effective blockade of oil terminals
(iv) New technology reducing the costs of 'cracking' oil into petroleum products

3 If product X in Figure 1.5 is again *petrol*, then the move from B to E could be caused by which *two* of the following:

(i) A fall in tax on petrol
(ii) A rise in tax on petrol
(iii) OPEC (Oil Producing and Exporting Countries) raising quotas for each member country
(iv) OPEC cutting quotas for each member country

4 Match the *letter* of each description on the left with the *number* for its correct term on the right.

Description
(a) Sometimes called a 'complement in production' with the production process for one product automatically resulting in more output of the other product (i.e. the by-product).
(b) Where the factors of production (land, labour, capital) could be used to produce either product.
(c) Has the effect of shifting the supply curve upwards and to the left (decrease in supply) by a constant amount (i.e. a parallel shift).
(d) Has the effect of shifting the supply curve upwards and to the left (decrease in supply) by a non-constant amount (i.e. a non-parallel shift).
(e) More can now be supplied at any given price or the same quantity can now be supplied at a lower price (increase in supply).

Terms
(i) Fall in costs of production
(ii) Imposing or raising a lump-sum tax
(iii) Substitute in production
(iv) Imposing or raising a percentage tax (e.g. VAT)
(v) Jointly supplied product

Answers to Checkpoints and Activities can be found on pp. 705–35.

Price determination

We shall initially assume that we have a *free market*, i.e. one in which demand and supply alone determine the price. Since our demand and supply curves have the same axes, i.e. price and quantity, we can put them on the same diagram. We do this in Figure 1.6 and we can see that at price P_1 the demand and supply curves intersect at the same quantity, Q_1. We call this price P_1 and quantity Q_1 the *equilibrium* price and quantity. Equilibrium means 'at rest', with 'no tendency to change'.

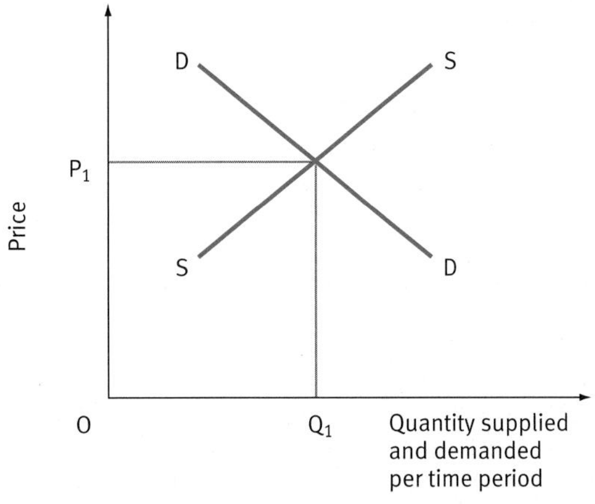

Fig 1.6 Equilibrium price and quantity

Restoring equilibrium price

At any price other than P_1 there will clearly be a tendency for change.

Excess supply

Suppose price is higher than P_1, then supply will exceed demand. At price P_2 in Figure 1.7 there is an *excess supply*. In a free market this excess supply will cause price to fall as suppliers try to dispose of their surplus stock.

- *As price falls* consumers find the product more attractive than substitutes in consumption and some will switch away from those substitutes so that we move rightwards along the demand curve D (expansion of demand).
- *As price falls* producers find the product less attractive than any substitutes in production and may switch resources to these alternatives so that we move leftwards along the supply curve (contraction of supply).

Price will continue to fall until we reach price P_1, where sellers and buyers are in harmony, with all that is offered for sale being purchased, i.e. we have equilibrium in the market.

Excess demand

Suppose price is lower than P_1, then demand exceeds supply. At price P_3 in Figure 1.7 there is an *excess demand*. In a free market excess demand will cause prices to be bid up, as at an auction, since there are more buyers than units of the product available.

- *As price rises*, consumers find the product less attractive than the substitutes in consumption and some will switch into those substitutes so that we move leftwards along the demand curve D (contraction of demand).

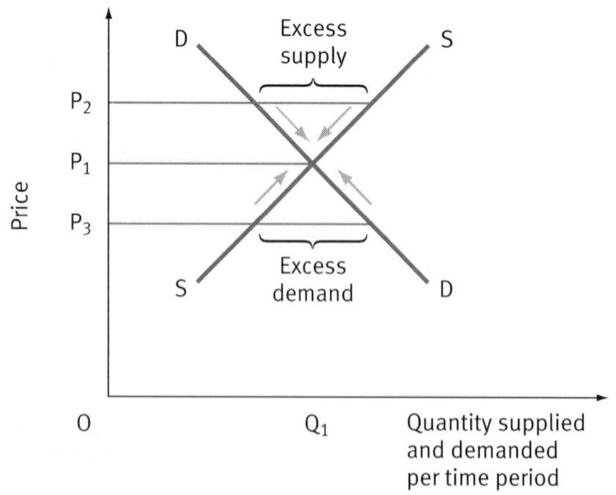

Fig 1.7 Restoring equilibrium price and quantity in a free market

- *As price rises*, producers find the product more attractive than any substitutes in production and may switch resources to this product so that we move rightwards along the supply curve S (expansion of supply).

Prices will continue to rise until we reach price P_1 where sellers and buyers are again in harmony, with all that is offered for sale being purchased, i.e. we have equilibrium in the market.

Remember

Price is acting as a *signal* to buyers and to sellers and helps direct them to take actions (expand or contract demand or supply) which bring about an equilibrium (balance) in the market.

Changes in market price and quantity

We have seen that changes in the conditions of demand or supply will *shift* the demand or supply curves. This in turn will cause changes in the equilibrium price and quantity in the market. It will be useful to consider how increases and decreases in both demand and supply will influence equilibrium price and quantity.

Increase in demand

We have seen that the demand curve may shift to the right (increase) for a number of reasons: a rise in the price of a substitute in consumption; a fall in the price of a complement in consumption; a rise in income for a normal product; a change of consumer tastes in favour of the product, etc.

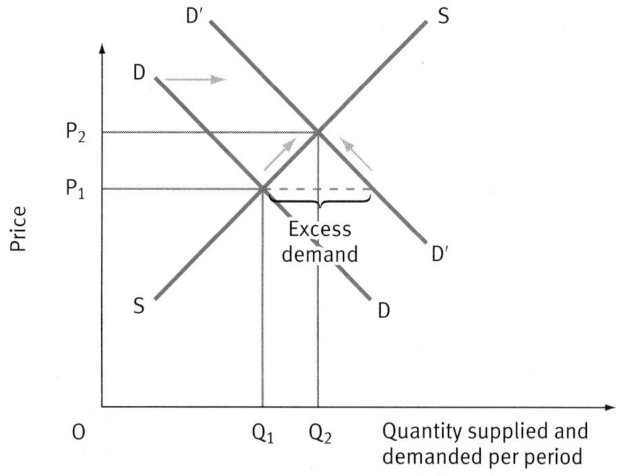

Fig 1.8 Increase in demand: rise in equilibrium price and quantity

In Figure 1.8 demand increases from D to D′, so that the original equilibrium price-quantity P_1–Q_1 can no longer continue. At price P_1 we now have a situation of *excess demand*. In a free market, price will be bid up. As price rises, supply *expands* along S and demand *contracts* along D′ until we reach the higher price P_2 at which demand and supply are again equal at Q_2. We call P_2–Q_2 the new price and quantity equilibrium.

Prediction An increase in demand will raise equilibrium price and quantity.

Decrease in demand

In the opposite case (Figure 1.9), where demand shifts leftwards from D to D″, we find the new price-quantity equilibrium to be P_2–Q_2. At price P_1 we now have a situation of *excess supply*. In a free market price will fall. As price falls, demand *expands* along the new demand curve D″ and supply *contracts* along S until we reach the lower price P_2 at which demand and supply are again equal at Q_2.

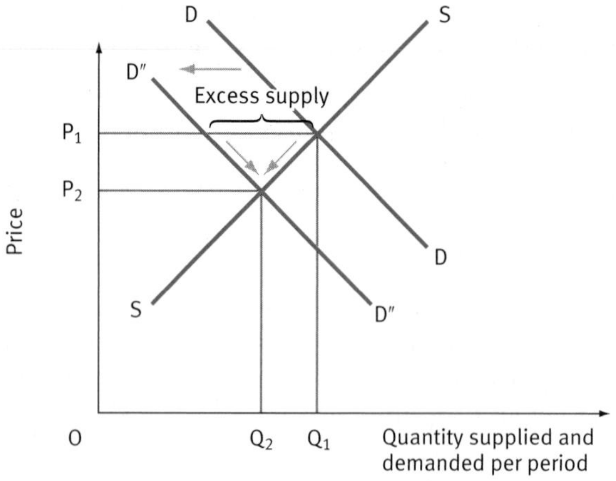

Fig 1.9 Decrease in demand: fall in equilibrium price and quantity

Prediction A decrease in demand will reduce equilibrium price and quantity.

Case Study 1.3 looks at the impacts of the Atkins diet on consumer tastes, and therefore on demand.

Case Study 1.3 **Consumer tastes and the Atkins diet**

In recent years there has been a major change in consumer tastes in the US and the UK which studies suggest have been linked to the popularity of the 'Atkins diet'. *The New Atkins Diet* has been a long-running bestseller on both sides of the Atlantic. This diet instructs those who wish to lose weight to eat more protein (e.g. eggs,

Case Study 1.3 continued

cheese, cream and meat) and fewer carbohydrates (e.g. bread, potatoes and pasta). For example, the demand for eggs has increased by around 4% in the UK, resulting in upward pressure on egg prices – especially free range eggs – whereas the demand for potatoes in the UK has begun to fall (in the US the fall was as much as 10% in 2003), creating downward pressure on potato prices.

The increase in demand for eggs has been associated with the growing popularity of Atkins-friendly salads loaded with eggs (also chicken and ham) in food chains throughout the UK and US. The increased demand for eggs has raised the equilibrium price and quantity of eggs (Figure 1.10a). In the meantime, the decrease in demand for potatoes has resulted in the price of potatoes falling by around 6% in the UK, together with a fall in equilibrium quantity (Figure 1.10b). A concerned Potato Council has launched a £1m marketing campaign in the UK with the slogan 'fab not fad', designed to shift the demand for potatoes back to their former level.

Interestingly, eggs and potatoes used to be seen as complements to each other in such classic meals as 'egg and chips' – now, with the impact of the Atkins diet, they seem to be regarded as substitutes by some sections of the consuming public!

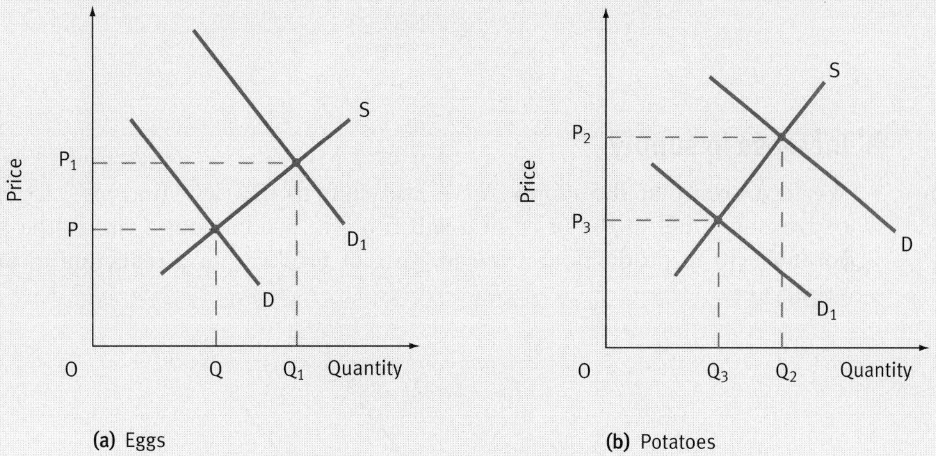

Fig 1.10 Equilibrium price/quantity for (a) eggs and (b) potatoes

Nor are the impacts of the Atkins diet confined to eggs and potatoes. The *National Bread Leadership Council* in the US found that 21% of Americans were reducing their carbohydrate intake and 40% were eating less bread in 2003 than in 2002. Global beef demand in early 2004 was up 10%, linked by many to Atkins diet effects, raising 'spot market' beef prices by some 40% – this sharp price increase aided by a decrease in beef supply from Canada linked to the US 'mad cow disease' in late 2003.

Case Study 1.3 continued

Whole ranges of low-carbohydrate products are being provided to meet these new consumer tastes. Anheuser Busch, the world's largest brewer, launched *Nichelob Ultra* in September 2002 under the slogan 'Lose the carbs not the taste'. Other brewers have followed. SAB Miller, the US number two brewer, is placing greater marketing emphasis on its low carb *Miller Lite* brand, and reported sales for Miller Lite up by 13.5% in 2003, compared to falling sales in 2002. Heinz is introducing its 'one carb' version of the market-leading Ketchup in 2004 and the Atkins company is itself introducing, under its own logo, a wide range of high-protein, low-sugar breakfast cereal bars, milkshakes, chocolate and baking mix for bread and muffins.

Questions

1 Can you use a diagram to explain why the market price of beef rose by a dramatic 40% in early 2004?

2 A recent and well-publicised study has severely criticised the Atkins diet on health grounds. Suggest how this might influence the equilibrium price and quantity of both eggs and potatoes. What other effects might there be on other products?

Increase in supply

We have seen that the supply curve may shift to the right (increase) for a number of reasons: a fall in the price of a substitute in production; a rise in the price of a complement in production; a fall in costs of production; a reduction in tax on the product etc.

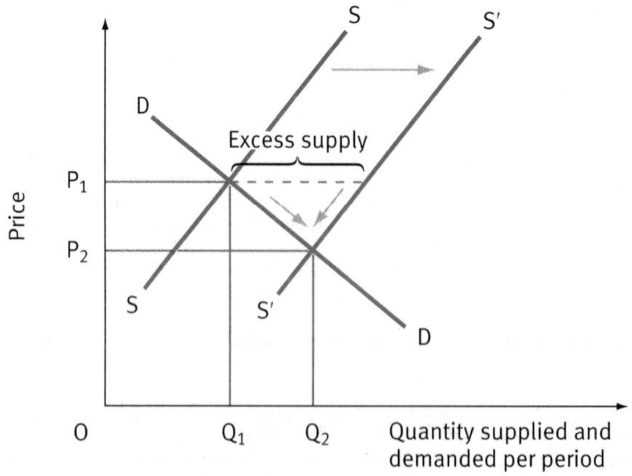

Fig 1.11 Increase in supply: fall in equilibrium price and rise in equilibrium quantity

In Figure 1.11 supply shifts from S to S′ so that the original equilibrium price-quantity P_1–Q_1 can no longer continue. At price P_1 we now have a situation of *excess supply*. In a free market, price will fall as producers try to dispose of surplus stock. As price falls, supply *contracts* along S′ and demand *expands* along D until we reach the lower price P_2, at which demand and supply are again equal at Q_2.

Prediction An increase in supply will lower equilibrium price but raise equilibrium quantity.

Decrease in supply

In the opposite case (Figure 1.12), where supply shifts leftwards from S to S″, we find the new price-quantity equilibrium to be P_2–Q_2. At price P_1 we now have a situation of *excess demand*. In a free market price will be bid upwards. As price rises, supply *expands* along the new supply curve S″ and demand *contracts* along D until we reach the higher price P_2 at which demand and supply are again equal at Q_2.

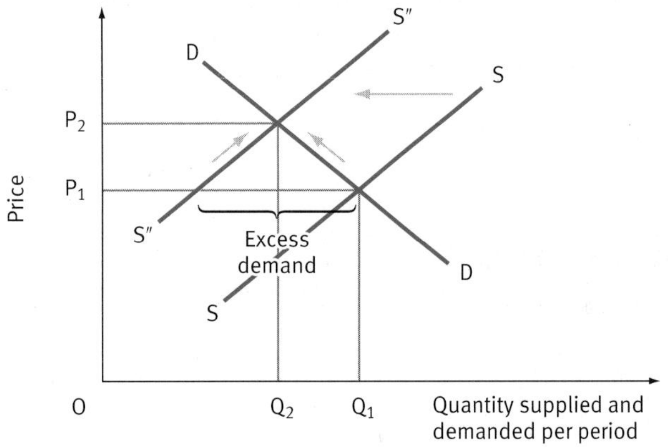

Fig 1.12 Decrease in supply: rise in equilibrium price and fall in equilibrium quantity

Prediction A decrease in supply will raise equilibrium price but reduce equilibrium quantity.

Case Study 1.4 examines the use of demand and supply analysis in discussing policies aimed at combating drug use.

Case Study 1.4 The drug war

There is a debate in the US and in Europe as to how to influence the market for drugs such as cocaine. Some argue that the answer is to *reduce the supply* of drugs from Colombia – which would otherwise eventually find their way onto the world markets – by giving aid to the Colombian government to fight the drug suppliers. If this is

Case Study 1.4 continued

successful, it will drive up the price of cocaine on the streets. Higher prices mean that fewer people will be willing and able to buy drugs, resulting in a fall in demand.

This scenario can be seen in Figure 1.13(a) where a successful anti-drug policy in Colombia would decrease supply, i.e. shift the supply curve for cocaine upwards and to the left so that there is an *excess demand* for cocaine at price P. This will result in a rise in the equilibrium price of cocaine from P to P_1. The quantity demanded will contract along the demand curve D from Q to Q_1 as price rises from P to P_1. Critics of these ideas argue that programmes designed to reduce the supply of cocaine from Colombia have failed in the past because the high price of drugs makes them very profitable to produce in other areas outside Colombia.

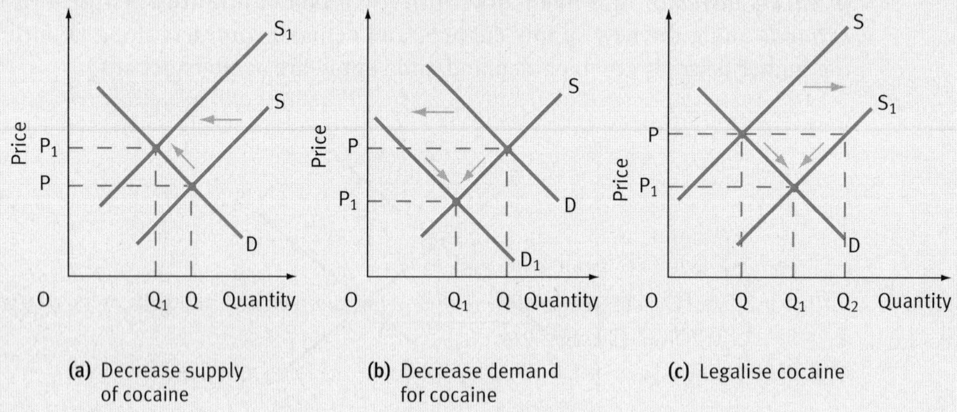

Fig 1.13 Supply and demand for cocaine.

Some argue that the answer is to *reduce the demand* for illegal drugs by various means such as improved education, or by advertising the damaging effects of drugs such as cocaine. This can be seen in Figure 1.13(b) where a successful education policy decreases demand, i.e. shifts the demand curve D downwards and to the left, so that there is an *excess supply* of cocaine at price P. This will result in a fall in the equilibrium price from P to P_1 and in quantity from Q to Q_1.

Another solution would be to *legalise the consumption of cocaine*. This would arguably increase supply, i.e. shift the supply curve downwards and to the right as in Figure 1.13(c), substantially reducing the price of cocaine in the streets from P to P_1. Proponents of legalisation argue that the very high price of cocaine forces many people into criminal activity to support their habit, so that the lowering of the price of cocaine after legalisation would reduce the pressure on addicts to use criminal activity to buy the drug.

However, it is often admitted that in the short run the equilibrium quantity of cocaine in use will rise from Q to Q_1 as the price of cocaine falls from P to P_1. Others

Case Study 1.4 continued

argue that the legalisation of the drug will reduce the 'thrill' of engaging in what is currently illegal, anti-establishment activity by taking drugs. If so, this would cause the demand curve D to decrease, shifting downwards and to the left of D. If this did happen the price of cocaine would fall below P_1 and the equilibrium quantity of cocaine use might fall below the original level Q if demand decreased sufficiently.

Further, if the lower price of cocaine squeezed the profits of suppliers, then they might use their resources elsewhere so that the supply curve decreased, shifting to the left from S_1.

Although the answer to this policy dilemma for governments is neither easy nor wholly clear, at least supply and demand analysis helps to put the fundamentals of the debate into perspective.

Questions

1 Use Figure 1.13(c) to show the extent to which the demand for cocaine must decrease to result in less cocaine being used *after* legalisation as compared to *before* legalisation.

2 How might the outcome in question 1 be affected by the now lower price for cocaine squeezing the profits of suppliers, so that supply decreases from the level S_1 reached immediately after legalisation?

3 How might the steepness of the demand and supply curves for cocaine be relevant to the outcome of legalisation?

4 What other issues might be raised by a policy of legalisation of cocaine use?

5 A major study from Loughborough University in 2004 argued that, whatever their faults, the Taliban had been effective in their policy of decreasing the supply of poppy growing and therefore of heroin and cocaine in 2001 (over 50% of the world supply of the poppies for these products comes from Afghanistan). Which of the three diagrams in Figure 1.13 best represents how they achieved this policy? How did the researchers know that the world supply of these drugs had fallen so sharply in 2001?

Maximum and minimum prices

LINKS

Maximum and minimum prices are sometimes referred to as 'market failure' since the market mechanism is prevented from using price signals to eliminate an excess demand or supply. A number of other types of 'market failure' are considered in some detail in Chapter 8 (pp. 278–282).

Of course, in reality governments or regulatory bodies may intervene in markets, as for example in setting maximum or minimum prices. In these cases prices are *prevented* from acting as the signals which guide buyers and sellers to an equilibrium outcome.

Maximum price

The government or agency may seek to establish a **maximum price** in the market, i.e. a *ceiling* above which price will not be allowed to rise. Again we can use demand and supply diagrams as in Figure 1.14 to show what will then happen.

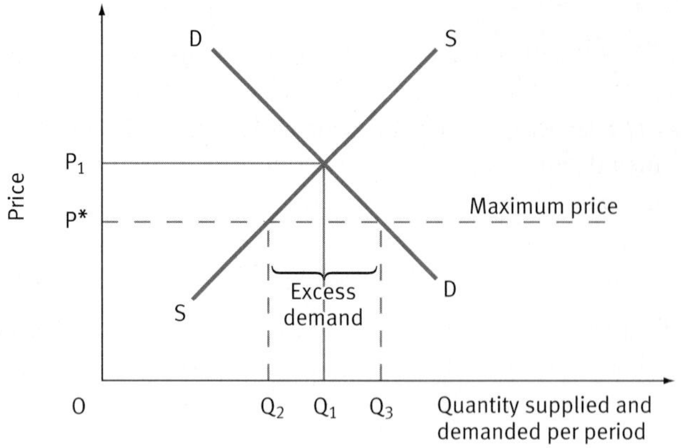

Fig 1.14 A maximum price P* set below the equilibrium price P_1

If the maximum price were set *above* the equilibrium price P_1, then the market would still be able to reach the equilibrium outcome of price P_1 and quantity Q_1. However, the market mechanisms would not be able to reach this equilibrium outcome if the maximum price (P^*) was set *below* the equilibrium price P_1. At price P^* there is an excess demand and price would have risen in a free market to P_1, encouraging producers to expand supply from Q_2 to Q_1 and discouraging consumers so that demand contracts from Q_3 to Q_1, until the equilibrium P_1–Q_1 was established. Here, however, price is prevented from providing such signals to sellers and buyers to bring their decisions into harmony, and we may be left with the **disequilibrium** outcome P^* in which excess demand persists.

Box 1.3 considers some of the possible ways in which resources might be allocated in the case of a maximum price set below the equilibrium price.

Box 1.3 **Non-market mechanisms and resource allocation**

How then will resources be allocated in a situation where excess demand exists?

- *Rationing*. Vouchers or coupons could be issued so that everyone got at least some of the quantity (Q_2) of the product available. The government or agency must still decide who qualifies for vouchers and how much product each voucher holder receives. Rationing is also costly to administer, with vouchers having to be printed, distributed, taken in, etc.
- *First come, first served* In other words, some sort of queuing system may be used to allocate the product available. Time is wasted by having to queue.
- *Ballots*. The limited supply of the product may be shared amongst potential purchasers by some sort of ballot. 'Tickets' may be issued and a draw made, with 'successful' individuals able to purchase the product at price P*. Again ballots can be costly to administer and are arguably less fair than rationing.
- *'Black market'*. Although not strictly a mechanism for allocating resources, a 'black market' invariably operates whenever a maximum price results in excess demand. In Figure 1.14, the demand curve DD tells us that some people are 'willing to pay' a very high price for the product, well in excess of P*. This, of course, is the basis for ticket touts being able to sell tickets to popular events at a price well above the official price of the ticket.

Minimum price

The government or agency may seek to establish a **minimum price** in the market, i.e. a *floor* below which the price will not be allowed to fall. We can use our familiar demand and supply diagrams as in Figure 1.15 to show what will happen in these circumstances.

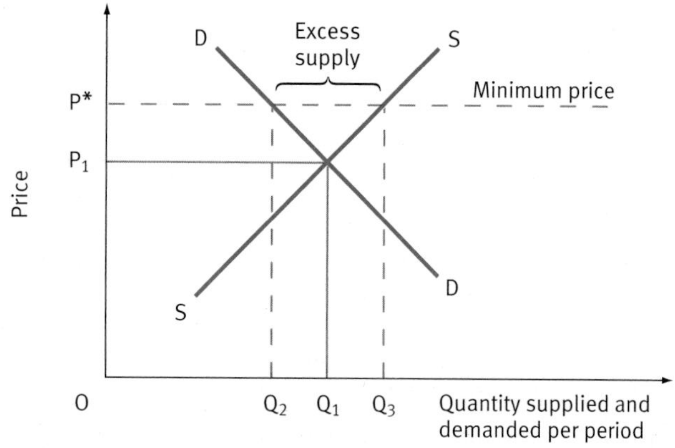

Fig 1.15 A minimum price P* set above the equilibrium price P_1

Suppose now that the government imposes a minimum price, P*, below which the price will not be allowed to fall. If that minimum price is set *below* the equilibrium price P_1 then there will be no problem. The market will already have reached its equilibrium at price P_1, and there will be no reason for P_1 to change. If, however, the minimum price is set *above* the equilibrium price P_1, then price will have to rise from P_1 to the new minimum, P*. We can see from Figure 1.15 that there will then be an excess supply at P* of Q_3–Q_2 units.

If the market had remained free, the excess supply would have been removed by the price system. However, the important point here is that the market is not free! Price cannot fall below the minimum that has been set, P*. The excess supply will therefore remain and the price system will not be able to remove it. Sellers will be unable to dispose of their surplus stocks, which will have to be stored, destroyed or disposed of in less orthodox ways which prevent the price falling below P*.

Checkpoint 3 Can you think of what these 'less orthodox ways' might be?

Case Study 1.5 investigates the market for oil to consider how changes in the conditions of demand and supply for oil have influenced the world price of oil.

Case Study 1.5 Oiling the wheels

In August 2004 the widely used measure for the price of crude oil, the West Texas Spot-rate, had reached $42 per barrel, some 44% higher than in August 2002. Indeed the crude oil price was as low as $11 a barrel as recently as summer 2001. Why has there been such volatility in price? Close examination of demand and supply conditions for oil may give us some clues!

Crude oil is refined into a vast number of products via the chemical process of 'cracking'. However, just three, namely petrol, diesel and fuel oil, account for around 75% of oil derivative products and are mainly used in transport and electricity-generating activities. Of course, the demand for transport and electricity is closely linked to economic growth; For example, every 1% rise in US national income has been estimated as raising US demand for crude oil by nine-tenths of 1%.

Few immediate substitutes exist for crude oil derivatives in transport and energy. Natural gas is perhaps the closest substitute and provides around 25% of total global energy. Estimates suggest that a 1% fall in price of natural gas leads to a three-quarters of 1% fall in demand for crude oil. However, other, less obvious substitutes for oil are becoming more important. For example, all types of renewable energy sources (wind, water, sun etc.) are increasingly seen as more environmentally desirable (if more expensive) substitutes for oil in energy production in that they do not emit the carbon dioxide (CO_2) and other greenhouse gases which result from using oil-based products. The scientific linkage of these emissions with global warming led to 93 countries (but not the US) having ratified the Kyoto Protocol by 2003, with the developed countries committing themselves to an overall 5% reduction in the emissions of greenhouse gases by 2012.

Climate itself can also influence the demand for oil. The OECD noted that in 2002 the Northern Hemisphere recorded the warmest-ever first quarter of the year, and linked this to demand for crude oil from countries in the Northern Hemisphere falling by 1.1 million barrels per year.

Whilst the demand for oil is capable of significant shifts, so too is the supply. Around one-third of total supply of crude oil is in the hands of a small group of well-organised oil producing and exporting countries (OPEC). Members of OPEC include Saudi Arabia, Iraq, Iran, Qatar, Libya, Kuwait, United Arab Emirates, Nigeria, Indonesia and Venezuela. These countries meet regularly to decide on the total supply they should collectively produce, seeking to limit the total supply in order to keep the world price of crude oil at a 'reasonable' level (said to be around $25 a barrel). Having fixed the total supply, OPEC then allocates a *quota* to each member state which specifies their maximum oil production in that year.

When OPEC increases or decreases the agreed total supply of oil, this clearly has a major impact on the oil price. It was the sharp cuts in OPEC oil production that resulted in the major world 'oil crises' of 1967 and 1973, with rapid rises in the oil price leading to global recession. However, another unpredictable variable has been

Case Study 1.2 continued

added to oil supply in recent years, namely the growing contribution of *non-OPEC* oil-producing countries. For example, Russia and the US are outside OPEC but each produces almost as much oil as the world's largest oil producer, Saudi Arabia, and many new oil resources in the former Soviet Republics such as Azerbaijan and Kazakhstan are now coming on stream. The top ten producers and consumers of oil in 2002 are listed below, with the OPEC and non-OPEC producers identified.

Top 10 oil producers (million barrels per day)		**Top 10 oil consumers (million barrels per day)**	
Saudi Arabia (OPEC)	8.8	US	19.6
USA (non OPEC)	7.2	Japan	5.4
Russia (non OPEC)	7.1	China	5.1
Iran (OPEC)	3.7	Germany	2.8
Mexico (non OPEC)	3.6	Russia	2.4
Venezuela (OPEC)	3.4	South Korea	2.2
Norway (non OPEC)	3.4	India	2.1
China (non OPEC)	3.3	France	2.0
Canada (non OPEC)	2.7	Italy	1.9
UK (non OPEC)	2.5	Canada	1.9

It is not only actual events but *possible future events* that can influence the price of oil. For example, in the months before the second Iraq War in 2003, it was claimed that there was a 'war risk premium' of $5 a barrel built into the then current price of over $30 a barrel.

Questions

1 (a) Discuss some of the factors suggested in the case study that might cause an *increase* in the world demand for oil.
(b) Now discuss possible reasons for a *decrease* in the world demand for oil.
(c) Can you think of reasons why there might be a fall in the equilibrium price of oil but a rise in the equilibrium quantity?

2 We have seen that OPEC has tried to restrict the total supply of crude oil from its member countries to keep the world price at a 'reasonable' level of around $25 a barrel. Suppose it now aims for a higher world price of around $35 a barrel.
(a) How might it achieve this new target? (You could use a diagram here.)
(b) What problems might OPEC encounter in trying to achieve this higher oil price?

3 Can you explain what was meant by those who argued that a 'war risk premium' raised the price of oil to over $30 a barrel before the second Iraq War in 2003?

CHECK THE NET

Useful data on demand and supply issues can be found at various websites, including:

http://thomasregister.com
http://www.foodanddrink.co.uk
www.cocacola.com
www.emigroup.com
www.virginrecords.com
www.bip.co.uk

Activity 1.4 gives you more practice in price determination.

Activity 1.4

1 Look at Figure 1.16 and answer the following questions.

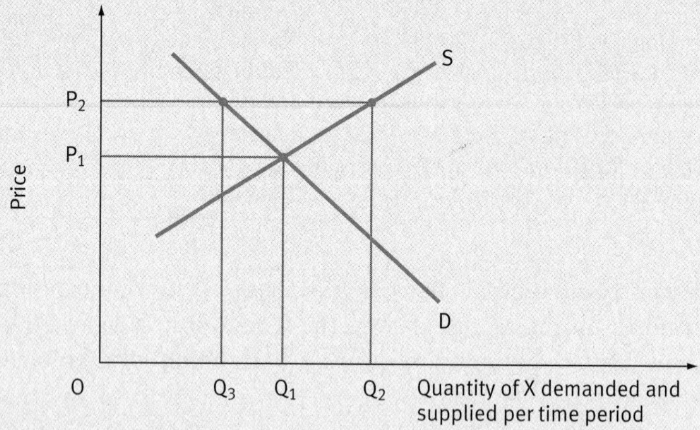

Fig 1.16

(a) Price P_2 is an 'equilibrium price'. True/False
(b) At price P_2 demand exceeds supply. True/False
(c) At price P_2 excess supply is the amount $Q_2 - Q_3$. True/False
(d) If the initial price is P_2, in a free market price will rise. True/False
(e) As price moves from P_2 towards the equilibrium price, demand will expand. True/False
(f) As price moves from P_2 towards the equilibrium price, supply will decrease. True/False
(g) In moving to an equilibrium, price is acting as a 'signal' to bring the decisions of producers and consumers into balance (harmony) with each other. True/False
(h) If price falls below P_1 then excess demand will result in price moving back to P_1. True/False

2 The market for designer trainers is currently in equilibrium. Other things equal, what will be the likely impact of each of the following events?

Event	Change in equilibrium price	Change in equilibrium quantity
(a) Successful TV advertising for designer trainers	Rise/Fall	Rise/Fall
(b) Report indicates foot damage from wearing designer trainers	Rise/Fall	Rise/Fall
(c) New factories in developing countries reduce costs of producing designer trainers whilst retaining quality	Rise/Fall	Rise/Fall
(d) Higher rate of VAT applied to designer trainers	Rise/Fall	Rise/Fall

3 Look carefully at Figure 1.17, which shows an increase in demand for Microsoft (X Box). Can you explain what is happening as regards Sony (PlayStation 2) in (b) and why?

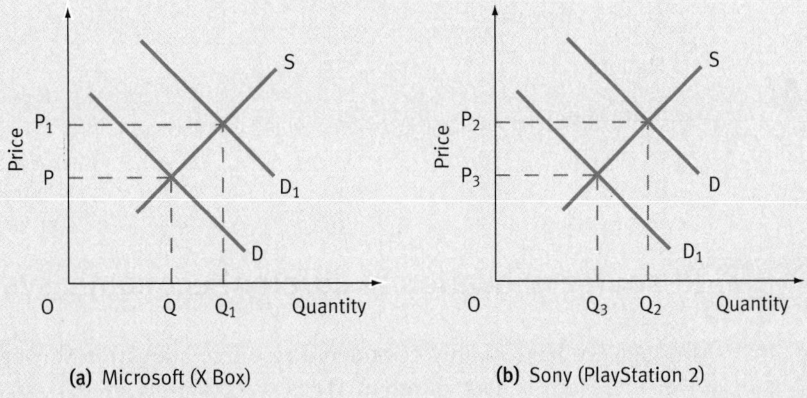

Fig 1.17

4 Look carefully at Figure 1.18, which shows an increase in demand for wool in (a). Can you explain what is happening to mutton in (b) and why?

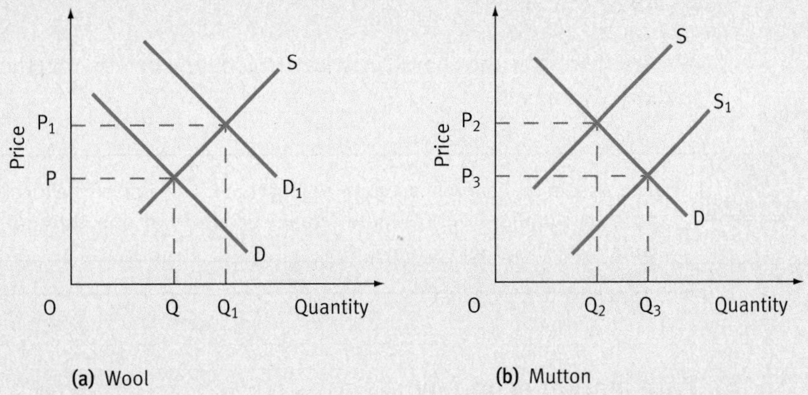

Fig 1.18

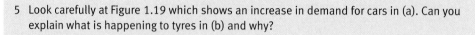

5 Look carefully at Figure 1.19 which shows an increase in demand for cars in (a). Can you explain what is happening to tyres in (b) and why?

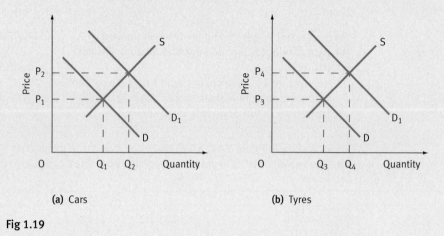

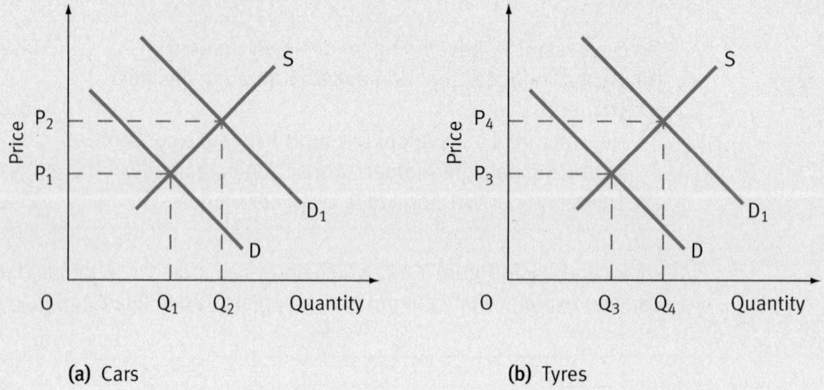

Fig 1.19

Answers to Checkpoints and Activities can be found on pp. 705–35.

Resource allocation in different economic systems

Although we have mainly considered resource allocation through the *market mechanism*, there are in fact different types of economic system for allocating resources. Three particular types of economic system are often discussed in the literature.

- Pure market economy
- Pure command economy
- Mixed economy

We briefly review the characteristics of each type below, together with their advantages and disadvantages.

Watch out! Of course, in reality most economies might more accurately be located somewhere along a *spectrum* running from the pure market economy at one extreme to the pure command economy at the other extreme.

Pure market economy

- Markets alone are used to allocate scarce resources of land, labour and capital.
- Prices (determined on markets) act as 'signals' to producers and consumers, bringing supply and demand into balance (equilibrium).

- No direct role for governments in resource allocation – their main task is to provide the infrastructure needed to allow markets to work (e.g. law and order, defence etc.).
- *Advantages* – markets co-ordinate (via price) the activities of millions of buyers and sellers without any need for an expensive bureaucracy of decision makers.
- *Disadvantages* – 'market failures' (see Chapter 8, p. 278) can result in a misallocation of resources.

Quote

It was the role of prices within the market mechanism that Adam Smith was referring to when, in his *Wealth of Nations* in 1776, he observed that each individual was 'led by an invisible hand to promote an end which was no part of his intention'.

Pure command economy

- Governments, not markets, allocate scarce resources of land, labour and capital.
- Comprehensive plans are drawn up to decide which products are to be produced and in what quantities.
- Prices, if they exist, are determined by governments. If there is excess demand at the ruling price, then 'rationing' may be used. If there is excess supply, then unwanted product may simply be stored or even destroyed.
- Governments retain ownership of the means of production (little or no private ownership).
- *Advantages* – production and consumption can be based on 'social' rather than 'private' needs and wants.
- *Disadvantages* – expensive bureaucracy needed to allocate resources; inappropriate decisions often made by bureaucrats, resulting in excess supply for unwanted products or excess demand for wanted products.

Mixed economy

CHECK THE NET

You can find up-to-date information on the US economy from the Economics Statistics Briefing Room of the White House at: http://www.whitehouse.gov/fsbe/esbr.html

Data on other advanced industrialised market economies can be found at: http://www.oecd.org

Data on the transition economies can be found from the European Bank for Reconstruction and Development website at: www.ebrd.com

- Uses both markets and government intervention to allocate scarce resources of land, labour and capital.
- Government intervention can be direct (e.g. nationalised industries, public sector services) and/or indirect (e.g. regulations, tax policies).
- Most modern economies are mixed – e.g. around 40% of UK expenditure and output involves the public sector.
- *Advantages* – government intervention can help offset various types of 'market failure' (see Chapter 8, p. 282); markets and prices can be used to co-ordinate large numbers of independent decisions.

- *Disadvantages* – high taxes may be needed to provide the revenues to support government intervention; these may reduce incentives and discourage output, investment and employment.

Case Study 1.6 gives a brief outline of the workings of the Russian economy in the years when it operated towards the 'command economy' end of the spectrum.

Case Study 1.6 Fulfilling the plan

The term 'communist bloc' was used in the West until the late 1980s to describe the operation of 25 economies under the Soviet sphere of influence. A characteristic of all these economies was an extensive central planning system, often termed a 'command economy'. The command economy dominated every aspect of life, telling factories where to buy their inputs, how much to pay their workers, how much to produce and where to sell their output. Individuals were trained in specialist schools and universities and directed to work at specific factories, which provided their wages, houses, health care – even holidays in enterprise-owned hotels and sanatoria. The national bank was told how much to lend to which factories and how much cash to print to pay wages.

As a theoretical concept, central planning was very elegant. Using 'input–output' analysis (a planning framework which calculated the inputs required for each factory in order for it to deliver its planned outputs to the next stage in the production process), the planning ministry could calculate precisely how much labour, capital and raw materials each enterprise required to achieve its production targets. The various production targets for raw materials and intermediate and final products all fitted together to ensure a perfectly balanced expansion of the economy. Input and output prices were carefully set to ensure that all firms could pay their wage bills and repay loans from the national bank, while at the same time pricing consumer goods to encourage consumption of socially desirable goods (e.g. books, ballet, theatre, public transport etc.) and discourage consumption of politically unfavoured goods (e.g. international telephone calls, cars, luxury goods).

The overall national plan was thus internally consistent. If each of the enterprises achieved its production targets, there could not be, by definition, shortages or bottlenecks in the economy. There would be full employment, with everyone working in an enterprise for which he/she had been specifically trained at school and university. The total wage bill for the economy, which was paid in cash, would be sufficient to buy all the consumer goods produced. There would be zero inflation and all the country's citizens would have access to housing, education and health care.

Of course, in practice things rarely worked out as planned and since the late 1980s the 'command economy' system has been progressively replaced with a more market-based system for allocating resources. However, decades of economic planning meant that these 25 so-called 'Transition Economies' began the reform process without having functioning markets for labour, goods or capital, since all three had been allocated by the central planner, in accordance with an internally coherent economic plan. Because

Case Study 1.6 continued

all the means of production had been in state hands, there was, moreover, no legislative framework for the enforcement of property rights, the valuation and disposal of assets or the liquidation of unprofitable enterprises. Nor in a system of directed labour was there any official unemployment and, hence, no need for a social security system.

Source: Healey, N. (2004) in Griffiths, A. and Wall, S. *Applied Economics* (10th edn), Harlow: Pearson Education, Chapter 30.

Questions

1 Why do you think the command economy failed to deliver many of the benefits claimed for it in this case study?

2 Can you find any clues in the case study to explain why the transition from a command economy to a market economy has proved to be so painful for many of these states?

3 What would you consider to be the potential advantages and disadvantages for these states seeking to move from a command to a market economy?

Activity 1.5 provides opportunities to think more about these different types of economic system.

Activity 1.5

1 Place each of the following countries into what you regard as the appropriate box below: Poland, US, UK, Cuba, France, China. Explain your reasoning.

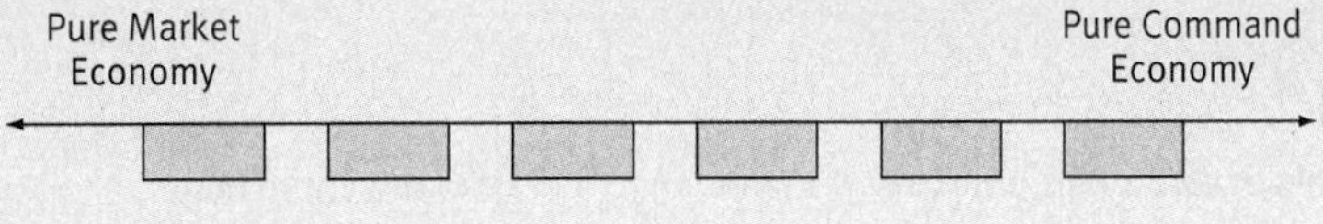

Fig 1.20

2 Look carefully at Figure 1.21 which involves two products, A and B, which are substitutes in production.

(a) Use appropriate words to fill in each of the six empty boxes (Note: boxes 1 and 4 refer to demand and boxes 2 and 5 to price.)

(b) Explain why this diagram might be useful in highlighting the role of prices as 'signals' in a market economy.

(c) Can you suggest why those who broadly support a market economy might still wish the government to intervene in this situation? What type of intervention might be proposed?

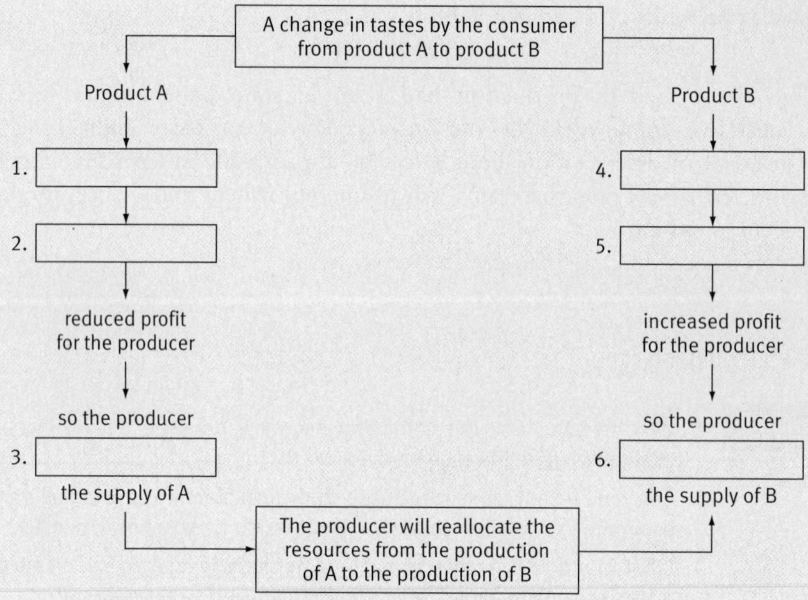

Fig 1.21 The market mechanism

Answers to Checkpoints and Activities can be found on pp. 705–35.

Exam hints!

Wherever appropriate, using demand/supply diagrams can help to clarify your answer to many assignments and exam questions on the topic areas of this chapter. However, do make sure that you draw the diagram neatly (use a rule!), label the diagram fully and, most important of all, write about the diagram in the text of your answer.

Key Terms

Complements in consumption Where consuming more of one product results in consuming more of some other product.

Complements in production Where producing more of one product automatically results in producing more of some other product (by-product). Sometimes called 'jointly supplied' products.

Conditions of demand The variables which result in the demand curve shifting to the right (increase) or left (decrease).

Conditions of supply The variables which result in the supply curve shifting to the right (increase) or left (decrease).

Demand curve Maps the relationship between the quantity demanded of some product and changes in its own price.

Demand function Expresses the relationship between the quantity demanded of some product and the main variables that influence that demand.

Equilibrium A state of balance or harmony. Equilibrium price is that price for which demand and supply are equal and there is no tendency for the price to change.

Inferior goods Cheap but poor-quality substitutes for other goods. As real incomes rise above a certain 'threshold', consumers tend to substitute more expensive but better-quality alternatives for certain products. In other words, inferior goods have negative income elasticities of demand over certain ranges of income.

Market failure Where one or more conditions prevent the market, via the price mechanism, from allocating resources in the best possible way.

Normal good One for which a rise in real income will always lead to an increase in demand.

Opportunity cost The next best alternative foregone, in a situation characterised by scarcity and choice.

Production possibility curve (or frontier) Maps the different output combinations from fully using all the resources available.

Scarcity The central 'economic problem', arising from the fact that wants are unlimited but the means to satisfy those wants are limited.

Substitutes in consumption Where the products are alternative purchases for consumers.

Substitutes in production Where the factors of production could produce either product.

Supply curve Maps the relationship between the quantity supplied of some product and changes in its own price.

Supply function Expresses the relationship between the quantity supplied of some product and the main variables that influence supply.

Key Points

- In a free market system, price co-ordinates the decisions of buyers and sellers to bring them into balance (equilibrium).
- Prices act as 'signals' to consumers – e.g. a higher price for X means that substitutes in consumption are now relatively more attractive, so that demand for X contracts.
- Prices act as 'signals' to producers – e.g. a higher price for X means that substitutes in production are now relatively less attractive, so that supply of X expands.
- Excess demand at any price can be expected to raise market price.
- Excess supply at any price can be expected to reduce market price.
- A change in the product's own price (other things equal) will result in a movement along the demand or supply curve (expansion or contraction).
- A change in the conditions of demand or supply will cause the respective curves to shift (increase or decrease).
- 'Market failures', such as maximum or minimum prices, may prevent the price mechanism from allocating resources, so that 'non-price' mechanisms for resource allocation are needed.
- In a 'mixed economy' both markets and governments play a role in the allocation of scarce resources (e.g. land, labour and capital).

Assessment Practice

The following questions will help to check your understanding of some of the key points raised throughout the chapter.

Multiple choice questions

1 Which *two* of these are examples of 'effective demand'?

(a) Sarah is struggling to survive on her grant but would love to go on a summer world tour.
(b) Bill Gates decides to buy 3 million WAP mobile phones this month.
(c) John has hit the jackpot in the national lottery and orders six new Ferraris.
(d) 'Guidelines', a small publishing consultancy, makes an offer for News International owned by Rupert Murdoch.

2 Other things remaining equal, which *one* of the following will result in a *movement along* the demand curve for petrol?

(a) A rise in the real income of consumers
(b) A fall in the price of cars
(c) A rise in the price of petrol
(d) A change of consumer tastes away from private transport and towards public transport

3 Other things remaining equal, which *two* of the following will result in the demand curve for petrol shifting downwards and to the left (i.e. *decrease in demand*).

(a) A fall in the price of new and old cars
(b) A rise in the price of petrol
(c) A 50% cut in the price of all forms of public transport
(d) A rise in the price of new and old cars

4 Other things remaining equal, which *two* of the following will result in the supply curve for petrol shifting downwards and to the right (i.e. *increase in supply*).

(a) Rise in the price of petrol
(b) More oil being produced per day by the oil producing and exporting countries (OPEC)
(c) Rise in the price of crude oil
(d) New technology which reduces the cost of converting oil into petrol products

5 Which *two* of the following would you expect to lead to a *fall* in the price of CDs?

(a) Napster losing a court case to the CD-producing companies involving the downloading and free distribution of music
(b) Napster winning an appeal giving it the right to provide software permitting the downloading and free distribution of music
(c) New technology which results in a fall in the costs of production for CDs
(d) An increase in value added tax (VAT) levied on CDs

6 Other things remaining equal, which *two* of the following would you expect to lead to a *rise* in the price of Levi jeans?

(a) A press revelation that the outsourcing of production of Levi jeans in developing countries has involved the use of child labour
(b) An increase in the costs of raw materials used in the production of Levi jeans
(c) A massive and successful worldwide marketing campaign by Levi
(d) Other designer label clothing companies moving into the production of jeans

7 Which *one* of the following would NOT result in an increase in demand for beer (a normal good)?

(a) Rise in real incomes
(b) Rise in price of spirits
(c) Rise in price of lager, a substitute in consumption for beer
(d) No smoking policy adopted in all pubs
(e) Successful TV advertising programmes by major breweries

8 Which *one* of the following would NOT result in an increase in supply of beer in the UK?

(a) Abundant harvest of hops in Kent
(b) New technologies reducing costs of beer production
(c) Reduction in UK excise duty on beer
(d) Opening of new breweries in UK after record profits in earlier years
(e) Rise in price of spirits after the major breweries had diversified into beer and spirit production

9 Which *one* of the following would NOT tend to raise the price of fuel in the UK (other things equal)?

(a) A reduction in oil supply quotas agreed by the OPEC countries
(b) A successful government campaign to reduce new car prices in the UK
(c) Release of oil from the US oil reserve stocks
(d) A fall in the rate at which the pound sterling exchanges for the US dollar
(e) Higher than expected rates of economic growth recorded in the advanced industrialised countries

10 Which *one* of the following is NOT likely to be a feature of a pure command economy?

(a) A five-year plan
(b) Government ownership of the means of production
(c) An extensive planning bureaucracy
(d) Frequent examples of excess supply in a range of commodities
(e) Contractual rights to own and transfer property

Data response and stimulus questions

1 Look at this recent data on tea drinkers in the UK:

Thirst of a nation

- In Britain we drink 165 million cups of tea every day, the equivalent of three per person.
- The UK tea market is worth £66m annually.
- Tea outsells coffee by 2 to 1 in tonnage.
- The average cup of tea contains 50 mg of caffeine – half the amount in filter coffee.
- 98% of people in the UK take milk in their tea.
- 93% of tea drunk is made from tea bags.
- 42% of the nation's fluid intake today will be tea.
- There are more than 3,000 tea varieties.

Suggest changes in the *conditions of demand* for tea that might result in each of the following:

(a) an *increase* in demand for tea
(b) a *decrease* in demand for tea.

2 The supply and demand situation for product X is as follows.

Price of X (£ per unit)	Quantity demanded of X (000 units per week)	Quantity supplied of X (000 units per week)
10	20	80
9	40	70
8	60	60
7	80	50
6	100	40

(a) Draw a diagram showing the demand and supply curves for X and identify the equilibrium price and quantity.
(b) Why is £9 not an equilibrium price? Use your diagram to explain how equilibrium will be restored in a market economy.
(c) The government now introduces a maximum price of £6 per unit. Using your diagram, explore the likely consequences of such a maximum price.
(d) Suppose the government introduced a minimum price of £10 per unit. Using your diagram, explore the likely consequences of such a minimum price.

3 Coffee bars have been accused of charging excessive prices and failing to pass on dramatic falls in coffee prices to their customers. For example, Brazilian coffee is one of the most popular types and as a result of an increase in supply from growers has fallen from around £2 per pound weight in 1997 to around 50 pence per pound weight today. Yet the average price of coffee in high street coffee bars such as Starbuck's have continued to rise, for example, by over 10% in the last 12 months.

Can you use demand and supply analysis to explain any of these findings?

4 **The Oil Producing and Exporting Countries (OPEC) indicated that they would not respond further to US-led calls from consuming nations for an increased supply of oil to bring prices down from the current $35 a barrel. Ali Rodriguez, OPEC's president and Venezuelan oil minister, said OPEC's analysis was that world supply actually exceeded the world demand of 76 million barrels per day (bpd) by 1.4 million bpd at the OPEC target price of $25 a barrel, but that prices were currently 'artificially' high because countries were now adding to their global stocks of crude oil which they had previously allowed to fall to extremely low levels.**

Use demand and supply diagrams to explain the analysis presented by Ali Rodriguez.

True/False questions

1 If the government sets a *minimum price* for a product which is lower than the equilibrium market price, this will have no effect on the equilibrium price and output.
True/False

2 If the government sets a *maximum price* which is higher than the equilibrium market price, this will have no effect on the equilibrium price and output.
True/False

3 If the government sets a *minimum price* higher than the equilibrium market price, we can (at least initially) expect price to rise and for there to be excess supply in the market.
True/False

4 A benefit of a pure command economy is that consumer preferences, expressed through the marketplace, determine resource allocation.
True/False

5 If OPEC members produce more than their quotas, then world oil price is likely to rise.
True/False

Essay-type questions

1 Use your knowledge of the price mechanism to explain why strawberries are cheaper in the summer in the UK than they are in the winter.
2 Explain how the price mechanism might be applied to easing the problems of traffic congestion in city centres.
3 Why is there a thriving 'black market' for tickets at Wimbledon? How might this problem be overcome?
4 Why have most countries adopted some form of the 'mixed economy' in allocating resources?

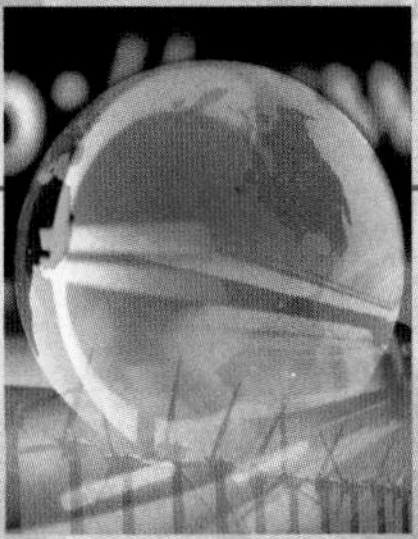

Chapter 2

Demand, revenue and consumer behaviour

Introduction

In this chapter we take further our discussions on the demand curve in Chapter 1. Why do some businesses claim that cutting prices is vital to their future prospects, whilst others insist on raising prices? How should a business respond to the price cuts or price rises of a rival? Is there any reason to link the future prospects of the business to changes in household or national income? We shall see that the 'elasticity' concept as applied to demand plays a key role in determining the firm's response to such questions and will help you understand the economic and business principles which influence many of the revenue-based strategies adopted by individual firms. The chapter concludes by examining those aspects of consumer behaviour which underpin the so-called 'law of demand' which predicts a rise in consumer purchases of a product as its price falls.

Learning objectives:

By the end of this chapter you should be able to:

- explain the meaning of price elasticity of demand and identify the factors influencing its value
- relate price elasticity of demand to business turnover (revenue)
- show how the impact on price from taxing a product (i.e. tax incidence) depends on the price elasticity of demand for that product
- outline other types of 'elasticity' of demand (such as cross elasticity and income elasticity) and assess their importance to a business
- consider the relevance of the 'Veblen effect' to consumer behaviour
- understand the relevance of utility to consumer behaviour, as in explaining the downward sloping demand curve (i.e. the 'law of demand')
- define and apply the idea of consumer surplus.

Price elasticity of demand (PED)

In Chapter 1 the demand curve for a product X was drawn sloping downwards from left to right, indicating a sensitivity of demand for the product to changes in its own price. But will demand for X change substantially or hardly at all as the price of X varies? It will obviously be helpful to have a broadly accepted *measure* of such responsiveness.

Price elasticity of demand (PED) is a measure of the responsiveness of demand for a product to a change in its own price. PED assumes that as the price of X changes, other things (the conditions of demand) remain equal, so it involves *movements along* the demand curve (expansion/contraction) rather than shifts in the demand curve (increase/decrease).

The PED for product X is given by the equation:

$$\text{PED} = \frac{\%\ \text{change in quantity demanded of X}}{\%\ \text{change in price of X}}$$

Strictly speaking, the sign of PED for a product is negative, since a fall in price of X will lead to an expansion of demand for X (+/− = −). For example, if a 2% fall in price of X results in a 6% expansion in demand, then PED is +6/−2 = −3. However, we usually ignore the sign of PED when expressing the numerical values.

Table 2.1 outlines the different numerical values (ignoring the sign) for price elasticity of demand, together with the terminology used and what it actually means.

Table 2.1 Price elasticity of demand: numerical value, terminology and description

Numerical value	Terminology	Description
0	Perfectly inelastic demand	Whatever the % change in price no change in quantity demanded (Figure 2.1a)
$> 0 < 1$	Relatively inelastic demand	A given % change in price leads to a smaller % change in quantity demanded (Figure 2.1b)
1	Unit elastic demand	A given % change in price leads to exactly the same % change in quantity demanded (Figure 2.1c)
$> 1 < \infty$	Relatively elastic demand	A given % change in price leads to a larger % change in quantity demanded (Figure 2.1d)
∞ (infinity)	Perfectly elastic demand	An infinitely small % change in price leads to an infinitely large % change in quantity demanded (Figure 2.1e)

Figure 2.1 gives a visual impression of each of these price elasticity situations.

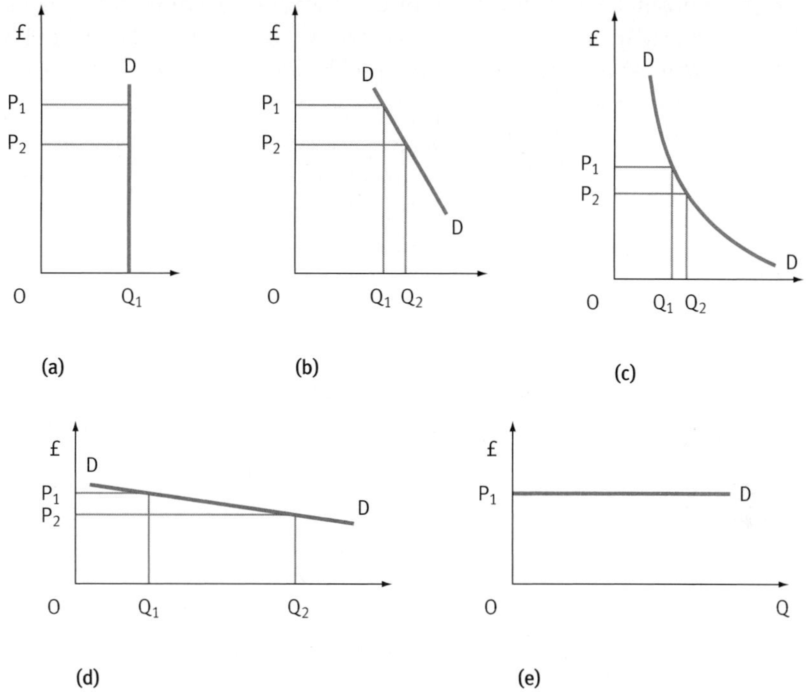

Fig 2.1 Visual presentations of price elasticity of demand

Checkpoint 1 Can you suggest why relying on visual presentation alone in Figures 2.1(b) and (d) might give a misleading impression of the true price elasticity of demand?

Factors affecting PED

The numerical value of PED depends on a number of factors, including:

1 *The availability of substitutes in consumption.* The more numerous and closer the substitutes available, the more elastic the demand. A small percentage change in price of X can then lead to a large percentage change in the quantity demanded of X as consumers switch towards or away from these substitutes in consumption.

2 *The nature of the need satisfied by the product.* The more possible it is to classify the need as being in the luxury category, the more price sensitive consumers tend to be and the more elastic the demand. The more basic or necessary the need, the less price sensitive consumers tend to be and the less elastic the demand.

3 *The time period.* The longer the time period, the more elastic the demand (consumers take time to adjust their consumption patterns to a change in price).

4 *The proportion of income spent on the product.* The greater the proportion of income spent on the product, the more elastic the demand will tend to be. A given percentage change in the price of a product which plays an important role in the consumer's total spending pattern is more likely to be noticed by the consumer and thereby to influence future purchasing intentions (see also the idea of 'income effect', p. 693).

5 *The number of uses available to the product.* The greater the flexibility of the product in terms of the number of uses to which it can be put, the more elastic the demand. Of course, the greater the number of uses available to the product, the more substitute products there will tend to be (point 1 above).

CHECK THE NET

The Business Owners Toolkit has a section on pricing and elasticity: www.toolkit.cch.com

Price elasticity of demand (PED) and revenue

For a business to make sensible decisions as to the price it should charge, it will help to be aware of the linkage between PED and total revenue (turnover). The 'box' diagram shown in Figure 2.2 helps explain this linkage using a straight line (linear) demand curve (DD).

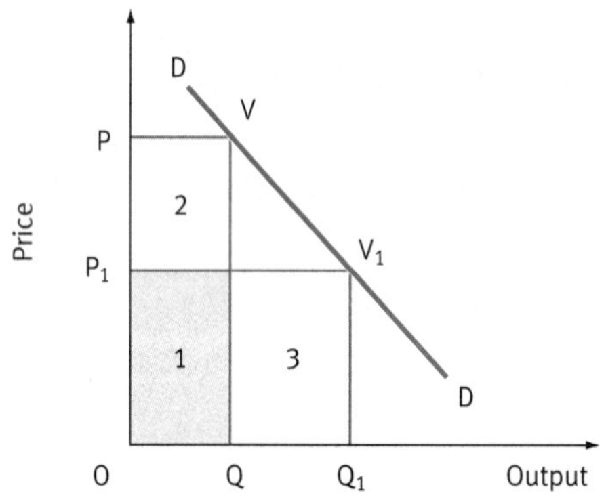

Fig 2.2 Box diagram to show how revenue varies with output for a linear demand curve

We can see that with the initial price at OP, total revenue (price × quantity) is shown by area OPVQ. A fall in price to OP_1 will lead to an expansion of demand to OQ_1 and a new total revenue indicated by area $OP_1V_1Q_1$. Clearly Area 1 is common to both total revenue situations, but here Area 2 is lost and Area 3 gained. The loss of Area 2 is due to selling the original OQ units at a now lower price; the gain of Area 3 is due to the lower price attracting new $(Q–Q_1)$ consumers for the product.

Watch out!

In this and other chapters of this book you will come across various signs which it is important to be familiar with.

$>$ greater than
$\geqslant$ great than or equal to
$<$ less than
$\leqslant$ less than or equal to
∞ infinity

The relationships listed in Table 2.2 will hold true for the box diagram.

Table 2.2 PED and revenue

Numerical value of PED	Relationship between Area 2 and Area 3
1	Area 3 = Area 2
>1	Area 3 $>$ Area 2
<1	Area 3 $<$ Area 2

We can now use these relationships to make a number of predictions involving price changes and total revenue.

Price changes and total revenue

- For *price reductions* along a **unit elastic** demand curve (PED = 1) or segment of a demand curve, there will be no change in total revenue (Area 3 = Area 2).
- For *price reductions* along a **relatively elastic** demand curve (PED $> 1 < \infty$) or segment of a demand curve, total revenue will increase as there is a more than proportionate response of extra consumers to the now lower price (Area 3 $>$ Area 2).
- For *price reductions* along a **relatively inelastic** demand curve (PED $> 0 < 1$) or segment of a demand curve, total revenue will decrease as there is a less than proportionate response of extra consumers to the now lower price (Area 3 $<$ Area 2).

Checkpoint 2 Now rework these predictions for a *price increase* in each of the three situations.

Example:

Price inelastic demand

In March 2004 it was reported that the *Daily Mirror* was to raise its price from 32p to 35p, which analysts said would increase revenues by £14m in the rest of 2004 whilst leaving its 19% market share unchanged. Clearly the presumption here is that the *Daily Mirror* has a price inelastic demand, with the price rise of over 9% expected to result in a much smaller percentage contraction in quantity demanded, thereby raising total revenue.

Case Study 2.1 shows how the link between price elasticity of demand and revenue is an important consideration when setting prices for cross-Channel crossings.

Case Study 2.1 Channel Tunnel revenues collapse

The Channel Tunnel in 2004 is still only carrying half the number of passengers it was built to carry some 10 years after it began operations. Price cuts in 2003 had been introduced by Eurotunnel, the operator of the Channel Tunnel, to raise revenues. These price cuts for using the Channel Tunnel reduced the costs for operators and resulted in around 20% cuts on average in fares on Le Shuttle, which is owned by Eurotunnel, and transports cars, buses and trucks through the tunnel. The result of these lower fares did indeed allow Le Shuttle to take a greater share of the cross-Channel market, with the number of cars on its shuttle services expanding by 4%, to around 1.1 million in the six months following the price cuts. However revenues did not rise, they actually fell by 11% to £149m. Eurotunnel expressed great disappointment at this outcome.

Eurotunnel, as well as operating Le Shuttle itself, is the owner of the Channel Tunnel and allows other train operators to use its infrastructure – including Eurostar, EWS and SNCF. These companies pay Eurotunnel a fee in proportion to the number of passengers and vehicles they carry – but they too have been unable to increase passengers and vehicles significantly even after passing on the lower costs of using the Channel Tunnel as lower fares to users. For example, Eurostar alone had been hoping to carry more than 13 million passengers annually by 2004 but by that date the figure had reached little more than 7 million passengers. Indeed the price cuts introduced by Eurostar following the reduction in Channel Tunnel costs seemed to have had little effect, with the Eurostar services between Waterloo and Paris carrying just 2.8 million passengers in the first half of 2003, compared with 3.2 million in the first half of 2002 when it charged higher prices for passengers.

Of course, one of the problems facing Eurotunnel is the competing means of crossing the Channel, in particular the use of ferries and low cost airlines. These have also been involved in price cutting strategies with what has in effect been a 'price war' between the tunnel, ferries and low-cost airlines to capture cross-Channel passengers.

Questions

1. Use your knowledge of price elasticity of demand to help explain the 'disappointment' of Eurotunnel and other Channel Tunnel transporting companies in seeing their revenues fall from price-cutting strategies.
2. As well as price elasticity of demand, what other reasons might explain this fall in revenue of Channel Tunnel transporting companies after cutting their prices?

Measuring price elasticity of demand (PED)

It is clearly vital that the firm has an accurate estimate of price elasticity of demand over the relevant segment of its demand curve if it is to correctly forecast the revenue consequences of any proposed price change.

So far we have tended to suppose that the *whole* demand curve is relatively elastic, relatively inelastic or unit elastic. However, this is rarely the case, except for the three situations of perfectly inelastic demand, unit elastic demand and perfectly elastic demand curves shown earlier in Figure 2.1(a), (c) and (e) respectively.

In most cases price elasticity of demand *varies along different segments* of the same demand curve. Box 2.1 presents the reasoning behind this important observation.

Box 2.1 **Variations in PED along a demand curve**

For simplicity we assume a straight-line (linear) demand curve, as in Figure 2.3(a).

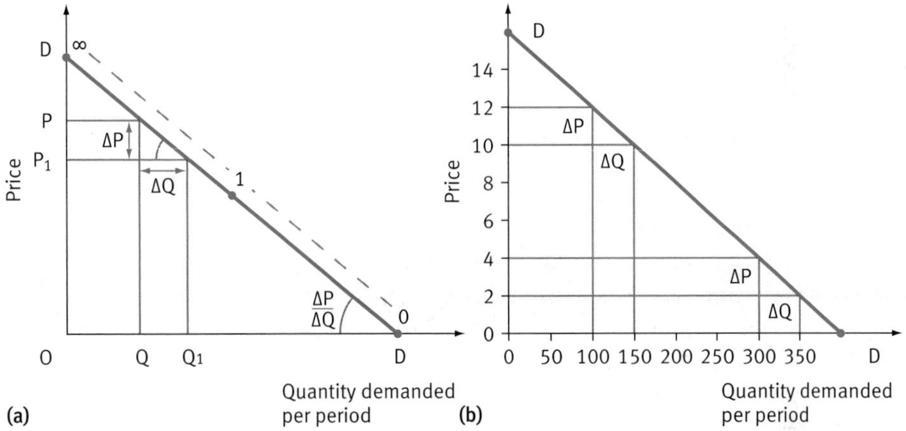

Fig 2.3 PED varies along the linear demand curve

P, Q is the initial price and quantity
P_1, Q_1 is the new price and quantity
Δ indicates the absolute change in the price or quantity

$$\text{PED} = \frac{\text{percentage change in quantity demanded}}{\text{percentage change in price}}$$

$$= \frac{(\Delta Q/Q) \times 100}{(\Delta P/P) \times 100}$$

$$= \frac{\Delta Q}{Q} \div \frac{\Delta P}{P} \quad \text{(100s cancel out)}$$

$$= \frac{\Delta Q}{Q} \times \frac{P}{\Delta P} \quad \text{(change} \div \text{to} \times\text{)}$$

$$= \frac{P}{Q} \times \frac{\Delta Q}{\Delta P} \quad \text{(rearranging)}$$

$$\boxed{\text{PED} = \frac{P}{Q} \times K \quad \text{(a constant)}}$$

Note that we are multiplying the ratio P/Q by a *constant value* (K), since the slope of the demand curve does not change over its entire length.*

We can use this expression to show that the value of price elasticity will vary all the way along the demand curve DD, from infinity (∞) to zero as we move down the demand curve from left to right.

- At the top end of the demand curve (DD), the ratio P/Q is close to infinity where the demand curve cuts the vertical axis (large P, infinitely small Q), and infinity times a constant (K) is infinity.
- At the bottom end of the demand curve (DD), the ratio P/Q is close to zero where the demand curve cuts the horizontal axis (infinitely small P, large Q), and zero times a constant (K) is zero.

We can apply our analysis to the actual demand curve shown in Figure 2.3(b).

For the straight-line demand curve $\Delta Q/\Delta P$ is a constant at $+50/-2 = (-)25$

- When P = 12, PED = $\frac{12}{100} \times (-)25 = (-)3$
- When P = 4, PED = $\frac{4}{300} \times (-)25 = (-)\frac{1}{3}$

* Note that $\frac{\Delta Q}{\Delta P} = 1 \div \frac{\Delta P}{\Delta Q}$ i.e. 1 ÷ the slope of the demand curve

1 divided by a constant is itself a constant (K)

Prediction For a straight-line demand curve, PED falls from infinity to zero as price falls, since the ratio P/Q falls and the ratio $\Delta Q/\Delta P$ is a constant.

Non-linear demand curve

If the demand curve is *not* a straight line (i.e. it is non-linear) then we have a further problem since the ratio $\Delta Q/\Delta P$ will no longer be a constant. Clearly the ratio $\Delta Q/\Delta P$ in Figure 2.4 will now vary depending on the *magnitude* of the price change from P and the *direction* of the price change from P. This is one of the reasons why alternative

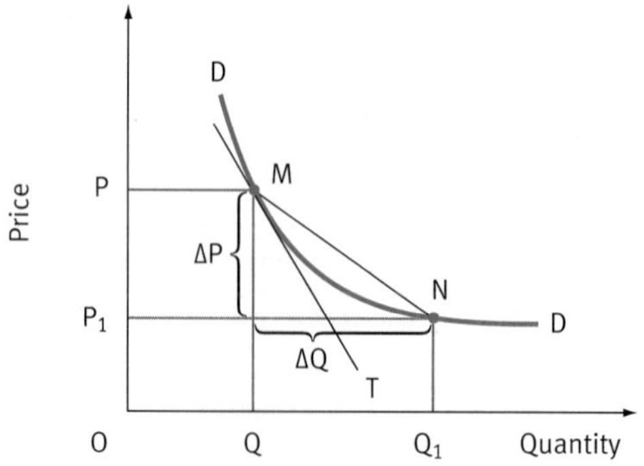

Fig 2.4 Arc and point elasticities for the non-linear demand curve

measures of price elasticity of demand are used, namely 'arc elasticity' and 'point elasticity'.

Arc elasticity of demand

As is shown in Figure 2.4, this measure is a type of 'average' elasticity between two points (i.e. two different price and quantity situations) on a demand curve. It is particularly useful when the demand curve is not a straight line.

Instead of using only the initial price and quantity values in measuring PED, the concept of *arc elasticity* uses the average of the initial and final values. If, using Figure 2.4, P and Q are the initial price and quantity respectively and P_1 and Q_1 are the final price and quantity, then we can write:

$$\text{Arc elasticity of demand} = \frac{\frac{P + P_1}{2}}{\frac{Q + Q_1}{2}} \times \frac{\Delta Q}{\Delta P} \qquad \text{(2s cancel out)}$$

$$\textbf{Arc elasticity of demand} = \frac{P + P_1}{Q + Q_1} \times \frac{\Delta Q}{\Delta P}$$

The arc elasticity is a measure of *average* elasticity. In Figure 2.4 it is the elasticity at the mid-point of the chord connecting the two points (M and N) on the demand curve corresponding to the initial and final price levels.

Clearly, arc elasticity is only an approximation to the true elasticity over a particular segment (MN) of the demand curve. The greater the curvature of the segment of the demand curve being measured, the less accurate will this approximation of the true elasticity be.

Box 2.2 Example of arc elasticity

Suppose that demand for widgets is non-linear and that in 2004, at a price of £4 per widget, the demand was 10 million widgets per annum. In 2005 let us suppose that the price falls to £2 and, other things being equal, the demand expands to 13 million widgets per annum.

To find arc elasticity of demand we can use the following formula.

$$e_p = \frac{P + P_1}{Q + Q_1} \times \frac{\Delta Q}{\Delta P}$$

e_p = arc elasticity of demand
P = the original price in 2004 (£)
P_1 = the new price in 2005 (£)
Q = the original quantity demanded in 2004 (in millions)
Q_1 = the new quantity demanded in 2005 (in millions)
Δ = absolute change

Thus the calculation is as follows:

$$e_p = \frac{4+2}{10+13} \times \frac{3}{-2}$$

$$= \frac{18}{-46}$$

$$= (-)0.39$$

Demand is relatively inelastic with respect to price and hence we can expect total revenue to fall as price falls, which indeed it does from £40m to £26m.

Point elasticity of demand

As is also shown in Figure 2.4, this is a measure of the price elasticity of demand *at a single point* (i.e. a single price and quantity situation) on a demand curve. Again it is a particularly useful measure when the demand curve is not a straight line. It involves finding the slope (–) $\frac{\Delta Q}{\Delta P}$ of the straight line that just touches the demand curve at that point (i.e. the slope of the *tangent* MT) as given by the angle formed at point M in Figure 2.4. Then, using our formula from Box 2.1 (p. 51), we multiply this slope by the price/quantity ratio.

Definition

Point elasticity of demand $= \frac{P}{Q} \times$ slope of tangent at point M.

Example:

Suppose we wish to estimate *point elasticity of demand* at the original price (P) in our widget example from Box 2.2. The slope of the tangent MT at point M (sometimes referred to as dQ/dP) is, say, (–)0.5.

Point elasticity of demand $= \frac{4}{10} \times (-)0.5 = (-)0.2$

The point elasticity of demand is even less elastic than arc elasticity of demand.

Total, average and marginal revenue

We have already mentioned total revenue (turnover) and linked this to price elasticity of demand. It may be useful at this stage to look a little more carefully at three widely used definitions of revenue, namely total, average and marginal revenue, before linking all of them to price elasticity of demand.

Total revenue

The firm's *total revenue* is its total earnings from the sale of its product. Where the firm's product is sold to all consumers at the *same* price, then total revenue is simply price (P) multiplied by quantity sold (Q).

$$\text{Total revenue} = \text{price} \times \text{quantity}$$
$$TR = P \times Q$$

Average revenue

The firm's *average revenue* is simply total revenue (TR) divided by quantity sold (Q). When the firm sells all its output at the same price, then price (P) and average revenue (AR) are identical.

$$\text{Average revenue} = \frac{\text{Total revenue}}{\text{Total output}}$$
$$AR = \frac{TR}{Q} = \frac{P \times Q}{Q} = P$$

It follows that in this situation the demand curve of the firm is the average revenue (AR) curve, since it tells us the price (AR) consumers are willing to pay for any given quantity of the product.

Marginal revenue

The firm's *marginal revenue* is the addition to total revenue from selling the last unit of output. Marginal revenue can also be defined as the rate of change of total revenue. As we see from Question 1 in Activity 2.1 below, the MR curve will lie inside a downward sloping demand (AR) curve.

Example:

Suppose 5 units of product can be sold at £100 per unit and 6 units of product can be sold at £90 per unit.

- The *total revenue* from 5 units (TR_5) would be £500 (P × Q) and the *average revenue* (P) £100.
- The *total revenue* from 6 units (TR_6) would be £540 (P × Q) and the *average revenue* (P) £90.
- The *marginal revenue* from selling the 6th unit (MR_6) would be £540 (TR_6) – £500 (TR_5) = £40. In other words selling the last (6th) unit of output adds £40 to total revenue.

CHECK THE NET

You can visit individual company websites to see how they project their future demand, revenue and pricing situations. For example:

Virgin's website is www.Virgin.com
Procter & Gamble's website is www.pg.com
Coca-Cola is www.cocacola.com
McDonald's website is www.mcdonalds.com

More generally, as regards the nth unit:

$$MR_n = TR_n - TR_{n-1}$$

PED and tax incidence

Having introduced the idea of price elasticity of demand (PED), it will be useful to consider its role in determining the extent to which a tax on a product (indirect tax) can be passed on to the consumer as a higher price. This is often referred to as the *incidence* of the tax on the consumer.

Types of tax

We saw in Chapter 1 (p. 16) that an increase in tax on a product will shift the supply vertically upwards (and to the left), i.e. a decrease in supply. This is because the producer will need to charge a *higher* price after the tax is imposed, in order to receive the same revenue per unit as was the case before the tax. In other words, any given quantity will now only be supplied at a higher price.

- *Lump-sum tax*. This is a constant absolute amount of tax (e.g. £1 per unit) irrespective of price. The supply curve shifts vertically upwards by £1 at all points, i.e. a parallel shift from S to S_1 in Figure 2.5(a).
- *Percentage (ad valorem) tax*. This is where the absolute amount of tax varies with the price of the product. For example, VAT at $17\frac{1}{2}$ per cent will mean more tax is paid as the price of the product rises. The supply curve shifts vertically upwards by an increasing amount as price rises, i.e. a non-parallel shift from S to S_2 in Figure 2.5(a).

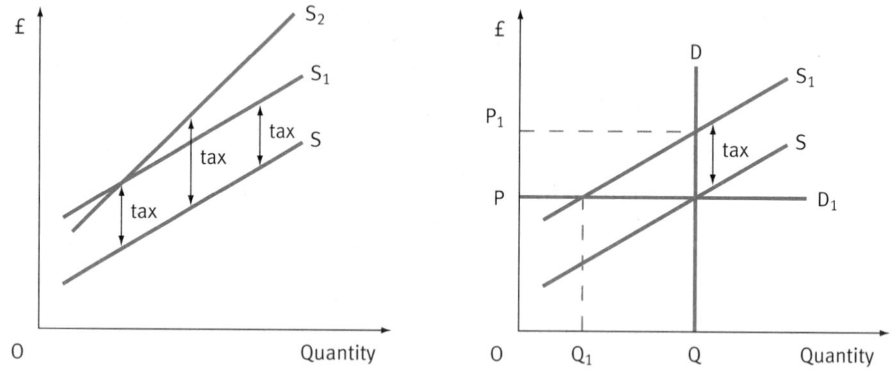

(a) Lump-sum and percentage taxes: impacts on supply (% tax results in increasing amounts of tax, ie S to S_2)

(b) Lump-sum tax: incidence of tax on consumer when demand is perfectly inelastic (D) and perfectly elastic (D_1)

Fig 2.5 Tax and tax incidence.

Tax and PED

In Figure 2.5(b) we assume, for simplicity, a lump-sum tax which shifts the supply curve S vertically upwards by the amount of the tax, giving the parallel curve S_1.

Perfectly inelastic demand

Where the demand curve is *perfectly inelastic* (D), the equilibrium price rises from P to P_1, i.e. by the full amount of the tax (equilibrium quantity is unchanged at Q).

We conclude that all the tax is passed on to the consumer, i.e.:

- 100% tax incidence on the consumer;
- 0% tax incidence on the producer.

Perfectly elastic demand

Where the demand curve is *perfectly elastic* (D_1), the equilibrium price is unchanged at P (equilibrium quantity falls to Q_1). We conclude that none of the tax is passed on to the consumer, i.e.:

- 0% tax incidence on the consumer;
- 100% tax incidence on the producer.

Relatively elastic or inelastic demand

Of course, in practice these two extreme price elasticity of demand situations are unlikely to occur. More usually the producer will be faced with *relatively inelastic demand* (Figure 2.6a) or *relatively elastic demand* (Figure 2.6b).

- Where the demand curve is *relatively inelastic* (Figure 2.6a), the producer is able to pass on the larger part of the lump sum tax *t* to the consumer in the form of a higher price. The producer only needs to absorb a small part of the tax.

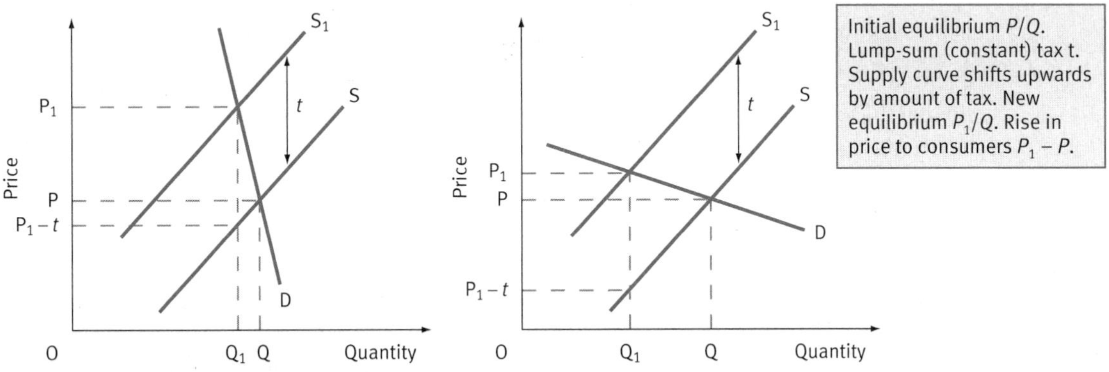

(a) Relatively inelastic demand (b) Relatively elastic demand

Fig 2.6 Lump-sum tax: incidence of tax on consumer when demand is relatively inelastic and relatively elastic.

- Where the demand curve is *relatively elastic* (Figure 2.6b), then the producer is less able to pass on the tax t to the consumer and instead the producer must absorb the larger part of the tax.

We conclude that:

- the *more inelastic* the demand, the greater the tax incidence on the consumer, and the smaller the tax incidence on the producer;
- the *more elastic* the demand, the smaller the tax incidence on the consumer, and the greater the tax incidence on the producer.

Case Study 2.2 provides some data on the impacts of higher taxes on French cigarettes.

Case Study 2.2 Taxing French smokers

President Chirac has called for 2004 to be a 'year of results' in terms of fulfilling his pledge to French electors in 2002 to cut smoking by 30% among young people and by 20% among adults within 5 years. To the delight of campaigners, cigarettes sales in France are estimated to have fallen 12–13% in 2003, following a 3.5% fall in 2002. The cumulative impact of tax rises, i.e. 8.6% in 2002, 11% in January 2003, 20% in October 2003 and 8–10% in January 2004 – is starting to bite. Studies consistently show that taxation and pregnancy are the two most effective ways of stopping smoking.

The chairman of the French Alliance Versus Tobacco, an umbrella organisation for 29 anti-smoking helplines, Gerard Dubois, said that it was unprecedented and that calls to quit-smoking helplines have risen seven-fold in the past year. Also, sales of nicotine gum and patches, made by pharmaceutical giants such as GSK and Pfizer, have increased 89% in the year to September, while turnover of Zyban, an anti-depressant taken by many people giving up smoking, is up 20%.

Campaigners regret, however, that the government is not pressing its advantage further. The political clout of France's 32,000 tobacconists, furious that French cigarettes are now the most expensive in the EU after those sold in the UK, has prompted Jean-Pierre Raffarin, prime minister, to promise a four-year freeze on cigarette duties. This is expected to apply from this year.

The concession to powerful *buralistes* is the latest measure to pacify this group of opinion formers ahead of this year's elections. As many of France's 11 million smokers pass through their local *tobac* on a regular basis, their owners, who often run bars and small bistros on the side, are in a position to bend the ear of a large proportion of the electorate.

After the January 2004 8–10% increase in cigarette taxes, the average pack of 20 costs around €5 ($5.85, £3.50) in France, compared with just €2.50 in neighbouring Spain and €2.90 in Luxembourg.

Case Study 2.2 continued

The French government estimates that more than a third of French adults smoke, of whom half want to stop. France also has the highest proportion of young smokers in Europe, with 53% of 15–24-year-olds counting themselves as regular smokers, compared with an EU average of 41%.

Questions

1. What does the case study tell us about the price elasticity of demand for cigarettes in France?
2. Consider some of the implications for other products of raising taxes sharply on French cigarettes.
3. Can you identify any constraints for the French government in seeking to raise cigarette taxes still further?

Tax and government revenue

A possible motive for raising indirect taxes on products is, of course, for the government to generate additional tax revenue. Price elasticity of demand for the taxed product will play a key role in determining the impact of such tax increases on government revenue. As we can see from Figure 2.7, the more inelastic the demand for the product, the smaller the impact of any given lump-sum tax on the quantity of the product purchased and therefore the greater the government tax-take (tax per unit × quantity purchased). The tax-take (government revenue) is indicated by the

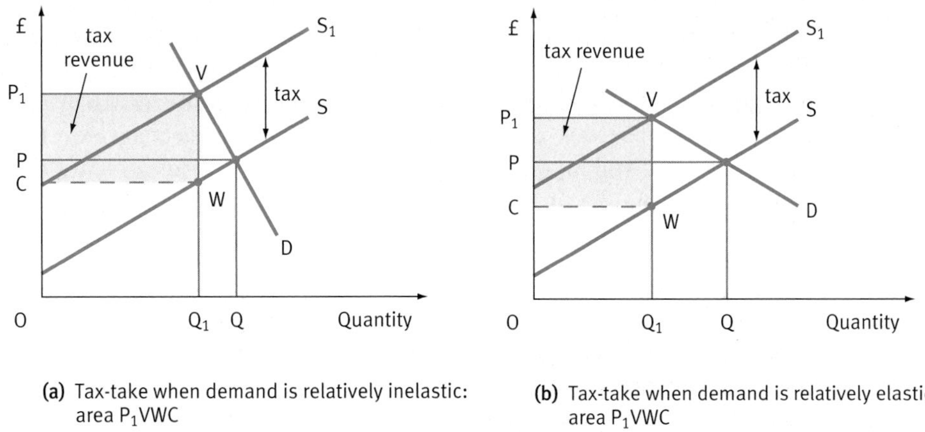

(a) Tax-take when demand is relatively inelastic: area P_1VWC

(b) Tax-take when demand is relatively elastic: area P_1VWC

Fig 2.7 Price elasticities of demand and government revenue from a lump-sum tax.

shaded rectangle P_1VWC, which is clearly greater when demand is relatively inelastic, as in Figure 2.7(a).

It is hardly surprising, therefore, that the Chancellor of the Exchequer has tended to impose higher taxes on goods and services such as cigarettes, alcoholic drinks and gambling, all of which have relatively inelastic demands. Not only can the Chancellor claim to be taxing unhealthy lifestyles (so-called 'sin taxes'), but he can rest assured that he will be raising much-needed revenue for the Exchequer. Or can he?

It is certainly true that most empirical estimates indicate relatively inelastic demands for tobacco, drink and gambling. For example, estimates of PED for cigarettes in both the US and UK are in the range (−)0.2 to (−)0.6. However there is increasing evidence that the impacts of globalisation which are considered throughout this book (e.g. Chapter 15, pp. 624–637) may be imposing new constraints on governments seeking to raise revenue via indirect taxation. Case Study 2.3 looks at the impacts of increased levels of smuggling on the revenue raised from tobacco taxes.

Case Study 2.3 Tobacco smuggling, price elasticity of demand and tax revenue

One of the impacts of the increased geographical mobility and more open borders which have accompanied globalisation has been a dramatic increase in smuggling activities. For example, tobacco smuggling features in many reports as Britain's fastest-growing category of crime. Customs and Excise estimate that around £3bn is lost in revenue each year from tobacco smuggling, including cross-Channel bootlegging, large-scale freight smuggling from outside the EU and the diversion to the home market of cigarettes officially designated for export. The VAT and excise duty lost has been estimated as equivalent to around 30% of the amount actually collected.

In fact the UK Chancellor of the Exchequer, Gordon Brown, was advised when preparing his recent Budgets to rethink any additional tax rises planned for tobacco. This advice was in recognition of the huge differences already existing between UK tobacco prices and those in other EU countries, thereby providing a huge incentive for smuggling. For example, a 50-gram pinch of hand-rolled tobacco which costs around £8 in British shops can be bought in Belgium for less than £2. The result of these price differences is that bootlegged sales now account for 80% of the UK market in hand-rolling tobacco. Customs and Excise also estimates that in the north of England around half of all packets of cigarettes sold are contraband. In the past three years trade in smuggled cigarettes has nearly doubled. The government has found that its revenue from tobacco is one-third less in 2004 than it was in 1999, largely due to smuggling.

Studies by the Treasury recommend the use of X-ray scanners at Channel ports, 'duty-paid' marks on packs, and heavier penalties for those caught smuggling, but have also told Mr Brown that such counter-measures would not work unless the price gap between legitimate and smuggled goods was narrowed. These studies also point to the fact that Canada, Sweden, Denmark and Switzerland have all reduced tobacco smuggling by cutting duty rates.

Case Study 2.3 continued

Questions

1 What does the case study imply is happening, as a result of increased smuggling, to the effective price elasticity of demand for tobacco in the UK?

2 Consider the advantages and disadvantages of the Chancellor following the advice to avoid raising taxes on tobacco.

3 Suggest any implications this case study might have for the French policy towards tobacco users outlined in Case Study 2.2 (p. 58).

Activity 2.1 gives you the opportunity to check your understanding of price elasticity of demand and its links to total revenue and to tax incidence.

Activity 2.1

1 (a) Complete the table.

Quantity (units)	AR (£)	TR (£)	MR (£)
1	100		
2	95		
3	90		
4	85		
5	80		
6	75		
7	70		
8	65		

(b) Draw the AR and MR curves. What do you notice?

2 In this question you'll see a lettered description of a particular situation involving PED. In each case try to match the letter for the description with the number (i) to (v) representing the correct term.

Descriptions

(a) A 5% fall in the price of lager leads to a 3% expansion in the amount of lager consumed.

(b) A 10% rise in the price of books leads to a 15% contraction in the number of books purchased.

(c) A 6% fall in the price of package tours leads to a 6% expansion in the number of package tours purchased.

(d) An infinitely small percentage change in the price of wheat leads to an infinitely large percentage change in world demand for wheat.

(e) A 10% rise in the price of kidney transplants in private sector hospitals leads to no change in demand for these transplants.

Terms

(i) Perfectly inelastic demand
(ii) Relatively inelastic demand
(iii) Unit elastic demand
(iv) Relatively elastic demand
(v) Perfectly elastic demand

3 True or false

(a) Demand for coach travel is relatively elastic, so lower fares can be expected to raise total revenue for the coach company. True/False

(b) Demand for rail transport is relatively inelastic so a rise in fares can be expected to reduce total revenue for the train operating company. True/False

(c) Price elasticity of demand for air travel has a numerical value (ignoring sign) of 3, so a 1% cut in price will lead to a 3% expansion of demand and a rise in total revenue. True/False

(d) A certain make of shoes has been found to have a unit elastic demand. A 5% rise in price can be expected to result in a 5% contraction of demand and an unchanged total revenue. True/False

4 Multiple choice questions

(a) Which *two* of these examples involve 'price elasticity of demand'?
(i) A fall in the price of beer has resulted in higher beer sales on campus.
(ii) The higher prices of books means that students are going to the cinema less often.
(iii) A fall in student income has led to fewer books being bought.
(iv) Rents in halls of residence have increased so less students are now applying for this type of accommodation.

(b) Which *one* of these statements is true?
(i) Price elasticity of demand tells us about shifts in the demand curve.
(ii) Price elasticity of demand tells us how demand for a product responds to changes in the price of substitutes in consumption.
(iii) Price elasticity of demand tells us about movements along the demand curve.
(iv) Price elasticity of demand tells us how demand for a product responds to changes in the price of complements in consumption.

(c) Which *two* of these statements are true?
(i) Strictly speaking, the sign of price elasticity of demand is negative.
(ii) Strictly speaking, the sign of price elasticity of demand is positive.
(iii) If a 5% fall in price results in a 10% expansion in quantity demanded, then demand is 'relatively inelastic'.
(iv) If a 5% fall in price results in a 10% expansion in quantity demanded, then demand is 'relatively elastic'.

(d) Which *one* of the following would be likely to result in a small percentage fall in price of Levi jeans, leading to a large percentage expansion in quantity of Levi jeans demanded.
(i) Few alternative makes of jeans are available to consumers.
(ii) Many alternative makes of jeans are available to consumers.
(iii) Levi jeans are withdrawn from high street shops and can only now be purchased by mail order.
(iv) The advertising budget for Levi jeans is sharply reduced.

(e) Which *one* of these statements is true?
  (i) The more inelastic the demand, the greater the incidence of a tax on the producer.
  (ii) The more elastic the demand, the smaller the incidence of a tax on the consumer.
  (iii) If demand is perfectly inelastic, the whole incidence of the tax will be on the producer.
  (iv) If demand is perfectly elastic, the whole incidence of the tax will be on the consumer.

Answers to Checkpoints and Activities can be found on pp. 705–35.

Other elasticities of demand

Here we consider a number of other elasticities which can have important impacts on the demand for a product.

Cross elasticity of demand (CED)

CED is a measure of the responsiveness of demand for a product (X) to a change in price of *some other product* (Y). It involves shifts in a demand curve (increase/decrease) for X rather than movements along a demand curve (expansion/contraction).

The CED for product X is given by the equation:

$$\text{CED} = \frac{\text{\% change in quantity demanded of X}}{\text{\% change in the price of Y}}$$

- The *sign* of CED will indicate the direction of the shift in demand for X (D_X) in response to a change in the price of Y (P_Y), which in turn will depend upon the relationship in consumption between products X and Y.
  - Where X and Y are **substitutes in consumption**, a fall in P_Y will result in an expansion of demand for Y and a decrease in demand for X, i.e. a leftward shift in D_X as some consumers switch to the now relatively cheaper substitute for X. Here the sign of CED will be positive (−/− = +).
  - Where X and Y are **complements in consumption**, a fall in P_Y will result in an expansion of demand for Y and an increase in demand for X, i.e. a rightward shift in D_X as consumers require more of X to complement their extra purchases of Y. Here the sign of CED will be negative (+/− = −).

- The *magnitude* of the shift in D_X will depend upon how close X and Y are as substitutes or complements in consumption. The closer the two products are as substitutes or complements, the greater will be the numerical value of cross-elasticity of demand. In other words, a given fall in price of Y will cause a larger shift to the left of D_X for close substitutes, and a larger shift to the right of D_X for close complements.

Income elasticity of demand (IED)

IED is a measure of the responsiveness of demand for a product to a change in income (household income or national income). Usually we use **real income** rather than nominal income for this measurement. IED involves shifts in a demand curve (increase/decrease) rather than movements along a demand curve (expansion/contraction).

The IED for product X is given by the equation:

$$\text{IED} = \frac{\%\text{ change in quantity demanded of X}}{\%\text{ change in income}}$$

- For a *normal product* the sign of IED will be positive: for example, a rise in income increases demand for X, i.e. a rightward shift in D_X, with more of X demanded at any given price.
- For an *inferior* product the sign will be negative over certain ranges of income: for example, a rise in income beyond a certain 'threshold' level may decrease demand for X as consumers use some of the higher income to switch away from the relatively cheap but poor-quality product X to a more expensive, better-quality substitute.

As a broad rule of thumb, some people regard income elasticity of demand as useful in classifying products into 'luxury' and 'necessity' groupings. A product is often considered a luxury if IED is > 1 and a necessity if IED is significantly < 1.

Factors affecting IED

Factors affecting the numerical value of IED for a commodity include the following:

1. *The nature of the need satisfied by the commodity.* For some basic needs, e.g. certain types of foodstuffs, the proportion of household income spent on products satisfying these needs falls as income increases. For other needs, the proportion of household income spent on products satisfying these needs rises as income increases, e.g. services such as healthcare and education.
2. *The time period.* The longer the time period, the more likely it is that consumer expenditure patterns will have adjusted to a change in income, implying a higher IED.
3. *The initial level of national income.* At low levels of national income, certain products will still be largely unattainable for the majority of the population. Changes in national income around such a low level will therefore have little effect on the demand for these products, implying a lower IED.

Box 2.3 provides a useful outline of some of the earliest work on income elasticity of demand.

Box 2.3

Income elasticity and Ernst Engel (1821–96)

Engel was appointed director of the Bureau of Statistics in Prussia and outlined what became known as Engel's Law in a paper published in 1857. The essential idea is that the proportion of income spent on food declines as income rises. In other words, food was being regarded as a necessity with an income elasticity of demand less than 1. Table 2.3 presents data on the spending patterns of 153 Belgian families he studied in 1853. This cross-sectional evidence has subsequently been verified in a range of time-series (longitudinal) data, and cross-country data. For example, in nineteenth-century America people spent some 50 per cent of their incomes on food compared to less than 20 per cent today. Again, people in the less developed countries spend higher proportions of their income on food than do people in, say, the advanced industrialised countries of the OECD.

Table 2.3 Percentage of total expenditure on various items by Belgian families in 1853

	Annual income		
Expenditure item	**\$225–\$300**	**\$450–\$600**	**\$750–\$1,000**
Food	62.0%	55.0%	50.0%
Clothing	16.0	18.0	18.0
Lodging, light and fuel	17.0	17.0	17.0
Services (education, legal, health)	4.0	7.5	11.5
Comfort and recreation	1.0	2.5	3.5
Total	100.0	100.0	100.0

Source: Reproduced in A. Marshall, *Principles of Economics*, 8th edn, London, Macmillan, 1920, p. 97. Some items have been aggregated

Engel himself was extremely cautious in interpreting his results at the time. Certainly the table data give early support for services of various forms having high income elasticities of demand.

Engel's relationship between income and the quantity demand of a product has been generalised and brought up to date in the so-called Engel curves shown in Figure 2.8.

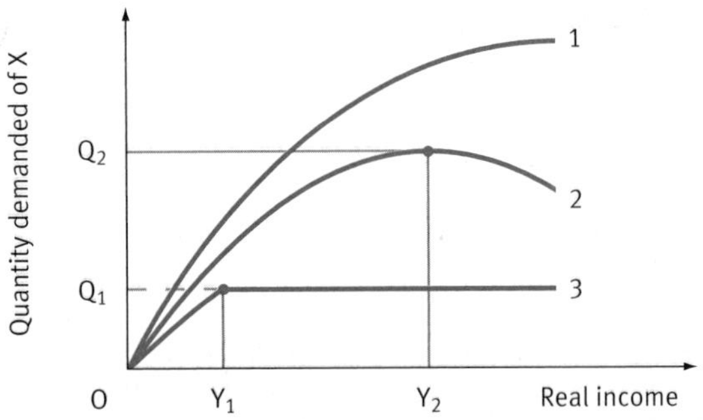

Fig **2.8** Engel curves

These Engel curves relate quantity demanded of a product to real income.

- Curve 1: a rise in real income increases demand for product X at all levels of income. X is a 'normal good'.
- Curve 2: a rise in real income increases demand for product X, but only up to the level of real income Y_2. Further rises in real income beyond Y_2 result in a decrease in demand for X. Product X is an 'inferior good'.
- Curve 3: a rise in real income increases demand for product X, but only up to the level of real income Y_1. Further rises in real income beyond Y_1 result in no change in demand for X. We say that demand for this product is 'fully satisfied' or 'satiated' at a relatively low level of real income.

Advertising elasticity of demand (AED)

This is a measure of the responsiveness of demand for product X to a change in advertising expenditure on the product. The intention of most forms of advertising is to reinforce the attachment of existing consumers to the product and to attract new consumers. In this latter case the advertising is seeking to change consumer tastes in favour of the product, i.e. shift the demand curve to the right with more of X bought at any given price.

$$\text{AED} = \frac{\%\text{ change in quantity demanded of X}}{\%\text{ change in advertising expenditure on X}}$$

A firm may also be interested in *cross-advertising elasticity*, which measures the responsiveness of demand for product X to a change in advertising expenditure on some other product Y. If X and Y are substitutes in consumption and extra advertising on the rival Y decreases demand for X substantially, then some counter-strategy by X to restore its fortunes (i.e. shift its demand curve to the right) might be of high priority, perhaps including an aggressive advertising campaign of its own.

Exam Hints!

So many questions depend on your knowledge of PED and these other elasticities. Do make sure that you are familiar with the 'box diagram' (Figure 2.2, p. 48) and that, should price be changed, you can relate the numerical value of PED to changes in total revenue.

Activity 2.2 uses a number of questions to check your understanding of these other elasticities of demand.

Activity 2.2

1 Which *two* of the following statements are true?

(a) A small rise in the price of student accommodation means that fewer books are bought, which suggests that the price elasticity of demand for books is high.

(b) A small rise in the price of student accommodation results in far fewer books bought, which suggests that there may be a high cross-elasticity of demand between the two items.

(c) The sign of the cross-elasticity of demand between two products can help indicate whether they are substitutes in consumption or complements in consumption.
(d) Cross-elasticity of demand involves movements along the demand curve for a product, not shifts in the demand curve for that product.

2 Which *two* of the following statements refer to 'income elasticity of demand'?

(a) A 1% rise in the UK's GNP will result in a 2% increase in demand for travel.
(b) A 1% fall in the price of travel will lead to a 2% expansion in the demand for travel.
(c) A 1% fall in the UK's GNP will result in a 3% decrease in demand for healthcare products.
(d) A 1% rise in the price of prescription drugs will lead to a 3% contraction in demand.

3 In this question you'll see a lettered description of a particular situation involving CED. In each case try to match the letter for the description with the number (i) to (v) representing the correct term.

Description

(a) The purchase of books from the campus bookshop falls dramatically every time the price of beer rises.
(b) A fall in the price of CDs has had no effect on the quantity of books sold.
(c) Every time the price of designer jeans falls there is a large increase in the sales of higher-quality trainers.
(d) A 5% rise in the price of cinema admissions leads to a 1% decrease in ice cream sales in the cinema.
(e) A 10% fall in the price of cigarettes leads to a 1% decrease in the purchase of cigars.

Terms

(i) Large negative value for CED
(ii) Large positive value for CED
(iii) Small negative value for CED
(iv) Small positive value for CED
(v) Zero value for CED

4 Which of the following situations would be most favourable for a company with an income elasticity of demand for its product of +3 to plan for an increase in output?

(a) Money incomes to rise by 2% and prices by 2%.
(b) Money incomes to rise by 3% and prices by 4%.
(c) Money incomes to rise by 4% and prices by 2%.
(d) Money incomes to rise by 5% and prices by 6%.
(e) Money incomes to rise by 6% and prices by 5%.

5 Football socks are found to have a cross-elasticity of demand of –2 with respect to product Y. Which of the following products is most likely to be product Y?

(a) Rugby boots
(b) Football boots
(c) Tennis socks
(d) Tennis shoes
(e) Cricket boots

6 Lager is found to have a cross-elasticity of demand of +2 with respect to product Y. Which of the following products is most likely to be product Y?
(a) Crisps
(b) Vodka
(c) Pub lunches
(d) Beer
(e) Wine

Answers to Checkpoints and Activities can be found on pp. 705–35.

The following case study uses transport to see how these different elasticity concepts can be relevant to practical policy making.

Case Study 2.4 Transport and elasticities of demand

In late 2003 fuel protests began to be heard again as the Chancellor raised the tax on petrol by 1.28 pence per litre (6 pence per gallon). Motorists and organisations such as the AA and RAC point to the fact that over 80% of the price paid at the pump now goes to the Treasury in tax, a dramatic rise on the much smaller 44% of the petrol price which went to the Treasury as recently as 1980.

Evidence from the developed economies suggests that for every 10% increase in real fuel prices, the demand for fuel will fall by around 6%. This consumer response to higher fuel prices may take several years to fully work through.

The demand for car ownership and for travel (and therefore the derived demand for fuel) is also closely related to the level of household income. Again, studies suggest that for every 10% increase in real income the demand for fuel eventually increases by around 12% within two years of the rise in real income.

Of course, the demand for fuel does not only depend on its own price and the level of real household income, but also on other factors. For example, whereas the real cost of motoring per kilometre travelled (fuel costs, car purchase, repairs, road tax etc.) has barely changed over the past 20 years (e.g. more efficient engines result in more kilometres per litre of petrol), the real costs of rail and bus per kilometre travelled have risen by more than 30% and 35% respectively over the same 20-year period. Clearly this change in *relative* costs has given a boost to demand for car ownership and travel, and therefore to the demand for fuel.

Many people argue that fuel taxes should rise even higher than they are now, since the private motorist imposes costs on society that he or she does not actually pay for. Extra motorists bring about congestion on our roads and increased journey times, increase the need for more road building with the inevitable loss of countryside, result in more carbon dioxide (CO_2) and other toxic gas emissions which damage the ozone layer and lead to global warming. In other words, many believe that the *private costs* of the motorist do not fully reflect the *social costs* imposed by the motorist.

Case Study 2.4 continued

Higher taxes on fuel will, as we have seen, raise the price of motoring and discourage road travel. For example, it has been estimated that a 10% increase in the price of fuel will lead to an extra 1% of rail passengers on rail services and an extra 0.5% of bus passengers on bus services.

Of course, demand for some products may actually *decrease* as fuel prices rise. With less car usage there may be a decrease in demand for garage-related services and products.

The *net* effect of a rise in fuel prices will depend on the sign and size of all these elasticities, namely own-price, income and cross-elasticities of demand.

Questions

1 Can you calculate any own-price, income and cross-elasticities of demand from the information given in the case study?

2 Why do some people believe that fuel taxes and fuel prices are too low?

3 Can you suggest why governments might be wary of making the motorist pay the full private and social costs of any journey?

'Veblen effect' and consumer behaviour

So far we have assumed that a fall in price will lead to an expansion of demand, and vice versa; in other words, that the demand curve slopes downwards from left to right. Later in this chapter and in Appendix 1 (p. 687) we use indifference curves to explain why this so-called 'law of demand' generally applies to most products.

However, it is worth noting at this point that there has long been a recognition that in some circumstances, the demand curve might actually slope upwards from left to right. In other words, that a rise in price results in an expansion of demand, and a fall in price a contraction of demand. For example, Thorstein Veblen, in his book *Theory of the Leisure Class* in 1899, pointed out that the key characteristic of some products is that they are ostentatious ('showy') and intended to impress. For such 'conspicuous consumption products', the satisfaction derived from their consumption derives largely from the effect this has on other people rather than from any inherent utility in the product itself.

What has become known as the 'Veblen effect' refers to the psychological association of price with quality by consumers, with a fall in price taken to imply a reduction in quality and therefore greater reluctance to purchase. Instead of expansion of demand, the fall in price may therefore result in a contraction of demand, giving us an upward-sloping demand curve. The 'Veblen effect' is more likely to operate for high-priced products in 'prestige' markets where accurate information on the true quality of these products is highly imperfect.

Case Study 2.5 looks at the issue of 'top-up fees' to be used in English universities from 2006 onwards and the suggestion that universities charging less than the maximum £3,000 per annum fee for a course may be deemed, by prospective students, to be offering poorer-quality courses even where that is not, objectively, the case.

Case Study 2.5 'Top-up fees' and the 'Veblen effect'

From September 2006 universities in England will be able to charge 'top-up fees' of between £0 and £3,000. They are called 'variable top-up fees' because the charge can vary between different courses in a given university and for the same course in different universities.

Most higher education institutions are expected to publish information on projected top-up fees by Summer 2005, with that information contained in prospectuses for entry in 2006. It is expected that most universities will charge the full £3,000 annual tuition fee on at least some courses. However, 'older' (the so-called Russell group) universities can be expected to charge this full fee across a higher proportion of courses and subjects than 'newer' universities.

A number of potential pricing (charging) principles are being actively discussed by universities.

- *Cost-plus pricing*. Here top-up fees are higher where the costs of course/subject delivery are higher. For example, science-based courses need expensive laboratories and equipment.
- *Revenue-based pricing*. Here top-up fees are higher for those courses/subjects where demand is greatest. This often means courses/subjects which are the most popular with students, sometimes because they are expected to increase employment opportunities the most and therefore raise the expected lifetime income from studying that course.
  Let us first review some studies indicating lifetime returns on undergraduate study. Considerable evidence exists to suggest that projected student lifetime returns and other benefits (e.g. lifetime employment prospects) are greater, on average, for graduates than for non-graduates.
  The *average* lifetime return for graduates vis-à-vis non-graduates has been calculated at various times in the recent past.
  - In 1988 the UK government claimed that the annual rate of return on human capital investment in the form of a degree – reflecting the additional lifetime earnings a graduate will accrue over and above those of a non-graduate – was around 25%.
  - In 1996, the Dearing Report brought this 'rate of return' estimate down to between 11% and 15%.
  - In 2001 the OECD estimated that the annual 'rate of return' on a UK degree was some 17% vis-à-vis non-graduates (higher than that in any of the ten countries studied, such as the 15% of France and 10% of the Netherlands).

Case Study 2.5 continued

- In the past few years the UK government has used a figure of £400,000 as the additional lifetime earnings for the average graduate vis-à-vis the average non-graduate.
- Data from the Department for Education and Skills 2003 focuses on comparing the lifetime earnings of those with a degree with a more specific comparator group than the 'average non-graduate'. When comparing the lifetime earnings of graduates with those who 'have the qualifications to get into higher education but choose not to go to university', the earnings premium falls from £400,000 to £120,000 over the average working lifetime.

The lifetime *employability* of graduates has also been emphasised in recent studies by the Council for Industry and Higher Education in 2003, which indicate that the overall demand for graduates is likely to exceed the growing number emerging with degrees, even should the 50% target be achieved.

Let us now review some studies indicating variations in lifetime returns by subject/course studied. Fragmentary data exists to show differential benefits to lifetime earnings of graduates by subject/course studied.

- R. Naylor and A. McKnight of the LSE (2002) showed that occupational earnings for a female graduate in law or politics were, on average, 26% higher than the earnings of an otherwise identical social science graduate.
- I. Walker of Warwick University (2002) showed that the rates of return to economics graduates were, on average, some 35% higher than for otherwise identical arts graduates.

■ *Prestige pricing*. Here price is itself associated with *quality* by users of the product. In situations where the information available to users is imperfect, price is often used as a proxy variable for quality. Student and parent assessment of educational courses characterised by differential top-up fees is an obvious candidate for such a 'Veblen' effect, reinforced by the fact that the 'older' universities (widely perceived by the general public to be of the highest quality) will be seen to charge the full £3,000 annual tuition fee for most of their courses.

A major cross-country study into higher education by IDP Education Australia in association with the British Council in 2003 strongly supports the existence of this Veblen effect as regards international student demand for higher education. Senior researcher Anthony Bohm comments: 'Students cannot make an informed choice about the exact quality of comparable products, so they use price as a proxy for understanding the value they will get out of an international programme.'

Questions

1. Suppose you were responsible for setting the top-up fees to be charged for the course you are studying. Use the ideas in the case study to suggest how you might go about making your decision.
2. Can you explain how the case study might provide some support for an upward-sloping demand curve for higher education?

Consumer surplus

LINKS

Pricing policies are discussed in many chapters of this book. However Chapter 13 (pp. 500–501) brings these various pricing approaches together in one section.

Before leaving our discussion of consumer behaviour, it is useful to consider the idea of **consumer surplus**. In its most widely used form it measures in value terms the difference between the amount of money that a consumer *actually pays* to buy a certain quantity of product X and the amount that he/she would be *willing to pay* for this quantity of X. In Figure 2.9 it is given by the area APC, where quantity X_1 is purchased at price P.

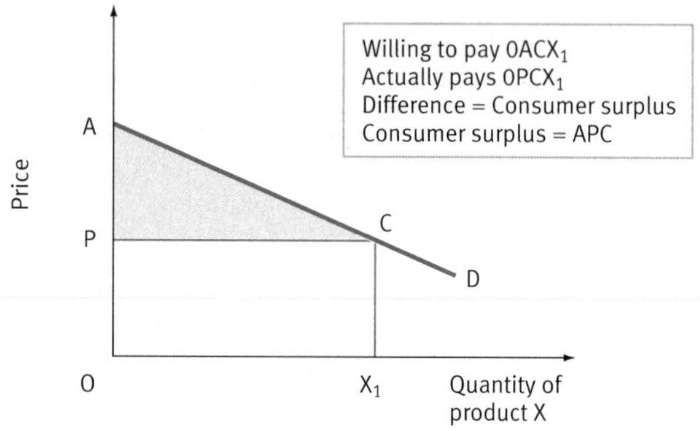

Fig 2.9 Consumer surplus

As we shall see in other parts of this book, the idea of consumer surplus is sometimes used when trying to put a value on the *economic welfare* from using resources in a particular way (e.g. Chapter 8, p. 295).

Utility and consumer behaviour

Utility refers to the satisfaction consumers derive from the consumption of goods and services (products). Utility is important because only those products which possess utility, i.e. which provide satisfaction, will be demanded. Of course, the amount of utility or satisfaction gained from consuming a product is different for different people. Nevertheless, to begin with, we simplify the situation by assuming that utility can be measured in 'units of satisfaction' as in Table 2.4.

Total and marginal utility

- **Total utility** represents the overall satisfaction from consuming a given amount of a product.
- **Marginal utility** represents the change in satisfaction from consuming an extra unit of the product.

Table 2.4 shows the different levels of total and marginal utility from consuming different amounts of drink.

Table 2.4 An individual's utility schedule

Drinks consumed	Total utility (units of satisfaction)	Marginal utility (units of satisfaction)
0	0	–
1	27	27
2	39	12
3	47	8
4	52	5
5	55	3
6	57	2
7	58	1
8	58	0
9	56	–2

We can see that *total utility* rises up to seven drinks consumed, remains unchanged for the eighth drink and actually falls for the ninth drink.

Figure 2.10 plots the data of Table 2.4 on a diagram showing the *total utility curve* and the marginal utility curve.

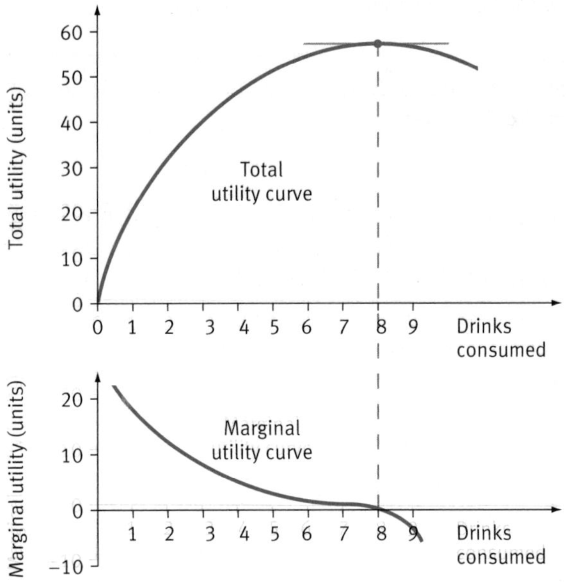

Fig 2.10 Total and marginal utility curves

Checkpoint 3

Comment on the relationship between total and marginal utility:

(a) when total utility is rising;
(b) when total utility is a maximum;
(c) when total utility is falling.

Law of diminishing marginal utility

This simply states that as extra units of a product are consumed, each extra (marginal) unit adds less and less to total utility (satisfaction). The second cold drink on a hot day may certainly increase your satisfaction, but *by less* than you gained from consuming the first cold drink! In other words, the marginal utility of the second cold drink was less than the first, and so on. Indeed the marginal utility of the eighth drink is zero in Table 2.4 and that of the ninth drink is actually negative (i.e. results in *disutility*).

Utility and the demand curve

The law of diminishing marginal utility helps to explain the general relationship between an individual's demand for a good or service and the price of that good or service. If each extra unit of a product gives less satisfaction to an individual than the previous unit, then it follows that the individual will often need the incentive of a lower price if he or she is to be encouraged to consume an extra unit. Because of this it is reasonable to assume that for an individual, as the price of a good or service falls, the amount demanded will rise (expand).

Remember

We are moving along a given demand curve as the price of the product changes – so we use the terms *expand* or *contract.*

A further assumption about utility is usually made, namely that consumers will choose between the different goods and services they might purchase in order to gain as much utility as possible, i.e. *maximise total utility*. Of course, the different combinations of goods and services actually available to the consumers will depend upon their levels of income and the prices of the goods and services.

Box 2.4 presents a more formal explanation of this linkage between marginal utility and the downward sloping demand curve.

Box 2.4 **Marginal utility and demand**

Since consumers aim to maximise their total utility, it follows that consumer equilibrium exists when a consumer cannot increase total utility by reallocating his/her expenditure. This occurs when the following condition is satisfied:

$$\frac{MU_A}{P_A} = \frac{MU_B}{P_B} = \cdots \frac{MU_n}{P_n}$$

In other words, when the ratios of marginal utility and price are equal for all products consumed.

When this condition is satisfied, it is impossible for the consumer to increase total utility by rearranging his/her purchases because the last pound spent on each product yields the same addition to total utility in all cases. This must maximise total utility because, for example, if the last pound spent on product B yielded more utility than the last pound spent on product A, then the consumer could increase total utility by buying more of B and less of A. This is impossible when the ratios of marginal utility and price are equal (see Table 2.5).

Table 2.5 Marginal utility and demand

	Product A			Product B		
Quantity consumed	**Price (£)**	**Total utility**	**Marginal utility**	**Price (£)**	**Total utility**	**Marginal utility**
1	2	15	15	4	25	25
2	2	27	12	4	48	23
3	2	37	10	4	68	20
4	2	46	9	4	86	18
5	2	53	7	4	102	16
6	2	56	3	4	116	14
7	2	57	1	4	128	12
8	2	55	−2	4	139	11

It is assumed that only two products, A which costs £2 per unit and B which costs £4 per unit, are available, and that the consumer has a total budget of £18.

Given the consumer's budget, the existing prices and the levels of utility available from consumption, equilibrium is achieved when 3 units of product A and 3 units of product B are purchased.

$$\frac{MU_A}{P_A} = \frac{MU_B}{P_B} \quad \text{with} \quad \frac{10}{2} = \frac{20}{4}$$

With a budget of £18 it is impossible to achieve a higher level of utility.

Checkpoint 4 Suppose the price of product B now falls from £4 to £2 per unit, other things equal; use the equilibrium condition to show that demand for B expands.

Whilst there are many problems in doing so, modern approaches are trying to measure the utility of different products to different people. Case Study 2.6 looks at recent attempts to put a value on a particular 'product' (namely time) as between different people.

Case Study 2.6 What is time worth?

Putting a value on time

Some recent calculations suggest that the average British minute is worth just over 10p to men and 8p to women. A mathematical formula for the monetary value of every minute of a person's working life has been devised by researchers at Warwick

Case Study 2.6 continued

University, showing the precise cost of a lie-in, an extra hour at the office or even brushing one's teeth.

The equation, according to its inventors, will allow people to work out whether they are getting a fair rate for overtime, as well as helping them to decide whether it is worth spending extra cash to save time. It can judge the financial cost of a takeaway meal against the time taken to cook dinner, or the relative benefits of paying for a taxi or saving money by taking the bus, and comes up with very different answers according to where people live and how much they earn.

The formula, which has been calculated by Ian Walker, a professor of economics at Warwick University, is

$$V = W\frac{\left(\frac{100 - t}{100}\right)}{C}$$

where V is the value of an hour, W is a person's hourly wage, t is the tax rate and C is an index of the local cost of living.

This means that an hour of a man on average earnings in 2003 was valued at £6.16, or just over 10p a minute, whilst an hour of a woman on average earnings in 2003 was valued at £4.87 or just over 8p per minute. An hour is most valuable to men in London, where it averages £7.35, and least valuable to women in the north of England, at £4.52.

People who earn the same amount of money, however, can find their time worth significantly more or less in different parts of the country. In the north of England, where the cost of living is lowest, someone with a salary of £20,000 puts a value of £6.80 on an hour compared with just £5.15 in London.

Professor Walker said that the formula would help people to work out whether they would benefit by spending money to save time, for example by employing a cleaner or by taking taxis. If the amount one pays for a service is less than the value of the time you would take to do it yourself, it is generally worth spending the money on buying the service.

For example, an accountant living in London on a salary of £60,000 with a cost of living index (C) of 1.32 will value each hour at £13.64 and each minute at 23p. It will cost the accountant 69p (3 minutes) to brush his/her teeth and £11.50 (50 minutes) to cook dinner. In contrast, an office worker on a salary of £20,000 in Sunderland with a cost of living (C) of 1.00 will value each hour at £6.80 and each minute at 11p. It will cost 33p to brush his/her teeth and £5.50 to cook dinner.

'This research is the first of its kind to take into account the overall picture of how highly our time is being valued,' he said. 'Traditionally, wages or salaries have given an indication of how we are valued at work; however, by looking at salaries against

Case Study 2.6 continued

taxation, the cost of living and regional variations we can see how much an hour of our time is worth whether at work or home.' Ian Barber of Barclaycard, which commissioned the research, said 'What this formula can do is help us to think about how to value and use our time more effectively, vital in an age when many people feel as though they have less time to spend in the way they want to.' An automatic 'time of money' calculator, based on the formula, is available on the Internet at www.barclaycard.co.uk/timeismoney.

Questions

1 Why is it suggested that for people earning the same amount the value of an hour is worth more in the North than in London?

2 What does it mean when C (index of the local cost of living) is stated as being 1.32 in London but 1.00 in the North?

3 Does the case study suggest that we can have a 'unit of utility' for time that is common to everyone?

Activity 2.3 checks your understanding of total and marginal utility.

Activity 2.3

1 Which *two* of these examples illustrate the idea of diminishing marginal utility?

(a) The third ice cream raises total utility by the same amount as the second ice cream.
(b) The third ice cream raises total utility by more than the second ice cream.
(c) The third ice cream raises total utility by less than the second ice cream.
(d) The addition to total utility from the second ice cream is more than the addition to total utility from the third ice cream.
(e) The addition to total utility from the second ice cream is less than the addition to total utility from the third ice cream.

2 Which *one* of these examples illustrates the idea of constant marginal utility?

(a) The third ice cream raises total utility by the same amount as the second ice cream.
(b) The third ice cream raises total utility by more than the second ice cream.
(c) The third ice cream raises total utility by less than the second ice cream.
(d) The addition to total utility from the second ice cream is more than the addition to total utility from the third ice cream.
(e) The addition to total utility from the second ice cream is less than the addition to total utility from the third ice cream.

3 Which *two* of the following refer to situations in which total utility is a maximum?

(a) Marginal utility is positive.
(b) Marginal utility is negative.
(c) Marginal utility is zero.
(d) The ratios of prices and marginal utilities are different for all the products consumed by an individual.
(e) The ratios of prices and marginal utilities are equal for all the products consumed by an individual.

Answers to Checkpoints and Activities can be found on pp. 705–35.

So far we have assumed that we can actually measure satisfaction (i.e. that utility is **cardinal**). In practice, many observers believe that there is no such thing as a 'unit of satisfaction (utility)' that is common to everybody, so that utility cannot be measured. If that is the case then we need a different approach to consumer behaviour. An alternative approach can also explain the downward sloping demand curve but using the much 'weaker' and more realistic assumption that consumers need only be able to *order* their preferences between different combinations (bundles) of products, preferring some bundles to other alternative bundles (i.e. utility is **ordinal**). This is the essential feature of **indifference curve analysis**, which is considered in detail in Appendix 1 (pp. 687–96).

Whatever our approach to utility, what is clear is that the tastes of consumers have changed considerably over time and continue to change. The resulting shifts in demand curves for various goods and services have had significant effects on patterns of output and employment in the UK. Case Study 2.7 documents some of the changes in tastes of UK consumers over the past 50 years or so.

LINKS

If your course involves indifference curves and budget lines, then turn to Appendix 1 (pp. 687–96) for an analysis of the 'law of demand' using these techniques.

Case Study 2.7 Changing tastes over time

We have seen that an indifference curve captures the different bundles of products that give the consumer a constant level of utility. There is no doubt that the bundles of products that yielded a certain amount of utility in the past are very different from the bundles that give a similar amount of utility today!

For example, each year the Office of National Statistics (ONS) monitors the most popular products in the nation's shopping baskets in the UK. The basket in 2003 contained 650 goods and services that a typical household bought over the last 12 months, and each year the basket is adjusted to reflect changing consumer behaviour. Table 2.6 presents the products that were included for the first time in 2003, and those products that were excluded.

The shopping basket was first introduced in 1947 as a basis for accurately calculating the rate of inflation. In the 1960s the products entering included sliced bread, fish fingers, crisps, jams and 'meals out' in restaurants. During the 1970s in came frozen

Case Study 2.7 continued

Table 2.6 Changes in the UK 'shopping basket' in 2003

Products in	Products out
Coffee shop caffe latte	Tinned spaghetti
Takeaway burger	Frozen fish in sauce
Takeaway kebab	Brown ale
Draught premium lager	Vinyl floor covering
Dried potted snack	Fixed telephone
Diet aid drink powder	Dog mixer
Single serve cat food	Dry cat food
Complete dry dog food	Women's shoe repair
Booster injection for dog	Men's belt
Designer spectacles	Battery powered clock
Dental insurance	Electronic keyboard
Hair gel	Leaded petrol
Shower gel	
Slimming club fees	
Aid fares	
Car CD	
Golf fees	
Horseracing admissions	

foods, aluminium foil, wine, hardboard for home improvements and the cost of visiting stately homes. The 1980s saw the introduction of microwaves, video recorders, CDs and CD players and low alcohol lager and the 1990s included for the first time the Internet, satellite dishes, camcorders, computer games, CD-Roms, Internet subscriptions and foreign holidays.

In 2003 it was caffe latte, takeaway burgers and kebabs and other convenience foods that made their first entry into this typical shopping basket. Indeed, expenditure on such foods has risen by 40% over the past five years, and they join the vegetarian and reduced-calorie ready meals which appeared for the first time in 2002. Spending on healthcare is also rising rapidly in the UK and even pre-prepared pet food is now in, replacing the effort previously made in preparing home-made foods for pets.

Questions

1 Look again at Table 2.6. Can you explain any of the patterns and trends in the UK which might help explain why some products are 'in' and some 'out' of the typical shopping basket?

2 Does your answer to Q.1 help explain the products in the shopping basket observed in the earlier decades of the 1960s, 1970s, 1980s and 1990s?

3 What products might you expect to appear in, and disappear from, the typical shopping basket over the next ten years? Explain your reasoning.

Key Terms

Arc elasticity of demand A measure of price elasticity of demand which uses the average of the initial and final values for price and quantity. It is the elasticity at the mid-point of the chord connecting the two points on the demand curve corresponding to the initial and final price levels.

Cardinal utility The cardinalist school supposed that utility could be measured, either in terms of some abstract quantity (e.g. utils) or in terms of money. In the latter case, utility is expressed in terms of the amount of money a consumer is willing to sacrifice for an additional unit of a commodity.

Cross-elasticity of demand (CED) Indicates the responsiveness of demand for a product to changes in the price of some other product.

$$\text{CED} = \frac{\%\text{ change in quantity demanded of X}}{\%\text{ change in price of Y}}$$

The CED for *substitutes in consumption* is positive (–/–). The CED for *complements in consumption* is negative (+/–). CED involves shifts in demand.

Income elasticity of demand (IED) The responsiveness of demand for a product to changes in consumer (national) income. Here, as for CED, we are considering shifts in the demand curve of the product.

$$\text{IED} = \frac{\%\text{ change in quantity demanded of X}}{\text{change in real income}}$$

Marginal utility The addition to total utility from consuming the last unit of a product.

Ordinal utility The ordinalist approach does not assume that consumer utility be measurable, merely that consumer preferences can be ranked in order of importance.

Price elasticity of demand (PED) A measure of the responsiveness of demand for a product to changes in its own price.

PED indicates the extent of movement along the demand curve for X in response to a change in price of X.

$$\text{PED} = \frac{\%\text{ change in quantity demanded of X}}{\%\text{ change in price of X}}$$

Relatively elastic demand Where a given % change in own-price of a product leads to a larger % change in quantity demanded of that product.

Relatively inelastic demand Where a given % change in own-price of a product leads to a smaller % change in quantity demanded of that product.

Tax incidence This involves measuring the proportion of any tax increase that is paid for by the consumer (in higher prices) or by the producer. For example, the tax incidence would be 100% on the consumer and 0% on the producer should the whole of the tax increase be passed on to the consumer (e.g. perfectly inelastic demand).

Turnover A term which refers to the total sales revenue of a business.

Unit elastic demand Where a given % change in own-price of a product leads to exactly the same % change in the quantity demanded of that product.

Veblen effect The psychological association of price with quality.

Key Points

- The numerical value of price elasticity of demand (PED) indicates to the business the likely impact of a change in the price of its product on total revenue.
- 'Arc elasticity of demand' is an *average* measure of PED over a range of the demand curve. 'Point elasticity of demand' is a measure of PED at a particular point on a demand curve.

- The incidence of a tax on a product will fall more on the consumer (and less on the producer) the less elastic is the demand for the product.
- The sign and size of cross-elasticity of demand (CED) indicates the closeness of substitutes or complements in consumption for product X. It tells us the direction and magnitude of shift in the demand curve for product X when some other product Y changes its price.
- The sign and size of income elasticity of demand (IED) tells us the direction and magnitude of shift in the demand curve for product X when real incomes rise.
- The law of 'diminishing marginal utility' can be used to help explain why the demand curve is negatively sloped (i.e. the 'law of demand').

Assessment Practice

Multiple choice questions

1 **A university decides to raise tuition fees to increase the total revenue it receives from students. This strategy will work if the demand for education at that university is:**

(a) Unit elastic
(b) Elastic
(c) Inelastic
(d) Inversely related to price
(e) Perfectly elastic.

2 **As you move down a straight-line-downward-sloping demand curve, the price elasticity of demand:**

(a) becomes more elastic
(b) may become more or less elastic depending on the slope of the demand curve
(c) remains constant because the slope is constant
(d) becomes less elastic
(e) is unit elastic the whole length of the demand curve.

3 **The bus fare charged by the local bus company is £2.00 during the morning rush hour, but only £1.50 during the early afternoon. This can be explained by the fact that the demand for bus rides during the morning rush hour is ____________; but during the early afternoon the demand for bus rides is____________:**

(a) less elastic; more elastic
(b) unit elastic; inelastic
(c) perfectly elastic; perfectly inelastic
(d) more elastic; less elastic
(e) perfectly inelastic; relatively inelastic.

4 **If the income elasticity of a demand for a good is negative, then the good is:**

(a) a normal good
(b) an income-neutral good
(c) an inferior good
(d) a Giffen good
(e) a luxury good.

5 At a price of £11.00, quantity demanded is 90; and at a price of £9.00, quantity demanded is 110. The price elasticity of demand is:

(a) −1.22
(b) −1
(c) −0.82
(d) 0
(e) 0.1

6 The government wants to reduce the consumption of electricity by 5%. The price elasticity of demand for electricity is −0.4. The government should:

(a) raise the price of electricity by 2%
(b) raise the price of electricity by 0.8%
(c) lower the price of electricity by 12.5%
(d) lower the price of electricity by 0.4%
(e) raise the price of electricity by 12.5%.

7 If the cross elasticity of demand between two goods is negative, then the two goods are:

(a) normal goods
(b) unrelated goods
(c) complements
(d) substitutes
(e) inferior goods.

8 If the government is seeking to raise revenue by increasing the rate of indirect tax on a product, it will be most successful where price elasticity of demand is:

(a) perfectly elastic
(b) relatively inelastic
(c) relatively elastic
(d) unit elastic
(e) perfectly inelastic.

9 The 'Veblen effect' refers to situations in which consumers tend to regard:

(a) price and quality being unrelated
(b) price and quality being inversely related
(c) price and quality being directly related
(d) rises in price indicating reductions in quality
(e) falls in price indicating increases in quality.

10 Total utility will be a maximum when:

(a) marginal utility is zero
(b) marginal utility is negative
(c) marginal utility is positive
(d) marginal utility equals average utility
(e) marginal utility equals total utility.

Data response and stimulus questions

1 **Look carefully at the data in the table.**

Estimated own-price elasticities of demand for tickets at football clubs in England

Club	Price elasticity of demand
Chelsea	−0.40
Everton	−0.97
Manchester United	−0.12
Newcastle	−0.39
Nottingham Forest	−0.57
Tottenham Hotspur	−0.44

Briefly comment on what the data suggests and on any policy implication for the clubs involved.

2 **Look carefully at Figure 2.11 which is a scatter diagram relating the percentage growth of UK imports (g_m) to the percentage growth of UK national income (g_y). The 'line of best fit' has the equation:**

$$g_m = 0.69 + 1.96g_y$$

How does the idea of income elasticity of demand apply to this situation?

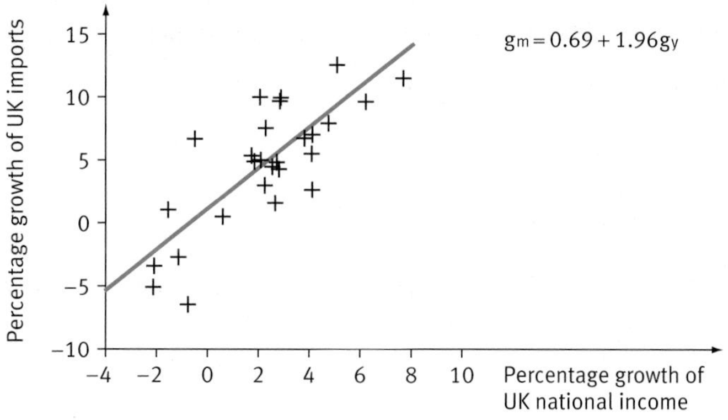

Fig 2.11 Growth of UK imports and national income 1978–2002

3 **A medium-sized publishing company produces a specialised journal for the electrical industry. Its monthly market demand schedule is described by the data shown in the table on the next page.**

(a) Draw the demand curve from the data given in the table.
(b) Show the amount of 'consumer surplus' on your diagram when the market price is £6.
(c) Can you calculate the value of the consumer surplus in (b)?
(d) Calculate the arc price elasticity of demand when the price rises from £5 to £6.

Price of journal (£)	Quantity demanded (per month)
11	0
10	100
9	200
8	300
7	400
6	500
5	600
4	700
3	800
2	900
1	1,000
0	1,100

4 A student has received a one-off unexpected extra monthly grant allowance of £38 and has decided to spend it on entertainment. She can spend the money on tickets to the cinema, concert hall and jazz club, and the prices of the tickets are £2, £4 and £8 respectively. Her marginal utility functions, measured in utils, are shown in the table.

No. of tickets	Cinema	Concert hall	Jazz club
1	10.0	12.0	25.0
2	8.0	8.0	18.0
3	4.0	6.0	16.0
4	3.5	4.0	12.0
5	3.0	2.0	10.0
6	2.0	1.5	7.0
7	1.0	0.5	5.0
8	0.5	0.25	3.0

(a) How many tickets should she buy for the cinema, concert hall and jazz club if she is to maximise her total utility, assuming that she wants to spend her extra money on a spread of entertainment? Explain why this is the only combination that fulfils all the necessary conditions for utility maximisation.

(b) If the student is told at the box office that there are only two jazz tickets available, how should she re-allocate the surplus money from the third jazz ticket between cinema and concert hall tickets in order to achieve a 'second best' alternative to her original choice?

(c) When the student purchases her tickets at the box office she is also told that, had she booked two months earlier, she could have bought any number of jazz tickets at an introductory offer of £6 per ticket. If the student had been able to book these cheaper tickets, would her total utility have been maximised at a higher level than in part (a) above?

Matching pair questions

Match each *lettered* term to its correct *numbered* description.

1 Terms

(a) Price elasticity of demand
(b) Cross-elasticity of demand
(c) Income elasticity of demand
(d) Inferior good (product)
(e) Unit elastic demand

Descriptions

(i) Responsiveness of demand for a product to changes in consumer income.
(ii) Rise in real income over certain ranges may cause demand to shift to the left.
(iii) Where a given % change in own-price of the product leads to the same % change (in opposite direction) in quantity demanded.
(iv) Responsiveness of demand for a product to changes in its own-price.
(v) Responsiveness of demand for a product to changes in the price of some other product.

2 Terms

(a) Negative cross-elasticity of demand
(b) Positive cross-elasticity of demand
(c) Unit elastic demand
(d) Relatively elastic demand
(e) Relatively inelastic demand

Descriptions

(i) Where any change in price leaves total revenue unchanged.
(ii) Where two products are substitutes in consumption.
(iii) Where a fall in price will reduce total revenue.
(iv) Where two products are complements in consumption.
(v) Where a fall in price will raise total revenue.

3 Terms

(a) Point elasticity of demand
(b) Arc elasticity of demand
(c) Engel's Law
(d) Perfectly elastic demand
(e) Perfectly inelastic demand

Descriptions

(i) Where an infinitely small change in price will lead to an infinitely large change in quantity demanded.
(ii) Where it is predicted that the proportion of income spent on food declines as income rises.
(iii) A measure of average elasticity over a range of the demand curve.
(iv) Where there will be no change in quantity demanded whatever the change in price.
(v) A measure of elasticity of demand which involves an infinitely small change from some initial price.

True/False

Which of the following statements are true and which false?

1 Price elasticity of demand refers to shifts in the demand curve for a product.
True/False

2 We might expect a fall in price for a product with a relatively price elastic demand to raise total revenue.
True/False

3 Tennis racquets and tennis balls are likely to have a positive cross-elasticity of demand.
True/False

4 We might expect the income elasticity of demand for health-related services to be positive in sign and relatively high in size.
True/False

5 The 'Veblen effect' supports a downward-sloping demand curve.
True/False

6 A positive income elasticity of demand will indicate that a rise in real income will shift the demand curve to the right (increase).
True/False

7 A government seeking to raise revenue should increase taxes on products with relatively elastic demands.
True/False

8 If the price of a product is unchanged, a rightward shift in the firm's demand curve will increase the consumer surplus available.
True/False

9 A rise in the price of a product is likely to raise total revenue where price elasticity of demand is unit elastic.
True/False

10 Different types of washing-up liquid are likely to have a positive cross-elasticity of demand.
True/False

Essay questions

1 Consider the relevance of price elasticity of demand to the firm's pricing policy.
2 Explain under what circumstances a producer will be able to pass on most of any increase in indirect tax to the consumer.
3 How relevant do you consider income elasticity of demand and cross-elasticity of demand to be when the firm is considering what price it should charge?
4 Examine the circumstances best suited to a government being able to raise revenue by taxing a product more heavily.
5 How can the idea that utility is measurable help to explain a downward (negatively) sloped demand curve for a product?

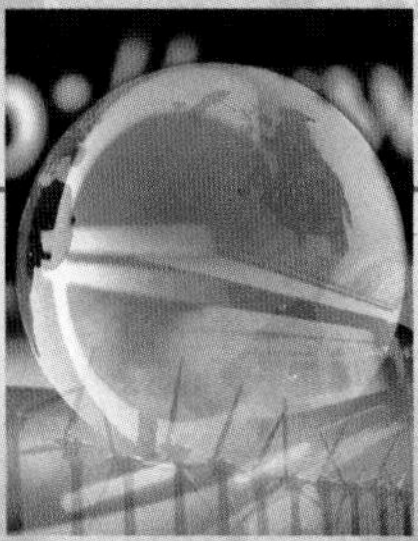

Chapter 3

Supply, production and cost

Introduction

When the price of a product rises, what extra quantity will the business supply and how long will this take? In other words, how responsive or 'elastic' is the quantity supplied of a product to changes in its own price and over what time period? The answer depends on how easily the business can acquire additional resources to use in production (such as raw materials, labour or capital equipment) and on the extra costs it incurs as output expands. In this chapter we review the production and cost issues which underpin the conventional upward (positive) sloping supply curves encountered in Chapter 1. We also assess the benefits to business from growing in size and operating at a larger scale of production. The growth of 'outsourcing' for parts of the production process is considered, although a more detailed assessment of outsourcing is left to Chapter 15.

Learning objectives:

By the end of this chapter you should be able to:

- outline some basic principles of production, in both short- and long-run time periods
- explain the linkages between production and cost
- assess the relevance of costs to business decision making
- distinguish between the different types of business cost and identify situations where the firm may cease production in short- and long-run time periods
- suggest why larger businesses often have a cost advantage over smaller businesses and why 'outsourcing' is becoming increasingly important
- show how government policies can play a key role in production decisions and cost outcomes for businesses
- explain the relevance of price elasticity of supply to business
- outline the idea of 'producer surplus' and consider its possible use in issues involving resource allocation

We begin the chapter by outlining the factors of production and identifying some well-established 'laws' of production in both short- and long-run time periods.

- *Short-run time period* is that period of time in which at least one factor of production is fixed and cannot be changed. The length of this time period will depend on the economic activity under consideration. It may take 20 years or more to plan, locate and make operational a new nuclear power station but only a few months to plan, locate and make operational a workshop producing knitwear or other types of clothing.
- *Long-run time period* is that period of time in which *all* factors of production can be varied. In our example above, the long run would be 20 years plus for the nuclear power sector since its capital infrastructure cannot be changed in less than that time period. However, the long run would only be a few months for our knitwear or clothing sector.

The factors of production

Factors of production are those inputs required to produce a particular product, and are often thought to include land, labour, capital and enterprise.

Land

This was defined by early economists to include 'all the free gifts of nature', i.e. all the natural resources with some economic value which do not exist as a result of any effort by human beings. It therefore includes the surface area of the planet as well as its mineral and ore deposits. These natural resources are sometimes classified as renewable and non-renewable. *Renewable* resources include sunlight, wind, water and other power sources which can be reproduced. *Non-renewable* resources include coal, oil, gas and other power sources which, once used, cannot be reused. As a factor of production, land has special characteristics as it cannot be moved from one place to another.

Labour

Labour not only refers to the number of people available for the production of goods or services, but also includes their physical and intellectual abilities. The *labour force* of a country is the number of people in employment plus the number unemployed. The size of the labour force depends on the age distribution of the population and the proportion of any age group actually engaged in work (i.e. the *participation rate*). An interesting issue is how best to organise work in order to get the most output from the available workforce.

Division of labour

'Division of labour' or 'specialisation' refers to the way in which economic activities are broken down into their various component parts so that each worker performs only a small part of the entire operation. The idea was developed as early as 1776 by Adam Smith in his *Wealth of Nations* when he demonstrated how the production of pins could be greatly increased by splitting the process down into separate tasks, each performed by a single person.

Advantages of division of labour

- *Increased productivity.* Division of labour leads to a greater average product per worker being achieved than is possible in the absence of specialisation. But why is this increase in productivity possible?
  - Someone who performs the same task every day becomes very skilled at it and is able to work much faster.
  - Most of the worker's day is spent on a particular task so that less time is wasted in moving from work area to work area or in changing one set of tools for another.
  - Workers can be trained more quickly since there are fewer skills to learn.
  - Breaking production down to a small number of repetitive tasks makes possible the use of specialist machinery which, in combination with the worker, can raise productivity (e.g. output per person hour).
  - Workers can specialise in performing tasks for which they have a particular aptitude.
- *Increased standard of living.* The greater levels of productivity achieved through division of labour have led to an increase in the volume and value of output per person, raising levels of money income and helping to reduce prices (raising 'real' income still higher).
- *Increased range of goods available.* The greater output, higher money incomes and lower prices achieved by division of labour have increased the range of goods and services available to most people.

Disadvantages of division of labour

Despite these advantages, the division of labour has several disadvantages.

- *Increased boredom.* Greater specialisation results in boredom as workers perform the same tasks throughout the working day. This can lead to low morale, which in turn leads to poor labour relations, higher absenteeism as well as carelessness and an increased number of accidents.
- *Lack of variety.* Output is standardised and large numbers of identical products are produced.
- *Worker interdependence.* Specialisation leads to interdependence, with each worker in the production process depending upon all other workers in the production process. A stoppage by a small group of workers can therefore cause considerable disruption.

- *Limited market size*. Division of labour is only possible if there is a large market. It is useless producing vast quantities of output, even at relatively low prices, if there is only a small market for what is produced.

Remember

A common expression is to say that division of labour or specialisation is 'limited by the size of the market'.

Capital

This is defined by economists as any man-made asset which can be used in support of the production of further goods and services. However, it is the *use* to which a particular asset is put which determines whether or not it is regarded as capital. For example, a vehicle used by a salesman would be classed as capital, but the same vehicle used for social and domestic purposes would be classed as a consumer product.

Economists sometimes distinguish between *fixed capital* and *circulating capital*. The former can be used time and again in the production process whereas the latter can only be used once. Fixed capital therefore includes such things as machinery and factory buildings, the road and rail networks, hospital and educational buildings and so on, whereas circulating capital (also known as *working capital*) consists of raw materials and other intermediate inputs into the production process.

Capital is created from scarce resources and therefore has an **opportunity cost** (see Chapter 1, p. 4). For example, in order to create more capital, it may be necessary to consume less so that resources can be released from producing consumer products and used instead for the production of capital. In other words, to accumulate capital a community may need to forego current consumption, i.e. the community as a whole must save. This is an issue we return to in Chapters 9 and 10.

Enterprise

This factor of production may also be referred to as *entrepreneurship*. The *entrepreneur* is seen as performing two important roles:

- hiring and combining factors of production;
- risk-taking by producing goods and services in anticipation of demand which may, or may not, materialise.

Whilst there is no universally accepted definition of the term 'entrepreneur', the *Oxford English Dictionary* defines an entrepreneur as 'a person who attempts to profit by risk and initiative'. There is considerable debate as to how to identify and develop entrepreneurial talent that can better fulfil the two roles identified.

Example: In 2004 the *Global Entrepreneurship Monitor*, the largest independent study of its kind, found that one in sixteen adults in the UK had set up their own business in 2003, a 20% jump on the previous year. One in six graduates in the UK will set up their own business and black males are twice as likely as white males to go it alone.

Combining factors of production: the laws of returns

All production requires the input of factors of production. However, these can often be combined in a variety of ways, sometimes by using more of one factor relative to another, and vice versa. Profit-maximising firms, i.e. firms which aim to make as large a profit as possible, will combine the factors of production so as to achieve the maximum output from a given amount of factor inputs or, put another way, to minimise the cost of producing any given output.

Measuring changes in output

Over time, firms vary the level of output they produce within any given period, such as a week or a month. Here we define some important concepts which are used to measure these changes in output.

- **Total product** (TP). This is simply the total output a firm produces within a given period of time. For example, the total product of a particular firm might be 1,000 units per week.
- **Average product** (AP). This is usually measured in relation to a particular factor of production, such as labour or capital.

$$\text{Average product of labour} = \frac{\text{Total product}}{\text{Total labour input}}$$

- **Marginal product** (MP). Marginal product is the change in total product when one more unit of the factor is used. For example, if total product when the firm employs 10 workers is 1,000 units per week, and this rises to 1,080 units per week when the firm employs an additional worker, then the marginal product of the last (11th) worker is 80 units per week.

$$\text{Marginal product of labour} = \frac{\text{Change in total product}}{\text{Change in labour input}}$$

Example: Each year the *Harbour Report* provides data on the average product of labour in car assembly in the US. In 2003 it noted that Japanese carmakers in the US maintained their lead in productivity, with Mitsubishi leading the overall company assembly rankings for the first time with 21.33 hours per vehicle at its sole North American facility, in Illinois. That compares to 36.67 hours for GM, 39.95 hours for Ford and 40.60 hours for Chrysler. Nissan recorded the best performance for a single assembly plant in the Harbour Report's history, with 15.74 hours per vehicle recorded at its sprawling plant at Smyrna, Tennessee.

Law of variable proportions

This 'law' applies to the short-run time period when at least one factor of production (usually capital) is fixed. It follows that as the variable factor is progressively increased, the *proportions* in which it is combined with the fixed factor will change. The result is that in the short-run time period the so-called 'law of variable proportions' applies. We can use Table 3.1 to illustrate this 'law'.

Table 3.1 Changing nature of returns to a variable factor

No. of workers	Total product	Average product	Marginal product
1	4	4	4
2	10	5	6
3	20	6.7	10
4	35	8.8	15
5	50	10	15
6	61	10.2	11
7	65	9.3	4
8	65	8.1	0
9	55	6.1	−10

Figures rounded to one decimal place

Increasing returns to the variable factor

The idea here is that prior to some optimum proportion of variable to fixed factor (e.g. 1 man: 1 machine), we initially have too little of the variable factor. Extra units of the variable factor, here labour, will then be highly productive, making fuller use of 'spare capacity' in the fixed factor. Output rises more than in proportion to the extra input of variable factor, and we say that *increasing returns* have set in.

Diminishing returns to the variable factor

Beyond the optimum proportion of variable to fixed factor, additional units of the variable factor, here labour, will be progressively less productive, and we now say that *diminishing returns* have set in.

As we can see from Table 3.1 where labour is the variable factor, it may be that **diminishing average returns** set in at a different level of input of the variable factor than is the case for **diminishing marginal returns**. Indeed we can see from Table 3.1 that diminishing average returns set in after six units of labour, but diminishing marginal returns set in earlier, after only five units of labour.

Figure 3.1 presents a stylised diagram to highlight some of these relationships between total, average and marginal product of the variable factor, here labour.

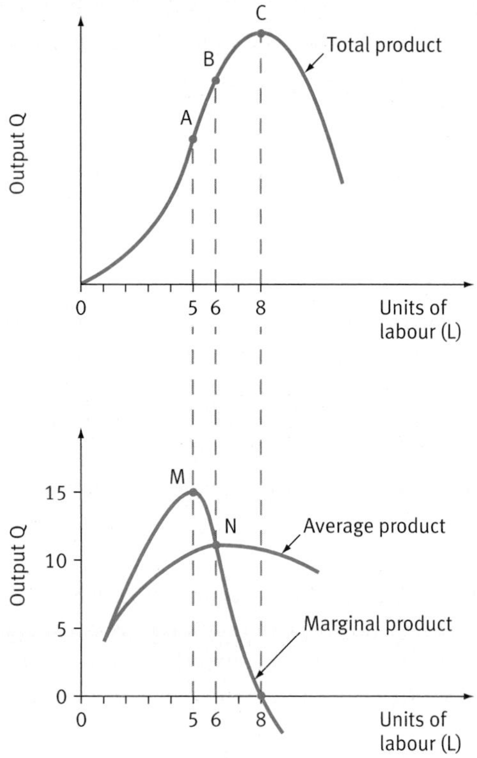

Fig 3.1 Total, average and marginal product curves for the variable factor (labour)

Now we can see visually that the marginal product of labour curve starts to fall after five units of labour, but that the average product of labour keeps rising until six units of labour are employed, after which it falls. In other words, diminishing marginal returns set in before diminishing average returns.

Watch out!

Even though the *marginal product* of labour is falling after five units (point M), it is still above the *average product* between five and six units so the average product of labour will keep rising. Think of a game of darts; if your last (marginal) score is higher than your average score, then your average will still rise, even if your marginal scores are falling. When your marginal score exactly equals your average score (point N), the average will neither rise nor fall. When your marginal score falls below the average, then the average will fall.

Note that when the last worker neither adds to, nor subtracts from, output (i.e. the marginal product is zero), then total product is a maximum (point C).

Costs of production: short run

We shall see that the ideas we have discussed for production are important for determining **costs**, particularly in the *short-run* time period when the law of variable proportion applies.

In the short-run time period, costs are usually defined as either fixed or variable costs corresponding to the fixed or variable factors of production previously discussed.

Fixed costs

It is impossible to vary the input of fixed factors in the short run, therefore fixed costs do not change as output increases. Additionally, it is important to realise that fixed costs are incurred even when the firm's output is zero. Fixed costs might include mortgage or rent on premises, hire purchase repayments, business rates, insurance charges, depreciation on assets, and so on. None of these costs is directly related to output and they are all costs that are still incurred in the short run, even if the firm produces no output. They are therefore sometimes referred to as *indirect costs* or *overheads*.

Variable costs

Unlike fixed costs, variable costs are directly related to output. When firms produce no output they incur no variable costs, but as output is expanded extra variable costs are incurred. The costs that vary directly with output include costs of raw materials and components, power to drive machinery, wages of labour and so on.

Checkpoint 1 Think of your own college, university or workplace. Can you identify the fixed and variable costs? Be as precise as you can.

Just as we defined total, average and marginal *product*, so it will be useful to define total, average and marginal *cost*, as can be seen from Box 3.1.

Box 3.1 Total, average and marginal cost

- **Total cost**

  Total cost = Total fixed cost + Total variable cost

  i.e. TC = TFC + TVC

- **Average total cost**

$$\text{Average total cost (ATC)} = \frac{\text{Total cost}}{\text{Total output}} = \frac{TC}{Q}$$

i.e. $$ATC = \frac{TFC + TVC}{Q} = \frac{TFC}{Q} + \frac{TVC}{Q}$$

$$ATC = AFC + AVC$$

- **Marginal cost** Marginal cost is the addition to total cost from producing one extra unit of output. Marginal cost is entirely variable cost.

$$\text{Marginal cost (MC)} = \frac{\text{Change in total cost}}{\text{Change in total output}} = \frac{\Delta TC}{\Delta Q} \text{ where } \Delta Q = 1$$

Table 3.2 presents an arithmetic example of short-run changes in costs as output expands. It gives us the opportunity to calculate total, average and marginal costs respectively.

Table 3.2 Relationship between cost (£) and output in the short run

Output	Total fixed cost	Total variable cost	Total cost	Marginal cost	Average variable cost	Average fixed cost	Average total cost
0	100	0	100		0	–	–
				50			
1	100	50	150		50	100	150
				45			
2	100	95	195		47.5	50	97.5
				40			
3	100	135	235		45	33.3	78.3
				30			
4	100	165	265		41.3	25	66.3
				15			
5	100	180	280		36	20	56
				10			
6	100	190	290		31.7	16.7	48.4
				5			
7	100	195	295		27.9	14.3	42.2
				10			
8	100	205	305		25.7	12.5	38.2
				20			
9	100	225	325		25	11.1	36.1
				40			
10	100	265	265		26.5	10	36.5
				60			
11	100	325	425		29.5	9.1	38.6
				85			
12	100	410	510		34.2	8.3	42.5

rounded to one decimal place

It is often helpful to plot the values for total, average and marginal costs on diagrams. Figure 3.2 presents stylised diagrams indicating the relationships between the various curves.

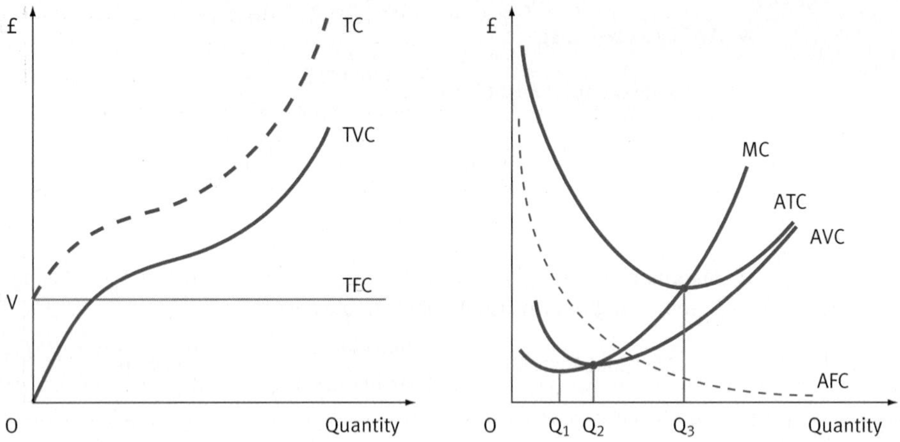

(a) Total cost curves

(b) Average and marginal cost curves

Fig 3.2 Short-run cost relationships.

Total cost curves

As we can see from Figure 3.2(a), the total cost (TC) curve is obtained by adding (vertically) the total fixed cost (TFC) and total variable cost (TVC) curves. TFC is a horizontal straight line at some given value, 'V', since the fixed costs do not vary with output. However, TVC is usually drawn as an inverted letter 'S', suggesting that *increasing returns* to the variable factor initially mean that total variable costs rise relatively slowly with output. However, as *diminishing returns* set in, the total variable costs rise at an increasingly rapid rate with output.

Average and marginal cost curves

Figure 3.2(b) presents the various average cost curves and the marginal cost curve.

- Note that average fixed costs (AFC) fall continuously as we divide an unchanged TFC with a progressively increasing quantity. (This is often referred to as 'spreading the overheads'.)
- Note that the marginal cost (MC) curve slopes downwards initially, with falling marginal costs the mirror image of *increasing marginal returns* to the variable factor in the short run (see the rising part of the marginal product curve in Figure 3.1, p. 93). At output Q_1 *diminishing marginal returns* set in (see the falling part of the marginal product curve in Figure 3.1, p. 93) and the MC curve begins to rise.
- Note that we initially have increasing average returns to the variable factor with the result that AVC falls. At output Q_2 *diminishing average returns* set in (again see Figure 3.1) and the AVC curve begins to rise.
- Note that the ATC curve is the vertical sum of AFC and AVC curves and this starts to rise after output Q_3 when the rise in AVC outweighs the fall in AFC.

- Note also that, for reasons identical to those previously explained, the MC curve cuts the AVC and ATC curves at their respective minima. As soon as the marginal is above the average, then of course the average must rise; the analogy with a game being that if your last (marginal) score is greater than your average, then your average must rise.

Case Study 3.1 Theatre costs in the West End

In 2003 *Umoja*, a celebration of African music, was performed at the New London Theatre, owned by the Really Useful Theatre (RUT) company, in London. In Chapter 2 we noted how the prices charged should take into account the price elasticity of demand for the product. However, they must also take some account of the cost structure for putting on the show. In the short run, revenue must cover the variable or running costs, and in the long run revenue must cover all costs, including 'normal profit'.

For *Umoja* the ticket prices ranged from £10 to £37.50 (average £20), depending on seating position. The New London Theatre has a seating capacity of 900 (average attendance 50%) and eight shows were performed per week. The producer of the show paid a fixed rent of £12,000 a week to the New London Theatre. The 'contra' costs (i.e. the costs of running the theatre, including wages of performers, cleaning and maintenance) were estimated to be between £20,000 and £25,000 per week. Wages of performers were set by Equity, the actors' union, at a minimum of £331.52 per week, with a cast of 40 needed for *Umoja*.

David Lister (2003) suggested a more general breakdown of the typical costs of putting on a West End show. The table below reflects his estimates of where the money received on each ticket actually goes.

		% of total costs
Fixed costs	Theatre rent 'Contra' (cost of running and maintenance of theatre)	Up to 50%
Variable costs	Ticket master (booking fees)	4%
	Theatre commission per ticket	10%
	Creative team pay (commission-based contract)	4.5%
	VAT	17.5%
Profit	(depending on attendance)	14%

Of course, as well as ticket revenue, extra revenue is possible to the producers of shows via the sales of merchandising. Even here, however, merchandising staff were required to pay a 25% commission to RUT, the owners of the New London Theatre.

Questions

1 Why are 'performers' wages regarded as a fixed cost in the table? Is this a usual practice?

Case Study 3.1 continued

2 Comment on the items placed under the 'variable cost' heading.
3 Look carefully at the actual figures given for *Umoja*. How do these compare with the more general percentage figures given in the table?
4 What constraints might the cost figure facing *Umoja* place on its ticket pricing strategy?

Activity 3.1 gives you the opportunity to check your understanding of production and costs in the short-run time period.

Activity 3.1

1 Complete the following table which shows how total product (TP) varies with the number of workers (L) employed, in the short-run time period when other factors of production are fixed. You need to work out the average product and marginal product for the variable factor, here labour.

No. of workers (L)	Total product (TP)	Average product (AP)	Marginal product (MP)
1	40		
2	140		
3	255		
4	400		
5	600		
6	720		
7	770		
8	800		
9	810		
10	750		

(a) After how many workers does:
  (i) diminishing marginal returns set in?
  (ii) diminishing average returns set in?
(b) Draw a diagram showing the marginal product (MP) and average product (AP) curves for the variable factor, labour.

Note: Put number of workers on the horizontal axis.

2 Look carefully at Figure 3.3 which shows production and cost curves in the short-run time period.

(a) Explain what is happening in the top diagram where MP is marginal product and AP is average product.
(b) Explain what is happening in the bottom diagram where MC is marginal cost and AVC is average variable cost.

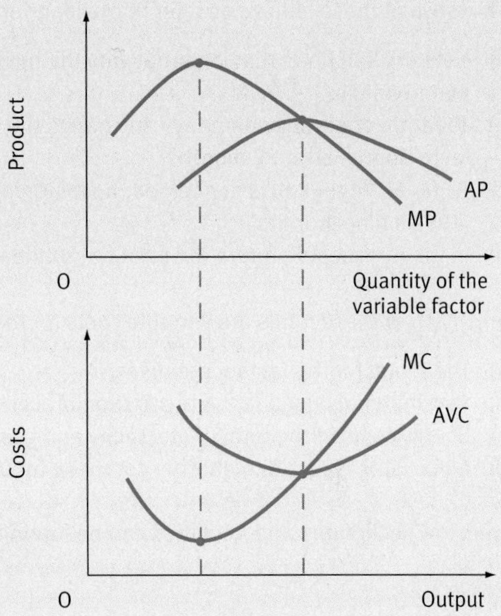

Fig 3.3

(c) How are the two diagrams linked? In other words, explain the relationship between marginal product (MP) and marginal cost (MC), and between average product (AP) and average variable cost (AVC).

3 Complete the following table.
Note: round, where needed, to 1 decimal place.

Output	TFC	TVC	TC	AFC	AVC	ATC	MC
0	50	0					
1	50	40					
2	50	75					
3	50	108					
4	50	138					
5	50	170					
6	50	205					
7	50	243					
8	50	286					
9	50	335					
10	50	390					

Now draw a diagram which includes the AFC, AVC, ATC and MC curves. What do you notice?

4 Which *two* of these situations refer to the long-run time period?

(a) Network Rail finds that it cannot vary the number of engineers employed in track maintenance.
(b) The train operating company can change the number of drivers, trains and any other factor inputs after 12 months.
(c) As far as Virgin Rail is concerned, no factor input need be regarded as fixed after as little as nine months.
(d) In the foreseeable future the total track mileage in the UK cannot be expanded.

5 Which *two* of these items are variable costs for the business?

(a) The rental for the factory premises.
(b) Raw materials used in the production process.
(c) Energy costs in the form of electricity and gas used in production.
(d) A licensing fee paid to another company for using a patented process.

Answers to Checkpoints and Activities can be found on pp. 705–35.

Costs of production: long run

The *long run* has been defined as the period of time in which all factors of production can be varied. We are now in the situation of **returns to scale**. We no longer need to add units of a variable factor to a fixed factor since, in the long run, there is no fixed factor. The average cost curves we considered in Figure 3.2(b) above were *short-run average cost* curves. How do these curves differ from **long-run average cost** curves? It is to this question that we now turn.

Long run average cost (LRAC)

Figure 3.4 shows the long-run average cost (LRAC) curve as an *envelope* to a family of short-run average cost curves (SRACs).

Each of the short-run average cost (SRAC) curves show how costs change with output at some given value/level of the fixed factor, here capital. For example, with capital fixed at $\overline{K}_1$, the lowest cost of producing output Q_1 would be C_1. However in the long run we can vary *all* factors, including capital. The lowest cost of producing output Q_1 in the long run would be to change capital to $\overline{K}_2$ when it would be possible to produce Q_1 at cost C_2. So C_2 (and not C_1) is a point on the **long-run average cost curve** (LRAC) which shows the lowest cost of producing any output, given that *all* factors (here including capital, K) can be adjusted to their optimal level.

In fact, the outer envelope to the family of short-run average cost curves in Figure 3.4 will constitute the long-run average cost curve (LRAC). Up to output Q* the LRAC is falling, and we refer to **economies of scale**; beyond output Q* the LRAC is rising, and we refer to **diseconomies of scale**.

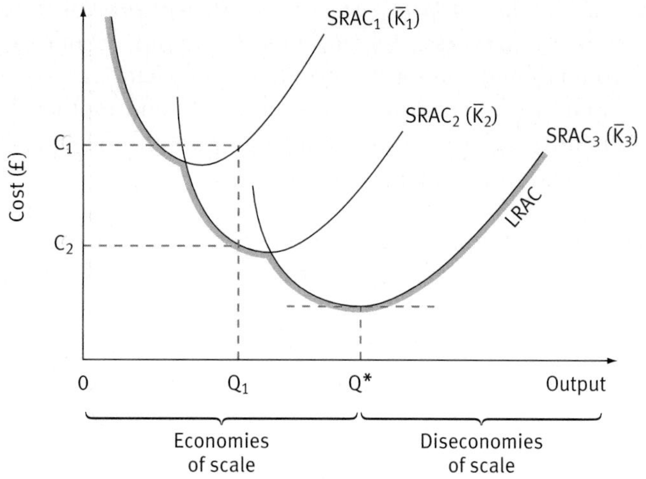

Fig 3.4 The long-run average cost (LRAC) curve as the outer 'envelope' to a family of short-run average cost (SRAC) curves

Reasons for economies of scale

In the long run the firm can increase all its factors of production and grow in size (scale) of output. This greater size may allow it to combine the factors of production in ways that reduce long-run average cost and yield economies of scale.

The economies of scale are many and varied, but they are usually grouped into certain categories.

1 Technical economies

These are related to an increase in size of the plant or production unit. Reasons include:

- *Specialisation of labour and capital* becomes more possible as output increases. Specialisation raises productivity per unit of labour/capital input, so that average variable costs fall as output increases. We have already seen that specialisation is 'limited by the size of the market' so that as output grows, more specialisation is possible.
- *'Engineers' rule'* whereby material costs increase as the square but volume (capacity) increases as the cube, so that material costs per unit of capacity fall as output increases. Wherever volume is important, as in sizes of containers, lorries, ships, aircraft etc., this 'rule' is important.
- *Dovetailing of linked processes* may only be feasible at high levels of output. For example, if the finished product needs processes A, B and C respectively, each with specialised equipment producing 10, 24, 30 items per hour, then only at 120 units per hour can all processes 'dovetail' in the sense that each process divides exactly into this level of output (120 is the lowest common multiple of 10, 24 and 30).

NOTE

Any output smaller than 120 units will incur the unnecessary cost of spare (unused) capacity. For example, if output was only 100 units per hour, then we need four items of specialised equipment for process C, but only one-third of the fourth item is used.

- *Indivisibility of large-scale, more efficient processes*. Certain processes of production, e.g. mass assembly techniques, can only be operated efficiently at large output volumes and cannot be operated as efficiently at lower outputs, even if all factor inputs are scaled down in proportion to one another. We call this inability to scale down the processes of production without affecting their efficiency of operation, *indivisibility* of the production process.

Take, for example, the three production processes outlined in Table 3.3. For all three processes, the capital:labour ratio is the same at 1:1 and each process is a scaled-down (or scaled-up) version of one of the other processes. However the larger-scale processes are clearly more productive or efficient than the smaller-scale processes.

Table 3.3 Indivisibility in the production process

	Factor inputs		Output
Type of process	L (men)	K (machines)	X (units)
A Small-scale process	1	1	1
B Medium-scale process	100	100	1,000
C Large-scale process	1,000	1,000	20,000

Example:

Microchip production

The global microchip producers are now seeking to build huge £3bn state-of-the-art chip fabrication factories ('Fabs') that can use the 12-inch wafers (also known as 300 mm wafers) which are replacing the 8-inch versions currently in use. Where chipmakers could produce 100 chips from an 8-inch wafer, a 12-inch wafer can produce 225 chips. This means substantial reductions of around 40% in the average cost of manufacturing a chip.

2 Non-technical (enterprise) economies

These are related to an increase in size of the *enterprise as a whole* rather than simply an increase in size of the plant or production unit. Reasons include:

- *Financial economies*. Larger enterprises can raise financial capital more cheaply (lower interest rates, access to share and rights issues via Stock Exchange listings, etc.).
- *Administrative, marketing and other functional economies*. Existing functional departments can often increase throughput without a pro-rata increase in their establishment. Case Study 3.2 looks in detail at the potential for gaining administrative economies.
- *Distributive economies*. More efficient distributional and supply-chain operations become feasible with greater size (lorries, ships and other containers can be despatched with loads nearer to capacity, etc).
- *Purchasing economies*. Bulk buying discounts are available for larger enterprises.

Case Study 3.2 looks in detail at the potential for gaining administrative economies.

Case Study 3.2 Head Office – some easy economies?

A smaller head office means more money for the company's real work: producing products and services and selling them to customers. Companies with slimmer headquarters are hungrier, more focused and financially more successful. It is an attractive notion. The only problem is that there is little evidence to support it.

Take a look at the size of head offices in different countries. Which part of the world would you imagine has the most streamlined corporate headquarters: the US or Europe? Wrong. The flabby, decadent Europeans have the leanest head offices. The median American head office has 14.8 staff members for every 1,000 employees in the company. In France the median is 10 headquarters staff for every 1,000 employees. In Germany the figure is 9.3. In the Netherlands it is 7.4 – half the US figure – and in the UK 7.3. Japan, on the other hand, is true to stereotype with a mean 38.7 head office staff for every 1,000 employees.

The figures are from a recent paper by David Collis of the Harvard Business School and Michael Goold and David Young of the Ashridge Strategic Management Centre in the UK. Their survey of 600 companies reveals, however, that those national averages hide huge differences within countries. In the US, the smallest corporate head office they looked at had seven members and the largest 13,030. In the UK the smallest corporate headquarters had 10 staff members, the largest 8,100.

The reason for the variations is that different head offices perform different tasks. Some are responsible for little more than the basic corporate functions: financial reporting, legal services, taxation and the like, with everything else handled in the operating companies. Other head offices have large research and development and information technology departments, serving the entire company.

Those familiar with Mr Goold's earlier work – carried out with his Ashridge colleague Andrew Campbell – will be aware of his finding that differences in corporate head offices reflect more than chief executives' attitudes to staffing levels; they are often the result of entirely different approaches to running companies.

In their 1987 book *Strategies and Styles*, Mr Goold and Mr Campbell identified three office philosophies. The first involved head offices being deeply involved in formulating operating subsidiaries' strategies and giving them time to reach their financial targets. The second philosophy was more distant – and less forgiving. Head offices did not involve themselves in their operating companies' business. They set operating managers demanding 12-month financial targets, rewarded them handsomely if they met them and got rid of them if they did not. These head offices were smaller than the first group. The third philosophy was somewhere between the first two: some financial target setting and some active interference.

The new research that Ashridge has done with Harvard builds on this work, looking at what makes different companies opt for different sorts of head offices. For

Case Study 3.2 continued

example, companies whose subsidiaries are in similar businesses have bigger head offices than conglomerates whose operating companies have less in common. This is because companies whose subsidiaries are in related fields find it more convenient to provide shared services from corporate headquarters.

The most important question is whether, as many cost-cutting chief executives appear to believe, companies with smaller headquarters are financially more successful. The answer appears to be No. The companies that have the highest return on capital employed have larger head offices than those that generate the lowest returns. The researchers are not altogether sure why this is. It could be because larger headquarters use their staff in ways that benefit the company, or it could be that highly profitable companies have more money to spend on head office staff. What is clear, however, is that large head offices are not necessarily a sign of corporate weakness.

That one successful company has a head office of a certain size does not mean that everyone else should have one too. 'The temptation to imitate competitors in the belief that there is a single best-demonstrated practice should be resisted,' the researchers say. 'It is more important for each company to develop a clear corporate strategy and reflect that strategy in the design of its corporate headquarters.' It may be that all those headquarters staff really are a waste of expensive space. Alternatively, strange as it seems, they may be doing something useful.

Questions

1 Why does the case study suggest that there may be fewer administrative economies available than is often supposed?

2 What policy implications follow from the case study?

Cost gradient

As can be seen from Figure 3.5, where economies of scale exist for these various reasons, then the long-run average cost (LRAC) curve will fall as output rises over the range $0–Q_1$. The *more substantial* these economies of scale the *steeper* the fall in the LRAC curve, which then means that any firm producing less output than Q_1 is at a considerable cost disadvantage vis-à-vis its competitors.

The *cost gradient* is an attempt to measure the steepness of the fall in LRAC up to the minimum efficient size (MES). Sometimes this 'cost gradient' is expressed over the range of the LRAC from $\frac{1}{2}$ MES to MES and sometimes from $\frac{1}{3}$ MES to MES.

For example, suppose the cost gradient for an industry is expressed as 20% from $\frac{1}{2}$ MES to MES. This means that a firm that is at output Q_2 in Figure 3.5 will have average costs at C_2 which are some 20% higher than a firm which has an output that is twice as large as Q_2 and which is benefiting from all the economies of scale available.

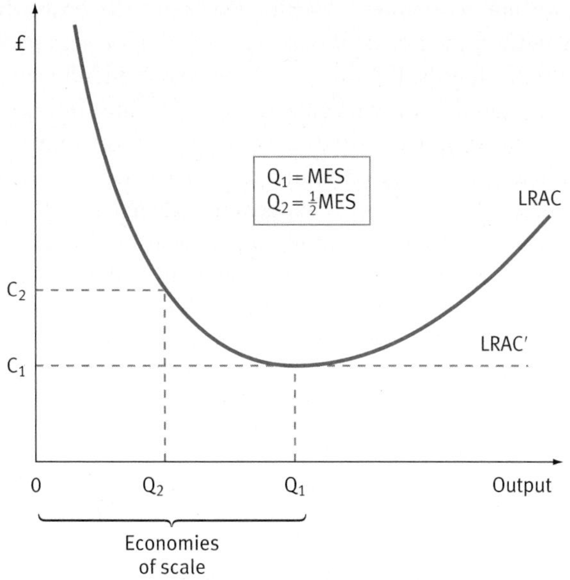

Fig 3.5 Economies of scale and minimum efficient size (MES)

Clearly the steeper (higher value) the cost gradient, the greater the disadvantages for a business in operating below the MES for that industry.

Also note that the larger MES (Q_1) is relative to total industry output the fewer efficient firms the industry can sustain. For example, if Q_1 is 50% of the usual UK output of glass, then arguably the UK can only sustain two efficient glass producers.

Diseconomies of scale

Some surveys suggest that if a firm attempts to produce beyond the MES (Q_1), then average costs will begin to rise and we have the 'U'-shaped LRAC curve in Figure 3.5. These higher average costs are called *diseconomies of scale* and are usually attributed to managerial problems in handling output growth efficiently.

However, other surveys suggest that while LRAC ceases to fall, there is little evidence that it actually rises for levels of output beyond Q_1. In other words, it flattens out to look less like the letter 'U' and more like the letter 'L', shown by LRAC' in Figure 3.5.

NOTE

As well as the various types of short- and long-run costs noted so far, there are other cost ideas you may encounter.

- *Opportunity cost*: the next best alternative forgone (see Chapter 1, p. 4).
- *Sunk costs*: those costs which cannot be recovered should the business fail and the assets be liquidated.

Internal and external economies of scale

- **Internal economies of scale.** These are the cost advantages from a growth in the *size of the business* itself over the long-run time period.

- **External economies of scale.** These are the cost advantages to a business from a growth in the *size of the sector of economic activity* of which the business is a part. In other words, the sources of the cost reductions are external to the business itself. For example, if a particular industry locates in a geographical area, a whole range of support services often develop to support that industry. Historically, the textile industry was located mainly in the north west of England and specialist textile markets (e.g. cotton exchanges), textile machinery suppliers, fabric and dye specialists, textile-related training and educational courses, and transport infrastructure (canals, railways, roads) were established to serve this localised industry. As the textile industry grew in size, the individual businesses which were part of that sector of economic activity benefited from these specialist support services which were often delivered at lower cost and higher quality, yielding 'external' economies of scale.

Checkpoint 2 Can you think of any other examples of external economies of scale?

Economies of scope and experience

We have considered costs that depend mainly on the size of output and the time period in question. Here we consider two other types of cost which may be important to the business.

- **Economies of scope.** This refers to changes in average costs as a result of changes in the *mix* of production between two or more products. The suggestion here is that there may be benefits from the joint production of two or more products. Such economies of scope may occur in various situations:
  - *Unrelated products*, as in the joint use of inputs such as management, administration, marketing, production or storage facilities, and so on which yield cost savings for all the products produced. One head office may be able to absorb the administrative responsibilities related to several products.
  - *Related products*, as in moving towards a mix of product for which there is an element of complementarity in production, such as teaching and research, beef and hides, cars and trucks.
  - *By-products* may play a role in generating economies of scope, as with heat from energy production being used in horticulture.
- **Economies of experience.** This refers to a fall in average costs as *cumulative output* rises (see Figure 3.6). For example, a small firm producing an average output of 5,000 units over 20 years has a cumulative output of 100,000 units. It may have learnt many useful 'lessons' over time to help it reduce costs and compete effectively with larger rivals.

Checkpoint 3 What policy implications might follow if there are extensive economies of experience in a sector of economic activity?

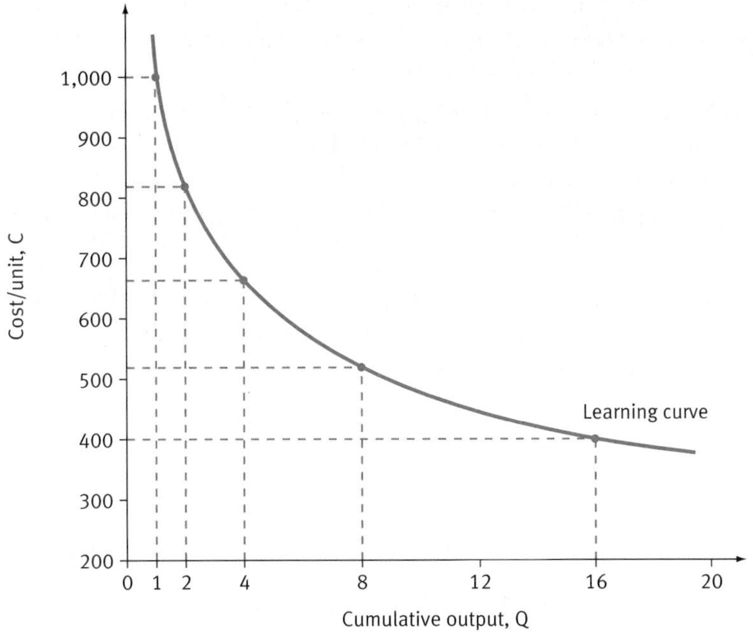

Fig 3.6 Experience or learning curve: declining average costs as a function of cumulative output

Exam hint!

Questions are regularly set in examinations and assignments which involve the reasons firms seek to grow in size and the methods they adopt (Chapter 5). It will help if you can explain economies of scale (technical and non-technical), scope and experience in some detail, using diagrams where appropriate to support your argument. Recent case-study examples will also help to 'deepen' your argument.

Case Study 3.3 **Scale economies in the skies**

In late 2005 we can expect the huge Airbus A380 super-jumbo jet to take off on its maiden test flight, before entering service in Spring 2006. Although the absolute costs of building the 555- to 650-seater A380 super-jumbos are dramatically higher than for today's 350–400-seater jumbos, the *cost per passenger seat* is estimated to be some 15% to 20% lower than for the widely used Boeing 747-400.

How can this be? Certainly the hugely expensive \$10.7 billion (£6.7 billion) programme will require 6,000 engineers at factories in Germany, France, Spain and Britain, with an assembly hall in Toulouse more than twice the size of a football pitch! To bring all the component parts of the A380 to Toulouse from the 15 different manufacturing plants in the four countries will also be hugely expensive. For example, purpose-built roll-on roll-off ferries, barges and road trailers have had to be designed and built to transport to Toulouse in southern France the huge wings (from Broughton, Wales), the rear and

Case Study 3.3 continued

forward fuselage (from Hamburg, northern Germany), the tail piece (from Cadiz, southern Spain) and the centre fuselage and cockpit (from St Nazaire, western France). Roads are having to be widened and secure overnight parking facilities provided (e.g. three nights of stops needed for transporting the slow-moving road convoys in France).

Nevertheless, a 'value chain' for production which involves specialising in these individual parts using firms in the different countries is thought to be cost and quality efficient and to more than compensate for the huge costs and logistical problems in transporting them for final assembly in Toulouse.

The design of the A380 has taken into account the views of numerous focus groups of potential users from many airlines. It has been designed with 20% of the airframe made from the most modern tough, light-weight plastic materials to keep within the maximum take-off weight of 560 tonnes. The basic version with 550 passengers will be able to travel some 8,000 miles without refuelling, and an extended version will carry 650 passengers an extra 1,000 miles (i.e. 9,000 miles in total).

Airbus will need to sell around 250 of these A380 jets to break even, and stated that it was over halfway to that total by late 2003, with orders from ten different airlines. Airbus estimate the total market for aircraft in the 400-plus seat category to be around 1,100 over the next 20 years. It also predicts that an air-freight version will be in demand, with some 300 extra customers attracted.

The annual traffic growth for air passengers has been predicted at around 4.7% per annum over the next 20 years. However, much of this growth will involve the Asia-Pacific region, and Airbus has yet to receive orders from Japan Air Lines or All Nippon Airways – both major carriers to that region. Other companies also challenge the Airbus strategy, with its main rival, Boeing, believing the market will be better met by flying smaller aircraft into a wider range of smaller airports, rather than huge aircraft into a few hub-to-hub centres.

Vital statistics of A380

Assembly	Toulouse
Price	\$260m
Capacity	556–650 seats
Range	8,000–9,000 miles
Take-off weight	560 tonnes
Entry into service	Spring 2006
Programme cost	\$10.7bn

Questions

1 What sources of economies of scale are helping the A380 achieve the projected 15% to 20% lower seat cost?

2 Can you identify some of the benefits and costs (e.g. risks) to Airbus in following this scale-economy strategy?

Deciding whether to produce in the short run and the long run

The distinction between fixed costs and variable costs is important in deciding whether firms should cease production. The firm is obliged to cover its fixed costs whether it undertakes production or not. For example, even when the firm produces no output it still incurs costs such as insurance charges, depreciation on assets, mortgage repayments, rent on premises, and so on. However, unlike these fixed costs, variable costs are incurred only when the firm undertakes production. When the firm produces no output it incurs no costs from purchasing raw materials, from charges for energy to drive the machinery, from overtime payments to existing workers or extra labour costs for hiring new workers, etc. All of these costs tend to rise only as output increases.

Once a firm has incurred fixed costs, its decision about whether to continue producing is therefore determined by the relationship between revenue and costs incurred over the time period in question.

Short-run

- If total revenue *just covers* the total variable (running) costs incurred by producing, then the firm is neither better off nor worse off if it continues production.
- If total revenue is *greater than* total variable costs, then the firm makes at least some contribution towards covering the fixed costs already incurred by continuing in production.
- If the total revenue is *less than* total variable cost then the firm will be better off by ceasing production altogether. If the firm shuts down, its total loss is equal to its fixed cost compared with a loss equal to its fixed costs *plus* the ongoing losses from failing to cover its variable costs.

Firms will therefore undertake production, in the short run, if the *price* (average revenue) at which their product is sold is at least equal to the *average variable cost* of production. When price (average revenue) and average variable cost are equal, total revenue is exactly equal to total variable cost.

Long run

In the long run, unless *price* (average revenue) at least covers the *average total cost*, firms will experience a loss. In other words, total revenue must cover total cost in the long run, including total variable costs and total fixed costs. By definition, when prices (average revenue) *exactly equal* average total costs, firms break even.

Watch out!

In the long run the total revenue of the firm must also cover 'normal profit', i.e. that level of profit regarded as just sufficient to keep a firm in that industry (line of economic activity) in the long run. Normal profit is often thought of as a long-run 'cost' of production in that if it is not made then the firm will move its scarce resources into another line of economic activity.

Whilst they may be prepared to accept losses in the short run (as long as total variable costs are covered), firms cannot accept losses in the long run. If firms are to continue in production in the long run, the price at which their product is sold must at least equal the average total cost of production. We return to this issue in Chapter 6 (p. 203).

Activity 3.2

1 Look carefully at the data on economies of scale in car production shown in the tables.

Car output per plant per year	Index of unit average production costs (car)
100,000	100
250,000	83
500,000	74
1,000,000	70
2,000,000	66

Optimum output per year (cars)	
Advertising	1,000,000
Sales	2,000,000
Risks	1,800,000
Finance	2,500,000
Research and Development	5,000,000

What does the data suggest about the benefits of size in the car industry?

2 In this question you'll see a letter giving a description of a particular situation and a number next to a term. Try to match each description with its correct term.

Description

(a) A larger firm can reduce the costs of raising finance by using a rights issue on the London Stock Exchange.

(b) The material costs of producing cargo ships increase as the square but the capacity increases as the cube.

(c) We can cut the costs of production by using the robotic assembly line for both cars and tractors.

(d) Robotic assembly techniques are highly efficient but can only be used by firms producing over 4 million cars per year.

(e) Even though the paint company only has around 1% of the market, it has been in the paint business for over 50 years and still manages to compete.

(f) Firms in 'Silicon Fen' around Cambridge benefit from a pool of highly skilled electronic experts, with their training needs well supported by local universities and colleges.

Terms

(i) Economy of scale: technical
(ii) Economy of scale: non-technical
(iii) Economy of scope
(iv) Economy of experience
(v) External economy of scale

Note: one of these terms is the answer to two of the descriptions.

3 Match the letter of each description with the correct number of each term.

Description

(a) A type of cost which falls continuously as output increases.
(b) A cost which cannot be recovered if the firm is liquidated.
(c) Costs over this time period result from adding variable factors to one or more fixed factors.
(d) A cost which refers to the next best alternative forgone.
(e) The addition to total cost from producing one extra unit of output.
(f) Costs over this time period result from changing the proportions in which all factors of production are combined.
(g) Found by dividing all the running costs by total output.

Terms

(i) Opportunity cost
(ii) Marginal cost
(iii) Sunk cost
(iv) Average fixed cost
(v) Average variable cost
(vi) Short-run cost
(vii) Long-run cost

4 Which *two* of the following long-run situations might be regarded as yielding economies of scale?
(a) Higher output results in lower average costs of production through greater specialisation of machinery and equipment.
(b) Managers find it more difficult to cope with higher levels of output.
(c) A firm producing containers finds that costs of production (area) increase as the square but capacity (volume) increases as the cube.
(d) New breakthroughs in information technology allow 'miniaturisation' of the production process, so that smaller firms can now introduce the more efficient techniques previously only available to larger firms.

5 If output of the firm rises from $\frac{1}{2}$ minimum efficient size to the minimum efficient size and average costs fall by 60% in the long run, we might say that:
(a) The cost gradient is steep, reflecting substantial economies of scale.
(b) The cost gradient is shallow, showing little evidence of economies of scale.
(c) Being below the minimum efficient size is of little consequence.
(d) The firm is likely to consider demerging its activities.
(e) Economies of scope would seem extremely attractive.

6 Which of the following is NOT a technical economy of scale?
   (a) Specialisation of labour and equipment is possible at larger output and raises factory productivity.
   (b) Dovetailing of separate but linked processes can only occur at larger outputs.
   (c) Material costs increase as the square but capacity as the cube.
   (d) The larger-scale processes of production tend to be the more productive but cannot easily be scaled down: i.e. they tend to be 'indivisible'.
   (e) Large factory output allows the firm's lorries to operate with smaller proportions of empty space.

7 A reduction in long-run average costs (LRAC) due to a different product mix being selected by the firm is an example of:
   (a) technical economies of scale
   (b) non-technical economies of scale
   (c) lower sunk costs
   (d) external economies of scale
   (e) economies of scope.

8 An increase in cumulative output of 10% reduces average costs by 5%. This is an example of:
   (a) technical economies of scale
   (b) experience economies
   (c) lower sunk costs
   (d) external economies of scale
   (e) economies of scope.

9 True/False
   (a) 'Normal profit' is that profit which is more than sufficient to keep the firm in the industry in the long run. True/False
   (b) When the 'long-run average cost' curve starts to rise we refer to economies of scale having set in. True/False
   (c) A rise in cumulative output leading to a reduction in average costs is an example of economies of scope. True/False
   (d) In the long run the firm will cease production unless average revenue is at least equal to average total cost (including 'normal profit'). True/False
   (e) Those who suggest that the long-run average cost curve is 'U'-shaped usually point to diseconomies of scale resulting from managerial inefficiencies as output rises. True/False

Answers to Checkpoints and Activities can be found on pp. 705–35.

Price elasticity of supply (PES)

Price elasticity of supply is a measure of the responsiveness of the supply of product X to changes in its own price. It refers to movement along the supply curve (expansion/contraction) rather than shifts in the supply curve (increase/decrease).

$$\text{PES} = \frac{\text{\% change in quantity supplied of X}}{\text{\% change in price of X}}$$

The numerical value, terminology and descriptions used for price elasticity of demand (PED) apply equally to supply, though for supply all the signs are strictly positive, since when the price of X rises the quantity supplied of X also rises (+/+ = +).

Table 3.4 presents the numerical values, terminology and descriptions for price elasticity of supply while Figure 3.7 presents diagrams to capture some of these PES situations.

Table 3.4 Price elasticity of supply, terminology and description

Numerical value of PES	Terminology	Description
0	Perfectly inelastic supply	Whatever the % change in price (Figure 3.7a), no change in quantity supplied
>0<1	Relatively inelastic supply	A given % change in price leads to a smaller % change in quantity supplied
1	Unit elastic supply	A given % change in price leads to exactly the same % change in quantity supplied (Figure 3.7b)
>1<∞	Relatively elastic supply	A given % change in price leads to a larger % change in quantity supplied
∞ (infinity)	Perfectly elastic supply	An infinitely small % change in price leads to an infinitely large % change in quantity supplied (Figure 3.7c)

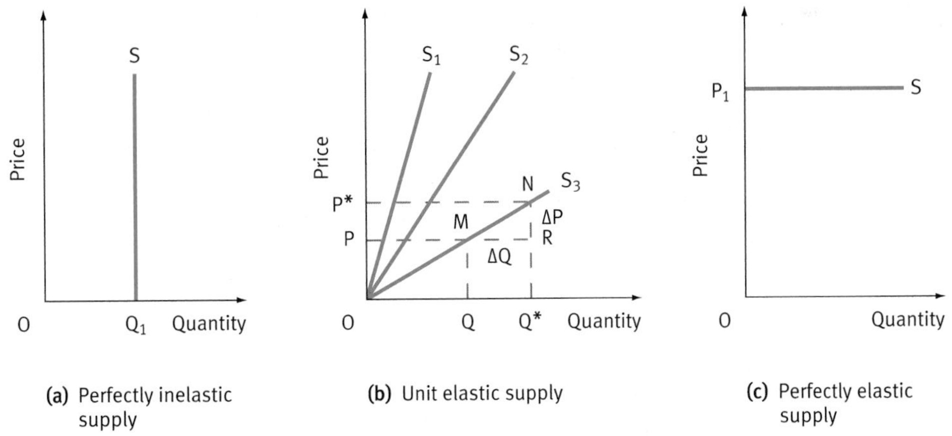

Fig 3.7 Some important price elasticities of supply.

Factors affecting PES

Factors affecting the numerical value of PES for a product include the following:

- *The mobility of factors of production.* The more easily the factors of production can be moved between product X and the supply of other products, the more elastic the supply.
- *The time period in question.* The longer the time period under consideration, the more elastic the supply (producers take time to redirect factors of production).
- *Producer's attitude towards risk.* The less risk-averse the producer, the more elastic the supply. In other words, if producers are more willing to take risks, they will be more responsive in redirecting factors of production to alternative uses in response to price changes in product X.
- *The existence of natural constraints on production.* The less inhibited is production as regards natural constraints (such as fertile land, climate, mineral deposit, etc.), the more elastic the supply is likely to be.

The diagram representing *unit elasticity of supply*, as in Figure 3.7(b), is any straight line supply curve through the origin. Box 3.2 explains this situation and presents more information on calculating PES.

Box 3.2 Calculating price elasticity of supply (PES)

The equivalent diagram for unit elastic demand was seen in Chapter 2 to be the rectangular hyperbola (Figure 2.1(c), p. 47). Before considering the principles behind the shape of the *unit elastic supply* curve it will be useful to follow the approach for expressing price elasticity of demand (PED) in Chapter 2 (p. 51).

We can devise an expression for price elasticity of supply (PES) in similar fashion as follows:

$$\text{PES} = \frac{P}{Q} \cdot \frac{\Delta Q}{\Delta P}$$

where P, Q refer to the original price and quantity supplied of X and ΔP, ΔQ to the change in price and quantity supplied of X.

Unit elastic supply curve

We can now see why any straight-line supply curve through the origin has unit elasticity of supply. From Figure 3.7(c):

Triangles OMQ, MNR are similar; therefore ratios of corresponding sides are equal, so

$$\frac{MQ}{OQ} = \frac{NR}{MR} \quad \text{i.e.}$$

$$\frac{P}{Q} = \frac{\Delta P}{\Delta Q}$$

$$\frac{P}{Q} \cdot \frac{\Delta Q}{\Delta P} = 1 \quad \text{(rearranging}\}$$

Point elasticity of supply

For a *non-linear* supply curve we can use the expression

$$PES = \frac{P}{Q} \cdot \frac{\Delta Q}{\Delta P}$$

where $\frac{\Delta Q}{\Delta P}$ is the slope of the tangent to that point on the non-linear supply curve.

Outsourcing and cost

Costs of production depend not only on the size of the production unit (plant) or enterprise (firm) but also on the geographical location of different elements of the 'value chain' (see Chapter 15, p. 627). This geographically dispersed supply chain must be carefully coordinated as it will influence the speed with which supply of the finished product can respond to changes in price (i.e. PES). In an increasingly global economy, we note in Chapter 15 that new outsourcing opportunities are available for many multinational enterprises (MNEs) which can reduce the costs of producing any given level of output. Case Study 3.4 looks at the impacts of *outsourcing* on production and costs for MNEs in the UK.

Case Study 3.4 Outsourcing, production and costs

The outsourcing of elements of the production process was widely used by UK firms in 2003. The list below indicates just some of the companies in the manufacturing sector using global competitiveness arguments for UK job losses in 2003.

Alexandra Workwear	170 jobs to Morocco
Black and Decker	950 jobs to Czech Republic
Compaq	700 jobs to Czech Republic
Dyson	800 jobs to Malaysia
Raleigh	300 jobs to Vietnam and South Korea
Sara Lee Courtaulds	500 jobs to China
Waterford Wedgewood	1,058 jobs to China

James Dyson, long associated with manufacturing his innovative products in the UK, shifted production of his revolutionary dual cyclone bagless vacuum cleaner to Malaysia in 2002/3 with the loss of over 800 jobs at his factory in Malmesbury, Wiltshire, which had produced some 8,000 vacuum cleaners per day. The company argues that its production costs will benefit from the much lower wages in Malaysia, equivalent to £1.50 per hour (despite its intention to pay twice the Malaysian

Case Study 3.4 continued

national average to its employees) as compared to the minimum wage of £4.50 per hour in the UK in 2003. Indeed the company estimates that lower wages will reduce its unit production costs by around 30%. Further cost savings will come from now having most of its component suppliers nearby (South East Asian component suppliers having progressively replaced those from the UK) and from now being much closer to emerging new markets in Japan, Australia and the Far East.

Similarly, Waterford Wedgwood, the china and crystal maker, suggested that outsourcing production to China will bring unit-cost savings of at least 70% without which it would be unable to compete in the mid- and lower-priced tableware market segments. However, Wedgwood would continue to produce its more up-market, higher value-added tableware in the UK, as low costs and low prices were less important in this market segment.

Similar announcements were made in 2003 in the *service sector*, as with BT's plans to open two call centres in India employing 2,200 people. Whilst BT itself denies that UK jobs will actually be lost, unions point out that the 2,200 new jobs in India exactly correspond to the number of jobs BT announced it was cutting from its UK call centre staff exactly a year ago. If this trend continues, a major UK sector will be put at risk, since around half a million people work in call centres in the UK.

BT is not the only service sector company to be seeking to cut costs by outsourcing their back-office jobs abroad. With Indian labour costing as little as £5 a day compared to £5.40 an hour in the UK, savings of up to 20% on running costs for back-office services are widely claimed for such outsourcing. HSBC, Prudential, Royal and SunAlliance, Citigroup, ABN Amro and Fidelity Investments are all financial services firms which have outsourced back-office and support staff to the subcontinent.

The call centre industry itself has become big business in India, with more than 100,000 people employed in Delhi, Bombay and Bangalore alone. National Rail Enquiries employs 2,000 workers in the UK and handles 60 million calls a year, but announced in 2003 that it will consider transferring its operations to India when its call centre contracts fall due for renewal in 18 months' time. Critics argue that the more complicated enquiries cannot be dealt with in India by workers who lack the tacit cultural and linguistic knowledge to deal with them. However, almost all Indian call centre workers are graduates, compared to less than a third in the UK, and the quality of their spoken English is high. New recruits in India also undergo intensive courses in British culture, including watching episodes of *Eastenders* and *Blackadder*.

Questions

1 How are the outsourcing opportunities influencing the production patterns in these firms?

2 Which cost curves will be affected by such outsourcing?

In fact this discussion brings into play the idea of *relative unit labour costs* (RULC) which we consider further in Chapter 15 (p. 634). Certainly we can expect service sector as well as manufacturing employment to be affected. For example, *Troika*, the retail financial services consultancy, predicted in November 2003 that over 100,000 British financial services jobs will be lost in the next five years by outsourcing back-office jobs to overseas locations, as insurers and banks struggle to cut costs. The report noted that the costs per financial or insurance policy in India and South Africa were less than £10 compared to over £30 in the UK. However, costs per policy in China are expected to fall to £0.50 per policy within five years! The report also noted that India produces 2.5 million English-speaking university graduates a year, more than the whole of Western Europe, with 70% of these graduates being IT specialists.

Even if some jobs are lost, the key idea underpinning free trade is that all countries will benefit when each country specialises in those activities in which it has a comparative advantage (see Chapter 14, p. 586) and trades the output of these activities with the rest of the world. This broader view is supported by a recent report from the consultants *McKinsey* in 2003 on outsourcing which concludes that it is a win–win arrangement for the countries involved. For example, the report estimates that for every $1 previously spent in America and now outsourced to India, there is a 'global impact' of $1.47. Of that, the US itself receives back $1.14 – as a result of cheaper services for consumers, redeploying labour to better paid jobs, additional exports of US goods to India, etc. India also receives an extra $0.33 via new wages, extra profits and extra taxes.

LINKS

For more on outsourcing see Chapter 15, pp. 631–635.

Governments, location and cost

Government influence on the macro business environment and therefore over a wide range of business activities is considered in some detail in Chapters 9, 10 and 12. Here the focus is government influence on the *micro business environment*, especially where government incentives are directed explicitly towards influencing locational decisions and the cost base of businesses.

Government aid and production: UK

The UK government, as with many others, has sought to support inward foreign direct investment (fdi) by overseas firms in order to raise UK output and employment and (via exports) improve the balance of payments. A variety of grants, subsidies and incentives have been provided by the UK government, many of which are related to the business operating in a particular region of the UK.

Regional Selective Assistance (RSA)

This is the main instrument of the UK in seeking to influence locational decisions for production activities in various regions. It is a discretionary grant towards projects of any size in both the manufacturing and service sectors, is open to both domestic and international firms and is available to help with the investment costs of projects with capital expenditures above £500,000. It has three overlapping objectives.

- first, to create and safeguard jobs;
- second, to attract and retain internationally mobile investments;
- third, to contribute to improving the competitiveness of disadvantaged regions.

The RSA is usually administered either as a capital-related or job-related grant.

- *Capital-related project grants* are normally used to help cover the costs of land purchase and site preparation or the acquisition of plant and machinery.
- *Job-related project grants* are normally used to help cover the costs of hiring and training staff.

The Department of Trade and Industry (DTI) administers the scheme and has spent over £750m over the past decade on the RSA, safeguarding or creating some 180,000 UK jobs. However, the cost per job has been estimated at around £4,000 during this period.

Example: Samsung, the Korean electronics firm, located a major manufacturing plant for electronic equipment in Teeside, UK in 1994. To encourage Samsung to locate in Teeside it received £86m of public money from the UK government, £58m in the form of RSA to support the development of infrastructure needed by the new plant, training and other project costs. It was expected that 3,000 new jobs would be created and £600m of new investment in a state-of-the-art electronic factory. In the event Samsung decided to close the manufacturing site in January 2004, claiming falling global prices for flat panel screens and microwaves, two of its key projects. Samsung announced that it would disperse production to China and Slovakia, where labour costs were only 50 pence and £1 per hour respectively, compared to £5.61 per hour in Teeside.

Not all UK experiences with state aid for inward investment have been so disappointing. Nissan established its Sunderland car plant in 1969, resulting in direct employment of 4,500 people (and many more indirectly) and a major contribution to UK car exports. Nevertheless, a Financial Times Survey in 2003 found that half the £750m of grants involved in 50 regional aid projects over the past decade went to 16 companies which have since closed or fallen well short of job creation targets promised in return for this state aid.

Case Study 3.5 highlights some of the problems faced by electronics businesses in general, and especially those attracted to relatively higher labour cost countries such as Britain.

Case Study 3.5 Low-cost goods rule out Britain

FT

The falling price of consumer electronics has buoyed demand for items from microwave ovens to flat-screen televisions, filling our living rooms with games consoles and DVD players. But lower price tags and margins also make it uneconomic to manufacture these goods in high-cost countries such as Britain.

Prices fall as volume production ramps up, enabling big manufacturers to take advantage of economies of scale. The cost of silicon chips, for example, has reduced steadily even though the power of such chips has risen greatly.

David Alker, senior industry analyst at SRI Consulting Business Intelligence, said: 'The retail cost does not reflect the actual cost of consumer electronics. A digital camera that sold for £300 a few years ago retails for £100 now, but the actual cost of production is identical. It's just that prices were higher at first in order to recoup the research and development costs.'

The electronics industry has always relied on a small proportion of early adopters, the people who must have new gadgets as they arrive, in order to defray the high initial costs until demand ramps up. At this point other manufacturers pile in with similar products, bringing down prices. This pattern is far from unique to the electronics industry: it can be seen in every piece of new technology, from light bulbs to cars.

New technology also causes disruption for suppliers of the old products. The Samsung plant mentioned earlier (p. 118) was planning to make fax machines at a time when few were predicting the rapid rise of e-mail.

Saturation in certain key markets also plays a part in lowering margins, as PC makers and mobile phone manufacturers have found to their cost.

But the most significant factor bringing down costs is the entry of manufacturers based in eastern Europe and China, where labour is much cheaper. Mr Alker points out the human cost of such 'slave labour'.

Source: *Financial Times*, 16 January 2004, p. 3

Questions

1 Why are electronic businesses in general coming under increased pressure to reduce costs?

2 What particular problems are facing electronics businesses located in Britain?

3 Can you suggest any implications of this case study for UK government policy towards state aid for incoming electronics (or other) businesses?

LINKS

You can find more on state aid in Chapter 8, pp. 307–308.

The issues of whether and to what extent state aid should be provided to business is important to many other countries as well as Britain.

Here we review attempts by other governments to aid business activities.

Government aid and production: global

Even countries which already have lower labour costs than the UK and other advanced industrialised economies are creating even stronger incentives for overseas businesses to locate production in their territories. For example, India is planning an aggressive drive to create special economic zones that would enable the country to compete better with China for foreign investment. Senior officials say New Delhi is planning to forgo India's restrictive labour laws within the country's planned 17 *special economic zones* (SEZs). This would be designed to allay foreign investor concerns about India's low labour productivity. In addition, New Delhi would remove remaining bureaucratic obstacles to creation of the zones.

India, which has roughly half the per capita income of neighbouring China, aims to increase its share of world trade to 1% by 2007, up from 0.7% in 2003. In 2002 India attracted roughly one-tenth the foreign investment that went to China. A senior government figure reported that they needed to create success stories in trade so that they can move forward in India. He also said that they need to increase foreign direct investment. The SEZs are key to this.

Producer surplus

This is an idea similar to that of consumer surplus considered in Chapter 2 (p. 72). Whereas consumer surplus involves the idea of individuals being willing to pay more than the market price for units of a product, here producers are seen as being willing to offer units of the product at less than market price. In Figure 3.8 the OQ_1th unit would have been supplied at a price of P_1, but the producer actually receives the higher market price of OP, giving a producer surplus of $P - P_1$ on that unit. Over all the OQ

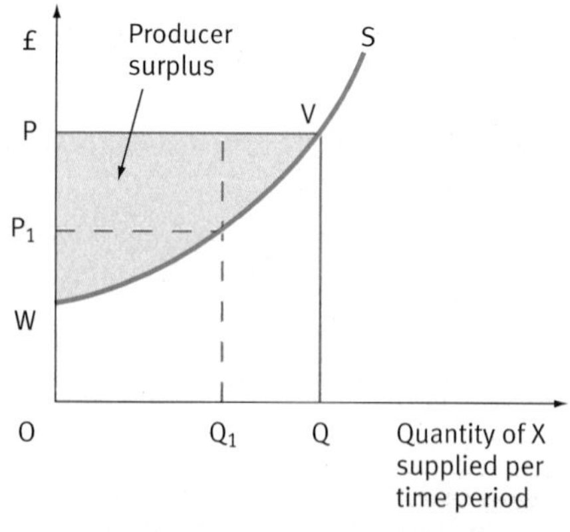

Fig 3.8 Producer surplus

LINKS

Check whether your course and syllabus includes the use of *isoquants* and *isocosts*. If it does then you can turn to Appendix 2 (pp. 697–700) to see how these can be used in identifying the process of production (combination of factor inputs) a firm might select to produce its target output at the lowest cost possible.

units, the shaded area PVW corresponds to the *excess* of revenue received by producers over and above the amount required to induce them to supply OQ units of the product.

It is this excess that we call the **producer surplus.**

Activity 3.3 checks some of the ideas involving price elasticity of supply and producer surplus.

Activity 3.3

1 In this question you'll see a description of a particular situation involving PES. Try to match the letter for the description with the number for its correct term.

Description

(a) A 2% fall in the price of a magazine leads to a 3% contraction in the quantity supplied.
(b) A 4% rise in the price of beer leads to a 4% expansion in the quantity supplied.
(c) An infinitely small percentage change in the price of microprocessors leads to an infinitely large percentage change in the quantity supplied.
(d) A 5% rise in the price of fuel leads to a 1% expansion in the quantity available at the refineries.

Terms

(i) Perfectly inelastic supply
(ii) Relatively inelastic supply
(iii) Unit elastic supply
(iv) Relatively elastic supply
(v) Perfectly elastic supply

2 'True' or 'false'

(a) The factors of production used in brick production are highly mobile, so that they can be varied quickly and easily. Price elasticity of supply will therefore be relatively inelastic. True/False
(b) We would expect the price elasticity of supply to be higher in the long-run time period than in the short run. True/False
(c) The managing director of the firm is so cautious he is unlikely to change his methods of operation. We can therefore expect price elasticity of supply to be rather low. True/False
(d) Since a 4% fall in price leads to a 3% contraction of supply, the value of PES will be −0.75. True/False

3 Price elasticity of supply for a commodity is a measure of the:

(a) ease with which one factor of production can be substituted for another in producing that commodity
(b) responsiveness of quantity supplied to a change in price
(c) responsiveness of price to a change in quantity supplied
(d) responsiveness of price to a change in quantity demanded
(e) responsiveness of quantity demanded to a change in price.

4 A relatively elastic supply is more likely when:
(a) factors of production are highly immobile
(b) factors of production are highly mobile
(c) the time period is very short
(d) producers are highly risk-averse and therefore extremely cautious
(e) recent natural disasters have severely constrained production.

5 At any given price P_1 the more inelastic the upward sloping supply curve is for all prices below P_1:
(a) the smaller will be producer surplus
(b) the smaller will be consumer surplus
(c) the greater will be producer surplus
(d) the greater will be consumer surplus
(e) will not affect either producer or consumer surplus.

Answers to Checkpoints and Activities can be found on pp. 705–35.

Key Terms

Cost gradient Represents the increase in costs as a result of the production (enterprise) unit being only a specified percentage of the optimum size.

Diminishing returns Usually refers to the short-run time period. The average/marginal product curves of a variable factor will eventually decline as more of the variable factor is applied to some fixed factor.

Diseconomies of scale The suggestion that, in the long run, long-run average costs rise as output rises beyond a certain level (MES).

Economies of experience Where increases in *cumulative output* reduce the average costs of the firm. Even smaller firms in business for many years can gain from economies of experience.

Economies of scale Changes in (long-run) average cost as a result of proportionate changes in all the factors of production. It describes the downward sloping segment of the LRAC curve.

Economies of scope Changes in average costs of production as a result of changes in the mix of output.

Increasing returns Usually refers to the short-run time period. The average/marginal product curves of a variable factor may at first rise as more of the variable factor is applied.

Long run The period of time in which all factors of production can be varied.

Minimum efficient scale (MES) That level of output which results in the lowest attainable average cost. Usually refers to the long-run time period.

Price elasticity of supply (PES) A measure of the responsiveness of supply of a product to changes in its own price.

$$\text{PES} = \frac{\%\text{ change in quantity supplied of X}}{\%\text{ change in price of X}}$$

Short run That period of time in which at least one factor of production is fixed.

Sunk cost A cost of acquiring an asset, whether tangible (e.g. plant) or intangible (e.g. reputation), which cannot be recouped by selling that asset or redeploying it to some other use.

Key Points

- The 'law of variable proportions' involves situations in which extra units of a variable factor of production are added to one or more fixed factors.
- Diminishing average and marginal returns to the variable factor will occur in the short-run time period, when at least one factor of production is fixed.
- In the long run, when all factors are variable, average cost may fall significantly with increased output for both technical and non-technical reasons.
- As well as such 'internal' economies of scale, costs may fall because of economies of scope and experience, or because 'external' economies of scale are available.
- Costs may also fall where multinationals take advantage of 'outsourcing' opportunities.
- The more mobile the factors of production are, the greater will tend to be the responsiveness of supply to a change in product price (i.e. price elasticity of supply).

Assessment Practice

Multiple choice questions

1 The long run is a period of time in which:

(a) the firm is able to maximise total profit
(b) the firm may want to build a bigger plant, but cannot do so
(c) the firm can hire all the workers that it wants to employ, but it does not have sufficient time to buy more equipment
(d) economic efficiency is achieved
(e) the quantities of all inputs can be varied.

2 The 'law of diminishing marginal returns' refers to the general tendency for __________ to eventually diminish as more of the variable input is employed, given the quantity of fixed inputs.

(a) average product
(b) marginal product
(c) capital
(d) marginal cost
(e) average total cost

3 Look carefully at the table which represents a firm's short-run total cost schedule. When output goes up from four to five shirts the marginal cost is:

(a) £20.00
(b) £25.00
(c) £30.00
(d) £4.00
(e) £4.25

Output	Total cost (£)
3	25
4	55
5	75
6	79

4 Which one of the following statements is false?

(a) Marginal cost is the increase in total cost resulting from a unit increase in output.
(b) Marginal cost depends on the amount of labour hired.
(c) Average fixed cost plus average variable cost equals average total cost.
(d) Average total cost is total cost per unit of output.
(e) Total cost equals total fixed cost plus total average cost.

Look carefully at Figure 3.9 which shows various short-run average cost curves.

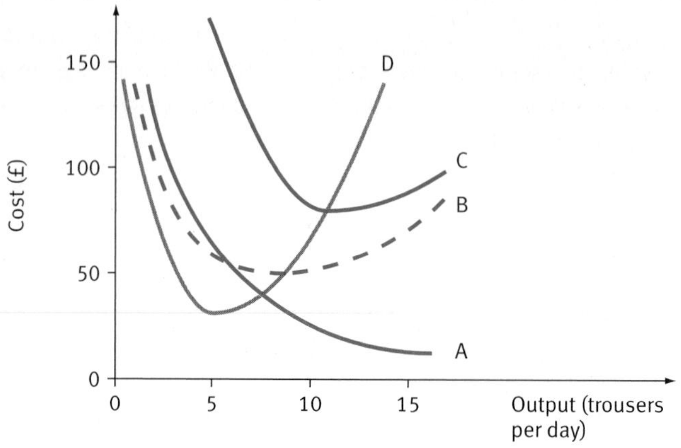

Fig 3.9 Output (trousers per day)

5 Which one of the following statements is false?

(a) Average fixed cost decreases with output.
(b) Curve B comes closer to curve C as output increases because of a decrease in average fixed costs.
(c) The vertical gap between curves B and C is equal to average fixed cost.
(d) Curve D represents marginal cost.
(e) The vertical gap between curves B and C is equal to average variable cost.

6 In Figure 3.9 the average variable cost curve is represented by the curve labelled:

(a) C
(b) B
(c) A
(d) D
(e) None of the above.

7 When the marginal product of labour is greater than the average product of labour:

(a) the marginal product of labour is increasing
(b) the total product curve is negatively sloped
(c) the firm is experiencing diminishing returns
(d) the firm is experiencing constant returns
(e) the average product of labour is increasing.

8 Economies of scale exist when:

(a) the firm is too small and too specialised
(b) a firm's decision to hire additional inputs does not result in an increase in the price of inputs
(c) the long-run cost of producing a unit of output falls as the output increases
(d) the firm is too large and too diversified
(e) the cost of finding a trading partner is low.

9 Economies of scope exist when:

(a) doubling factor input doubles output
(b) increasing returns applies in the short run
(c) greater experience in producing the product reduces average cost
(d) a fall in wages reduces average cost
(e) changing the mix of production reduces average cost.

10 The marginal cost (MC) curve intersects the:

(a) ATC curve at its maximising point
(b) ATC, AVC and AFC curves at their minimum points
(c) AVC and AFC curves at their minimum points
(d) ATC and AVC curves at their minimum points
(e) ATC and AFC curves at their minimum points.

Data response and stimulus questions

1 Complete each column of the table below.

(1) Output per month (units)	(2) Total fixed costs (£)	(3) Total variable costs (£)	(4) Total costs (£)	(5) Average fixed costs (£)	(6) Average variable costs (£)	(7) Average total costs (£)	(8) Marginal costs (£)
0	500	0					
1	500	400					
2	500	600					
3	500	750					
4	500	1,200					
5	500	1,800					
6	500	2,700					
7	500	3,800					
8	500	5,200					
9	500	6,900					
10	500	8,700					

2 Look carefully at the data in the table which refers to the average cost of processing different quantities of blood samples by a company.

What does the data suggest?

Average total costs for blood samples at different scales of activity

Cost per test in pence
Throughput: 000s samples

Item	50	100	200	400	500
Labour	2.5	2.5	2.5	2.5	2.5
Materials	2.5	2.5	2.5	2.5	2.5
Equipment	10	5	2.5	1.25	1
Overheads	25	25	25	25	25
Average total cost	40	35	32.5	31.25	31

3 Mini-case study: organic farming

Recent studies show that the organic food sector has great potential for expansion. Surveys show nearly 80% of consumers, traumatised by a series of food-contamination scandals, would buy organic produce if it cost the same as conventional food. British production falls well short of meeting that demand. Britain lies in only tenth place in terms of land given over to organic production, with less than 2%, compared with Liechtenstein's 17%, Austria's 8.4% and Switzerland's 7.8%.

As a result, Britain imported about 75% of the £550m of organic food it consumed last year; much of that – humiliatingly – was root crops, cereals and dairy produce, all ideally suited to the British climate and soil. With the annual 40% growth rate in British sales of organic foods likely to continue, and every supermarket now offering a range of products, local farmers have, belatedly, been queuing up to fill that vacuum.

Nevertheless, organic farmers are worried that recent attempts by supermarkets to drastically reduce the 25% premium on prices currently charged for organic products will be passed down the line to themselves. Many believe that if the price premium over non-organic products disappears, then it will be uneconomic for the many small organic farmers to continue production. The pity is that in the long term, organic producers argue, organic farming could supply the mass market relatively cheaply. Yields will gradually increase as the size of organic farms increases, crop rotation kicks in and soil fertility rises. The gradual transformation of what is, in effect, a cottage industry into a serious commercial concern will allow economies of scale, both technical and non-technical. Steady government support, including aid that recognises the rural 'stewardship' provided by organic farmers, would narrow the cost differences with conventional farming.

Only when a certain critical mass has been attained – and many organic advocates believe it must wait until 30% of British land (currently 2%) and 20% of British food is organic – can organic farm prices be expected to fall of their own accord. Until that point, their message will be: please buy organic, but be prepared to pay for it.

Question

Why might the small scale organic farmer seek to grow larger? What opportunities and threats are posed to the organic farmer by large retailers reducing the prices of organic food?

True/False questions

1 The supply of toys is relatively elastic, which suggests that the factors of production used in producing toys can easily be switched between different uses.

True/False

2 In the long-run time period it is variable costs that the firm must be able to cover in order to remain solvent (avoid bankruptcy).

True/False

3 'Normal profit' is that profit which is more than sufficient to keep the firm in the industry in the long run.

True/False

4 If the firm earns more profit than is necessary to keep it in the industry in the long run, we call this 'super-normal' profit.

True/False

5 When the 'long-run average cost' curve starts to rise we refer to economies of scale having set in.

True/False

6 A rise in cumulative output leading to a reduction in average costs is an example of economies of scope.

True/False

7 The marginal cost curve must cut the average variable cost curve at its lowest point.

True/False

8 When the producer receives a price higher than that needed to bring about his/her supply of the product, we call the difference 'producer surplus'.

True/False

9 The 'indivisibility of large scale, more efficient processes of production' is a source of technical economies of scale.

True/False

10 If a 5% increase in scale of output results in a 40% fall in average cost, we speak of a steep 'cost gradient'.

True/False

Essay-type questions

1 Assess the possible advantages and disadvantages to a business from a growth in size.
2 Under what circumstances might a business think it worth while to continue in production: (a) in the short-run and (b) in the long-run time periods?
3 Consider the factors which will determine how responsive the quantity supplied of a product will be to changes in its own price.
4 Examine the reasons for firms increasingly looking to outsource parts of their production process.

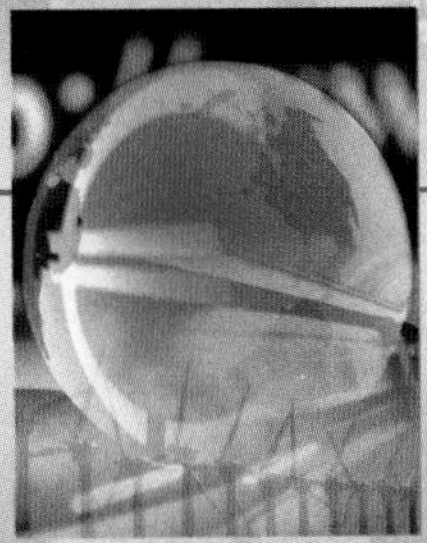

Chapter 4

Business organisation, objectives and behaviour

Introduction

What types of business organisation are typical in advanced industrial economies such as the UK? After considering the various types we note that most organisations, whether they are in the public sector or the private sector, have mission statements which give an indication of what the organisation wants to achieve through its operations, both in the short and long term.

The chapter examines a number of alternative objectives open to the firm. It begins with those of a *maximising* type, namely profit, sales revenue and growth maximisation, predicting firm price and output in each case. A number of *non-maximising* or behavioural objectives are then considered. The chapter also reviews recent research into actual firm behaviour, and attempts to establish which objectives are most consistent with how firms actually operate. We see that although profit is important, careful consideration must be given to a number of other objectives if we are accurately to predict firm behaviour. The need for a perspective broader than profit is reinforced when we consider current management practice in devising the corporate plan.

Issues involving corporate governance, executive remuneration and social and corporate responsibility are also reviewed.

Learning objectives:

By the end of this chapter you should be able to:

- outline the advantages and disadvantages of different types of business organisation, such as sole traders, partnerships, private and public limited companies
- examine the so-called 'principal–agent' problem and its implications for firm behaviour
- identify the various types of maximising and non-maximising (behavioural) objectives the firm might pursue and assess their implications for price and output policy

- assess the empirical evidence used in support of the various firm objectives and relate these objectives to current management practice
- evaluate the suggestion that ethical, environmental and ecological considerations are increasingly influencing firm behaviour
- consider issues of corporate governance and executive remuneration
- review the impact of the 'product life cycle' on business behaviour.

Types of business organisation

Business organisations take various forms, which we now consider. However, it will be useful first to outline certain terms often used when discussing business behaviour.

- **Unincorporated businesses**. These are sole traders and partnerships. This form of ownership is called *unincorporated* because:
  - *They have no separate legal identity*. It is the owner who makes contracts on behalf of the business and it is the owner, not the business, that is liable for the debts of the company.
  - *There is unlimited liability* for business debts, which means that the owner or owners can be declared bankrupt and any personal possessions may be taken and sold to pay off the debts of the business.
  - *There are few formalities* when it comes to setting up the business.
- **Incorporated businesses**. These mainly include private and public limited companies. They are said to be *incorporated* because:
  - *They have a separate identity* from the owner and consequently can sue and be sued in their own right (i.e. under the name of the company).
  - *There is limited liability* for business debts, which means that the owners are liable only up to the amount they have themselves invested in the business. For example, if a company becomes insolvent, and a shareholder owns £1,000 of shares in the company, then he or she will only lose the £1,000 invested.
  - *There are many formalities* required to establish a company.

Sole traders

Sole traders or sole proprietors are the most common form of business organisation in the UK. Many sole traders work on their own, although they sometimes employ other people. They are to be found in all sectors of the economy, such as manufacturing, retailing and services.

Table 4.1 outlines the advantages and disadvantages of operating as a sole trade (or as self-employed).

Table 4.1 Advantages and disadvantages of the sole trader

Sole trader	
Advantages	**Disadvantages**
Needs only a small amount of capital to start up	Lack of capital can limit expansion if the trader wants to grow
Can start the business easily – no need for elaborate legal requirements	May therefore fail to benefit from any economies of scale
Trader keeps all the profit so that there is an incentive to work hard	Liability is unlimited so that the owner's personal wealth is always at risk
Can make decisions quickly and so is relatively flexible	Lack of innovative ideas for expansion because there is only one main owner
Is in sole charge of the business so it is clear who makes the decisions	Long hours and lack of continuity should the owner not be able to carry on the business

Partnerships

Partnerships have virtually the same characteristics as sole traders. This form of business relationship is usually entered into by individuals who wish to take advantage of the combined capital, managerial skills and experience of two or more people.

Ordinary partnerships

These are allowed to have up to 20 partners (see Table 4.2), although banks are not allowed to have more than 10 partners while professional firms, such as accountants and solicitors, are allowed more than 20 partners. Within a partnership there can be a 'sleeping partner', i.e. a person who invests money in the partnership but has nothing to do with the daily running of the partnership.

Most partnerships will begin with a *deed of partnership*, which is a written agreement that covers specific aspects of mutual interest to the partners. These often include:

- the amount of capital provided by the partners;
- the division of labour and profits;
- the rules for taking on new partners;
- how the partnership could be dissolved;
- the allocation of votes to each partner.

Limited partnerships

There is also a form of business organisation known as a limited partnership in which the liability of at least one of the partners is limited to the amount of money invested in the partnership. These partners have a share in the profits but have no say in the running of the business. However, at least one other partner must have unlimited liability, i.e. be liable for the debts of the partnership. Limited partnerships are rare and have to be registered with the Registrar of Companies.

Table 4.2 Advantages and disadvantages of the ordinary partnership

Ordinary partnerships	
Advantages	**Disadvantages**
Easy and cheap to set up Financial base is greater than that of the sole trader Costs, risks and responsibility can be shared	Unlimited liability The capital base is still relatively small and this limits future expansion Profits have to be shared and each partner is liable for the debts of the company, even if not responsible for those debts
No requirement to publish full financial details, so more privacy for partners. Finances need only be declared to the income tax and VAT authorities	Partners can individually make decisions in respect of the partnership which are binding on all the partners
Continuity of ownership on a day-to-day basis as partners cover for each other	Lack of continuity in that if a partner dies or resigns or is made bankrupt the partnership is automatically dissolved
No requirement to publish full financial details. More privacy for partners	
Unlike a limited company, a partnership cannot be taken over against its will by another partnership	Disagreement between partners could cause difficulties in decision making and even the break-up of the partnership

In April 2001 a *Limited Liability Partnership (LLP)* also became formally available in order to combine the benefits of limited liability with the flexibility of organising the business as a traditional partnership. However, the LLP has similar disclosure requirements to a company, including the filing of company accounts.

Limited company

The structure of a limited company is different from that of sole traders and partnerships in that ownership and control are separated. Ownership is in the hands of the shareholders (principals) who appoint directors to report, usually on an annual basis, at the Annual General Meeting (AGM). However, the directors and managers (agents) are responsible for the day-to-day running of the business and report back to the shareholders (principals) at the AGM.

A limited company (whether private or public) must issue a *Memorandum of Association* defining its relationship with the outside world and *Articles of Association* defining its internal government.

The AGM is the occasion where shareholders can elect directors and also vote to dismiss directors and auditors. Since 2003 UK shareholders have also been given the right to vote on proposed remuneration packages for senior executives, although the vote is only 'advisory' (see p. 141). Shareholders are rewarded for investing in companies by receiving a dividend on each share. In some cases, shareholders do not check the performance of managers very rigorously and managers who control the company on a day-to-day basis may have motives which are different from those of shareholders. We consider these different motives below (pp. 137–146). Here we merely note that where we have a manager disagreement resulting from the separation between ownership and control, we call this the *principal–agent problem*.

Private limited company (Ltd)

This is a company whose shares cannot be sold to the general public (see Table 4.3). The name always ends with 'Ltd'. The minimum number of members is one and the minimum number of directors is one. There is no minimum requirement for the value of issued share capital. Shareholders are usually family members, existing business partners and employees.

Table 4.3 Advantages and disadvantages of the private limited company

Private limited company (Ltd)	
Advantages	**Disadvantages**
Limited liability – personal possessions of the owners are protected as they cannot lose more than they have invested	Shares cannot be sold on the open market – harder for investors to get money back if they want to sell their shares
The owners keep control and choose the shareholders	Difficult to raise much money as shares cannot be sold to the general public
The business has its own legal identity so that the survival of the company does not depend on the personal circumstance of its shareholders	There is a limit to the amount of capital that can be raised from friends and family
Accounts need only be published in summarised form, thus preserving some privacy	Unless the founder members own the majority of shares, they may lose control over the business

There is another type of private limited company, i.e. the *private company limited by guarantee* – which is a company where the members' liabilities are limited to the amount they have undertaken to contribute to the company's assets should it be wound up. These companies are usually formed by professional, trade or research associations and are not as common as the private limited company.

Case Study 4.1 looks at the reasons a computer services company chose to change from a partnership to a private limited company in 2003.

Case Study 4.1 **Partnership or Ltd company?**

In 2003 Gandlake Computer Services, which develops business software in Newbury, Berkshire, changed to a private limited company (Ltd) after trading as a partnership since 1971. It became a limited company after managing director John Gandley decided that it would help to grow the business. Gandley argued that although the partnership was doing well and had a strong cash flow, because, as a partnership, it

Case Study 4.1 continued

was not publishing accounts at Companies House, that aspect of the business was invisible to its clients. His preference was for the market to see that Gandlake was very solvent and profitable and had good reserves of working capital so that people could compare it with its competitors. This visibility as to its competitive edge would then be used as a strong selling point in marketing the company. He added: 'I also wanted to become a limited company because, as the business grew and we got bigger clients and bigger contracts, our lawyers advised us that it would be wise to move from having unlimited status to limited liability. Another reason was that all our clients were either limited companies, plcs or big government departments and they didn't really understand the concept of partnerships. It was always a potential obstacle to doing business that had to be overcome'.

In Gandley's view, making the switch was time-consuming but straightforward. 'There was a lot of paperwork. It took about six months of preparation with lawyers and accountants. We also had to have the whole operation valued by external company valuers to put a market price on the enterprise'. Gandley estimated that the whole process cost between £100,000 and £120,000, but he expects to recover this in his first year through tax savings and business expansion.

John Lisby, regional director of the business adviser Numerica, said that every sole trader or partnership should now be seriously looking into the option of becoming a limited company because the tax position for the latter was so much more beneficial. He explained that owners of small businesses that make a profit of less than £300,000 could benefit in two ways – from lower corporation tax rates and lower National Insurance payments. 'As a sole trader you are liable for tax on all the profits that you make, whether or not you actually take them out of the business. So even if you decide to retain the profits in the business, you'll still be liable for corporation tax of up to 40% on them. If, however, you are a limited company, then any profit you retain in the business will be taxed only up to a maximum of 19%.'

Lisby said owners of limited companies also benefited if they decided to take some profits out of the business because they had the option of getting it in the form of a dividend instead of a salary. Dividends carry a lower tax rate and also do not require payment of National Insurance.

Questions

1. Identify the advantages to Gandlake of changing from a partnership to a private limited company.
2. What might be the disadvantages of such a move?

Public limited company (PLC)

This is a company which has its shares listed on the London Stock Exchange. The name must always end with 'PLC' (see Table 4.4). The minimum number of members is two and the minimum number of directors is two. The company must have an authorised share capital of at least £50,000. Shareholders usually include large institutions such as insurance companies, pension funds and trade unions as well as the general public.

Table 4.4 Advantages and disadvantages of the public limited company (PLC)

Public limited company (PLC)	
Advantages	**Disadvantages**
Limited liability	The company must pay for an auditor to independently check the accounts
Continuous existence as the survival of the company does not depend on personal circumstances of its shareholders	Many legal formalities have to be completed before the company can be set up
Large amounts of cash can be raised in a relatively short time because of the company's size and the security it offers	Requires a solicitor to register the company and this makes it more expensive to set up than a sole trader or partnership
Can specialise by setting up separate departments etc.	Activities are closely controlled by company law
Company has a separate legal existence from its owners	The real performance of the company may not always be reflected in the price of its shares
People are willing to invest in shares because it is easy to sell their shares on the stock exchange if they want cash	Company can become too large and bureaucratic, resulting in poor communications and inefficiency
Banks are willing to lend them money	Divorce of ownership from control can lead to conflict of interest
The company is able to enjoy economies of scale	Accounts are public so this means lack of privacy
Company accounts have to be published in detail each year. Potential shareholders and those wishing to do business with them can check to see if they are financially sound	They may be subject to takeover bids as there is no way of preventing other companies buying their shares
Very large companies can compete worldwide	In practice the small shareholder has very little influence on how the company is run

The most important features of a public limited company are:

1. *Access to funding* – much more funding is available than is the case with a sole trader or a partnership. This makes the growth of the company more feasible.
2. *Shareholders* – jointly own the business through the purchase of shares.
3. *Limited liability* – for each shareholder.
4. *Separate legal existence* – which means the company can sue or be sued under its own name.

5 *Continuity* – the running of the business is not affected by events and the personal circumstances of the individual shareholders.

Holding company

This type of business organisation operates under section 736 of the UK Companies Act 1985 and is known as a holding company. It is said to be a 'holding' or 'parent' company in that it owns a majority (over 50%) of the voting shares in a subsidiary firm or group of firms. In this way the holding company can control the management and operations of any constituent firm by having the right to appoint its board of directors.

Activity 4.1 reviews some of the aspects of business organisation.

Activity 4.1

1 Look around any local town or village (e.g. for sole traders and partnerships) and look through recent copies of the financial press (e.g. *Financial Times*, *The Economist* etc.) for Ltd and PLC companies. Name *five* examples of each of the following types of companies. What do you notice?

Company type	Example
Sole trader	1
	2
	3
	4
	5
Partnership	1
	2
	3
	4
	5
Private limited company (Ltd)	1
	2
	3
	4
	5
Public limited company (PLC)	1
	2
	3
	4
	5

2 Look carefully at the table below. What does the table suggest?

Number of VAT-based enterprises by category 2003 (UK)

Sector	Total	Sole proprietors	Partnerships	Companies and public corporations	General government and non-profit making bodies
Agriculture	140,175	59,980	68,610	11,065	525
Production	144,575	32,770	21,190	90,465	155
Construction	178,580	81,885	29,780	66,305	45
Services	1,160,395	376,970	216,150	541,815	26,005
Total	**1,623,725**	**551,605**	**335,730**	**709,650**	**26,730**

Source: Adapted from ONS (2003) PA 1003 *Size Analysis of United Kingdom Business*

Answers to Checkpoints and Activities can be found on pp. 705–35.

Business objectives: maximising

The objectives of an organisation can be grouped under two main headings: *maximising objectives* and *non-maximising objectives*. We shall see that marginal analysis is particularly important for maximising goals. This is often confusing to the student who, rightly, assumes that few businesses or organisations can have any detailed knowledge of marginal revenue or marginal cost. However, it should be remembered that marginal analysis does not pretend to describe *how* firms maximise profits or revenue. It simply tells us what the output and price must be if firms do succeed in maximising these items, whether by luck or by judgement.

Profit maximisation

For most firms **profit** is the major concern, with total profit defined as total revenue minus total cost. A profit objective is often the principal reason for the original formation of the company. The traditional economist's view is that firms in the private sector are profit maximisers, with each business decision based on the need to increase profits. This may be the case for small operations that are under the direct control of the owner but, as we note later, large companies may be equally concerned with objectives such as turnover, market share or growth.

Profit, however, remains an important objective because:

- it ensures the long-term survival of the business;
- it provides a source of finance for future investment;

- it provides rewards for stakeholders (dividends for shareholders, wage increases for employees, price reductions or improved products for the consumer etc.);
- it provides a measure of the efficiency and effectiveness of management policies;
- it allows comparison with other forms of investment.

Figure 4.1 shows the output (Q_p) at which total profit is a maximum. We return to this diagram from time to time as we consider other maximising objectives.

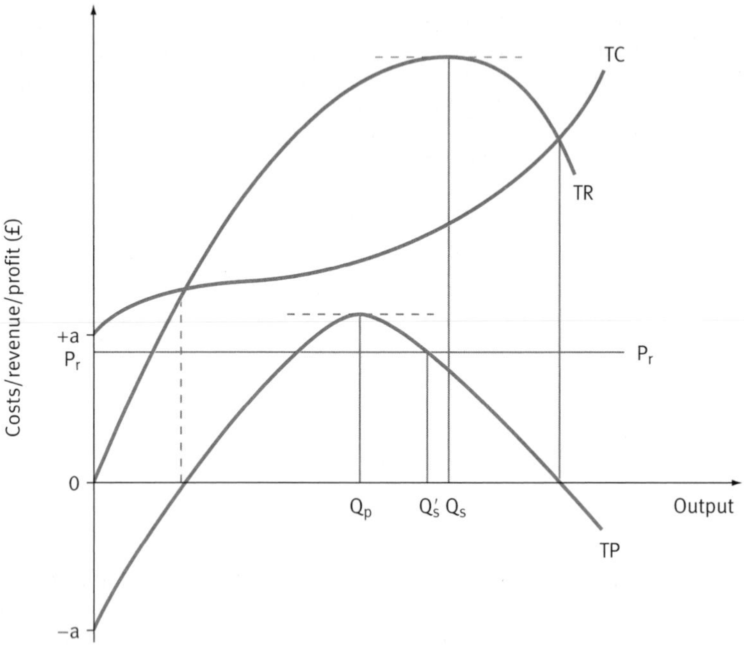

Fig 4.1 Variation of output with firm objective

Checkpoint 1 Had the marginal revenue and marginal cost curves been presented in Figure 4.1, where would they have intersected?

It may be useful at this stage to look at Box 4.1 which explains why profit can only be a maximum where marginal cost equals marginal revenue.

Box 4.1 Profit maximisation and marginal analysis

Does Stephen Hendry or Jimmy White stop to calculate the angle of incidence and angle of reflection before trying to pot each snooker ball? Of course not, they use their experience, skill and judgement, although when they do pot the ball it will be *as if* they had made the calculation. Similarly, when a firm uses its experiences and judgement to maximise its profit it will be equating marginal cost (MC) with marginal revenue (MR). Even if it is entirely unaware of these terms, it will be acting *as if* it had made such a calculation.

In Figure 4.2 we show that total profit can only be a maximum when MR = MC.

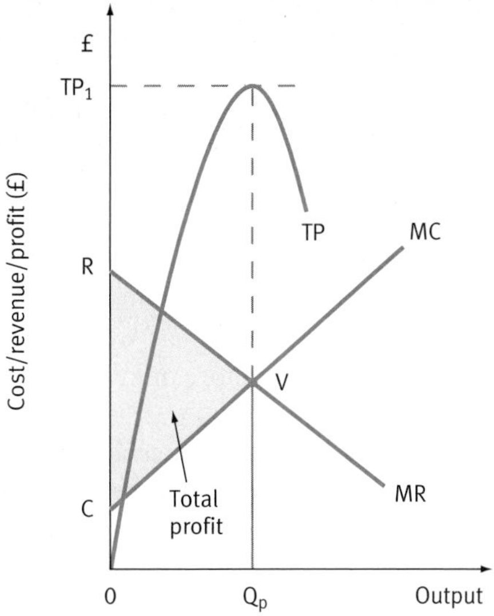

Fig 4.2 Total profit is a maximum (RVC) at the output (Q_p) for which MR = MC

Before using Figure 4.2 to demonstrate this point, we might note the following expressions for profit:

- Total profit = Total revenue – Total cost (TP = TR – TC)
- Average profit = Average revenue – Average total cost (AP = AR – ATC)
- Marginal profit = Marginal revenue – Marginal cost (MP = MR – MC)

In Figure 4.2, for every unit of output up to Q_P, MR is greater than MC and each unit adds something to total profit (i.e. marginal profit is positive).

For the Q_Pth unit of output, MR = MC and that unit adds nothing to total profit (i.e. marginal profit is zero).

For every unit of output beyond Q_P, MR is less than MC and each extra unit reduces total profit (i.e. marginal profit is negative).

It follows that only at output Q_P is total profit (area RVC) a maximum. If we draw the total profit (TP) curve, it will have reached a maximum value (TP_1) at output OQ_P.

Note: At output Q_P the rate of change of Total profit (i.e. marginal profit) is zero. We can see this from the fact that the gradient to the TP curve is horizontal at output Q_P (i.e. TP has reached a maximum turning point).

The profit-maximising theory is based on two key assumptions: first, that owners are in control of the day-to-day management of the firm, so that there is no 'principal–agent' problem (see below); second, that the main desire of owners is for higher profit. The case for profit maximisation as 'self-evident' is, as we shall see, undermined if either of these assumptions fails to hold.

Principal–agent problem

To assume that it is the owners who control the firm neglects the fact that the dominant form of industrial organisation is the public limited company (PLC) which is usually run by managers rather than by owners. This may lead to conflict between the owners (shareholders) and the managers whenever the managers pursue goals which differ from those of the owners. This conflict is referred to as a type of *principal–agent problem* and emerges when the shareholders (principals) contract a second party, the managers (agents), to perform some tasks on their behalf. In return, the principals offer their agents some compensation (wage payments). However, because the principals are divorced from the day-to-day running of the business, the agents may be able to act as they themselves see fit. This independence of action may be due to their superior knowledge of the company as well as their ability to disguise their actions from the principals. Agents, therefore, may not always act in the manner desired by the principals.

Indeed, it may be the agents' objectives that predominate and that may shift the focus away from profit. This has led to a number of managerial theories of firm behaviour, such as sales revenue (turnover) maximisation and growth maximisation.

Sales revenue maximisation

It has been suggested that the manager-controlled firm is likely to have sales revenue (turnover) maximisation as its main goal rather than the profit maximisation favoured by shareholders. W. J. Baumol argued that the salaries of top managers and other perquisites (perks) are more closely correlated with sales revenue than with profits, giving managers an incentive to prioritise sales revenue in situations where managers had effective control of the firm.

O. E. Williamson developed a theory of 'managerial utility maximisation' which, like Baumol's, suggested that managers would seek to maximise sales revenue. Williamson's theory was, however, more broadly based, with the manager seeking to increase satisfaction through the greater expenditure on both staff levels and projects made possible by higher sales revenue. Funds for greater expenditure on staff levels and projects can come from profits, external finance and sales revenue. In Williamson's view, however, increased sales revenue is the easiest means of providing such additional funds, since higher profits have in part to be distributed to shareholders, and new sources of finance imply greater accountability. Baumol and Williamson are actually describing the same phenomenon, though they approach it from somewhat different perspectives.

If management seeks to maximise sales revenue without any thought to profit at all (i.e. **pure sales revenue maximisation**), then this would lead to output Q_s in Figure 4.1. This last (Q_sth) unit is neither raising nor lowering total revenue, i.e. its marginal revenue is zero and total revenue is a maximum.

Constrained sales revenue maximisation

Both Baumol and Williamson recognised that some constraint on managers could be exercised by shareholders. Maximum sales revenue is usually considered to occur well above the level of output that generates maximum profits. The shareholders might demand at least a certain level of distributed profit, so that sales revenue can only be maximised subject to this constraint.

The difference a profit constraint makes to firm output is shown in Fig. 4.1 (p. 138):

- If P_r is the minimum profit required by shareholders, then Q'_s is the output that permits the highest total revenue whilst still meeting the profit constraint.
- Any output beyond Q'_s up to Q_s would raise total revenue TR – the major objective – but reduce total profit TP below the minimum required (P_r).
- Therefore Q'_s represents the **constrained sales revenue maximisation** output.

Case Study 4.2 looks at the recent rise in shareholder power and its impacts in strengthening the links between executive remuneration packages and profit targets.

Case Study 4.2 The rise of shareholder power

Every single shareholder in a PLC, whether an individual with one share or an institutional investor with tens of thousands of shares, can attend the Annual General Meeting (AGM). It is the opportunity for the owners of the company to challenge those directing the company. In 2003 the government introduced a ruling compelling a vote by shareholders at each AGM on executive remuneration packages proposed by PLCs for their senior executives.

Although these votes are, as yet, only 'advisory', it may be that they have begun to influence company policies on executive remuneration. For example, a new pay deal was arranged for Jean-Pierre Garnier, the chief executive officer (CEO) of GlaxoSmithKline (GSK) in December 2003 after the original deal was humiliatingly defeated at the AGM six months previously. That remuneration package had offered as much as £22m over two years for Mr Garnier should he choose to leave GSK during that two-year period. He would receive this £22m even if the company's share price continued to fall. Institutional shareholders were outraged and voted against the remuneration package, seeing it as 'reward for failure'.

A much warmer welcome has been given by these shareholders to what they see as a more rigorous and more profit-related *revised* remuneration package submitted six months later in December 2003. This established a 'low' basic salary of £1m per year, with profit-related incentivised payments for 'success'. For example, if the share price rises from the current £12.60 to £15 and the company's earnings-per-share growth exceeds current forecasts of 4.9%, then Mr Garnier would receive 50% of his potential share options worth around £1.1m. This figure would double to £2.2m if the full 100% of share options were received, but this would only happen if GSK earnings per share rose by 5% *on top of the retail price index*.

Case Study 4.2 continued

Should the same share price rise to £15 be achieved, but with total shareholder return at least half as good as the average for its competitor group (the 15 largest pharmaceutical companies), then Mr Garnier receives a further bonus of £2.1m. Other potential bonuses bring the estimated total remuneration package to just under £6m per annum for his new one-year (rather than two-year) contract.

Questions

1 Why have some analysts seen the events in the case study as marking a new beginning in shareholder power?

2 What implications do you think the revised remuneration package might have for GSK's business objectives?

Growth maximisation

Some of the main reasons for firms seeking **growth** include:

- *Cost savings*: firms can benefit from economies of scale.
- *Diversification of product*: reduces the risk of dependence on one product or service.
- *Diversification of market*: reduces dependence on one economy and one set of customers.
- *Market power*: increased power in the market allows firms to influence prices and to obtain better margins through reduced competition.
- *Risk reduction*: larger firms are less likely to suffer in market downturns and are less likely to be taken over by competitors. In an increasingly competitive market, firms are pressured into continually reducing costs and improving efficiency. One way of achieving this is to expand either by internal or by external growth.
- *Internal growth*: this is when the firm expands without involving other businesses. It is organic growth achieved by increasing sales of its existing products to a wider market.
- *External growth*: this can be achieved by either a takeover (gaining at least a 51% share in another firm) or a merger (two firms agreeing to join in creating a new third company).

Marris model of growth

So far we have assumed that the goals of owners (profits) have been in conflict with the goals of management (sales revenue). R. Marris, however, argues that the overriding goal which *both* managers and owners have in common is growth:

- Managers seek a growth in demand for the firm's products or services, to raise sales revenue and firm size, and thereby managerial income, power and status.
- Owners seek a growth in the capital value of the firm to increase personal wealth.

It is important to note, therefore, that it is only through the growth of the firm that the goals of both managers and owners can be achieved.

Also central to the analysis of Marris is the ratio of retained to distributed profits, i.e. the '*retention ratio*':

- If managers distribute most of the profits (*low retention ratio*), shareholders will be content and the share price will be sufficiently high to deter takeover.
- If managers distribute less profit (*high retention ratio*), then the retained profit can be used for investment, stimulating the growth of the firm. In this case shareholders may be less content, and the share price lower, thereby increasing the risk of a takeover bid.

The major objective of the firm, with which both managers and shareholders are in accord, is then seen by Marris as maximising the rate of growth of both the firm's demand and the firm's capital ('*balanced growth*'), subject to an acceptable retention ratio. Figure 4.3 shows the trade-off between higher balanced growth and the average profit rate:

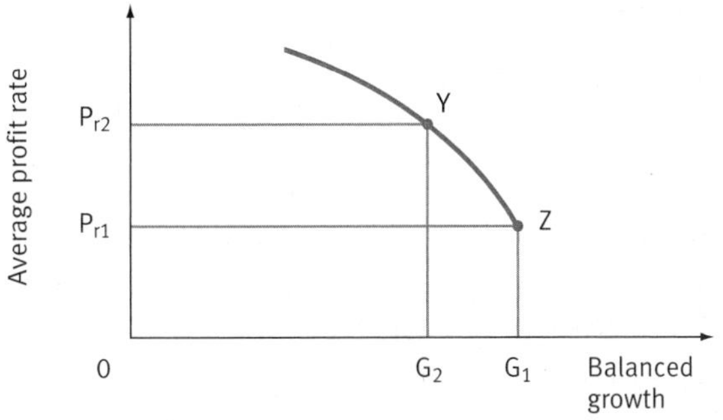

Fig 4.3 Trade-off between average profit and balanced growth

- For 'balanced growth' to increase, more and more investment in capital projects must be undertaken. Since the most profitable projects are undertaken first, any extra investment must be reducing the average profit rate.
- Point Z is where the balanced growth rate is at a maximum (G_1), with an implied retention ratio so high that all profitable investment projects have been pursued, giving an average profit rate P_{r1}.
- Risk avoidance by managers may, however, enforce a lower retention ratio with more profits distributed. Point Y is such a constrained growth-maximising position (G_2), with a lower retention ratio, lower investment and higher average profit (P_{r2}) than at point Z.

How close the firm gets to its major objective, Z, will depend on how constrained management feels by the risk of disgruntled shareholders, or a takeover bid, should the retention ratio be kept at the high rates consistent with points near to Z.

Business objectives: non-maximising behaviour

The traditional (owner control) and managerial (non-owner control) theories of the firm assume that a single goal (objective) will be pursued. The firm then attempts to achieve the highest value for that goal, whether profits, sales revenue or growth.

The **behaviouralist** viewpoint is rather different and sees the firm as an organisation with various groups, such as workers, managers, shareholders and customers, each of which has its own goal, or set of goals. The group that achieves prominence at any point of time may be able to guide the firm into promoting its 'goal set' over time. This dominant group may then be replaced by another giving greater emphasis to a totally different 'goal set'.

The traditional and managerial theories which propose the maximisation of a single goal are seen by behaviouralists as being remote from the organisational complexity of modern firms.

Satisficing theories

One of the earliest behavioural theories was that of H. A. Simon who suggested that, in practice, managers cannot identify when a marginal point has been reached, such as maximum profit with marginal cost equal to marginal revenue. Consequently, managers set themselves *minimum acceptable levels of achievement*. Firms which are satisfied in achieving such limited objectives are said to '**satisfice**' rather than 'maximise'.

This is not to say that satisficing leads to some long-term performance which is less than would otherwise be achieved. The achievement of objectives has long been recognised as an incentive to improving performance and is the basis of the management technique known as management by objectives (MBO).

Figure 4.4 illustrates how the attainment of initially limited objectives might lead to an improved long-term performance. At the starting point 1, the manager sets the objective and attempts to achieve it. If, after evaluation, it is found that the objective has been achieved, then this will lead to an increase in aspirational level (3B). A new and higher objective (4B) will then emerge. Thus, by setting achievable objectives, what might be an initial minimum target turns out to be a prelude to a series of higher targets, perhaps culminating in the achievement of some maximum target or objective.

If, on the other hand, the initial objective is *not* achieved, then aspirational levels are lowered (3A) until achievable objectives (4A) are set.

Simon's theory is one in which no single objective can be presumed to be the inevitable outcome of this organisational process. In fact, the final objective may, as we have seen, be far removed from the initial one.

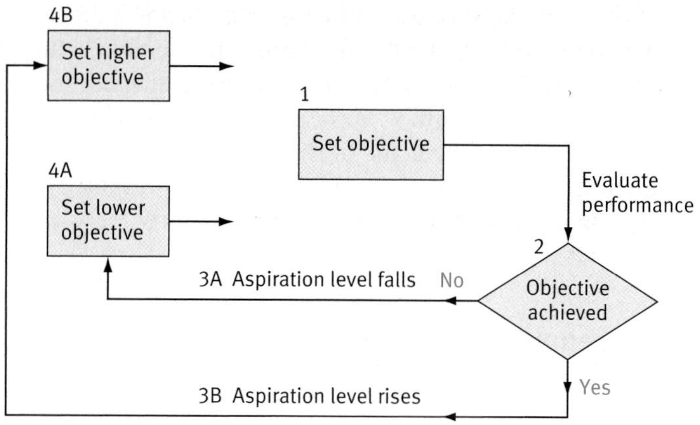

Fig 4.4 Development of aspiration levels through goal achievement

Coalitions and goal formation

If a firm is 'satisficing', then who is being satificed – and how? R. M. Cyert and J. G. March were rather more specific than Simon in identifying various groups or coalitions within an organisation. A **coalition** is any group that, at a given moment, shares a consensus on the goals to be pursued.

Workers may form one coalition, wanting good wages and work conditions and some job security; managers want power and prestige as well as high salaries; shareholders want high profits. These differing goals may well result in group conflict, e.g. higher wages for workers may mean lower profits for shareholders.

The behavioural theory of Cyert and March, along with Simon, does not then view the firm as having *one* outstanding objective (e.g. profit maximisation), but rather *many*, often conflicting, objectives.

Cyert, March and others have suggested that different coalitions will be in effective control of firms (i.e. be *dominant)* at different times. For example, in times of recession the dominant coalition may be that which has formed around the cost and management accountants with the agreed objective of avoiding bankruptcy. In more prosperous times the dominant coalitions may involve marketing or promotion directors and others seeking objectives such as higher turnover, market share or growth. Clearly, different objectives may be followed depending on the coalitions that are dominant at any point in time.

The following are just some of the multiple objectives or goals which are identified by Cyert and March:

- *profit goals* (e.g. rate of return on capital employed);
- *sales goals* (e.g. growth of turnover or market share);
- *production goals* (e.g. to achieve a given level of capacity or to achieve a certain unit cost of production);
- *financial goals* (e.g. to achieve a sustainable cash flow).

Within the organisation different groups will pursue different priorities. In order to achieve success the firms' managers have to compromise and 'trade off' some goals or objectives against others. For example, a single-minded pursuit of production goals can obviously conflict with sales goals (if the production levels exceed market demand), inventory goals (if the unsold production piles up in warehouses), financial goals (if the firm's cash is tied up in unsold output) and profit goals (if, in order to sell the output, prices are slashed to below cost).

Stakeholder approaches

It is not just internal groups that need to be satisfied. There is an increasing focus by leading organisations on **stakeholders**, i.e. the range of both internal and external groups which relate to that organisation. Stakeholders have been defined as any group or individual who can affect or be affected by the achievement of the organisation's objectives. Cyert and March suggest that the aim of top management is to set goals that resolve conflict between these opposing stakeholders groups.

Does firm objective matter?

The analyst is continually seeking to predict the output and price behaviour of the firm. Figure 4.1 (p. 138) has already indicated that *firm output* does indeed depend upon firm objective, with the profit-maximising firm having a lower output than the sales-revenue-maximising firm (pure and constrained).

If we remember that price is average revenue (i.e. total revenue/total output), we can see from Figure 4.5 that *firm price* will also vary with firm objective.

$$\text{Price in the pure sales-maximising firm} = \tan\theta_s = R_1/Q_s$$
$$\text{Price in the profit-maximising firm} = \tan\theta_p = R_2/Q_p$$
$$\tan\theta_s < \tan\theta_p$$

Price of the pure sales-maximising firm is below that of the profit-maximising firm. It is clear that it really does matter what objectives we assume for the firm, since both output and price depend on that objective.

Activity 4.2 gives an opportunity to self-check your understanding of material covered so far in this chapter.

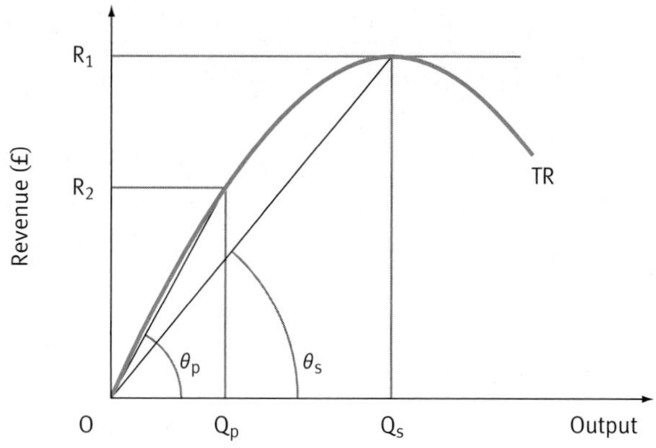

Fig 4.5 Variations of price with firm objective

Activity 4.2

1 Look carefully at the diagram (Figure 4.6).

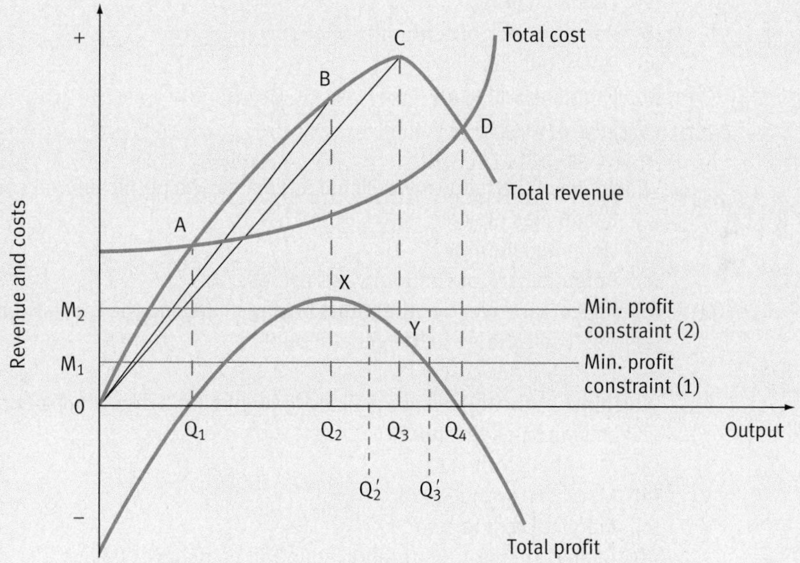

Fig 4.6

(a) At what output is total profit a maximum? What is the value of total profit at this output?

(b) At what output is total revenue a maximum? What is the value of total revenue at this output?

(c) What is the situation at both output Q_1 and Q_4?

(d) If the firm is seeking to maximise sales revenue subject to the minimum profit constraint (1), what output should it produce? Would anything change if the minimum profit constraint rises from (1) to (2)?

2 Look carefully at the table below which reflects the results of a major questionnaire survey by Shipley (1981) on business objectives. Some 728 firms responded to his questionnaire, with two particular questions giving the following results (percentages).

1 Does your firm try to achieve:	%
(a) Maximum profits	47.7
(b) 'Satisfactory' profits?	52.3
2 Compared to your firm's other leading objectives, is the achievement of a target profit ... regarded as being	
(a) of little importance	2.1
(b) fairly important	12.9
(c) very important	58.9
(d) of overriding importance?	26.1
Those responding with both 1(a) and 2(d)	15.9

Source: Adapted from Shipley (1981) Sample of 728 firms

What conclusions might you draw from these results?

3 Which *two* of the following are characteristics of a sole trader?
(a) Limited liability
(b) Potential lack of continuity of business
(c) Unlimited liability
(d) Economies of scale
(e) Ease of access to capital.

4 Which *two* of the following are characteristics of a public limited company (PLC)?
(a) Economies of scale
(b) Unlimited liability
(c) Potential lack of continuity of business
(d) Risk of takeover by other firms buying shares on the Stock Exchange
(e) Can't sell shares to the general public.

5 Which *two* of the following are likely to be true for a firm which succeeds in maximising sales revenue?
(a) Marginal profit is zero.
(b) Marginal revenue is zero.
(c) Marginal cost is zero.
(d) At any other output, total revenue will be rising or falling.
(e) At any other output, total profit will be rising or falling.

6 Which *two* of the following are likely to be true for a firm which succeeds in maximising total profit?
(a) Marginal profit is zero.
(b) Marginal revenue is zero.
(c) Marginal cost is zero.
(d) At any other output, total revenue will be rising or falling.
(e) At any other output, total profit will be rising or falling.

7 Which *two* of the following are likely to be true for a firm which can be said to be a 'satisficer'?
(a) Marginal profit is zero.
(b) The firm will revise its objectives if achievement fails to match aspiration.
(c) The firm produces at break-even output.
(d) It is extremely difficult to predict the firm's output and pricing policy.
(e) The difference between total revenue and total cost is a maximum.

8 Which *two* of the following are characteristics of the 'principal–agent' problem?
(a) Ownership and control in hands of same people.
(b) Ownership and control in hands of different people.
(c) Shareholders and managers pursue different objectives.
(d) Shareholders and managers pursue same objectives.
(e) Sole traders are the dominant form of business organisation.

9 Which *two* of the following are characteristic of a constrained sales revenue maximising firm?
(a) Total profit is zero.
(b) Total revenue is the highest it can be whilst still meeting the profit constraint.
(c) Total profit is the highest it can be whilst still meeting the revenue constraint.
(d) Any extra output will raise total revenue but reduce total profit below the constraint.
(e) Any extra output will raise total profit but reduce total revenue below the constraint.

Answers to Checkpoints and Activities can be found on pp. 705–35.

Profit, ethics and the environment

It is often suggested that firm behaviour which seeks to be more than usually ethical or to give considerable weight to environmental concerns must do so at the expense of profit. However, many firms are now seeing ethical and environmentally responsible behaviour as being in their own self-interest. Indeed, attempts are now being made to incorporate ethical/environmental considerations into formal stock exchange indices in the UK and other financial markets. A new FTSE 4 Good Index was launched in July 2001, using social and ethical criteria to rank corporate performance. All companies in three sectors were excluded, namely tobacco, weapons and nuclear power (representing 10% of all FTSE companies). Of the remaining companies, three criteria were applied for ranking purposes: environment, human rights and social issues. If a company 'fails' in any one of these criteria, it is again excluded. Of the 757 companies in the FTSE All Share Index, only 288 companies have actually made it into the index.

CHECK THE NET
KPMG has a section devoted to business ethics: www.kmpg.com/ethics

The FTSE itself has produced figures showing that if this new FTSE 4 Good Index had existed over the previous five years, it would actively have outperformed the more conventional stock exchange indices. The same has been found to be true for the Dow Jones Sustainability Group Index in the US. This is a similar ethical index introduced in the US in 1999. When backdated to 1993 it was found to have outperformed the Dow Jones Global Index by 46%.

Checkpoint 2 Can you think of reasons why ethical/environmental considerations might actually increase, rather than reduce, business profitability?

Case Study 4.3 looks further into this linkage between social/environmental responsibility and business performance.

Case Study 4.3 **Brand value and social responsibility**

In December 2003 the annual report of the Co-operative Bank into ethical purchasing included the results of a survey of 1,000 consumers. This survey sought to assess the extent of ethical boycotting of various products (goods and services) and its impact on the industries involved. The results suggested that over the previous 12 months the cost in the UK of consumers switching brands for ethical/environmental reasons was over £2.6bn in lost business.

As many as 52% of consumers surveyed claimed to have boycotted at least one product during that period, and over 66% claimed that they would never return to a product once it had been associated with unethical/environmentally damaging practices.

There is also extensive evidence to support those who claim that *positive* associations with ethical/environmental initiatives are good for business. For example, the total sales of ethical/environmental products rose by 44% from £4.8bn to £6.9bn between 1999 and 2002 according to the Co-op Bank annual report. Indeed the market share of such products was estimated as rising by 30% over the same period.

Food, household appliances, cosmetics and tourism were among the purchases most frequently influenced by ethical/environmental concerns. Around £1.8bn was spent in the UK in 2003 on Fairtrade and organic products. A further £1.5bn was spent in the UK in 2003 on 'green' household products, including environment-friendly cleaning products and energy-efficient appliances, with £200m on cosmetics that were not tested on animals and £110m on 'responsible' tourism. A Mori poll in 2002 revealed that 92% of people believed 'multinational companies should meet the highest human health, animal welfare and environmental standards' *wherever they are operating*.

Apart from commercial pressures, legal pressures on business are moving in this direction. The UK government included proposals for a Companies Bill in the 2003 Queen's Speech, which will require businesses to produce environmental and social reviews of their actions on an annual basis.

Questions

1. What incentives does this study give to businesses considering becoming more ethically/environmentally 'friendly'?
2. Can you think of any considerations which might caution a business against becoming too preoccupied with such an approach?

CHECK THE NET

www.maketradefair.com Oxfam, Make Trade Fair campaign
www.labourbehindthelabel.org Labour behind the Label pressure group
www.cleanclothes.org Clean Clothes, European campaign
www.Guardian.co.uk/fairtrade

Firms are increasingly aware of the benefits of aligning themselves with ethical and ecological initiatives. Various 'kitemarks' exist for firms to certify that their product confirms to ethical standards in production, as for example 'Rug-Mark' for carpets and rugs, 'Forest Stewardship Council' mark (to certify wood derived from sustainable forestry extraction methods) and 'Fairtrade' mark (guarantees a higher return to developing country producers).

At the sectoral level, many of Britain's biggest retail names have joined the *Ethical Trading Initiative* (ETI) which brings together companies, trade unions and non-governmental organisations in seeking to ensure that the products sold in their retail outlets have not been produced by 'sweatshop' labour working for next to nothing in hazardous conditions.

At the corporate level Exxon Mobil seems to be an example of a company that has accepted the linkage between ethical/environmental practices and corporate profits. It announced in late 2003 that it had been holding discreet meetings with environmentalists and human rights groups worldwide in an effort to change its unfavourable image in these respects. The charm offensive has been linked to fears at Exxon's Texas headquarters that a negative public image is threatening to damage its Esso petrol brand, which has faced 'stop Esso' boycotts in the EU and elsewhere following its being linked to supporting President Bush's boycott of the Kyoto agreement on protecting the climate.

Example:

Fairtrade

It was reported in 2004 that annual sales of *Fairtrade* food and drink in Britain have reached over £100m, having grown at over 40% per year over the past decade. It has expanded from one brand of coffee ten years ago to 130 foodstuffs, including chocolate, fruit, vegetables, juices, snacks, wine, tea, sugar, honey and nuts. A Mori poll in January 2004 found that two-thirds of UK consumers claim to be green or ethical and actively look to purchase products with an environmental/ethical association.

Business behaviour

We now turn our attention to the ways in which companies actually behave and consider some of the implications of such behaviour.

Control in practice

Profit maximisation is usually based on the assumption that firms are *owner-controlled*, whereas other theories as to firm objective often assume that there is a *separation* between ownership and control. The acceptance of these alternative theories was helped by early research into the ownership of firms.

- Studies in the US by Berle and Means in the 1930s, and by Larner in the 1960s, suggested that a substantial proportion of large firms (44% by Berle and Means and 85% by Larner) were manager-controlled rather than owner-controlled.
- Later research has, however, challenged the definition of 'owner-control' used in these early studies. Whereas Berle and Means assumed that owner-control is only present with a shareholding of more than 20% in a public limited company, Nyman and Silberston (1978) used a much lower figure of 5% after research had indicated that effective control could be exercised by owners with this level of shareholding.
- This lower figure would suggest that owner-control is far more extensive than previously thought. For example, Leech and Leahy (1991) found that 91% of British public limited companies are owner-controlled using the 5% threshold figure, whereas only 34% are owner-controlled using a 20% threshold figure.
- Clearly the degree of control by owners of firms is somewhat subjective, depending crucially on the threshold figure assigned to shareholding by owners in order to exercise effective control.
- A further aspect of owner-control involves the role of financial institutions and pension funds. Between them they now own over 76% of the shares of public companies in the UK, compared to only 36% in 1963, while individual share ownership has declined from 54% in 1963 to around 20% today.
- Financial institutions are more likely than individuals to bring influence to bear on chief executives, being experienced in the channels of communication and sensitive to indices of firm performance. The increase in share ownership of these institutions is seen by many as moving the firm towards the profit-maximising (owner-controlled) type of objective.

Profit-related behaviour

In a major study, Shipley (1981) had concluded that only 15.9% of his sample of 728 UK firms could be regarded as 'true' profit maximisers (see p. 148). A similar study by Jobber and Hooley (1987) found that 40% of their sample of nearly 1,800 firms had profit maximisation as their prime objective. In a more recent study of 77 Scottish companies by Hornby (1994), 25% responded as 'profit maximisers' to the 'Shipley test'.

Given the significance of the profit-maximising assumption in economic analysis, these results may seem surprising, with less emphasis on profits than might have been expected. However, some consideration of the decision-making process may serve to explain these low figures for profit maximisation.

Firms in practice often rely on *pre-set 'hurdle' rates of return* for projects, with managers given some minimum rate of return as a criterion for project appraisal. As a result, they may not consciously see themselves as profit maximisers, since this phase suggests marginal analysis. Yet in setting the hurdle rates, top management will be keenly aware of the marginal cost of funding, so that this approach may in some cases relate closely to profit maximisation. In other words, the response of management to questionnaires may understate the true significance of the pursuit of profit.

Profit as part of a 'goal set'

Although few firms appear to set out specifically to maximise profit, profit is still seen (even in response to questionnaires) as an important factor in decision making. In the Shipley study the firms were asked to list their principal goal in setting price (see Table 4.7, p. 166). Target profit was easily the most frequently cited, with 67% of all firms regarding it as their principal goal when setting prices. Even more firms (88%) included profit as at least part of their 'goal set'.

Profit and reward structures

There has been a great deal of concern over recent years that managers in large firms have paid too little regard to the interests of shareholders, especially as regards profit performance of the company. Indeed, a number of celebrated cases in the press have focused on the apparent lack of any link between substantial rises in the pay and bonuses of chief executives and any improvements in company performance.

The majority of empirical studies have indeed found little relationship between the remuneration of top managers and the profit performance of their companies. In the UK, Storey *et al.* (1995) found no evidence of a link between the pay of top managers and the ratio of average pre-tax profits to total assets, with similar results for studies by Jensen and Murphy (1990) and Barkema and Gomez-Meija (1998) in the US.

However, the absence of any proven link between the profitability of a firm and the reward structures it offers to its CEO and other top managers does not necessarily mean that profit-related goals are unimportant. Firms increasingly offer top managers a total remuneration 'package' which often involves bonus payments and share options as well as salary. In this case higher firm profitability, and therefore dividend earnings per share, may help raise the share price and with it the value of the total remuneration package. Indeed Ezzamel and Watson (1998) have suggested that the total remuneration package offered to CEOs is directly related to the 'going rate' for corporate profitability. It may therefore be that top management have more incentives for seeking profit-related goals than might at first be apparent.

To summarise, therefore, although there may be no open admission to profit maximisation, the strong influence of owners on managed firms, the use of preset hurdle fates and the presence of profit-related reward structures may in the end lead to an objective, or set of objectives, closely akin to profit maximisation.

Sales revenue-related behaviour

Sales revenue maximisation

Baumol's suggestion that management-controlled firms will wish to maximise sales revenue was based on the belief that the earnings of executives are more closely related to firm revenue than to firm profit. A number of studies have sought to test this belief. For example, in a study of 177 firms between 1985 and 1990, Conyon and Gregg (1994) found that the pay of top executives in large companies in the UK was most strongly related to a long-term performance measure (total shareholder returns) and not at all to current accounting profit. Furthermore, growth in sales resulting from takeovers was more highly rewarded than internal growth, despite the fact that such takeovers produced on average a lower return for shareholders and an increased liquidity risk. These findings are in line with other UK research (Gregg *et al.*, 1993; Conyon and Leech 1994) and with a study of small UK companies by Conyon and Nicolitsas (1998) which also found sales growth to be closely correlated with the pay of top executives.

Sales revenue as part of a 'goal set'

The results of Shipley's analysis tell us little about sales revenue maximisation. Nevertheless, Shipley found that target sales revenue was the fourth-ranked principal pricing objective (see Table 4.7, p. 166), and that nearly half the firms included sales revenue as at least part of their set of objectives. Larger companies cited sales revenue as an objective most frequently; one-seventh of companies with over 3,000 employees gave sales revenue as a principal goal compared to only one-fourteenth of all the firms. Since larger companies have greater separation between ownership and management control, this does lend some support to Baumol's assertion. The importance of sales revenue as part of a set of policy objectives was reinforced by the study of 193 UK industrial distributors by Shipley and Bourdon (1990), which found that 88% of these companies included sales revenue as one of a number of objectives. However, we see below that the nature of planning in large organisations must also be considered and that this may temper our support for sales revenue being itself the major objective, at least in the long term.

Strategic planning and sales revenue

Current thinking on strategic planning would support the idea of short-term sales maximisation, but only as a means to other ends (e.g. profitability or growth). Research in the mid-1970s by the US Strategic Planning Institute linked market share – seen here as a proxy for sales revenue – to profitability. These studies found that high market share had a significant and beneficial effect on both return on investment and cash flow, at least in the long term. However, in the short term the high investment and marketing expenditure needed to attain high market share reduces profitability and drains cash flow. Profit has to be sacrificed in the short term if high market share, and hence future high profits, are to be achieved in the long term.

Constrained sales revenue maximisation

The fact that 88% of all companies in Shipley's original study included profit in their 'goal set' indicates the relevance of the profit constraint to other objectives, including sales revenue. The later study by Shipley and Bourdon (1990) reached a similar conclusion, finding that 93% of the UK industrial distributors surveyed included profits in their 'goal set'.

Non-maximising behaviour

We have seen that the non-maximising or behavioural theories concentrate on how firms actually operate within the constraints imposed by organisational structure and firm environment. Recent evidence on management practice broadly supports the behavioural contention, namely that it is unhelpful to seek a single firm objective as a guide to actual firm behaviour. This support, however, comes from a rather different type of analysis, that of portfolio planning.

Portfolio planning

Work in the US by the Boston Consulting Group on the relationship between market share and industry growth gave rise to an approach to corporate planning known as 'portfolio planning'. Firms, especially the larger ones, can be viewed as having a collection or 'portfolio' of different products at different stages in the product life cycle. If a product is at an early stage in its life cycle, it will require a large investment in marketing and product development in order to achieve future levels of high profitability. At the same time another product may have 'matured' and, already possessing a good share of the market, be providing high profits and substantial cash flow.

The usual strategy in portfolio planning is to attempt to balance the portfolio so that existing profitable products are providing the funds necessary to raise new products to maturity. This approach has become a classic part of strategic decision making.

If a firm is using the portfolio approach in its planning then it may be impossible to predict the firm's behaviour for individual products or market sections on the basis of a single firm objective. This is because the goals of the firm will change for a given product or market sector depending on the relative position of that product or market sector within the overall portfolio. Portfolio planning, along with other behavioural theories, suggests that no single objective is likely to be useful in explaining actual firm behaviour, at least in specific cases.

'Managing for value' (MFV)

The non-maximisation behaviour of large companies can be seen clearly in the approach taken by some large companies (Griffiths, 2000). For example, between 1997 and 2000 Cadbury Schweppes, the chocolate and confectionery multinational, explained its objectives in terms of 'managing for value' (MFV). To meet the MFV criterion the company stressed the importance of:

- increasing earnings per share by at least 10% every year;
- generating £150m of free cash flow every year;
- doubling the value of shareholders' investment in the four years to 2000;
- competing in the world's growth markets by effective internal investment and by value-enhancing acquisitions;
- developing market share by introducing innovations in product development, packaging and routes to market;
- increasing commitment to value creation in managers and employees through incentive schemes and share ownership;
- investing in key areas of air emissions, water, energy and solid waste.

From the above list it is clear that the first three preoccupations are related to the profit objectives while the fourth and fifth relate to company growth and market share. In addition, the final two objectives encompass both human resource and environmental issues. In this context, it can be seen that maximising a single corporate goal seems unrealistic in the dynamic world of multinationals.

Reviewing business behaviour

The traditional theory of the firm assumes that its sole objective is to maximise profit. The managerial theories assume that where ownership and control of the organisation are separated, the objective that guides the firm will be that which the management sets. This is usually thought to be maximisation of either sales revenue or growth. It is important to know which, if any, of the maximising objectives are being pursued, since firm output and price will be different for each objective. Behavioural theory tends to oppose the idea of the firm seeking to maximise any objective. For instance, top management may seek to hold the various stakeholder groups in balance by adopting a set of minimum targets. Even where a single group with a clear objective does become dominant within the firm, others with alternative objectives may soon replace it.

In practice, profit maximisation in the long term still appears to be important. Sales revenue seems quite important as a short-term goal, though even here a profit target may still be part of the goal set. The prominence of the profit target may be an indication that ownership is not as divorced from the control of large firms as may once have been thought. One reason why sales revenue may be pursued in the short term is found in an analysis of current strategic planning techniques, which link short-term sales revenue to long-term profit. Sales revenue may therefore be useful for explaining short-term firm behaviour.

Those who, like Marris, argue that growth is a separate objective from profit find some support in the lack of any clear relationship between growth and profitability. Growth may also be a means of securing greater stability for the firm. It may reduce internal conflict, by being an objective around which both owner-shareholders and managers can agree, and possibly reduces the risk of takeover. Also, large firms experience, if not higher profits, then less variable profits. A widely used technique in the management of larger firms, portfolio planning, would seem to support the behaviouralist view, that no single objective will usefully help predict firm behaviour in a given market.

Corporate governance

Corporate governance refers to the various arrangements within companies which provide both authority and accountability in its operations. In other words, the various rules and procedures which are in place to direct and control the running of the company. However, there has been much concern in recent years as to the ways in which the larger public limited companies (PLCs) have been governed, especially in view of high-profile company collapses such as Enron in the US in 2001 and Parmalat in Italy in 2004.

Before turning to the problems encountered by such companies and the remedies proposed, it may be useful to consider the issue of *executive remuneration* in rather more detail. This has itself been a major source of concern to shareholders and other corporate investors.

Executive remuneration

In Europe, 84% of companies place decisions about executive pay in the hands of their compensation, or remuneration, committee, according to a survey by consultants Hewitt, Bacon and Woodrow. So, ultimately, it is remuneration committees that are as responsible as anyone when executive pay appears to bear scant relationship to corporate performance. *Pensions and Investment Research Consultants* (PIRC), the UK corporate governance watchdog, reported that the pay of executive directors at FTSE 100 companies spiralled high above inflation, rising by 10.3% during 2003, spurred by bonuses rising by 14.5%.

The rapid rise in executive pay, when the companies themselves have been performing modestly at best, has created widespread criticism from shareholders and others. *Stock options* have been a particular source of criticism – the practice whereby senior executives have been given the 'option' of buying company shares at a heavily discounted price (i.e. lower than the market price) and then selling them at a profit should they succeed in raising the share price above an agreed target. Often, exercising these options has given far more income to executives than their basic salaries.

So who sits on the remuneration committee which decides the executive remuneration schemes? In the UK the *Combined Code* of corporate governance states that members should be drawn 'exclusively' from non-executives due to the potential for conflicts of interest. By and large, this is so. However, says PIRC, some 14% of FTSE 100 companies continue to include executives on their remuneration committees.

Arguably, excessive executive pay is even more widespread in the US. For example, the gap between the earnings of ordinary Americans and top executives has grown far wider in the past 25 years. A statistic commonly quoted by the labour group AFL-CIO shows that a chief executive made $42 for every dollar earned by one of his or her blue-collar workers in 1980. Today, chief executives were earning $531 for every dollar taken home by a typical worker.

Corporate 'scandals'

Corporate scandals, such as those at Enron, WorldCom and Global Crossing in the US, have become well known in the past few years. However, such problems are by no means confined to the US, as Case Study 4.4 on the Italian dairy company, Parmalat, clearly indicates.

Case Study 4.4 Crisis at Parmalat

In little more than a fortnight in December 2003, the Italian dairy conglomerate became engulfed in Europe's biggest financial fraud as some €10bn to €13bn were found to have disappeared from its accounts.

Deloitte, Parmalat's chief auditor, did not do its own checks on some big bank accounts at one of the Italian dairy group's subsidiaries that turned out to be fakes. As a result, in December 2003, a major scandal broke after the disclosure that Bonlat, a Parmalat subsidiary in the Cayman Islands, did not have accounts worth almost €4bn (£2.8bn) at Bank of America (B of A). Eventually this 'lost' money was found to be three times greater. Bonlat's auditor is Grant Thornton and B of A told it in January 2004 that a document purportedly showing accounts with cash and securities worth €3.95bn was fake. The document was used by Grant Thornton as part of its work on Bonlat's 2002 accounts, which were then consolidated into Parmalat group's 2002 financial statements.

Deloitte, one of the big four global accounting firms, did not make independent checks on the authenticity of Bonlat's supposed accounts with B of A, according to people close to Parmalat and familiar with the investigations into the company. These people said Deloitte believed it was entitled to rely on Grant Thornton's work on Bonlat, rather than do its own checks, and such an arrangement was permitted by Italian law and regulators. They also said that the division of work between Deloitte, as chief auditor, and Grant Thornton, as auditor to Parmalat's subsidiaries, was agreed with the company and notified to Consob, Italy's chief financial regulator.

Deloitte strongly denies any wrongdoing. It denies acting negligently or being complicit in the alleged massive fraud at Parmalat, according to people close to Parmalat and familiar with the investigations. These people said that Deloitte believed it had been misled by Parmalat. Deloitte's relationship with Grant Thornton, a medium-sized accounting firm, appears to have become strained during the second half of 2003. Deloitte raised concerns about Parmalat's 2003 interim results because of issues initially raised by Deloitte, rather than Grant Thornton, according to people close to Parmalat.

In October 2003, Deloitte declined to authenticate the value of Bonlat's mutual fund in Cayman. It also refused to approve a gain on a derivatives contract held by the fund. Deloitte's concerns about Parmalat's accounts focused on its financial companies such as Bonlat. It qualified the accounts of Parmalat Soparfi, a Luxembourg subsidiary, in 1999, 2000 and 2001. Parmalat personnel systematically created assets and records to accompany them, which were non-existent, according to people close to the company. Deloitte said it did not know if the €3.95bn of cash and securities supposedly held by Bonlat was fictional or had been placed somewhere other than B of A.

Deloitte was increasingly reliant on Grant Thornton for verification of Parmalat's consolidated assets. In 1999, Grant Thornton certified 22% of Parmalat's assets, but it rose to 49% in 2002. But Deloitte had to verify at least 51% of Parmalat's assets because of its role as chief auditor.

Case Study 4.4 continued

Questions

1. What were the causes of the collapse of Parmalat?
2. Why have some blamed the auditors for the collapse, as well as dishonesty at Parmalat itself?
3. What lessons might be learned from this case study?

Lessons for corporate governance

These high-profile company collapses, together with shareholder concerns as to the often 'excessive' remuneration packages of company directors in poorly performing companies, have resulted in changes in the rules of corporate governance in recent years. These have involved changes in both internal and external practices, as for example in the companies' dealings with auditors and accountants. Box 4.2 reviews some recent changes and proposals for change in the UK and elsewhere.

Box 4.2 Corporate governance

In the UK the *Higgs Committee* in 2002 has sought to improve corporate governance in the wake of the bitter experiences for shareholders and investors in the collapse of Enron, WorldCom, Global Crossing and other high-profile companies. The Higgs proposals include the following:

- At least 50% of a company's board should consist of independent non-executive directors.
- Rigorous, formal and transparent procedures should be adopted when recruiting new directors to a board.
- Roles of Chairman and Chief Executive of a company should be separate.
- No individual should be appointed to a second chairmanship of a FTSE 100 company.

In the US the *Sarbanes–Oxley Act* in 2002 was also directed at strengthening corporate governance.

- If officers of a company are proved to have intentionally filed false accounts, they can be sent to jail for up to 20 years and fined $5m.
- Executives will have to forfeit bonuses if their accounts have to be restated.
- A ban on company loans to its directors and executives.
- Protection for corporate whistleblowers.
- Audit committees to be made up entirely of independent people.
- Disclosure of all off-balance-sheet transactions.

Other suggestions for improving corporate governance include the following:

- The European Commission wants to ensure that group auditors take responsibility for all aspects of companies' accounts and is considering requiring each European Union member state to set up US-style accounting oversight boards.

- Italy's government wants a stronger regulator to replace Consob, the existing securities and markets authority.
- The OECD has drafted a revision of its principles of corporate governance, including calls for shareholders to be able to submit questions to auditors.
- Auditors should be seen as accountable to shareholders and not to management, as has often been the case. The draft proposals also call on boards to protect whistleblowers.

Product life cycle

Most products go through four stages in their life cycle, namely introduction, growth, maturity and decline, as indicated in Figure 4.7. As we see below, business behaviour in terms of price-setting and other product-related policies will depend upon the stage the product has reached in its life cycle.

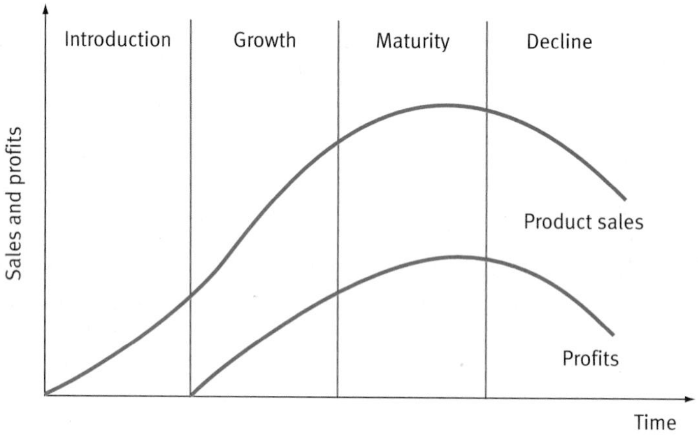

Fig 4.7 Stages in the product life cycle

1 *Introduction.* This is a stage in which the product is relatively unknown, sales are low, and profits are not yet being made. The promotion strategy will be designed to inform people that the product is available. The product would normally be stocked in a limited number of outlets but the firm would try to ensure that there was maximum exposure at these points of sale. Price might be relatively low at this time in an attempt to gain a market 'foothold' (*penetration pricing* strategy). Alternatively, price might be relatively high where the producer faces little competition for a new product with unique characteristics (*price skimming* strategy).

2 *Growth.* In this stage there is extremely rapid growth which attracts the first competitors to the market. Prices are likely to be lowered to attract a wider base of customers and the number of outlets likely to be increased. The firm will also be seeking the new products that will replace this one, or modifications to some existing

products that will extend their life cycle. The profits which are starting to be made can be used to support such investments.

3 *Maturity*. The majority of sales are repeat orders in this stage rather than first-time purchases. Fierce competition often forces the firm to reduce prices further. Advertising seeks to persuade customers to buy this, rather than some other, brand of product. The firm will be looking to see if the product can be sold in other markets – often abroad. Refinements and cosmetic changes are introduced to provide a competitive edge and maintain sales levels. Replacement products are likely to be introduced. Economies of scale resulting from large volume production will help to keep unit costs low and profits high.

4 *Decline*. As sales decline, advertising and promotion cease. Prices may be reduced as much as possible to keep at least some sales. Eventually, as the product moves into loss, it is withdrawn from the market. However, as price is relatively inelastic for those fewer 'loyal' customers who still purchase it, prices may sometimes be increased during the decline stage for some products.

Checkpoint 3 What might be the reasons for increasing the price of a product during its decline stage?

Table 4.5 summarises this discussion on how price and non-price behaviour of a business might vary with the product life cycle.

Table 4.5 Business behaviour and the product life cycle

Introduction	Growth	Maturity	Decline
Characteristics ■ High failure rate ■ Little competition ■ Frequent modifications ■ Make losses	*Characteristics* ■ More competitors ■ Rising sales ■ Possibly acquired by larger company	*Characteristics* ■ Sales increase at reduced rate ■ Product line widened ■ Prices fall as market share is lost ■ Difficult for new entrants ■ Marginal producers drop out	*Characteristics* ■ Falling industry sales ■ Falling product sales ■ Some producers abandon market ■ Falling profits
Strategies ■ Create product awareness ■ 'Skim' pricing or penetration pricing ■ Shake-out policy – quickly drop unsuccessful products	*Strategies* ■ Promote brand image ■ Acquire outlets ■ Obtain economies of scale	*Strategies* ■ Encourage repeat buys ■ Seek new customers by repositioning and brand extension strategies ■ Seek to hold or increase market share by greater efficiency ■ Use price discounting to hold or win market share ■ Hold on to distributors	*Strategies* ■ Strict cost control ■ 'Run out' sales promotion with low price to get rid of stocks prior to introduction of replacement ■ Higher prices charged to fewer, but still loyal customers

LINKS

Business behaviour involving product, price, promotion and place for both single product and multi-product firms is considered more fully in Chapter 13, p. 497.

Key Terms

Articles of Association Sets out the rules by which the company will be administered (e.g. voting rights of directors).

Behavioural objectives Objectives influenced by the dynamics of firm behaviour: often non-maximising.

Coalitions Groups which have a consensus on a particular objective/goal.

Constrained sales revenue maximisation Firm seeks to maximise sales revenue (turnover) but subject to meeting some minimum profit target.

Corporate governance The various rules and procedures used to direct and control the running of the company.

Growth This can be expressed in various forms: e.g. the rate of increase of output per annum, or rate of increase of the firms capitalised value per annum, and so on.

Managerial objectives Objectives set by managers (agents) rather than shareholders (principals). Profit will tend to be less important; sales revenue, market share, growth will tend to be more important.

Memorandum of Association Document which forms the basis of registration of a company. Lists the subscribers to the capital of the company and the number of shares they hold. May also list company objectives etc.

Partnership Unincorporated business of between 2 and 20 people who share risks and profits. Partnerships usually have unlimited liability for debts of other partners (though limited partnerships can be formed).

Penetration pricing A low-price strategy in the introduction stage of the product life cycle.

Price skimming A high-price strategy in the introduction stage of the product life cycle.

Principal–agent problem Where agents (managers) pursue different objectives from principals (shareholders).

Private limited company (Ltd) A limited number of shareholders (2–50) with limited liability. Cannot offer shares to general public.

Product life cycle The stages a typical product will go through during its 'life cycle', namely introduction, growth, maturity and decline stages.

Public corporations Government owned; sometimes called nationalised industries.

Public limited company (PLC) Unlimited number of shareholders (with limited liability). Can offer shares to general public.

Sales revenue maximisation Firm seeks to maximise sales revenue (turnover).

Satisficing A theory which suggests that objectives constantly change, depending on whether previous aspirations have (or have not) been met.

Sole trader One-person business.

Key Points

- Separation between ownership by shareholders (principals) and control by managers (agents) makes profit maximisation less likely.
- Maximisation of sales revenue or asset growth (as well as profit) must be considered in manager-led firms.

- The objectives pursued by the firm will influence the firm's price and output decisions.
- Different groupings (coalitions) may be dominant within a firm at different points of time. Firm objectives may therefore change as the coalitions in effective control change.
- Organisational structure may result in non-maximising behaviour; e.g. the presence of diverse stakeholders may induce the firm to set minimum targets for a range of variables as a means of reducing conflict.
- Shipley's seminal work (supported by later studies) found less than 16% of the firms studied to be 'true' profit maximisers. However, Shipley found that 88% of firms included profit as part of their 'goal set'.
- Separation between ownership and control receives empirical support, though small 'threshold' levels of shareholdings may still secure effective control in modern PLCs.
- Profit remains a useful predictor of long-term firm behaviour, though sales revenue may be better in predicting short-term firm behaviour.
- Profit maximisation may not be acknowledged as a goal by many firms, yet in setting 'hurdle rates' senior managers may implicitly be following such an objective.
- Profitability and executive pay appear to be largely unrelated, suggesting that other managerial objectives might be given priority (sales revenue, growth, etc.). However, total remuneration 'packages' for top executives may be linked to profitability, helping to align the interests of managers more closely to the interests of shareholders.
- Businesses may be able to raise revenue and profit by adopting ethical and environmentally sustainable policies.
- Business behaviour, both price and non-price, may depend on the stage the product has reached in its life cycle.
- Portfolio planning points to a variety of ever-changing objectives guiding firm activity rather than any single objective.

Assessment Practice

Multiple choice

1 *Limited liability* describes a situation where:

(a) all shareholders are equally responsible for all the debts of the company
(b) the responsibility of shareholders for the debts of a company is limited to the amount they agreed to pay for the shares when they bought them
(c) the responsibility of shareholders for the debts of a company is limited to the number of debentures they hold in the company
(d) the responsibility of shareholders for the debts of a company is limited to the value of their personal wealth
(e) all shareholders must hold a minimum of 20 shares in a company.

2 **Which of the following is a quality enjoyed by a form of enterprise called a *partnership*?**

(a) Shares can be issued to the general public.
(b) The partnership usually consists of up to 30 people.
(c) The owners are not jointly liable for the repayment of the debts of the partnership.
(d) The owners of such enterprises do not need to publish their accounts.
(e) The action of one partner is not binding on another.

3 **Which of the following describes a *holding company* form of business organisation?**

(a) A company that controls more than 33% of the equity of another company
(b) A company that usually acts as market leader in an industry
(c) A company that often exists only to hold over 50% of the equity of a group of subsidiary companies
(d) A single company that organises its activity into a matrix format
(e) A single company that has been divided into many divisions

4 **A difference between a public limited company (PLC) and a private limited company (Ltd) is that:**

(a) the PLC has limited liability
(b) the PLC has shareholders
(c) the PLC has a limited number of shareholders
(d) the PLC can only raise a limited amount of capital
(e) the PLC can sell shares on the open market such as the London Stock Exchange.

5 **The *principal–agent problem* describes a situation where:**

(a) firms fail to maximise long-term investment
(b) firms fail to achieve market power because of managerial incompetence
(c) managers follow their own inclinations, which often differ from the aims of shareholders
(d) managers disagree with employees on production issues
(e) shareholders prevent managers from maximising profits.

6 **Which document issued by a limited company defines its internal government?**

(a) Articles of Association
(b) Memorandum of Association
(c) Shareholder Certificate
(d) Profit and Loss Accounts
(e) Balance Sheet

7 **If profits are maximised, then:**

(a) marginal revenue is zero
(b) marginal cost is zero
(c) marginal revenue is greater than marginal cost
(d) marginal revenue equals marginal cost
(e) marginal revenue is less than marginal cost.

8 This describes a situation where firms are seen as adopting different strategies for products at different stages in their product life cycle.

(a) Satisficing
(b) Principal–agent problem
(c) Coalition
(d) Portfolio planning
(e) Sales revenue maximiser

9 A 'penetration pricing strategy' is most likely to be used in which stage of the product life cycle?

(a) Maturity
(b) Decline
(c) Introduction
(d) Growth
(e) Stagnation

10 A 'price skimming' strategy is sometimes used in the introduction stage of the product life cycle because:

(a) charging low prices helps to gain market share
(b) charging low prices when demand is elastic raises revenue
(c) charging high prices when demand is unit elastic raises revenue
(d) charging high prices when demand is elastic raises revenue
(e) charging high prices when demand is inelastic increases revenue.

Data response and stimulus questions

1 Look carefully at the following text and data.

Co-op Bank, ethics and profits

In 2001 the Co-op Bank sought to put a value on the costs and benefits of its ethical stance over the past year. It argued that its support for ethical policies in areas such as renewable energy and the arms trade gave it an extra profit of £16m in 2000 (around 16% of all pre-tax profits) even after taking into account the extra £2.5m of net costs incurred.

The list below itemises some of the cost outlays and cost savings related to its ethical policies in 2000, identified in the Bank's fourth annual 'Partnership Report'.

Ethics tally

Extra costs	(£000s)
Income lost through turning down unacceptable business	1,696
Ethical audit	144
Staff salaries and overheads	370
Best practice, e.g. environmentally safe air conditioning	792
Community investment	2,520
Electricity from renewable sources	41
Replacing PVC in plastic cards	15
Recycling	6
Environmentally sound paper	52

Cost savings	(£000s)
Energy saved	112
Waste reduction	7
Re-use of furniture	7
Lower paper use	2,901
Net cost (before profit from extra business)	£2,587,000

On the revenue side, the bank stresses the benefit from having ethics as an important element of the bank's brand image. Its marketing and finance specialists have estimated that ethical values can be linked to substantial revenue growth responsible for between 15% and 18% of the £96m pre-tax profit declared in 2000. Mori (the poll experts) conducted research for the Co-op Bank and concluded that over 25% of its current account customers cited ethics or the environment as the main reason for banking with the Co-op.

Question

What implications might this study have for corporate business objectives?

2 Look carefully at the results from two major questionnaire surveys in the UK on firm objectives (Tables 4.6 and 4.7). What do these results suggest?

Table 4.6 Important objectives identified by 77 Scottish firms

Objectives	Number	Per cent
No single objective	23	29.9
Maximising profit	22	28.6
Maximising sales revenue	1	1.3
Increasing shareholder value	11	14.3
Target rate of return on capital employed	7	9.1
Other	13	16.9
Total	77	100.0

Source: Hornby (1994)

Table 4.7 Objectives in price setting of 723 UK firms surveyed

	Principal goal	Part of goal set
Target profit or ROCE*	486	639
Prices fair to firm and customers	94	353
Price similarity with competitors	56	350
Target sales revenue	54	342
Stable volume of sales	37	182
Target market share of sales	16	129
Stable prices	11	120
Other	10	38

* Return on Capital Employed
Source: Shipley (1981)

Matching pairs

1 **Match the *lettered* term to the correct *numbered* description.**

Term

(a) Private limited company
(b) Public limited company
(c) Sole trader
(d) Ordinary partnership
(e) Holding company

Description

(i) In which type of business it is most likely that ownership of the business ensures control of the business.
(ii) In which type of business there is unlimited liability but a sharing of costs, risks and responsibility.
(iii) In which type of business there is a restriction on selling shares to the general public.
(iv) This type of business owns a majority of the voting shares in a subsidiary company or group of firms.
(v) In which type of business the principal–agent problem most commonly occur.

2 **Match the *lettered* term to the correct *numbered* description.**

Term

(a) Profit maximiser
(b) Sales revenue maximiser
(c) Constrained sales revenue maximiser
(d) Coalition
(e) Satisficer

Description

(i) A firm which produces output until marginal revenue is zero.
(ii) A firm for which future objectives depend on the extent to which previous aspirations have been achieved.
(iii) A firm for which the additional cost of producing the last unit exactly equals the additional revenue from producing the last unit.
(iv) A firm which is mainly interested in turnover but recognises the need to provide a reasonable return for shareholders.
(v) A firm for which the group which effectively runs the company has a consensus on the objectives to be pursued.

True/False questions

1 A group which cannot agree a consensus as to the goals it should pursue is called a 'coalition'.

True/False

2 Firms may seek to maximise sales revenue because the salaries and status of managers may be more closely related to turnover than to profit performance.

True/False

3 Firms may follow a constrained sales-revenue-maximising approach because managers recognise that they must achieve at least a minimum level of profit to keep shareholders content.

True/False

4 The stakeholders of a firm are those who hold equity in the firm.

True/False

5 When total revenue exactly matches total costs (both variable and fixed), then break-even output has been reached.

True/False

6 Output is likely to be lower and price higher for the profit-maximising firm than would be the case for the sales-revenue-maximising firm.

True/False

7 Marginal revenue equals marginal cost is the condition required for the level of output which maximises sales revenue.

True/False

8 Total revenue is a maximum and total cost a minimum for the profit-maximising level of output.

True/False

9 In times of recession a 'coalition' is likely to be formed based around the objective of the firm remaining solvent.

True/False

10 A benefit of pursuing 'growth' as the firm's main objective is that it may help reduce risk, for example by allowing more product and market diversification.

True/False

Essay questions

1 Does business objective matter to the price and output behaviour of a firm? Explain your reasoning.
2 Assess the advantages and disadvantages of forming a public limited company (PLC).
3 Why might a business itself consider it to be worth while to adopt high standards in terms of ethical/environmental considerations?
4 Why has the issue of corporate governance received such a high profile in recent years? Suggest how such governance might be improved.
5 Consider the relevance of the product life cycle to business behaviour.

Chapter 5

Firm size, mergers and the 'public interest'

Introduction

How do we define small and medium-sized enterprises (SMEs)? Why has the small firm continued to survive and how important is it to the whole economy? Why do many SMEs wish to grow larger, what methods do they use and what problems do they encounter? Under what circumstances are mergers likely to be in the 'public interest' and in any case what do we mean by the 'public interest'. What patterns and trends are taking place in merger activities and why and how do governments seek to regulate such activity?

The contents of this chapter will help you to understand these issues and take further the discussions on economies of scale, scope and experience in Chapter 3. A more detailed analysis of competition policy in the UK and EU, including mergers and restrictive practices legislation, is presented in Chapter 8.

Learning objectives:

By the end of this chapter you should be able to:

- outline the various definitions of SMEs and their contribution to the UK economy
- explain the reasons why small firms continue to exist
- understand why SMEs often seek to grow larger, the methods they use and the government support programmes available
- assess the contribution of larger firms to the UK economy
- identify the patterns and trends in merger activity and understand why governments seek to regulate merger activity in the 'public interest'.

Small to medium-sized enterprises (SMEs)

Before assessing the contribution of small and medium-sized enterprises (SMEs) to the UK and the EU economy, it will be helpful if we first define them.

Definition of SMEs

There are a number of different ways of defining small and medium-sized firms.

- *Bolton Committee Report of 1971*. This had recognised the difficulty of defining the small firm. Rather than depending solely on numbers of employees or other data, it suggested that the emphasis be placed on the characteristics which make the performance of small firms significantly different from those of large firms. Three such characteristics were identified as being of particular importance:
  - having a relatively small share of the market;
  - being managed by owners in a personalised way rather than via a formalised management structure;
  - being independent of larger enterprises, so that its owner-managers are free from outside control when taking their decisions.
- The *1985 Companies Act*. This was more specific and defined a company in the UK as small if it satisfied any *two* of the following:
  - turnover less than £2m;
  - net assets under £975,000;
  - fewer than 50 employees.
- *The Department of Trade and Industry* (DTI). This defines SMEs in terms of numbers of employees as follows:
  - micro firm (0–9 employees);
  - small firm (10–49 employees);
  - medium-sized firms (50–249 employees);
  - large firm (over 250 employees).
- *European Union* (EU). This definition of an SME involves four criteria, as listed in Table 5.1.

Table 5.1 Defining micro, small and medium-sized firms

	Micro firm	Small firm	Medium firm
Turnover		Not exceeding €7m	Not exceeding €40m
Balance sheet total		Not exceeding €5m	Not exceeding €27m
Employees	Fewer than 10	Fewer than 50	Fewer than 250
Independence criteria	–	25% or less	25% or less

To qualify as an SME both the employees and independence criteria must be satisfied together with either the turnover or the balance sheet criteria. An SME is defined as an 'independent enterprise' when the amount of capital or voting rights in that firm held by one or more non-SME firms does not exceed 25%. The values shown in the table for turnover and balance sheet are liable to be changed over time as the absolute monetary values require adjustment because of inflation.

Importance of SMEs

Table 5.2 indicates the shares of different-sized enterprises in the total number of enterprises, total employment and total turnover, both for the UK and the EU.

Table 5.2 Shares (%) of enterprises, employment and turnover: UK and EU

	Micro (0–9)	Small (10–49)	Medium (50–249)	Large (250+)
Enterprises:				
UK	95.0	4.2	0.6	0.2
EU	93.1	5.9	0.8	0.2
Employment				
UK	30.3	13.4	11.4	44.9
EU	34.0	19.0	13.0	34.0
Turnover				
UK	22.8	14.5	13.9	48.8
EU	18.0	17.4	19.3	45.3

Sources: Adapted from *European Commission* (2002): *Small Business Service* (2002)

The 'micro' firm, employing fewer than 10 people, makes up 95% of all UK enterprises, provides 30.3% of all UK employment and 22.8% of all UK turnover. While the figures for the contribution of micro enterprises were similar in the UK and the EU, it is interesting to note that small and medium-sized enterprises tended to contribute rather less to employment and turnover in the UK than in the EU. The mirror image of this can be seen in the greater contribution that large firms make to employment and turnover in the UK as compared to the EU.

Although large firms with over 250 employees are few in number in both the UK and EU, their contribution to employment and turnover is highly significant. In the UK, whilst large firms are only 0.2% (i.e. 1 in 500) of all enterprises, they contribute 44.9% of UK employment and 48.8% of UK turnover. We return to consider the large firm in more detail later in this chapter (p. 177).

Small firm survival

As we saw in Chapter 3 (pp. 101–105), economic theory suggests that large firms should be more efficient than small firms owing to the existence of **economies of scale**. Despite this, small firms continue to survive for the following reasons.

- *Supply a small (niche) market* either geographically (e.g. corner shop) or by producing a specialist item or service.

- *Provide a personal or more flexible service*, e.g. local solicitor, accountant or builder.
- *Allow entrepreneurs the opportunity to start their own business and to test their ideas in the marketplace.* Many of these people are dissatisfied with working for large companies and desire to be their 'own boss'.
- *The owners have made a conscious decision not to grow* because they do not want to undertake the inherent risks and workload associated with growth.
- *Benefit from government support programmes* directed towards helping the small firm survive and grow.

Checkpoint 1 Can you identify *three* different sectors of economic activity in which you would expect small firms to thrive?

'Problems' facing SMEs

Despite the importance of SMEs to the UK and EU economies noted in Table 5.2, they face a number of obstacles to their survival and growth.

- *Small firms and the banks.* One of the most common concerns of SMEs has been to secure adequate financial backing at reasonable interest rates. Smaller firms rely on personal savings at the start-up stage but then obtain some 60% of external finance from banks, although very small firms also use hire purchase and leasing arrangements. The relationship between smaller firms and banks is therefore of vital importance for this sector of UK industry. As has been noted in many surveys, the central problem of financial support for small firms is not necessarily the availability of finance but its cost. For example, the rate of interest for small firms employing fewer than 30 employees in the UK is currently between 3% and 5% above base rates and this is often doubled if the overdraft is exceeded, even if only briefly.
- *Debt structure.* Another issue for UK small firms relates to the structure of their debt. As can be seen from Table 5.3, the UK dependence on overdraft finance accounts for 59% of total external funding, which is above the EU average. Such dependence often restricts the ability of smaller firms to take a long-term view

Table 5.3 Sources of SME external funding (%) and lengths of loans

		Length of loan (%)		
Country	Overdraft (%)*	Up to 3 years	3–5 years	Over 5 years
UK	59	24	29	47
EU average	50	25	37	37

Adapted from Bank of England (2002)
* Repayable on demand

because overdrafts are repayable on demand. As far as the length of loans is concerned, some 24% of UK companies have loans of up to three years, which is similar to the EU average. On the other hand, a smaller proportion of UK firms have loans of three to five years, and a larger proportion of UK firms have loans of over five years, as compared to the EU average.

- *Lack of training*. Surveys in the past decade have shown that between 80% and 90% of small companies in the UK had no business training and received no formal preparation for company board responsibility. The continued need for such support was highlighted in a major study of 1,300 SMEs by the Centre for Business Research of Cambridge University (Cosh and Hughes, 2000). This study found that less than half of all the firms investigated had formal structures for their management organisation and less than half provided formal training within their companies.
- *Low turnover and cash flow* are frequently identified as problems in regular surveys, such as the National Westminster/SBRT Quarterly Survey of Small Business.
  - *Low turnover* was identified by almost 45% of firms as the most important problem in the immediate aftermath of the economic slowdown of the early 1990s and is still cited as such by around 25% of UK SMEs.
  - *Cashflow payments* problems are seen as the main source of concern by around 10% of UK SMEs. Sometimes the source of this problem may be high interest rates on loans or the lack of demand in times of recession. However the linkage of cashflow problems in SMEs to late payments is sometimes exaggerated. For example, UK SMEs currently have an average payment delay of 41 days, longer than countries such as Denmark (33 days), Norway (30 days) and Germany (31 days), but shorter than France (58 days) and Italy (78 days).
- *Government regulations and paperwork*. These are cited as a problem by nearly 15% of respondents to the NatWest/SBRT surveys. Valuable time and resources are taken up responding to a host of paperwork reflecting new initiatives and directives from the UK, EU and other regulatory bodies. Nor is the problem confined only to SMEs. The Institute of Chartered Accountants produced a survey in late 2003 estimating that such 'red tape' cost the UK economy over £6bn each year.

It may be useful to review how successive governments in the UK have introduced various support programmes, especially as the small firm has become more widely perceived as a source of growth for both national output and employment.

Government support programmes

Small firm support has focused on three main areas.

1 Easier access to equity and loan capital

- *Small Firms Loan Guarantee Scheme*. First introduced in 1981 to encourage financial institutions to lend to (higher risk) SMEs. The government now guarantees 70% of loans by 'authorised' financial institutions to companies trading for less than two years and 85% to companies trading for more than two years.

- *Enterprise Investment Scheme*. Introduced in 1994 as a successor to earlier schemes, it encourages equity investment in small unquoted companies by offering various tax allowances on shares to investors.

Other government schemes to provide funds for small businesses include Regional Venture Capital Funds, High Technology Funds, Phoenix Funds, Venture Capital Trusts and support for the Alternative Investment Market (AIM). Case Study 5.1 looks in more detail at the contribution of AIM to SME financial support.

2 Increased tax allowances and grants

- *Corporation tax*. Small companies pay a reduced rate of 10% on the first £10,000 of taxable profits compared to a standard rate of 30%.
- *Enterprise grants*. Grants up to the value of 15% of the costs of fixed capital equipment (with a maximum grant of £75,000) can be claimed by small firms to help investment.

Other such schemes include Small Firms Training Loans (SFTL) and a host of small firm support services via Training and Enterprise Councils (TECs), Chambers of Commerce, Business Links, Small Business Service etc.

3 Less government interference

Various attempts have been made to reduce 'red tape' and government bureaucracy for small firms, with mixed results.

Case Study 5.1 reviews survey evidence on the contribution of the Alternative Investment Market to the growth of small firms in the UK economy.

Case Study 5.1 Alternative Investment Market (AIM)

In June 1995 the *Alternative Investment Market* (AIM) was opened to meet the demand for a low-cost and accessible investment market for small and growing companies. Its trading rules are less demanding than those for a full listing on the London Stock Exchange, as indicated in Table 5.4.

Table **5.4** The differences between the main market and AIM

Listing criteria	Main market	AIM
% of free-floating shares	Minimum 25% in public hands	No minimum
Trading history	Three years trading record normally required	No prior trading record required
Listing fees	Companies required to pay a listing fee of between £5,125 and £256,250, depending on market capitalisation	Flat fee of £4,000 per company
Shareholder participation	Prior shareholder approval needed for certain transactions	No prior shareholder approval required
Reporting requirements	Required to report profits twice a year	Required to report profits twice a year

Case Study 5.1 continued

By early 2004, there were 693 companies trading on the AIM, with a total of £5bn having been raised since 1995. Companies on the AIM include Centre Parcs, Peel Hotels, Majestic Wine and Ask Central (restaurants), Hardy Amies (fashion house), Pixology (photographic software) and Aberdeen Football Club. In 2003 almost as much money was raised by SMEs on AIM (£1.6bn) as on the London Stock Exchange.

Question How might you justify government support for the Alternative Investment Market?

It may be useful at this stage to review some survey evidence on the contribution of small firms to the UK economy.

Small firms and the UK economy

The current interest in small firms is due partly to a growing recognition of their ability to create new jobs and provide innovative products and services. However, there is a danger in placing too heavy an emphasis on the role of small firms in rebuilding the UK's industrial base. Figures from the Department of Trade and Industry (DTI) in 2002 showed that 45% of VAT registered businesses failed to survive the first three years. Storey (1982) had already shown that most small firms stay static or die. In his study of all the new manufacturing firms started in Cleveland, County Durham and Tyne and Wear from 1965 to 1978 he found that only 774 survived out of 1,200. Of the survivors, more than half still had fewer than 10 employees in 1982, and nearly three-quarters had fewer than 25. In fact, the probability of a new business employing more than 100 people after a decade was less than 0.75%. For every new job created by a small firm in these three counties over the 13-year period, four jobs were lost from large companies employing over 1,000 persons.

Storey *et al.* (1987) found that in their survey of single-plant independent manufacturing companies in northern England, one-third of the new jobs were found in less than 4% of the new starters. Further research (Storey, 1994) also showed that it is incorrect to assume that countries which have experienced the most rapid increase in new firm formation (measured in terms of increase in self-employment) are those which have experienced the fastest growth of employment creation. The same survey also pointed out that investment in government training schemes for small company entrepreneurs at the start-up or at later stages is not necessarily related to the future success of small companies. The evidence shows that success is more closely related to the original educational attainment of the business owner. In other words, it may be more important to improve the level of the UK's general education as a whole, if small firms are to thrive.

For all these reasons, the net advantages of small firms may be less than is commonly supposed. Nevertheless, small firms are able to find market niches, especially where economies of scale are not easily obtained, as in providing specialised items for small markets, and in developing products used as components by large firms. Also, the movement towards a higher proportion of employment being in the service sector, where traditionally smaller firms have been dominant, suggests an increasingly important role for small firms in the UK economy. For example, a recent report has shown that UK-based SMEs performed relatively well over the period 1988–2001 as compared to large companies when measured in terms of growth in real value added, employment and profitability (European Commission, 2002).

However, in absolute terms there are still major gaps between small and large firms. For example, in the UK at the beginning of the new millennium, the value added per occupied person (labour productivity) in small firms was still only 87% of the UK average as compared to 120% for large firms (TUC, 2000). In addition, larger firms should not be neglected since although only 1 in 500 UK firms have 250 or more employees, large firms currently contribute around 52% of total employment and 49% of total turnover in the UK.

Activity 5.1 gives an opportunity to further check your understanding of SMEs.

Activity 5.1

1 Look carefully at Table 5.5. What does the table suggest about the contribution of: (a) SMEs in the UK, (b) large firms in the UK?

Table 5.5 Number of businesses, employment and turnover share by size band in the UK (2001)

Employment size band	Number of businesses (thousands)	Share of total (%)		
		Businesses	Employment	Turnover
0	2,634	68.2	10.6	6.8
1–4	797	20.6	8.4	8.9
5–9	216	5.6	5.6	5.8
10–19	119	3.1	6.0	7.1
20–49	59	1.5	6.3	7.6
50–99	19	0.5	4.8	6.6
100–199	8	0.2	4.3	6.2
200–249	2	–	1.5	2.1
250–499	4	0.1	4.7	7.4
500+	4	0.1	47.7	41.5
Total	3,860	100.0	100.0	100.0

Small Business Service (2003) SME Statistics: UK

2 Which of these sectors is likely to contain the highest proportion of small firms?

(a) Public utilities
(b) Personal services
(c) Manufacturing
(d) Industrial construction
(e) Telecommunications

3 In which type of market is a small firm most likely to survive?

(a) Mass market
(b) Global market
(c) National market
(d) Niche market
(e) Common market

4 Which type of situation is *least favourable* to the small firm's survival?

(a) Few economies of scale
(b) Market involves personal services
(c) Many small competitors exist
(d) Considerable product differentiation (i.e. non-homogeneous product)
(e) Substantial economies of scale

5 Which of the following is NOT a reason why small firms may want to grow?

(a) Cost savings through economies of scale
(b) Diversification of product portfolio to reduce risk
(c) Diversification of market to reduce dependence on one set of customers
(d) To ensure that ownership continues to provide control of the firm
(e) To increase market power and, with it, control over price

Answers to Checkpoints and Activities can be found on pp. 705–35.

Growth in firm size

Important though SMEs are, Table 5.5 shows that large firms also make a vital contribution to the UK economy. Although only 0.2% (i.e. 1 in 500) of the businesses have 250 or more employees, these large firms contribute some 52.4% of total employment and 48.9% of total turnover.

Reasons for firm growth

In Chapter 3 (p. 100–105) we noted that there are potential cost savings from the growth in firm size. However, as Table 5.6 notes, these economies of scale are only one of a number of possible reasons why firms may seek to grow in size.

Table 5.6 Reasons for growth in firm size

Reasons for growth	Description
Cost savings	Firms can benefit from economies of scale, both technical and non-technical economies (see Chapter 3, pp. 101–105)
Diversification of product	Firms reduce the risk of dependence on one good or service
Diversification of market	Firms reduce their dependence on one economy and one set of customers
Market power	Firms increase their power in the market as they grow larger, which allows them to influence prices and to obtain better profit margins through reduced competition
Risk reduction	Firms of larger size with a more diversified product portfolio and market presence are less likely to suffer in market downturns and are less likely to be taken over by competitors

Methods of firm growth

The methods by which firms seek to grow are many and varied. It will be useful to review some of the most usual methods adopted.

Organic growth

This is where the firm uses its own resources to support growth, for example reinvesting its own profits ('ploughed-back profits'). Of course, the firm may also seek to raise investment finance by borrowing from financial intermediaries or by issuing share or paper assets. As we noted in Chapter 4, the sources of finance available to the firm will depend on whether it is a sole trader, partnership, private limited company or public limited company.

Checkpoint 2 What are the advantages and disadvantages of organic growth?

Franchising and licensing

- *Franchising*. Here one firm (the franchisee) purchases the right to undertake business activity from another firm (the franchisor) using that firm's name or trademark rather than any patented technology. The scale of this activity varies from so-called 'first-generation franchising' to 'second-generation franchising' in which the franchisor transfers a much more comprehensive business package to the franchisee to help establish a 'start-up position'. This may include detailed guidance on how to operate the franchise, even extending to specialist staff training.

  In *first-generation* franchising, the franchisor usually operates at a distance. However, in *second-generation* franchising, the franchisor exerts far more control on the day-to-day running of the local operations. This type of franchising is common in the hotel, fast food restaurant and vehicle rental industries, such as Holiday Inn, McDonald's and Avis respectively.

LINKS

Joint ventures and alliances may also be used as a mechanism for expanding the activity base of a firm. However, some would argue that these do not, strictly, contribute to growth of firm size. Chapter 15 (pp. 638–641) looks at the strategic benefits of joint ventures and alliances.

- *Licensing*. At its simplest, licensing can mean permission granted by one firm (*licensor*) to another firm (*licensee*) in the form of a contract to engage in an activity that would otherwise be legally forbidden. The licensee buys the right to exploit a fairly limited set of technologies and know-how from the licensor, who will usually have protected the intellectual property rights involved by a patent, trademark or copyright. This tends to be a low-cost strategy for growth since the licensor makes little or no resource commitment. The licensor benefits from the licensee's local knowledge and distribution channels which would otherwise be difficult and time-consuming to develop and maintain.

Mergers and acquisitions

Mergers and acquisitions have become two of the most widely used methods of firm growth in recent years, accounting for about 50% of the increase in firm assets and 60% of the increase in industrial concentration in the UK.

- *Merger*. This takes place with the mutual agreement of the management of both companies, usually through the merging firms exchanging their own shares for shares in the new legal entity. Additional funds are not usually required for the act of merging, and the new venture often reflects the name of both the companies concerned.
- *Takeover (or acquisition)*. This occurs when the management of Firm A makes a direct offer to the shareholders of Firm B and acquires a controlling interest. Usually the price offered to Firm B shareholders is substantially higher than the current share price on the stock market. In other words, a takeover involves a direct transaction between the management of the acquiring firm and the stockholders of the acquired firm. Takeovers usually require additional funds to be raised by the acquiring firm (Firm A) for the acquisition of the other firm (Firm B) and the identity of the acquired company is often subsumed within that of the purchaser.

As we consider in more detail below, it is often suggested that merger activity brings potential benefits for the new, enlarged enterprise via both cost savings and revenue opportunities.

Mergers: who benefits?

A key question, not as yet fully answered, is who exactly benefits from the regular surges in merger activity experienced throughout the world? Undoubtedly the many financial and legal advisers earn huge fees, but have the owners of the company (shareholders) found that merger activity adds value or destroy value? It is to this important issue that we now turn.

The managerial theories considered in Chapter 4 would suggest that fast-growing firms, having already adopted a growth-maximisation approach, are the ones most likely to be involved in merger activity. These theories would also suggest that fast-growing firms will give higher remuneration to managers, and will raise job security by being less prone to takeover. Is it then the managers (agents) rather than the shareholders (principals) who have most to gain from merger activity?

Case Study 5.2 considers the issue of who, if anyone, actually benefits from the frequently observed surges in mergers and acquisitions activity in the UK and elsewhere.

Case Study 5.2 Mergers – for managers or shareholders?

A number of surveys in recent years have suggested that the owners of companies, the shareholders, rarely benefit from mergers. For example, Buckingham and Atkinson (1999) note that only 17% of mergers and acquisitions produced any value for shareholders while 53% of them actually destroyed shareholder value. However, there is ample evidence (Fuller, 2004) that managers' remuneration packages may be more closely related to variables such as growth in corporate turnover and growth in company size than to corporate profitability. This misalignment of incentives between senior management seeking growth and shareholders seeking profit may be an important factor in the continued drive towards M&A as a strategic focus, with managers seeing M&A as the quickest way to grow both turnover and company size.

Another reason for mergers often failing to increase profitability and therefore shareholder value may be put down to the overconfidence and lack of judgement of senior management and the self-interested city financiers who advise them. These flaws can show up in all three phases of any merger activity, namely the planning implementation and operational phases.

For example, in the *planning phase* the top management of the merging firms invariably see benefits from combining operations which are rarely actually achieved. Steve Case, the founder of America Online, stunned the world in 2000 by announcing his intention to acquire Time Warner, a merger completed in January 2001 with the birth of the new combined company AOL Time Warner. When AOL revealed its intention to acquire Time Warner the Internet boom was at its peak and AOL's sky-high share value gave it the paper wealth to make its £97bn offer, despite the fact that Time Warner's revenues were four times higher than AOL. The expected benefits of combining the companies were seen in terms of linking, for the first time, a major Internet company with a major media company. Ted Turner, vice chairman of the new company, said 'I have not been so excited since I first had sex 42 years ago.' Yet just two years later, in January 2003, Steve Case announced his intention to stand down as chairman, with the new company valued at less than one-quarter of the £162bn value placed on it at the time of the merger.

In the *implementation phase* culture clashes at corporate or national levels may also occur, preventing potential benefits being realised. For example, at the corporate level, acquisitions involving a traditional bureaucratic company with an innovative entrepreneurial company will invariably bring conflicts, with the result that for some employees there will be a loss of identification with, and motivation by, the new employer. High-quality human resources are extremely mobile and key knowledge,

Case Study 5.2 continued

skills, contacts and capabilities are embedded in these employees, whose loss as a result of the M&A activity will seriously diminish the prospects of the new corporate entity.

Finally, in the *operational phase* the hoped-for economies of scale and scope may fail to materialise, for a variety of reasons, not least problems of coordination and control when new, integrated computer systems fail to work as intended. In surveying 253 horizontal mergers in manufacturing in the EU and US, Laurence Capron (1999) found that only 49% of companies believed that the implementation of the merger had created any positive net value in terms of the overall outcome.

Questions

1 How has the separation between ownership and control acted as a stimulus to merger activity?

2 Why do so few mergers seem to create extra value for shareholders?

Recent merger evidence

A study by Sara Moeller *et al.* (2004) of mergers in the US between 1998 and 2001 also questions whether shareholders benefit from such activity. After examining some 4,136 US mergers and acquisitions during this time, the combined stockmarket value of the merging firms was found to have fallen by an astonishing $158bn. Shareholders of the *buying firms* lost the most, the value of their shares falling by $240bn – some 12% of the purchase price.

However, this data may overstate the losses of shareholders! Moeller and her co-authors point out that the buying shareholders often used their own, over-valued shares in helping to fund the deals. In other words, they knowingly exchanged their own over-valued shares (equity) for the real assets of the companies bought, hardly a true loss of shareholder value! Further, most of the shareholder losses could be linked to 87 huge merger deals, representing less than 2% of the mergers investigated. The remaining 98% of mergers actually increased shareholder value for both buyers and sellers.

Within this broad picture, *The Economist* (2004) notes that two further patterns are identifiable:

- The value created by mergers and takeovers has been almost twice as high when there has been more than one bidder. Arguably, when the opportunities to create value are greatest, this tends to be recognised by several would-be buyers.
- The value created has been larger for mergers within the same industry than for diversifying acquisitions (see p. 185). This suggests that chief executive officers should focus on mergers within sectors of economic activity with which they are familiar.

Merger avoidance

Companies have become quite skilled in placing barriers in the way of unwanted takeover bids. Two of the most widely used involve the so-called 'poison pill' and 'staggered board' barriers.

'Poison pill' barrier

This often involves company rules that allow the shareholders to buy new shares in their company at a large discount, should that company be threatened by a hostile takeover. The now enlarged pool of shareholders makes it more difficult and more expensive for the acquiring firm to complete the takeover. In the US, some 40% of the 5,500 companies tracked by *Institutional Shareholder Service*, a research organisation, have been found to employ the 'poison pill'.

'Staggered board' barrier

These involve company rules which allow different groups of directors to be elected in different years. This is likely to deter hostile takeovers since it may be many years before the acquiring company will be able to dominate the existing boardroom of the target company. *Institutional Shareholder Service* estimate that some 60% of US companies have a staggered board. Lucian Bebchuk (2004) of Harvard Business School argues that staggered boards cost shareholders around 4–6% of their firm's market value by allowing entrenched managers and directors to resist takeover bids which would be attractive to the majority of shareholders.

Types of merger activity

Four major forms of merger activity can be identified: horizontal integration, vertical integration, the formation of conglomerate mergers, and lateral integration.

Horizontal integration

This occurs when firms combine at the same stage of production, involving similar products or services. Some 80% of mergers in the UK over the past decade have been of this type. The Hong Kong and Shanghai Banking Corporation's acquisition of Midland Bank to become HSBC in 1992, the merger of Royal Insurance and Sun Alliance to form Royal SunAlliance in 1996, the merger of Carlton and Granada broadcasting companies to form ITV PLC in 2004, and Air France merging with the Dutch carrier KLM in 2004 are all examples of horizontal mergers.

Horizontal integration may provide a number of cost-based economies at the level both of the plant (productive unit) and the firm (business unit).

- *Plant economies* may follow from the rationalisation made possible by horizontal integration. For instance, production may be concentrated at a smaller number of enlarged plants, permitting the familiar technical economies of greater specialisation, the dovetailing of separate processes at higher output, and the application of the 'engineers' rule' whereby material costs increase as the square but capacity as the cube. All these lead to a reduction in cost per unit as the size of plant output increases.

Example:

Microchip manufacture

The huge fabricated chip manufacturing plants ('Fabs') cost over $3bn each, roughly twice as much as previous plants, but are able to produce over three times as many silicon chips per time period. These 'plant economies' have reduced the unit cost per chip by over 40%.

- *Firm economies* result from the growth in size of the whole enterprise, permitting economies via bulk purchase, the spread of similar administrative costs over greater output, the cheaper cost of finance, various distributive and marketing economies etc.

Example:

Air France–KLM merger

The newly named and expanded Air France–KLM airline formed in 2004 has estimated cost savings from 'firm economies' of around €300m (around £200m) over the next five years from functional areas such as sales and distribution, IT and engineering.

Watch out!

Plant economies are sometimes called 'technical economies' and firm economies are sometimes called 'non-technical economies' or 'enterprise economies'.

As well as these cost-based economies, new revenue opportunities may present themselves for the now enlarged company.

- *Revenue-based synergies*. Horizontal (or vertical – see below) acquisitions may enable companies to develop new competencies which may in turn enable them to command a price premium (via increased market power, higher innovation capabilities) or to increase sales volume (via increased market presence – both geographically and in terms of an extended product line).

Example:

Carlton–Granada merger

The new ITV PLC formed by this merger estimates that it can innovate to increase advertising revenues. With extra TV time now available, requiring an enlarged output of programmes, and with over 50% of TV advertising time, ITV plc intends to match more closely its commissioning and scheduling of new programmes to the needs of its advertisers. By making TV content and its scheduling more appealing to key advertisers, ITV PLC believes that it can sell a more coherent package to its advertisers and therefore charge higher (premium) prices for its advertising slots, further increasing sales revenue.

Below is a list of some more recent examples of horizontal integration.

- *Cadbury Schweppes* acquiring *Adams* confectionery business for £2.6bn in 2003, making *Cadbury Schweppes* the largest confectionery business in the world.
- *British American Tobacco* (BAT) acquiring *RJReynolds*, America's second largest tobacco group for $6.2bn in 2003.
- *SAB Miller*, the London-listed second largest brewer in the world, acquiring *Birra Peroni*, Italy's number two brewer in 2003.
- *Logica*, the UK IT service company, merging with *CMG*, another IT service company, in 2003 to form *LogicaCMG*.
- *Morrison's*, the UK supermarket, acquiring Safeway, another UK supermarket, for £3bn in 2004, almost doubling its market share to 20% in the UK.

Vertical integration

This occurs when the firms combine at different stages of production of a common good or service. Only about 5% of UK mergers are of this type.

- *Backward vertical integration.* Firms might benefit by being able to exert closer control over quality and delivery of supplies if the vertical integration is 'backward', i.e. towards the source of supply. Factor inputs might also be cheaper, obtained at cost instead of cost + profit.
- *Forward vertical integration.* Of course, vertical integration could be 'forward' – towards the retail outlet. This may give the firm merging 'forward' more control of wholesale or retail pricing policy, and more direct customer contact. An example of forward vertical integration towards the market was the acquisition by the publishing company Pearson PLC of National Computer Services (NCS) in 2000 for £1.6bn. NCS was a US global information service company providing Internet links and curriculum and assessment testing facilities for schools. The takeover allowed Pearson to design integrated educational programmes for schools by providing students with customised learning and assessment testing facilities. It could also use the NCS network to reach both teachers and parents. In this way, Pearson was able to use its NCS subsidiary to sell its existing publishing products while also developing new online materials for the educational marketplace.

Vertical integration can often lead to increased control of the market, infringing monopoly legislation. This is undoubtedly one reason why they are so infrequent. Another is the fact that, as Marks & Spencer (M&S) have shown, it is not always necessary to have a controlling interest in suppliers in order to exert effective control over them. Textile suppliers of M&S send over 75% of their total output to M&S, which has been able to use this reliance to their own advantage. In return for placing long production runs with these suppliers, M&S have been able to restrict supplier profit margins whilst maintaining their viability. Apart from low costs of purchase, M&S are also able to insist on frequent batch delivery, cutting stockholding costs to a minimum.

Conglomerate integration

This involves each firm adding different products and activities to those with which it was previously involved. The major benefit is the spreading of risk for the respective firms and shareholders. Giant conglomerates like Unilever (with interests in food, detergents, toilet preparations, chemicals, paper, plastics, packaging, animal feeds, transport and tropical plantations – in 75 separate countries), are largely cushioned against any damaging movements which are restricted to particular product groups or particular countries.

Example:

Procter & Gamble moves into beauty products

Procter & Gamble (P&G), the US multinational, is the world's largest consumer group conglomerate, owning brands such as Pringles crisps, Pampers nappies and Crest toothpaste. In recent years it has broadened its portfolio of products still further into haircare, acquiring Clairol for £3.1bn in 2001 and the German haircare company, Wella, in 2003.

The various 'firm (enterprise) economies' outlined above may also result from a conglomerate merger. P&G expects to save €300m annually from its purchase of Wella by economies from combining back-office activities, media buying, logistics and other purchasing activities.

The ability to buy companies relatively cheaply on the stock exchange and to sell parts of them off at a profit later is another important reason for some conglomerate mergers. The takeovers by Hanson PLC of the Imperial Group, Consolidated Goldfields and the Eastern Group, in 1986, 1989 and 1995 respectively, provide good examples of the growth of a large conglomerate organisation which subsequently demerged the acquired businesses. Similarly, P&G has developed a strategy of divesting itself of brands in slower growth markets and focusing on sectors with faster future growth potential, such as beauty products.

Despite these benefits of diversification, times of economic recession (e.g. the early 1990s in the UK) often result in firms reverting back to their more familiar 'core' businesses. Only some 10% of UK mergers over the past decade can be classified as conglomerate mergers and some conglomerates have moved in the opposite direction. For example, the de-merger of Hanson PLC in 1996 produced four businesses with recognisable 'core' activities, namely tobacco, chemicals, building and energy.

Lateral integration

This is sometimes given separate treatment, though in practice it is difficult to distinguish from a conglomerate merger. The term 'lateral integration' is often used when the firms that combine are involved in different products, but in products which have some element of *commonality*. This might be in terms of factor input, such as requiring similar labour skills, capital equipment or raw materials; or it might be in terms of product outlet. For example, the takeover of Churchill Insurance by the Royal

Bank of Scotland (RBS) for £1.1bn in 2003 is arguably an example of lateral integration. Churchill will give RBS a presence in the *general household insurance* business for the first time, complementing its existing presence in motor insurance via its earlier acquisition of Direct Line. Direct Line dominates the market in selling insurance to careful, budget-conscious motorists, whilst Churchill is widely used by buyers of household insurance in which Direct Line is less strong. For example, in 2003 Direct Line insured 6 million motorists but only 1.6 million households, whereas Churchill insured 5 million households but only 2 million motorists.

The takeover of Clerical Medical, the life assurance company, by Halifax Building Society for £800m in 1996 was also an example of lateral integration, involving the linking of companies with different products but within the same financial sector. The increase in savings by an ageing population, together with a reduction in mortgage business, meant that the Halifax had surplus funds which it could now direct into insurance policies using Clerical and Medical's strong presence amongst independent financial advisers. These advisers could also act as distribution channels for other Halifax products as well as for those of its Clerical Medical subsidiary.

However, the Swiss company TetraLaval's offer for the French company Sidel in 2001 (which was finally cleared by the EU competition authorities in 2002) provides an example of the difficulty of distinguishing the concepts of conglomerate and lateral integration. TetraLaval designs, manufactures and sells packaging for liquid food products as well as manufacturing and marketing equipment for milk and farm products. Sidel designs and sells machines used in the manufacture of plastic bottles and packaging. The European Commission regarded the merger as conglomerate in that the companies operated in different sectors of the market and were to be organised, post-merger, into three distinct entities within the TetraLavel Group. However, it was still the case that the merger would resemble a case of lateral integration in that the companies had a commonality of experience in the package and container sector.

Checkpoint 3 Can you find additional examples of these four different types of integration?

Explanations of merger activity

A number of theories have been put forward to explain the underlying motives behind merger activity. However, when these various theories are tested empirically the results have often been inconsistent and contradictory.

The value discrepancy hypothesis

This theory is based on a belief that two of the most common characteristics of the industrial world are imperfect information and uncertainty. Together, these help explain why different investors have different expectations of the prospects for a given firm.

The *value discrepancy hypothesis* suggests that one firm will only bid for another if it places a greater value on the firm than that placed on the firm by its current owners. If Firm B is valued at V_A by Firm A and V_B by Firm B then a takeover of Firm B will only take place if $V_A > V_B$ + costs of acquisition. The difference in valuation arises through Firm A's higher expectations of future profitability, often because A takes account of the improved efficiency with which it believes the future operations of B can be run.

It has been argued that it is in periods when technology, market conditions and share prices are changing most rapidly that past information and experience are of least assistance in estimating future earnings. As a result, differences in valuation are likely to occur more often, leading to increased merger activity. The value discrepancy hypothesis would therefore predict high merger activity when technology change is most rapid, and when market and share price conditions are most volatile.

The valuation ratio

Another factor which may affect the likelihood of takeover is the *valuation ratio*, as defined below:

$$\text{Valuation ratio} = \frac{\text{market value}}{\text{asset value}} = \frac{\text{no. of shares} \times \text{share price}}{\text{book value of assets}}$$

If a company is 'undervalued' because its share price is low compared to the value of its assets, then it becomes a prime target for the 'asset stripper'. If a company attempts to grow rapidly it will tend to retain a high proportion of profits for reinvestment, with less profit therefore available for distribution to shareholders. The consequence may be a low share price, reducing the market value of the firm in relation to the book value of its assets, i.e. reducing the valuation ratio. It has been argued that a high valuation ratio will deter takeovers, while a low valuation ratio will increase the vulnerability of the firm to takeover. In the early 1990s, for example, the property company British Land purchased Dorothy Perkins, the womenswear chain, because its market value was seen as being low in relation to the value of its assets (prime high street sites). After stripping out all the freehold properties for resale, the remainder of the chain was sold to the Burton Group.

In recent years the asset value of some companies has been seriously underestimated for other reasons. For example, many companies have taken years to build up brand names which are therefore worth a great amount of money; but it is often the case that these are not given a money value and are thus not included in the asset value of the company. As a result, if the market value of a company is already low in relation to the book value of its assets, then the acquirer gets a double bonus. One reason why Nestlé was prepared to bid £2.5bn (regarded as a 'high' bid, in relation to its book value) for Rowntree Mackintosh in 1988 was to acquire the 'value' of its consumer brands cheaply, because they were not shown on the balance sheet. Finally, it is interesting to note that when the valuation ratio is low and a company would appear to be a 'bargain', a takeover may originate from within the company; in this case it is referred to as a management buyout (MBO).

Checkpoint 4 Can you name any recent examples of management buyouts?

Case Study 5.3 looks at value-related aspects of the AOL/Time Warner merger in 2000.

Case Study 5.3 AOL and Time Warner merger

FT

When the AOL, Time Warner merger was announced in January 2000, Ted Turner, then Time Warner vice-chairman, said he had approved the deal with 'as much enthusiasm' as when he had first made love 42 years earlier. Many shared his excitement. But how would things have been different had the merger never happened?

Ambitious media executives drew two lessons from the deal: first, that big was better; and second, that convergence – the marriage of old and new media, content and the Internet – was the future. This created panic in the sector; the result would be two or three media mega-monopolies and any company that did not move fast would be left out in the cold. The result was a flurry of similar – ultimately disastrous – deals. Most important was Vivendi's acquisition of Seagram, owner of Universal. At the very least, the AOL merger weakened the scepticism that one hopes the Vivendi board would have shown for the $34bn (£19bn) deal, which brought together a hotchpotch of ill-assorted assets.

AOL shareholders are clearly better off than they would have been had they pursued another Internet deal. On 7 January 2000, the last day of trading before the Time Warner deal was announced, AOL shares traded at $73.75, giving it a market capitalisation of $179bn. By December this year, the combined company had a market value of only $79bn. How would AOL shareholders have fared had their company continued to be valued as an Internet stock? Since 7 January 2000, the Morgan Stanley Internet index has fallen 86% – so AOL's market capitalisation could well have dropped to just under $24bn. Yet AOL shareholders retained 55% of the combined AOL Time Warner, a stake today worth about $45bn – not a bad showing.

It is a very different story for Time Warner shareholders. On the eve of the deal their shares were trading at $64.75, valuing the company at $90bn. A portfolio of comparable media companies has dropped 16% since the announcement of the deal, so Time Warner would now be worth about $76bn. Instead, based on their 45% stake of the combined company, Time Warner investors' holding is now worth only $36bn – a loss of $40bn.

Time Warner could have invested that $40bn in a completely different future, perhaps even making money for shareholders rather than losing it. It could, for example, have bough Seagram, sold the spirits business and kept the Universal studios, theme parks, music business, cable channels and enormous library of film and television programmes. These would have mapped neatly on to its existing businesses. Instead of having to sell Warner Music – as Time Warner did recently – the company might have become of the music sector's winners.

Case Study 5.3 continued

Perhaps the best Time Warner could have done would have been to consolidate the still fragmented cable business. Cable is one of the few remaining natural monopolies with huge economies of scale and its importance is growing as the connection for broadband. Many local cable systems require heavy capital investment if they are to be maintained, digitised for interactive services and upgraded for broadband. Time Warner had the capital to do this.

The irony is that these are precisely the things being talked about today by Dick Parsons, chairman and chief executive of Time Warner (the AOL part of the name has been dropped). He recently told the FT: 'We like the business we are in. We like the cable business, we like cable networks, we like publishing and like the motion picture business. We look to grow in these businesses.' Enlarging the cable business, adding television channels and expanding Warner Brothers' film library were his three priorities. Imagine what Time Warner's core businesses might look like if the AOL deal had not diverted its attention for almost four years.

Source: *Financial Times*, 30 December 2003, p. 15

Questions

1 Does the study suggest that AOL benefited from the merger? Explain your reasoning.

2 Does the study suggest that Time Warner benefited from the merger? Explain your reasoning.

The market power theory

The main motive behind merger activity may often be to increase monopoly control of the environment in which the firm operates. Increased *market power* may help the firm to withstand adverse economic conditions, and increase long-term profitability.

Three situations are particularly likely to induce merger activity aimed at increasing market power:

1 Where a fall in demand results in excess capacity and the danger of price-cutting competition. In this situation firms may merge in order to secure a better vantage point from which to rationalise the industry.

2 Where international competition threatens increased penetration of the domestic market by foreign firms. Mergers in electronics, computers and engineering have in the past produced combines large enough to fight off such foreign competition.

3 Where a tightening of legislation makes many types of linkages between companies illegal. Firms have in the past adopted many practices which involved collusion in order to control markets. Since restrictive practices legislation has made many of these practices illegal between companies, merger, by 'internalising' the practices, has allowed them to continue.

For these reasons merger activity may take place to increase a firm's market power. However, the very act of merging usually increases company size, both in absolute terms and in relation to other firms. It is clear, therefore, that increased size will be both a by-product of the quest for increased market power and itself a cause of increased market power.

Economies of scale and other synergies

It is often argued that the achievement of lower average costs (and thereby higher profits) through an increase in the scale of operation is the main motive for merger activity. As we noted in Chapter 3 (p. 101) and in this chapter (p. 178), such economies can be at two levels:

- first, at the level of the plant, the production unit, including the familiar technical economies of specialisation, dovetailing of processes, engineers' rule, etc;
- second, at the level of the firm, the business unit, including research, marketing, administrative, managerial and financial economies.

To these plant- and firm-level economies we might add the 'synergy' effect of merger, the so-called '2 + 2 > 4' effect, whereby merger increases the efficiency of the combined firm by more than the sum of its parts. Synergy could result from combining complementary activities as, for example, when one firm has a strong R&D team whilst another firm has more effective production control personnel.

Managerial theories

In all the theories considered so far, the underlying reason for merger activity has been related, in one way or another, to the pursuit of profit. For example, market power theory suggests that through control of the firm's environment, the prospects of higher revenues and therefore profit, at least in the long run, are improved. Economies of scale theory concentrates on raising profit through the reduction of cost. Managerial theories on the other hand (see also Chapter 4) lay greater stress on non-profit motives. Some theories see the growth of the firm in terms of revenue, asset size, etc. as raising managerial utility by bringing higher salaries, power, status, and job security to managers. Managers may therefore be more interested in the rate of growth of the firm than in its profit performance.

Demerging

Whilst the focus has been on merger activity, in recent times there has been a renewed interest in the alleged benefits of *demerging*. Case Study 5.4 considers this in more detail.

Case Study 5.4 Demergers boost value

In the UK telecom giant BT demerged its mobile phone unit BT Cellnet. Shares in the unit, now called mmO_2, started trading independently of their parent on the stock market in November 2001. Corporate demergers create significant value for shareholders in both the parent company and the demerged, or separated, entity within a year of the deal being completed, a recent survey has found. The Deloitte & Touche survey in 2002 was based on an analysis of the 118 biggest demergers carried out worldwide between 1990 and 1999.

The survey noted that while demerger announcements are usually greeted at the outset with a 2–10% drop in share price, there is a dramatic turnaround within a year of the demerger. The share price of most parent companies increases within the year by from 12% to more than 52%, while the separated business also fares well, with share price rises of between 13% and more than 46%.

'Currently there is a lack of understanding about demergers, which partly explains the dip in share price on announcement, with investors fearing a loss of scale and that assets will be sold cheaply,' said Angus Knowles-Cutler, a partner in merger integration services at Deloitte & Touche. 'In reality, the potential diseconomies of a loss of scale for both separating entities are far outweighed by the extra clarity of purpose provided by the demerger. Management is able to focus on the core business, decision making becomes easier, and motivation rises with greater sense of ownership of the smaller business and shared sense of direction,' he said.

Conversely, he believes the opposite can be true of mergers. Acquiring businesses that are greeted with share price rises of 3% or more following the merger announcement usually fail to increase share value in year one, while those greeted with a share price drop under-perform even further.

'The frequent hike in share price on announcement of a merger is often justified because the rationale behind the deal is well founded. The problems often come from clumsy integration, which has a habit of destroying focus and motivation – the factors that make demergers successful,' said Mr Knowles-Cutler.

Questions

1 On what basis are proposed merger deals often seen as attractive by investors, resulting in immediate rises in share prices?

2 Why does the share price of the merged entity often fall after its earlier rise?

3 What is the evidence for suggesting that demergers have been successful, and why?

Mergers and the public interest

Although there is clearly much debate about the motivation behind merger activity, there is a broad consensus that the resulting growth in firm size will have implications for the 'public interest'. It may be helpful to consider the potential impacts of a merger on productive efficiency and allocative efficiency, which are two key elements in any definition of the 'public interest'.

- *Productive efficiency*. This involves using the most efficient combination of resources to produce a given level of output. Only when the firm is producing a given level of output with the least-cost methods of production available do we regard it as having achieved 'productive efficiency'.
- *Allocative efficiency*. This is often taken to mean setting a price which corresponds to the marginal cost of production. The idea here is that consumers pay firms exactly what it costs them to produce the last (marginal) unit of output: such a pricing strategy can be shown to be a key condition in achieving a so-called 'Pareto optimum' resource allocation, where it is no longer possible to make someone better off without making someone else worse off. Any deviation of price away from marginal cost is then seen as resulting in 'allocative inefficiency'.

What may pose problems for policy makers is that the impacts of proposed mergers may move these two aspects of economic efficiency in opposite directions. For example, economies of scale may result from the merger having increased firm size, with a lower cost of producing any given output thereby improving productive efficiency. However, the greater market power associated with increased size (see Chapter 6, p. 214) may give the enlarged firm new opportunities to raise price above (or still further above) its costs of production, including marginal costs, thereby reducing allocative efficiency.

We may need to balance the gain in productive efficiency against the loss in allocative efficiency to get a better idea of the overall impact of the merger on the 'public interest'.

LINKS

Chapter 8, pp. 300–306, examines the issue of mergers and the public interest in more detail, including the approach of the UK and EU competition authorities to this issue.

Activity 5.2 helps you self-check many of the issues involved in the growth of firm size.

Activity 5.2

1 Match each *lettered* term to the correct *numbered* description.

Term

(a) Cost savings
(b) Diversification of product
(c) Diversification of market
(d) Market power
(e) Organic growth
(f) Forward vertical integration
(g) Backward vertical integration

Description

(i) Firm wishes to grow in order to gain control over prices and to obtain better margins through reduced competition.
(ii) A small shoe manufacturer acquires a leather works.
(iii) A song-writing partnership acquires a music publishing company.
(iv) A firm wishes to grow in order to reduce its dependency on one good or service.
(v) A firm decides to increase output by 50% since it expects to benefit from both technical and non-technical economies of scale.
(vi) A firm decides to build a new factory rather than take over a smaller competitor.
(vii) A firm decides to establish a subsidiary company overseas since home market demand is 'saturated'.

2 Match each *lettered* term to the correct *numbered* description.

Term

(a) Conglomerate integration
(b) Lateral integration
(c) Horizontal integration
(d) Forward vertical integration
(e) Backward vertical integration

Description

(i) Involving a firm in the same business and at the same stage of production.
(ii) Involving a firm in a totally unrelated business.
(iii) Towards the final consumer.
(iv) Towards the raw material supplier.
(v) Involves firms in different product areas but with some common element (e.g. common factor inputs or product outlets).

3 (a) A car battery firm acquiring a firm producing acidic materials for those batteries is an example of forward vertical integration. True/False
(b) A soft drinks producing firm acquiring a chain of stores to distribute its products is an example of backward vertical integration. True/False
(c) A car assembly firm merging with another car assembly firm is an example of conglomerate integration. True/False
(d) A holiday company merging with a financial services provider in order to spread risk is an example of conglomerate integration. True/False
(e) A ferry operator merging with a food export/import company because its ships can be used in both functions is an example of lateral integration. True/False
(f) A company 'ploughing back' its own profits to fund new investment projects is an example of organic growth. True/False
(g) A high gearing ratio means that the company is at little risk, since external borrowing is a small percentage of total capital employed. True/False
(h) The market for personal services is one in which small firms typically operate at a competitive disadvantage. True/False

Answers to Checkpoints and Activities can be found on pp. 705–35.

Key Terms

Allocative efficiency Where price is set equal to marginal cost and resources are allocated so no one can be made better off without making someone else worse off (i.e. a 'Pareto optimal' resource allocation).

Alternative Investment Market (AIM) Low-cost and accessible market for SMEs seeking to raise share capital.

Backward vertical integration Towards the raw material supplier.

Conglomerate integration Involving firms in a totally unrelated business.

Demergers Where a company breaks itself up into smaller units.

Economies of scale Achieving lower long-run average cost by growth in size.

Forward vertical integration Towards the final consumer.

Gearing ratio Reflects the financial risk to which the company is exposed via external borrowing. Ratio of external borrowing to total capital employed.

Horizontal integration Involves firms in the same business and at the same stage of production.

Large firm Over 250 employees.

Lateral integration Involves firms in different product areas, but with some common elements (e.g. factor inputs, product outlets).

Liquidity ratios Give an indication of the company's short-term financial position in terms of the availability of cash or marketable assets with which to meet current liabilities.

Medium sized firm 50–249 employees.

Micro firm 0–9 employees, includes sole traders.

Organic growth Where the firm uses its own resources (e.g. 'ploughed-back profits').

Productive efficiency Producing at the level of output where average total cost is a minimum.

Small firm 10–49 employees.

SME Small and medium-sized enterprises, include micro, small and medium-sized firms.

Valuation ratio The ratio of market value/asset value.

Value discrepancy hypothesis Suggests that one firm will only bid for another if it places a greater value on the firm than that placed on the firm by its current owners.

Key Points

- Across all sectors in the UK, firms with fewer than five employees account for around 90% of the total number of firms. However, such firms account for only around 19% of total employment and 15% of total turnover.
- The small firm is increasingly seen by governments as a focus of new growth and employment opportunities, therefore justifying government support. Such small firm support has focused on three main areas: easier access to equity and loan capital, increased tax allowances and grants, and less government interference.
- Banks provide the main source (59%) of external finance for small firms (via overdraft) in the UK, increasingly in the form of medium- to longer-term loans, though high exposure to such overdraft finance remains a problem in the UK.

- Small firms in the UK see interest rate policy, general macroeconomic policy and taxation policy as the governmental policies with most impact on themselves.
- Low turnover is by far the most important single problem identified by small firms in the UK.
- Types of merger activity include horizontal, vertical, conglomerate and lateral.
- Suggested reasons for merger include at least one company believing it can add value beyond the costs of merger (value discrepancy hypothesis), a low valuation of share price relative to assets (valuation ratio) and the desire for greater market power.
- Other reasons include the securing of substantial economies of scale at plant and/or enterprise level. The former would be mainly technical economies by rationalisation of production into larger plants and the latter mainly non-technical economies related to functional areas such as administration, finance, marketing, distribution, purchasing, etc.
- There is little evidence to suggest that merger activity increases shareholder value but considerable evidence to suggest that merger activity may diminish profitability and shareholder value.

Assessment Practice

Multiple choice questions

1 Which *two* types of situation are most favourable to the small firm's survival?

(a) Serve 'niche' markets, often too small for large firms to service profitably
(b) Allow 'outsourcing' of functions which can more efficiently be conducted within larger firms
(c) Large economies of scale
(d) Few economies of scale
(e) Large 'bulk purchase' economies available

2 Which *two* of the following are accurate statements about the small firm in the UK?

(a) Over 99% of all UK firms have fewer than 50 employees.
(b) Over 99% of all UK employment is in firms with fewer than 50 employees.
(c) Over 99% of all UK turnover is in firms with fewer than 50 employees.
(d) Over 60% of all UK businesses are sole traders or partnerships.
(e) Over 60% of all UK turnover is from businesses which are sole traders or partnerships.

3 Which *two* of the following government policies seek to provide the small firm with easier access to equity and loan capital?

(a) Reduction in extent of government regulations on small firms
(b) Government guarantees to financial institutions giving loans to small firms
(c) Extra tax allowances to firms employing over 500 people
(d) Extra tax allowances for those buying shares in small firms
(e) Withdrawal of government guarantees to financial institutions giving loans to small firms

4 Which *two* of the following are often cited by small firms as problems they face?

(a) High turnover restricting cash flow available to finance expansion
(b) Excessive government regulations
(c) Over-supply of potential sources of lending
(d) Lack of government involvement with small firm sector
(e) Low turnover restricting cash flow available to finance expansion

5 The £120bn merger of Glaxo Wellcome and Smithkline Beecham in 2000 to form GlaxoSmithKline, one of the largest pharmaceutical companies in the world, is best described as:

(a) backward vertical integration
(b) conglomerate merger
(c) lateral integration
(d) forward vertical integration
(e) horizontal integration.

6 Which of the following is NOT generally regarded as a possible reason for merger/take-over activity?

(a) Major benefits available from increased market power
(b) Managers want to maximise the size of their company to get greater status and power
(c) Diversification into new activities shows great promise
(d) Synergistic benefits are limited
(e) The introduction of government legislation against collusive behaviour

7 A conglomerate merger is a merger of:

(a) firms producing the same product
(b) firms producing unrelated products
(c) firms at various stages in a production process
(d) firms producing complementary products
(e) firms producing consumer goods.

8 Which theory of merger activity suggests that a merger will occur only if firm A places a greater value on firm B than is placed on B by its current owners?

(a) Valuation ratio
(b) Value discrepancy hypothesis
(c) Retention ratio
(d) Market power theory
(e) Economies of scale theory

9 Which type of merger involves a firm merging with another which is nearer to the final consumer?

(a) Horizontal integration
(b) Lateral integration
(c) Conglomerate integration
(d) Forward vertical integration
(e) Backward vertical integration

10 **Which type of merger involves firms in different product areas, but with some common element (e.g. common factor inputs or product outlets)?**

(a) Horizontal integration
(b) Lateral integration
(c) Conglomerate integration
(d) Forward vertical integration
(e) Backward vertical integration

Data response and stimulus questions

1 **The following output/cost data was observed for a bakery, with 1,000 loaves per day given the cost per unit index number 100.**

Loaves per day	Cost per unit (index)
1,000	100
2,000	90
3,000	75
4,000	55
5,000	30

If the bakery currently produces 1,000 loaves per day, is there an argument for it seeking to grow in size?

2 **The following data on changes in cost per unit as *cumulative* output doubles is recorded for various products.**

Product	Decrease in costs per unit as cumulative output doubles
Electrical components	30%
Microcomputing	30%
Ball bearings	27%
Industrial plastics	25%
Equipment maintenance	24%
Life assurance	23%
Aerospace	20%
Electricity	20%
Starters for motor vehicles	15%
Oil refining	10%

(a) What might the data suggest?
(b) Are there any implications for merger or takeover activity?

True/False questions

1 The 'Small Firms Loan Guarantee Scheme' is an example of a government measure aiming to give small firms easier access to equity and loan capital.

True/False

2 Small firms may seek to grow larger to achieve diseconomies of scale.

True/False

3 'Large' firms with over 250 employees make up less than 1% of all businesses in the UK but contribute around 40% of total employment and total turnover.

True/False

4 Sole traders are the most common type of small firm in the UK.

True/False

5 BP acquiring a chain of garage outlets is an example of backward vertical integration.

True/False

6 Interbrew of Belgium, owners of the Stella Artois brand, purchasing another brewery, AmBev of Brazil in 2004, is an example of horizontal integration.

True/False

7 If a firm is 'productively efficient' it will set price equal to marginal cost.

True/False

8 The value discrepancy hypothesis suggests that demerging is more likely than merging.

True/False

9 If the valuation ratio is high for a company then it will be an attractive takeover target.

True/False

10 If a firm is 'allocatively efficient' then it will charge consumers exactly what it costs to produce the last unit of output.

True/False

Essay questions

1 Why do small firms continue to exist despite the benefits associated with size?
2 Explain the possible reasons which might help to explain merger activity.
3 Do you agree with those who advocate demerging? Explain your reasoning.
4 Consider the different methods by which a small firm might grow in size. Identify the advantages and disadvantages of the various methods.
5 To what extent would you agree with the suggestion that mergers are almost always in the interests of managers and not shareholders?

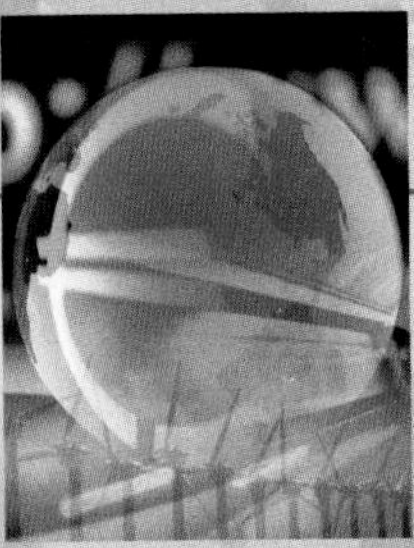

Chapter 6

Market structures

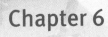

Introduction

We saw in Chapter 1 that prices in free markets are determined by the interaction of supply and demand. However, this does not imply that price determination is completely beyond the influence of all firms (or consumers). If firms are able to influence supply and/or demand conditions for their product, they can clearly influence the price at which that product is sold. The level of control that a particular firm has over the price of its product will depend to a large extent on the *structure* of the particular market in which it operates, i.e. on:

- the number of other firms producing that product;
- the number of other firms producing a close substitute for that product;
- the relative ease with which firms can enter or leave the market for that product.

Differences in these three market characteristics produce different market structures that are usually categorised as *perfect competition*, *monopolistic competition*, *monopoly* and *oligopoly*, all of which are reviewed in this chapter.

Learning objectives:

By the end of this chapter you should be able to:

- explain why perfect competition is often suggested to be the 'ideal' form of market structure in terms of resource allocation
- understand that 'contestable market' analysis is an attempt to relate the ideas of perfect competition to actual market situations
- outline the major barriers to market entry and discuss their contribution to 'market power'
- examine the 'classical' case against monopoly (higher price/lower output than perfect competition) and identify circumstances when this may or may not apply

- compare and contrast the outcomes of monopolistic competition with those from other market structures.
- evaluate the key characteristics of oligopoly markets and the relevance of competitor actions and reactions to different market outcomes.

An industry, sector or market (these terms are used interchangeably) can be defined as a group of firms that produce close substitutes, whether goods or services, as for example in the case of the cosmetics industry, the motor industry, the healthcare sector, the educational sector and so on. These industries or sectors have different numbers of firms operating within them, different levels of substitutability by other products, and different barriers (if any) to the entry of new firms. This chapter examines how these three market characteristics may affect the price and output behaviour of firms and therefore how resources are allocated under a particular market structure. As we shall see, the allocation of resources resulting from one type of market structure might, under certain circumstances, be regarded as preferable to that resulting from another type of market structure.

Figure 6.1 shows that perfect competition and monopoly fall at the opposite ends of the spectrum of market structures. Perfect competition, on the extreme left, is often said to represent the 'ideal' market structure in which producers have no control over price and resources are allocated most efficiently. The further to the right our position on the spectrum in Figure 6.1, the greater the extent to which the firm can influence price and output, and the less competitive the market structure.

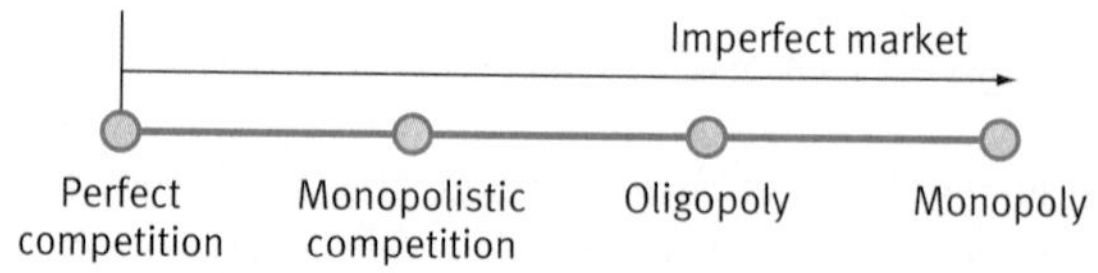

Fig 6.1 Spectrum of market structures

We begin by reviewing the 'perfect competition' model of market structure, although we should remind ourselves that all the models of market structure described in this chapter are a simplification of reality.

Perfect competition

In this type of market structure, there are a large number of small firms producing identical products with none of these firms having any 'market power', in the sense of being able to influence market price or output. Strictly speaking, for a market to be defined as 'perfectly competitive' a number of conditions must all be met simultaneously:

- *large number of small firms* supplying the product, none of which is able, by itself, to influence overall (market) supply;
- *each small firm is a 'price taker'* in the sense that it recognises that it is too small to influence the ruling market price, which must therefore simply be accepted;
- *large number of buyers*, none of whom is sufficiently large to influence overall (market) demand;
- *perfect information* for both sellers and buyers;
- *homogeneous product* so that the product offered by one firm is identical in all respects to the product offered by the other firms;
- *freedom of entry and exit* so that firms can either enter or leave the market at will, with no 'barriers' to discourage such entry or exit.

These assumptions are extremely restrictive and it would be difficult to find an example of a market structure that fulfils all these assumptions simultaneously. However, some markets display many of the features of perfect competition. For example, an individual farmer has little influence over the price of carrots since the farmer produces only a small proportion of the total market supply. Nothing makes these carrots any different from any other farmer's carrots, and all the buyers of carrots are well informed about prices.

As we shall see, the perfectly competitive market structure makes certain predictions as to firm and industry price and output in both short-run and long-run time periods. However, before undertaking this analysis it will be useful to consider the individual firm's *demand curve* in rather more detail.

Firm's demand curve

We have noted that each perfectly competitive firm recognises that, by itself, it cannot influence market supply and therefore market price. It is therefore in the situation shown in Figure 6.2.

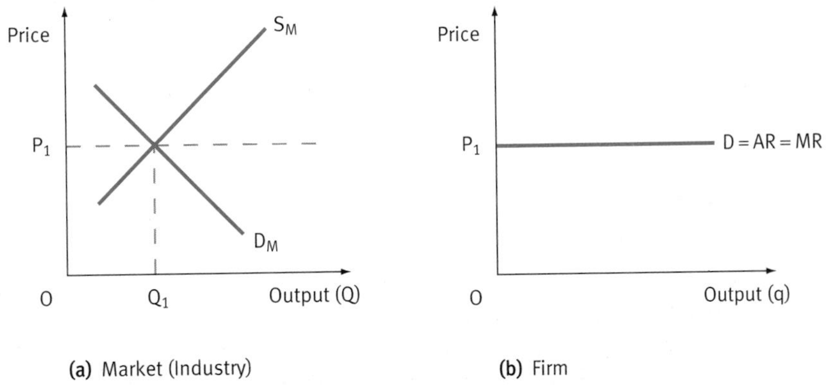

Fig 6.2 The firm as a 'price taker'.

The equilibrium price (P_1) is determined in Figure 6.2(a) by the intersection of the market demand curve (D_M) with the market supply curve (S_M) for this identical product. At this market price P_1 the small firm can reasonably suppose that it can sell *all* its output, knowing that it is so small that any extra output will have no impact on market supply and therefore no impact on price. It is as though the firm's demand curve is perfectly elastic at the going market price P_1, as we can see in Figure 6.2(b).

When the firm sells all its product at an identical price, then the firm's demand curve tells us the revenue per unit or average revenue (AR) from any given output. When the firm's demand (D = AR) curve is horizontal or perfectly elastic (see Chapter 2, pp. 46–55), then each additional unit of output adds exactly the same amount to total revenue as did each previous unit. In other words, the marginal revenue (MR) is constant at the going market price P_1. We can say that:

D = AR = MR

Example:

AR and MR for a 'price taker'

Suppose our small firm is faced with the following situation as it seeks to raise output from four units:

Price (AR)	Quantity (Q)	TR	MR
£5	4 units	£20	£5
£5	5 units	£25	£5
£5	6 units	£30	£5
£5	7 units	£35	£5

The small firm is a 'price taker' at £5. Raising output from four units to five units will raise total revenue (TR) from £20 to £25. Average revenue is still £5 (TR/Q) and the marginal revenue (MR) of the fifth unit is also £5 (£25 – £20).

So £5 = AR = MR

This perfectly elastic demand curve for the firm will ensure that it charges an identical price for its product to that charged by other firms. Since the product is homogeneous, consumers will have no preference for a particular firm's product, so that if a firm sets a price *above* that of its competitors it will face a total loss of sales.

Alternatively, the firm has no incentive to set a price *below* that of its competitors since it can sell its entire output at the existing market price. The firm in perfect competition is therefore a 'price taker', i.e. it accepts the market price as given and beyond its control.

Firm's supply curve

In Chapter 4 we noted (p. 138) that the profit-maximising firm must equate marginal cost with marginal revenue (MC = MR). It follows that, under perfect competition, the *marginal cost curve* will, in effect, be the firm's supply curve. This is shown in Figure 6.3.

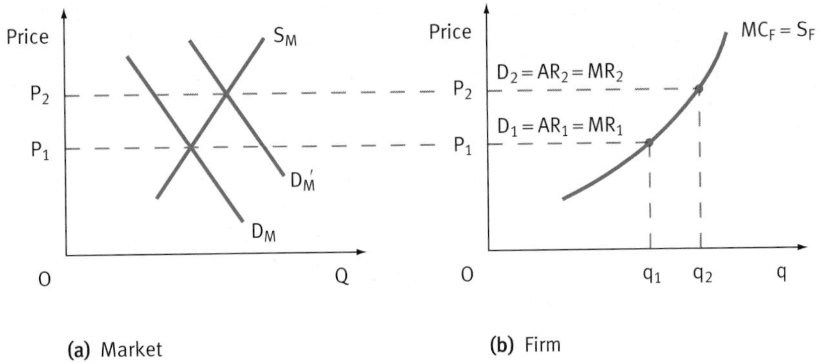

Fig 6.3 Under perfect competition the firm's supply curve (S_F) is the firm's marginal cost (MC_F).

We start with market demand D_M and market supply S_M in Figure 6.3(a), giving an initial market price P_1. At this price P_1 the price-taking small firm in Figure 6.3(b) is faced with the horizontal demand curve $D_1 = AR_1 = MR_1$. The profit-maximising firm will then produce output q_1, where marginal cost equals marginal revenue.

However, should market demand increase to D'_M in Figure 6.3(a), then market price rises to P_2 and the price-taking small firm in Figure 6.3(b) is faced with the horizontal demand curve $D_2 = AR_2 = MR_2$. The profit-maximising firm will now produce output q_2, where marginal cost equals marginal revenue.

What we can see in Figure 6.3(b) is that at each price, the small firm will *supply* that output where price (= AR = MR) = marginal cost (MC). Put another way, the *firm's marginal cost curve* is the *firm's supply curve*, telling us how much output the profit-maximising firm will supply at each and every price.

Box 6.1 looks at the firm's supply curve under perfect competition in the short-run and long-run time periods.

Box 6.1 Short- and long-run supply curves

We noted in Chapter 3 (p. 97) that the marginal cost (MC) curve will always intersect the average variable cost (AVC), and average total cost (ATC) curves at their lowest points. Here we use this knowledge to identify the firm's short- and long-run supply curves.

Firm's short-run supply curve

In the short-run time period, the firm must at least earn enough revenue to cover its *total variable costs*, thereby making some contribution to the total fixed costs already incurred. In other words, price (AR) must be greater than or equal to average variable cost (AVC).

- At any price *below* P_1, we have AR < AVC so that TR < TVC. The firm is better off shutting down, since it is not even covering its total variable costs. No output will be supplied in the short run at prices less than P_1.
- At any price *above* P_1, we have AR > AVC so that TR > TVC and the firm is making some contribution to the total fixed costs already incurred. The firm will therefore produce output in the short run.

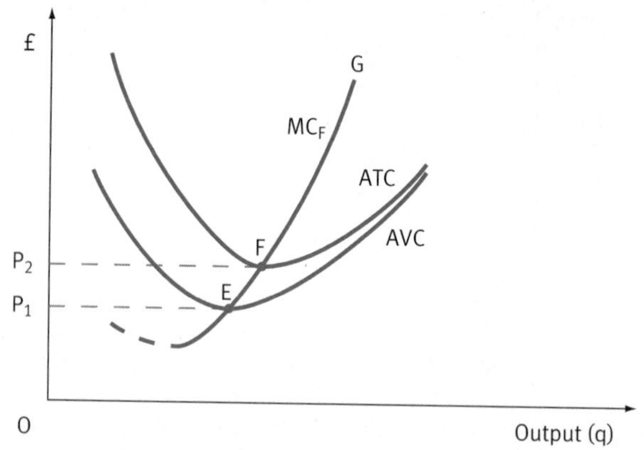

Fig 6.4 Under perfect competition EG is the firm's *short-run* supply curve and FG the firm's *long-run* supply curve

Note: 'Normal profit' (defined as that just sufficient to keep the firm in the industry in the long run) is included in ATC

In Figure 6.4 the segment of the firm's marginal cost curve EG represents the firm's *short-run supply curve.*

Firm's long-run supply curve

In the long-run time period all costs, whether variable or fixed, must be covered, including the 'normal profit' (see p. 109) often included in cost.

- At any price *below* P_2, AR < ATC so that TR < TC and no supply is worthwhile.
- At any price *above* P_2, AR > ATC, so that TR > TC and supply is worthwhile.

In Figure 6.4 the segment of the firm's marginal cost curve FG represents the firm's *long-run supply curve.*

Having identified the firm's supply curve, we can now identify the industry (market) supply curve.

Industry supply curve

Clearly, segments of the MC curve of the firm constitute the supply curve of the firm, depending on the time period in question. If we aggregate the MC curves for each and every firm (summing horizontally), we derive the industry MC curve. Since by aggregating the MC curves of each firm we are aggregating their supply curves, we also derive the industry supply curve. Figure 6.5 outlines this procedure in a simplified situation in which three firms constitute the industry.

The industry supply curve is therefore the sum of the individual firm MC curves in a competitive industry.

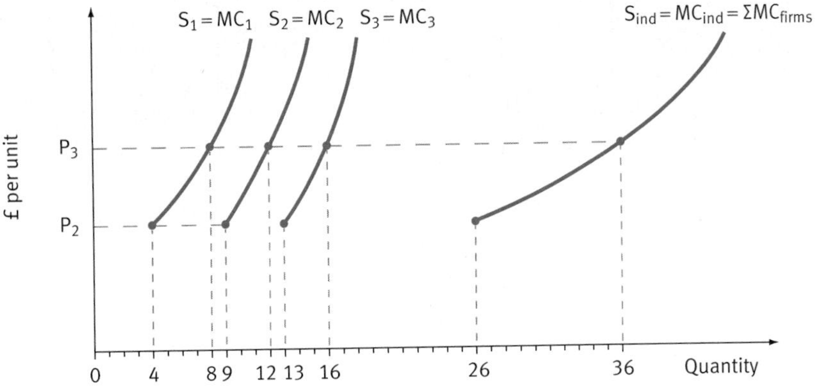

Fig 6.5 The industry supply curve is the industry MC curve, which in turn is the sum of the firm MC curves

Short-run equilibrium

We have already defined (p. 94) the short run as that period of time in which at least one factor of production is fixed. Therefore no new firms can enter the market/industry, being unable to acquire all the factors of production needed to supply the product over this time period.

Definition

Normal profit is the level of profit that is just enough to persuade the firm to stay in the industry in the long run, but not high enough to attract new firms. It can, therefore, be considered as a 'cost' to the firm in that this minimum acceptable rate of profit must be met if the firm is to stay in the industry in the long run.

As we shall see, in the short-run time period the market (industry) and the firm may earn either above normal (*super-normal*) or below normal (*sub-normal*) profits. Figure 6.6(a) indicates the former and Figure 6.6(b) the latter.

Making super-normal profit

In Figure 6.6(a) the profit-maximising firm equates MC with MR (see Chapter 4, p. 139), produces output q_1, earns total revenue (price × quantity) of Oq_1bP_1, incurs total cost of Oq_1ad and therefore makes a super-normal profit of abP_1d. In the short run no new firms can enter and this excess profit can be retained.

Making sub-normal profit

In Figure 6.6(b) the profit-maximising firm produces output q_2, earns total revenue of Oq_2bP_2 but incurs total costs of Oq_2ad, and therefore makes a sub-normal profit (loss) of abP_2d. In the short run, no existing firms exit the industry (unless they are not even covering their variable costs, see p. 94) and so these losses will remain.

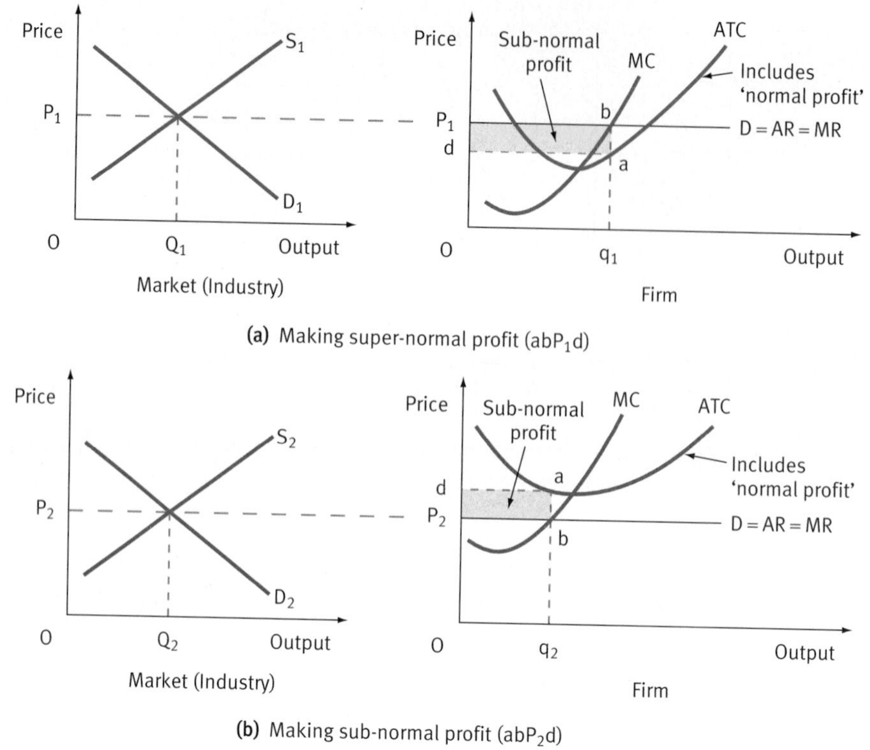

Fig 6.6 Short-run equilibrium.

In summary, in the short-run profit-maximising equilibrium

$$P = AR = MR = MC$$

Long-run equilibrium

In the long run *all* factors can be varied, new firms can enter and existing firms (*incumbents*) can leave the market/industry. It will be helpful to see how we move from our short-run equilibrium positions of super-normal and sub-normal profits, respectively, to the long-run equilibrium where only normal profits are earned.

Short-run super-normal profits

If a large number of new (small) firms are attracted into the industry by super-normal profits, then this will have an effect on the (long-run) industry supply curve, shifting it to the right in Figure 6.6(a). New firms will continue to enter the industry until any super-normal profit is competed away: i.e. only normal profit is earned.

The mechanism by which the super-normal profit is eroded is indicated in Figure 6.7 and involves the industry price falling (P_1 to P^*) as industry supply increases (S_1 to S^*). What has happened is that new firms have been encouraged to enter the industry by the super-normal profits and industry supply has increased (shifted to the right). Price will continue to fall until the super-normal profits are competed away.

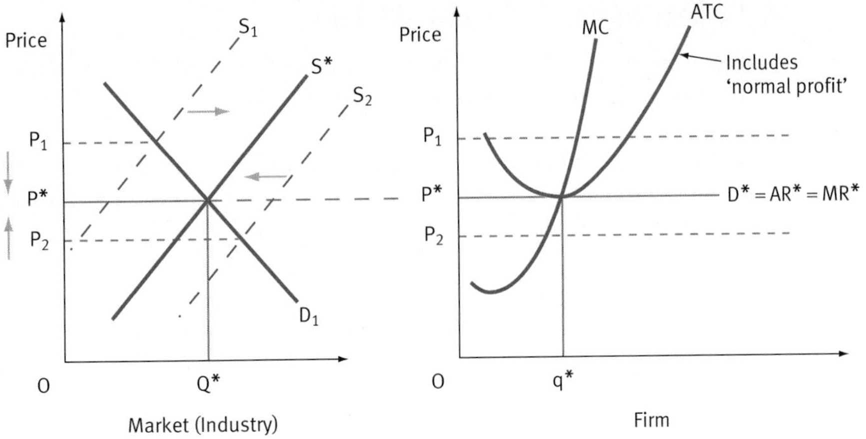

Fig 6.7 Long-run equilibrium for a profit-maximising firm in perfect competition (P^*q^*): normal profit earned

Long-run equilibrium will only be achieved when the profit-maximising firm (MC = MR) is just earning normal profit (ATC = AR), i.e. when the following condition holds true:

$$P = AR = MR = MC = ATC$$

This can only occur (see Figure 6.7) when the price-taking firm faces a perfectly elastic demand curve that just touches (is a tangent to) the bottom of its ATC curve. Here, and here only, is the above condition satisfied (remember MC intersects ATC from below at the lowest point of ATC). The profit-maximising firm (MC = MR) is now earning only normal profit (ATC = AR), and no further incentive exists for new firms to enter the industry. We are in *long-run equilibrium.*

Short-run sub-normal profits

In our earlier Figure 6.6(b), where firms earned sub-normal profits, a large number of (small) firms would leave the industry, shifting industry supply to the left in Figure 6.7 (S_2 to S^*), raising industry price (P_2 to P^*) and restoring profits to the normal level. What has happened here is that existing firms have failed to achieve the level of profit (normal profit) needed to keep them in this industry in the long run and have left the industry. Again we are in *long-run equilibrium.*

In summary, the long-run profit-maximising equilibrium will only occur when firms are neither entering nor leaving the industry. This will occur when normal profits are being earned, i.e. when the following condition is fulfilled.

$$P = AR = MR = MC = ATC$$

Perfect competition and efficiency

Some ideas of 'efficiency' were considered in Chapter 5 (p. 192) and are considered further in Chapter 8. Here we identify two types.

- *Productive efficiency.* To achieve productive efficiency (or cost efficiency) a firm must use its resources in such a way as to produce at the lowest possible cost per unit of output. Therefore, productive efficiency is achieved at the lowest point on a firm's long-run average total cost curve. In other words, costs per unit of production in the long run are as low as technically possible. Productive efficiency is achieved by the firm in Figure 6.7 at output q* (and price P*).
- *Allocative efficiency.* To achieve allocative efficiency it *should not be possible* to make someone better off by a reallocation of resources without, at the same time, making someone worse off. If you could make someone better off and no one worse off, then you should obviously reallocate resources. To achieve this situation (called a 'Pareto optimum' resource allocation, see Chapter 8, p. 295), one key condition is that price should equal marginal cost. In other words, consumers should pay a price for the last unit of output that just covers the extra cost of producing that last unit of output. Allocative efficiency is achieved by the firm in Figure 6.7 at price P* (and output q*).

NOTE

Strictly, it can be shown that the long-run equilibrium in Figure 6.7 will be one in which the bottom of both the short-run *and* long-run average total cost curves (see Chapter 3, p. 101) just touch the perfectly elastic demand curve at P*.

In other words, the long-run equilibrium of the firm (and of the market/industry) under perfect competition results in both productive and allocative efficiency. This is why the perfectly competitive market structure is often thought to be 'ideal' in terms of resource allocation.

We consider these 'efficiency' or resource allocation aspects of competitive markets further in Chapter 8. We also look at the impacts of various types of 'market failure' in preventing these 'efficiency' outcomes.

Case Study 6.1 applies our ideas of perfect competition to the Internet.

Case Study 6.1 Perfect competition and the Internet

It has been argued in recent years that the explosive growth of retailing on the Internet has made this form of retailing resemble an almost perfectly competitive market. Consumers appear to have perfect information about both prices and products at their fingertips by merely logging onto the net in search of the best deals. In a perfectly competitive market products are identical; there are a large number of buyers and sellers; there are no search costs; customers are perfectly informed; there is free entry into and exit out of the industry; and profit margins would be 'normal' in the long run.

The Internet does seem to have some of these attributes of a perfect market. For example, studies have shown that online retailers tend to be cheaper than conventional retailers and that they adjust prices more finely and more often. The Internet

Case Study 6.1 continued

has also led to the growth of people who use 'shopbots', i.e. computer programs that search rapidly over many websites for the best deal. These provide customers with a more complete knowledge of the market, hence minimising search costs. In addition, entry and exit from Internet sites is relatively easy for sellers so there are no obvious barriers to entry. Under these conditions one would expect prices for the same or similar products to be virtually identical on the Internet, as under perfect competition.

However, a closer study of the Internet retail market shows that there may still be important elements of imperfection in the market. Studies in the US by the Sloan School of Management have shown that there is still an element of price dispersion (i.e. difference between the highest and lowest prices for a given product or service) in Internet retail markets. This would tend to indicate that the Internet retail market is inefficient, with some retailers still being able to charge more than others. For example, price dispersion for identical books and for CDs and software amongst different online retailers can differ by as much as 33% and 25% respectively. Researchers at the Wharton School in Pennsylvania found that airline tickets from online travel agents differed by an average of 28%!

Questions

1 Why does a degree of price dispersion suggest that we do not have a perfect market?

2 What factors might explain why various retailers can still charge different prices for the same product over the Internet, despite the claim that it resembles a perfect market?

Contestable market theory

The theory of 'contestable markets' indicates how the principles we have discussed might generally apply to markets which are not, strictly, perfectly competitive. The emphasis here is on the threat of new entrants resulting in existing firms in non-perfectly competitive markets acting *as if* they were in a perfectly competitive market.

The idea of *contestable markets* broadens the application of competitive behaviour beyond the strict conditions needed for perfect competition. In other words, instead of regarding competitive behaviour as existing only in the perfectly competitive market structure, it could be exhibited in any market structure that was contestable. Generally speaking, the fewer the barriers to entry into a market, the more contestable that market. In this sense, some monopoly and oligopoly markets could be regarded as contestable.

The absence of entry barriers increases the *threat* of new firms entering the market. It is this threat which is assumed to check any tendency by incumbent (existing) firms to raise prices substantially above average costs and thereby earn super-normal profit.

Checkpoint 1 Can you identify any product markets which have few, if any, entry barriers?

Perfectly contestable market

It may be useful to illustrate this approach by considering the extreme case of perfect contestability. In a *perfectly contestable market* there are no barriers to entry so that incumbent firms are constrained to keep prices at levels which, in relation to costs, earn only normal profits. Incumbents in perfectly contestable markets therefore earn no super-normal profits, are cost efficient, cannot cross-subsidise between products or in any way set prices below costs in order to deter new entrants.

At least three conditions must be fulfilled for a market to be perfectly contestable.

1 *An absence of sunk costs* (see p. 105). Sunk costs are the costs of acquiring an asset (tangible or intangible) which cannot be recouped by selling the asset or redeploying it in another market should the firm exit the industry. The presence of sunk costs, by increasing the costs of exiting the industry, can be assumed to make incumbent firms more determined to avoid being forced to exit the industry and therefore more aggressive towards new entrants. They might then seek to resist new entrants by adopting a variety of strategies which essentially constitute a barrier to entry.

2 *The potential entrant must be at no disadvantage compared to incumbents as regards production technology or perceived product quality*. Any lack of access to equivalent production technology utilised by incumbents might prevent new entrants competing on the same cost base or quality of product base. This would inhibit the threat of potential new entrants, thereby permitting incumbents to earn and retain super-normal profits. Similarly, perceptions of consumers (via branding etc.) as to the superiority of incumbent product quality would also inhibit the threat of new entrants and permit incumbents to earn and retain super-normal profits.

3 *The entrant must be able to engage in 'hit and run' tactics;* i.e. to enter a market, make a profit and exit before incumbents can adjust their prices downwards. Put another way, existing suppliers can only change their prices with time-lags whereas consumers respond immediately to any lower prices offered by new entrants.

Under these conditions there is a total absence of barriers to entry, and exit from the market is costless. Such a *perfectly contestable market* will ensure that incumbents are unable to earn super-normal profits in the long run, and that price will equate with long-run average total cost (including normal profit). Any rise in price above long-run average cost will attract new entrants which, by undercutting the price of incumbents, can attract their customers and make a profit before the incumbent can react by reducing price. The new entrant can exit the market at zero cost by such 'hit and run' tactics, having benefited by earning super-normal profits prior to the reaction of incumbents, namely the curbing of their prices back to long-run average cost.

Although such perfect contestability is an ideal rarely, if ever, achieved, it sets the context for competitive behaviour in all types of market structure. Even highly monopolistic or oligopolistic markets could, in principle, experience a high degree of contestability, thereby achieving a competitive-type market solution with price close to long-run average costs and profits close to normal. The policy implication of such an approach is to encourage the removal of entry barriers and the lowering of exit costs in all types of market structure in order to increase the degree of contestability.

A rather weaker, but more pragmatic, approach to contestability focuses on cost rather than price contestability. Here the suggestion is that the threat of entry may be more likely to induce incumbents to be *cost efficient* than to set prices equal to long-run average costs. By 'cost efficient' is meant the delivery of a given level of output at the lowest cost technically feasible. As we shall see (Chapter 8), the perspective of 'cost contestability' is a widely used argument in support of deregulation, i.e. the opening up of specified markets to potential new entrants as a means of securing efficiency gains via cost cutting by incumbents.

Monopoly

In this section we move the analysis to the opposite end of the spectrum from pure perfect competition to look at what happens to price and output decisions in a *monopoly* market structure.

Pure monopoly

This occurs in the extreme case when there is a *single* seller of the product, with no close substitute available, so that the firm is, in effect, the industry.

It follows that under 'pure monopoly' the downward sloping demand (AR) curve of the *industry* is now the downward sloping demand curve of the *firm*. As we saw in Chapter 2 (p. 55), this means that there will be a marginal revenue (MR) curve lying inside the downward sloping demand (AR) curve, as in Figure 6.8 (p. 213).

Barriers to entry

Any monopoly situation, 'pure' or otherwise, can only exist in the long run because of barriers to new firm entry. These barriers can take various forms.

- *Substantial scale economies*, so that large firms have a significant cost-advantage over smaller new entrants. In the extreme case the *minimum efficient size* (MES) of production (see p. 105) may be so large that the industry can only sustain one technically (productively) efficient firm. This is the 'natural monopoly' argument, which we return to below (p. 213).
- *Control over scarce resources needed for production*, such as raw materials, key components, skilled labour etc.
- *Possession of patents or copyrights* for products or for processes of production.
- *Awarding of franchises* giving firms the exclusive rights to sell a particular good or service in a specified location.

- *Government regulations*, such as those creating the nationalised industries or other public sector bodies.

Checkpoint 2 Choose *three* separate products and for each identify any barriers to entry that might exist.

Case Study 6.2 shows how the *absence* of serious barriers to entry is likely to influence the price of flat-top TV screens in the long-run time period, even when the industry has elements of market power in the sense that large-scale producers are dominant.

Case Study 6.2 **New entry and profit rates**

During 2004 there was a significant increase in the demand for flat-panel TVs which Scott McGregor, the boss of Philips semiconductors, said was irrational since conventional TV could produce just as good an image. However, the real reason for such an increase in demand for flat-panel TVs was that manufacturers saw the possibility of a lucrative new market. LCD screens for desktop and laptop computers have become relatively common and so profit margins have fallen. However, in the TV market, although the larger LCD screens cost more to make, they also command much higher profit margins.

The interesting thing about this new TV market is that both new firms and also old established firms such as Motorola and Westinghouse (who stopped making TVs decades ago) are entering the market because of the higher margins. So too are computer makers such as Dell and Gateway who already sell LCD computer monitors and can undercut traditional consumer electronics firms by selling direct over the Internet. For example, in January 2004 a 30-inch flat-panel TV from Sony cost $3,999 whereas the equivalent Dell flat-panel TV cost $2,999 over the Internet.

The market for flat-panel TVs accounted for 3% of all TV sets sold in 2004 but is set to rise to 55% by 2005. Therefore, the market is experiencing the 'early adopter' phase of product sales which comprises the early part of the flat-panel's 'life-cycle'. The market research company, iSuppli, believes that as more suppliers enter the market and new factories are built, the prices of flat-panel TVs will probably fall by around 40% in 2004, resulting in decreased profit margins all round.

Questions

1. What does the above account tell us about the nature of the 'barriers to entry' in the flat-panel TV market?
2. How does the flat-panel TV market help us understand the concepts of 'normal profit' and 'super-normal profit' in an industry?
3. What would you expect potential buyers of flat-panel TVs to do, given the information in the above account?

Equilibrium price and output

Because of these barriers to entry, any super-normal profits earned in the short run can be retained in the long run. Figure 6.8 outlines the equilibrium situation for a pure monopoly setting a single price.

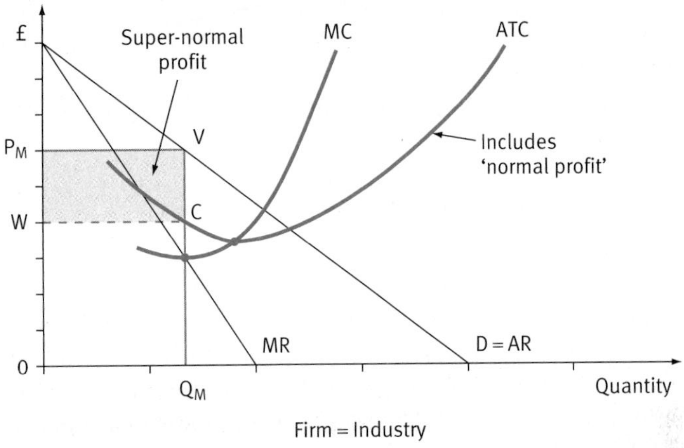

Fig 6.8 Price (P_M) and output (Q_M) for the 'pure monopoly'

In Figure 6.8 the profit-maximising monopolist equates MC with MR, giving output Q_M and price P_M in equilibrium. Under 'pure monopoly' strict barriers to entry allow the super-normal profit (P_MVCW) to be retained in the long run, so this is both a short-run and a long-run equilibrium.

Notice here how, unlike perfect competition, monopoly fails to achieve either productive or allocative efficiency.

- Output (Q_M) is lower than that at which ATC is a minimum, so no 'productive efficiency'.
- Price (P_M) is higher than marginal cost (MC), so no 'allocative efficiency'.

Natural monopoly

Figure 6.9 provides a useful illustration of the natural monopoly argument which suggests that, in terms of our earlier analysis (Chapter 5, p. 190), the minimum efficient size (MES) is so large that only one efficient firm producing at minimum long-run average cost (LRAC) can be sustained by that particular industry.

Checkpoint 3 Can you identify any natural monopoly situation?

The falling long-run average total cost curve (LRAC) indicates that economies of scale occur as output rises. When there is only one firm operating in the market the industry

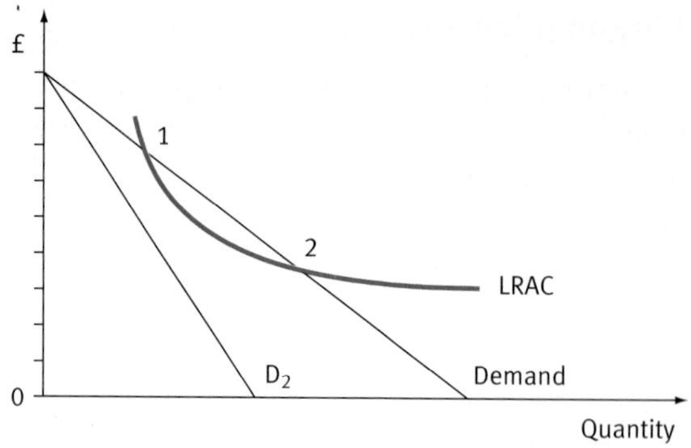

Fig 6.9 'Natural monopoly' situation

and the firm's demand curve is the same. Here output can occur between points 1 and 2 profitably. Suppose a second firm enters the market and the industry demand is now divided between the two firms (in this case each firm has 50% of the market). Each firm now faces the same individual demand curve, i.e. D_2 in Figure 6.9. In this situation long-run costs (LRAC) are greater than revenue at all levels of output. Consequently, one firm must leave the market, leaving us with a single (natural) monopoly.

LINKS
The natural monopoly argument is further considered in Chapter 8, p. 298).

'Classical' case against monopoly

The so-called 'classical' case against monopoly is that price is higher and quantity lower than under perfect competition. We now evaluate this case, for simplicity keeping our assumption of a pure monopoly.

Under perfect competition, price is determined for the industry (and for the firm) by the intersection of demand and supply, at P_C in Figure 6.10. We have already seen (p. 205) that the supply curve, S, of the perfectly competitive industry is also the marginal cost (MC) curve of the industry.

Suppose now that the industry is taken over by a single firm (pure monopoly), and that both costs and demand are initially unchanged. It follows that the marginal cost curve remains in the same position; also that the demand curve for the perfectly competitive industry now becomes the demand (and AR) curve for the monopolist. The marginal revenue (MR) curve must then lie inside the negatively sloped AR curve.

The profit-maximising price for the monopolist is P_M, corresponding to output Q_M where MC = MR. Price is higher under monopoly than under perfect competition ($P_M > P_C$) and quantity is lower ($Q_M < Q_C$). This is the so-called 'classical' case against monopoly.

This criticism of monopoly is additional to the fact that, as we noted from Figure 6.8 earlier, output is *not* at minimum average total cost and price does *not* equal marginal cost, breaking the respective conditions for productive and allocative efficiency (productive and allocative inefficiency).

However, these criticisms of monopoly may not be as strong as they first appear. We have already seen that the increased size which underpins monopoly power

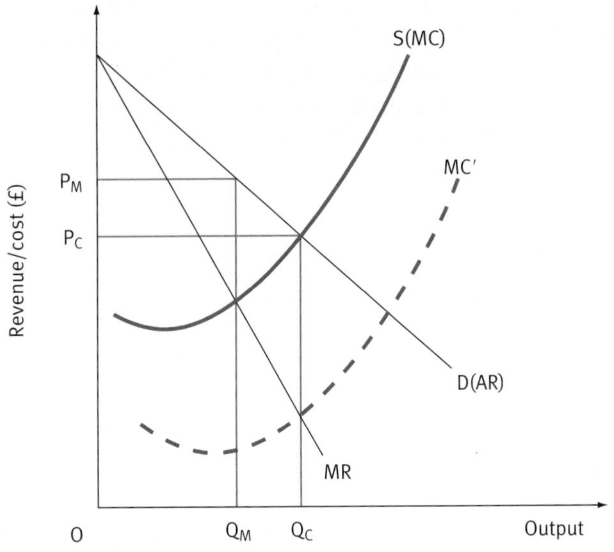

Fig 6.10 Price under perfect competition and monopoly

may yield *economies of scale*, both technical and non-technical (see Chapter 3, pp. 101–105). Where these economies of scale are significant, it may even be that the 'classical' case against monopoly fails to hold true, with the firm now able to move to a lower short-run average cost curve and with it a lower marginal cost curve.

Remember

The marginal cost (MC) curve must cut the bottom (p. 97) of each short-run average cost curve (SRAC). If economies of scale allow the firm to move to a lower SRAC curve, then the firm will also have a lower MC curve (see Chapter 3, p. 101).

In Figure 6.10, if economies of scale were sufficiently large to lower the MC curve to MC′ then the profit-maximising monopoly price P_M and quantity Q_M would be *identical* to those achieved under perfect competition. If economies of scale were even greater, lowering the MC curve *below* MC′, then the monopoly price (P_M) would be below that of perfect competition and the monopoly output (Q_M) would be higher than that of perfect competition. The key question is therefore how substantial are the economies of scale for the monopoly industry, and it is this *empirical* question which will determine whether or not the 'classical' case against monopoly still holds true.

Checkpoint 4

1 Why might the demand curve be different for the monopoly than for the perfectly competitive industry?
2 What might this mean for the 'classical case' against monopoly?

Throughout this discussion of monopoly we have simplified the analysis by contrasting 'pure monopoly' with perfect competition. In fact, industries in which more than one-third of the output is in the hands of a single seller or group of linked sellers can technically be called 'monopoly' in the UK. However, such 'general' monopoly situations are in practice difficult to distinguish from the oligopoly form of market structure which we consider later in the chapter.

Activity 6.1 gives you the chance to self-check some of the material on perfect competition and monopoly.

Activity 6.1

1 Figure 6.11 shows the cost and revenue curves of a firm under conditions of pure monopoly. Answer the following questions with reference to this figure.

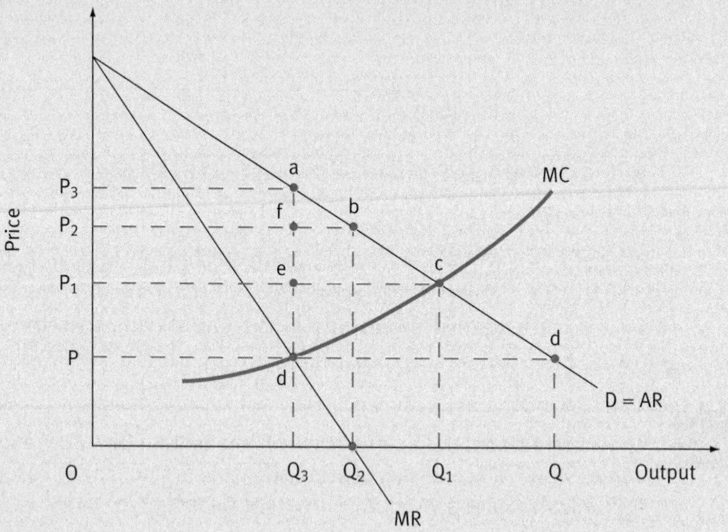

Fig 6.11

(a) What would be the price and output if the market was perfectly competitive?
(b) What price would a monopolist charge if it wished to maximise profit and what output would it produce?
(c) Marginal revenue becomes negative beyond what output level?
(d) At what point on the demand curve is the price elasticity of demand equal to unity?
(e) If the 'classical case' against monopoly holds true, how much *consumer surplus* and how much *producer surplus* is lost as compared to the perfectly competitive equilibrium?
(f) If the monopoly was seeking to maximise *total revenue*, what price would it charge and what output would it produce?

2 Put the *letter* for each of the following types of barrier to entry in the box next to its correct description.

(a) Geographical distance
(b) Brand image
(c) Restrictive practices by incumbents

(d) Economies of scale
(e) Government regulations
(f) Ownership of resources

Type of barrier	Description
	The minimum efficient size (MES) at which average costs are a minimum may be a large output, preventing smaller firms from competing effectively
	Access to scarce raw materials or scarce intellectual property rights (patents/copyright) may be in the hands of a few large firms
	Expensive advertising has created strong consumer loyalty to products which may deter new firm entry
	The creation of nationalised industries or the imposition of tariff barriers, quota restrictions etc. may restrict competition in national markets
	High transport costs may discourage competition from outside a particular region or nation
	Existing firms may use various devices to discourage new firm entry, e.g. setting artificially low prices, parallel pricing (all set similar prices), etc.

3 Which *two* of the following are key assumptions of perfect competition?

(a) The firm has perfect information about the market in which it operates.
(b) Firms find it easy to leave the industry but difficult to enter.
(c) Some firms are able to influence market price by making an individual decision.
(d) Firms produce differentiated products so there is no need for advertising.
(e) Each firm faces a perfectly elastic demand curve at the going market price.

4 Which *two* features refer to a perfectly competitive firm operating in the long run?

(a) Earns super-normal profit
(b) Earns normal profit
(c) Produces at the technical optimum (minimum average cost)
(d) Earns sub-normal profit
(e) Produces at an average cost above the minimum level technically feasible

5 Which *two* of the following features will help to make a market more contestable?

(a) There are few barriers to entry.
(b) There are many barriers to entry.
(c) Incumbent firms find it easy to erect new entry barriers.
(d) Incumbent firms find it difficult to erect new entry barriers.
(e) The industry is a 'natural monopoly'.

6 Which *two* of the following characteristics apply to pure monopoly?

(a) All units of the product are sold at an identical price.
(b) The firm is the industry.
(c) The firm faces a horizontal demand curve.
(d) The firm faces a downward sloping demand curve.
(e) Price = marginal revenue = average revenue.

Answers to Checkpoints and Activities can be found on p. 705–35.

Monopolistic competition

This type of market structure is sometimes called 'imperfect competition'.

- It contains elements of a competitive market structure in that it assumes:
  - a large number of small firms in the industry;
  - freedom of entry into, and exit from, the industry.
- It contains elements of an 'imperfect' market structure in that it assumes:
  - each small firm supplies a product which is not homogenous but *differentiated* in some way from that of its rivals. Put another way, the product of each small firm is a close but not perfect substitute for the product of other small firms in the industry.

Examples: There are many Chinese takeaway restaurants in most cities and towns. The menus are very similar but each one arguably cooks or presents its food in ways which differ from its rivals. Similarly, orange growers in Australia differentiate their orange juice concentrate from domestic and foreign rivals by designating the region of Australia in which the oranges were grown.

Downward sloping demand curve

Because the product is differentiated from that of its rivals, the firm's demand curve will no longer be the perfectly elastic (horizontal) demand curve of perfect competition. In fact, it will be the downward (negatively) sloping demand curve shown in Figure 6.12(a).

- If the firm lowers the price of its (differentiated) product it will capture some, but not all, consumers from other firms.
- If the firm raises its price it will lose some, but not all, of its consumers to rival firms.

Loyalty to the differentiated products of the respective firms means that price, while important, is not the sole influence on consumer choice. Hence we have a negatively sloped demand curve for the firm's products. Of course, the greater the loyalty to the firm's differentiated product, the greater the price rise needed to induce consumers to switch away from the product to that of a rival. Similarly, the greater the price cut needed to attract (loyal) consumers attached to its rival firm's products. It follows that the greater the product differentiation and consumer loyalty to the product, the *less price elastic* the demand curve for a particular firm will be, and of course the greater the monopoly power over price available to the firm.

Short-run equilibrium

In Figure 6.12(a) the profit-maximising firm (MC = MR) will, in the short run, produce output Q_S and sell this at price P_S, yielding super-normal profit P_SVWC. This excess profit will, given freedom of entry into the market, attract new entrants.

Unlike perfect competition, the new entrants do not increase the overall market supply of a single, homogenous product. Rather, the new entrants will partly erode the consumer demand for an existing firm's (differentiated) product, i.e. the new entrants will capture some of the customers of the existing firm by offering a still wider variety of differentiated products. We show this by a leftward shift (decrease) in the existing firm's demand curve in Figure 6.12(a).

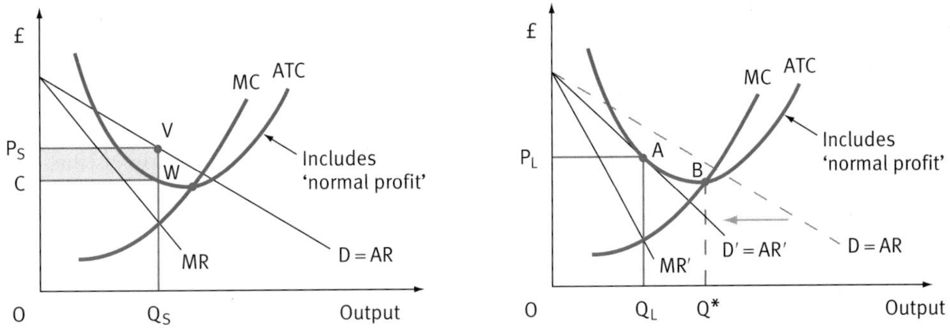

(a) Short-run equilibrium: super-normal profit (P_SVWC)

(b) Long-run equilibrium: normal profit

Fig 6.12 Short-run and long-run equilibrium under monopolistic competition.

Long-run equilibrium

Only when profit is reduced to normal for firms already in the market will the attraction for new entrants be removed, i.e. when ATC = AR, with normal profit included in ATC. In other words, the demand (AR) curve for the existing firm will shift leftwards until it just touches the ATC curve. This long-run equilibrium occurs in Figure 6.12(b) with demand curve D′ at price P_L and output Q_L.

- If the demand curve is still to the right of D′ in Figure 6.12(b) then super-normal profits will still be made and new entry will continue.
- If the demand curve has shifted to the left of D′ then sub-normal profits will be made and some firms will leave the industry (bankruptcy) and the demand curve will shift back to the right.
- Only at D′, when normal profits are earned, will there be no long-run tendency for firms to enter or leave the industry.

In this analysis, the firm will produce an output of Q_L and charge a price of P_L, making normal profit – there is no further entry of firms into the industry. The firm will operate where the average cost is tangential to the demand curve (point A) but technically the firm is able to operate at point B with an output of Q*. In other words, the firm has a capacity to produce more at a lower average cost. Consequently, a criticism of monopolistic competition is that each firm is serving a market that is too small and has the capacity to serve more customers. The firm in monopolistic competition therefore operates with *excess capacity* in the long run, equivalent to the difference between Q_L and Q^* in Figure 6.12(b). The excess capacity leads to higher average costs than would exist if output were expanded and to higher consumer prices.

Monopolistic competition and efficiency

We might usefully summarise the 'efficiency' aspects of long-run equilibrium for monopolistic competition.

- *Normal profits*. Only normal profits are earned in the long run, as with perfect competition.
- *Higher price, lower output*. Price is higher and output lower than would be the case in the long run for perfect competition (which would be at the price and output corresponding to point B).
- *Productive efficiency*. ATC (at A) is higher than the minimum level technically achievable (B), so productive efficiency is *not* achieved.
- *Excess capacity*. In Figure 6.12(b) output is Q_L but for minimum ATC output should be higher at Q^*. This shortfall in actual output (Q_L) below the productively (technically) efficient output (Q^*) is often called excess capacity.
- *Allocative efficiency*. Price is higher than marginal cost, so allocative efficiency is *not* achieved.

Activity 6.2 gives you the opportunity to consider further some aspects of monopolistic competition.

Activity 6.2

1 Put the letter for each of the following statements in the correct box.

(a) Downward sloping demand curve
(b) Perfectly elastic demand curve
(c) Differentiated product
(d) Homogeneous product
(e) Average cost a minimum in long run
(f) Average cost above minimum in long run
(g) No monopoly power
(h) Some monopoly power
(i) Price taker
(j) Some non-price consumer loyalty

Perfect competition	Monopolistic competition

2 If a firm in monopolistic competition is in its long-run equilibrium position, then which one of the following is untrue?

(a) Profits are normal.
(b) P > MC
(c) AR = AC
(d) AC is not at its minimum.
(e) No excess capacity.

3 Which one of the following does *not* hold true for a firm operating under monopolistic competition?

(a) Price is the sole influence on consumer choice.
(b) The greater the product differentiation, the more inelastic the demand.
(c) The firm will maximise profits in the short run where MR = MC.
(d) In the long run the firm will not produce at the technical optimum (minimum average cost).
(e) Only normal profits will be earned in the long run.

4 Refer to Figure 6.13. If this profit maximising firm is in monopolistic competition, then it will produce an output level:

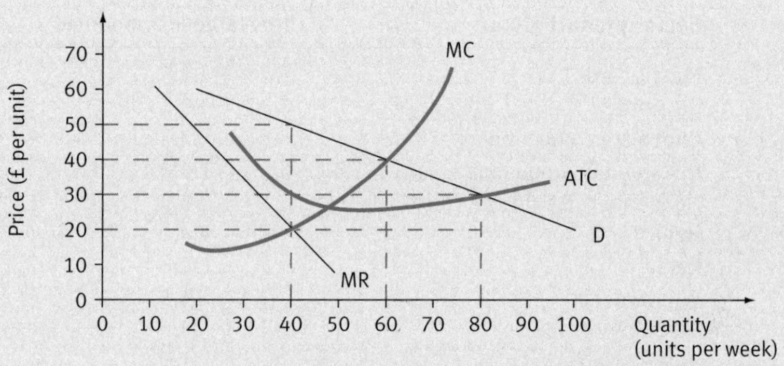

Fig 6.13

(a) of 40 units
(b) of 60 units
(c) of 80 units
(d) that is impossible to determine without information concerning the rival firms
(e) that is lower than 40 units.

Answers to Checkpoints and Activities can be found on pp. 705–35.

Oligopoly

Oligopoly refers to a situation in which a few firms dominate the market. Crucially, these few firms recognise their rivalry and interdependence, fully aware that any action on their part is likely to result in counter-actions by their rivals. Firms will therefore be drawn into devising strategies and counter-strategies taking into account their rivals' expected actions and reactions.

The three- and five-firm *concentration ratios* are often used as an indicator of the presence of oligopoly markets. These ratios tell us the proportion of the total value of output or of employment contributed by the three and five largest firms, respectively, in the market or industry. For example, the largest five firms in the tobacco industry in the UK contribute 99% of output and 98% of employment, clearly suggesting an oligopoly market.

Table 6.1 presents some data at the 'product group' level, showing both three- and five-firm concentration ratios in terms of product output in the UK.

Table 6.1 Company shares of the UK market by sector/product group

	Percentage share of UK market by volume	
Sector/product group	**Three largest companies**	**Five largest companies**
Plastic cards	83.5	99.6
Cigarettes	80.6	99.0
Chocolate confectionery	77.5	81.9
Refrigeration appliance	56.0	68.2
Household cleaning products	55.2	62.1
Beer	54.1	68.6
Cars	38.8	53.1
Wristwatches	34.5	45.0
Stationery products	33.0	37.4
Bottled water	31.9	39.9

Another feature of oligopoly markets is *product differentiation*. There are often many brands of a particular product, with extensive advertising by rival firms emphasising the difference between their product and that of their rivals, whether real or imagined.

As we shall see, the greater uncertainty of oligopoly markets makes it more difficult to predict short-run and long-run equilibrium situations, as we did for the previous market structures. Nevertheless, we can analyse various types of oligopoly situations, using two broad categories.

- *Non-collusive oligopoly*. Here the oligopoly firms compete against each other using strategies and counter-strategies, but do not seek to make agreements, whether formal or informal, to 'fix' the market outcome.
- *Collusive oligopoly*. Here the oligopoly firms do seek various arrangements between themselves in an attempt to remove some of the market uncertainty they face.

Quote

People of the same trade seldom meet together, even for merriment and diversion, but the conversation ends in a conspiracy against the public or in some contrivance to raises prices.

(*Adam Smith, The Wealth of Nations*, 1776)

Non-collusive oligopoly

First we consider situations in which each firm decides upon its strategy without any formal or even informal collusion with its rivals.

Kinked demand curve

In 1939 Hall and Hitch in the UK and Sweezy in the US proposed a theory to explain why prices often remain stable in oligopoly markets, even when costs rise. A central feature of that theory was the existence of a *kinked demand curve*.

To illustrate this theory, we take an oligopoly market which sells similar, but not identical products, i.e. there is some measure of product differentiation. If one firm raises its price, it will then lose some, though not all, of its customers to rivals. Similarly, if the firm reduces its price it will attract some, though not all, of its rivals' customers. How many customers are lost or gained will depend partly on whether the rivals follow the initial price change.

Extensive interviews with managers of firms in oligopoly markets led Hall and Hitch to conclude that most firms have learned a common lesson from past experience of how rivals react.

- If the firm were to *raise* its price above the current level (P in Figure 6.14), its rivals *would not follow*, content to let the firm lose sales to them. The firm will then expect its demand curve to be relatively elastic (dK) for price rises.

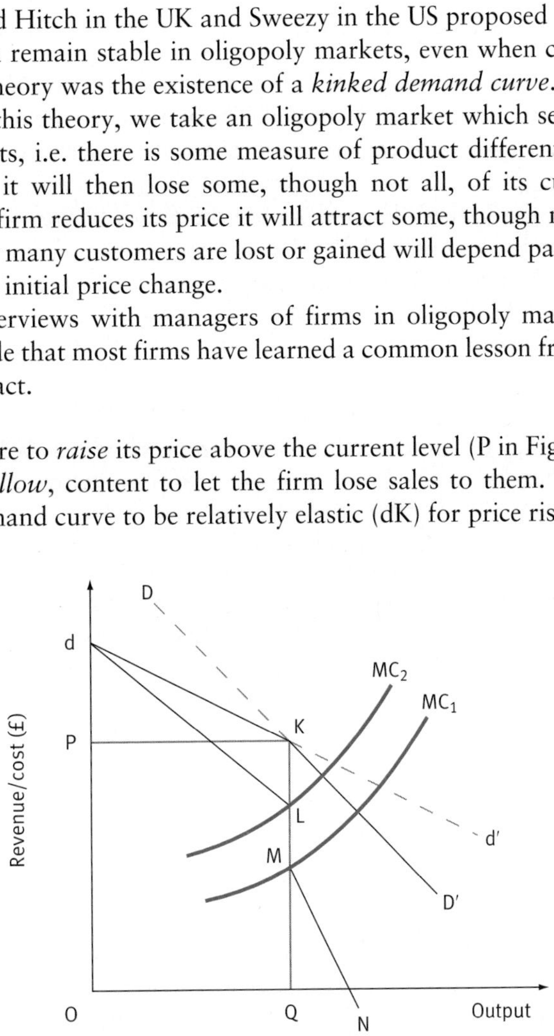

Fig 6.14 Kinked demand curve and price stability

Notes: d–d' = Demand curve when rivals *do not* follow price changes; D–D' = Demand curve when rivals *do* follow price changes; dKD' = Kinked demand curve; dLMN = Associated marginal revenue curve

- However, if the firm were to *reduce* its price, rivals would follow to protect their market share, so that the firm gains few extra sales. The firm will then expect its demand curve to be relatively inelastic (KD′) for price reductions.

Overall, the firm will believe that its demand curve is kinked at the current price P, as in Figure 6.14.

Remember

Associated with each demand (AR) curve in Figure 6.14 will be an associated marginal revenue (MR) curve which lies inside it.

- **For price rises *above* P, dL is the relevant marginal revenue curve.**
- **For price reductions *below* P, MN is the relevant marginal revenue curve.**

As we can see in Figure 6.14, there is a *vertical discontinuity*, LM, in the overall marginal revenue curve dLMN. The marginal cost curve could then vary between MC_1 and MC_2 without causing the firm to alter its profit-maximising price P (or its output Q).

In the kinked demand model the firm assumes that rivals will react to its own strategies, and uses past experience to assess the form that reaction might take. In this case the firm assumes that price increases will largely be ignored but price decreases will tend to be matched.

Example:

Price reductions matched by tabloid newspaper

The assumption that firms in oligopoly markets will tend to match price reductions by rivals is certainly supported by many examples of price 'warfare' as amongst the tabloid newspapers.

The *Daily Mirror* has around 19% of total tabloid ('popular') newspaper sales in the UK whilst the *Sun* (owned by Rupert Murdoch) has around 34%. They have been engaged in matching one another's price reductions for much of the past decade – though this has often damaged profitability! It was reported in 2003 that the *Daily Mirror* had lost £22m of revenue over the past year alone in matching price reductions by the *Sun*.

Non-price competition

We have seen that kinked-demand theory predicts relatively stable prices in oligopoly markets, and that the assumption is made, based on past experience, that the rival will react to a price cut, but not react to a price rise.

However, instead of using past experience to assess future reactions by rivals, the firm itself could try to identify the *best possible moves* the opposition could make to each of its own strategies. The firm could then plan counter-measures if the rival reacts in these predicted ways. As we see below, this is the essence of game theory and can involve both price and non-price competition.

Game theory

This terms refers to various theories which analyse oligopoly situations as though they were 'games' in which 'players' can adopt various strategies and counter-strategies in order to improve their position. Many of these oligopoly 'games' were developed from an early, non-economic problem known as the *Prisoners' Dilemma*, which is considered in some detail in Box 6.2.

Box 6.2 Prisoners' Dilemma

Alf and Bob (the 'players') have been caught stealing cars. The case against them is watertight and enough to imprison them for five years apiece. The police also suspect the pair of stealing the Crown Jewels – a serious crime warranting 30 years in the Tower of London. In order to get a conviction, the police need confessions, so Alf and Bob are interviewed separately and each given the following alternatives:

1 If both say nothing, each will receive a five-year sentence.

2 If one confesses to stealing the Crown Jewels but the other does not, the confessor will receive an incredibly lenient two years but his partner will get the full 30 years.

3 If both confess, both receive a reduced sentence of 10 years.

What strategy should each adopt? The options or strategies are shown in Table 6.2, which is a special table known as a *pay-off matrix.*

Table 6.2 Pay-off matrix for the Prisoners' Dilemma

		Bob's strategies	
		Confess	*Doesn't confess*
Alf's strategies	*Confess*	(a) Alf gets 10 years Bob gets 10 years	(c) Alf gets 2 years Bob gets 30 years
	Doesn't confess	(b) Alf gets 30 years Bob gets 2 years	(d) Alf gets 5 years Bob gets 5 years

The pay-off matrix shows all the possible outcomes (pay-offs) for each combination of strategies that Alf and Bob could choose. In this case there are four possible combinations:

1 Both confess.

2 Neither confesses.

3 Alf confesses but Bob does not.

4 Bob confesses but Alf does not.

- Here, Alf's strategies are read along the rows, whilst Bob's are read down the columns.
- The intersections of rows and columns form *cells* which display the pay-off for that combination of strategies.
- By convention, the player with strategies along the rows has his or her pay-off listed first.

Alf's point of view

If Alf decides to confess, we must read along the top row to work out his pay-offs. If Bob also confesses, the outcome in cell (a) shows us that they both can expect 10 years in prison.

Now move along the top row to cell (c) which shows the pay-off if Alf confesses but Bob remains stubbornly silent. This time Alf gets two years but poor Bob spends the next 30 years in the Tower of London.

Checkpoint 5 What are the pay-offs to Alf if he doesn't confess?

Bob's point of view

Now look at the matrix from Bob's point of view and assume that he also decides to confess. This time we must read down the first column to work out Bob's pay-offs. Once again we come across cell (a) where both players receive 10 years' imprisonment. Moving down the column to cell (b) we see what happens when Bob confesses but Alf remains silent. We see that this time it is Bob who receives two years whilst silent Alf will get the full 30 years' imprisonment – the exact opposite of cell (c) when we were following Alf's pay-offs.

Checkpoint 6 What are the pay-offs to Bob if he doesn't confess?

Arguably, the best outcome for their common good is if both don't confess and receive five years (cell d). This is the optimal (best possible) solution. Any other combination will either result in 10 years apiece (a) or with at least one of them serving 30 years (cells b and c).

The prisoners cannot speak to one another so cannot collude; each must make his own decision. Game theory assumes that Alf and Bob are rational human beings whose sole aim in life is to maximise their own rewards (thus to minimise their sentences) regardless of other people. Alf and Bob will also assume that their partner will act equally selfishly.

Looking at the matrix, we can see that remaining silent ('doesn't confess') will result in either five years or thirty years in prison. On the other hand, confessing could bring as little as two years in prison and at worst no more than ten years.

Both realise that for their common good they should both remain silent – but can they trust one another to do so? This is indeed a dilemma. Some questions and answers will help to highlight various aspects of this prisoner's dilemma.

LINKS

Cell (d) is often called the *Pareto optimal* solution, since one prisoner cannot be made any better off without making the other prisoner worse off. We consider Pareto optimal solutions further in Chapter 8, p. 295.

Question	*If Alf and Bob act selfishly, as game theory predicts, what will they do?*
Answer	Alf will confess. He is prepared to let Bob spend 30 years in prison if he can get away with only two. Alf knows he may still receive 10 years if Bob confesses, but that is preferable to the 30 years he could receive if he remains silent and Bob confesses. Even if the police hinted that Bob was not talking, Alf will still confess; Alf is rational and prefers two years in prison to the five he would receive if he remained silent like his partner. Bob will also confess – for the same selfish reasons as outlined for Alf. Thus both prisoners confess, the game is 'solved' and equilibrium is reached at (confess, confess). Each player has the same '*dominant strategy*' (see below). What happens if Alf confesses and Bob does not? Alf serves a mere two years whilst Bob is in prison for 30 – surely that is not fair? But game theory is not about fairness; game theory assumes that all players act rationally and selfishly – even to the detriment of the common good.
Question	*Would the outcome be any different if Alf and Bob had agreed on a vow of silence before their arrest?*
Answer	Yes, provided they both stuck to their agreement, the outcome would be five years apiece. Collusion is in their mutual interest.
Question	*Supposing Alf and Bob return to their life of crime once they have served their 10 years. They are rearrested and face a similar scenario as before. Will they confess this time?*
Answer	This is known as a *repeated game*, a situation where we would expect players to learn from their previous mistakes. Alf and Bob should realise that silence is the best policy – but can they trust one another?

Game theory can readily be applied to firms in oligopoly situations as they also face uncertainty in terms of the actions and reactions of rivals, just like Alf and Bob. We might usefully review some important terms and definitions widely used in game theory, before turning to some business examples.

Types of game

- *Zero sum*: where any gain by one player must be matched by an equivalent loss by one or more other players. A market share game is zero sum, since only 100% is available to all players.
- *Non-zero sum*: where gains and losses need not cancel out across all players. The *Prisoners' Dilemma* was one example (the four cells in the matrix did not have the same net value) and a *profits game* is another.

Types of decision rule

- *Maxi-min*: where the best of the worst-possible outcomes from any strategy is selected.

- *Mini-max*: where the worst of the best-possible outcomes from any strategy is selected.

Dominant strategy

The term 'dominant strategy' is sometimes used in game theory. It is often used where a firm is able to identify *one* policy option as being best for it, regardless of the reactions of any rivals. In Table 6.2 Alf has 'confess' as his dominant strategy, since whatever Bob's reaction, he gets less time in prison (10 years or 2 years) than if he doesn't confess (30 years or 5 years). The same is true for Bob.

Nash equilibrium

Where each firm is doing the best that it can in terms of its own objectives, taking into account the strategies chosen by the other firms in the market.

We can illustrate the application of game theory to business situations taking a zero-sum (market share) game involving two firms (duopoly). By its very nature, a market share game must be 'zero sum', in that any gain by one 'player' must be offset exactly by the loss of the other(s).

Example: **duopoly (two firm) market share game**

Suppose Firm A is considering choosing one of two possible policies in order to raise its market share, a 20% price cut or a 10% increase in advertising expenditure. Whatever initial policy Firm A adopts, it anticipates that its rival, Firm B, will react by using either a price cut or extra advertising to defend its market share.

Firm A now evaluates the market share it can expect for each initial policy decision and each possible reaction by B. The outcomes expected by A are summarised in the pay-off matrix of Table 6.3.

Table 6.3 Firm A's pay-off matrix

		Firm B's strategies	
		Price cut	**Extra advertising**
Firm A's strategies	Price cut	60*#	70#
	Extra advertising	50*	55

* 'Worst' outcome for A of each A strategy
\# 'Worst' outcome for B of each B strategy

If A cuts price, and B responds with a price cut, A receives 60% of the market. However, if B responds with extra advertising, A receives 70% of the market. The 'worst' outcome for A (60% of the market) will occur if B responds with a price cut.

If A uses extra advertising, then the 'worst' outcome for A (50% of the market) will again occur if B responds with a price cut.

We will assume that both players adopt a *maxi-min* decision rule, always selecting that policy which results in the best of the worst possible outcomes.

Firm A will select the price-cut policy since this gives it 60% market share rather than 50%, i.e. the best of these 'worst possible' outcomes.

If firm B adopts the same *maxi-min* decision rule as A, and has made the same evaluation of outcomes as A, it also will adopt a price-cut strategy. For instance, if B adopts a price-cut policy, its 'worst' outcome would occur if A responds with a price cut – B then gets 40% of the market (100% minus 60%), rather than 50% if A responds with extra advertising. If B adopts extra advertising, its 'worst' outcome would again occur if A responds with a price cut – B then receives 30% rather than 45%.

The best of the 'worst possible' outcomes for B occurs if B adopts a price cut, which gives it 40% of the market rather than 30%.

In this particular game we have a *stable equilibrium*, without any resort to collusion. Both firms initially cut price, then accept the respective market shares which fulfil their maxi-min targets, i.e. 60% to A, 40% to B.

The problem with game theory is that it can equally predict unstable solutions. An unstable solution might follow if each firm, faced with the pay-off matrix of Table 6.3, adopts an entirely different decision rule. Firm B might not use the maxi-min approach of A, but a *mini-max* approach, choosing the worst of the 'best possible' outcomes.

A mini-max approach is arguably a more optimistic but riskier approach to the game. You assume your rival does not react in the worst way possible to each decision you make, but in the best way for you. You then introduce a note of caution by selecting the 'worst' of these 'best possible' outcomes.

Checkpoint 7

What would happen in Table 6.3 if A adopts a maxi-min decision rule and B a mini-max decision rule?

An unstable solution might also follow if each firm evaluates the pay-off matrix differently from the other. Even if they then adopt the same approach to the game, one firm at least will be 'disappointed', possibly provoking action and counteraction.

If we could tell before the event which oligopoly situations would be stable, and which unstable, then the many possible outcomes of game theory would be considerably narrowed. At present this is beyond the state of the art. However, game theory has been useful in making more explicit the interdependence of oligopoly situations.

We can equally apply our terms and definitions to a *non-zero sum* game, namely a profits game. This is done in Box 6.3.

Box 6.3 **Profit game**

Alpha and Beta are two rival firms and each must choose whether to charge relatively high or relatively low prices for their products. Market research suggests the pay-off matrix (profits) shown in Table 6.4. For simplicity we assume that both firms evaluate the pay-off matrix as shown in this table.

Table 6.4 Pay-off matrix showing profits in £millions for Alpha and Beta

		Beta's strategies	
		Low price	*High price*
Alpha's strategies	*Low price*	(a) Alpha 200 Beta 200	(c) Alpha 40 Beta 260
	High price	(b) Alpha 260 Beta 140	(d) Alpha 100 Beta 100

Pay-off matrices invariably have some outcomes that are worse than others. The maxi-min decision rule is to adopt the policy option that gives the 'best of the worst' of these outcomes.

- *Alpha's maxi-min approach*. Alpha looks at its policies and asks 'what is the worst that can happen?'
  - For Alpha's low price policy, the worst that could happen would be for Beta to charge a high price and reduce Alpha's profits to £40m (cell c).
  - For Alpha's high price policy, the worst that could happen would be for Beta to charge a high price, giving Alpha £100m profit (cell d).
  - The best of these 'worst possible outcomes' is £100m, thus Alpha's maxi-min strategy would be to charge the higher price.

- *Beta's maxi-min approach*:
  - Beta's low price policy gives £140m (cell b) as the worst possible outcome.
  - Beta's high price policy gives £100m (cell d) as the worst possible outcome.
  - The best of these 'worst possible outcomes' is £140m, thus Beta's maxi-min policy would be to charge a low price.

Cell (b) would be the outcome from Alpha and Beta both adopting a maxi-min strategy. Alpha will be pleasantly surprised by doing better than expected (£260m compared to £100m) and Beta will do as expected (£140m). This could therefore be a stable (Nash) equilibrium, with neither firm seeking to change its policies.

As we noted earlier, the term 'dominant strategy' is sometimes used in game theory to refer to situations in which a firm is able to identify *one* policy option as being best for it, regardless of the reactions of any rivals. In Table 6.4 Alpha would identify 'high price' as the policy option which corresponds to a 'dominant strategy', since this gives Alpha the highest profit whether or not Beta reacts with low price (£260m > £200m) or high price (£100m > £40m).

Checkpoint 8

1 Does Beta have a 'dominant strategy'?

2 How might we expect Beta to react if it has identified a high price policy as Alpha's dominant strategy?

Collusive oligopoly

When oligopoly is non-collusive, the firm uses guesswork and calculation to handle the uncertainty of its rivals' reactions. Another way of handling that uncertainty in markets which are interdependent is by some form of *central coordination*; in other words, 'collusion'. The methods that are used to promote collusion may be formal, as in a cartel, or informal, via tacit understandings or arrangements.

Formal collusion: cartels

Formal collusion involves establishing and maintaining some kind of organisation which seeks to direct the policy of its members to reach some agreed end. For example, OPEC (Oil Producing and Exporting Countries) seeks to control the output of its member countries in order to keep the oil price above a target level previously agreed.

The operation of a cartel can be illustrated in terms of Figure 6.15.

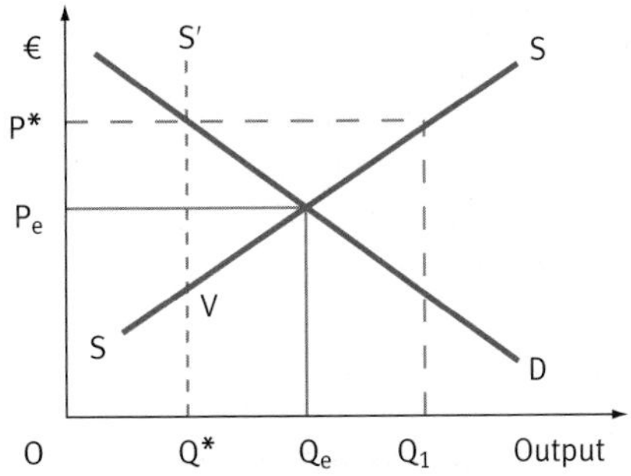

Fig 6.15 Operation of a cartel seeking minimum price P*

If no agreement is reached among suppliers, the suggestion in Figure 6.15 is that an equilibrium price P_e and quantity Q_e will result from the market. However, suppose the producers establish an organisation which seeks to prevent prices falling below P*. In effect the cartel must prevent output rising above Q*. It can do this by capping output at Q*, causing the original supply curve SS to take the shape SVS′ in Figure 6.15.

An obvious problem is that at price P* the producers would (in the absence of the cartel) have supplied quantity Q_1, giving *excess supply* Q* – Q_1. In order to limit the output of members to Q*, big cartels often allocate quotas, i.e. a maximum production level for each member such that, when aggregated, no more than Q* is produced in total. Of course, if members cheat and produce more than their quota, overall supply will rise above Q* and price will fall below P*.

Case Study 6.3 reviews a number of cartels found to have operated in the UK and EU in recent years.

Case Study 6.3 Cartels and collusion

Companies in oligopolistic markets such as Coke and Pepsi, or Exxon Mobil and Shell, can generally set prices at levels that match mutual profit requirements, with neither price wars nor secret meetings. However, cartels still happen and the following examples will help show the degree of formal collusion which often occurs.

In 2000, the three largest UK producers of ordinary Portland cement (OPC), namely Blue Circle PLC, Castle Cement Ltd and the Rugby Group, refused to supply OPC in bulk to concrete producers such as Readymix when they heard that the concrete producers intended to resell the cement themselves in bag form to builders' merchants. This was because they, themselves, sold OPC in bag form to other customers. However, the three producers were forced to supply cement after the Office of Fair Trading (OFT) found that refusing to supply OPC in bulk for ultimate resale in bags was anti-competitive.

In December 1999 the OFT had discovered that Vitafoam Ltd of Rochdale, Carpenter PLC of Glossop, Derbyshire, and Reticel Ltd of Alfreton, Derbyshire, had met to agree on the price rises of 8% for foam rubber and 4% for reconstituted foam which they supplied to the upholstery business. Cartel members agreed that the price rises announced by Vitafoam, the market leader, would be matched by similar announcements from Carpenter and Reticel.

On a much larger scale, the European Commission identified a 'vitamin cartel' in 2001, when eight pharmaceutical companies led by the Swiss firm, Hoffman La Roche, were found to have been operating secret market sharing and price fixing cartels in the supply of vitamins throughout the 1990s. These vitamins were used in a multitude of products from cereals and biscuits to cosmetics. The Commission found that the companies led by Hoffman La Roche allocated sales quotas, agreed on and implemented price increases, and engaged in regular meetings between the senior executives of the companies. The Commission imposed a record fine of £534m on the companies for operating an illegal cartel.

Questions

1 In what ways do the examples above show that cartel activity can take various forms?

2 Why are cartels widely believed to be against the public interest?

3 Draw a simple supply and demand diagram to illustrate a supply-based cartel and indicate what conditions are necessary for the cartel to be successful.

LINKS
For more on the legality of cartels in the UK, see Chapter 8, p. 305.

The governments of most advanced industrialised nations subscribe to the view that formal (or informal) agreements to restrict output are harmful and therefore have passed legislation making cartels illegal. However, certain international cartels have not been prohibited, covering commodities such as oil, tin and coffee and indeed services such as air transport and telecommunications.

Informal collusion

Certain forms of informal (tacit) collusion are also illegal in many countries (see Chapter 8, p. 304). However, other forms are legal, including various types of 'price leadership'. In these situations one or more firms become recognised as the main price-setters for the industry and the other firms tend to act as followers.

Three different type of price leadership are often identified, namely dominant, barometric and collusive.

- *Dominant firm price leadership*. This is when the firm widely regarded as dominating the industry or market is acknowledged by others as the price leader. Ford has frequently acted as the dominant price leader in the motor vehicle industry by being first to announce price increases for various models of car.
- *Barometric price leadership*. In some cases the price leader is a small firm, recognised by others to have a close knowledge of prevailing market conditions. The firm acts as a 'barometer' to others of changing market conditions, and its price changes are closely followed.
- *Collusive price leadership*. This is a more complicated form of price leadership; essentially it is an informal cartel in which members arrange to introduce price changes almost simultaneously. Such 'parallel' price changes have been noticed in the wholesale petrol market from time to time. In practice it is often difficult to distinguish collusive price leadership from types in which firms follow price leaders very quickly. Collusive price leadership is actually illegal in many countries.

Other oligopoly practices

A number of other practices are widely associated with oligopoly.

Deterrence of new entrants by limit pricing

A major threat to long-run profit is the potential entrance of new firms into the industry. The '*limit price*' can be defined as the highest price which the established firms believe they can charge without inducing new firm entry. Its precise value will depend upon the nature and extent of the 'barriers to entry' for any particular industry. The greater the barriers to entry, the higher the 'limit price' will be.

The principle of 'limit-pricing' can be illustrated from Figure 6.16. Let us make the analysis easier by supposing that each established firm has an identical average total cost (ATC) curve, and sells an identical output, Q_F, at profit-maximising price P^* which the established firms have identified as appropriate for the industry. Suppose a new firm, with an identical cost profile, is considering entering the industry, and is capable of selling E units in the first instance. Despite the initial cost disadvantage, the new firm believes it can survive.

One way of preventing the survival of the new firm, perhaps even deterring its entry, would be for the established firms to agree to reduce the industry price to P_L. Although this would reduce their own excess profits in the short run (by VW per unit), the new entrant would make a loss selling E at price P_L, since price would be less than

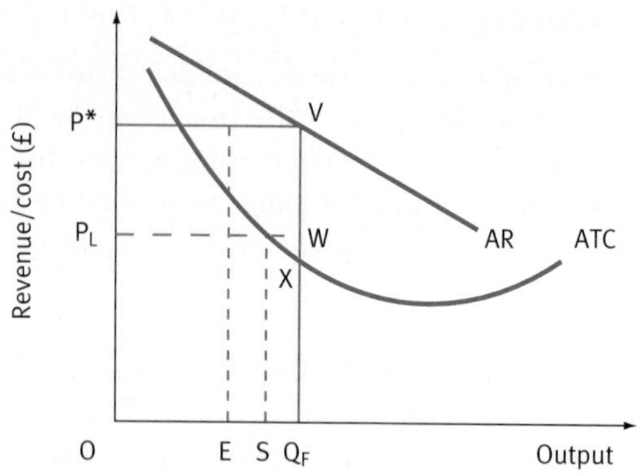

Fig 6.16 Limit pricing as a barrier to entry

average cost at that output. It would have needed to produce as much as output S immediately at the price P_L, even to have just covered its average costs.

The greater the barriers to the entry of new firms, the higher the 'limit price', P_L, can be, i.e. the closer P_L can be to P*. The most favourable situation for established firms would be if barriers were so great that P_L were at, or above, P*. In other words, established firms could set the joint profit-maximising price without inducing entry.

Price discrimination

Another strategy often associated with oligopoly (though equally available to monopoly) is that of *price discrimination*. So far we have assumed that firms charge only one price for their product. In practice, firms may charge different prices for an identical product – which is what 'price discrimination' refers to. If the product is differentiated in some way, then charging different prices to reflect a different quality of good or different standard of service *is not* price discrimination. For example, price discrimination does not occur when an airline company charges a higher price for a business class seat since the price premium over an economy class seat reflects different quality of service.

Examples of price discrimination might include:

- manufacturers selling an identical product at different prices in different geographical locations (e.g. different regions of a country, different national markets, etc.);
- electricity, gas and rail companies charging higher prices at peak hours than at off-peak hours for the same service;
- cinemas, theatres and transport companies cutting prices for both younger and older customers;
- student discounts for rail travel, restaurant meals and holidays;
- hotels offering cheap weekend breaks and winter discounts.

A key reason for price discrimination is to increase revenue and profit (revenue minus cost) for the firm. Suppose that if, instead of charging the single, uniform price OP in Figure 6.17(a), the firm were to charge what each consumer is *willing to pay*, as indicated by the demand curve.

- It follows that an additional PP_WV of revenue will result. Total revenue would be OP_WVQ as compared to OPVQ with a single, uniform price OP.

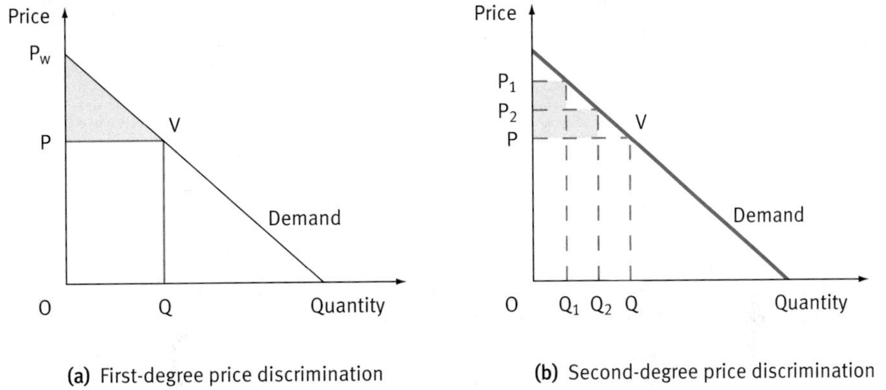

Fig 6.17 First- and second-degree price discrimination.

Remember **This type of price discrimination is capturing all the consumer surplus that occurs at price OP and converting it into revenue for the producer.**

This type of price discrimination is sometimes called 'first degree' price discrimination. In fact, three types of price discrimination are often identified in the literature.

- *First-degree price discrimination.* Where, as in Figure 6.17(a), the firm charges a different price to every consumer, reflecting each consumer's willingness to pay.
- *Second-degree price discrimination.* Where different prices are charged for different quantities or 'blocks' of the same product. So, for example, in Figure 6.17(b) the quantity OQ is split into three equal-sized blocks ($O–Q_1$, $Q_1–Q_2$, $Q_2–Q$) and a different price is charged for each block (P_1, P_2, P respectively). The idea is that whilst consumers cannot, in practice, be identified in terms of individual willingness to pay, different prices might be charged to groups of consumers. Again, total revenue (shaded area) is greater than would have occurred with a single uniform price (OPVQ).
- *Third-degree price discrimination.* Where the market is separated into two or more groups of consumers, with a different price charged to each group. Box 6.4 looks in more detail at this type of price discrimination.

Box 6.5 Third-degree price discrimination

For third-degree price discrimination to be undertaken it must be both possible and profitable to segment the market into two or more groups of consumers, with a different price charged to each group.

- *To be possible*, the firm must be able to prevent consumers moving from the higher-priced market segment to the lower-priced market segment. In other words, there must be 'barriers' separating the respective market segments. Such barriers could include geographical distance (domestic/overseas markets), time (peak/off-peak), personal identification (young/old) etc.
- *To be profitable*, the price elasticity of demand must be different in each separate market segment.

Figure 6.18 outlines the situation of third-degree price discrimination.

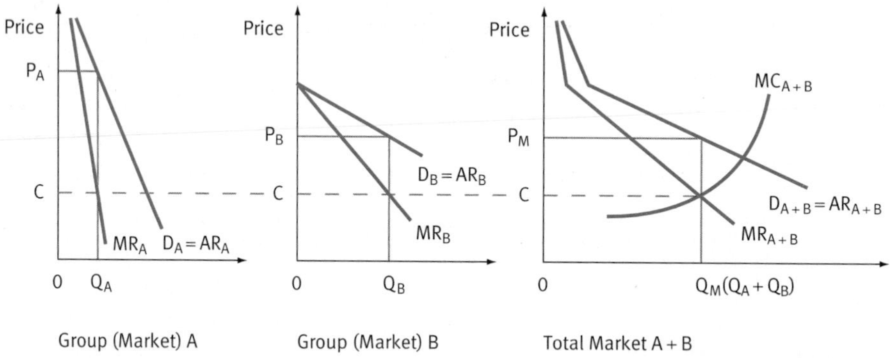

Fig 6.18 Third-degree price discrimination: charging different prices to different groups of customers

In Figure 6.18 we assume that the large oligopoly firm produces in one location and sells its output to two separate markets, A and B, with different price elasticities of demand in each market. Market B has a much higher price elasticity of demand than Market A. The corresponding *total market* marginal and average revenue curves are obtained by summing horizontally the *individual market* marginal and average revenue curves.

With production in a single location there is one MC curve, giving the overall profit-maximising output of Q_M, which might be sold at a single price P_M. However, total profit can, in this situation, be raised by selling this output at a different price to each group (market).

The profit-maximising condition is that MC for whole output must equal MR in each separate market:

$$\text{i.e. } MC_{A+B} = MR_A = MR_B$$

In Figure 6.18 total output Q_M will be allocated so that Q_A goes to group (market) A and Q_B to group (market) B, resulting in the respective prices P_A and P_B.

Any other allocation of total output Q_M must reduce total revenue and therefore, with unchanged costs, reduce total profit.

We can illustrate this by considering a single unit reallocation from market A to market B. The addition to total revenue (MR_B) of this unit when sold in market B is less than C, whereas the loss to total revenue (MR_A) of not selling this unit in market A is C. The overall change in total revenue from this unit reallocation is clearly negative, which, with total costs unchanged, must reduce total profit.

As we can see from Figure 6.18, the implication of third-degree price discrimination is a higher price in the market with lowest price elasticity of demand ($P_A > P_B$).

Case Study 6.4 looks at a particular case of third-degree price discrimination in the UK.

Case Study 6.4 Price discrimination in pharmaceuticals

In April 2001 the Office of Fair Trading (OFT) in the UK imposed a penalty on Napp Pharmaceuticals Holdings Ltd, a Cambridge-based pharmaceutical company, for abuse of its dominant position in the market for a drug called MST, a slow-release morphine product used to treat severe pain in cancer patients. The company controlled 94% of the overall sales of the drug, which was sold to two distinct markets – the community segment and the hospital segment. The community segment involved MST sold to pharmacies who, in turn, supplied them to patients through GP prescriptions, while the hospital segment involved sales of MST direct to hospitals.

The OFT Report commented that GPs were strongly influenced by the reputation of the product and were reluctant to experiment with new products of which they had no direct experience. In addition, for GPs, cost seemed to be 'rarely considered in terminal care pain relief'. On the other hand, hospital doctors were found to be more willing to accept 'intra-molecular substitution' – that is, they were willing to use any brand of a single molecular product to treat their patients. The OFT Report found that the price which Napp charged for its 5 mg tablets of MST to the *community market* was 70% higher than its price to the *hospital market* – where prices were set at below average variable cost (AVC). The OFT found that Napp had engaged in anti-competitive activity and proposed that the company should immediately reduce the price of MST tablets to the community sector. It was estimated that this would save the NHS around £2m annually.

Questions

1 What indicators are there that Napp had monopoly power in the market for MST?

2 Identify the factors which would ensure that Napp could apply price discrimination policies in this market.

3 How was Napp keeping other rivals out of the market?

Activity 6.3 looks at various aspects of oligopoly markets.

Activity 6.3

1 Try to match the *lettered* term with the correct *numbered* description.

Term

(a) Zero-sum game
(b) Kinked demand theory
(c) Maxi-min decision rule
(d) Mini-max decision rule
(e) Cartel
(f) Barometric leadership
(g) Parallel pricing

Description

(i) Where the industry strategy is set by a small firm recognised as having good market intelligence.
(ii) Selecting the best of the worst possible outcomes.
(iii) Where any gain for one firm is offset by an equivalent loss for some other firm (or firms).
(iv) A central body responsible for setting the industry price or output.
(v) Selecting the worst of the best possible outcomes.
(vi) Where any change in price by one firm is simultaneously matched by other firms.
(vii) Where rivals match the firm's price cuts but do not match the firm's price rises.

2 Which one of the following is *not* a characteristic of an oligopolistic market?

(a) Prices can become 'sticky' or rigid.
(b) There are a few sellers of a good or service.
(c) Entry is relatively easy.
(d) Firms consider the possible reactions of rivals.
(e) Firms are often drawn into game-playing situations.

3 Which of the following statements does *not* refer to a method of deterring entry into an industry?

(a) Where incumbent firms set a price that is below the average long-run costs of the potential new entrant.
(b) Where incumbent firms advertise extensively in order to make their demand curves more inelastic.
(c) Where incumbent firms agree to decrease prices almost simultaneously in response to the threat of potential new entrants.
(d) Where incumbent firms decide to leave a cartel that had previously sought to maximise joint profits.
(e) Where incumbent firms purchase all known sources of supply of a vital raw material.

4 Which of the following is a feature of a two-firm zero sum game?

(a) A loss for one firm can lead to an equivalent loss for the other firm.
(b) A gain by one firm can lead to a gain for the other firm.
(c) If both of the firms select the worst of the best possible outcomes for each initial strategy, they are said to be adopting a maxi-min approach to the game.
(d) In a market share duopoly game, +3% to one firm must be matched in reality by −3% to the other firm.
(e) In a profits game, +£1m to one firm is matched by +£1m to another firm.

Answers to Checkpoints and Activities can be found on pp. 705–35.

Key Terms

Barometric-firm leadership Here the price leader is a small firm, recognised by others as having a close knowledge of prevailing market conditions.

Barriers to entry Various deterrents to new firm entry into a market.

Contestable markets Markets in which the threat of new firm entry causes incumbents to act as though such potential competition actually existed.

Dominant strategy One in which the respective firms seek to do the best they can in terms of the objectives set, irrespective of the possible actions/reactions of any rival(s).

Long-run Period of time in which all factors of production can be varied.

Maxi-min An approach in game theory whereby the firm selects from the best of the worst possible outcomes identified in a pay-off matrix.

Mini-max An approach in game theory whereby each firm selects the worst of the best possible outcomes identified in a pay-off matrix.

Monopolistic competition A market structure which contains elements of both monopoly and competitive market forms. Differentiated (or non-homogeneous) products give firms an element of market power, but the existence of large numbers of relatively small firms, with freedom of entry/exit, provides an element of competition.

Monopoly Where over 25% of the output of a product is in the hands of a single firm or group of linked firms.

Nash equilibrium Occurs when each firm is doing the best that it can in terms of its own objectives, given the strategies chosen by the other firms in the market.

Natural monopoly Situation where the minimum efficient size of the productive unit or enterprise is so large that the industry can sustain only a single operator.

Normal profit That profit just sufficient to keep the firm in the industry in the long run.

Pareto optimal A resource allocation for which it is no longer possible to make anyone better off without making someone else worse off.

Perfectly contestable market Situation in which no barriers to entry exist so that incumbent firms are constrained by the threat of new firm entry to keep prices at levels that, in relation to costs, earn only normal profits. Incumbents in perfectly contestable markets earn no super-normal profits, are cost efficient, and cannot cross-subsidise between products or set prices below costs in order to deter new entrants.

Price discrimination Situation in which different prices are charged for identical units of a product.

Pure monopoly A single supplier of the product.

Short-run Period of time in which at least one factor of production is fixed.

Stable equilibrium Situation in which any movement away from an equilibrium initiates changes that move the situation back towards that equilibrium.

Zero-sum game A game in which any gain for one or more players is offset by an equivalent loss for some other players.

Key Points

- Concentration ratios for both product and industry groups have risen over time, implying a more oligopolistic market structure.
- 'Recognised interdependence between the few' is a key feature of oligopoly markets.
- Where firms develop their own strategies independently we speak of 'non-collusive behaviour'.
- Even in this case firms will seek to anticipate how their rivals might react to any strategy they might adopt.
- Past experience might be a guide to rival reactions, as in the 'kinked demand' model. Firms learn that rivals match price cuts but not price rises. The model predicts price stability.
- Even where there is little price competition, there may be extensive non-price competition.
- 'Game' simulations may be used to predict the outcomes of different combinations of action/reaction. Games may or may not have stable equilibriums depending on the strategies each firm adopts.
- To avoid uncertainty, collusion may occur, whether formal (cartels) or informal (tacit).
- To be successful firms must abide by the rules of a cartel, e.g. producing no more than their allocated quotas.
- Informal collusion may include various types of price leadership models as well as agreements of various kinds.

Assessment Practice

Multiple choice questions

1 **Perfect competition occurs in a market where there are many firms each selling:**

(a) an identical product
(b) a similar product
(c) a unique product
(d) a capital intensive product
(e) a competitive product.

2 **Which one of the following does NOT occur in perfect competition?**

(a) No single firm can exert a significant influence on the market price of the good.
(b) There are many buyers.
(c) There are significant restrictions on entry into the industry.
(d) Firms and buyers are completely informed about the prices of the products of each firm in the industry.
(e) Firms already in the industry have no advantage over potential new entrants.

3 **In perfect competition, a firm's marginal revenue equals its:**

(a) price
(b) total revenue
(c) supply curve
(d) average revenue
(e) both (a) and (d).

4 **Refer to Figure 6.19. What price will the monopolist charge in order to maximise profit?**

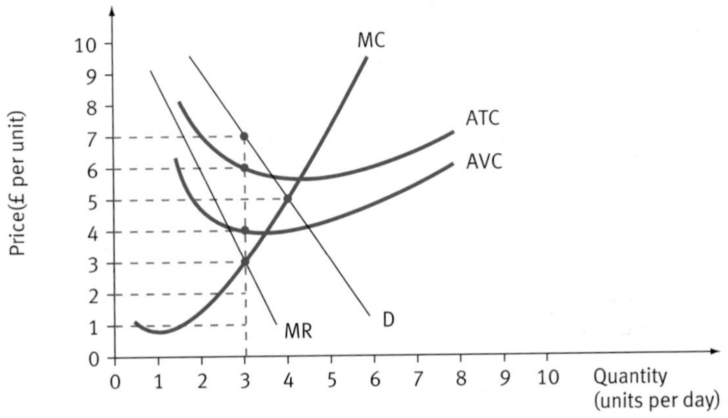

Fig 6.19

(a) £3
(b) £5
(c) £10
(d) £4
(e) £7

5 **Refer to Figure 6.19 in question 4 above. At the profit-maximising price and output, the total revenue is:**

(a) £10
(b) £16
(c) £18
(d) £21
(e) £7

6 Which *three* of the following characteristics apply to oligopoly?

(a) A few large firms account for a high percentage of industry output.
(b) Many small firms account for a high percentage of industry output.
(c) Each firm faces a horizontal demand curve.
(d) Each firm faces a downward sloping demand curve.
(e) The industry is often characterised by extensive non-price competition.

7 One difference between perfect competition and monopolistic competition is that:

(a) There are a smaller number of firms in perfectly competitive industries.
(b) In perfect competition, the products are slightly differentiated between firms.
(c) Monopolistic competition has barriers to entry, whereas perfect competition has none.
(d) Firms in monopolistic competition have some degree of market power.
(e) There are a larger number of firms in monopolistic competition.

8 To achieve more market power, firms can:

(a) lobby the government to eliminate barriers to entry
(b) reduce their costs of production
(c) advertise that they charge low prices
(d) differentiate their products from the products of their rivals
(e) raise their profit margin on prices.

9 Under which type of market structure is price rigidity (stickiness) often predicted?

(a) Perfect competition
(b) Pure monopoly
(c) Imperfect competition
(d) Oligopoly
(e) Natural monopoly

10 Which *two* of the following assumptions apply to 'kinked-demand' analysis in oligopoly markets?

(a) Rivals' reactions are irrelevant.
(b) Rivals will raise prices in response to the firm's higher prices.
(c) Rivals will tend not to raise prices in response to the firm's higher prices.
(d) Rivals will reduce prices in response to the firm's lower prices.
(e) Rivals will tend not to reduce prices in response to the firm's lower prices.

Data response and stimulus questions

1 Study Tables 6.5 and 6.6 and answer the following questions.

(a) What conclusions can be drawn from the data shown in Table 6.5?
(b) Define more closely the 'property and business services' sector by entering the ONS site and finding an in-depth definition of this sector.
(c) How can you integrate the information in both tables to show that elements of *monopolistic competition*, with its need to differentiate products and services, is still a feature of UK businesses?

Table 6.5 Number of VAT enterprises 2003 in selected sectors

Sector	Enterprises employing 0–9 people	Total number of enterprises
Construction	160,658	178,303
Retail	171,820	188,610
Property and business services	399,440	441,450
Hotel and catering	90,390	110,145
All industries	1,419,810	1,620,200

Adapted from ONS (2003) PA 1003 *Size Analysis of United Kingdom Businesses*, London: HMSO

Table 6.6 UK media advertising expenditure 2002 (%)

TV	26	Direct Mail	7
Regional Press	21	Posters	6
National Press	14	Radio	4
Magazines	13	Internet	1
Directories	7	Cinema	1

Adapted from *Advertising Association* (2003) *Advertising Statistical Yearbook*, London: World Advertising research Centre (WARC)

2 Look at Figure 6.20 then answer the questions which follow.

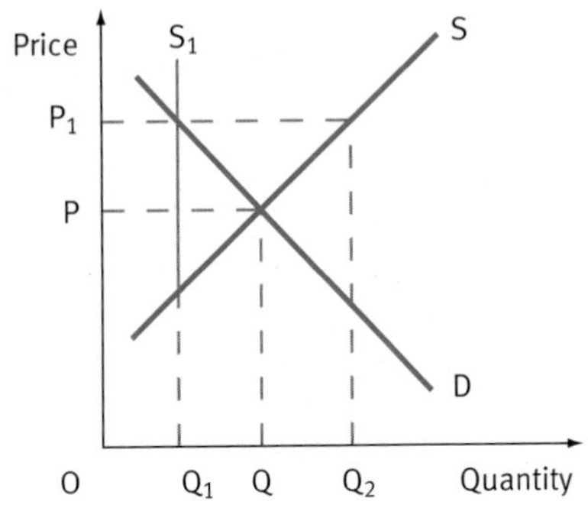

Fig 6.20

(a) What would be the price and output per barrel of oil if the market were competitive?
(b) What would be the shape of the supply curve if oil countries formed a cartel to limit the supply of oil to Q_1?
(c) What would the new price of oil be if the cartel achieved its output objective in (b)?
(d) With reference to price elasticity of demand, explain the conditions under which a cartel might want to keep price above the competitive price.

3 Read the following text, then answer the question.

Car prices in the UK

Britain is still the most expensive car market in the European Union despite price cuts by some producers, according to a survey by the European Commission. Prices in the UK are more than 50% higher than in Denmark, where pre-tax car prices are the lowest in the EU.

In the UK, a Volkswagen Passat is 49% more expensive than the cheapest euro-zone market in Portugal. In fact there is a variation of more than 30% in EU car prices for the same models in different countries. The European Commission believes there is no justification for prices varying by more than 12% between countries.

Direct Line, the insurance group that sells cars through its jamjar.com subsidiary, said UK consumers were paying £1bn a year too much for new cars.

Question

Why do you think car prices are higher in the UK than in other EU countries?

True/False questions

1 A major threat to longer-term profits exists when barriers to entry into an industry are high.
True/False

2 Extensive advertising can be a powerful barrier to entry into an industry.
True/False

3 In a non-zero-sum game, any benefit to one firm must be offset by an equivalent loss to some other firm.
True/False

4 In the long run, the monopolist can remain in the industry at a price that is just below long-run average costs.
True/False

5 Under perfect competition the marginal cost curve for the industry is the supply curve for the industry.
True/False

6 Under monopoly the marginal cost curve for the industry is the supply curve for the industry.
True/False

7 A maxi-min decision rule means selecting the best of the worst possible outcomes in the pay-off matrix.
True/False

8 Under kinked demand theory the prices of oligopolists are predicted to be rather rigid or ‘sticky’.
True/False

9 Price discrimination refers to charging different prices for different products in different markets.
True/False

10 A 'natural monopoly' is said to exist when the minimum efficient size for the firm is a small percentage of industry output.
True/False

11 Normal profits are more than sufficient to keep the firm in the industry in the long run.
True/False

12 In the long run, firms under monopoly or oligopoly must only earn normal profits.
True/False

Essay questions

1 Why is perfect competition often described as the 'ideal' market structure?
2 Consider the suggestion that monopoly will invariably result in a higher price and lower output than a competitive market structure.
3 Compare and contrast long-run equilibrium under monopolistic competition with that under perfect competition.
4 Can you explain why prices often show less variation under oligopoly than under other types of market structure?
5 Explain why price discrimination may be regarded as being in the best interest of the firm.
6 Use game theory to illustrate how recognised interdependence between sellers may still result in equilibrium outcomes.

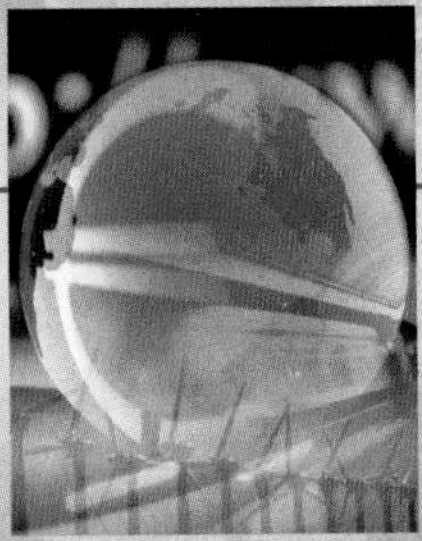

Chapter 7

Labour and other factor markets

Introduction

In this chapter we consider how the price and output of the factors of production are determined, paying particular attention to the labour market. We begin by discussing the idea that the return to all factors of production is 'derived' from the demand for the product or service they help produce. Attention then switches exclusively to labour as a factor of production and to those elements influencing the wage rate and the level of employment for various occupations. We go on to review many of the policy issues affecting work in modern societies. These include a wide variety of attempts to impose regulations on working conditions by both national and supra-national (e.g. EU) bodies. The minimum wage, maximum working hours directives and issues involving work–life balance are amongst those covered in this chapter, together with ageism and gender issues in the labour market. The circumstances in which payments to some factors of production can be regarded as 'surplus' are then considered.

Chapter 11 takes further a number of issues involving working patterns and conditions.

Learning objectives:

By the end of this chapter you should be able to:

- explain the idea of 'derived demand' for a factor of production
- account for variations in earnings between different occupations
- examine the impacts on occupational earnings and employment of 'monopoly' and 'monopsony' conditions in imperfectly competitive labour markets
- evaluate the costs and benefits of various types of labour market regulation, including the minimum wage
- assess the implications for the UK labour market of the EU Social Chapter and various work-related Directives

- discuss issues of gender and age discrimination in labour markets
- identify the circumstances in which the returns to factors of production include an element of surplus payment ('economic rent').

Factor payments and derived demand

We noted in Chapter 3 (p. 88) that a conventional listing of factors of production often includes land, labour and capital, though some might include 'entrepreneurship' as a factor in its own right.

Derived demand

Whatever our list, what is generally true is that factors of production are not demanded for purposes of ownership, as is arguably the case with consumer goods, but rather because of the stream of services they provide. For example, in the case of labour, workers are demanded for their mental and physical contribution to the production process. We therefore say that the demand for a factor of production is a *derived demand* rather than a direct demand. It is derived from the demand for the product, whether a good or a service, which the factor helps to produce.

It may be useful to begin by outlining the *marginal productive theory* of wages, which is often used to explain the demand for a particular occupation and therefore the wage it can command in the marketplace. As we shall see, this theory makes a number of assumptions which are broadly unrealistic (such as perfectly competitive product and labour markets), which we relax later in the chapter.

Marginal productivity theory

According to this theory, firms will continue to employ labour until the employment of the marginal worker adds as much to revenue as it does to costs. For simplicity, it is sometimes assumed that there is perfect competition in the market in which the product is sold so that firms can sell their entire output at the ruling market price.

We noted in Chapter 3 (p. 92) that the 'law of variable proportions' applies in the short run when at least one factor of production is fixed. This 'law' predicts that when labour is the variable factor being applied to some fixed factor (such as land or capital), the marginal physical product of labour at first rises but subsequently falls as the employment of workers increases, as is shown in Table 7.1.

- *Marginal physical product* of labour (MPP_L) refers to the additional (physical) output contributed by the last person employed. We can see from Table 7.1 that MPP_L begins to fall after the sixth worker has been employed. However, employers are less concerned with marginal physical product than with marginal revenue product.

Table 7.1 Returns to labour in the short run

No. of workers	Total physical product	Marginal physical product (MPP_L)	Marginal revenue product (MRP_L)	Marginal cost (MC_L)	Total revenue product	Total variable cost	Total profit
1	12	12	60	100	60	100	−40
2	26	14	70	100	130	200	−70
3	50	24	120	100	250	300	−50
4	90	40	200	100	450	400	50
5	140	50	250	100	700	500	200
6	200	60	300	100	1,000	600	400
7	254	54	270	100	1,270	700	570
8	304	50	250	100	1,520	800	720
9	340	36	180	100	1,700	900	800
10	358	18	90	100	1,790	1,000	790
11	374	16	80	100	1,870	1,100	770
12	378	4	20	100	1,890	1,200	690

- *Marginal revenue product* of labour (MRP_L) is the addition to total revenue contributed by the last person employed. In a perfectly competitive product market, MRP_L is found by multiplying the MPP_L by the price of the product; in Table 7.1 the MRP_L is calculated assuming a constant product price of £5 per unit.

$$MRP_L = MPP_L \times \text{product price}$$

Under marginal productivity theory the profit-maximising firm will continue to employ workers until the last person employed adds exactly the same value to revenue as he or she adds to costs, i.e. until MRP_L from employment = MC_L of employment.

$$MRP_L = MC_L \text{ for profit maximisation}$$

For illustrative purposes, as well as assuming a constant product price of £5, Table 7.1 assumes a constant wage rate per person of £100 so that the employer can hire as many people as he/she wants at £100 per person (i.e. $AC_L = MC_L = £100$). The only cost in Table 7.1 is labour, i.e. variable cost.

It is clear from Table 7.1 that after the employment of the second person and up to the employment of the ninth person, each worker adds more to revenue than to cost ($MRP_L > MC_L$). After the employment of the ninth worker the situation is reversed and each additional employee adds more to costs than to revenue ($MRP_L < MC_L$). It follows that profit is maximised (at £800) when nine people are employed.

NOTE

In terms of a diagram, at a wage of £100 the supply of labour curve (S_L) is perfectly elastic (see Figure 7.1). It follows that £100 = wage = MC_L = AC_L. For example, if three people are employed, total cost of labour is £300, average cost of labour is £100. If four people are employed, total cost of labour is £400, average cost of labour is £100 and the marginal cost of labour is £100 (i.e. £400 − £300).

MRP_L as the firm's demand curve for labour

The demand curve for any factor, including labour, is seen as being *derived* from the demand for the product or service it produces. Additional labour will always be required if the revenue gained from selling the output produced by the last person, the marginal revenue product of labour (MRP_L), is greater than the extra cost of employing that person, the marginal cost of labour (MC_L). In a competitive labour market (see Figure 7.1), the supply of labour (S_L) to each firm would be perfectly elastic at the going wage rate (W_1), so that the wage rate is itself both the average and the marginal cost of labour.

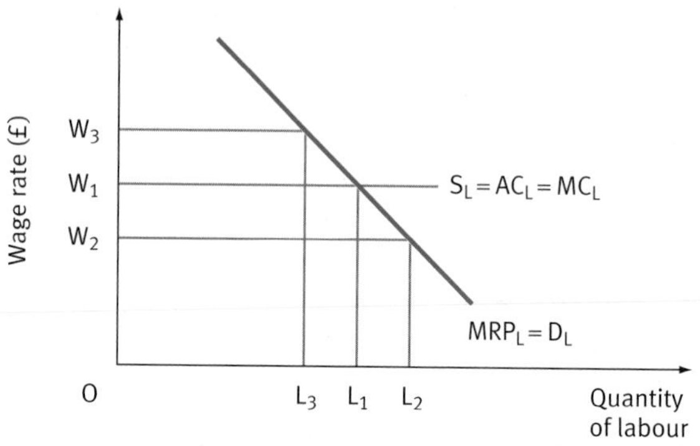

Fig 7.1 Wage determination in a competitive market

The profit-maximising firm would then hire people until MRP_L equalled MC_L, i.e. L_1 persons in Figure 7.1.

- If *more than* L_1 people were hired, then the extra revenue from hiring an extra person would be less than the extra cost. Profit will rise by hiring less people.
- If *fewer than* L_1 people were hired, then the extra revenue from hiring an extra person would be greater than the extra cost. Profit will rise by hiring more people.

Under these conditions the MRP_L curve becomes the demand curve for labour (D_L), since at any given wage rate the profit-maximising firm will employ labour until MRP_L equals that wage rate. For example, if the wage rate falls to W_2 in Figure 7.1 then demand for labour expands to L_2.

Example:

Productivity lags in the UK

The marginal physical productivity of labour (MPP_L) is clearly a key element in labour demand. Professor Michael Porter was commissioned by the UK Department of Trade and Industry to investigate the UK's comparative productivity in 2003. His results showed that in Germany and France output per hour worked was some 20% higher and in the US 40% higher than in the UK. One of the key reasons, in Porter's view, was the higher capital to labour ratio in these countries; the amount of capital per hour worked being 25% lower in the UK than in the US, 32% less than in France and a remarkable 60% less than in Germany.

Market (industry) demand for labour

If we know the number of workers each *firm* in an industry demands at any given wage rate, then we can derive the overall *market* (industry) demand for labour by adding together the individual firm's demand curves. Because each individual firm's demand for labour will vary inversely with the wage rate, the overall market demand for labour will also vary inversely with the wage rate. In other words, market demand for labour will expand as the wage rate falls (see Figure 7.1).

Of course, the firm and market demand for a *particular occupation* will be different from that for an entirely different occupation. In moving to market demand we are therefore aggregating firm demands for a particular skill level or occupational type, rather than for all skill levels or all occupational types.

Elasticity of demand for labour

As with (price) elasticity of demand for products (Chapter 2, p. 46), so we can define (price) elasticity of demand for factors such as labour.

$$\text{Elasticity of demand for labour} = \frac{\%\text{ change in quantity of labour demanded}}{\%\text{ change in price of labour}}$$

It is clearly useful to know how responsive the demand for labour will be to a change in its price (e.g. wage rate). Clearly the demand for labour will vary *inversely* with the wage rate, with the demand for labour expanding as the wage rate falls. However, as with price elasticity of demand, we usually ignore the sign. The range of numerical possibilities and terminology are in fact the same as in Table 2.1 (p. 46) for price elasticity of demand.

Influences on the elasticity of demand for labour

We can say that the elasticity of demand for labour will depend upon the following:

- *The price elasticity of demand (PED) for the product produced by labour.* If PED for the product is relatively inelastic, then elasticity of demand for labour will tend to be relatively inelastic, with a given percentage rise in the price of labour resulting in a smaller percentage fall in the demand for labour. The reasoning is that employers will be able to pass on the higher wage costs as higher product prices in the knowledge that consumer demand will be little affected.
- *The proportion of the total costs of production accounted for by labour.* Where this is relatively small, then the demand for labour will tend to be relatively inelastic. Even a large percentage rise in the price of labour will have little effect on the price of the product and therefore on the demand for labour.
- *The ease with which other factors of production can be substituted for labour.* Where it is difficult to substitute capital equipment or other factors of production for the now more expensive labour input, then elasticity of demand for labour will tend to be relatively inelastic, with any given percentage rise in the price of labour having little effect on the demand for labour in the production process.

Checkpoint 1 Outline the situations which will tend to make the demand for labour relatively elastic.

Elasticity of supply of labour

We have seen that the equilibrium price (wage rate) and quantity of labour employed depend on both demand and supply conditions. The supply of labour to any particular industry or occupation will vary *directly* with the wage rate. At higher wage rates more workers make themselves available for employment in this particular industry or occupation and vice versa. At the higher wage, extra workers are attracted to this occupation since they now earn more than in the next best paid alternative employment.

Again it will be useful to know how responsive the supply of labour will be to a change in its price (e.g. wage rate). The (price) elasticity of supply for labour can be expressed as follows:

$$\text{Elasticity of supply for labour} = \frac{\%\ \text{change in quantity of labour supplied}}{\%\ \text{change in price of labour}}$$

Influences on the elasticity of supply for labour

We can say that the elasticity of supply of labour will depend upon the following:

- *The degree to which labour is mobile, both geographically and occupationally.* The less mobile a particular type of labour (e.g. occupation) is between geographical regions and occupations, then the less responsive (less elastic) will be its supply to a change in the wage rate.
- *The time period in question.* The supply of labour to all industries or occupations will tend to be less responsive (less elastic) in the short run than in the long run since it may take time for labour to acquire the new skills and experience required for many occupations. This is especially true where the nature of the work is highly skilled and requires considerable training. In this case the supply of labour to the occupation will not rise substantially, at least initially, as wage rates increase, as for example with doctors and barristers.

Activity 7.1

Look back at Table 7.1 (p. 249).

(a) Use this table to identify and draw the *demand curve for labour* when there is perfect competition in both factor and product markets.
(b) Use your demand curve to identify how many people would be employed at a wage rate of:
(i) £250
(ii) £80.
Explain your reasoning.
(c) Under what conditions might this demand curve for labour become *more elastic*?

(d) Suppose the price of the product produced by labour now rises from £5 per unit to £8 per unit.
  (i) How would this affect Table 7.1?
  (ii) Would your answers in part (b) of this question remain the same?

Answers to Checkpoints and Activities can be found on pp. 705–35.

Occupational differences in wages and employment

We now seek to apply what we have learned to the key question of why some occupations achieve higher levels of earnings and higher rates of employment than others. That differences in occupational earnings exist and are actually widening is evident from recent data.

Example:

Widening gap between high earners and others

Researchers at *Incomes Data Services* report that since 1990 pay rises for higher-earning occupations have outstripped those for the rest of the workforce. As a result of this 'skew' (to the right) in the occupational earnings distribution, the average (arithmetic mean) wage has been pulled upwards, leaving more and more occupations beneath it. In 2004 some 65% of the workforce earned less than the average weekly wage of £495 before tax, compared to only 60% in 1990.

We first approach this question assuming no imperfections in the labour market before relaxing this assumption and examining the labour market as it really is in practice.

Competitive labour market

In competitive labour markets, wage rates are determined by the forces of supply and demand for labour. In these circumstances, different wage rates between occupations will reflect differences in the respective conditions of supply and demand, as in the two hypothetical labour markets shown in Figure 7.2.

In Figure 7.2(a) the higher wage rate (W_1) in one of these competitive labour markets is due to the fact that, at any given wage rate, demand for labour is greater (D_1D_1) and supply of labour is lower (S_1S_1) in this, as compared to the other competitive labour market. This wage difference can be maintained over time if the labour markets are separate, i.e. little or no mobility between the two occupations (e.g. surgeons and nurses).

However, if workers can easily move between the two occupations, then any initial wage difference is unlikely to be maintained over time (e.g. bus and lorry drivers).

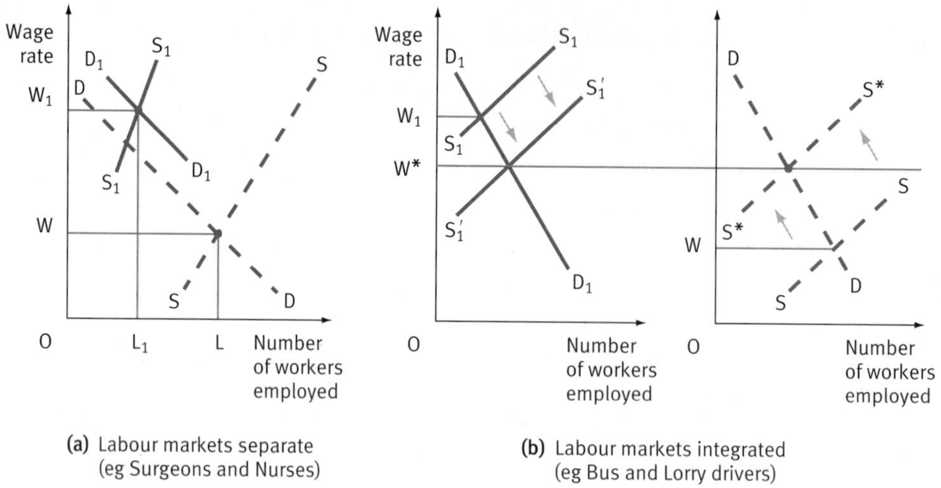

Fig 7.2 Equilibrium wage rates and levels of employment in two competitive labour markets.

Checkpoint 2

- Use Figure 7.2(a) to explain the circumstances under which the wage rate for the occupation described by the DD and SS curves respectively might rise *above* W.
- How might the level of employment be affected at this now higher wage?
- Use Figure 7.2(b) to explain why the initially higher wage (W_1) for bus drivers may not

Given a competitive labour market and a particular set of supply and demand conditions for labour, we can now make a number of assertions:

- Only one wage rate is sustainable (i.e. in equilibrium), namely that which equates supply of labour with demand for labour.
- Wages in a particular industry or occupation can only change if there is a change in the conditions of supply or in the conditions of demand, or in both.

Case Study 7.1 Pop idols

Madonna is not quite the box-office hit today that she has been in the past. Her 2003 album *American Life was* a relative disappointment, despite notching up 3.5 million sales. This figure was only half that achieved in 2000 by Madonna with her *Music* album.

Nevertheless, Madonna is seeking a payout of £36m from Time Warner in 2004 to add to her annual royalty income on record sales, past and present, estimated to be over £18m in 2003 alone. The one-off £36m payment relates to the value placed on

Case Study 7.1 continued

her own recording label, *Maverick*. This was created in 1992 with her manager, Freddy DeMann. Time Warner bought out Madonna with a contract that also guaranteed financial support for *Maverick* until 2004. In fact *Maverick* has been one of the more successful of the so-called 'vanity labels', having released records from stars such as Alanis Morissette and Prodigy. Nevertheless, Time Warner have only offered some £11m as final settlement for *Maverick*, some £25m short of Madonna's own valuation.

Nor is this the only disagreement with Time Warner. Madonna is threatening to sue Time Warner for the dramatic fall in value of the £25 million of options in Time Warner shares granted to her in 1999. She blames the disastrous Time Warner–America On-Line merger in 2001 (see Case Study 5.3, p. 188) for so reducing the paper value of these options that they have become virtually worthless. Some reports suggest that Madonna is threatening to sue Time Warner for misleading her as to the likely future value of these stock options.

Questions

1. With Figure 7.2 in mind, use demand–supply analysis to suggest how the huge annual earnings of Madonna and similar pop idols might be explained.
2. Explain why the stock-option deal of 1999 with Time Warner failed to yield Madonna the future income she expected.

Of course, in reality the labour market may not be competitive at all. We now turn to consider the impacts of different types of 'market failure' in labour markets.

Imperfectly competitive labour markets

We turn first to the presence of monopoly conditions in the supply of labour.

Monopoly in labour markets: trade unions

If the labour force is now unionised, then the *supply* of labour to the firm (or industry) may be regulated. However, even though unions bring an element of **monopoly** into labour supply, theory suggests that they can only influence price or quantity, but not both. For example, in Figure 7.3(a) the union may seek wage rate W_3, but must accept in return lower employment at L_3. Alternatively, unions may seek a level of employment L_2, but must then accept a lower wage rate at W_2. Except (see below) where unions are able to force employers off their demand curve for labour (MRP_L), unions can only raise wages at the 'cost' of reduced employment.

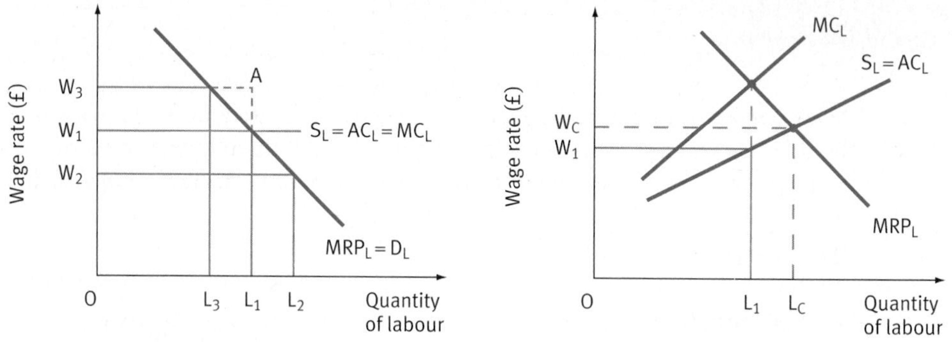

(a) Monopoly power: Trade Unions force employers off their demand curve (ie point A)

(b) Monopsony power: Employers Associations exert power in the hiring of labour

Fig 7.3 Imperfections in the labour market.

A given rise in wages will reduce employment by less, under the following circumstances:

1 the less elastic is final demand for the product;
2 the less easy it is to substitute other factors for the workers in question;
3 the lower the proportion of labour costs to total costs of production.

All of these circumstances, as we have already noted, will make the demand curve for labour, MRP_L, less elastic (i.e. steeper).

Unions and bargaining power

Unions may seek to force employers *off* their demand curve for labour so that they make less than maximum profits. It may then be possible for wages to rise from W_1 to W_3 with no loss of employment, i.e. point A in Figure 7.3(a). How effective unions will be in such strategies will depend upon the extent of their 'bargaining power'. Chamberlain defines union bargaining power as:

$$\text{Union bargaining power} = \frac{\text{Management costs of disagreeing (to union terms)}}{\text{Management costs of agreeing (to union terms)}}$$

Although the ratio cannot be measured, as it relies on subjective assessments, it is a useful analytical tool. If unions are to exert effective influence on management the ratio must exceed unity. That is to say, it must be more costly for management to disagree (e.g. loss of profits or loss of market share as a result of industrial action) than to agree (e.g. higher labour costs and higher employment levels) to the union's terms. The higher the ratio, the more likely it is that management will agree to the union's terms.

Example:

Union density and bargaining power

The 'management costs of disagreeing' to union terms are likely to be greater, the higher the proportion of total workers in a union. For the UK as a whole this 'union density' has fallen dramatically in recent times and with it, arguably, the 'bargaining power' of unions. For example, union density in the UK reached a peak of 55% in 1979 but is only around 28% in 2004.

Monopsony in labour markets: employer associations

It may, however, be the case that market power lies not with the 'suppliers' of labour (e.g. the trade unions) but with the 'buyers' of labour. In this case we use the term **monopsony** to refer to market power in the hands of those who demand labour.

Employer associations are groups of employers who come together to create an element of monopoly on the *demand* side of the labour market (i.e. 'monopsony'). These associations bring together the employers of labour in order to exert greater influence in collective bargaining. Standard theory suggests that monopsony in the labour market will, by itself, reduce both wages and employment in the labour market.

Example:

Employer associations

Altogether there are about 150 employer associations in the UK which negotiate the national collective agreements for their industry with the trade unions concerned. Most of these belong to the *Confederation of British Industry (CBI).*

In Figure 7.3(b), under competitive labour market conditions the equilibrium would occur where the supply of labour ($S_L = AC_L$) equalled the demand for labour (MRP_L), giving wage W_C and employment L_C. If monopsony occurs, so that employers bid the wage rate up against themselves, then it can be shown that the MC_L curve will lie *above* the $S_L = AC_L$ curve. For example, if by hiring the fourth worker, the wage (= AC_L) of all three existing workers is bid up from £5 to £6, then the AC_L for the fourth worker is £6 but the MC_L for the fourth worker is higher at £9 (£24 – £15). The profit-maximising employer will want to equate the extra revenue contributed by the last worker employed (MRP_L) to the extra cost of employing the last worker (MC_L). In Figure 7.3(b) this occurs with L_1 workers employed.

Note, however, that the employer only has to offer a wage of W_1 in order to get L_1 workers to supply themselves to the labour market. The wage W_1 is *below* the competitive wage W_C and the level of employment L_1 is *below* the competitive level of employment L_C. This is the standard case against monopsony in a labour market, namely lower wages and lower employment as compared to those in a competitive labour market.

Activity 7.2 gives you the chance to review the presence of monopsony and monopoly in the labour market.

Activity 7.2

1 Look at the following table for a monopsony labour market.

Wage rate (AC_L) (£)	Number of workers supplied (per day)	Total cost of labour (£)	Marginal cost of labour (MC_L) (£)
50	1		
60	2		
70	3		
80	4		
90	5		
100	6		
110	7		
120	8		

(a) Complete the table.
(b) Draw the labour supply (AC_L) curve.
(c) Draw the marginal cost of labour (MC_L) curve.
(d) What do you notice?
(e) How will your answer to (d) influence the equilibrium level of wages and employment under monopsony? Draw a sketch diagram to illustrate your answer.

2 Assume that a trade union is important in a particular labour market.

(a) Draw a sketch diagram and use it to show how the union might be able to raise wages *without* reducing employment.
(b) What will determine the ability of the union to achieve the outcome in (a)?

Answers to Checkpoints and Activities can be found on pp. 705–35.

UK labour market regulations

We first consider the introduction of the National Minimum Wage in the UK, before moving to a variety of other important labour market regulations.

The National Minimum Wage

In the UK the Low Pay Commission for the first time recommended the introduction of a National Minimum Wage (NMW) as from October 2000, at that time set at £3.70 per hour for those 21 years and over, with a lower 'development' wage of £3.20 for 18–21 year olds. There has been much controversy over the level at which the NMW should be set. The unions had pushed for a rate considerably above £4.00 per hour in

2000, but the Low Pay Commission eventually recommended a lower rate. By October 2004 the over-21 minimum wage rate had risen to £4.87 per hour, with a new minimum of £3 per hour introduced for 16–18-year-olds.

Figure 7.4(a) illustrates the problem of setting too high a minimum wage. If the NMW is set *above* the competitive wage (W_C) for any labour market, then there will be an excess supply of labour of L′–L*, with more people supplying themselves to work in this labour market than there are jobs available. In Figure 7.4(a) the actual level of employment falls from L_C to L*.

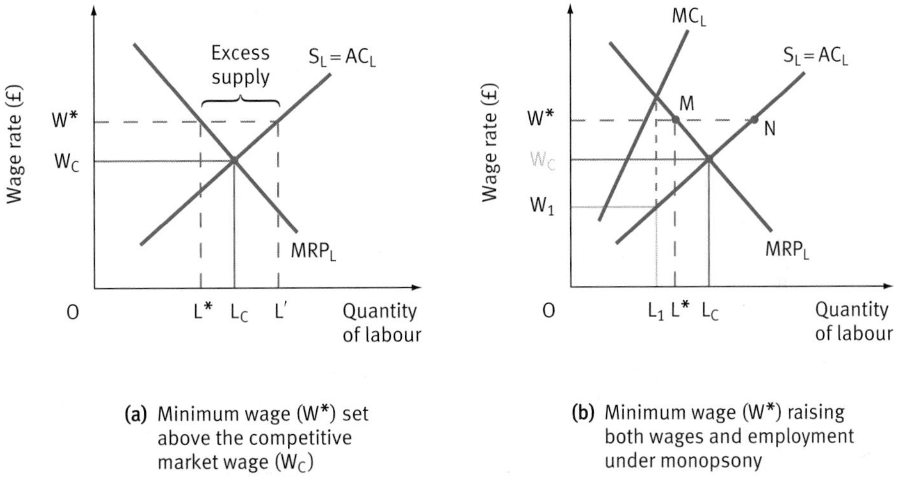

Fig 7.4 Impacts of a minimum wage.

However, there have been a number of studies suggesting that in the US, a higher minimum wage has actually increased *both* wages and employment, although it has been noted that many of the US studies have involved labour markets (e.g. the fast food sector) which are dominated by a few large employers of labour, i.e. *monopsonistic* labour markets.

In fact our earlier analysis of monopsony might have led us to expect this. For example if, in Figure 7.4(b), the initial monopsony equilibrium was wage W_1 and employment L_1, then setting a minimum wage of W* would result in a rise in both wages (W_1 to W*) and employment (L_1 to L*). It will be helpful to explain this outcome using Figure 7.4(b).

Since no labour is supplied *below* the minimum wage W*, then W^*NS_L becomes the effective labour supply curve. Along the horizontal segment, W*N, we then have $W^* = AC_L = MC_L$ (as in Figure 7.1). The profit-maximising situation is at point 'M' on the MRP_L curve, where the marginal cost of hiring the last person (MC_L) exactly equals the extra revenue resulting from employing that last person (MRP_L). So imposing a minimum wage on a labour market that is already imperfect (here monopsony) can increase both wages and levels of employment.

Case Study 7.2 reviews some recent discussions on the implications of the minimum wage for small businesses in the UK.

Case Study 7.2 Concerns over the NMW

FT

For six years it was the dog that didn't bark, but business concern about the government's minimum wage is slowly mounting, thanks to an unlikely alliance of hairdressers, hoteliers and fish-friers. The national hourly rate for adults over 21 was increased in October 2003 from £4.20 to £4.50, the fourth upward adjustment since the measure was proposed by the incoming Labour government in 1997. Gordon Brown, the chancellor, won applause at the Labour Party's conference by predicting it would soon rise to over £5.

Until now, the steadily rising rate has caused nothing like the backlash among employers that was predicted by its early opponents. Most economic studies have also shown little, if any, negative impact on job creation. But the smooth ride enjoyed by the government may be coming to an end as a growing number of smaller employers and industries in poorer parts of the country begin to voice opposition to further increases. Stephen Alambritis, of the Federation of Small Business, says his members are worried that any economic downturn could worsen the problem and would like to see more consideration of regional economic variations.

'The government have been lucky; because of the strength of the economy no one is really against the idea of a minimum wage any more,' he said. 'However, the problem is that the level is creeping up to a point that certain regions and sectors are beginning to find it very difficult.'

One such industry is hairdressing, traditionally one of the lowest-paid occupations in the country. Thousands of low-paid employees have benefited, but smaller salons fear they cannot continue to meet wage increases. Ray Seymour, general secretary of the National Hairdressers' Federation, said a particular worry is the Low Pay Commission's proposal to extend the slightly lower minimum wage for 18–21-year-olds to trainees *under* the age of 18. 'The trouble with fighting this is it's very hard to single out the minimum wage as directly causing problems,' he said. 'It's the totality of new costs on employers like the Working Time Directive that really add up.'

Others warn that the increases are encouraging some businesses to break the law. 'It's becoming very common among smaller hoteliers to keep employees off the books,' said Roland Haywood, chairman of the Blackpool Private Hotels Association. He estimates that the black market wage rate in the town's hotels – where a room can cost as little as £10 per night – is actually around £3.50 per hour.

Despite this, few trade bodies argue for an end to the minimum wage entirely – they just worry where the increases are leading. David Audley, vice president of the National Federation of Fish Friers, said: 'we don't have any problem with it in principle, but the government needs to be careful about increasing it beyond the rate of inflation, otherwise most self-employed fish friers will end up paying themselves less than their staff.'

Case Study 7.2 continued

Research by the Organisation for Economic Co-operation and Development, the rich-country think-tank, suggests that workers in their teenage years and early twenties have seen their job prospects suffer when the minimum wage has been set too high. The clearest example of this was Spain, where employment was hit when the adult rate was extended to 16-year-olds.

Source: *Financial Times*, 3 October 2003, p. 3

Questions

1 What are the main concerns raised in the case study?

2 How does this case study relate to our earlier analysis of the NMW?

Other UK labour market regulations

Apart from the National Minimum Wage, a number of other changes have been made in recent years to the regulations governing the UK labour market. These regulations have involved particular aspects of labour market activity.

Closed shop

This is a situation where employees obtain or retain a job only if they become a member of a specified trade union. This practice was progressively weakened by legislation in the 1980s and 1990s making unions liable to legal action from both employees and management if they tried to enforce the closed shop.

Strikes and other industrial action

- *Secondary action*. An important provision in the *1982 Employment Act* restricted 'lawful trade disputes' to those between workers and their own employer, making 'secondary action' unlawful, i.e. action against an employer who is not part of a dispute.
- *Picketing*. This is where striking workers approach non-strikers as they enter their place of work. Picketing is now restricted in law to the union members' 'place of work', often even excluding another plant of the same employer. If illegal picketing occurs, unions are now liable to pay damages in civil actions brought against them by employers.
- *Secret ballots*. Official industrial action, i.e. that approved by the union leadership, must be sanctioned by a secret ballot of the membership. The ballot must be held no more than four weeks before the event, and a majority of union members must be in favour of the action. If the action takes place without majority consent, then the union loses any legal immunity for organising industrial action that it may have enjoyed in the past. These provisions were strengthened by the *1988 Employment*

Act which gave the individual union member the right not to be called out on strike without a properly held secret ballot and the right not to be disciplined by his or her union for refusing to strike or for crossing a picket line.

- *Unofficial action.* The *1990 Employment Act* and *1992 Trade Union and Labour Relations Act* took the control of union behaviour even further by requiring that the union leadership must take positive steps to repudiate 'unofficial action', i.e. actions undertaken by union members without union consent (that is, of the executive committee or president or general secretary). For instance, the union must do its best to give written notice to all members participating in the unofficial action that it does not receive the union's support. Failure by the union to take such steps could mean loss of immunity for the union, even though the action is unofficial.
- *Postal ballots.* The *Trade Union Reform and Employment Rights Act 1993* passed two main provisions relating to the organisation of industrial action. First, ballots held in support of action should be fully postal and subject to independent scrutiny, effectively restricting the ability of the 'rank-and-file' to initiate action. Second, unions are to be required to give seven days' written notice before industrial action can be taken. This gives a longer waiting period which may help in settling any dispute.

Example:

Unions must be sincere in opposing unofficial strikes

Although trade unions can avoid potential liability for unofficial strikes by making it clear that the union does not support them, union officials must not behave in a manner inconsistent with the union's repudiation. For example, in 1985 the Newspaper Group Express & Star Ltd took on the printers' union, the NGA, in an early test case of the Conservatives' trade union legislation involving a strike by printers. The court held that any repudiation of unofficial action must be 'clear and unambiguous'. In this case it was ruled that the repudiation was a 'sham'. The court ruled that two officials were 'paying lip service to the order but plainly breaking it', and that it was 'inconceivable that they would do this unless encouraged from above'. The union was fined £15,000.

Large unions can be fined up to £250,000 for fomenting action, with the smallest unions liable for fines of up to £10,000.

Trade union democracy

The various Trade Union Acts already mentioned have also sought to strengthen trade union democracy:

- The main executive committee of a trade union must now be elected in a secret ballot of the union's members within the previous five years.
- Trade union members have the right to a postal vote in elections for all members of union-governing bodies and for key national leaders.

Recognition of trade unions

The *Employment Relations Act 1999* gives union rights to workers in organisations with at least 21 employees where a trade union has made a request to be recognised as the representative of employees for bargaining purposes. If an employer rejects the request, the union can apply to the Central Arbitration Committee (CAC) which has to decide whether the union has the support of the majority of the workforce that comprises the proposed 'bargaining unit', i.e. the group of employees to be covered by collective bargaining. If 50% or more of the bargaining unit are members of the union applying for recognition, then the CAC may award automatic recognition. If this criterion is not met, then a ballot can be held. In this case recognition will depend on the union receiving a majority of the votes in a ballot in which at least 40% of the workers entitled to vote have done so. The recognition agreement lasts for three years.

CHECK THE NET

Many interesting articles on labour issues are included in:

www.peoplemanagement.co.uk
www.tomorrowscompany.com
www.croner.co.uk

Before looking at other work-related issues in the UK, it will help to review EU legislation which itself has a major impact on the UK labour market.

EU Social Chapter

The 'Social Chapter' was the name given to the bringing together in the 1992 *Maastricht Treaty* of many work-related provisions contained in earlier EU treaties. It was made clear in the Maastricht Treaty that these provisions would be further developed by a series of 'Directives' and other EU regulations (see Chapter 12, p. 466). The idea was to provide minimum agreed working conditions for all employees in EU firms, creating a 'level playing field' when those firms compete in the Single European Market. It was expected that these minimum working conditions might then be improved throughout the EU over time.

After initially 'opting out' of the Social Chapter, the new Labour government agreed to join it shortly after its election in 1997, though reserving the right to delay implementation of certain specified Directives.

Main Directives of the Social Chapter

Over 30 Directives have so far been adopted by the EU.

- *Parental Leave Directive*. Women, regardless of length of service, are to have 14 weeks' *maternity leave* during which their jobs will be protected and firms will have to find replacements. Various rights to take time off after the birth or adoption of a child have now been extended to fathers. Prior to this Directive there was a length of service requirement with the employer of two years for full-timers and five years for part-timers. Women with over 26 weeks' service have the right to *maternity pay*.
- *Working Hours Directive*. A maximum of 48 hours is imposed on the working week (with exceptions for hospital doctors and for workers with 'autonomous decision making powers' such as managers). Other requirements include a four-week paid annual holiday, and an eight-hour limitation on shifts.
- *Part-time Workers Directive*. This extends equal rights and pro-rata benefits to part-time staff.

- *European Works Council Directive*. Companies employing over 1,000 workers, with at least 150 in two or more member states, are required to install a *transnational worker council* with information and consultation rights over the introduction of new production processes, mergers and plant closures.
- *Information and Consultation Directive*. In 2002 these rights were extended to any establishments in EU states with at least 50 employees. These now have the right to information and consultation on the performance of the business and on decisions relevant to employment, particularly where jobs are threatened. The Directive will only be introduced in the UK in 2008.
- *Young Workers Directive*. There is a ban on work for those under 15. For those who are 17 or under and in education, work must be less than three hours a day: if out of education, the limit is eight hours a day; five weeks' paid holiday is also required and there is a ban on night work.

As far as the Social Chapter of the Maastricht Treaty was concerned, the UK had been opposed to many of the regulations and directives associated with the Social Chapter and secured an opt-out from its provisions. Successive Conservative governments had argued that attempting to impose regulations in such areas as works councils, maternity/paternity rights, equal pay, part-time workers' issues and so on merely increased labour costs and decreased UK competitiveness. Nevertheless, the Labour government in the UK has adopted many parts of the Social Chapter in order to provide basic minimum standards across Europe, even if this does result in some increase in labour costs. In any case, even if the UK had remained outside the Social Chapter it would still have been subject to a great deal of EU social and health and safety legislation introduced as part of other programmes for which there is no UK 'opt-out'.

We have already noted that the Working Hours Directive imposes a 48-hour limit on the number of hours worked per week. However, all Social Chapter Directives seek to set 'minimum' working conditions and individual EU countries can always impose improved working conditions. In the context of weekly hours worked, an 'improvement' would imply a still *lower limit*. France is one EU country which has done just this, imposing a 35 hours per week limit on weekly working.

Case Study 7.3 Working hours in France

There is much debate in France as to whether improving on the EU Working Hours Directive has been of benefit to France. This issue usefully points out why there are supporters and critics of many of the EU Social Chapter Directives. In 2004 Jean-Pierre Raffarin, the Prime Minister, and his centre-right Cabinet planned the shortened working week, which was hailed by the Left as an act of pioneering social progress for many of the ills now besetting France. Originally cast as an antidote to unemployment and a boost to workers' rights, the law is being blamed for pushing the budget deficit over the maximum allowed under the EU stability rules for the single currency.

Case Study 7.3 continued

Acknowledging for the first time that France is on the brink of recession, M Raffarin has approved a parliamentary inquiry into the damage inflicted by the law. An official inquest into the huge death toll from the August 2003 heatwave has found already that the shorter hours for medical staff left hospitals unable to handle the emergency.

While the Left and Right argue about the cost of the shorter working week, which is estimated at more than £20bn, M Raffarin wants to restore the value of work and ensure that 'the future of France is not to be a huge leisure park'. The idea that a work-shy France risks relegating itself to the second industrial rank is now being widely discussed, with much criticism of RTT (Reduction de temps de travail) as the reduced working time is known.

Even heavyweight leftwingers have joined the criticism of the experiment in social engineering brought in under the leadership of Lionel Jospin. Jacques Attali, former chief adviser to Francois Mitterand, President Chirac's Socialist predecessor, said in 2004 that RTT sent the French a harmful message about the merits of work when they should be striving harder to compete in the global economy.

The government is drawing encouragement from unexpected quarters. Industrial workers are unhappy with antisocial shift times and a restraint on wage demands that were agreed as a condition of shorter hours. Their frustrations, together with contempt for RTT amongst small businesses, were reflected in an opinion poll that found that 54% of the country was in favour of doing away with, or suspending, the law.

RTT has proved most popular among white-collar workers in larger businesses and, to the surprise of the champions of the old class war, amongst executives in large companies. As well as providing free time, in the form of longer holidays or periodic four-day weeks, the law has helped to keep down wages and forced new flexibility in France's rigid shop floor practices.

M Raffarin has backed away from any attempt to rescind the law, preferring to neuter it through gradual measures, such as exempting smaller businesses from having to apply it.

Questions

1 Consider the advantages and disadvantages of the 35-hour working week to:
 (a) employers;
 (b) employees.

2 Why is the new French government and prime minister keen to increase working hours in France?

The UK in 2004 has the longest working hours in the EU, with the 'usual hours worked per week' being 45 hours in the UK, compared to an average of 39.8 hours for the EU as a whole.

The UK is the only EU country to have insisted on an 'opt-out' clause for the *Working Hours Directive* whereby individual workers in any occupation can voluntarily agree to work more than 48 hours. In 2004 the EU reported that about 4 million people, or 16% of the UK workforce, claim to work over the 48-hour limit and expressed concern that many of these 'voluntary' agreements to work longer are in fact the result of pressure by employers.

Work–life balance

The *Employment Act 2002* introduced further individual rights for employees, the most significant of which address certain 'family friendly' practices to promote 'work–life balance'. Box 7.1 looks at this issue in more detail.

Since April 2003, maternity leave was increased and working fathers have been given the right to two weeks' paternity leave. Employees are also able to request flexible working from their employers, such as job-sharing, flexi-time, home-working and part-time working. Employers have the right to refuse such requests, but must explain their reasons for this to the employee in writing. Box 7.1 outlines the main provisions involving work–life balance in the UK.

Box 7.1 Work–life balance

The changes which came into effect in the UK in April 2003 are outlined below.

- Parents of children under six have the right to ask employers to let them work flexibly.
- Employers are obliged to take their request seriously. Bosses who fail to pay proper heed to requests could face claims at employment tribunals.
- Employees have to take reasonable account of the business interests of the firm, including the size of the firm, production deadlines and so on.
- The right to ask to work flexibly applies to parents of disabled children up to the age of 18.
- Fathers are entitled to two weeks' paid paternity leave, paid at £100 a week, within eight weeks of the birth or adoption of a child.
- Entitlement to maternity leave is extended up to a year, comprising 26 weeks' paid and 26 weeks' unpaid leave.
- Standard statutory maternity pay is to be increased from £75 to £100 a week, with most firms able to reclaim the cash from the government.
- Parents adopting a child are entitled to go on leave when a child is newly placed with them.

Perhaps not surprisingly, there are different perspectives as to who will benefit from these new flexible working opportunities. Case Study 7.4 looks at some of these different viewpoints.

Case Study 7.4 **Flexible working – opportunity or threat**

There is certainly evidence to suggest that flexible working is popular with employees. A survey of over 4,000 jobseekers in 2003 by the recruitment website reed.co.uk found that almost a third put flexible hours above an extra £1,000 a year. Even more, about 46%, said that flexible working was the benefit they would most look for in their next job.

Yet fewer than 60 out of over 100,000 posts advertised on the recruitment website used for the study specifically offered flexible working conditions to attract employees. James Reed, whose website conducted the study, suggested that this research was a real wake-up call for employers. He suggested that too many organisations seemed to be missing out on one of the most effective ways to attract top talent.

However, employers have voiced some concerns. Swapping shifts, altering rotas at the last minute and ensuring that there are enough staff in to do the work would not be an easy task.

The first step for all employers is to get to grips with the legislation. Murray Fairclough of Abbey Legal Protection says: 'When an employee makes a request for flexible working you need to know whether they are eligible for it, whether you can turn them down and what process you need to follow.'

Valid reasons for refusing a request include inability to meet customer demand, to reorganise existing staff or to hire replacements. These reasons cannot be queried in an employment tribunal – unless the employer's facts were inaccurate or he/she failed to follow the correct legal process after the request was made.

That process involves 'seriously considering' all requests for flexi-working. In practice, says James Davies of the law firm Lewis Silkin, that means sitting down and talking with the employee. The employer should then go away, make a practical assessment of how it can be arranged and deliver a detailed written answer explaining his reasons within 14 days, he says. If a request is rejected, the employee must be allowed to appeal against the decision.

Experts agree that the key for the employer is to create a paper trail – a written record of all consultations and meetings – in case of a dispute. Practical issues of the new law are important. For example, there is a need to talk to suppliers and clients to alert them to changes and discuss what situations they see as acceptable. Health and safety issues may need checking, for example can machinery usually manned by two people legally be manned by one?

Firms can gain by the new law. They need to promote their family-friendly practice in their literature.

Questions

1 Why are employees in favour and employers concerned about the new flexible working rights?

2 How can the suggestion that 'firms can gain by the new law' be supported?

Gender and ageism

It will be useful at this stage to review two other issues often raised in labour market discussions, namely gender and ageism issues.

Gender issues

In the UK in 2003, the gap between the *hourly pay* of men and women narrowed to its smallest yet, with women's hourly pay at 82% of that for men. However, the gender gap for *annual earnings* was wider, with the average annual salary of women in 2003 around 72% of that for men.

Checkpoint 3 Can you think of reasons why the gender gap in favour of men is greater for annual earnings than for hourly earnings?

That such a gender gap still exists would disappoint those who framed two key Acts of Parliament seeking to reduce gender inequalities in the UK.

- *Equal Pay Act* (1970): women performing similar tasks to men, or performing work of equal value to that of men, must be treated equally to men.
- *Sex Discrimination Act* (1975): men and women should have equal opportunities.

Possible reasons for lower female earnings

Of course, for any particular task, to the extent that men/women present *different characteristics* to the labour market, some of the observed pay differential might be justified, i.e. not be 'discrimination' as such.

1 *Less continuous employment* is more likely to be the experience of women than men, given child-bearing and rearing responsibilities. For example, some 28% of women graduates leave the labour force for family reasons within five years of joining it.
   - Continuous employment is associated with an earnings premium of around 3% per year for both men and women in the UK.
   - Continuous employment implies being more up to date with changing technologies and work practices, thereby raising marginal productivity.
   - Continuous employment implies greater opportunities to receive in-firm education and training, acquiring skills which raise marginal productivity.

2 *Less geographical mobility* for women when partners'/husbands' jobs take priority. Where this is the case, an oversupply of women in a given geographical location may depress female wages.

3 *Less unionisation of women workers*, especially for the higher proportion of part-time employment, reduces female bargaining power. Statistically, union membership is associated with an hourly wage some 7% higher than for non-unionised labour.

4 *Less unsocial working hours* for women than men, with such unsocial hours receiving, on average, an extra 11% in earnings per hour in the UK.

Where these different labour market characteristics are presented by women, then it might be argued that at least some of the gender pay gap actually observed may be 'justified' rather than 'discriminatory'.

Other gender inequalities

In 2004 the *Equal Opportunities Commission* (EOC) published new research indicating that women are still 'massively under-represented' in positions of influence in business, the police, the media and the senior judiciary, despite more females working than ever before. Table 7.2 presents some of these findings.

Table 7.2 Percentage of women in high places

Job description	% of women
Editors of national newspapers	9
Senior judiciary (high court judge and above)	7
Local authority chief executives	13
Headteachers in secondary schools	29
Chief executives of national sports bodies	14
Directors in FTSE 100 companies	9
University vice-chancellors	12
Members of parliament	18
Senior police officers	7
Senior ranks in armed forces	1

Source: Adapted from Equal Opportunities Commission (2004) 'Sex and power: Who runs Britain', available from http://www.eoc.org.uk/cseng/policyandcampaigns/whorunsbritain.pdf

CHECK THE NET
Equal Opportunities Commission is found at www.eoc.org.uk.

The EOC Report encourages employers to promote flexible working and to employ 'positive action' where women are under-represented.

Checkpoint 4 What might such 'positive action' by employers involve?

Ageism issues

LINKS
Chapter 11 reviews demographic aspects such as an increasing proportion of older people in the economies of most advanced industrialised economies, including the UK.

Until recently, the 'norm' in the UK was for men to work until 65 years and women until 60 years. However, changes in the law now permit women to work until 65 years and only at that age to qualify for the retirement pension and men no longer have to retire compulsorily at 65 years.

Nevertheless, there are still complaints of 'age discrimination' in the workplace. For example, although men can legally work beyond the age of 65 years, they have no legal rights to do so. If employers choose to dismiss workers beyond the official retirement age, then these older workers have less protection in law. Age Concern is committed to providing people over 65 years with exactly the same workplace rights and protection as those under 65 years.

Example:

No rights for over-65s!

In 2002 John Rutherford, 72, and Samuel Bentley, 75, had won a key case for unfair dismissal by their employers. They had claimed that their dismissal from their jobs in the clothing industry on the grounds of age had been 'discriminatory' since more men than women work beyond 65. However, in October 2003 this earlier judgement in their favour was overturned by the Employment Appeals Tribunal, thereby removing any hopes from the earlier judgement that the over-65s might after all have workplace protection.

However, the UK government is obliged by a European Directive to introduce laws to prevent age discrimination in the workplace in 2006, although it is as yet unclear as to what these laws will include.

Checkpoint 5

Why might it be in the interests of employers themselves to provide more incentives for workers over 65 years?

Transfer earnings and economic rent

These ideas apply to any factor of production:

- **Transfer earnings** are defined as the payments that are absolutely necessary to keep a factor of production in its present use.
- **Economic rent** is any extra (surplus) payment to the factor over and above its transfer earnings.

For example, if David Beckham (factor – labour) currently receives £100,000 a week as a footballer but could earn £40,000 a week in his next best paid alternative employment as, say, a celebrity host on television, then we might regard £60,000 per week as *economic rent* and £40,000 per week as *transfer earnings*. If he were to receive less than £40,000 per week as a footballer he might be expected to 'transfer' to his next best paid alternative employment, i.e. celebrity host on television.

Watch out!

'Economic rent' is used here to mean a surplus payment to *any* factor over and above its next best paid alternative (transfer earnings). This can be confusing since 'rent' is a word usually applied in everyday use to the return on the factor land or payment on a property let to tenants.

We can use the demand and supply diagrams of Chapter 1 to illustrate these ideas further.

In Figure 7.5(a) SS and DD represent the relevant supply and demand curves for any factor of production. In this market the equilibrium price is P. However, all but the last unit employed would have been prepared to accept a *lower price* than P to offer themselves to this factor market. In fact, the very first unit would have been supplied at a price of approximately equal to S. All units except the last unit supplied therefore receive an amount *in excess* of their supply price or transfer earnings. Because of this, the area PRS is referred to as *economic rent* (surplus) and the area OSRQ is referred to as *transfer earnings*.

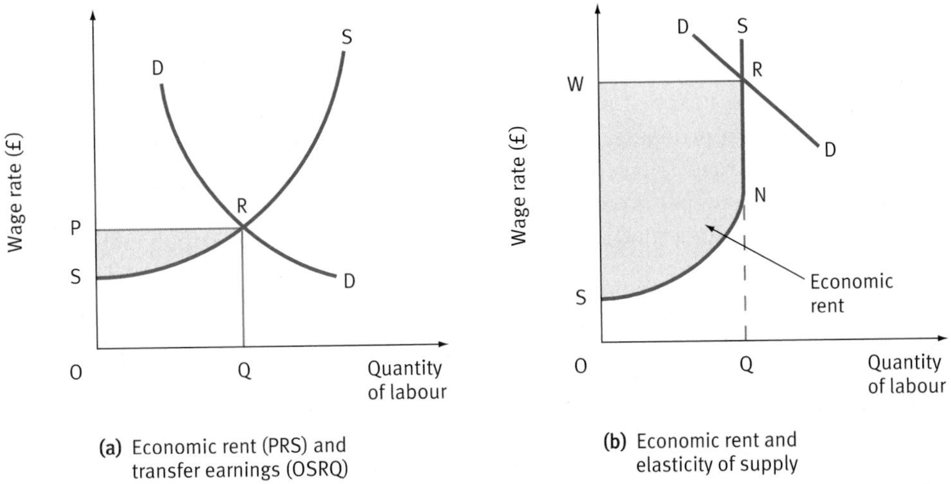

Fig 7.5 Economic rent and transfer earnings.

Definition

Transfer earnings refer to the payments necessary to keep the factor in its present use. *Economic rent* is any surplus payments over and above these 'transfer earnings'.

To earn relatively high reward it is necessary to possess those abilities which are in scarce supply and which are demanded by others and for which people are prepared to pay. It is, therefore, both supply and demand that account for the relatively large earnings of pop singers, film stars and some individuals from the sporting and entertainment world. Figure 7.5(b) is used to illustrate this point. Above some relatively low rate of pay, the supply of this individual's services becomes totally inelastic (at N). The actual rate of pay is determined by the intersection of supply and demand at W. Because of the inelastic supply and high level of demand, the bulk of this person's earnings consist of economic rent, equal to WRNS.

It is clear that any factor of production can earn economic rent and that the main determinant of such rent involves both the supply and demand curves for the factor of production.

Short and long run: quasi rent

Sometimes factors of production earn economic rent in the *short run* which is eliminated in the *long run*. In this case economic rent is referred to as **quasi rent**.

Should economic rent by taxed?

It is often suggested that economic rent should be taxed. The reasoning behind this is that since economic rent is a surplus rather than a cost of supply, a tax on economic rent will be borne entirely by the factor of production receiving economic rent. This will leave the supply of that factor, and therefore the output it produces, unchanged.

The case for taxing economic rent is therefore a powerful one. However, there are major difficulties with implementing such a tax. In the first place, it is extremely difficult to identify economic rent. If a tax exceeds the value of the surplus, then the supply of the factor of production will be reduced and its price, along with the price of whatever it produces, will be increased. Another problem is that not all economic rent that is earned is true economic rent; it might simply be quasi rent. Quasi rent refers to income that is entirely a surplus in the short run, but part of which is transfer earning in the long run. Taxing this will reduce the long-run supply of the factor of production.

Key Terms

Diminishing returns Usually refers to the short-run time period. The average/marginal product curves of a variable factor will eventually decline as more of the variable factor is applied to some fixed factor.

Economic rent A surplus payment to a factor of production in the sense of being over and above the minimum price at which that factor would be supplied.

Increasing returns Usually refers to the short-run time period. The average/marginal product curves of a variable factor may at first rise as more of the variable factor is applied.

Marginal physical product of labour The additional physical output contributed by the last unit of factor input.

Marginal revenue product of labour The additional value contributed by the last unit of factor input. Often refers to labour as factor input. In a perfectly competitive product market, MRP of labour is found by multiplying the MPP of labour by the price of the product.

Monopoly In the labour market context this usually refers to the presence of trade unions who seek to regulate the supply of labour in one way or another.

Monopsony Occurs when a firm is a significant purchaser of labour. Any additional hiring of labour potentially forces up the price of labour against itself.

Quasi rent That part of the earnings of a factor of production that is economic rent in the short run but transfer earnings in the long run.

Transfer earnings A necessary payment to a factor of production in that it is the minimum payment required for the factor to be supplied.

Union bargaining power The ability of unions to influence the bargaining process. Can be represented by the following ratio:

$$\frac{\text{Management costs of disagreeing (to union terms)}}{\text{Management costs of agreeing (to union terms)}}$$

Union density The proportion of the workforce who are members of a trade union.

Key Points

- Demand for and supply of labour will determine wage rates and levels of employment in competitive labour markets.
- Unions can usually secure higher wages only at the 'cost' of less employment unless their bargaining power is strong. If this is the case, they may be able to force employers off their labour demand curves, securing higher wages with no loss of employment.
- Chamberlain defined union 'bargaining power' as the ratio between the management costs of disagreeing and of agreeing to union terms. The larger the ratio, the greater the union bargaining power.
- A given rise in wages will usually reduce employment by less: (a) the less elastic the demand for the final product, (b) the less easy it is to substitute labour by other factors of production, (c) the lower the proportion of labour costs in total production costs.
- The government has legislated to reduce union power in various ways, e.g. removing the closed shop, imposing conditions on strikes and other union activities, deregulating the setting of wages and other working conditions and promoting trade union democracy. It has also legislated to introduce a national minimum wage.
- Where buyers of labour have market power, we refer to *monopsony* in the labour market. Monopsony can be expected to reduce both wages and employment.
- Governments may intervene in labour markets to prevent 'market failure'. For example, a national minimum wage may be introduced to protect the low paid. Both theory and evidence suggest that a higher minimum wage in monopsony labour markets might raise both wages and employment.
- The EU Social Chapter seeks to create *minimum standards* for working conditions in all member states.

Assessment Practice

Multiple choice questions

1 **In a competitive labour market, the *demand curve for labour* is given by which *one* of the following?**

(a) Total physical product
(b) Total revenue product
(c) Marginal physical product
(d) Marginal revenue product
(e) Marginal cost

2 **A *monopsony* type of market failure is said to occur for which *one* of the following?**

(a) Suppliers of labour have market power.
(b) Suppliers of products have market power.
(c) Buyers of labour have market power.
(d) Buyers of products have market power.
(e) There is a natural monopoly.

3 **Which *two* conditions are most likely to lead to a rise in union bargaining power?**

(a) Rise in the percentage of the workforce in the union
(b) Increased competition in the product market
(c) A sustained rise in GDP
(d) Relatively high elasticity of demand for labour
(e) Monopsony in the labour market

4 **A European directive which helps establish employer/employee consultation procedures for multinational companies in the EU is which *one* of the following?**

(a) The Working Time Directive
(b) The Part-time Workers Directive
(c) The Young Workers Directive
(d) The European Works Council Directive
(e) The Parent Leave Directive

5 **Which *one* of the following describes a state of the labour market which is often linked to a lower wage for those employed?**

(a) Higher cost of living
(b) National minimum wage
(c) Strong trade unions
(d) Highly skilled occupation
(e) Monopsony

6 **Where the return to the factor is greater than is needed for it to supply itself:**

(a) Quasi rent
(b) Transfer earnings
(c) Interest
(d) National minimum wage
(e) Economic rent

7 **Where the return to the factor is economic rent in the short run but transfer earnings in the long run:**

(a) Quasi rent
(b) Transfer earnings
(c) Interest
(d) National minimum wage
(e) Economic rent

8 **A situation in which the marginal cost of labour curve will lie above the average cost of labour curve:**

(a) Monopoly
(b) Bargaining power
(c) Monopsony
(d) Bilateral monopoly
(e) Oligopoly

9 **The addition to total revenue from employing the last person:**

(a) Marginal physical product
(b) Marginal utility
(c) Marginal social benefit
(d) Marginal revenue product
(e) Marginal profit

10 **That return to the factor just sufficient to cause it to supply itself:**

(a) Economic rent
(b) Quasi rent
(c) Marginal revenue product
(d) Transfer earnings
(e) Marginal physical product

Data response and stimulus questions

1 **Look carefully at the data in the table.**

Earnings of occupational groups: average (gross weekly) earnings of full-time male employees in selected occupations, as a percentage of average (gross weekly) earnings of all full time male employees (April 2003)

Non-manual	
Managers and administrators	152
Professional occupations	132
Associate professional and technical	113
Sales	76
Personal and protection services	76
Clerical and secretarial	63
Manual	
Craft and related occupations	78
Plant and machine operators	71
Other occupations	60

Adapted from ONS (2003) New Earnings Survey, London: HMSO

Question

Can you explain the earnings differentials given in the table?

2 **It was reported in 2004 that the gap between the earnings of ordinary workers and top executives has grown even larger in recent years. For example, in the US 20 years ago, a chief executive made $42 for every dollar earned by one of his or her blue-collar workers. Today, chief executives in the US earn $531 for every dollar taken home by a typical worker.**

Question

Can you use the analysis of this chapter to suggest some of the reasons which might help to explain this growing inequality?

True/False questions

1 The National Minimum Wage can lead to higher wages and employment in monopsonistic markets.

True/False

2 A given rise in wages will usually reduce employment by less the easier it is to substitute labour by other factors of production.

True/False

3 A trade union has more bargaining power the larger the ratio between the management costs of disagreeing and management costs of agreeing to union terms.

True/False

4 If unions have little bargaining power they are more likely to secure higher wages with no loss of employment.

True/False

5 The average cost of labour curve will lie above the marginal cost of labour curve under monopsony.

True/False

6 The more inelastic the supply of labour for an occupation, the greater the proportion of the wage that is likely to be transfer earnings.

True/False

7 The National Minimum Wage (NMW) in the UK only applies to those over 21 years.

True/False

8 EU Directives usually establish minimum labour market conditions which member states must implement unless they have an agreed 'opt-out' clause.

True/False

9 In the UK the *Equal Pay Act* makes it illegal for employers to pay women less than men.

True/False

10 A rise in marginal physical productivity or in the value of any goods and services produced will tend to raise the marginal revenue product of labour.

True/False

Essay questions

1 How would you explain the difference in earnings between consultants and healthcare workers in a hospital?
2 Examine the case for and against the National Minimum Wage.
3 To what extent would you support the use of Directives in the European Social Chapter?
4 Under what circumstances might a union be able to raise both wages and the level of employment?
5 Consider the arguments for and against raising the retirement age for workers.

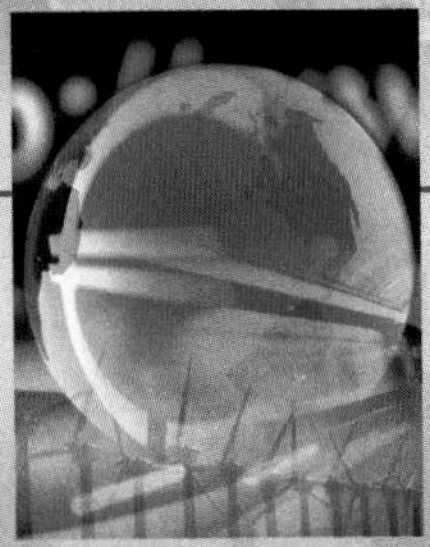

Chapter 8

Market failure, regulation and competition

Introduction

Chapter 6 introduced elements of market failure by considering types of market structure other than perfect competition. For example, both monopoly and oligopoly market structures give producers a degree of market power, enabling them to influence price or output (but not both!). We also noted in Chapter 7 various types of market failure in the labour market, affecting both the supply (trade unions) and demand (employer confederations) for labour.

In this chapter we consider a broad range of types of market failure and the impact of these on resource allocation. Policy responses to these various types of market failure are examined, including regulation, deregulation and privatisation. The approach to competition policy in both the UK and EU is reviewed, with particular reference to the control of mergers and acquisitions and various restrictive practices.

Learning objectives:

By the end of this chapter you should be able to:

- identify the various types of 'market failure'
- examine the impact of these market failures on resource allocation
- review the arguments for government intervention to 'correct' these market failures and discuss the policy instruments that might be used
- understand the case for and against deregulation and privatisation
- assess the need for and the role of the 'regulators' such as OFGAS, OFWAT and OFTEL
- explain the main features of competition policy in the UK and the EU, particularly in the context of mergers and restrictive practices.

Types of market failure

Strictly speaking, any departure from the conditions necessary for the perfectly competitive *product* markets of Chapter 6 or the perfectly competitive *factor* markets of Chapter 7 can be regarded as 'market failure'. However, four broad types of market failure are often identified, namely externalities, imperfect information, monopoly power and 'public good' types of market failure. Here we consider each of these types and their possible impacts on resource allocation.

Quote

> Enhancing markets will mean reducing government but ... we must also have the courage to recognise where markets do not work.
>
> *Gordon Brown, UK Chancellor of the Exchequer, 4 February 2003*

Externalities

Externalities occur when economic decisions create costs or benefits for people other than the decision taker: these are called the *external costs* or *external benefits* of that decision.

- *External costs.* For example, a firm producing paint may discharge various chemicals into a nearby river, polluting the river, spoiling its use for leisure activities and damaging the health of those coming into contact with it. The true cost to society is then more than the (scarce) resources of labour and capital used up by the firm in producing paint. To these *private costs* of firm production, reflected by wage bill, raw material costs, lease of premises, interest payments etc., we must add any *external costs* that do not appear in the firm's balance sheet but which have resource implications for society, if we are to assess the true *social costs* of production.

$$\text{Marginal social cost} = \text{Marginal private cost} + \text{Marginal external cost}$$
$$\text{MSC} = \text{MPC} + \text{MEC}$$

- *External benefits.* For example, a firm developing a successful drug to treat motor neurone disease may spend large amounts on research but will only be able to sell the drug to the relatively few people suffering from this severe affliction. The true benefit to society is arguably more than the (small) revenue stream to the firm selling the drug. To these *private revenues* from firm production we must add any *external benefits* that do not appear in the firm's balance sheet (such as the value to society of being able to improve the quality of life of those with the disease) if we are to assess the true *social benefits* of production.

$$\text{Marginal social benefit} = \text{Marginal private benefit} + \text{Marginal external benefit}$$
$$\text{MSB} = \text{MPB} + \text{MEB}$$

Externalities and resource allocation

It will be useful to consider how the presence of externalities may distort the signals conveyed by prices in a market economy and lead to a misallocation of resources. Here we use an example where marginal social cost is higher than the marginal private cost (MSC > MPC), because of the presence of a marginal external cost (MEC > 0).

Watch out!

Although at first sight it may seem a contradiction, when marginal social cost is higher than marginal private cost (MSC > MPC) because of the existence of a *positive marginal external cost* (MEC > 0), we use the term *negative externality*. This is the situation shown in Figure 8.1 where we can see that the marginal social cost of production lies above the marginal private cost.

Negative externalities

We shall see that when negative externalities are present, the firm that seeks to maximise its *private surplus* (profit) will fail to act in the best interests of society. Put another way, when private surplus (profit) is a maximum, *social surplus* is not as high as it could be.

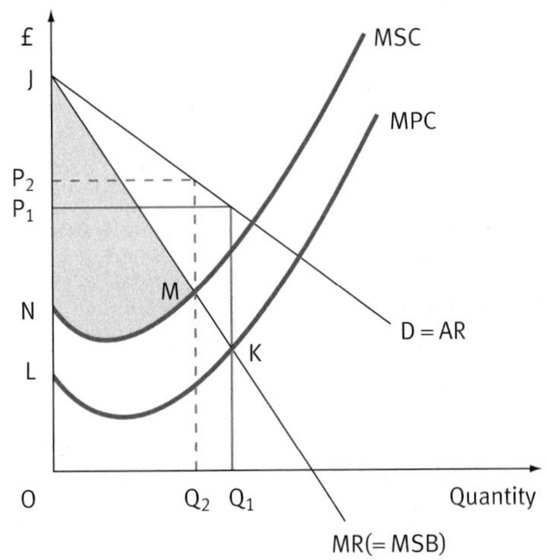

Fig 8.1 With negative externalities (MSC > MPC), the output Q_1 maximising private surplus (profit) differs from the output Q_2 maximising social surplus

Note: MEC is the vertical difference (at each level of output) between MSC and MPC

The profit-maximising firm in Figure 8.1 will produce output OQ_1 at price OP_1 since marginal private cost = marginal revenue (marginal private benefit) at this output. Total profit can be regarded as *total private surplus*, and this is a maximum, given by area JKL in the diagram. To produce one extra unit beyond OQ_1 would reduce total private surplus as the extra unit would incur a loss (MPC > MR); to produce one fewer unit than OQ_1 would also reduce this total private surplus, since that unit would have yielded a profit (MR > MPC) had it been produced.

Unfortunately, this output Q_1 which maximises total private surplus (profit) is *not* the output that maximises *total social surplus*. This occurs where the marginal social benefit of production, MSB (here shown as being the same as MR), equals the marginal social cost of production, MSC. This occurs at output OQ_2 with total social surplus a maximum given by area JMN, using the same reasoning as before.

Checkpoint 1 Explain in your own words why total social surplus is a maximum at output OQ_2.

Clearly, a situation in which output Q_1 and price P_1 result will, if uncorrected, be one in which prices are conveying inappropriate signals to producers. They are leading to profit maximisers producing too much of the product and selling it at too low a price, as compared with the needs of society as a whole.

Example:

CO_2 emissions and global warming

Excessive emissions of CO_2 in the use of energy by businesses and households have been linked directly to climate change, which in turn is imposing major external costs on society. For example, a report by the *World Health Organisation* (WHO) in December 2003 estimated that over 1 million extra cases of malaria per year could be linked to an increase in global temperatures via CO_2 and other greenhouse gas emissions.

Externalities of both a negative (adverse) and even positive (beneficial) type can have major impacts on resource allocation if left uncorrected.

Positive externalities

You should be able to use Figure 8.1 to consider the implications of a *positive externality* (MSC < MPC) on firm output, as for example, when a firm uses its scarce resources to support some type of environmental improvement. If marginal social costs (MSC′) were now *below* marginal private costs in the diagram, then the target output for society would need to be raised above OQ_1 if social surplus is to be a maximum, and price would need to be reduced below OP_1. This time, price signals, if uncorrected, are leading to profit maximisers producing too little of the product and selling it at too high a price, as compared with the needs of society as a whole.

Imperfect information

Firms may have information on their product which is not available to the purchasers. For example, a number of court cases brought by cancer sufferers have shown that cigarette companies knew from their own research about the dangers to health of smoking cigarettes decades ago but concealed this information from the general public. Similarly, recent court cases involving the mis-selling of pensions have shown that the companies involved withheld information from purchasers. Where one party has information not available to another party, this is often called ‘information asymmetry’. This can again lead to a misallocation of resources.

Example:

Enron deceives employees and investors

Enron, the Houston-based energy company which once dominated the market for trading of natural gas and electric power, filed for bankruptcy in December 2001 after it emerged that the company had long hidden its true financial state, eventually revealed as \$67bn of outstanding debt with a \$20bn 'black hole' in the accounts. Subsequently, investigations have shown how misleading information given to employees and investors alike had led to major losses for over 20,000 investors and creditors of the company, with shares falling in value by over \$60bn once the true information was known.

We can again illustrate the effect of imperfect information using Figure 8.1. For example, smoking has been shown to damage the health of those who smoke (via increased risks of cancer, heart and lung diseases) and of those ('passive smokers') who inhale the air polluted by smokers. In other words, the marginal social cost of the cigarettes produced by a tobacco company is considerably higher than the marginal private costs of producing those cigarettes. We are in the *negative externality* situation of Figure 8.1, with the cigarette companies seeking to profit-maximise (MPC = MR) at output Q_1 but with society preferring output Q_2 (MSC = MSB) where *social surplus* is maximised at JMN.

Monopoly power

Chapter 6 has shown how monopoly power can lead to a higher price and lower output as compared to a perfectly competitive market structure. This is the so-called 'classical case against monopoly' (Chapter 6, p. 214). The same situation can arise under an oligopoly market structure, where a few large firms dominate the market.

Nor is the problem of 'market power' leading to a misallocation of resources confined to product markets! We noted in Chapter 7 that when the trade unions have market power over the supply of labour (monopoly), wages can be higher and employment lower than might have been the case under competitive labour market conditions (Chapter 7, p. 256). Similarly, where the purchasers of labour have market power (monopsony), the wages can be lower and employment lower than under competitive labour market conditions (Chapter 7, p. 257).

Public goods

The term 'public goods' is used to refer to goods (or services) which have particular characteristics of a type which makes it impractical for private markets to provide them. It follows that if they are to be provided, only the 'public' sector will be able to fund them out of general tax revenues, hence the name 'public good'.

Pure public goods

Two particular characteristics must be present for what is called a 'pure' public good.

- *Non-excludable.* This refers to the difficulty of excluding those who do not wish to pay for the good (or service). For example, how could you charge individuals a price for police or army protection? If you tried to use a national referendum, only charging those who say 'yes' in the referendum to wanting a police or defence force, you will encounter the so-called 'free rider' problem. This refers to people who, while they do want this protection, may vote 'no' hoping that sufficient others vote 'yes' for them still to have the protection but not have to pay for it themselves. The non-excludable condition prevents a free market developing since it is difficult to make 'free riders' actually pay for the public good, which means that it can only be provided by the 'public' sector out of tax revenue.
- *Non-exhaustible.* This refers to the fact that the marginal cost of providing the 'pure' public good is essentially zero. To protect an extra person in the country using the police or army effectively costs nothing. If marginal cost is zero, then the price set under perfect competition (see Chapter 6, p. 207) should also be zero. But private markets guided by the profit motive are hardly in the business of charging zero prices! The non-exhaustible condition implies that any price that is charged should, for 'allocative efficiency' (see also Chapter 6, p. 208), equal marginal cost and therefore be zero, which means that it can only be provided by the 'public' sector out of tax revenue.

Both conditions imply that when the market failure involves a 'pure public good', then it is best supplied by the public sector at zero price, using general tax revenue to fund provision.

Mixed (quasi) public goods

The suggestion here is that a broader category of products (goods or services) will have elements of these characteristics, while not fully meeting the criteria for a 'pure' public good. For example, many products may be *non-exhaustible* in the sense that (at least up to the congestion point) extra people can consume that product without detracting from existing consumers' ability to benefit from it: e.g. use of a motorway, a bridge or a scenic view. However, the *non-excludable* condition may not apply, since it may be possible to exclude consumers from that product: e.g. tolls on motorways and bridges, or fencing (with admission charges) around scenic views. So a private market could be established for such a *mixed* or *quasi public good*, with a non-zero price charged.

Correcting 'market failures'

Here we consider the various policy instruments that can be used by governments to correct the four types of 'market failure' we have identified. Such corrective policies can include a number of different policy instruments.

Government intervention to correct various 'market failures' can take many different forms. It can involve the application of maximum or minimum prices, the imposition of various types of standards, taxes, quotas, procedures, directives etc., whether issued by national bodies (e.g. the UK government or its agencies) or international bodies (e.g. the EU Commission, the World Trade Organisation etc.)

Correcting an externality

It may be useful to illustrate the ways in which government intervention can improve resource allocation by first considering how the *negative externality* situation might be approached.

Correcting a negative externality

Again we can illustrate the situation using Figure 8.1 (p. 279). It shows that with the firm producing a *negative externality* (MSC > MPC) society's best interests are served with an output of OQ_2 (where MSC = MSB) which maximises *social surplus* at JMN. However the profit-maximising firm is given inappropriate 'signals' in the market, so that it seeks an output of OQ_1 (where MPC = MR) which maximises its own *private surplus* at JKL. Sometimes those who impose external costs in this way can be controlled by regulation (e.g. pollution controls such as Clean Air Acts with fines for breaches of minimum standards) or can be given incentives to reduce pollution through the tax mechanism.

- *Regulations.* The government could impose a regulation setting a *maximum level of output* of OQ_2, so that the firm is prevented from producing the extra Q_2–Q_1 output which would have raised profit still further.
- *Taxes.* The government can set a tax on the product to make the firm pay for the external cost it imposes on society. The 'ideal' tax would be one which exactly captures the marginal external cost at each level of output. This would now make the firm pay for its own internal costs *and* for the external costs it imposes. In other words, the tax policy is 'internalising the externality' so that the (previous) externality now shows up as a private cost on the firm's own balance sheet. In terms of Figure 8.1 the new MPC curve after this 'ideal' tax will be the same as the MSC curve. It follows that the profit-maximising firm will itself now want to produce output Q_2 at which the new MPC (= MSC) exactly equals MR, with both private surplus (profit) and social surplus maximised at JMN.

NOTE

This 'ideal' tax which is exactly equal to the marginal external cost is sometimes called a 'Pigouvian tax', after the economist A. C. Pigou who proposed such a tax.

An example of using a type of tax to correct a negative externality is the *London Congestion Charge* introduced in February 2003 and considered further in Case Study 8.1.

Case Study 8.1 The London Congestion Charge

A congestion charge of £5 has been levied on drivers in an eight square mile zone in inner London since 17 February 2003. The charges operate from 7.00 am to 6.30 pm, Mondays to Fridays, excluding public holidays, and must be paid in advance (at selected retail outlets or by Internet or by SMS text) or by 10.00 pm on the day your vehicle entered the zone. An £80 penalty charge is imposed on those who fail to pay and have been identified by cameras recording their vehicle registration plates. Discounts of up to 90% are available for residents and other designated (e.g. blue badge holders) individuals. Any monies received by 'Transport for London' from the charge must, by law, be spent on transport.

Twelve months after the introduction of the London Congestion Charge, some interesting results have been noted:

- cars in the charging zone are down by 30%;
- journey times in the charging zone are 10–15% faster;
- bus journeys in the zone are up by 15%;
- taxi journeys in the zone are up by 20%;
- cycles entering the zone are up by 30%;
- 108,000 congestion charge payments are made each day.

Supporters of the scheme also point to less air pollution as being a further benefit of the scheme. The Mayor of London, Ken Livingstone, considers the congestion charge such a success that he intends to double the area of the charging zone in London as soon as practicable.

Although widely acclaimed, some criticisms have been made of the London Congestion Charge. The company, Capita, running the scheme had admitted that limited resources result in it identifying and sending penalty notices to only 83% of those failing to pay the fee – with the remaining 17% (around 1,650 drivers daily) not pursued. Transport for London (TFL) originally estimated that the charge would raise some £200m for other transport projects each year, but only £68m was raised in the first full year of operation. Around 25% of London traders responding to a Mori poll in 2004 have blamed the congestion charge for a decline in business, though some 58% regarded it as broadly positive and to be welcomed.

Nor is there much evidence to suggest that traffic congestion has increased in the areas bordering the charging zone, as critics argued would be the case. The RAC Foundation concluded that congestion outside the zone has also been reduced because fewer people are driving towards the centre of the capital. However, all is not perfect – the RAC Foundation noted that traffic is still averaging only 7.4 mph at peak hours inside the zone.

Case Study 8.1 continued

Questions

1 Mr Livingstone claimed that the London Congestion Charge has caused a change in travel habits in favour of public transport. What evidence is there to support this claim and what consequences might follow from it?

2 Why do you think London businesses claim to be broadly supportive of the scheme?

3 How might the current London congestion charge be modified if it is to move more closely towards a Pigouvian tax which charges individual drivers according to the negative externalities they themselves impose?

Case Study 8.2 looks at a rather unusual way of dealing with the admitted presence of a negative externality.

Case Study 8.2 Town bought by power company

In 2002 America's largest power generator found a unique way to avoid legal challenges from a town it has polluted – buy it, lock, stock and barrel, for \$20m (£13.7m). American Electric Power (AEP), which also runs the UK's coal-fired Ferrybridge power station, is buying Cheshire, Ohio, which found itself under brown and blue clouds from AEP's coal-burning General James M. Gavin plant that looms over the town.

All 221 residents will leave after accepting a deal that gives 90 homeowners cheques for three times the assessed value of their homes, about \$150,000 each, totalling \$13.5m. Those renting homes in the town will each get \$25,000. And in true American style the three lawyers hired by residents to negotiate the deal will share \$5.6m between them. AEP gets 200 acres of property, several businesses and 90 homes to use as temporary housing for plant employees.

More importantly, it gets non-disclosure agreements that prevent residents disclosing the terms of the deal and signed pledges that townsfolk will never sue the power company for property damage or health problems. No one yet has sued AEP for the asthma attacks, grime, headaches, burning eyes, sore throats and lips, mouth blisters or white-coloured burns on lips, tongues and insides of mouths caused by sulphur dioxide and sulphuric acid emissions.

These emissions worsened in 2001 after the installation of a new \$195m emissions-control system meant to cut nitrogen oxide emissions. That is when the blue plumes arrived – because the new technology did not work very well and a blue acid haze fell on Cheshire, usually on hot, humid days when exhaust fumes from the 830 ft smokestacks fell down into the town rather than going up into the sky.

The Environmental Protection Agency (EPA) of the US had accused AEP two years earlier of violating the Clean Air Act and threatened to force the plant to stop burning cheaper high-sulphuric coal. The EPA and environmental groups ranging

Case Study 8.2 continued

from the Sierra Club to the Edison Electric Institute all now seem happy with this new deal, which is thought to be the first takeover offer for a whole town. The EPA has even backed off from plans to force the burning of more expensive coal at the 2,600-megawatt General James M. Gavin plant by AEP, the nation's largest utility with annual revenues of $61bn.

But some of the townsfolk seem to have regrets. Helen Preston, the town's oldest resident, who still lives in the house where she was born, reportedly thinks her fellow residents sold out too cheaply by accepting the first offer. Others acknowledged that legal action might have taken a decade and there might not have been another chance to get away from the health hazards falling from the skies from the Gavin plant.

Questions

1 How does the idea of negative externalities apply to this case study?

2 Consider the advantages and disadvantages of this approach to solving the negative externality problem.

Correcting a positive externality

On the other hand, firms creating positive externalities (MSB > MPB) may be rewarded by the receipt of *subsidies*. For instance, it can be argued that railways reduce road usage, creating external benefits by relieving urban congestion, pollution and traffic accidents. This is one aspect of the case for subsiding railways so that they can continue to offer some loss-making services.

Checkpoint 2

Draw a diagram and use it to explain how a positive externality might be 'corrected' by a government subsidy.

Of course, the government may wish to intervene to correct market failures other than those involving externalities.

Correcting imperfect information

Regulations may force firms to give more information to consumers or to employees, or to shareholders. For example, regulations on the labelling of ingredients in foodstuffs helps increase consumer information. Other regulations may establish maximum levels for known toxins in various situations (e.g. CO_2 and other air pollutants near airports) or minimum standards to meet health and safety requirements at work (e.g. number and width of fire-exits in a building). Still other regulations require secret ballots before employees can be asked to take industrial action by unions or give rights to shareholders to vote on executive remuneration packages at Annual General Meetings.

> **LINKS**
> If your course includes indifference curves, Appendix 1 (p. 696) uses these to show how imperfect information reduces consumer welfare.

Governments can be even more proactive in this area, as for example, in providing job centres to help those without jobs be aware of vacancies or training opportunities. In all these cases the objective is to give more information to the various parties than would otherwise be available, thereby helping reduce any 'information asymmetry' that might exist. The general approach is that better informed decisions are likely to be in both the private and public interest.

Correcting monopoly power

In Chapter 5 we noted some of the benefits from increased firm size, as with various technical and non-technical economies of scale (Chapter 5, pp. 177–178). However, we also noted the potential for increased size and greater market power in the case of monopoly and oligopoly market structures to be used to raise prices and lower outputs (Chapter 6, pp. 211–239). Governments are well aware of the tensions created by a desire, on the one hand, to support large, efficient firms and on the other to protect consumers and employees from any abuse of such monopoly (or oligopoly) power.

To this end both the UK government and the EU have set certain rules and regulations to establish the institutions and procedures used for investigating proposed mergers and acquisitions, and the conditions under which approval is likely to be given or withheld. We consider such mergers and restrictive practices regulation for the UK and EU later in this chapter (pp. 300–308).

Correcting public and merit good situations

In recognition of the need to provide certain goods and services largely through the public sector, *general taxation* is used in the UK to support the provision of important services such as the police, the defence forces (army, navy, airforce), health and social services, education, transport and so on. Some of these are 'mixed' (quasi) public goods rather than 'pure' public goods, which means that some private market provision may take place alongside the public sector provision.

Box 8.1 looks in more detail at policies involved in correcting situations of 'pure' and 'mixed' public goods.

Box 8.1 Public goods and policy responses

Pure public goods

We noted earlier that products which satisfy the two key characteristics of being non-excludable and non-exhaustible are called 'pure' public goods. In this case we should have a situation similar to that shown in Figure 8.2(a), with two consumers for simplicity. Strictly speaking, the marginal social cost (MSC) of providing an extra unit of the pure public good to another consumer is zero. This follows from the non-exhaustive or non-rivalry characteristic:

once provided for one person, someone else can also consume that unit at no extra cost and without reducing the first person's ability to consume that same unit. In this case we can regard the MSC curve as zero, coinciding with the horizontal axis.

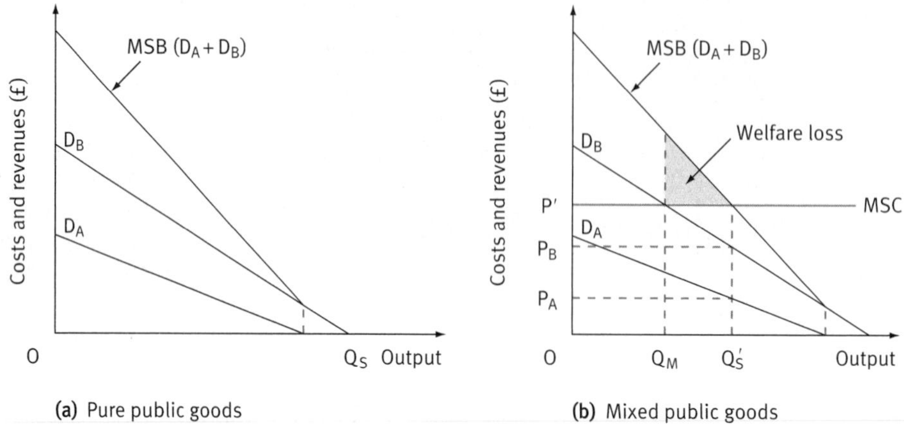

Fig 8.2 'Pure' and 'mixed' public goods and the socially optimum output

The socially optimum solution is where MSB = MSC, i.e. output Q_S in Figure 8.2(a). In this extreme case we can see that the appropriate target is the output level demanded at zero price. Clearly private markets, driven by the profit motive, will have no incentive to be established under these conditions (zero price); hence the suggestion that these are public goods. Only if general tax receipts are used to fund such products will they be provided.

Mixed (quasi) public goods

The suggestion here is that a broader category of products (goods or services) will have elements of these characteristics, while not fully meeting the criteria for a pure public good. For example, many products may be *exhaustible* in the sense that (at least up to the congestion point) extra people can consume that product without detracting from existing consumers' ability to benefit from it: e.g. use of a motorway, a bridge or a scenic view.

However, the *non-excludable* condition may not apply, since it may be possible to exclude consumers from that product: e.g. tolls on motorways and bridges, or fencing (with admission charges) around scenic views. So a market could be established for such a *mixed or quasi public good*, with a non-zero price charged. Moreover, at least beyond the congestion point, the marginal social cost of provision is also non-zero, since extra cars cause existing users to slow down on roads and bridges, and extra people hinder the enjoyment of the scenic view. As a result MSB = MSC above the horizontal axis, implying a non-zero price at P′ and target output of Q'_S.

In Figure 8.2(b) the socially optimum output (MSB = MSC) occurs at Q'_S with market price P′. This price might be composed of two parts (where price discrimination is possible in the market) equivalent to the individual valuation of each consumer of output Q'_S, namely P_A and P_B. Of course there is the practical problem of identifying what sum of money each person is really willing to pay for this output. If consumers want the product but understate their true preferences in the hope that they can 'free ride', then this social optimum output Q'_S may not occur. For example, if only consumer B reveals his true preference/willingness to pay market price P′ in Figure 8.2(b) (perhaps via response to a questionnaire) then the market solution might be output Q_M, with the shaded area corresponding to the welfare loss resulting from the free-rider problem.

This analysis highlights one of the problems with public goods: namely, that everyone has an incentive to rely on their neighbours to provide them, rather than provide them themselves. A shipping company may desire lighthouses to guide its ships, as may other shipping companies. Unfortunately, all may delay investment decisions, hoping that a rival builds the lighthouses, on which they can then 'free ride'. Eventually perhaps one company for whom the lighthouses have most value may relent and begin construction, but the level of provision may be less than optimal. This is because it is only the (vertical) sum of the marginal valuations of all consumers of the good that can help to determine the social optimum solution. If any consumer fails to express their true marginal valuation (i.e. attempts to free ride), then we have the suboptimal type of solution shown at Q_M in Figure 8.2(b).

Merit goods

This term refers to goods and services which tend to create positive externalities, i.e. benefiting society as well as the firms and individuals providing the good or service. Education is a well-used example of a merit good, since a better educated population not only benefits the *individual* (via higher lifetime earnings) but also *society* as a whole. For example, labour productivity is likely to be higher for better educated workers, raising income levels not only for the worker but for the firm (higher profits) and the government (higher tax revenue from higher employee incomes and higher corporate profits). In addition, a better educated population raises levels of employment, saving the government expenditure on unemployment and other benefits. A better educated workforce is also likely to be a healthier workforce, reducing spending on health and related services.

In all these ways, the positive externalities associated with 'merit goods' argues in favour of their receiving government support (e.g. *subsidies*) to encourage a higher output of these 'merit goods' than might otherwise occur. We are in a situation in which marginal social benefit (MSB) is greater than marginal private benefit (MR) in our earlier Figure 8.1 (p. 279).

Checkpoint 3 Go back to Figure 8.1 and re-draw the diagram for a merit good (MSB > MR).

Regulation

In seeking to 'correct' market failures we have seen that governments can use a wide variety of policy instruments, one of which is to use *regulations*. These usually involve rules setting minimum standards for products or processes.

Types of regulation

It is very difficult to classify all the different types of regulation or rules that can be imposed on firms by the UK government or by the EU. However, two broad types are often identified:

1. regulations aimed at protecting the consumer from the consequences of market failure;
2. regulations aimed at preventing the market failure from happening in the first place.

We might illustrate these two types using regulations imposed by the EU on business. In terms of the financial sector, the *Deposit Guarantee Directive* of the EU is of the first type. This protects customers of accredited EU banks by restoring at least 90% of any losses up to £12,000 which might result from the failure of a particular bank. In part this is a response to 'asymmetric information', since customers do not have the information to evaluate the credit worthiness of a particular bank, and might not be able to interpret that information even if it were available.

The *Capital Adequacy Directive* of the EU is of the second type. This seeks to prevent market failure (such as a bank collapse) by directly relating the value of the capital a bank must hold to the riskiness of its business. The idea here is that the greater the value of capital available to a bank, the larger the 'buffer stock' it has in place should it need to absorb any losses. Various elements of the Capital Adequacy Directive force the banks to increase their capital base if the riskiness of their portfolio (indicated by various statistical measures) is deemed to have increased. In part this EU regulation is in response to the potential for negative externalities in this sector. One bank failure can invariably lead to a 'domino effect' and risk system collapse, with incalculable consequences for the banking system as a whole.

In these ways the regulatory system for EU financial markets is seeking to provide a framework within which greater competition between banks can occur, while at the same time addressing the fact that greater competition can increase the risks of bank failure. It is seeking both to protect consumers should any mishap occur and at the same time to prevent such a mishap actually occurring.

Whilst regulations are usually imposed to protect consumers or producers from one or more types of 'market failures', they can have unexpected consequences, sometimes positive, as in Case Study 8.3, and sometimes negative.

Case Study 8.3 Tighter rules help to lift SIG sales

SIG is confident of delivering full-year profits in 2004 exceeding market expectations as tighter building regulations on thermal efficiency helped boost sales at Europe's largest supplier of insulation products.

The group, which also supplies roofing and commercial interior products, said in a trading update in January 2004 that it had achieved record sales of more than £1.26bn, or an increase of 9% from its combined operations in the UK and Ireland, mainland Europe and the US.

Case Study 8.3 continued

According to the Energy Saving Trust:

- Insulating roof and walls reduces heat loss by 50%.
- Loft insulation cuts up to 25% off heating bills.
- A hot water tank jacket costing £10 eliminates some 75% of heat loss.
- Draught-proofing windows and doors can save £10–£15 a year in heating bills.
- Underfloor insulation can save £15–£25 a year.

Questions How might tighter regulations have helped SIG to boost its sales?

Table **8.1** Top ten red tape burdens in the UK in 2004

Working time regulations	The cumulative cost for 1999–2004 is £11.1bn. Business fears further changes in these regulations as Britain's 48-hour opt-outs come under challenge
Data protection rules	The cumulative cost for 1998–2004 is £4.6bn. Businesses could face unlimited fines if they hold information on customers and do not comply with the law. Employees can be fined if they misuse data
Vehicles excise duty (reduced pollution) regulations	Cumulative cost since 2001 is £4.3bn. The recurring annual cost for firms is £1.2bn, according to official estimates
Control of asbestos at work	New regulations were introduced in December 2002. About 500,000 business premises in Britain contain asbestos. The new rules cover repair, dismantling and inspection. Cost so far: £1.4bn
Disability discrimination rules	Firms have to accommodate people with disabilities in the workplace by making existing facilities suitable, perhaps by modifying present equipment. The cumulative cost is £1bn since 1999
Employment Act 2002	Intended to help parents devote more time to children, it provides for 26 weeks of paid maternity leave (plus an optional 26 weeks unpaid), increased maternity payments and two weeks of paid paternity leave for new fathers. Cost so far: £565m
IR35 tax rule	This requires contractors, particularly in the IT industry, to be subject to National Insurance payments. It has been blamed for an exodus of IT specialists abroad. The cumulative cost since 2000 is £465m
The Tax Credits Act 1999	This requires firms to administer the government's tax credits, including Gordon Brown's flagship working families tax credit (now renamed the working tax credit). The cost so far is £465m
Stakeholder pensions	Companies with five employees or more are required to provide workers with access to a stakeholder scheme. The rule, which came into force in October 2001, is policed by the Occupational Pensions Regulatory Authority. The cost so far is £404m
Flexible working regulations, 2002	New rules, which came into effect in April 2003, cover parents of children aged under six years and parents of disabled children aged up to 18. The rules allow them to apply for flexible working arrangements. The government expects 500,000 such requests annually at a cost of £444m over several years

Adapted from Smith, D. (2004)

On the other hand, businesses often complain about the time they waste filling in forms and complying with a vast number of regulations, many of which they claim are unnecessary.

A National Audit Office (NAO) report on 'Better Regulation' estimated that around £11,000 a year was spent on average by small companies in the UK in implementing new regulations. Table 8.1 above indicates the ten most expensive regulations identified by small and medium-sized companies in the UK in 2004.

Nor do regulations always have the impact expected by those who devise them.

Example:

Regulation and unintended consequences

The EU *Gender Equality Directive* of 2004 is intended to reduce gender discrimination but critics argue that it is having the opposite effect. For example, Direct Line, the insurer, argues that it will have to charge young women drivers £500 more than before to avoid discriminating *in their favour*. Prior to the Directive the better driving record for young women allowed the actuaries (statisticians) of Direct Line to charge young women drivers lower premiums because they made fewer insurance claims for accidents. Young women drivers make 20% fewer claims in total than young men and their claims cost 40% less in value. For female drivers there are 17% fewer claims than for male drivers and these cost 32% less.

Overall, we can say that those who support any or all of these forms of government intervention, in whatever sector of the economy, usually do so in the belief that they improve the allocation of resources in situations characterised by one or more types of market failure.

Table 8.2 outlines a number of EU horticultural regulations involving fresh produce which have been widely criticised by growers and distributors.

Table 8.2 EU horticultural regulations

Product	Regulations
Bananas	Under EU regulation 2257/94 bananas must be at least 13.97 cm (5.5 inches) long and 2.96 cm (1.06 inches) round. They must not have 'abnormal curvature' as defined in an eight-page directive of 1994
Cucumbers	Any that curve more than 10 mm per 10 cm in length cannot be sold as 'Class 1'
Peaches	Must not be less than 5.6 cm in diameter between July and October to be sold as 'Class 1'
Red apples	Cannot be so described if less than 25% of the surface is red
Carrots	Cannot be less than 1.9 cm wide at the thick end, except in 'baby' varieties

Activity 8.1 reviews material involving the various types of market failure and policy responses to 'correct' those failures.

Activity 8.1

1 Here you will see a *lettered* description of a particular type of 'market failure' and a *numbered* list of terms. Try to match the description with its correct term.

Description

(a) Extra output of the firm emits CO_2 and pollutes the environment.
(b) The firm is aware of a design fault, the buyer is not.
(c) The firm employs almost all the labour force in a particular town.
(d) The firm finds it impossible to exclude people from consuming the product even if they don't pay.
(e) Extra output of the firm creates employment opportunities in a deprived area.
(f) The firm erects 'barriers to entry' to prevent any competition from rival firms.

Terms

(i) Positive externality
(ii) Negative externality
(iii) Monopoly power
(iv) Monopsony power
(v) Information asymmetry
(vi) Public good

2 Place 'M' next to those situations which might be described as leading to further market failure and 'P' next to those which might be seen as improving market efficiency.

(a) The Internet providing consumers with up-to-date information about new car prices.
(b) A report indicating that some multinationals have used child-labour to increase the production of sportswear.
(c) The UK Competition Commission preventing a merger between two companies on the basis that their combined output would be over 60% of the total supply of car batteries.
(d) New research suggesting that power lines increase the risk of developing leukaemia.
(e) A firm which already employs 40% of the labour force in a town merging with another local firm which currently employs around a quarter of the town's remaining labour force.
(f) The appointment of a new body to regulate the Financial Services industry after a report indicating the misuse of pension funds.
(g) Directors of various companies in an industry distributing copies of their proposed prices for next year to each other in order to avoid price competition.

3 Which *two* of the following might lead the government to increase tax on an activity?

(a) Marginal private cost exceeds marginal social cost.
(b) Marginal social cost exceeds marginal private cost.
(c) Marginal private benefit exceeds marginal social benefit.
(d) Marginal social benefit exceeds marginal private benefit.
(e) Marginal private benefit equals marginal social benefit.

4 Which *two* of the following might lead the government to subsidise an activity?

(a) Marginal private cost exceeds marginal social cost.
(b) Marginal social cost exceeds marginal private cost.
(c) Marginal private benefit exceeds marginal social benefit.
(d) Marginal social benefit exceeds marginal private benefit.
(e) Marginal private benefit equals marginal social benefit.

5 A negative externality can be said to occur where:

(a) private revenue falls short of private costs;
(b) private costs fall short of social costs;
(c) private costs exceed social costs;
(d) private and social costs are identical;
(e) providing extra output of the products creates a useful by-product.

Answers to Checkpoints and Activities can be found on pp. 705–35.

Deregulation and privatisation

Governments can intervene to correct 'market failures' by imposing rules and regulation. They can also intervene by *removing* rules and regulation, i.e. by using policies of deregulation.

Deregulation

Deregulation can be supported from a number of viewpoints:

- *Opening markets up to competition.* If removing regulations helps bring more competition into a market, then consumers arguably benefit from the extra choice and lower prices that usually result.
- *Removing unnecessary obstacles to business efficiency.* Firms, small, medium and large, regularly complain about the time and money 'wasted' having to comply (e.g. form-filling) with what they regard as unnecessary bureaucratic regulations.
- *Raising economic welfare.* If regulations have themselves become so complex, time-consuming and expensive for businesses and employees to comply with, then there may be a case for removing at least some of them. 'Public interest theory' would propose removing regulations where it can be shown that 'economic welfare', defined as consumer surplus plus producer surplus, is increased by removing the regulations.

Deregulation and public interest theory

We can define *economic welfare* as consumer surplus plus producer surplus.

- The *consumer surplus* is the amount consumers are willing to pay over and above the amount they need to pay.
- The *producer surplus* is the amount producers receive over and above the amount they need for them to supply the product.

In Figure 8.3 we start with an initial demand curve DD and supply curve SS giving market equilibrium price P_1 and quantity Q_1.

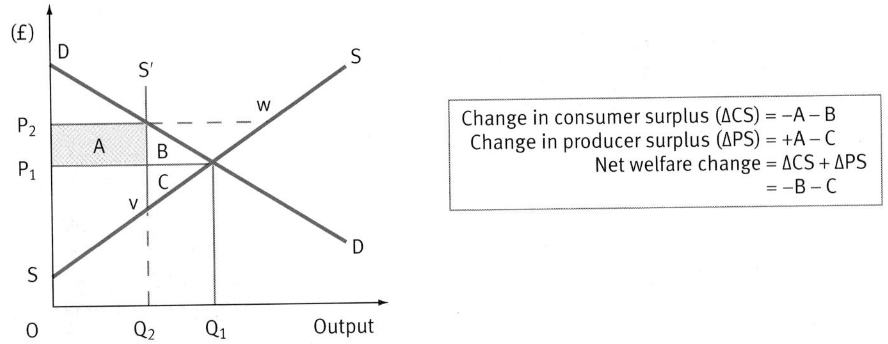

Fig 8.3 Welfare loss with a quota scheme OQ_2 raising price (P_2) above the market clearing level P_1

Suppose that a *regulation* has been introduced whereby, in order to prevent price falling below P_2, the government has set a *quota* restricting output of the product to OQ_2. In terms of Figure 8.3, if the quota is set at Q_2, then the effective supply curve becomes SvS', since no more than Q_2 can be supplied whatever the price.

The result is to raise the 'equilibrium' price to P_2 and reduce the 'equilibrium' quantity to Q_2.

- The quota regulation has resulted in a loss of economic welfare equivalent to the area B plus area C. The reduction in output from Q_1 to Q_2 means a loss of area B in consumer surplus and a loss of area C in producer surplus.
- However, the higher price results in a gain of area A in producer surplus which exactly offsets the loss of area A in consumer surplus.
- This means that the *net* welfare change is negative, i.e. there is a 'deadweight loss' of area B + area C.

'Public interest theory' suggests that deregulation should occur whenever the net welfare change of removing regulations is deemed to be positive. In terms of Figure 8.3 it might be argued that removing the regulation whereby the government restricts output to keep price artificially high at P_2 will give a net welfare change which is *positive*, namely a net gain of area B + area C.

In other words, allowing the free market equilibrium price P_1 and quantity Q_1 to prevail restores the previous loss of economic welfare via regulation. Put another way, public interest theory is suggesting that deregulation should occur whenever the outcome is a net welfare gain, so that those who gain can, at least potentially, more than compensate those who lose.

Privatisation

Privatisation is usually used to refer to a situation in which a good or service previously provided wholly or mainly by the public sector can now be provided by private sector firms. In the UK some important nationalised industries such as coal, telecommunications, gas, water and railways were until recently run by public corporations, not private firms. In 1979, with the election of Margaret Thatcher, these *nationalised industries* were privatised, with shares (ownership) now offered in most cases to the general public.

Privatisation in the UK has reduced the number of nationalised industries to a mere handful of enterprises accounting for less than 2% of UK GDP, around 3% of UK investment and under 1.5% of UK employment. By contrast, in 1979 the then nationalised industries were a very significant part of the economy, producing 9% of GDP, being responsible for 11.5% of UK investment and employing 7.3% of all UK employees.

Table **8.3** Major privatisations in the UK: a sectoral breakdown

Mining, Oil, Agriculture and Forestry	**Manufacturing, Science and Engineering**
British Coal	AEA Technology
British Petroleum	British Aerospace, Short Bros, Rolls-Royce
Enterprise Oil	British Shipbuilders, Harland and Wolff
Land Settlement	British Rail Engineering
Forestry Commission	British Steel
Plant Breeding Institute	British Sugar Corporation
	Royal Ordnance
Distribution, Hotels, Catering	Jaguar, Rover Group
British Rail Hotels	Amersham International
	British Technology Group Holdings (ICL, Fairey, Ferranti, Inmos)
Transport and Communication	
British Railways	**Electricity, Gas and Water**
National Freight, National and Local Bus Companies	British Gas
Motorway Service Area Leases	National Power, PowerGen
Associated British Ports, Trust Ports, Sealink	Nuclear Electric
British Airways, British Airways Authority (and other airports)	Northern Ireland Electric
British Telecommunication, Cable and Wireless	Northern Ireland Generation (4 companies)
	Scottish Hydro-Electric
Banking, Finance etc.	Scottish Power
Girobank	National Grid
	Regional Electricity Distribution
	Regional Water Holding Companies

The scale of the transfer of public sector businesses since 1979 to private ownership is indicated in Table 8.3, which lists the businesses privatised by their sector of operations.

We might usefully consider the arguments for and against privatisation.

Case for privatisation

1 *Greater efficiency*. The suggestion here is that breaking up the state monopoly and allowing private companies to provide the good or service makes resource allocation more efficient. Two main points are often made in this respect.
   - *Public choice theory*. This sees politicians and civil servants seeking to maximise their own interests (utility functions) in the nationalised industries. Politicians seek votes, civil servants support their departments which are lobbied by pressure groups, such as trade unions. As a result, objectives pursued in nationalised industries tend to be confused and inconsistent, resulting in inefficient management and operation of the industry.
   - *Property rights theory*. This emphasises the inability of the public to exercise control over nationalised industries. For example, the public (unlike private shareholders) have limited property rights over the company even though the public 'owns' them. In contrast, the private shareholders buying and selling shares, attending AGMs, the threat of takeovers, all resulting from private share ownership, are thought to increase the 'efficiency' of corporate activity.
   - *X-inefficiency* is the term often given to the result of these shortcomings; i.e. management failing to minimise cost in producing a given output – or failing to maximise output from a given set of resources.

2 *Greater managerial freedom*. The nationalised industries, being dependent on the Treasury for finance, had long complained of insufficient funds for investment. When the industry is privatised these constraints no longer apply, and management can now seek to raise finance for investment from the capital market (e.g. share issues).

3 *Wider share ownership*. In 1979, before the major privatisations took place, only 7% of UK adults owned shares. Today around 20% own shares, many having for the first time bought shares in some of the major privatisations. In this view, privatisation has helped create a 'property-owning democracy', resulting in more shareholders so more people sympathetic to a capitalist/market-based economy and a more committed and efficient workforce as a result of owning shares in the company.

4 *More government revenue*. The privatisation programme since 1979 has raised well over £50bn in revenue for the Treasury.

Case against privatisation

1 *Simply converts a state monopoly to a private monopoly*. The argument here is that economies of scale are so large for many of the industries and sectors privatised (see Table 8.3) that it will only ever be efficient to have one, or at most a few, large firms in those sectors. Box 8.2 looks at the *natural monopoly* argument which suggests that only a single efficient firm may be regarded as viable in that industry. This

criticism of privatisation points to the fact that one merely changes a 'state monopoly' for a 'private monopoly' by privatisation, with few if any benefits of lower price and extra choice for consumers.

2 *Need for industry regulation and extra bureaucracy.* Related to the previous point, governments have appointed industry regulators to protect the public from the market power of large private companies that have replaced the nationalised industries. So we have OFGAS, OFWAT, OFTEL, OFCOM and many other regulators who try to limit price increases and impose conditions on the operations of the now large private companies in gas, water, telecommunications and many other industries. Firms in these industries often complain of their lack of freedom to manage, excessive 'red tape' and bureaucracy from these industry regulators.

3 *Concentration of share ownership.* Whilst more individuals own shares, the larger shareholding institutions such as pension funds, insurance companies and unit trusts have increased their shareholdings and together own almost 60% of all shares in the UK. Only those shareholders who have a significant stake in the company can, in practice, influence company policy. Having some extra individuals with a few shares each does little to bring about a true 'property-owning democracy', in this view.

4 *Loss of government revenue.* At the time of privatisation, the new shares were offered to the public at largely 'knock-down' prices to create public interest in the privatisation. This undervaluation of shares lost the Treasury considerable potential revenue at the time of these privatisations.

Box 8.2 'Natural monopoly' argument

The *natural monopoly* argument is often advanced in favour of public ownership of certain industries. Economies of scale in railways, water, electricity and gas industries are perhaps so great that the tendency towards monopoly can be termed 'natural'. In terms of our earlier analysis (Chapter 6, p. 213) the *minimum efficient size* (MES) is so large that the nation can only sustain one efficient firm in that particular industry. It then follows that creating competition in providing such goods and services, with duplication of investment, would, in this view, be wasteful of resources.

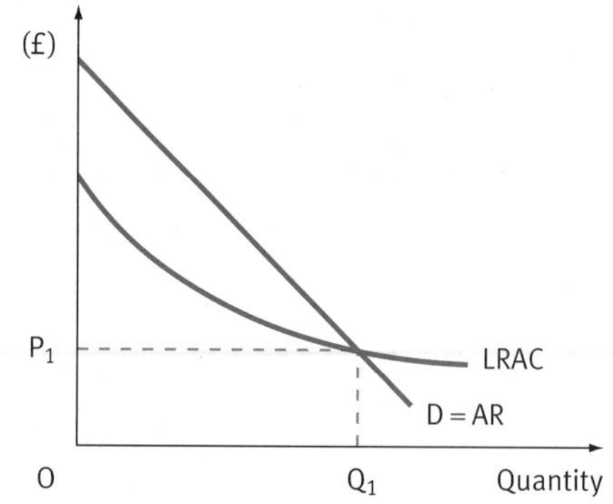

Fig 8.4 'Natural monopoly' with continuously falling long-run average cost (LRAC) curve

Figure 8.4 provides a useful illustration of the natural monopoly argument. The falling long-run average total cost curve (LRAC) indicates that significant economies of scale occur as output rises.

The demand (AR) curve for the product is such that it is not possible for this industry to have even one firm producing at the minimum efficient size (MES). Output Q_1 is the highest output the nationalised industry could produce and still break even (Price = AR = AC). However, even at this output the LRAC curve is still falling. To create private sector competition in such a 'natural monopoly' situation would mean smaller outputs than OQ_1 at higher average costs and higher prices than is needed to break even, a policy hardly likely to commend itself to consumers!

Regulation of privatised companies

The privatisation of public utility companies with 'natural' monopolies creates the possibility that the companies might abuse their monopoly power. In these cases UK privatisations have offered reassurance to the public in the form of regulatory offices for each privatised utility, For example, OFTEL for telecommunications and OFWAT for the water industry.

Objectives of regulators

Regulators have two fundamental objectives.

First, they attempt to create the constraints and stimuli which companies would experience in a competitive market environment. For example, companies in competitive markets must bear in mind what their competitors are doing when setting their prices and are under competitive pressure to improve their service to consumers in order to gain or retain market share. Regulations can stimulate the effects of a competitive market by setting price caps and performance standards.

Second, regulators have the longer-term objective of encouraging actual competition by easing the entry of new producers and by preventing privatised monopoly power maintaining barriers to entry.

An ideal is the creation of markets sufficiently competitive to make regulation unnecessary. The market for gas has moved substantially in this direction. British Gas, when first privatised, had an apparent classic natural monopoly in the supply of gas to industry, but by the end of 2003 the British Gas market share was below 30% for industrial users and since 1998 the company has faced nationwide competition in the supply of gas to domestic consumers. Similarly, the regulator insisted on the introduction of competition into the supply of electricity to domestic consumers by 1998.

Problems facing regulators

Regulators have an unenviable role as they try to create the constraints and stimuli of a competitive market. Essentially they are arbitrating between the interests of consumers and producers. Other things being equal, attempts by regulators to achieve improvements in service levels will cause increases in costs and so lower profits, whilst price caps (see below) on services with price inelastic demand will also reduced profits by preventing the regulated industries raising prices and therefore revenue.

The privatised company subject to a price cap may well look for ways of lowering costs to allow profits to be at least maintained, or perhaps raised. In most organisations there are economies to be gained by reducing staffing levels, and the utility companies have dramatically reduced their numbers of employees. Investment in new technology may also enable unit costs to be lowered so that profits are greater than they otherwise would have been.

Establishing a price cap

In deciding on a price cap the regulator has in mind some 'satisfactory' rate of profit on the value of assets employed. A key issue is then the valuation of the assets. If the basis of valuation is historical, using the market value at privatisation plus an estimate of investment since that date, then the company will face a stricter price cap than if current market valuations are used for assets. This is because historical valuations will usually be much smaller than the current valuations and so will justify much smaller total profits and therefore lower prices to achieve that profit.

Price caps are often associated with job losses. In an economy with less than full employment it may then be argued that such cost savings in the privatised companies are only achieved at the expense of extra public expenditure on welfare benefit. However, a counter-argument is that lower public utility prices benefit all consumers, with lower costs of production across the economy stimulating output and creating employment

Costs of regulation

Whilst regulation should produce clear benefits for the consumers of each privatised company, there are inevitable costs involved in running regulatory offices and also costs for the regulated company which has to supply information and present its case to the regulator. It is likely that companies will go further than this and try to anticipate the regulator's activities, so incurring further costs.

UK competition policy

Our particular concern in this section is with mergers and acquisitions policy in the UK. We have noted in Chapter 5 the potential benefits of increased size via various economies of scale. However, we have also noted in Chapter 6 that the extra market power from increased size can lead to higher prices, lower outputs and reduced choice for consumers. Competition policy in the UK seeks to balance the potential benefits of mergers with the need to protect the public from possible excesses of market power.

Before examining how UK competition policy has been conducted, it will be helpful to review the role of some of the key institutions and bodies which are involved.

UK merger policy: key 'players'

- *Office of Fair Trading* (OFT). This is an independent statutory body which has been given the task of keeping markets under review and promoting competition. In the *Enterprise Act of 2002* it was given the key role in deciding which mergers should be permitted and which should be investigated further. For those mergers to be investigated further it advises the *Secretary of State for Trade and Industry* on whether, and under what conditions, the proposed mergers should be allowed.
  - Sometimes the OFT bases that advice on in-depth investigations conducted by the *Competition Commission* (CC) to which it can refer proposed mergers. For a proposed merger to be referred to the Competition Commission, two key conditions must apply, and if they do it becomes a '*relevant merger*'.
    1. *Either* that the enterprise being taken over has a UK turnover exceeding £70m (the 'turnover test') *or* that the merged enterprises together supply at least 25% of the UK market (the 'share of supply' test). It is implicit in this criterion that at least one enterprise must trade within the UK.
    2. If the above condition is satisfied, the OFT will still only refer the proposed merger to the Competition Commission (CC) for further scrutiny if it is expected to result in a substantial 'lessening of competition' within the UK. 'Lessening of competition' would generally mean a situation where it is expected that product choice or quality would be reduced, prices raised, or innovation restricted as a result of the merger activity.
  - Sometimes the OFT might decide *not* to make a reference to the CC if the OFT itself believes that the 'public benefits' (e.g. higher choice, lower prices, higher quality or innovation) resulting from the merger outweigh the substantial 'lessening of competition' noted above.
- *Competition Commission* (CC). This replaced the previous Monopolies and Mergers Commission in 1998. It is an independent statutory body which conducts in-depth investigations of any potential merger situations referred to it by the OFT or the Secretary of State for Trade and Industry. The CC, when considering a merger in more depth, will weigh the 'lessening of competition' effect against the 'public benefits' effect before making its final decision.
- *Secretary of State for Trade and Industry*. This is a cabinet minister in the UK and in 2004 Patricia Hewitt held this position. The 2002 *Enterprise Act* has reduced the role of the Secretary of State in mergers policy. Most decisions as to which mergers should be referred to the Competition Commission (CC) are to be made by the Office of Fair Trading following the conditions and guidelines outlined above.
- *Competition Appeals Tribunal* (CAT). There is also a new appeals mechanism giving a right to those parties involved in the merger to apply to the Competition Appeals Tribunal (CAT) for a statutory judicial review of a decision of the OFT, CC or the Secretary of State.

- *Court of Appeal*. There is also a further right of appeal (on a point of law only) to the Court of Appeal.

Putting merger policy into practice

To understand the main procedures for merger investigation in the UK, a brief account will be given here of the process.

- *First stage*. When the OFT is made aware of a proposed merger which meets its conditions (a 'relevant merger'), it may choose to undertake a 'first stage' investigation. For example, it might seek to assess the potential effect of the merger on market structure. This market structure assessment could be followed by an examination of whether the entry of new firms into the market is easy or difficult and whether any 'lessening of competition' is likely to occur.
- *Second stage*. The OFT will then make its own decision on the case without reference to the Secretary of State. The OFT will give one of three possible decisions:
  - First, the merger is given an unconditional clearance.
  - Second, the merger is given a clearance only if the parties agree to modify any behaviour identified as 'uncompetitive' or decrease their market share and market power by selling off specified businesses.
  - Third, the merger may turn out to be serious enough to refer it directly to the CC for a 'second-stage' investigation. At this point the Secretary of State can intervene in the proceedings, but under the new *Enterprise Act* of 2002 this intervention can take place only in very specific circumstances involving mergers with media, national security or other narrowly specified implications.
- *Third stage*. If the OFT refers the merger to the CC, the Commission will consider the evidence of the OFT but will also make its own in-depth report on the merger. After consideration of the evidence and basing its views on both the 'lessening of competition' and 'customer benefits criteria', the CC will recommend that one of three possible actions be taken: (i) an unconditional clearance, or (ii) a clearance subject to conditions proposed by the CC, or (iii) an outright prohibition.
  - If the CC recommends conditional clearance then the companies involved may be asked to divest some of their assets or to ensure in some specified way that competition is maintained (e.g. giving licences to their competitors).
  - If the CC recommends prohibition of the merger, the parties can appeal to the *Competition Appeals Tribunal* (CAT). This is a three-person tribunal which seems to be an important new 'player' in mergers policy.

Case Study 8.4 indicates the growing importance of the Competition Appeals Tribunal (CAT).

Case Study 8.4 OFT loses power in merger decisions

FT

Mergers stand to cost more and take longer after a ground-breaking decision in December 2003 by the *Competition Appeals Tribunal*, which urged the Office of Fair Trading to refer more takeovers to the *Competition Commission*. In comments about the first merger decision to be challenged before the three-person tribunal, Sir Christopher Bellamy, its president, said that 'only exceptionally' should the OFT try to resolve mergers where there was a 'real question as to whether there is a substantial lessening of competition'.

Competition lawyers said the decision was likely to encourage competitors to take more merger challenges to the tribunal and would probably lead to more references to the *Competition Commission*. 'We're going to see a much higher level of contention,' predicted Chris Bright, lawyer at Shearman & Sterling. The decision came after the OFT cleared a planned £800m merger in November 2003 between Torex and iSoft, which supply software to hospitals and healthcare companies. Under rules brought in by the *Enterprise Act* of 2003 ministers have been taken out of the merger decision process and a new appeals procedure against OFT decisions has been introduced.

Both Torex and iSoft are bidding to participate in the modernisation of the National Health Service's computer system, the world's biggest IT project. The OFT itself decided, without reference to a more thorough investigation by the Competition Commissions, that the merger was not likely substantially to reduce competition. That view was challenged by IBA Health, an Australian-listed healthcare software provider. It claimed the OFT's decision was unlawful because of the anti-competitive implications. It pointed out that, for example, the combined group would have a market share of 46% in the electronic patient record sector and 100% of the installed base in Scotland.

The Competition Appeals Tribunal also took issue with the OFT's approach. 'We are not satisfied the OFT applied the right test or ... reached a conclusion that was reasonably open to them,' it said.

'In a merger case where it is clear that there are material and complex issues relating to what is potentially a substantial lessening of competition between horizontal competitors in a sector (of) national importance, we do not think it likely that parliament intended that those issues were to be resolved at the stage of the OFT,' Sir Christopher added in his remarks.

The tribunal quashed the OFT's decision and referred the matter back. This could either involve a fresh decision from the OFT or see it handed to the Competition Commission.

Source: *Financial Times*, 4 December 2003

Questions

1 Why did the Competition Appeal Tribunal overrule the OFT in this particular case?

2 What implications does this have for merger policy in the UK?

The OFT was concerned that the action of the Competition Appeals Tribunal would open up a 'two part' test, in that it would have to refer any proposed merger to the *Competition Commission* (a) if the OFT thought a deal might result in a 'substantial lessening of competition' or (b) if there was a possibility that the *Competition Commission* might take a different view to the OFT. In practice, almost every proposed merger would then be liable to be referred, implying huge time delays, extra costs and greater uncertainty.

In its judgement in February 2003, however, the Appeals Court rejected the need for such a 'two part' test by the OFT. However, it did criticise the OFT for making a hasty ill-thought-out judgement in the particular case of the iSoft and Torex proposed merger, which must now be re-investigated. Many lawyers believe the case will have made the OFT more cautious in its assessments, perhaps resulting in a small rise in reference to the *Competition Commission*.

CHECK THE NET

For information on past decisions of the UK *Competition Commission* go to: www.competition-commission.org

So far our concern has been with mergers policy in the UK. However, UK competition policy also includes dealing with various 'restrictive practices'.

Restrictive practices legislation

The *Restrictive Trades Practices Act* of 1956 specified that restrictive practice operated by groups of firms had now to be registered with a *Registrar of Restrictive Practices*. It was his responsibility to bring cases to the *Restrictive Practices Court*, consisting of five judges and ten lay members with the status of a High Court.

Such restrictive practices were deemed against the public interest unless they could satisfy at least one of seven 'pathways':

1 that it protects the public against injury;
2 that it confers special benefits on consumers;
3 that it prevents local unemployment;
4 that it counters existing restrictions on competition;
5 that it maintains exports;
6 that it supports other acceptable restrictions;
7 that it assists the negotiations of fair trading terms for suppliers and buyers.

Even having satisfied one or more of the 'gateway' conditions, the firms had still to show that the overall benefits from the restrictive practice were clearly greater than the costs incurred. This 'tail piece' was largely responsible for the prohibition of many restrictive practices. Between 1956 and 2004, over 12,000 restrictive agreements have been registered. However, few of these have been brought before the court; the majority of such practices have been 'voluntarily' ended by the parties themselves in anticipation of an unfavourable decision by the court.

In 1968, 'information agreements' (i.e. agreements whereby information concerning prices, conditions etc. are formally exchanged) were for the first time considered a restrictive practice. Also in 1968 an eighth 'gateway' was added, namely 'that the agreement neither restricts nor deters competition'.

The 1973 Fair Trading Act gave permission for restrictive practices legislation to be extended to cover services as well as the production of goods. The *1976 Restrictive Practices Act* consolidated previous legislation.

Despite these changes, the adequacy of restrictive practices legislation has been questioned. For example, under the Restrictive Practices Act there were no financial penalties for failing to register a restrictive agreement and many such practices were able to continue. Of particular concern was the legislation dealing with *cartels*, which has been considerably strengthened in recent years.

Cartels in the UK

The UK approach to cartels (Chapter 6, p. 231) has been considerably strengthened in recent years.

- Under the *1998 Competition Act* the OFT was given civil powers to fine companies for anti-competitive behaviour involving formal or informal cartels.
- Under the *2002 Enterprise Act* the OFT was given additional *criminal powers* when investigating such cartels. The OFT now has the power to investigate people suspected of price-fixing, bid-rigging or limiting production or supply of goods dishonestly. Regulators from the OFT can now use force to enter offices or homes under a search warrant and can bring in the Serious Fraud Office to prosecute any criminal offence suspected. In effect the OFT can do much more than impose fines; it can now take actions which result in the possible imprisonment of directors and others involved in cartel-related activity.

EU competition policy

European competition policy has been criticised for its lack of comprehensiveness, but in December 1989 the Council of Ministers agreed for the first time on specific cross-border merger regulations. The criteria for judging whether a merger should be referred to the European Commission covered three aspects.

- First, the companies concerned must have a combined world turnover of more than €5bn (though for insurance companies the figure was based on total assets rather than turnover).
- Second, at least two of the companies concerned in the merger must have an EU-wide turnover of at least €250m each.
- Third, if all parties to the merger have two-thirds of their business in one and the same member state, the merger was to be subject to national and not EU controls.

The European Commission must be notified of merger proposals which meet the criteria noted above within one week of the announcement of the bid and it will vet each proposed merger against a concept of '*a dominant position*'. Any creation or strengthening of a dominant position will be seen as incompatible with the aims of the EU if it significantly impedes '*effective competition*'.

The European Commission has one month after notification to decide whether to start proceedings and then four months to make a final decision. If a case is being investigated by the European Commission it will *not* also be investigated by national bodies such as the UK Competition Commission, for example.

LINKS
The operation of various EU institutions is considered in more detail in Chapter 12, pp. 466–469.

Member states may prevent a merger which has already been permitted by the EU only if it involves public security or some aspects of the media or if competition in the local markets is threatened.

Review of EU merger regulations

A number of reservations were expressed about this EU legislation on cross-border mergers and acquisitions.

First, a main aim of the legislation was to introduce a 'one-stop shop', which meant that merging companies would be liable to *either* European *or* national merger control, but not both. However, as can be seen above, in some situations national merger control could override EU control – a 'two-stop shop'!

Second, it was not clear how the rules would apply to non-EU companies. For example, it was quite possible that two US or Japanese companies, each with the required amount of sales in the EU but with no actual EU presence, could merge. While such a case would certainly fall within the EU merger rules, it was not clear how seriously the EU could exercise its powers in such cases.

Third, guidelines were needed on joint ventures.

New EU cross-border merger regulations

In March 1998 a number of amendments were made to the scope of EU cross-border merger regulations. The result of these amendments was that the three original criteria for exclusive reference to the European Commission remain, but other criteria were added to give the EU jurisdiction over smaller-sized mergers which would not be large enough to qualify under the €5bn and €250m rules described earlier.

As regards joint ventures, the new regulations also make a distinction between 'concentrative' joint ventures and 'cooperative' joint ventures, with the new European Commission rules applying to the first type (which was seen to concentrate power) but not to the second type (which was seen merely as a method to coordinate competitive behaviour).

In 2000, a review of the merger approval system was instigated by the EU. By November 2002 it was announced that a package of reforms would be introduced that would take effect from May 2004. One aspect of the reforms includes the retention of the rule that a merger is unlawful if it 'creates or strengthens a dominant position' but also adds an amendment to the merger regulation to include situations where a merger may be deemed unlawful if it creates 'collective dominance' in a market. This situation might occur when a merger results in the formation or strengthening of an oligopolistic market structure within which a few large firms can coordinate their activities to the detriment of consumers. To date, the European Commission has handled around 80 merger cases per year over the past decade.

Restrictive practices and EU legislation

As in the UK, the EU competition policy seeks to deal with much more than merger activity. The reasoning behind European competition policy is exactly that which created the original European Economic Community (EEC) over 40 years ago. Competition is viewed as bringing consumers greater choice, lower prices and higher quality goods and services.

Promoting 'fair and free' competition

The European Commission has a set of *directives* in this area which are designed to underpin 'fair and free' competition. They cover cartels (price fixing, market sharing etc.), government subsidies (direct or indirect subsidies for inefficient enterprises – state and private), the abuse of dominant market position (differential pricing in different markets, exclusive contracts, predatory pricing etc.), selective distribution (preventing consumers in one market from buying in another in order to maintain high margins in the first market), and mergers and takeovers.

Avoiding excessive use of state aid and subsidies

One of the most active areas of competition policy has involved *state aid*. The Commission has attempted to restrict the aid paid by member states to their own nationals through Articles 87 and 88 which cover various aspects of the distorting effect that subsidies can have on competition between member states. However, it is likely that the progressive implementation of Single Market arrangements will result in domestic firms increasing their attempts to obtain state aid from their own governments as a means of helping them meet greater Europe-wide competition. Overall, the amount of aid given by member states to their domestic industry has been running at around 2% of their respective GNPs during the 1990s and early years of the millennium.

However, it is not only aid and subsidies given to one's own national companies that is the target of the European Commission. Case Study 8.5 shows how important the issue of EU rulings on state aid and similar subsidies is to the European-wide operations of Ryanair.

Case Study 8.5 **Ryanair and Charleroi**

The wide-ranging problems resulting from EU rulings on the legitimacy of state aid and subsidies is usefully illustrated by the recent experience of Ryanair, the Irish carrier. In February 2004 the European Commission ruled that Ryanair had received around £11m (€15m) in state aid from the Belgian authorities to fly to and from Charleroi airport in southern Belgium and ordered the no-frills airline to return up to £3m (€4m) of the money. According to the judgement, Ryanair's controversial benefits from the Walloon regional government which owns Charleroi included €1.92m in subsidies to launch new routes, €768,000 for pilot training, €250,000 towards hotel costs and a landing charge of only €1 per passenger, compared to the standard rate of €8 to €13.

Case Study 8.5 continued

Loyola de Palacio, the EU transport commissioner, said she thought the ruling would force Ryanair to put up its prices by an average of up to €8 (£6) per return ticket but Mr O'Leary, Ryanair's owner, said it was likely to be double that.

The ruling is also expected to affect Ryanair's cut-price fares to other destinations since it has similar subsidy arrangements with 19 state-owned airports in France which include popular second-home destinations for British travellers such as Montpellier, Biarritz, Carcassonne and Pau.

Ms de Palacio made it clear that some forms of aid were acceptable, including one-off help from airports to provide marketing support for new routes. She also indicated that introductory discounts for new airlines could be acceptable for up to five years, rather than the 15 years agreed at Charleroi.

The ruling is only applicable to state-owned airports, which means that destinations in countries such as Britain and Germany, where airports are privatised, will be unaffected.

The European Low Fares Airline Association, which represents nine low-cost carriers, also criticised the European Commission ruling. The AEA's secretary general, Ulrich Schulte-Strathaus, said: 'Are we expected to believe that there is a natural market at Charleroi that can support three Boeing 737 services a day to London, and two a day to Venice? The Charleroi routes only make economic sense if, firstly, they are represented as serving Brussels and, secondly, they are supported by subsidies.'

Questions

1 Why have the regional governments owning these airports been willing to offer such aid and subsidies to Ryanair?

2 What is the European Commission's attitude to such aid and subsidies?

3 Consider some of the implications that might follow from this ruling against Ryanair.

Key Terms

Externality Where economic decisions create costs or benefits for people other than the decision taker.

Information asymmetry Where one person or firm knows more than another person or firm.

Marginal social benefit Defined as marginal private benefit plus marginal external benefit.

Marginal social cost Defined as marginal private cost plus marginal external cost.

Merit goods Goods/services that add to the quality of life but are not, strictly, public goods. For example, education/healthcare can be withheld from consumers (i.e. they do not possess the public good quality of non-excludability), and so private markets can be established to provide them.

Mixed (quasi) public goods Involves some aspect of non-excludability or non-exhaustibility, but not both.

Negative externality Where marginal social cost exceeds marginal private cost.

Pareto optimality A situation is said to be Pareto optimal when it is no longer possible to reallocate resources in such a way that we can make one person better off, without at the same time making someone else worse off.

Pigouvian tax A tax exactly equal to the marginal external cost at each level of output.

Price gap Maximum price set by an industry regulator.

Public good A good (or service) that involves two key characteristics: non-excludability and non-exhaustibility. Non-excludability means that, once provided, it is difficult to exclude people from consuming the good/service. Non-exhaustibility means that consumption of an extra unit by one person does not diminish the amount available for consumption by others.

Public interest theory An approach that seeks to assess the impacts of regulation or deregulation in terms of whether or not it raises economic welfare in such a way that gainers can potentially compensate losers. Usually involves the ideas of consumer and producer surplus.

Key Points

- Regulations are widely used in all economic sectors in order to protect consumers from 'market failure' and to prevent such failures actually occurring.
- There is considerable momentum behind removing regulations (i.e. deregulation) where this can be shown to be in the 'public interest'. However, evaluating the welfare change from deregulation is a complex exercise.
- Privatisation is the transfer of assets or economic activity from the public sector to the private sector.
- The term 'privatisation' is often used to cover many situations: the outright sale of state-owned assets, part-sale, joint public/private ventures, market testing, contracting out of central/local government services etc.
- The case for privatisation includes allegedly greater productive efficiency (lower costs) via the introduction of market pressures. These are seen as creating more flexibility in labour markets, higher productivity and reduced unit labour costs.
- The case against privatisation includes suggestions that state monopolies have often merely been replaced by private monopolies, with little benefit to consumers, especially in the case of the public utilities.
- Regulators have been appointed for a number of public utilities in an attempt to simulate the effects of competition (e.g. limits to price increases and to profits), when there is little competition in reality.

Assessment Practice

Multiple choice questions

1 **Which *two* of the following reasons are often used to support a policy to nationalise certain industries?**

(a) More difficult to take into account any divergence between private cost and social cost.
(b) Easier to take into account any divergence between private cost and social cost.
(c) Few economies of scale exist in the industry.
(d) Economies of scale are so large that the industry is a 'natural monopoly'.
(e) It is expensive and inefficient to establish a bureaucracy of civil servants to run the industry.

2 **Which *two* of the following reasons are often used to support a policy to privatise certain industries?**

(a) Firms exposed to market forces are likely to be more efficient.
(b) Firms insulated from market forces are likely to be more efficient.
(c) Firms can more easily take into account any negative externalities in their decision making.
(d) The stock market can exert a useful discipline on the firm, with less successful firms being more likely to be taken over by more successful ones.
(e) The public finances are likely to deteriorate.

3 **Which *two* of the following are problems which often confront regulators of particular industries?**

(a) Setting the price floor
(b) Setting the price cap
(c) Establishing the share price
(d) Restricting competition
(e) Encouraging competition

4 **Which *one* of the following comes closest to being a 'pure' public good?**

(a) Defence
(b) Education
(c) Electricity supply
(d) Health service
(e) Postal service

5 **Which *one* of the following refers to a situation in which those who purchase a product are less able to appreciate its quality than those who supply it?**

(a) Natural monopoly
(b) Public good
(c) Positive externality
(d) Negative externality
(e) Asymmetric information

6 **Which *one* of the following refers to a situation in which the minimum efficient size for firm output is greater than the current output of the industry?**

(a) Natural monopoly
(b) Public good
(c) Positive externality
(d) Negative externality
(e) Asymmetric information

7 **The optimum level of economic activity and associated pollution from society's point of view occurs where:**

(a) Marginal private benefit = Marginal private cost
(b) Marginal social benefit > Marginal social cost
(c) Marginal social benefit < Marginal social cost
(d) Marginal social benefit = Marginal social cost
(e) Marginal social benefit = 0

8 **Marginal social cost can be defined in which *one* of the following ways?**

(a) Marginal private cost plus Marginal external cost
(b) Marginal private cost minus Marginal private revenue
(c) Marginal private cost plus Marginal social cost
(d) Marginal external cost
(e) Marginal private cost

9 **Which *one* of these is an independent statutory body which conducts in-depth investigations of potential merger situations referred to it?**

(a) Office of Fair Trading
(b) Secretary of State for Trade and Industry
(c) Competition Appeals Tribunal
(d) Competition Commission
(e) Court of Appeal

10 **Which *one* of these has the initial task of deciding whether the potential merger should be classified as a 'relevant merger' and investigated further?**

(a) Office of Fair Trading
(b) Secretary of State for Trade and Industry
(c) Competition Appeals Tribunal
(d) Competition Commission
(e) Court of Appeal

Data response and stimulus questions

1 Read the text then answer the questions

State aid

One of the most active areas of competition policy has involved state aid. Currently some 45bn ECU per year is spent on state aid to EU manufacturing. Germany tops the league of aid recipients as it tries to help its new *Länder* in the former East Germany to restructure their industry. The main problem with state aid is that the big, industrially powerful countries – Germany, France, the UK and Italy – account for some 85% of the total state aid given by EU countries to their domestic industry. This arguably gives such economies considerable advantages over the four 'cohesion' countries – Greece, Portugal, Spain and Ireland – and the recent new entrant countries.

To counter some of these trends, the EU Commission has begun to scrutinise state aid much more closely – especially where the aid seems to be more than is needed to ensure the ultimate viability of the recipient organisations. For example, in April 1998 the Commission decided that aid paid to the German porcelain firm, Triptis Porzellan GmbH, should be recovered because it believed the aid to be more than was needed to restore the firm's viability, thereby distorting competition in the market.

Article 87 determines all state aid to be illegal, unless it conforms to one or more of a number of exceptions:

- Aid to promote improvements of a social character.
- Aid to promote economic development in areas with high unemployment or low living standards.
- Aid to promote a project of common EU interest.
- Aid to the former German Democratic Republic.
- Aid to disaster areas.
- Sectoral aid to assist in the restructuring of an individual sector in structural decline, e.g. shipbuilding.

Questions

1 Consider the case in favour of 'state aid' as a policy to correct market failure.

2 Now consider the problems with such a policy.

2 Read the text, then answer the questions which follow.

Charging the motorist

Until recently, the idea of charging for scarce road space was dismissed as political suicide, but some politicians have advocated road pricing and lived to tell the tale. Ken Livingstone, London's mayor, for instance, introduced road pricing in the capital in 2003. Now a new study for the European Commission takes the argument further. Enticingly entitled 'Revenues for Efficient Pricing', it argues that current transport taxes should be replaced by charges to reflect the true marginal costs of different forms of transport – not only the additional cost of each journey, but also the costs of pollution, congestion and accidents. On this basis the London car driver and truck driver should be charged three times as much than Ken Livingstone's £5 daily congestion charge for rush-hour journeys.

Marginal social-cost pricing, the economic jargon for this form of charging, would produce 50% more revenue than current taxes on fuel and vehicles. It would also recover the full costs of transport infrastructure. The cost burden would shift from rail to road because the marginal cost of each additional car journey is greater than that of an additional rail journey.

Questions

1 What is meant by marginal social-cost pricing?

2 Outline the benefits and problems of introducing a comprehensive scheme of marginal social cost pricing.

True/False questions

1 If the social costs of providing a product exceed the private costs, then there is a case for imposing taxes or looking for other ways of restricting output.
True/False

2 A 'natural monopoly' refers to monopoly power in the provision of natural resources.
True/False

3 A benefit of nationalisation is that it encourages wider share ownership.
True/False

4 If regulation can be shown to result in a net welfare loss, then this may be used as an argument in favour of deregulation.
True/False

5 A pure public good is non-excludable and non-exhaustible.
True/False

6 A positive externality would occur where marginal social benefit is greater than marginal private benefit.
True/False

7 Information asymmetry is where we both have the same knowledge.
True/False

8 A 'Pigouvian tax' is one which is exactly equal to the marginal external cost at all levels of output.
True/False

9 The Office of Fair Trading (OFT) is responsible in the UK for deciding whether or not to refer a proposed merger to the Competition Commission (CC).
True/False

10 The OFT can only refer 'relevant mergers' to the Competition Commission, i.e. mergers which fulfil either the 'turnover test' (>£70m in the UK) or the 'share of supply test' (at least 25% of the UK market).
True/False

Essay questions

1. Under what circumstances might you support government intervention in the economy?
2. What do you understand by a 'negative externality'? Consider the impacts of a negative externality on resource allocation and the policies which might be used to 'correct' it.
3. Why is it often suggested that imperfect information will result in a misallocation of resources? How can such a misallocation be avoided?
4. Examine the arguments for and against deregulation, using examples to support your points wherever appropriate.
5. Why does the UK government seek to influence merger activity? Briefly review the ways in which it seeks to influence merger activity.

Part II

Macro Business Environment

Chapter 9

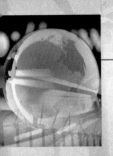

National income determination

Introduction

National income is, as the name implies, the income of the whole nation. However, it can be measured in three different ways, only one of which involves income, the other two using output and expenditure. Measuring national income is important since individuals, businesses and the government all have an interest in raising the real (after inflation) value of national income. Individuals can use their higher income to purchase more goods and services and thereby improve their standard of living. Businesses will now be able to sell more output so that they can raise revenue and profit. Governments will be more likely to retain the electoral support of their citizens where they benefit from a rising standard of living and the provision of improved public services. National income is thus of vital importance to the whole country and must therefore be carefully measured and monitored.

At first sight it might appear that the material in this chapter is a little technical and complex and has little real effect on the everyday life of consumers or businesses. This is not the case at all! The ideas, components and equilibrium levels of national income are extremely important, because what we are measuring here is the total economic activity inside an economy, and this is of crucial importance to us all.

It is of such importance that almost all large companies will employ economists and analysts to examine very closely any available data that might indicate future trends in the national income. Firms want to know this information in order to be able to judge when and by how much they should change target levels of output, hire or fire workers, invest in plant and machinery, hold inventories (stocks) and so on.

To illustrate how important national income is, one only needs to think of the consequences when it fails to grow, as occurred in the UK during the period 1990–1992. If expenditure by households falls for some reason, then output too will start to fall and fewer workers will be needed to produce that output. Unemployment may not occur immediately, as initially businesses may cut back on overtime and abandon investment plans. However, eventually, in order to remain in business, lay-offs may well become necessary and unemployment will rise and household incomes will fall. Spending may not at first fall by much but eventually may fall substantially, leading to less demand for goods and services, making output fall even further. This downward spiral of economic activity is called the *deflationary multiplier*: businesses fail, profits fall, output falls, unemployment rises. Of course, this process can be reversed and become a self-reinforcing upward spiral of recovery for output and employment, as in the case of the *expansionary multiplier*. We consider both such possibilities during the course of this chapter.

Always remember that behind national income data lie real people, and the impact of changing economic circumstances on the human beings involved should not be underestimated!

Learning objectives:

By the end of this chapter you should be able to:

- understand how national income is measured and what is meant by the various definitions of national income
- outline the relevance of national income data to international comparisons of standards of living
- consider the relevance of the various components of national income for business activity
- explain the meaning of 'equilibrium' national income and show how such an equilibrium is brought about
- use both the withdrawal/injection diagram and the 45° aggregate expenditure diagram to assess changes in the equilibrium levels of national income
- explain the meaning and importance of the 'national income multiplier'
- show how the government can respond to inflationary and deflationary 'gaps'.

Chapter 10 reviews government policy instruments and objectives in still more detail. It also develops the withdrawal/injection and 45° aggregate expenditure approaches into the aggregate demand and aggregate supply analysis, which is then applied to a range of policy issues.

National income

National income is a measure of the value of the *output* of the goods and services produced by an economy over a period of time, usually one year. It is also a measure of the *incomes* which flow from that output and the *expenditure* involved in purchasing that output. It follows that all three methods can be used to measure national income and we briefly review each in turn. However, before doing so it will help to introduce the so-called 'circular flow of income' and define some terms widely used when discussing national income.

Circular flow of income: simplified

NOTE
We use the term 'domestic' throughout to refer to firms and households *located within* the domestic economy (e.g. within the UK).

Figure 9.1 presents a simplified approach to the circular flow of income within a domestic economy characterised by firms (producers) and households (consumers). It is 'simplified' in that we initially assume no savings, no investment, no government expenditure or taxation and no international trade (so no exports or imports). Nevertheless, this approach is useful in indicating that output, income and expenditure are all involved in the circular flow of income.

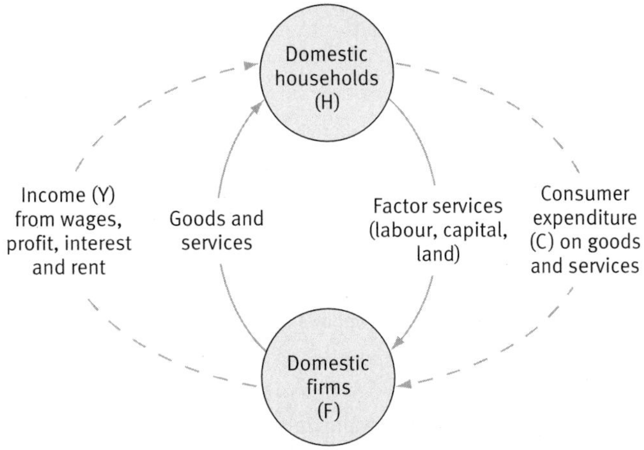

Fig 9.1 Circular flow: no withdrawals and no injections

Domestic households provide factor services (labour, loan capital, entrepreneurship, land) to domestic firms which use their services to produce an *output* of goods and services. These factor services from households are rewarded by *income* in the form of wages, dividends, interest and rent. With no savings in our simplified economy, no tax and no spending on imports, all the income received by domestic households goes in *consumption expenditure* (C) on the output of domestic firms.

In this simplified circular flow, any initial money value of income can be sustained indefinitely, since there are no withdrawals and no injections. In Figure 9.1 the dashed lines refer to 'monetary' flows, involving income and expenditure, whereas the solid lines refer to 'real' flows of factor services and the resulting output of goods and services.

It will be useful to consider a more realistic model of the circular flow of income before exploring the *three* alternative methods of measuring national income.

Circular flow of income: withdrawals and injections

We now relax our assumptions of no saving or investment, no government involvement and no international trade. As we can see from Figure 9.2, we now have certain *withdrawals* (W) from the circular flow of income, shown by a minus (–) sign, and certain *injections* (J), shown by a plus (+) sign.

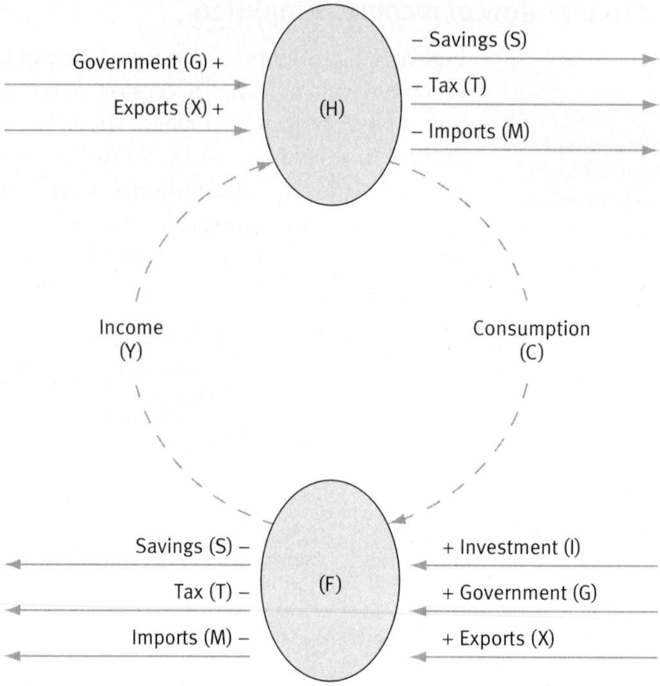

Fig 9.2 Circular flow: withdrawals and injections

Withdrawals (W)

Although it may seem over-fussy, it is very important to define carefully the terms we use in the circular flow.

We define a *withdrawal* (W) from the circular flow as either:

- any income received by a domestic household (H) not passed on to a domestic firm (F); or
- any income received by a domestic firm (F) not passed on to a domestic household (H).

Components of withdrawals (W)

As we see in Figure 9.2, some income received by domestic households (H) or domestic firms (F) is *not passed on* in the circular flow. In other words, it is saved (S), taxed (T) or spent on imports (M).

- *Savings* (S). These can be either personal savings by domestic households (H) or business savings (e.g. undistributed profits) by domestic firms (F).

- *Taxes* (T). These can be either taxes paid by domestic households (H), such as income tax, council tax, VAT etc. or taxes paid by domestic firms (F), such as corporation tax, business rates, VAT etc.
- *Imports* (M). These can be imports either by domestic firms (F) or domestic households (H) of goods or services from *overseas* firms or households.

In all the above cases, income received by domestic firms or households *is not passed on* in the circular flow to other domestic firms or households.

$$\text{Withdrawals} = \text{Savings} + \text{Taxes} + \text{Imports}$$
$$\text{i.e.}\quad W = S + T + M$$

Injections (J)

We define an *injection* (J) into the circular flow as either:

- any income received by a domestic household (H) that does not come from a domestic firm (F); or
- any income received by a domestic firm (F) that does not come from a domestic household (H).

Components of injections (J)

From Figure 9.2 we can identify investment (I), government expenditure (G) and exports (X) as meeting this definition of an injection.

- *Investment* (I). Here income is received by domestic firms (F) which does not come from domestic households (H) but from *other domestic firms* who purchase capital equipment, buildings etc. for investment purposes.
- *Government expenditure* (G). Here income is received by domestic firms (F) which does not come from domestic households (H) but from *the government* (e.g. government contracts). Alternatively, income is received by domestic households (H) which does not come from domestic firms (F) but from *the government* (e.g. public sector workers).
- *Exports* (X). Here income is received by domestic firms (F) which does not come from domestic households (H) but from *overseas households and firms*. Alternatively, income is received by domestic households (H) not from domestic firms (F) but from *overseas firms and households* (e.g. interest and dividends from overseas, consultancy overseas etc.).

$$\text{Injections} = \text{Investment} + \text{Government expenditure} + \text{Exports}$$
$$\text{i.e.}\quad J = I + G + X$$

Figure 9.2 (p. 320) brought these components of withdrawals (W) and injections (J) together on one diagram.

NOTE

Strictly speaking, the *equals* (=) signs used above should be *identity* (≡) signs. We use identity signs whenever we have defined a situation in such a way that the left-hand side must equal the right-hand side for *all* values of the variables.

National income: definitions and measurement

Having introduced the various withdrawals from, and injections into, the circular flow, we are now in a better position to consider the different definitions of national income and the three methods for measuring national income.

National income definitions

Gross domestic product (GDP)

This is the value of output produced (and incomes received) by domestic residents (firms and households) using resources located within the domestic economy (e.g. within the UK).

Gross national product (GNP)

This is the value of output produced (and incomes received) by domestic residents from their *ownership of resources*, wherever these resources happen to be located, whether inside or outside the domestic economy. For example, GNP takes account of the fact that some UK residents (firms and households) earn incomes such as profits, interest and rent from owning resources located abroad. The *net* value to UK residents of such receipts from abroad and the equivalent payments abroad is called 'net property income from abroad' in the national accounts.

$$\text{GDP} + \text{Net property income from abroad} = \text{GNP}$$

Net national product (NNP)

Gross national product is the total value of output produced and incomes received by UK residents in the course of a year. It therefore includes the full value of *new* plant and equipment produced during the course of the year (i.e. gross domestic fixed capital formation). However, over this period *existing* plant and equipment will have depreciated (i.e. declined in value due to wear and tear and obsolescence). In order to obtain a true measure of national income an appropriate deduction for capital depreciation must be made, i.e.

$$\text{GNP} - \text{Depreciation} = \text{NNP}$$

'Market prices' and 'factor cost'

All these measures of national income can be expressed either at 'market prices' or at 'factor cost'.

- *Market prices*. Here the value placed on any output uses the prices observed in the marketplace (where these are available). Such prices may, however, be distorted by taxes and subsidies. For example, the market prices of some products may be higher than they otherwise would be due to the taxes levied on them. Alternatively, the market prices may be lower than they otherwise would be due to subsidies received on them. 'Market prices' is a valuation approach which includes these impacts on price of taxes and subsidies.

- *Factor cost.* Here the value placed on any output seeks to *exclude* the 'distorting' impacts on the prices of product of any taxes or subsidies.
  - Taxes are subtracted from the valuation at market prices.
  - Subsidies are added to the valuation at market prices.

National income measurement

We now briefly consider the output, income and expenditure methods for measuring national income.

Strictly speaking, the national income accounts are defined in such a way that the three methods of measurement should give exactly the same result.

The output method

A country's national income can be calculated from the output figures of all firms in the economy. However, this does not mean that we simply add together the value of each firm's output. To do so would give us an aggregate many times greater than the national income because of *double counting*.

NOTES

If your syllabus requires a detailed treatment of the output, income and expenditure methods for measuring national income, read about these methods on pages 323–327, otherwise move on to page 328.

- *Avoiding double counting.* The outputs of some firms are the inputs of other firms. For example, the output of the steel industry is used in part as an input for the automobile industry and so on. To avoid including the total value of the steel used in automobile production twice (double counting) we sum only the *value added* at each stage of production. Alternatively, we sum only the *final value* of output produced for the various goods and services.

Example:

- A logger chops down trees and sells them to the sawmill for £500.
- At the sawmill the wood is cut into usable sizes, and sold to the timber merchant for £800.
- The timber merchant acts as the 'middleman' to B & Q and sells the wood to them for £900.
- B&Q sells the wood to the consumer for £1,500.

If we simply added all the outputs together it would add up to £3,700.
BUT the original logging work has been added several times.
To avoid double counting we calculate the value added at each stage:

Logger	£500
Saw mill	£300
Timber merchant	£100
B&Q	£600
Total value added	£1,500

Or, we only include the value of output at the final stage, £1,500.

- *Inventories.* We must also ensure that any additions to 'stock and work in progress' (inventories) are included in the output figures for each industry, since any build-up in stock during a year must represent extra output produced during that year.
- *Public goods and merit goods.* We have already seen in Chapter 8 that the government provides many goods and services through the non-market sector, such as education, healthcare, defence, police and so on. Such goods and services are clearly part of the nation's output, but since many of these are not sold through the market sector, strictly they do not have a market price. In such cases, the value of the output is measured at resource cost or factor cost. In other words, the value of the service is assumed to be equivalent to the cost of the resources used to provide it (although in 2004 new attempts are being made to measure value added for the public sector services.
- *Self-provided commodities.* A similar problem arises in the case of self-provided commodities, such as vegetables grown in the domestic garden, car repairs and home improvements of a do-it-yourself type. Again, these represent output produced, but there is no market value of such output. The vast majority of self-provided commodities are omitted from the national income statistics.
- *Exports and imports.* Not all of the nation's output is consumed domestically. Part is sold abroad as exports. Nevertheless, GDP is the value of *domestically produced* output and so export earnings must be included in this figure. On the other hand, a great deal of domestically produced output incorporates imported raw materials and components. Hence the value of the import content of the final output must be deducted from the output figures if GDP is to be accurately measured.
- *Net property income from abroad.* This source of income to domestic residents will not be included in the output figures from firms. We have already noted that the net inflow (+) or outflow (−) of funds must be added to GDP when calculating the value of *domestically owned* output, i.e. GNP.

The income method

When calculating national product as a flow of incomes it is important to ensure that only the rewards for factor services are included. In other words, only those incomes paid in return for some productive activity and for which there is a corresponding output are included. Of course, it is the *gross value* of these factor rewards which must be aggregated, since this represents the value of output produced. Levying taxes on factor incomes reduces the amount the factors receive, but it does not reduce the value of the output produced!

- *Transfer payments.* These are simply transfers of income within the community, and they are *not* made in respect of any productive activity. Indeed, the bulk of all transfer payments within the UK are made by the government for social reasons. Examples include social security payments, pensions, child allowances, and so on. Since no output is produced in respect of these payments they must be excluded from the aggregate of factor incomes.
- *Undistributed surpluses.* Another problem in aggregating factor incomes arises because not all factor incomes are distributed to the factors of production. For example, firms might retain part or all of their profits to finance future investment.

Similarly, the profits of public bodies may accrue to the government rather than to private individuals. Care must be taken to include these undistributed surpluses as factor incomes.

- *Stock appreciation*. Care must be taken to *exclude* changes in the money value of inventory or stock caused by inflation. These are windfall gains, and do not represent a real increase in the value of output.
- *Net property income from abroad*. When moving from GDP to either GNP or NNP we have seen that it is necessary to *add* net property income from abroad to the aggregate of domestic incomes.

The expenditure method

The final method of calculating national income is as a flow of expenditure on domestic output.

- *Final output*. It is only expenditure on final output that must be aggregated, otherwise there is again a danger of double counting, with intermediate expenditure on raw materials and components being counted twice.
- *Current output*. It is only expenditure on current output that is relevant. Second-hand goods are not part of the current flow of output, and factors of production have already received payment for these goods at the time they were produced. We should note, however, that any income earned by a salesperson employed in the second-hand trade, or the profits of second-hand dealers, *are* included in the national income statistics. The service these occupations render is part of current production!

Using the symbols of Figure 9.2 (p. 320) we can say that, using the expenditure method:

$$GDP = C + I + G + X - M$$

where C = Consumer expenditure
I = Investment
G = Government expenditure
X = Exports expenditure
M = Imports expenditure

As with the output and income methods, the value of expenditure in the economy must be adjusted if it is to measure national income accurately.

- *Consumer expenditure* (C). This is the major element in expenditure and in 2004 accounted for over 50% of total domestic expenditure in the UK.
- *Investment expenditure* (I). Expenditure on fixed capital, such as plant and machinery, must obviously be included in calculations of total expenditure. Gross domestic fixed capital formation incorporates this item and in 2004 this was around 12% of total domestic expenditure. What is not so obvious is that additions to stock and work in progress also represent investment. The factors of production which have produced

this, as yet, unsold output will still have received factor payments. To ignore additions to stock and work in progress would therefore create an imbalance between the three aggregates of output, income and expenditure. Additions to stock and work in progress are therefore treated as though they have been purchased by firms. Care must be taken to include them in the aggregate of total domestic expenditure.

- *Government expenditure* (G). Since only domestic expenditure on goods and services is relevant, care must be taken to deduct any expenditure on transfer payments by the government or other public authorities. Transfer payments do not contribute directly to the current flow of output and, therefore, we must only include that part of government current expenditure which is spent directly on goods and services. In 2004 government (central and local) expenditure on goods and services was just over 20% of total domestic expenditure.

- *Exports* (X) *and imports* (M). We have already seen that it is important to include exports and exclude imports from our calculation of national income. Care must be taken to ensure this when aggregating total expenditures.

- *Net property income from abroad.* As before, when moving from GDP to GNP or NNP, it is important to include net property income from abroad when aggregating total expenditures.

- *Taxes and subsidies.* In measuring the value of expenditure, we are attempting to measure the value of payments made to the factors of production which have produced that output. Indirect taxes raise total expenditure on goods and services relative to the amount received by the factors of production. Subsidies have the opposite effect. In order to avoid a discrepancy between the income and expenditure totals, it is necessary to remove the effects of taxes and subsidies from the latter. The expenditure total is adjusted to *factor cost* by deducting indirect taxes and adding subsidies

NOTE: THE 'BLACK ECONOMY'

One way in which the so-called 'black economy' can be estimated is through the difference between national income when measured by the *income* method and when measured by the *expenditure* method. Apart from errors and omissions, these are defined in the national accounts in such a way that they come to the same value. If, however, people receive income and do not declare it in tax returns, it will not appear on the income side, though expenditure will increase as the unrecorded income is spent on goods and services. In recent years the 'income' valuation – based on tax returns – has fallen short of the 'expenditure' valuation by progressively larger amounts. Some estimates have the 'black economy' as high as 10–12% of GDP.

Case Study 9.1 looks at various problems with using time series of GDP data to measure changes in the standard of living, especially at times of rapid technological change.

Case Study 9.1 GDP, technical progress and living standards

What has been the overall effect of technological progress on economic well-being? The standard method economists use to address this issue has historically been to use the national income accounts to estimate the rate of growth of real GDP per person. Over the past 25 years this has grown at a little under 2% per year in the UK.

Increasing awareness of the idea of 'sustainable national income' (SNI) has led to proposals to adjust GDP measurement downwards to allow for depletion of natural resources and environmental damage. The idea here is that the loss of these 'non-

Case Study 9.1 continued

renewable' resources will make it more difficult for future generations to enjoy the same benefits as the present generation, i.e. the measure of value of current national income is 'not sustainable'. The implementation of these adjustments is difficult – given the uncertainties involved in, say, identifying climate change and putting an economic value on the *net* impacts of climate change. But looking at recent trends in energy consumption, it seems likely that while the *level* of 'sustainable national income' is less than that of GDP, its *rate of growth* is much the same.

Whilst the discussion so far suggests that the GDP figure is an *overestimate* of SNI, on the other hand there are at least two reasons for arguing that it is an *underestimate* of SNI. First, the contribution made by new goods and services which incorporate technical advances is seriously undervalued. This problem is particularly serious in the context of advances that give fundamentally novel benefits to consumers – for instance, computer applications and mobile phones. The Boskin Commission in the US found that UK growth has been underestimated by perhaps 0.5 to 1.0 percentage points per year since the 1970s because these new products give consumers more output for ever-decreasing prices.

Second, a major gain in well-being has accrued through reduced risk of mortality. The empirical evidence shows that people value this highly, and estimates by Nicholas Crafts suggest the value of improvements since 1973 in terms of equivalent consumption may be about £8,000 per person at 1995 prices.

Incorporating these ideas into the national income measure would roughly double the post-1973 growth rate, raising it from 2% per year to about 4.5% per year from 1973 to the present day.

This has two important implications. First, we are in danger of undervaluing the contribution improvements in technology have made to our standard of living. Second, our failure to include consumer valuations of increased life expectancy in conventional measures of economic growth is potentially skewing policy – say in favour of tax cuts, as opposed to increased health spending.

Source: Adapted from N. Crafts (2002), *Public Lecture to the Royal Economic Society*, 4 December

Questions

1. Why might conventional GDP data be criticised for *overstating* the true increase in living standards?
2. Why might conventional GDP data be criticised for *understating* the true increase in living standards?

We now turn to other problems encountered when using GDP data to make international comparison of standards of living.

National income data: international comparisons

Real GDP per head is often used when comparing the standard of living between countries. Table 9.2 presents some recent data for the (then) 15 members of the European Union in 2002.

Table 9.2 Standards of living in the EU

Member country	Population (millions)	GDP euro (bn)	GDP per capita euro (000s)	Inflation (%)
Austria	8.2	216.4	26.4	2.4
Belgium	10.3	261.4	25.4	1.8
Denmark	5.4	186.6	34.5	2.3
Finland	5.2	139.5	26.8	2.0
France	61.2	1,505.0	24.6	1.6
Germany	82.4	2,107.0	25.6	1.3
Greece	11.0	139.9	12.7	3.1
Ireland	3.9	124.8	32.0	4.7
Italy	58.0	1,252.0	21.6	2.7
Luxembourg	0.4	21.7	54.3	1.9
Netherlands	16.2	446.3	27.5	3.4
Portugal	10.3	129.7	12.5	3.5
Spain	40.5	689.8	17.0	3.6
Sweden	8.9	246.9	27.7	2.0
UK	60.2	1,645.0	27.3	0.9
Total EU	382.1	9,111.0	23.8	1.9

Adapted from *European Commission* (2003), European Commission

- *Absolute levels of GDP.* Clearly there is considerable variation between the EU 15, with Germany, the UK, France and Italy having the four highest *absolute* levels of national income (GDP) measured in euros in 2002, with Luxembourg in last position.
- *GDP per head.* However, when we divide by population size to get GDP per head, Luxembourg moves into first position, having a very small population, with Denmark second, Ireland third and Sweden fourth.
- *Real GDP per head.* Although the 'real' value is not formally given in Table 9.2, we can see why we need to remove inflation from the comparison. Clearly inflation in 2002 was higher in Ireland, Spain, Portugal and Greece than in other EU countries, so the actual *purchasing power* of the 'GDP per head' figure is overstated in these countries as compared to those with lower rates of inflation.

Problems in comparing international standards of living

Even when we do have the official 'real GDP per head' figure for each country, there are still problems in using this data for international comparisons.

- Aspects of one's quality of life may not be reflected in a monetary value, e.g. feelings of safety from attack, access to the countryside, freedom to express one's viewpoint without fear of retribution.
- The same income in one country does not buy the same as in another. For example, even within the EU the prices of goods vary. A recent survey by the Greek tourist board showed that the price of a cup of coffee in Athens was €3.4 while in Paris it cost €1.85.
- Needs vary between countries, for example in hot countries such as Greece and Spain the people do not need to spend as much on clothes or food as those who live in colder climates, though they might have to spend more on water or air conditioning.

Other factors that make international comparisons difficult might include variations between countries in any or all of the following:

- the level of unrecorded activity, such as activity in the informal ('black') economy;
- number of hours that people work;
- the level of public provision of goods and services;
- the distribution of national income (i.e. levels of inequality);
- the levels of negative externalities such as road congestion/pollution.

Such problems in comparing 'quality of life' increase still further when we are using real GDP per head to compare very different countries, such as the EU countries with developing economies in Africa.

Measuring 'well-being' in developing economies

We have suggested that real GDP per head is an important measure of economic well-being (standard of living). However, although this value gives an average figure for income (or output) per head of population, it is particularly unhelpful for measuring 'well-being' in developing economies.

(a) *Inappropriate exchange rates*. Unlike eurozone countries which have a common currency (the euro), converting the value of GDP expressed in a local currency into a $ equivalent using the *official exchange rate* may misrepresent the actual purchasing power in the developing economy. This is because the official exchange rate is influenced by a range of complex forces in the foreign exchange markets and may not accurately reflect the purchasing power of one country's currency in another country.

Watch out! **A more accurate picture is given if we use *purchasing power parities* (PPPs) rather than official exchange rates when making this conversion. Purchasing power parities measure how many units of one country's currency are needed to buy exactly the same basket of goods as can be bought with a given amount of another country's currency.**

(b) *Differing degrees of non-market economic activity*. GDP per capita only includes the money value of recorded (market) transactions involving goods and services. Non-market transactions are excluded. For example, the output of subsistence agriculture, whereby farmers grow food for their own consumption, is excluded from GDP figures. In many less developed economies, where there is often a greater degree of non-market economic activity, this fact may lead GDP figures to underestimate the true living standards.

(c) *Varying levels of inequality*. GDP per capita gives an indication of the 'average' standard of living in a country. However, this may reflect the experience of only a small number of people in that country because its income distribution may be highly unequal, being skewed in the direction of the wealthier sections of society.

(d) *Incidence of externalities*. Externalities occur where actions by an individual or group impose costs (or benefits) on others which are not fully 'priced' (see Chapter 8). Increased pollution is a by-product of many industrial processes, reducing the quality of life for those affected. However, this negative externality may not be reflected in the GDP calculations. Similarly, the GDP figure makes no allowance for the depletion and degradation of natural resources and for the social costs these may impose, e.g. deforestation as a factor in global warming etc.

For these and other reasons (differing accounting conventions, economic and social practices etc.) there has been a move towards the use of indicators *other than* the GDP per capita figure to reflect the 'true' standard of living in developing countries. For example, various 'quality of life' indicators such as life expectancy, medical provision (number of people per doctor or nurse), educational opportunities (age of leaving school) are now widely used. The United Nations has published a Human Development Report since 1990 in which a new method of classification is presented, namely the *Human Development Index*, which incorporates both quality of life indicators and GDP per head data.

Case Study 9.2 looks in rather more detail at why official national income statistics need to be supplemented by other indicators if the true 'quality of life' of those in developing countries is to be assessed. The focus here is particularly on families and children in these developing countries.

Case Study 9.2 Quality of life in developing countries

HIV/Aids, and the poverty associated with it, is hitting children with a force no one foresaw, according to a new study prepared by Unicef for the United Nations Special Session on Children in May 2002. In Africa, in particular, it has already undone the achievements in social development of the last half century. Life expectancy has fallen by between 18 and 23 years in the worst-affected countries; malnutrition has risen; immunisation rates have dropped; more than 13 million children have been orphaned by Aids, 95% of them in Africa; and 4 million children have died of Aids since the epidemic began.

Beyond Africa, in Asia, eastern Europe and the Caribbean, decades of hard-won gains in child development and education are also unravelling. In all these places, where there is increasing poverty, sex is a currency and HIV/Aids has made it a deadly one. In Jamaica girls aged 15 to 19 are three times as likely to contract HIV/Aids as boys in the same age group. While deaths from traditional causes in under-fives are dropping, HIV/Aids has become the second leading cause of death in that age group. In the former Soviet Union 'child poverty has sky-rocketed', according to Unicef. 'Some 18 million of the region's 107 million people are living in poverty. A million and a half children are living in public care because their families are unable to provide for them. This is not what democracy and the market economy was supposed to bring.'

The death of teachers, health workers and other social service staff from Aids is a vicious circle, ravaging services that are crucial to children's welfare and development. Thirty-six million people are living with HIV/Aids, and nearly 22 million have already died. But the stigma associated with Aids makes denial of the disease common. In Mozambique they call it 'the century disease', and most death certificates for Aids patients bear the words 'cause unknown'. Mozambique is typical of the countries where poverty and Aids form a vicious circle, with dramatic consequences for the next generation. Poverty results in sexually transmitted infections going untreated, magnifying 20-fold the risk of HIV transmission; poverty keeps children out of school; and lack of education multiplies the chances of girls selling sex as their only viable economic option.

A report from the World Bank calls education 'crucial to the reduction of world poverty' and promised £1bn new money to countries making progress. But it warned that the goal of getting all children into elementary school by 2015 was unlikely to be met by a quarter of the countries in Africa and South Asia. Poverty is also at the root of the exploitation of children, and another of the session's goals is to raise the awareness of their need for protection. Between 50 million and 60 million children do what the International Labour Organisation considers 'intolerable kinds of work'. A million a year are trapped in sex work; and 300,000 child soldiers fight in 30 wars.

Other goals set in the previous 'World Summit on Children' in 1990 are being reached, such as a drop in infant mortality by one-third in 63 countries; the eradication of polio and guinea-worm disease; a cut of 50% in the 470,000 deaths from neo-natal tetanus; the prevention of a million deaths from diarrhoea and a

Case Study 9.2 continued

million child deaths from vitamin A deficiency; and the protection of 90 million newborns from loss of learning ability from iodine deficiency.

Questions

1. Why might it help to supplement national income data with other indices of quality of life in such countries? What other indices might be used?
2. In what ways does HIV/Aids, and the poverty associated with it, make sustainable development all but impossible for such developing countries?
3. What types of policy interventions might help restore the possibilities of sustainable development?

Despite these problems, national income data is still of great importance to governments and policy makers. We now look in more detail at the various components of the circular flow of income before examining how the equilibrium level of national income is determined in a country.

Components of the circular flow

It will be useful at this point to look at the various components of the circular flow in general terms and consider their relevance for business activity. In the next section we consider these same components rather more technically in terms of their role in determining the equilibrium value of national income.

Savings (S) and Investment (I)

Savings (S)

In the UK household savings have varied considerably over time, from around 2% of household income just after the Second World War to over 12% in the early 1980s and early 1990s. In 2004 this *household savings ratio* had fallen to around 4% of household income.

Of course, *national savings* depend on households, business and the government, all of whom may choose to save part of any extra income rather than spend it. When we aggregate all these savings, some 15% of the UK's national income is saved, which is a lower national savings ratio than that of any other OECD country today except for Turkey (13%) and Portugal (3%).

In the first instance, savings withdraws income from the circular flow, so that excessive savings may discourage business activity by reducing demand for goods and services.

Of course, should these national savings be re-injected back into the economy, as for example by being used for investment purposes, then the situation may be quite different.

Examples:

Thrifty Japan

Worried that the government may not be able to afford to pay for their future pensions, Japan's ageing population prefers to save rather than spend. Even with interest rates effectively zero per cent, this concern for the future has meant that Japanese banks are awash with savings. Unfortunately, over the past decade so few firms want to borrow these savings for investment that with so much saving and so little consumer spending the Japanese economy has barely grown.

Investment (I)

Investment expenditure is around 12% of total expenditure in the UK, i.e. around one-quarter the value of consumption expenditure (see p. 344). Nevertheless, investment is arguably one of the most significant components of total expenditure. It is highly volatile and through its impacts on productivity affects both the supply and demand sides of the economy.

Quote

> In discussing the volatility of investment, John Maynard Keynes noted that expectations of business people could change dramatically at the first sign of good or bad news, using the phrase 'animal spirits' to describe the unpredictable temperament of investors. He went on to state that the prospective yields of investment projects were based on: '... partly future events which can only be forecasted with more or less confidence'.
>
> *(Keynes, 1936, p. 147)*

In practice, a number of important variables may influence the firm's desire to invest in new projects. These are explored further in Box 9.1.

Box 9.1

What determines investment

Rate of interest

Lower rates of interest will encourage firms to invest more since the expected returns on some projects will now exceed the costs of borrowing to fund these projects. This is the reasoning behind the so-called *marginal efficiency of investment* (MEI) theory.

The MEI approach uses a rate of discount (i) to derive the *present value* (PV) of various investment projects. Strictly, the MEI of a particular project is that rate of discount which would equate the PV of the expected future income stream from a project with its initial capital outlay (the supply price):

$$S = PV = \frac{R_1}{(1+i)} + \frac{R_2}{(1+i)^2} + \frac{R_3}{(1+i)^3} + \cdots \frac{R_n}{(1+i)^n}$$

where S = the supply price
PV = present value
R = the expected yearly return; and
i = that rate of discount necessary to equate the present value of future income with the initial cost of the project.

The curve relating the marginal efficiency of investment (i) to the level of investment in Figure 9.3 is negatively sloped, for two main reasons.

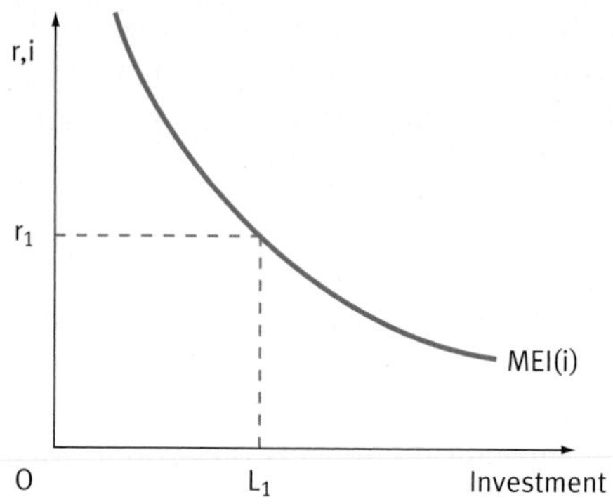

Fig 9.3 The investment demand schedule

- First, the earliest investment projects undertaken are likely to be the most profitable, i.e. offering the highest expected yearly returns (r) and therefore having the highest marginal efficiencies of investment (i). As more projects are initiated, they are likely to be less and less profitable, with lower expected yearly returns, and therefore lower MEIs.
- Second, a rise in the level of investment undertaken is, at least in the short run, likely to raise the supply price (S), which in turn will reduce the MEI. This could follow if the industries producing capital goods faced capacity constraints in their attempt to raise output in the short run.

The decision on whether to proceed with an investment project will depend on the relationship between the rate of interest (r) and the marginal efficiency of investment (i). If r is less than i then the annual cost of borrowing funds for an additional project will be less than the expected annual return on the initial capital outlay, so that the project will be profitable to undertake.

In Figure 9.3 with interest rate r_1 it will be profitable to invest in all projects up to i_1 with i_1 itself breaking even. The MEI schedule is therefore the *investment demand schedule*, telling us the level of investment that will be undertaken at any given rate of interest.

Expectations play an important role in this theory of investment. If, as is often the case, expectations are volatile, then the expected yearly returns (r) on any project will change, causing substantial shifts in the MEI schedule At any given rate of interest investment demand will therefore be changing, which will reduce the closeness of any statistical fit between the interest rate and investment.

In fact, it may be via expectations that interest rates exert their major influence on investment. A fall in rates is often a signal to investors of better times ahead, raising expected returns, shifting the MEI curve to the right, and raising investment (and conversely).

Accelerator theory

This suggests that if the existing capital stock is being fully used, then any *change in output* (ΔY) can only be achieved by new (net) investment (I_n). It also assumes that the capital/output ratio is some constant representing the extra value of capital needed on average to secure £1 of additional output.

$$\text{i.e.} \quad I_n = a\Delta Y$$

Suppose national output is at full capacity and rises (ΔY) by £4m during the year, with £5 of new investment in capital needed, on average, for each extra £1 of output ($a = 5$) to be produced. New investment (I_n) will then be 5 × £4m = £20m according to this accelerator theory.

An obvious weakness is that if there is spare capacity, then new investment will not be needed to raise output.

Profitability

There are at least two reasons why changes in profitability might be associated with changes in investment.

1 Higher profits may improve business confidence and raise the expected future return on any project. An outward shift of the MEI schedule (see Figure 9.3) might then raise investment at any given rate of interest.
2 Higher profits may raise investment by reducing its cost, as funds generated internally are cheaper than those obtained from any other source.

Taxation (T) and government expenditure (G)

Taxation (T)

Around 38% of all UK national income is currently taken in various forms of taxation on household income (income tax and National Insurance payments), company income (corporation tax) and household and company expenditure (VAT, customs and excise duties) etc. Such taxes represent, at least initially, a withdrawal from the circular flow of income and the total tax take is likely to rise as household and corporate incomes and expenditures increase.

Example: **National rates of taxation**

The UK is only a middle-ranked country in terms of taxation. Whereas some 38% of UK national income is taken in all types of tax, the figure is much higher for countries such as Sweden (53%), Denmark (49%), Austria (46%), Belgium (45%) and many others, although the US has a much smaller tax take at only 30% of national income.

Government expenditure (G)

Government expenditure is currently around 41% of total expenditure in the UK and is planned to rise to over 42% by 2005. Extra government spending will result in extra

LINKS
A more detailed treatment of both taxation and government expenditure can be found in Chapter 10, pp. 371–384).

income for those employed in the growing public sector or for the private firms used in providing public sector goods and services. These households and firms will in turn spend some of their extra income on the output of other businesses, further raising incomes and employment (see the 'multiplier', p. 354).

Imports (M) and exports (X)

Imports (M)

Imports, like savings and taxation, are treated as a withdrawal from the circular flow since income received is not passed on as expenditure to domestic firms or households. Imports of goods and services have risen substantially in the UK in recent years, and in 2003 exceeded exports of goods and services by around £36bn. As national income rises in the UK so does consumer expenditure (see p. 344), but much of this extra spending is going on imported goods and services.

It is on the goods side that imports have risen the fastest. In fact, imports exceeded exports of goods in the UK by around £50bn in 2003, whereas imports fell short of exports of services in the UK by around £14bn.

Example:

Increased import penetration in goods

Whereas imports made up 54% of total UK sales of computers in 1998, by 2003 that figure had risen to over 60%. For TVs and radios this import penetration ratio increased from 47% in 1998 to over 54% in 2003, and for motor vehicles from 43% in 1998 to around 46% in 2003.

There is strong evidence to suggest that a high proportion of any extra national income is spent on imported goods and services, particularly the former. Estimates indicate that the income elasticity of demand (see p. 64) for imported goods and services is around +2 for the UK, suggesting that for each 1% rise in real income, total demand for imported goods and services rises by 2%.

Our assumption throughout this chapter that imports rise with national income (as do savings and taxes) is therefore quite realistic. These three items, savings, taxes and imports, comprise 'total withdrawals' in the circular flow model, since in all cases income received is *not* passed directly on to domestic households and firms.

Exports (X)

As we have already noted, exports of goods and services fell short of imports by some £36bn in the UK in 2003. As with investments and government spending, exports result in a demand for goods and services from domestic households and businesses. Therefore these three items of expenditure, together with consumer expenditure, are regarded as 'aggregate expenditure' in the circular flow model. However, these three items (I + G + X) are treated separately as 'injection' expenditures (J) which do not vary with the level of national income, unlike consumer expenditure (C) which is assumed to vary with the level of national income (see p. 344).

Equilibrium in the circular flow: W/J approach

NOTE
This time it is strictly correct to use an equals (=) sign because W will only equal J for certain values of the variable (national income), not for all values of that variable.

'Equilibrium' or balance in the circular flow will occur, using this approach, when the value of withdrawals (W) from the circular flow exactly matches the value of injections (J) into the circular flow.

i.e. W = J is the equilibrium condition

Finding the equilibrium value of national income

To make the analysis simple, it is often assumed that the value of withdrawals (W) and of all its components (S, T and M) are *directly related* to the level of national income (Y). In other words, as national income (Y) rises, so does the value of savings (S), taxes (T) and imports (M) and therefore of withdrawals (W), defined as S + T + M. This situation is shown in Figure 9.4 and is further explored on pages 339–342 below.

Checkpoint 1

1 Can you explain why it is reasonable to suppose that the W schedule will rise as national income (Y) rises?

2 Can you explain why the W schedule intersects the vertical axis at a negative value in Figure 9.4?

However, it is often assumed in the W/J approach that the value of injections (J) is *unrelated* to the level of national income (Y). As we can see from Figure 9.4, this means that the injections schedule (J) is shown as a horizontal straight line, suggesting that the values of investment (I), government expenditure (G) and exports (X) are unchanged as national income rises or falls.

Checkpoint 2

Can you explain why this assumption for injections (J), while it helps to make the analysis easier, is actually unrealistic?

All the relationships in Figure 9.4 are assumed to be linear, so that the 'curves' can be drawn as straight lines.

In terms of the circular flow, we say that the various injections (I, G and X) are *exogenous variables*, determined outside the model, as these are independent of national income (Y). However, the various withdrawals (S, T and M) are *endogenous* variables, determined inside the model as they are dependent on national income (Y).

Before examining the individual components in Figure 9.4 more carefully, we can use the diagram to indicate why the *equilibrium* value for national income is Y_1. To do this we might look at values for national income that are *not* equilibrium values.

- *National income level* Y_2. Here withdrawals exceed injections (by g – h) so the value of the circular flow of income (Y) will fall. It will continue to fall until

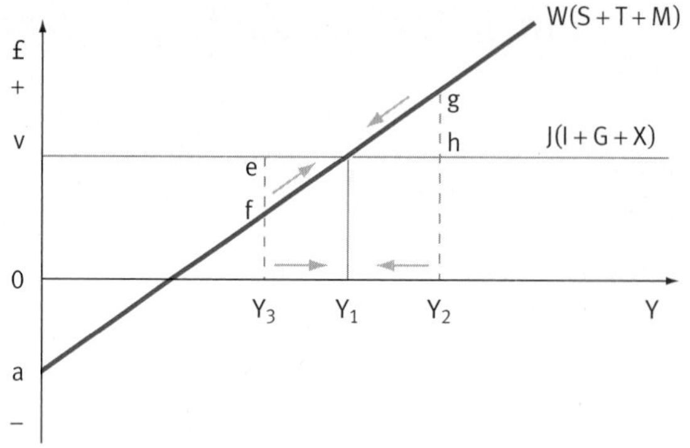

Fig 9.4 Equilibrium in the circular flow: W/J approach

withdrawals have fallen sufficiently to exactly equal the unchanged value of injections at national income level Y_1.

- *National income level* Y_3. Here injections exceed withdrawals (by e – f) so the value of the circular flow of income (Y_3) will rise. It will continue to rise until withdrawals have risen sufficiently to exactly equal the unchanged value of injections at national income level Y_1.

Only at national income level Y_1, where W = J, is there no further tendency for national income to change. We then say we have an equilibrium (balanced) level of income at Y_1 only.

We have seen that *investment* is an important component of injections into the circular flow. However, Case Study 9.3 points out that it may be possible to have 'too much of a good thing'!

Case Study 9.3 China's $29 test

FT

The fact that Wal-Mart can sell Chinese-made DVD players in the US for $29 (£16) is not just a testament to the miraculous productivity of the Chinese economy and the cheapness of its labour. It is also a warning of the dangers of over-investment. Chinese policy makers, justifiably proud of the announcement that the economy grew 9.1% in 2003, should consider the wider implications of the DVD phenomenon as they struggle to guide China in the right direction.

Dong Tao of Credit Suisse First Boston in Hong Kong is among economists predicting a Chinese slowdown in the next three years – to 7% growth or less, he says – as investment stalls after a period of extraordinary exuberance. The oversupply of DVD machines as a result of too much investment three years ago is now being replicated in many other industries.

China's already substantial output of steel, cars, textiles, ethylene, mobile telephones and much else besides is expected to double in the next three years, with unpredictable

Case Study 9.3 continued

and probably damaging results for prices. The country is on a wild, wild capex ride, says Mr Tao. 'China is in a situation of severe over-investment.' Fortunately, Chinese leaders seem to agree. They are tackling the problem by trying to limit investment in overheated 'bubble' sectors such as vehicle assembly and urban property. One of the most encouraging signs is that credit growth slowed in the fourth quarter of 2003, limiting the vulnerability of state banks already burdened with bad debts.

As China enters a phase of more moderate growth the government is also right to shift the focus from investment to consumption, and to favour the neglected rural and inland provinces. In spite of the cheapness of manufactured goods, yesterday's data showed that China had pulled itself out of deflation thanks to rising food prices – a boon to productive peasants and an effective form of wealth redistribution from city to countryside.

China's impressive economic performance in 2003, the best for seven years, was good for the country's 1.3bn inhabitants and good for the world, prompting the statistics chief who unveiled the figures to hail 'a milestone in Chinese economic history'. For the first time, China's gross domestic product exceeded $1,000 per capita. In purchasing power parity terms, the country contributed 1.1% of the world's 3.2% growth last year, against 0.7% from the US and 0.2% each from Japan and Europe.

Beijing even has a cushion to fall back on if growth slows faster than predicted, since most economists believe official figures are underestimates. Power consumption, transport statistics and other indicators suggest an actual 2003 growth rate of more than 11%. The tale of the throwaway DVD player, however, may yet return to haunt Chinese industry.

Source: Financial Times, 21 January 2004

Questions

1 What is meant by 'the danger of over-investment'?

2 What are the benefits of 'shifting the focus from investment to consumption'?

It will be useful at this point to look rather more carefully at the withdrawals and injections schedules. We will come across the important ideas of *marginal propensities* and *average propensities* in this part of our analysis.

Withdrawals schedule (W)

It will be useful at this stage to consider in greater detail the *direct* relationship we have assumed to exist between each component of withdrawals (i.e. S, T and M) and the level of national income (Y).

Withdrawals (W) and national income (Y)

Here we examine in more detail the suggestion of Figure 9.5 that each component of W (i.e. S, T and M) varies directly with the level of national income (Y), i.e. rising as Y rises, falling as Y falls.

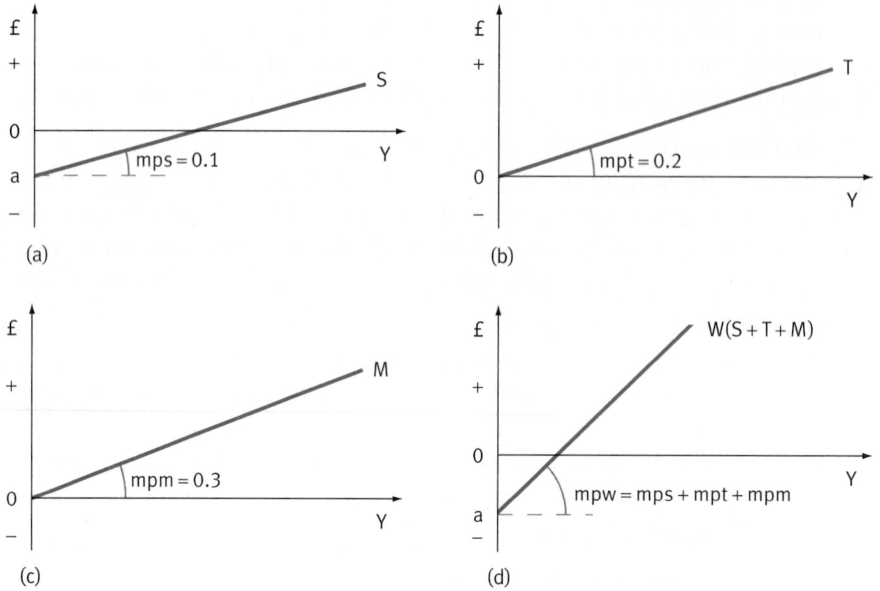

Fig 9.5 How savings (S), taxes (T), imports (M) and withdrawals (W) vary with national income (Y)

The savings (S), taxes (T) and imports (M) schedules are all drawn as straight lines, which assumes a *linear* relationship between each component and national income (Y). However, one difference is immediately apparent, namely that the savings schedule (S) does *not* go through the origin (zero). Rather Figure 9.5(a) shows S as having a negative value (–a) when national income (Y) is zero. The suggestion here is that at zero income, households will still have to spend some money on consuming various goods and services, and this can only come from running down past savings (i.e. *dissaving* or negative savings).

However, it is often assumed, as in Figure 9.5(b), that at zero income the government receives no tax revenue and, as in Figure 9.5(c), that at zero income there is no spending on imports. It follows that the T and M schedules go through the origin (zero).

In Figure 9.5(d) the withdrawals schedule (W) is shown as the aggregate of the three previous schedules (S + T + M).

For example, suppose we have the following relationships for S, T and M with respect to national income (Y).

$$S = -5 + 0.1Y$$
$$T = 0.2Y$$
$$M = 0.3Y$$

Then $\underline{W = -5 + 0.6Y}$

We can use this last relationship to explore the ideas of *marginal propensity to withdraw* and *average propensity to withdraw*. This important but rather technical material is considered in Box 9.2.

Box 9.2 Marginal and average propensity to withdraw

Marginal propensity to withdraw (mpw)

This is a ratio of the change in total withdrawals (ΔW) to the change in national income (ΔY). For example, if the household withdraws 60 pence out of an extra £1 of income, then *mpw* = 0.6. For any straight line (linear) withdrawals schedule this is given by the slope of the line, and is a constant over its entire length.

- Marginal propensity to withdraw (*mpw*) $= \dfrac{\text{Change in Withdrawals}}{\text{Change in National Income}} = \dfrac{\Delta W}{\Delta Y}$

where Δ = 'change in'

The *mpw* is shown in Figure 9.5(d) as the slope of the straight line withdrawals schedule (W). We have found this to be 0.6, suggesting that for every £1 rise in national income, 60 pence is withdrawn.

Other marginal propensities

You should be able to see that:

- Marginal propensity to save (*mps*) $= \dfrac{\text{Change in Savings}}{\text{Change in National Income}} = \dfrac{\Delta S}{\Delta Y} = 0.1$
- Marginal propensity to tax (*mpt*) $= \dfrac{\text{Change in Taxation}}{\text{Change in National Income}} = \dfrac{\Delta T}{\Delta Y} = 0.2$
- Marginal propensity to import (*mpm*) $= \dfrac{\text{Change in Imports}}{\text{Change in National Income}} = \dfrac{\Delta M}{\Delta Y} = 0.3$

mpw = *mps* + *mpt* + *mpm*

Average propensity to withdraw (*apw*)

However, we are often interested in the *average* as well as marginal propensities. The difference between *apw* and *mpw* is shown in Figure 9.6.

$$\text{Average propensity to withdraw } (apw) = \frac{\text{Total Withdrawals}}{\text{Total National Income}} = \frac{W}{Y}$$

Using the withdrawals (W) schedule in Figure 9.6:

$$W = -5 + 0.6Y$$

At, say, $Y_1 = 20$

$$W_1 = -5 + 0.6\,(20)$$

i.e. $W_1 = 7$

We can therefore say that at a level of national income (Y_1) of 20:

$$apw = \tfrac{7}{20} = 0.35$$

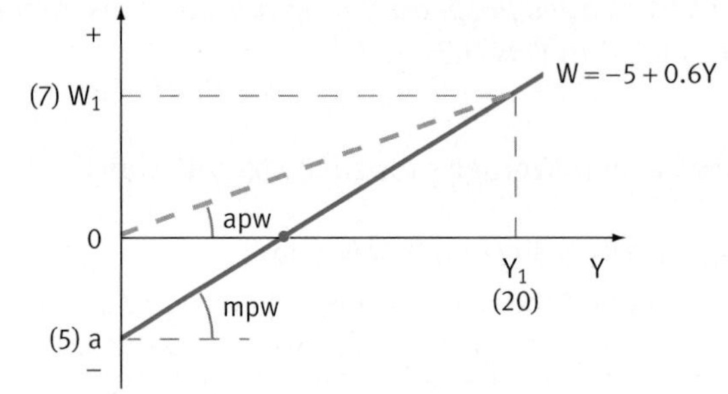

Fig 9.6 The withdrawals function (W), average propensity to withdraw (*apw*) and marginal propensity to withdraw (*mpw*)

We should be able to see from Figure 9.6 that *apw* is the slope of the straight line drawn from the origin to the relevant point on the withdrawals schedule (W). We should also be able to see that *apw* (unlike *mpw*) will rise continuously as the level of national income rises.

Checkpoint 3 gives you the opportunity to think about the other average propensities to save, tax and import.

Checkpoint 3

1 Define average propensity to save (*aps*)
average propensity to tax (*apt*)
average propensity to import (*apm*).

2 Using Figure 9.5(a), (b) and (c) on p. 340, calculate the respective average propensities when national income (Y) is 20 (assume the vertical intercept is −5 in Figure 9.5 (a)).

3 Using Figure 9.5(a), (b) and (c), suggest how the following relate to each other:
(a) *mps* and *aps*;
(b) *mpt* and *apt*;
(c) *mpm* and *apm*.

Injections schedule (J)

As already mentioned, we assume that each component of J (i.e. I, G and X) does *not* vary with national income, even though this may be something of an oversimplification. The injection schedule (J) is therefore drawn as a horizontal straight line at some given value *v* in Figure 9.4 (p. 338).

Put another way, we are treating each component of injections (i.e. I, G and X) as an *exogenous variable*, i.e. one that affects the equilibrium value of the circular flow but whose value is determined outside the circular flow.

Equilibrium in the circular flow: 45° diagram approach

An alternative approach to the W/J diagram in finding the equilibrium level of national income involves the 45° diagram. This approach makes use of the expenditure method (p. 325) of calculating national income.

The term *aggregate expenditure* (E) (or *aggregate demand*) is sometimes used to describe (C + I + G + X).

Under this approach, the equilibrium level of national income occurs where the value of aggregate expenditure (E) exactly equals the value of national output (Y).

$$E = Y$$
$$\text{i.e. } C + I + G + X = Y \text{ in equilibrium}$$

Figure 9.7 represents this situation, with equilibrium national income at Y_1 (where $E_1 = Y_1$). Notice that the 45° line represents all the values in the diagram for which E = Y.

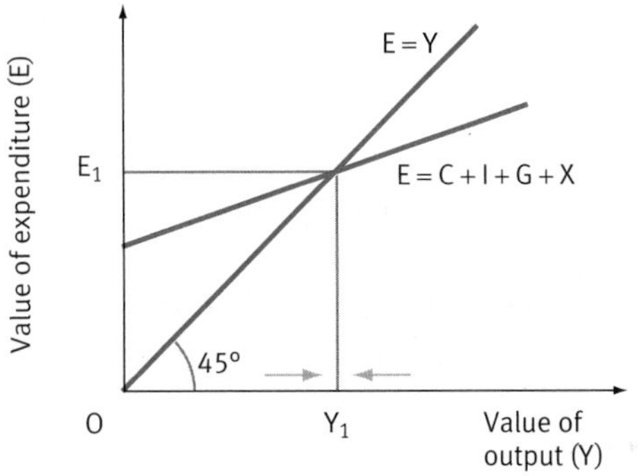

Fig 9.7 Equilibrium in the circular flow: 45° diagram approach

Checkpoint 4

Can you use the idea of a right-angled triangle to prove why E = Y at all points along the 45° diagram?

It follows that only where the aggregate expenditure schedule E *intersects* the 45° diagram do we fulfil the equilibrium condition E = Y.

- At levels of national income *above* Y_1, the value of expenditure *is less than* the value of output (i.e. $E < Y$), so the value of output falls.
- At levels of national income *below* Y_1, the value of expenditure *is greater than* the value of output (i.e. $E > Y$), so the value of output rises.
- Only at Y_1 where the aggregate expenditure schedule intersects the 45° line do we have the value of expenditure *exactly equal* to the value of output, i.e. an equilibrium ($E_1 = Y_1$) at which the value of output does not change.

The *aggregate expenditure* schedule (E) in Figure 9.7 includes the *consumption schedule* (C), sometimes called the *consumption function*. We now consider this consumption function in rather more detail, together with the important ideas of the marginal propensity to consume (*mpc*) and the average propensity to consume (*apc*).

The consumption function

Consumption is the most important single element in aggregate expenditure in the UK, accounting for around half its total value. John Maynard Keynes related consumption to current disposable income, and his ideas are embodied in the so-called consumption function.

Quote

In the *General Theory*, Keynes argued that

> 'the fundamental psychological law ... is that men are disposed, as a rule and on the average, to increase their consumption as their income increases, but not by as much as the increase in their income'.
>
> *(Keynes 1936, p. 96)*

From this statement can be derived the Keynesian consumption function.

The *consumption function* shows how consumer expenditure (C) varies directly with the level of national income (Y). In Figure 9.8 we can see that at zero national income consumption (C) is +a. Consumer spending with zero income can only be achieved by running down past savings (i.e. *dissaving*), as we noted in Figure 9.5(a) previously. Again we assume a straight-line (linear) relationship between consumption (C) and national income (Y).

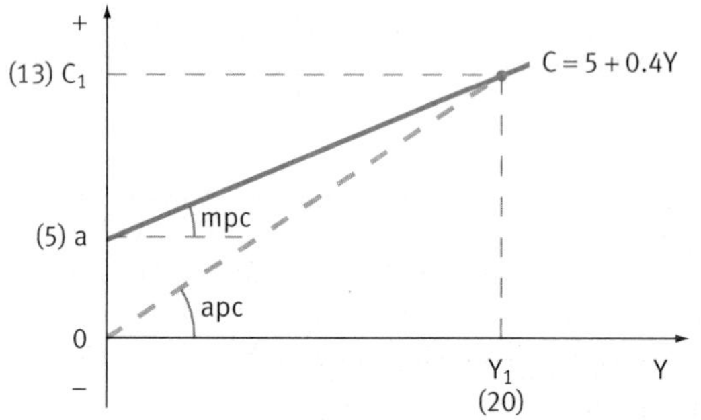

Fig 9.8 The consumption function C, average propensity to consume (*apc*) and marginal propensity to consume (*mpc*)

Case Study 9.4 looks a little more closely at the *consumption function* which plays such an important role in the circular flow of income.

Case Study 9.4 Consumer behaviour and indebtedness

The 'consumption function' in Figure 9.8 (p. 344) relates consumer spending to the current level of income of individuals and the nation. As we noted above, it is assumed that consumer spending will rise as national income rises. However, in reality, consumer spending may depend on much more than the current level of national income.

Certainly the consumer has been widely seen as sustaining the UK economy by continuing to purchase goods and services, creating extra output and employment. However, there is major concern that the growing 'debt overhang' may reduce consumer spending sharply in the near future. Figures from the Bank of England in 2004 showed that the average indebted household in Britain owed £3,516 in *unsecured debt* (hire purchase, credit cards, personal loans, overdrafts).

'Richer households' – defined as those earning more than £17,500 a year – owed an average of £4,991 in unsecured debt, while the 'poorer households' – defined as those earning less than £9,500 a year – owed an average of £1,936. Credit card debt was a major source of debt at all income levels, but (with student loan debt) especially for the 'poorer' income household.

A major concern for analysts is that any sustained rise in interest rates will make it extremely difficult for UK households to keep up their repayments on all types of debt, secured and unsecured. For example, in September 2003, almost £11bn was borrowed in one month alone, some £9bn of this being borrowed against property in the form of mortgages. This extra borrowing in just one month amounted to the equivalent of 1% of the country's entire annual wealth in just 30 days!

Mortgage debt is *secured debt* but will create major problems for consumers should interest rates rise. In October 2003, London and Country Mortgage brokers estimated the following impact of rises in mortgage rates above the then 3.5% per annum. Table 9.3 indicates the *increases* in monthly payments on different values of mortgages if interest rates rose by specified amounts.

Table 9.3 How mortgage payments could rise

Mortgage	Current monthly payments	Increase if base rate rises to		
		4.0%	4.5%	5.0%
£100,000	£292	£42	£83	£125
£250,000	£729	£103	£208	£313
£500,000	£1,458	£208	£417	£625
£750,000	£2,198	£313	£625	£938

Many people are projecting that UK interest rates will indeed rise to 5.0% or more during 2004/5 and beyond.

Case Study 9.4 continued

Questions

1 What impact would higher interest rates have on the consumption function in Figure 9.8 (p. 344)?

2 How would this influence the equilibrium level of national income?

3 Are there any policy measures which government might take to help reduce this potential problem?

It may be useful at this point to explore the ideas of *marginal propensity to consume* and *average propensity to consume*. This important but rather technical material is considered in Box 9.3.

Box 9.3 Marginal and average propensity to consume

Marginal propensity to consume (mpc)

The marginal propensity to consume (*mpc*) is a ratio of the change in total consumption (ΔC) to the change in national income (ΔY). For example, if the consumer spends 40 pence out of an extra £1 of income, then *mpc* = 0.4. For any straight-line (linear) relationship this is given by the slope of the line, and is a constant over its entire length.

$$\text{Marginal propensity to consume } (mpc) = \frac{\text{Change in consumption}}{\text{Change in national income}} = \frac{\Delta C}{\Delta Y}$$

where Δ = 'change in'

The *mpc* is shown in Figure 9.8 as the slope of the straight-line consumption function (C), and has the value 0.4. This suggests that for every £1 rise in national income, 40 pence is consumed.

mpc and mpw

It is worth noting an important relationship between *mpc* and *mpw* (strictly speaking, this is an identity ≡)

$$mpc + mpw \equiv 1$$

This must follow from our earlier Figure 9.2 (p. 320) which showed that any income received by domestic households (H) is either consumed (passed on in the circular flow) or withdrawn from the circular flow.

It follows that any change in Y(ΔY)

$$\Delta Y = C + W$$

$$\Delta Y = \Delta C + \Delta W$$

and dividing throughout by ΔY

$$\frac{\Delta Y}{\Delta Y} = \frac{\Delta C}{\Delta Y} + \frac{\Delta W}{\Delta Y}$$

$$\underline{1 = mpc + mpw}$$

We can therefore also say that

$$1 - mpc = mpw$$

Average propensity to consume (apc)

However, we are often interested in the average propensity to consume (*apc*). This is shown in Figure 9.8.

$$\text{Average propensity to consume } (apc) = \frac{\text{Total consumption}}{\text{Total national income}} = \frac{C}{Y}$$

Using the consumption function (C) in Figure 9.8:

$$C = 5 + 0.4Y$$

$$\text{At, say, } Y_1 = 20$$

$$C_1 = 5 + 0.4\,(20)$$

$$\text{i.e.} \quad C_1 = 13$$

We can therefore say that at a level of national income (Y_1) of 20:

$$apc = \frac{13}{20} = 0.65$$

We should be able to see from Figure 9.8 that *apc* is the slope of the straight line drawn from the origin to the relevant point on the consumption function (C). We should also be able to see that *apc* (unlike *mpc*) will fall continuously as the level of national income rises.

apc and apw

$$\text{If} \quad C + W = Y \text{ (see above)}$$

$$\text{Then } \frac{C}{Y} + \frac{W}{Y} = \frac{Y}{Y} \quad (\div \text{ by } Y)$$

$$apc + apw = 1$$

Other influences on consumer spending

As well as current income, other variables have been suggested as influencing current consumption expenditure. A number of theories have focused on the real value of *wealth* as influencing current consumption, therefore bringing other variables into play.

- *Interest rates*. If interest rates rise, then individuals are assumed to feel more secure as to the future returns from their asset holdings. If so, they may be inclined to spend more at any given level of current disposable income. In terms of Figure 9.8, the consumption function (C) will shift vertically upwards.
- *Price level*. If there is a rise in the general level of prices (inflation) then the value of people's money balances (wealth) will fall. They may therefore spend less of their current income in order to increase their money balances in an attempt to restore their initial real value. In terms of Figure 9.8, the consumption function (C) will shift vertically downwards as a result of this so-called 'real balance' effect.

Equivalence of the two approaches

Suppose we are faced with the situation shown in Table 9.4.

Table **9.4** National income equilibrium

National income (Y) (£bn)	Planned consumption (C) (£bn)	Planned withdrawals (W) (£bn)	Planned injections (J) (£bn)	Planned expenditure (E = C + J) (£bn)	Change in national income
0	12	−12	4	16	Increase
10	18	−8	4	22	Increase
20	24	−4	4	28	Increase
30	30	0	4	34	Increase
40	36	4	4	40	No change
50	42	8	4	46	Decrease
60	48	12	4	52	Decrease
70	54	16	4	58	Decrease
80	60	20	4	64	Decrease

Figure 9.9 presents the data in Table 9.4 using both the W/J and 45° diagrams.

- *W/J approach*
  - At all levels of national income *below* £40bn, planned injections exceed planned withdrawals (J > W). More is being added to the circular flow than is being withdrawn from it, so the value of that flow (national income) must rise.
  - At all levels of national income *above* £40bn, the opposite is true (J < W), and national income must fall.
  - At £40bn national income planned injections of £4bn exactly equal planned withdrawals of £4bn (J = W), and the level of national income is stable, i.e. in equilibrium.
- *45° diagram (aggregate expenditure) approach*
  - At all levels of national income *below* £40bn, planned aggregate expenditure (E = C + J) exceeds the national output/national income (i.e. E > Y). The value of Y must rise – either quantity of output rises or prices rise or both.
  - At all levels of national income *above* £40bn, the opposite is true (E < Y), and national income (Y) must fall.
  - At £40bn national income planned aggregate expenditure of £40bn exactly equals the value of national output/income of £40bn (E = Y), and the level of national income is stable, i.e. in equilibrium.

Activity 9.1 gives you the chance to self-check your understanding of the material discussed so far.

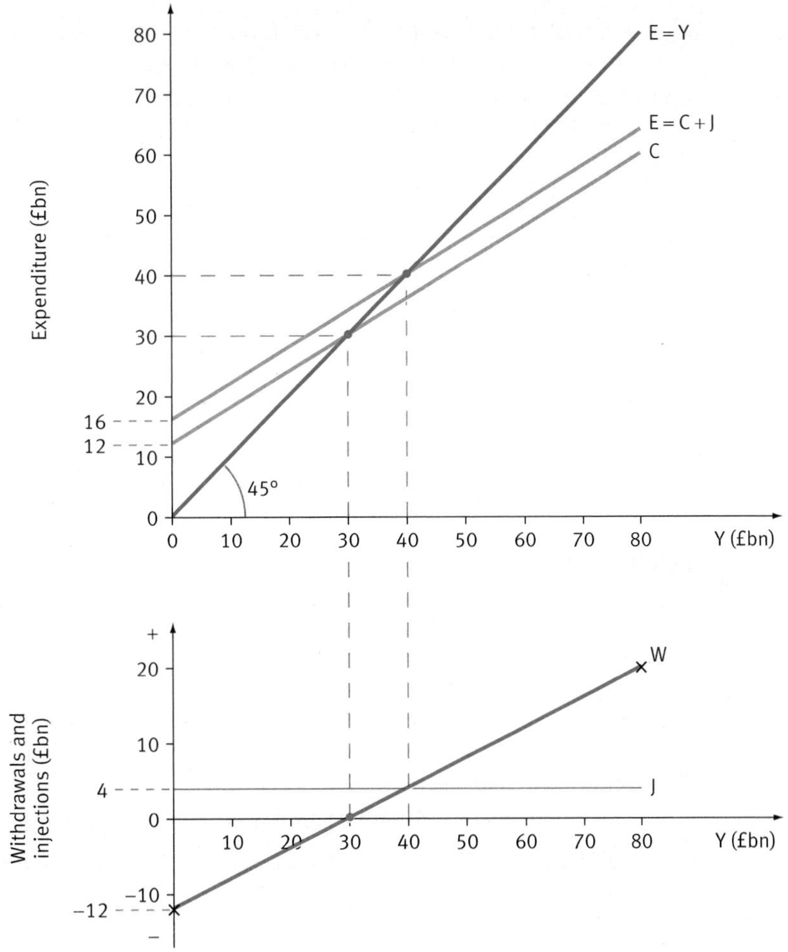

Fig 9.9 Equilibrium national income using W/J and 45° diagrams

Activity 9.1

1 In this question you have a description of a particular type of transaction in the circular flow of income. Try to match the *lettered* description with the correct *numbered* term.

Descriptions

(a) Ford, UK sells 50,000 Range Rovers to South Africa.
(b) A successful advertising campaign by Virgin Cola results in greater sales in its domestic (UK) market.
(c) A rise in the pound : euro exchange rate causes Toyota UK to switch from UK-based component suppliers to those located in the Eurozone.
(d) The main GlaxoSmithKline production plant in the UK purchases new machinery from another UK firm to produce its pharmaceuticals.

(e) A rise in UK interest rates raises the amount of money placed by domestic residents in various types of interest-bearing deposit accounts.
(f) A government contract to build a major trunk road is withdrawn because of environmental protests.

Terms

(i) Consumption expenditure (C)
(ii) Investment expenditure (I)
(iii) Government expenditure (G)
(iv) Exports (X)
(v) Savings (S)
(vi) Taxes (T)
(vii) Imports (M)

2 In this question you'll see a description of a particular type of measurement used for national output/income and a list of terms. Try to match the *lettered* description with its correct *numbered* term.

Descriptions

(a) The value of incomes received by residents located within a country (including indirect taxes and subsidies).
(b) Pensions paid by the government to residents of that country.
(c) The gross income received by residents minus the direct taxes they pay.
(d) The value of incomes received by residents of a country from their ownership of resources, wherever these are located (but excluding direct taxes and subsidies).
(e) Inward payments received by residents from their ownership of overseas property minus outward payments made by residents from their ownership of domestic property.
(f) GNP minus the depreciation of physical assets.

Terms

(i) Transfer payment
(ii) Net property income from abroad
(iii) GDP at market prices
(iv) GDP at factor cost
(v) GNP at market prices
(vi) GNP at factor cost
(vii) Net national product (NNP)
(viii) Disposable income

3 The value of national income (output) can be expressed in a number of different ways. Try to match the *lettered* description with its correct *numbered* term.

Descriptions

(a) Value of output produced (and incomes received) by factors of production located within that country.
(b) Value of output produced (and incomes received) by residents of that country wherever they are located.

(c) This measure takes into account the fact that some capital equipment will have depreciated over the year via wear and tear or because technological change has made it obsolescent.
(d) Measures of national output/income which *include* indirect taxes and subsidies.
(e) Measures of national output/income which *exclude* indirect taxes and subsidies.

Terms

(i) Factor cost
(ii) Gross national product (GNP)
(iii) Net national product (NNP)
(iv) Market prices
(v) Gross domestic product (GDP)

4 Look carefully at the table below:

National income (Y)	Planned savings (S)	Planned taxation (T)	Planned expenditure on imports (M)	Planned investment (I)	Planned government expenditure (G)	Planned export sales (X)	Tendency to change in national income
0	−1,000	0	0	600	900	500	
1,000	−800	200	100	600	900	500	
2,000	−600	400	200	600	900	500	
3,000	−400	600	300	600	900	500	
4,000	−200	800	400	600	900	500	
5,000	0	1,000	500	600	900	500	
6,000	200	1,200	600	600	900	500	
7,000	400	1,400	700	600	900	500	
8,000	600	1,600	800	600	900	500	

(a) Fill in the last column, using *one* of the three terms 'increase', 'decrease', 'no change'.
(b) Use the information in the table to complete the following.

National income (Y)	Withdrawals (W)	Injections (J)
0		
1,000		
2,000		
3,000		
4,000		
5,000		
6,000		
7,000		
8,000		

(c) Draw the W/J diagram.

(d) Can you express each of the following as a schedule? The first has been done for you. (Check back to Figure 9.5, p. 340).

Savings (S) $= -1000 + 0.2Y$
Taxes (T) =
Imports (M) =
Withdrawals (W) =

(e) Now use the information given in the table at the beginning to complete the following table:

National income (Y)	Consumption (C)	Injections (J)	Aggregate expenditure (E)
0			
1,000			
2,000			
3,000			
4,000			
5,000			
6,000			
7,000			
8,000			

Hint: Any income received by domestic households is either passed on in the circular flow (consumed) or withdrawn.

i.e. $Y = C + W$
so $\underline{Y - W = C}$

(f) Draw the 45° diagram.
(g) What is equilibrium national income using this 'aggregate expenditure' approach? What do you notice?

Answers to Checkpoints and Activities can be found on pp. 705–35.

Changes in national income

We can use our earlier Figure 9.4 (p. 338) to consider the effect of changes in withdrawals (W) or injections (J) on the *equilibrium* level of national income.

Changes in injections (J)

Increase in J (I + G + X)

As Figure 9.10(a) indicates, an *increase* in injections (ΔJ) from J_1 to J_2, will (other things equal) result in an increase in national income (ΔY) from Y_1 to Y_2. This upward shift in the injections schedule may result from an increase in investment (ΔI), government expenditure (ΔG), exports (ΔX) or in all three components.

At the original equilibrium Y_1, injections now exceed withdrawals, so the value of national income must rise. As national income rises, withdrawals rise (move along W). National income will continue to rise until withdrawals have risen sufficiently to match the new and higher level of injections (J_2). This occurs at Y_2, the new and higher equilibrium level of national income.

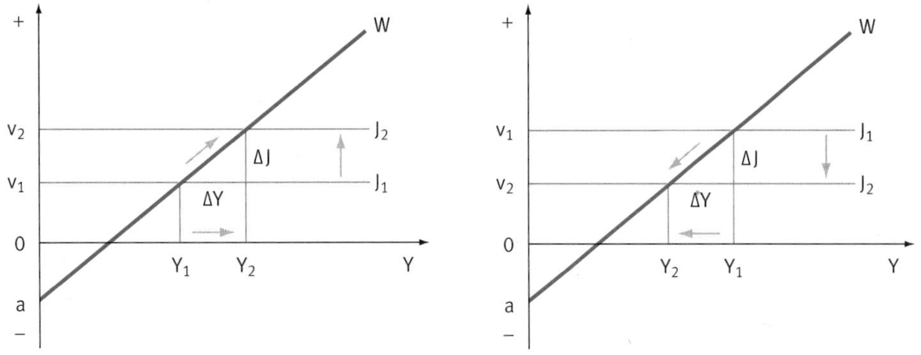

(a) Increase in injections from J_1 to J_2

(b) Decrease in injections from J_1 to J_2

Fig 9.10 Changes in national income (ΔY) following a change in injections (ΔJ = ΔI + ΔG + ΔX)

Decrease in J (I + G + X)

As Figure 9.10(b) indicates, a *decrease* in injections (ΔJ) from J_1 to J_2, whether from a decrease in investment (ΔI), government expenditure (ΔG), exports (ΔX) or decrease in all three components, will (other things equal) result in a *decrease* in national income (ΔY) from Y_1 to Y_2.

Checkpoint 5

1 Can you explain the mechanism involved in moving from the original equilibrium Y_1 to the new equilibrium Y_2 following a decrease in J from J_1 to J_2?

2 Draw a 45° diagram and use the aggregate expenditure approach in each of the following situations to show how equilibrium national income will be affected by:
(a) an increase in injections;
(b) a decrease in injections.

Changes in withdrawals (W)

Increase in W (S + T + M)

As Figure 9.11(a) indicates, an *upward shift* in the withdrawals schedule from W_1 to W_2 will result in a decrease in national income (ΔY) from Y_1 to Y_2. With the new withdrawals schedule W_2 there is now a higher level of withdrawals from any given level of national income (i.e. higher *apw*). This may be due to an upward shift in any or all of the savings (S), taxation (T) or imports (M) schedules shown in Figure 9.5 (p. 340).

At the original equilibrium Y_1, withdrawals now exceed injections, so the value of national income must fall. As national income falls, withdrawals fall (move along W_2). National income will continue to fall until withdrawals have fallen sufficiently to match the original level of injections (J). This occurs at Y_2, the new and lower equilibrium level of national income.

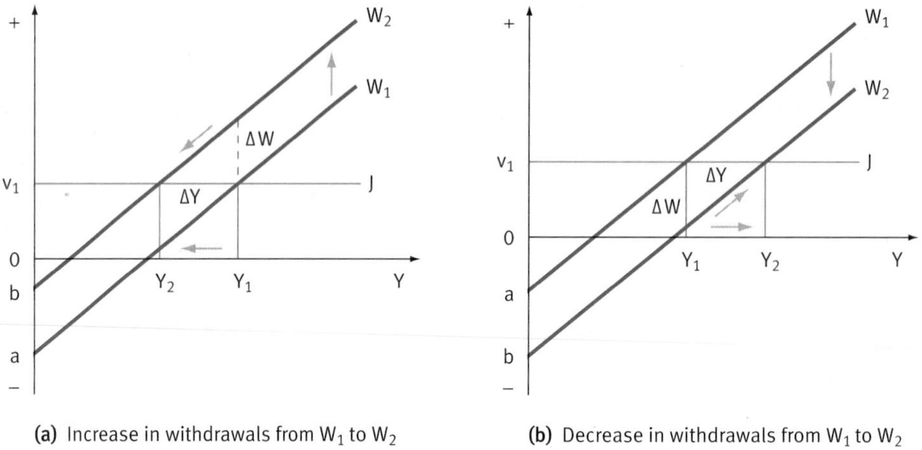

Fig 9.11 Changes in national income (ΔY) following a change in withdrawals ($\Delta W = \Delta S + \Delta T + \Delta M$)

Decrease in withdrawals W (S + T + M)

As Figure 9.11(b) indicates, a *downward shift* in the withdrawals schedule from W_1 to W_2 will result in an *increase* in national income (ΔY) from Y_1 to Y_2.

Checkpoint 6

1. Can you explain the mechanism involved in moving from the original equilibrium Y_1 to the new equilibrium Y_2?
2. How would a change in withdrawals be captured on the 45° diagram? For example, how would an increase in withdrawals affect the aggregate expenditure schedule (E) and why?

National income multiplier

The *national income multiplier* seeks to explain why any given change in injections (or withdrawals) may result in a change in national income which is often larger than (some multiple of) that initial change. In Figure 9.12 we see that an increase in injections of £10m results in an increase in national income of £40m, suggesting a national income multiplier (K) of 4.

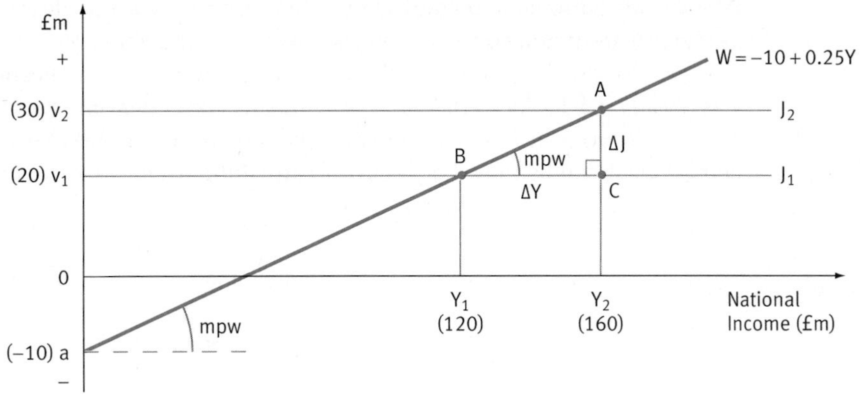

Fig 9.12 Finding the national income multiplier

The original equilibrium national income is $Y_1 = £120m$ at which withdrawals exactly equal injections at £20m.

$$\begin{aligned} W &= -10 + 0.25Y \\ J &= 20 \\ W &= J \text{ in equilibrium} \\ -10 + 0.25Y &= 20 \\ 0.25Y &= 30 \\ Y &= \frac{30}{0.25} \\ \underline{Y} &\underline{= £120\text{m in equilibrium}} \end{aligned}$$

Now injections rise by £10m, from £20m to £30m.

$$\begin{aligned} W &= -10 + 0.25Y \\ J &= 30 \\ W &= J \text{ in equilibrium} \\ -10 + 0.25Y &= 30 \\ 0.25Y &= 40 \\ Y &= \frac{40}{0.25} \\ \underline{Y} &\underline{= £160\text{m in equilibrium}} \end{aligned}$$

We define the national income multiplier (K) as:

$$K = \frac{\Delta Y}{\Delta J} = \frac{40}{10} = 4$$

Of course, the national income multiplier can work both ways:

- *raising* national income by some multiple of a given increase in injections or decrease in withdrawals (i.e. 'expansionary multiplier');

- *reducing* national income by some multiple of a given decrease in injections or increase in withdrawals (i.e. 'deflationary multiplier').

Case Study 9.5 looks at the ways in which a 'multiplier' effect can influence business activity. It looks at the London Olympic bid for 2012 and shows how incomes and employment can be raised well beyond any initial money injected into a project.

Case Study 9.5 The multiplier and the London Olympic bid

It is important to remember that people and businesses are at the centre of the workings of the so-called national income multiplier. Take, for example, London's bid for the 2012 Olympic Games. If successful, there will be a huge boost to London and surrounding areas in terms of extra income (and jobs) well beyond the initial £2.4bn of extra government spending promised for the project. The organisers have stated their intention to stage the most compact games in the history of the Olympics, with 17 of the 28 sports to be held in venues within a 15-mile radius of the Olympic Village to be constructed in Stratford, East London. Some 70,000 extra people will be hired to work in and around London before and during the games to provide support services at the various venues, all receiving an income and spending part of it on food, drink, leisure activities, accommodation, transport and so on. Those selling these goods and services to those extra workers will in turn expand output, hire new employees and generate still further employment and income.

Of course, many more firms and individuals will benefit. Barbara Cassani, the first Chairman of the London bid, said: '2012 will be a powerful catalyst for regeneration. It will lead to massive development with new sports facilities, new jobs and new housing. There will be massive benefits for the construction industry.'

One of the biggest beneficiaries of the games will be the east London borough of Newham, one of the most deprived areas in the country, where the main Olympic venues will be built, leading to major regeneration with new parks and community facilities. Once the games are over, the athletes' village will be used for affordable housing for the local community.

Around £17bn will be spent on improving road, train and underground links if London secures the 2012 games; the government has already given guarantees that the work will be carried out.

A new rail link from King's Cross to Stratford will be constructed for the Olympics, with the journey taking six and a half minutes. Major refurbishment work will be carried out on tube lines to Stratford while a £115m extension will be built to City airport in east London. The government and the Mayor of London have agreed a package that allows for nearly £2.4bn of public funding. This will comprise £1.5bn from the National Lottery and up to £625m from an increase in the London council tax. The London Development Agency has agreed to give £250m if it is needed.

Case Study 9.5 continued

Questions

1 Suggest how incomes are likely to rise by much more than the £2.4bn injected by the government into the games.

2 Will all the benefits of this multiplier effect occur in London?

3 What might help the final multiplier effect from the proposed £2.4bn of government expenditure to be larger or smaller?

We noted above that the multiplier effect can work in both directions – upwards (expansionary multiplier) as in the case of the London Olympic bid or downwards (deflationary multiplier).

Example:

Levi jeans and the deflationary multiplier

The good life has come to an end for workers at Levi Strauss's last two factories in America. In October 2003 members of the 2,000 strong workforce of the plant in San Antonio, Texas, queued up to collect their last pay cheques. Over the past few weeks, as well as sewing labels, zippers and rivets, they have been attending workshops and a job fair to help them prepare for life after Levi Strauss.

The closure ends a momentous chapter in the history of the jeans company, established 150 years ago by a 24-year-old Bavarian immigrant to clothe miners in the goldrush. The jeans with signature red tag, considered as American as Coca-Cola, Ronald Reagan and mom's apple pie, will from now on be made in Mexico and China. Levi Strauss, which in the 1980s had more than 60 factories in the US, has outsourced all its manufacturing to Latin America, Asia and the Caribbean in the face of fierce competition and price pressures from companies such as Wal-Mart.

Around half of these workers are expected to remain unemployed and those who do get a job are likely to find their earnings are much lower. Data from the Bureau of Labour Statistics in the US shows that while around 70% of all displaced US workers find a job eventually, for manufacturing the figure is only around 35%.

It is estimated that the 'ripple effects' of these job losses and earnings reductions on the whole economy of the towns affected will bring about many more job losses and threaten a downward spiral in the fortunes of these communities.

Of course, important objectives of most governments usually involve raising employment opportunities and prosperity for their populations. We consider the policy instruments which governments might use to achieve these objectives in Chapter 10.

Box 9.4 looks at how we can calculate the national income multiplier.

Box 9.4 Calculating the national income multiplier

As we see in the next section, it is very important for policy purposes to be able to calculate the value of K, the national income multiplier.

We defined K as the ratio $\frac{\Delta Y}{\Delta J}$, i.e. the ratio of the change in national income (ΔY) to the change in injections (ΔJ) which brought about that change in national income.

Of course, K could equally be expressed as the ratio $K = \frac{\Delta Y}{\Delta W}$.

Using this last expression allows us to return to Figure 9.12 (p. 355).

We have seen (p. 341) that the *slope* of the withdrawals schedule (W) is the marginal propensity to withdraw (*mpw*). Since the withdrawals schedule (W) is a straight line, *mpw* is a constant along its entire length.

Here we concentrate on the right-angled triangle ABC shown in Figure 9.12.

From the trigonometry of right-angled triangles we can say that:

$$\text{Tan of angle ABC} = \frac{\text{Side opposite}}{\text{Side adjacent}}$$

$$\text{i.e. } mpw = \frac{\Delta J}{\Delta Y}$$

$$\text{but } K = \frac{\Delta Y}{\Delta J}$$

$$\text{i.e. } K = 1 \div \frac{\Delta J}{\Delta Y} \left(= 1 \times \frac{\Delta Y}{\Delta J} \right)$$

$$\text{i.e. } K = \frac{1}{mpw}$$

Multiplier and the marginal propensities to save, tax and import

Remember that the marginal propensity to withdraw is the sum of the marginal propensity to save, tax and import (see p. 341).

$$\text{i.e. } mpw = mps + mpt + mpm$$

$$\text{so. } K = \frac{1}{mpw} = \frac{1}{mps + mpt + mpm}$$

For example, if $mps = 0.1$, $mpt = 0.2$ and $mpm = 0.3$

$$K = \frac{1}{0.1 + 0.2 + 0.3} = \frac{1}{0.6} = 1\frac{2}{3}$$

We can now find the value of the national income multiplier (K) by dividing 1 by the marginal propensity to withdraw (*mpw*).

In our previous example we could have calculated K directly from our knowledge of the withdrawals schedule.

$$W = -10 + 0.25Y$$
$$mpw = 0.25$$
$$K = \frac{1}{mpw} = \frac{1}{0.25} = 4$$

Watch out!

As well as the national income multiplier there is also the *employment multiplier*. This compares the *total* (direct and indirect) increase in employment to the *initial* increase in employment (direct) which begins the multiplier process. Suppose a building project initially employs 100 extra people but, when all the 'ripple' effects of their extra spending works through the economy, a total of 500 extra people are employed, then the 'employment multiplier' is 5.

Inflationary and deflationary gaps

Chapter 10 looks in more detail at a variety of policy issues involving national income determination. Here, in order to illustrate our earlier analysis, we briefly review the policy issues involved for governments when seeking to 'correct' the so-called inflationary and deflationary gaps.

As already noted, most issues involving national income can be expressed in terms of either the W/J diagram or the 45° diagram. Here we use the W/J diagram by way of illustration.

Inflationary gap

When injections exceed withdrawals we suggested that the 'value' of national income will rise. Of course, using the output method, the 'value' of a given quantity of output can be found, on a market, by price × quantity.

It follows that the rise in 'value' of national income could involve:

- a rise in quantity of output;
- a rise in price of output;
- some combination of rise in price and/or quantity of output.

The extent to which a rise in national income is likely to involve *prices* rather than output will depend in part on how much (if any) spare capacity exists in the economy.

LINKS

We return to unemployment in Chapter 10, p. 401, where we see that any economy will always have a certain level of unemployment, so that 100% employment is impossible.

Here we use Y_F to represent the 'full employment level of output', i.e. the level of output beyond which it will be difficult to produce any extra quantity of output because of resource (here labour) constraints. In practice, Y_F need not be 100% employment! Even with, say, 96% employment (i.e. 4% unemployment) it may be difficult in practice to raise the quantity of output.

Defining the 'inflationary gap'

We can now define an 'inflationary gap', using the W/J approach as:

The extent to which injections exceed withdrawals at the 'full employment' level of national income (Y_F).

In Figure 9.13(a) we have the 'full employment' level of national income (Y_F) *below* the equilibrium level (Y_1). The 'inflationary gap' in terms of our definition is represented by AB. The equilibrium level of national income will be above Y_F at Y_1, but we can expect most or all of this rise in 'value' to be due to higher prices rather than extra physical output.

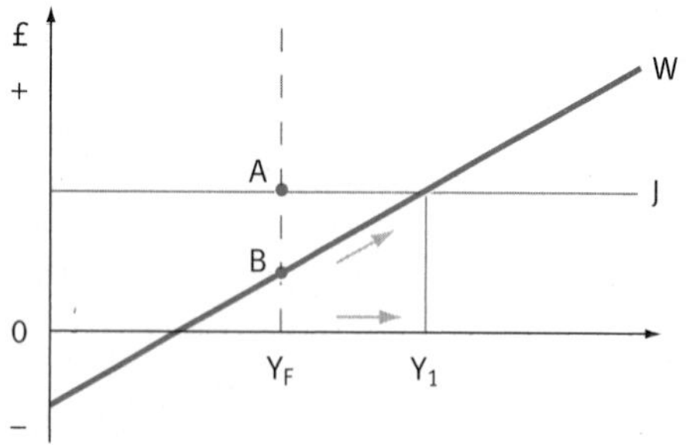

(a) Inflationary gap (AB) with Y_F as 'full employment' level of National Income

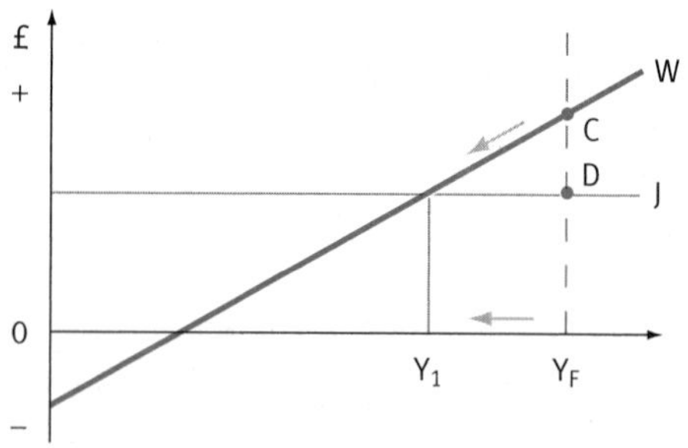

(b) Deflationary gap (CD) with Y_F as 'full employment' level of National Income

Fig 9.13 Inflationary and deflationary gaps.

Checkpoint 7

How might the government seek to close the inflationary gap AB, i.e. make Y_F the equilibrium level of national income and avoid the inflationary pressures from the gap AB?

Deflationary gap

When injections fall short of withdrawals the value of national income will fall. This might involve a fall in quantity of output, in the prices charged for that output, or both. Terms such as 'deflation' or 'recession' are often applied to situations when the value of national income is falling.

Defining the 'deflationary gap'

We can define a 'deflationary gap', using the W/J approach as:

The extent to which injections fall short of withdrawals at the 'full employment' level of national income (Y_F).

In Figure 9.13(b), we have the 'full employment' level of national income (Y_F) *above* the equilibrium level (Y_1). The 'deflationary gap' in terms of our definition is represented by CD. The equilibrium level of national income will be below Y_F at Y_1. It may be that most of this fall in 'value' is due to less physical output rather than lower prices; for example, if employment falls below Y_F we can expect less physical output to be produced by fewer workers (at least at present levels of technology!).

Checkpoint 8 How might the government seek to eliminate the deflationary gap CD, i.e. make Y_F the equilibrium level of national income and avoid the deflationary pressures from the gap CD?

We return to these issues of inflation and unemployment in more detail in Chapter 10, using a more realistic aggregate demand-aggregate supply model to examine their causes and consequences.

Key Terms

Circular flow of income A model to show how the 'equilibrium' level of national income is determined in an economy.

Consumption expenditure Where domestic households purchase the output of domestic firms.

Deflationary gap Shortfall of injections below withdrawals at the 'full capacity' level of national income.

Demand-pull inflation Inflation seen mainly by an increase in the components of aggregate demand (i.e. C, I, G or X).

Endogenous variable One which is determined *inside* the model or system.

Exogenous variable One which influences the system or model but which is determined *outside* that system or model.

Expenditure method Where national income is measured by expenditures on the final output of goods and services.

Factor cost The various measures of national output/income *exclude* indirect taxes and subsidies.

Full capacity That level of national income/output at which resources (land, labour, capital) are fully utilised.

Gross domestic product (GDP) Value of output produced (and incomes received) by firms and households using resources located within that country.

Gross national product (GNP) Value of output produced (and incomes received) by residents of that country from the ownership of resources, wherever those resources are located. The ownership of resources causes some UK residents to receive income from abroad (e.g. interest, dividends) or pay income abroad. In other words: GNP = GDP + *net* property income from abroad.

Income method Where national income is measured by adding incomes which correspond to productive activities.

Inflationary gap Excess of injections over withdrawals at the 'full capacity' level of national income.

Injections Additions to the circular flow of income (e.g. I, G, X).

Market prices The various measures of national output/income *include* indirect taxes and subsidies.

Multiplier The change in total national income as a multiple of the initial change in injections (or withdrawals) which brought it about. For a rise in national income the term 'expansionary multiplier' is often used, and 'deflationary multiplier' for a fall in national income.

National income Total value of income (output or expenditure) generated within the economy in a particular year.

National output *see* 'National income'.

Net national product (NNP) NNP takes into account the fact that some capital equipment will have depreciated over the year via wear and tear or because technological change has made it obsolescent. In other words:
NNP = GNP – depreciation.

Net property income from abroad Inward payments received by residents from their ownership of overseas resources minus outward payments made by residents to the overseas owners of resources located in the domestic economy.

Output method Where national income is measured by taking the value added at each stage of production.

Transfer payments Payments received out of tax revenue without production taking place (e.g. pensions).

Withdrawals Leakages from the circular flow of income (e.g. S, T, M).

Key Points

- National income can be measured using income, output, expenditure approaches.
- In the 'circular flow of income', *injections* (J) consist of investment (I), government expenditure (G) and exports (X), whilst *withdrawals* (W) consist of savings (S), imports (M) and taxes (T).
- 'Equilibrium' or balance in the circular flow occurs where injections into the flow (J) are exactly matched by withdrawals from the flow (W).
- 'Equilibrium' national income can be shown using *either* the withdrawals/injections diagram or the aggregate expenditure (45° diagram).
- We define aggregate expenditure (E) as consumer expenditure (C) *plus* injection expenditure (J).
- Any given change in withdrawals (W) or injections (J) will change national income by some *multiple* of the initial change in W or J.
- The national income multiplier is given by the reciprocal of (one divided by) the marginal propensity to withdraw.
- Inflationary or deflationary gaps are defined, respectively, in relation to the 'full capacity' level of national income.

Assessment Practice

1 **Which *two* of the following are likely to raise the value of national output/income?**

(a) Rise in withdrawals exceeding the rise in injections
(b) Rise in withdrawals matching the rise in injections
(c) Rise in withdrawals falling short of the rise in injections
(d) Rise in the combined value of investment, public expenditure and exports, withdrawals unchanged
(e) Rise in the combined value of savings, taxes and imports, injections unchanged

2 **Which *two* of the following are likely to reduce the value of national output/income?**

(a) Rise in withdrawals exceeding the rise in injections
(b) Rise in withdrawals matching the rise in injections
(c) Rise in withdrawals falling short of the rise in injections
(d) Rise in the combined value of investment, public expenditure and exports, withdrawals unchanged
(e) Rise in the combined value of savings, taxes and imports, injections unchanged

3 **The value of national output produced by residents located within the country, before depreciation and including the influence of taxes and subsidies, is known as:**

(a) GDP at market prices
(b) GDP at factor cost
(c) GNP at market prices
(d) GNP at factor cost
(e) NNP at factor cost.

4 **The value of national output produced by residents of a country, whether located at home or overseas, after depreciation and excluding the influence of taxes and subsidies, is known as:**

(a) GDP at market prices
(b) GDP at factor cost
(c) GNP at market prices
(d) GNP at factor cost
(e) NNP at factor cost.

5 **Which of the following represents the difference between GNP at market prices and GDP at market prices?**

(a) The value of depreciation
(b) The value of taxes and subsidies
(c) Exports
(d) Imports
(e) Net property income from abroad

6 Which of the following is a widely used measure of the standard of living?

(a) Nominal output (income) per employed person
(b) Nominal output (income) per head of population
(c) Real output (income) per head of population
(d) Real output (income) per employed person
(e) Real output (income) per unit of capital

7 Which *two* of the following situations are likely to increase the rate of inflation when the economy is already at full capacity?

(a) An increase in savings
(b) An increase in consumer spending
(c) A reduction in rates of income tax
(d) An increase in rates of income tax
(e) A reduction in government spending

8 Increases in which *two* of the following would be likely policies for a government trying to close a 'deflationary' gap?

(a) Savings
(b) Imports
(c) Consumer spending
(d) Taxes
(e) Government spending

9 Increases in which *two* of the following would be likely policies for a government trying to eliminate an 'inflationary gap'?

(a) Savings
(b) Government spending
(c) Investment
(d) Exports
(e) Taxes

10 Which *one* of the following will make the value of the national income multiplier equal 4?

(a) $mps = 0.1$, $mpt = 0.1$, $mpm = 0.1$
(b) $mps = 0.2$, $mpt = 0.1$, $mpm = 0.2$
(c) $mps = 0.2$, $mpt = 0.1$, $mpm = 0.1$
(d) $mps = 0.15$, $mpt = 0.2$, $mpm = 0.05$
(e) $mps = 0.1$, $mpt = 0.1$, $mpm = 0.05$

Data response and stimulus questions

1 Look carefully at Tables (i) and (ii) below which show national income in the UK in 2000, using the *income* and *expenditure* approaches respectively.

(i) Income method		(ii) Expenditure method	
UK National Account 2000 (£bn)		**UK National Account 2000 (£bn)**	
Income from employment	521.4	Expenditure by households	594.8
Income from profit and rent	213.2	Expenditure by government and non-profit organisations	197.7
Other	78.6		
GDP factor cost	813.2	Investment spending	167.1
Indirect taxes less subsidies	130.2	Exports–Imports	(–16.2)
GDP at market prices	943.4	GDP at market prices	943.4
Net property income from abroad	3.0	Net property income from abroad	3.0
GNP at market prices	946.4	GNP at market prices	946.4

Adapted from ONS, *Economic Trends*: *Annual Supplement*

Questions

(a) What do you notice?
(b) From Table (i), explain why GDP at market prices is higher than GDP at factor cost.
(c) From Table (i), explain why GNP at market prices differs from GDP at market prices.
(d) What types of income have not been included in Table (i) when measuring GDP or GNP?
(e) From Table (ii), identify 'aggregate expenditure'.
(f) From Table (ii), explain what contribution 'Exports–Imports' is making to calculating GDP at market prices.
(g) What types of expenditure have *not* been included in Table (ii) when measuring GDP or GNP?

2 Read the following text and try to answer the question.

Paradox of thrift

A paradox is a contradiction, something that is against logic or expectation. A very commonly discussed paradox revolves around time travel: If I went back in time and killed my mother when she was a child, then I would never have been born. If I was never born I would never have been alive to go back in time! The paradox of thrift doesn't give rise to quite so many interesting novels and films but it is rather more useful. It was put forward by the economist John Maynard Keynes and goes something like this:

A thrifty person is a careful person who wishes to spend within their means and always be able to pay their way. Being thrifty is considered to be a good thing, a virtue. However, Keynes pointed out two very important points about being thrifty.

- First, what may be a virtue in one person is not necessarily virtuous if *everyone* does it. What is good for one is not necessarily good for all.
- Second, the more savings that people intend to make, the less savings that may actually occur.

Thriftiness would therefore seem indeed to be a paradox, leading to possibly unexpected outcomes.

Question
Can you use the W/J schedules to explain why the above might occur?

3 **You are the managing director of a large sportswear company. The Chancellor of the Exchequer is about to announce his public expenditure and taxation plans in his budget. What measures would be particularly helpful to you as you seek to expand your business?**

4 **Read the text below and answer the question.**

Backward linkages

The purchase of services for use as inputs by manufacturing firms is a much larger proportion per unit of gross output than is the purchase of manufactured goods for use as inputs by service sector firms. Whereas a recent study found that each £1 spent on manufacturing gross output created £1.61 of employment income in all sectors, that same £1 spent on service gross output created only £0.56 of employment income in all sectors.

Question
What is the relevance of these findings to the use of the national income multiplier?

True/False questions

1 If national income rises by £10bn after an injection of £2bn, then the 'national income multiplier' is one-fifth.
True/False

2 If everyone saves more, then (other things equal) withdrawals from the circular flow will increase and national income will fall.
True/False

3 If injections exceed withdrawals at the 'full capacity' level of national income, then we have a 'deflationary gap'.
True/False

4 If withdrawals fall short of injections at the 'full capacity' level of national income, then we have an 'inflationary gap'.
True/False

5 An increase in pension-related incomes will increase GDP.
True/False

6 We use 'value added' in the output method to avoid double counting.
True/False

7 Measuring national income at 'factor cost' means that we have taken account of the distortions caused by taxes and subsidies on product prices.
True/False

8 An increase in the average propensity to withdraw will, other things equal, reduce the equilibrium level of national income.

True/False

9 A decrease in the average propensity to consume will, other things equal, increase the equilibrium level of national income.

True/False

10 An increase in government expenditure will, other things equal, increase the equilibrium level of national income.

True/False

Essay questions

1 Explain how GDP at factor cost can be found using the *expenditure* method.
2 Why are national income measures inadequate when comparing the standard of living between developed and developing countries?
3 Using any model you wish, explain what might be the consequences for the circular flow of income of:
   (a) an increase in government spending;
   (b) an increase in tax revenue.
4 What is the 'national income multiplier'? How useful is it for policy purposes?
5 Explain how the government can eliminate:
   (a) an inflationary gap;
   (b) a deflationary gap.

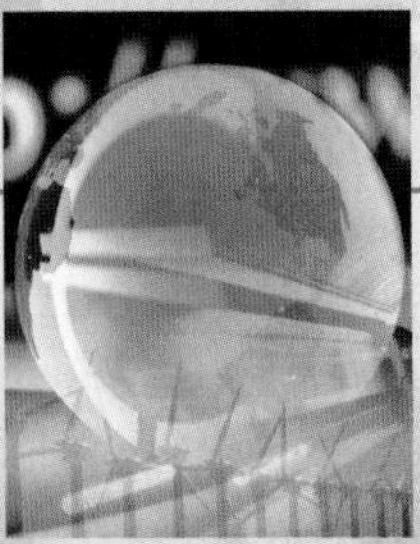

Chapter 10

Government policies: instruments and objectives

Introduction

This chapter takes forward the broad analysis of Chapter 9 into the more specific areas of government policy making. Such policies play a key role in shaping the macro-environment in which businesses and households must operate. Government policies on tax rates and allowances, levels and types of expenditure, interest rates and credit availability, public service provision, pension entitlement and on many other issues will have a major impact on businesses and households.

This chapter introduces the aggregate demand and aggregate supply schedules to help deepen our understanding of issues such as inflation, unemployment and economic growth.

Learning objectives:

By the end of this chapter you should be able to:

- identify the key policy instruments available to governments in seeking to influence the macroeconomic environment and review their relative effectiveness
- consider in some detail fiscal policy, monetary policy and exchange rate policy in the UK and other economies and assess their impacts on businesses and households
- explain what is meant by 'built-in stabilisers' and show how these can help avoid excessive increases or decreases in economic activity
- understand how and why governments seek simultaneously to achieve the objective of price stability, low unemployment, balance of payments equilibrium and sustained economic growth and the implications for business and households
- use aggregate demand and aggregate supply curves to analyse issues involving inflation, unemployment and economic growth.

We begin by looking in some detail at the use by governments of fiscal policy, paying particular attention to its role in the UK.

Fiscal policy

'Fiscal policy' is the name given to government policies which seek to influence government revenue (taxation) and/or government expenditure. We have already seen how changes in either can influence the equilibrium level of national income, with implications for output, employment and inflation.

Major changes in fiscal policy in the UK are normally announced at the time of the Budget, which in the UK traditionally takes place just before the end of the tax year on 5 April. Both revenue raising and expenditure plans are presented together at the Budget.

Budget terminology

A number of terms are often used to describe a Budget.

- *Budget deficit.* When tax revenues fall short of public expenditure (T < G).
- *Budget surplus.* When tax revenue exceeds public expenditure (T > G).
- *Balanced budget.* When tax revenue equals public expenditure (T = G).

Similarly, a number of terms are often used to describe the *consequences* of these budget situations.

- *Public sector borrowing requirements* (PSBR). Until recently, this term has been widely used to describe the outcome of a budget deficit, since the government will have to borrow to cover the excess of government spending over tax revenue (G > T), at least in the short run. This borrowing may involve issuing government bills and bonds to the financial markets.
- *Public sector net cash requirement* (PSNCR). In recent years this has been the term more usually used in the UK to refer to situations previously described by the PSBR.

Watch out! The PSNCR is sometimes described as the *public sector net borrowing* requirement (PSNBR).

Fiscal 'rules'

Further terms are often used in seeking to describe the government's fiscal policy. For example, in 1998 the Labour government committed itself to the following two important 'fiscal rules'.

- *The 'golden rule'*: over the economic cycle the government will only borrow to invest and will not borrow to fund current expenditure. In effect the 'golden rule' implies that current expenditure will be covered by current revenue over the economic cycle. Put another way, any borrowing to cover the PSNCR (public sector net cash requirement) must be used only for investment purposes, in effect for spending on infrastructure, such as roads and railways, capital equipment and so on.

- *The 'public debt rule'*: over the economic cycle the ratio of public debt to national income will be held at a 'stable and prudent' level. The 'public debt rule' is rather less clear in that the phrase 'stable and prudent' is somewhat ambiguous. However, taken together with the 'golden rule' it essentially means that, as an *average* over the economic cycle, the ratio of PSNCR to national income cannot exceed the ratio of investment to national income. Given that, historically, government investment has been no more than 2% to 3% of national income, then clearly the PSNCR as a percentage of national income must be kept within strict limits.

Checkpoint 1 What do you think is meant by the 'economic cycle'?

It will be useful to consider government taxation and government expenditure in turn and consider their impacts on businesses and households.

Taxation

Taxation is the major source of government revenue, with a 'tax' being a compulsory charge laid down by government. You must remember that the government is spending your money; it has no money of its own. Apart from government borrowing, it only has the money which it generates from taxation. Don't forget that everyone pays taxes. Even those who do not work pay expenditure taxes (e.g. VAT).

Example:

Taxation in various economies

It is often said that the UK is overtaxed. Currently around 38% of all UK national income is taken in various forms of taxation, which actually places the UK as only a middle-ranked country in terms of tax burden. Of the 20 largest world economies, ten have a higher tax burden than the UK. For example, over 53% of national income is taken in tax in Sweden, 49% in Denmark, 46% in Austria, 45% in Belgium, Norway and Finland, though only around 30% in the US.

Types of taxation

As long ago as the eighteenth century, Adam Smith laid down the rules for a 'good tax' in his so-called 'canons of taxation'. A tax should be:

1 *equitable* (fair); those who can afford to pay more should do so;
2 *economic*; more should be collected in tax than is needed to cover the costs of administration;
3 *transparent*; individuals should know how much tax they are paying;
4 *convenient*; the taxpayer should not find it difficult to pay the tax.

Direct and indirect taxes

Taxes are often grouped under these headings depending on the administrative arrangements for their collection.

- *Direct taxes*. These taxes are paid directly to the Exchequer by the taxpayer, whether by individuals (e.g. Income Tax, Employee's National Insurance, Capital Gains Tax) or by companies (e.g. Corporation Tax, Employer's National Insurance). Most of the revenue from direct taxes comes from taxing the *income* of the individuals and companies.
- *Indirect taxes*. These taxes are paid indirectly to the Exchequer by the taxpayer, e.g. via retailers. Other indirect taxes include a range of excise duties (on oil, tobacco and cars) and import duties. Most of the revenue from indirect taxes comes from taxing the *expenditure* of individuals and companies.

Table 10.1 Types of tax: % of tax revenue in 2003

Direct taxes	% of total tax revenue
Income Tax	29%
National Insurance (Employers + Employees)	16%
Corporation Tax	7%
Capital Gains, Inheritance	3%
Total Direct	***55%***
Indirect tax	**% of total tax revenue**
VAT	16%
Fuel duties	6%
Tobacco	2%
Alcohol	2%
Other indirect	2%
Total Indirect	***28%***

Table 10.1 shows that *direct taxes* contribute some 55% of total tax revenue, when we include employers' and employees' National Insurance Contributions, corporation taxes on company profits and capital gains and inheritance taxes. Indirect taxes

contribute some 28% of total tax revenues, with VAT the most important of these, and 'other taxes' (e.g. council tax, Business rates etc.) make up the other 17%.

There is a danger in discussing tax issues to forget that households and businesses are affected by tax in *general* (via the circular flow) and sometimes by taxes in *particular*. Some 30 years of VAT in the UK has had different implications for Blackpool Pleasure Beach and United Biscuits, as is indicated in the example below.

Example:

VAT, Blackpool Pleasure Beach and United Biscuits

VAT was invented in 1965 by Maurice Laure, a French civil servant, for use in the then European Common Market. The UK adopted the system in 1973. Because VAT is not supposed to be levied on 'essential' products but only on 'luxuries', various businesses have sought to be VAT exempt, sometimes with controversial results (e.g. cakes are VAT exempt, biscuits are not).

In 1974 Blackpool Pleasure Beach brought one of the first claims against Britain's new tax. They said their Big Dipper rollercoaster was a form of transport (VAT exempt) and argued that passengers should therefore be exempt from VAT. Customs and excise didn't agree. United Biscuits got into a wrangle with the authorities when it claimed its Jaffa Cakes snacks were cakes and not biscuits, thereby making them exempt from VAT. After taking the case to a tribunal the company won.

Total revenues since the introduction of VAT in 1973 add up to £826bn. The annual revenue for this tax in 2004 was around £645bn, up from £2.5bn in 1973. At 25% Denmark and Sweden have the highest VAT rates in Europe.

At the end of this section (p. 376) we look in more detail at the advantages and disadvantages of both direct and indirect taxation.

Specific and percentage taxes

- *Specific tax*. This is expressed as an *absolute* sum of money per unit of the product and is sometimes called a 'lump-sum' tax. Excise duties are often of this kind, being so many pence per packet of cigarettes or per proof of spirit or per litre of petrol.

LINKS

Chapter 2 (p. 56) looks at the impact of specific (lump-sum) and percentage taxes on business costs and supply curves.

- *Percentage tax*. This is levied not on volume but on value; e.g. in the UK in 2004/5 VAT was 17.5% of sales price, and corporation tax was 30% of assessable profits for larger companies and 19% of assessable profits for smaller companies. These percentage taxes are sometimes called *ad valorem* (to vary) since the absolute sum of money paid per unit of the product varies with the price.

Progressive and regressive taxes

- *Progressive taxes*. These occur when, as incomes rise, *the proportion of total income paid in tax rises*. Income tax is progressive, partly because of allowances for low-paid workers before any tax is paid, and partly because tax rates rise for higher income groups.

- *Regressive taxes*. These occur when, as incomes rise, *the proportion of total income paid in tax falls*. VAT is regressive, since the same absolute amount is paid by rich and poor alike, which means that for those on higher incomes a lower proportion of higher incomes is paid in VAT and most other indirect taxes.
- *Proportional taxes*. These occur when, as incomes rise, *the proportion of total income paid in tax remains unchanged*.

Those who suggest that more tax revenue should come from indirect taxes on expenditure are, according to this analysis, supporting a more regressive tax regime.

Hypothecated taxes

A recent approach favoured by many as a means of raising the tax take, whilst retaining public support, involves the idea of *hypothecation*. This is the allocation of monies received from current or additional taxes to specific *spending* outcomes.

Individual taxes

Here we consider some of the different taxes in a little more detail.

Income tax in the UK

Not all income is taxed; everyone is allowed to earn a certain amount before paying tax, which is shown in the tax code. For example, in 2004/5 each single person in the UK under 65 years had a *tax allowance* of £4,745 before tax.

Most workers have their tax paid for them by their employer using PAYE (Pay As You Earn). This conforms to the third and fourth 'canons of taxation', namely that taxes should be *transparent* and *convenient*. Employers have to give the worker a salary advice form showing the amount of tax deducted for the current time period (a week or a month) and the amount of accumulated tax deducted in the current tax year.

Table 10.2 shows how UK income tax rates have been simplified and lowered in the 16 years from 1987/8 to 2004/5.

Table 10.2 UK income tax schedules 1987/8 and 2004/5

Rate of tax (%)	1987/8 Taxable income (£)	2004/5 Taxable income (£)
10	–	0–1,960
22	–	1,961–30,500
27	0–17,900	
40	17,901–20,400	over 30,500
45	20,401–25,400	–
50	25,401–33,300	–
55	33,301–41,200	–
60	over 41,200	–

Other direct taxes in the UK

- *National Insurance*. A tax on employment, paid by both employees and employers. In 2004/5 this is levied at 0% on employees earning up to £91 per week, rising sharply to 11% on earnings between £91 and £610 per week, but only 1% on additional earnings over £610 per week.
- *Capital Gains Tax*. A tax on the increased value of an asset when it is sold. Capital gains above £7,790 are taxable at rates rising from 10% to 40%.
- *Inheritance Tax*. A tax on inheritance or gifts. In 2004/5 inheritance tax at a rate of 40% is only paid on estates valued at over £263,000.
- *Corporation Tax*. A tax on company profits at 30% as the standard rate, but a lower 19% for small firms.

Indirect taxes in the UK

- *Value Added Tax* (VAT). A tax on expenditure on most goods and services (currently 17.5% in the UK). Some items (e.g. children's clothes) are VAT exempt. VAT is a tax on expenditure levied by all EU countries, though at different rates.
- *Excise duties*. A specific tax of an absolute amount levied at different rates on goods such as tobacco, petrol, alcohol.

Other taxes in the UK

Some UK taxes are difficult to define or put into neat categories, such as the BBC licence; Road Fund Licence; Council Tax; Stamp Duty; Airport Tax; fees paid by local residents to the council for parking; prescription charges.

Checkpoint 2

1 Use either the W/J diagram or the 45° diagram to show how each of the following might influence the national income:
   (a) a 1% rise in the basic rate of income tax;
   (b) a £1 increase per item in a specific tax (e.g. excise duty).

2 Would either of these extra taxes influence the national income multiplier?

Taxes and economic incentives

There is an ongoing debate as to whether or not taxes are 'excessive' in the UK and whether current tax rates act as a disincentive to UK households and businesses.

Taxes and incentives to work

Many empirical studies have been conducted on tax rates and incentives, with no clear results. However, one widely accepted approach does warn governments against imposing too high an *overall tax rate*.

Laffer curve

Professor Laffer derived a relationship between tax revenue and tax rates of the form shown in Figure 10.1. The curve was the result of econometric techniques, through which a 'least square line' was fitted to past US observations of tax revenue and tax rate. The dotted line indicates the extension of the fitted relationship (continuous) line, as there will tend to be zero tax revenue at both 0% and 100% tax rates. Tax revenue = tax rate × output (income), so that a 0% tax rate yields zero tax revenue, whatever the level of output. A 100% tax rate is assumed to discourage all output, except that for subsistence, again yielding zero tax revenue. Tax revenue must reach a maximum at some intermediate tax rate between these extremes.

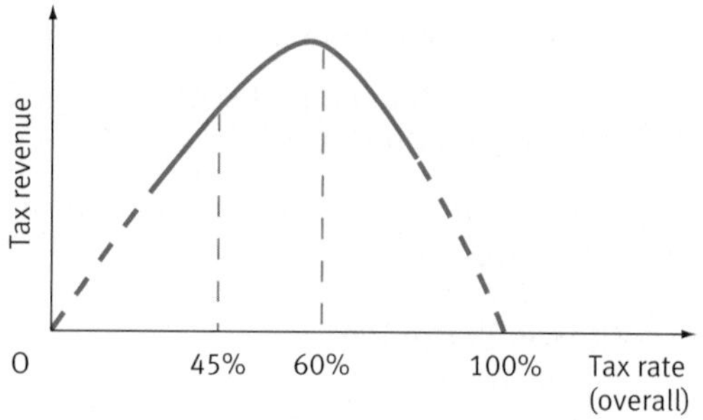

Fig 10.1 The 'Laffer' curve

LINKS

Our indifference analysis of Appendix 1 introduced the ideas of 'income' and 'substitution' effects. A higher tax on income will have two effects, which pull in opposite directions.

- An 'income effect', with real income reduced via higher taxes, which means less consumption of all items, including leisure, i.e. more work is performed.
- A 'substitution effect', with leisure now cheaper via higher taxes, since less real income is now sacrificed for each unit of leisure consumed. The substitution effect leads to cheaper leisure being substituted for work, i.e. less work.

On grounds of theory alone we cannot tell which effect will be the stronger, i.e. whether higher taxes on income will raise or lower the time devoted to work rather than leisure (where, of course, the worker has some choice).

The London Business School has estimated a Laffer curve for the UK using past data. Tax revenue was found to reach a peak at around a 60% 'composite tax rate', i.e. one which includes both direct and indirect taxes, as well as various social security payments, all expressed as a percentage of GDP. If the composite tax rate rises above 60%, then the disincentive effect on output is so strong (i.e. output falls so much) that tax revenue (tax rate × output) actually falls, despite the higher tax rate.

The Laffer curve in fact begins to flatten out at around a 45% composite tax rate. In other words, as the overall tax rate rises to about 45%, the disincentive effect on output is strong enough to mean that little extra tax revenue results. Econometric studies of this type have given support to those in favour of limiting overall rates of tax. In fact the reduction in the top income tax rate to 40% in the UK in 1988/9 was inspired by the Laffer curve.

Direct versus indirect taxes

It might be useful to consider in more detail the advantages and disadvantages of direct and indirect systems of taxation. For convenience we shall compare the systems under four main headings, with indirect taxes considered first in each case.

Macroeconomic management

Indirect taxes can be varied more quickly and easily, taking more immediate effect, than can direct taxes. Since the Finance Act of 1961, the Chancellor of the Exchequer has had the power (via 'the regulator') to vary the rates of indirect taxation at any time between Budgets. Excise and import duties can be varied by up to 10%, and VAT by up to 25% (i.e. between 13.13% and 21.87% for a 17.5% rate of VAT). In contrast direct taxes can only be changed at Budget time. In the case of income tax, any change involves time-consuming revisions to PAYE codings. For these reasons, indirect taxes are usually regarded as a more flexible instrument of macroeconomic policy.

Economic incentives

We have already seen how, in both theory and practice, direct taxes on income affect incentives to work. We found that neither in theory nor in practice need the net effect be one of disincentive. Nevertheless, it is often argued that if the same sum were derived from indirect taxation, then any net disincentive effect that did occur would be that much smaller. In particular, it is often said that indirect taxes are less visible (than direct), being to some extent hidden in the quoted price of the product. However, others suggest that consumers are well aware of the impact of indirect taxes on the price level. Certainly for products with relatively inelastic demands (Chapter 2, p. 57) any higher indirect taxes will be passed on to consumers as higher prices, and will therefore not be less visible than extra direct taxation.

Economic welfare

It is sometimes argued that indirect taxes are, in welfare terms, preferable to direct taxes, as they leave the taxpayer free to make a choice. The individual can, for instance, avoid the tax by choosing not to consume the taxed commodity. Although this 'voluntary' aspect of indirect taxes may apply to a particular individual and a particular tax, it cannot apply to all individuals and all taxes. In other words, indirect taxes cannot be 'voluntary' for the community as a whole. If a chancellor is to raise a given sum through a system of indirect taxes, individual choices not to consume taxed items must, if widespread, be countered either by raising rates of tax or by extending the range of goods and services taxed.

Another argument used to support indirect taxes on welfare grounds is that they can be used to combat 'externalities'. In Chapter 8 we noted that an externality occurs where private and social costs diverge. Where private costs of production are below social costs, an indirect tax could be imposed, or increased, so that price is raised to reflect the true social costs of production. Taxes on alcohol and tobacco could be justified on these grounds. By discriminating between different goods and services, indirect taxes can help reallocate resources in a way that raises economic welfare for society as a whole.

On the other hand, indirect taxes have also been criticised on welfare grounds for being regressive, the element of indirect tax embodied in product prices taking a higher proportion of the income from lower-paid groups. Nor is it easy to correct for this. It would be impossible administratively to place a higher tax on a given item for those with higher incomes, although one could impose indirect taxes mainly on the goods and services consumed by higher-income groups, and perhaps at higher rates.

In terms of economic welfare, as in terms of economic incentives, the picture is again unclear. A case can be made, with some conviction, both for and against direct and indirect taxes in terms of economic welfare.

Administrative costs

Indirect taxes are often easy and cheap to administer. They are paid by manufacturers and traders, which are obviously fewer in number than the total of individuals paying income tax. This makes indirect taxes such as excise and import duties much cheaper to collect than direct taxes, though the difference is less marked for VAT, which requires the authorities to deal with a large number of mainly smaller traders.

Even if indirect taxes do impose smaller administrative costs than direct taxes for a given revenue yield, not too much should be made of this. It is, for instance, always possible to reform the system of PAYE and reduce administrative costs; for example, the computerisation of Inland Revenue operations may, in the long run, significantly reduce the administrative costs associated with the collection of direct taxes.

In summary, there is no clear case for one type of tax system compared to another. The macroeconomic management and administrative cost grounds may appear to favour indirect taxes, though the comparison is only with the current system of direct taxation. That system can, of course, be changed to accommodate criticisms along these lines. On perhaps the more important grounds of economic incentives and economic welfare the case is very mixed, with arguments for and against each type of tax finely balanced.

Government expenditure

Government expenditure was almost 49% of national income in the UK in 1981, but in 2004 it had fallen to around 41% of national income. However, major increases in government spending over the period 2003–05 were announced in the *Comprehensive Spending Review* of November 2002, raising the projected ratio of government spending to over 42% of national income by 2005/6.

Table 10.3 gives a broad breakdown of the share of various departments and programmes in UK total government spending in 2003/4.

Clearly, Social Security, Health and Education are the key spending areas, taking around 56% of all government expenditure. The impact on business of extra government spending will depend on the sectors in which the money is spent. Obviously, defence contractors will benefit directly from extra spending on the armed services. However, as we noted in Chapter 9 (p. 354), the 'multiplier effect' from the extra government spending will increase output, employment, income and spending indirectly in many sectors of economic activity.

We have already considered (p. 371) the various 'rules' the Labour government has established for broadly controlling the growth of government expenditure over the economic cycle. Given the criticism that is often made of allegedly 'excessive' government spending in the UK, it is interesting to note that the UK is below average on most cross-country indices of government spending.

Table 10.3 UK government expenditure: % shares in 2003/4

Department/Programme	%
Social Security	28
Health	17
Education	11
Debt interest	7
Defence	6
Law and order	6
Industry and employment	4
Housing/environment	3
Transport	2
Contributions to EU	1
Overseas aid	0.5
Other	5

Example:

Government spending in various economies

Although the UK government is sometimes criticised for excessive spending, at 41% of national income, government spending is less than the 44% average across the EU countries, but more than the 31% of national income recorded for government spending in the US. In fact, in 2003, out of 14 major countries, the UK was only tenth highest in terms of the share of national income given to government expenditure.

Case for controlling public expenditure

The arguments used by those in favour of restricting public expenditure include the following.

More freedom and choice

The suggestion here is that excessive government expenditure adversely affects individual freedom and choice.

- First, it is feared that it spoonfeeds individuals, taking away the incentive for personal provision, as with private insurance for sickness or old age.
- Second, that by impeding the market mechanism it may restrict consumer choice. For instance, the state may provide goods and services that are in little demand, whilst discouraging others (via taxation) that might otherwise have been bought.
- Third, it has been suggested that government provision may encourage an unhelpful separation between payment and cost in the minds of consumers. With government provision, the good or service may be free or subsidised, so that the amount paid by the consumer will understate the true cost (higher taxes etc.) of providing him or her with that good or service, thereby encouraging excessive consumption of the item.

Crowding out the private sector

The previous Conservative government had long believed that (excessive) public expenditure was at the heart of Britain's economic difficulties. It regarded the private sector as the source of wealth creation, part of which was being used to subsidise the public sector. Sir Keith Joseph clarified this view during the 1970s by alleging that 'a wealth-creating sector which accounts for one-third of the national product carries on its back a State subsidised sector which accounts for two-thirds. The rider is twice as heavy as the horse.'

Bacon and Eltis (1978) attempted to give substance to this view. They suggested that public expenditure growth had led to a transfer of productive resources from the private sector to a public sector producing largely non-marketed output and that this had been a major factor in the UK's poor performance in the post-war period. Bacon and Eltis noted that public sector employment had increased by some 26%, from 5.8 million workers to 7.3 million, between 1960 and 1978, a time when total employment was being squeezed by higher taxes to finance this growth in the public sector – the result being deindustrialisation, low labour productivity, low economic growth and balance of payments problems.

Control of money

Another argument used by those who favour restricting public expenditure is that it must be cut in order to limit the growth of money supply (see p. 387) and to curb inflation. The argument is that a high PSBR (now PSNCR – public sector net cash requirement), following public expenditure growth, must be funded by the issue of Treasury bills and government stock, which increase liquidity in the system and can lead to a multiple expansion of bank deposits (money), with perhaps inflationary consequences.

A related argument is that public expenditure must be restricted, not only to limit the supply of money, but also its 'price' – the rate of interest. The suggestion here is that to sell the extra bills and bonds to fund a budget deficit, interest rates must rise to attract investors. This then puts pressure on private sector borrowing with the rise in interest rates inhibiting private sector investment and investment-led growth. A major policy aim of governments has, therefore, often been to control public sector borrowing.

Incentives to work, save and take risks

There are also worries that increased public spending not only pushes up government borrowing, but also leads to higher taxes, thereby reducing the incentives to work, save and take risks. However, we have already noted that the evidence to support the general proposition that higher taxes undermine the work ethic is largely inconclusive.

Balance of payments stability

A further line of attack has been that the growth of public expenditure may create problems for the balance of payments (see p. 407). The common sense of this argument is that higher public spending raises interest rates and attracts capital inflow, which in turn raise the demand for sterling and therefore the exchange rate. A higher pound then makes exports dearer and imports cheaper so that the balance of payments deteriorates.

The debate on the role of public expenditure continues. However, the present government has placed great emphasis on containing such expenditure by setting out its 'fiscal rules', which we considered earlier (p. 371).

Checkpoint 3

1 Use either the W/J diagram or the 45° diagram to show how a major increase in government expenditure might influence the equilibrium level of national income.

2 Can you suggest any other possible consequences from such an increase in government expenditure?

Fiscal policy and stabilisation

Business cycle

The terms *business cycle* or *trade cycle* are often used to refer to the tendency for economies to move from economic boom into economic recession, or vice versa. Economic historians have claimed to observe a five- to eight-year cycle of economic activity between successive peaks (A,C) or successive troughs (B,D) around a general upward trend (T) of the type shown in Figure 10.2.

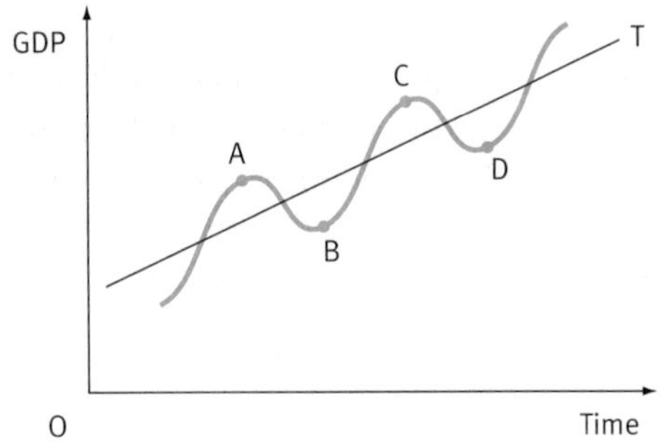

Fig 10.2 Business (trade) cycle

From a business perspective it is clearly important to be aware of such a business cycle, since investment in extra capacity in boom year A might be problematic if demand had fallen relative to trend by the time the capacity came on stream in the recession year B.

Example:

Microchip manufacture

In the boom dot.com years of the late 1990s many of the major chip-making firms such as Intel, Samsung, Fujitsu and Siemens invested in extra chip-making plants. Unfortunately, by the time many of these were ready for operation, the dot.com boom had turned to bust and many of these state-of-the-art plants had to be closed when excess chip supply resulted in plunging prices.

From a business perspective, investment might be better timed to take place at or around points B or D in Figure 10.2, depending on the time lags involved. Even better would be a situation in which government fiscal policies had 'smoothed' or stabilised the business cycle around the trend value (T) by making use of 'built-in' stabilisers or by using 'discretionary' fiscal policy. It is to this policy objective that we now turn.

Built-in stabilisation

Some of the tax and spending programmes we have discussed will act as built-in (or automatic) stabilisers. They do this in at least two ways.

- Bringing about an *automatic* rise in withdrawals and/or fall in injections in times of 'boom'. For example, when the economy is growing rapidly, individual incomes, business incomes and spending on goods and services will all be rising in value, thereby increasing the government's revenue from both direct and indirect taxes. At the same time, unemployment is likely to be falling, reducing the government's spending on social security, unemployment and other benefits.

  This 'automatic' rise in withdrawals and reduction in injections will help to dampen any excessive growth in national income which might otherwise result in rapid inflation and unsustainable 'boom' conditions.

- Bringing about an *automatic* fall in withdrawals and/or rise in injections in times of recession. For example, when the economy is contracting, individual incomes, business incomes and spending on goods and services will all be falling in value, thereby reducing the government's tax revenue from both direct and indirect taxes. At the same time, unemployment is likely to be rising, increasing the government's spending on social security, unemployment and other benefits.

  This 'automatic' fall in withdrawals and rise in injections will help to stimulate the economy and prevent national income from falling as far as it otherwise might have done.

Checkpoint 4

How can the government use fiscal policy to increase the extent of built-in (automatic) stability in the economy?

Discretionary stabilisation

On occasions, governments will intervene in the economy for specific purposes, such as reinforcing the built-in stabilisers already described.

- If an 'inflationary gap' is identified (Chapter 9, p. 359) then the government may seek to reduce G or raise T to eliminate it.
- If a 'deflationary gap' is identified (Chapter 9, p. 360) then the government may seek to raise G or reduce T to close it.

These are examples of *discretionary* fiscal policy, where the government makes a conscious decision to change its spending or taxation policy. As compared to built-in stabilisers, discretionary fiscal stabilisation policy faces a number of difficulties.

Time lags

At least two time lags can be identified.

- *Recognition lag*. It takes time for the government to collect and analyse data, recognise any problem that may exist, and then decide what government spending and taxation decisions to take.
- *Execution lag*. Having made its fiscal policy decisions, it takes time to implement these changes and it also takes time for these changes to have an effect on the economy.

In terms of discretionary fiscal policy these time lags can result in the government reinforcing the business cycle, rather than stabilising it, as indicated in Figure 10.3.

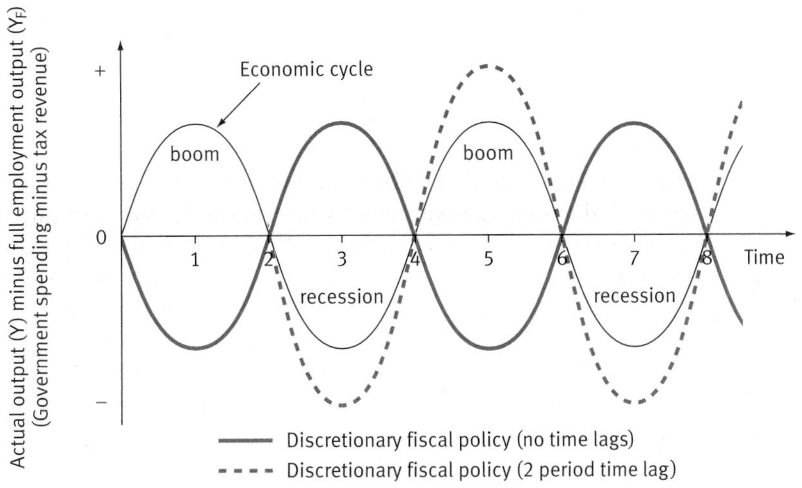

Fig 10.3 Stabilisation of the business cycle and discretionary fiscal policy

- *The business (trade) cycle* is shown as a continuous line in the diagram, with a complete cycle (peak to peak) lasting four time periods. For the business cycle the relevant variable on the vertical axis is 'Actual output (Y) minus full employment output' (Y_F).
  - Where this is *positive*, as in time periods 1 and 2, we have our familiar 'inflationary gap' (since $Y > Y_F$).
  - Where this is *negative*, as in time periods 3 and 4, we have our familiar 'deflationary gap' (since $Y < Y_F$)

- *Discretionary fiscal policy* is shown as both a coloured continuous line (no time lag) and a dotted line (two-period time lag) in the diagram. For discretionary fiscal policy the relevant variable on the vertical axis is 'Government spending minus tax revenue'.
  - Where the business cycle is experiencing an 'inflationary gap' (time periods 1 and 2), the appropriate discretionary fiscal policy is a *budget surplus* ($G < T$). This is the case with the coloured continuous line.
  - Where the business cycle is experiencing a 'deflationary gap' (time periods 3 and 4), the appropriate discretionary fiscal policy is a *budget deficit* ($G > T$). This is again the case with the coloured continuous line.

If the timing of the discretionary fiscal policy is correct, as with the coloured continuous line (no time lag), then intervention by the government will help to 'stabilise' the business cycle, with discretionary fiscal policy resulting in a net withdrawal in times of 'boom' and a net injection in times of recession.

However, when the recognition and execution time lags are present, discretionary fiscal policy can actually turn out to be 'destabilising'. This is the case in Figure 10.3 if these time lags cause a *two-time-period delay* in discretionary fiscal policy coming into effect. The dotted line of Figure 10.3 shows government intervention resulting in a budget surplus at times of recession (time periods 3 and 4) and a budget deficit at times of boom (time periods 5 and 6). This is exactly the opposite of what is needed for a discretionary fiscal policy to help stabilise the business cycle.

Checkpoint 5

Why might an inaccurate estimate of the national income multiplier by government also pose a problem for the use of discretionary fiscal policy?

Although fiscal policy is widely regarded as the most important policy approach in the UK, monetary policy can also have important impacts on national income and therefore on the prospects for businesses and households.

Monetary policy

Monetary policy has been defined as the attempt by government to manipulate the supply of, or demand for, money in order to achieve specific objectives. Since the rate of interest has an important role in determining the demand for money, monetary policy often concentrates on two key variables:

- money supply;
- rate of interest.

Money supply

If government is to control the money supply it must know what money is!

Definition of money

This may seem obvious but in a modern economy it is not. Money has been defined as anything that is generally acceptable in exchange for goods and services or in settlement of debts. Box 10.1 looks at the functions which an asset must fulfil if it is to be regarded as 'money'.

Box 10.1 What is money?

There are four key functions which money performs.

1 *To act as a medium of exchange* or means of payment. Money is unique in performing this function, since it is the only asset which is universally acceptable in exchange for goods and services. In the absence of a medium of exchange, trade could only take place if there was a *double coincidence of wants*; in other words, only if two people had mutually acceptable commodities to exchange. (I want yours, you want mine.) Trade of this type takes place on the basis of *barter*.

Clearly barter would restrict the growth of trade. It would also severely limit the extent to which individuals were able to specialise. By acting as a medium of exchange money therefore promotes specialisation. A person can exchange his/her labour for money, and then use that money to purchase the output produced by others. We have seen in Chapter 3 that specialisation greatly increases the wealth of the community. By acting as a medium of exchange money is therefore fulfilling a crucial function, enhancing trade, specialisation and wealth creation.

2 *To act as a unit of account.* By acting as a medium of exchange, money also provides a means of expressing value. The prices quoted for goods and services reflect their relative value and in this way money acts as a unit of account.

3 *To act as a store of wealth.* Because money can be exchanged immediately for goods and services it is a convenient way of holding wealth until goods and services are required. In this sense money acts as a store of wealth.

4 *To act as a standard for deferred payment.* In the modern world, goods and services are often purchased on credit, with the amount to be repaid being fixed in money terms. It would be impractical to agree repayment in terms of some other commodity; for example, it may not always be easy to predict the future availability or the future requirements for that commodity. It is therefore money which serves as a standard for deferred payments.

In the UK, notes, coins, cheques and credit cards are all used as a means of payment and all help to promote the exchange of goods and services and help to settle debts. However, cheques and credit cards are *not* strictly regarded as part of the money supply. Rather it is the underlying *bank deposit* behind the cheque or credit card which is regarded as part of the money supply. Cheques are simply an instruction to a bank to transfer ownership of the bank deposit, and of course a cheque drawn against a non-existent bank deposit will be dishonoured by a bank and the debt will remain; this will also be the case if an attempt is made to settle a transaction by using an invalid credit card.

Therefore a general definition of money in the UK today is notes, coins and bank and building society deposits.

Money and liquidity

One term frequently used in connection with money is *liquidity*. An asset is more liquid the more swiftly and less costly the process of converting the asset into the means of payment. It follows that money is the most liquid asset of all.

Creating money

When we say that banks and other financial institutions 'create money', what we mean is that at any one time these financial institutions only need to keep a small percentage of their deposits to fulfil their commitments to provide cash for their customers; the rest they can lend out as overdrafts or loans. Since deposits taking the form of overdrafts and loans are generally acceptable as a means of payment, they are part of the money supply.

- Each month the salaries of millions of people are paid into their *current accounts* (often called *sight deposits*) for use throughout the month. The banks know that during the month much of this money will lie idle, so they can lend some of the money out to people.
- Each month millions of people pay money into their *deposit accounts* (often called *time deposits*). This money tends to remain with the financial institutions for much longer periods than is the case with current accounts, so an even higher proportion of this money too can be lent out.

The amount of money that a financial institution does need to keep to fulfil its obligations to its customers is often called its 'cash ratio'.

As well as creating money by providing overdrafts and loans, the financial institutions also buy and sell *government securities*, such as Treasury Bills and Gilts (Government bonds). They also buy and sell *private securities* issued by firms, such as shares (equities) and debentures (company bonds). Box 10.2 looks more carefully at these various types of security.

Box 10.2 **Various types of bills, bonds and other securities**

- *Sterling commercial paper.* This term covers various securities (7–364 days) issued by companies seeking to borrow. The company promises to pay back a guaranteed sum in sterling at the specified future date.
- *Certificates of deposit.* A certificate of deposit (CD) is a document certifying that a deposit has been placed with a bank, and that the deposit is repayable with interest after a stated time. The minimum value of the deposit is usually £50,000 and CDs normally mature in twelve months or less, although they have been issued with a five-year maturity.
- *Treasury bills.* Treasury bills are issued by the Bank of England on behalf of the government and normally mature (are repayable) 91 days after issue. These again are a promise to pay a fixed sum of money at a specified future date. The purchaser of the Treasury bill earns a return by 'discounting' it, i.e. by offering to buy it at less than 'face value', the sum which is actually paid back at the future date. The rate of interest the government pays on its short-term borrowing is therefore determined by the price at which Treasury bills are

bought at the weekly tender. The higher the bid price, the lower the rate of interest the government pays on its short-term borrowing.

- *Equities*. These are the various types of shares issued by companies.
- *Bonds*. These are longer-term securities (usually three years and upwards) issued by governments and companies seeking borrow money. They pay an interest payment on the nominal (face) value of the bond. When issued by the government they are often called 'gilts', based on the belief that they are 'gilt-edged' (entirely secure). When issued by private companies they are often called 'debentures'.

By buying and selling these various securities, the financial intermediaries influence the general 'liquidity' of the financial system.

Near money

Figure 10.4 shows how, as well as those assets strictly included in our definition of 'money', a range of assets can be ranked in terms of their 'liquidity', i.e. the relative ease with which they can be converted into cash.

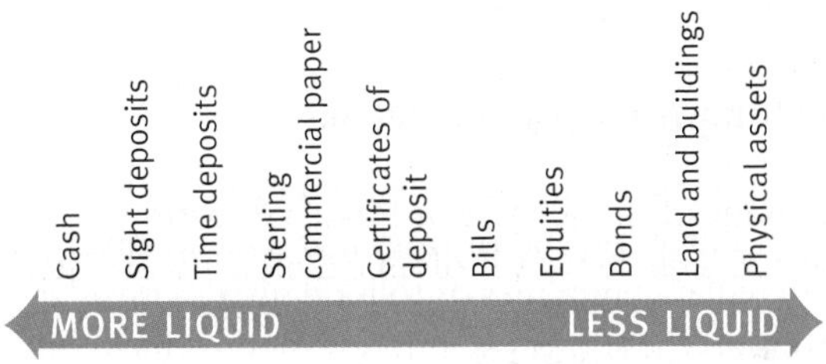

Fig 10.4 Liquidity spectrum

In seeking to influence the 'money supply', the government will be trying to influence not only the amount of 'money' available, strictly defined, but also the availability of many of these 'near money' assets. The more available are those assets at the 'more liquid' end of the spectrum in Figure 10.4, the more purchasing power will tend to be available in an economy.

Controlling the money supply

- When the government wishes to stimulate the economy, it is likely to seek to *increase* the money supply.
- When the government wishes to dampen down the economy, it is likely to seek to *reduce* the money supply.

The government can influence the supply of money by various techniques, including:

- *Issuing notes and coins*. The government can decide on the value of notes and coins to be issued through the Bank of England and by the Royal Mint.
- *'Open market' and other operations*. Making available more liquid assets in the financial system (e.g. Treasury bills). For example, the Bank of England might be instructed to buy securities in the 'open market' with cheques drawn on the government. This will increase cash and liquidity for the financial institutions and individuals selling their bonds and bills.

Checkpoint 6

Consider the likely effects of an increase in the money supply on:
(a) the W/J diagram;
(b) the 45° diagram.

Today, less emphasis is placed on controlling the money supply than was the case in the past. Instead, rather more attention is now given to controlling the demand for money using interest rates.

Controlling the rate of interest

There are, in fact, many rates of interest charged by different lenders. For example, a loan for a longer period of time will tend to carry a higher rate of interest, as might a loan to smaller companies or to individuals considered to be 'higher risk' by the lender. However, all these rates of interest tend to move upwards or downwards in line with the monthly rate of interest set by the Bank of England.

Since 1997 the Bank of England has been given independence by the government, and is now responsible for setting the interest rate each month. This is done at a monthly meeting of the nine members of the *Monetary Policy Committee* (MPC) at the Bank of England. The MPC takes into account the 'inflation target' the government has set and projections for future inflation when deciding upon the rate of interest.

Interest rates and the economy

Changing the interest rate affects the economy in a number of ways.

- *Savings*. Higher interest rates encourage saving, since the reward for saving and thereby postponing current consumption has now increased. Lower interest rates discourage saving by making spending for current consumption relatively more attractive.
- *Borrowing*. Higher interest rates discourage borrowing as it has now become more expensive, whilst lower interest rates encourage borrowing as it has now become cheaper. Borrowing on credit has played an important role in the growth of consumer spending and Chapter 9 (p. 345) showed how relatively small changes in interest rates in the UK result in major changes in the costs of borrowing.

- *Discretionary expenditure.* For many people their mortgage is the most important item of expenditure. To avoid losing their home, people most keep up with the mortgage repayments. Most people are on variable rate mortgages, so that if interest rates rise they must pay back more per month, leaving less income to spend on other things. Similarly, if interest rates fall, there will be increased income left in the family budget to spend on other things.
- *Exchange rate.* Increasing interest rates in the UK tends to make holding sterling deposits in the UK more attractive. As we see below (p. 409), an increased demand for sterling is likely to raise the exchange rate for sterling. Raising the exchange rate will make exports more expensive abroad and imports cheaper in the UK. Lowering interest rates will have the opposite effect, reducing the exchange rate for sterling, thereby making exports cheaper abroad and imports dearer in the UK.

Checkpoint 7 Can you suggest how a change in the interest rate will affect some businesses more than others?

Direct controls

LINKS

Later in this chapter (p. 390) we consider the impacts of both fiscal and monetary policy on businesses and households using 'aggregate demand' and 'aggregate supply' analysis.

As well as using fiscal and monetary policy, the government has the ability to change many rules and regulations which influence UK households and businesses. These so-called 'direct controls' were considered in more detail in Chapter 8.

Activity 10.1

1 Fill in the grid below with one or more of the letters, each representing a policy instrument.

(a) Increase tax allowances.
(b) Reduce interest rates.
(c) Increase interest rates.
(d) Reduce the top rate of income tax.
(e) Help given to firms moving to less developed areas.
(f) Reduce the basic rate of income tax.
(g) Increase VAT.
(h) Reduce VAT.
(i) Increase excise duties.
(j) Decrease excise duties.
(k) Increase restrictions on credit cards.
(l) Decrease restrictions on credit cards.
(m) Increase cash base.
(n) Decrease cash base.

Objective	Fiscal policy	Monetary policy
Increase economic growth		
Reduce inflationary pressures		
Reduce B of P deficit		
Reduce unemployment		
Reduce unemployment in the North East		

2 Consider some of the problems that might occur when trying to introduce the policies you identified as helping 'increase economic growth'.

3 Look carefully at the table below, which shows how indirect taxes influence groups of UK households arranged in quintiles (20% groups) from poorest to richest.

Quintile groups of households	Indirect taxes as percentage of disposable income per household		
	VAT	Other indirect taxes	Total indirect taxes
Bottom fifth	12.9	21.8	34.7
Next fifth	9.0	14.5	23.5
Middle fifth	8.5	12.9	21.4
Next fifth	7.5	10.7	18.2
Top fifth	5.9	7.2	13.1

Adapted from ONS (2003) *The Effects of Taxes and Benefits on Household Income*

Question

What does the table suggest?

Answers to Checkpoints and Activities can be found on pp. 705–735.

In the definitions we used at the beginning of our sections on both fiscal policy and monetary policy, the phrase 'in order to achieve specific objectives' was used. The rest of this chapter looks at a number of such *objectives*, including unemployment, inflation, economic growth and the balance of payments, paying particular attention to the impact of policies in these areas on businesses and households.

It will be useful at this stage to introduce an approach which develops further our earlier work on finding the equilibrium value of national income. This approach makes use of aggregate demand and aggregate supply curves, rather than the W/J or 45° diagrams used in Chapter 9.

Aggregate demand and aggregate supply analysis

In using these schedules we are seeking to establish linkages between the level of national output (income) and the general level of prices.

Aggregate demand schedule

We have already considered *aggregate expenditure* as consisting of consumption plus injection expenditure, C + I + G + X using the symbols of Chapter 9, p. 320. However, in this analysis we take the *net* contributions to aggregate demand from overseas trade, i.e. exports (injection) *minus* imports (withdrawal).

This gives us our expression for *aggregate demand* (AD).

$$AD = C + I + G + X - M$$

where C = consumer expenditure
I = investment expenditure
G = government expenditure
X = exports
M = imports

Aggregate demand and the price level

Another difference from our previous analysis is that we plot the general *price level* on the vertical axis and *national output* on the horizontal axis, as in Figure 10.5. Just as the *firm* demand curve shows an inverse (negative) relationship between price and demand for its output, the suggestion here is that the *aggregate* demand curve shows a similar inverse relationship between the average level of prices and aggregate demand in the economy.

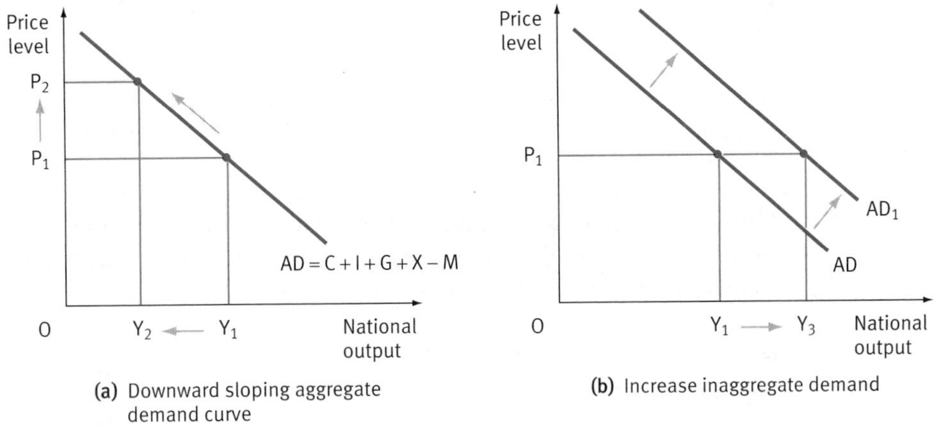

Fig 10.5 Aggregate demand (AD) schedules

In Figure 10.5(a) we can see that a rise in the average price level from P_1 to P_2 reduces AD from Y_1 to Y_2. For example, a higher price level reduces the real value of money holdings which (via the 'real balance' effect, p. 347) is likely to cut consumer spending (C), whilst a higher price level is also likely to result in interest rates being raised to curb inflationary pressures, with higher interest rates then discouraging both consumption (C) and investment (I) expenditures. As a result, as the average price level rises from P_1 to P_2, aggregate demand falls from Y_1 to Y_2.

In Figure 10.5(b) a rise in any one or more of the components of aggregate demand C, I, G or (X − M) will shift the AD curve rightwards and upwards to AD_1. Aggregate demand is now higher (Y_3) at any given price level (P_1).

The impact of changes in aggregate demand on equilibrium national output and inflation are considered further after we have introduced the aggregate supply curve (AS).

Aggregate supply schedule

We have previously noted a direct (positive) relationship between price and *firm* supply (e.g. Chapter 1) with a higher price resulting in an expansion of supply. The suggestion here is that the aggregate supply (AS) curve shows a similar direct relationship between the average level of prices and *aggregate* supply in the economy.

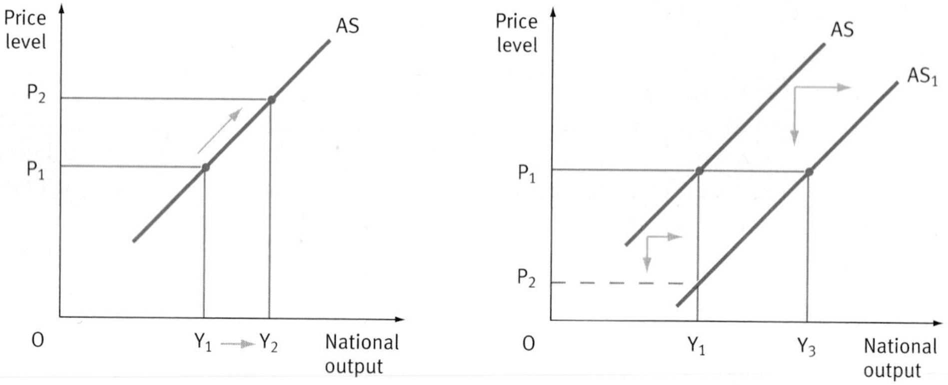

(a) Upward sloping aggregate supply curve

(b) Increase in aggregate supply

Fig 10.6 Aggregate supply (AS) schedules in the short-run time period

However, for aggregate supply we often make a distinction between the *short-run* and *long-run* time periods. In the short run at least one factor of production is fixed, whereas in the long run all factors can be varied.

Short-run aggregate supply

Figure 10.6(a) shows the upward sloping short-run aggregate supply curve (AS). It assumes that some input costs, particularly money wages, remain relatively fixed as the general price level changes. It then follows that an increase in the general price level from P_1 to P_2, whilst input costs remain relatively fixed, increases the profitability of production and induces firms to expand output, raising aggregate supply from Y_1 to Y_2.

There are two explanations as to why an important input cost, namely wages, may remain constant even though prices have risen.

- First, many employees are hired under fixed-wage contracts. Once these contracts are agreed it is the firm that determines (within reason) the number of labour hours actually worked. If prices rise, the negotiated *real wage* (i.e. money wage divided by prices) will fall and firms will want to hire more labour time and raise output.
- Second, workers may not immediately be aware of price level changes, i.e. they may suffer from 'money illusion'. If workers' expectations lag behind actual price level rises, then workers will not be aware that their real wages have fallen and will not adjust their money demands appropriately.

Both these reasons imply that as the general price level rises, real wages will fall, reducing costs of production and raising profitability, thereby encouraging firms to raise output.

In Figure 10.6(b) a rise in the productivity of any factor input or fall in its cost will shift the AS curve rightwards and downwards to AS_1. Aggregate supply is now higher (Y_3) at any given price level (P_1). Put another way, any given output (Y_1) can now be supplied at a lower price level (P_2).

Long-run aggregate supply

In the long run it is often assumed that factor markets are more flexible and better informed so that input prices (e.g. money wages) fully adjust to changes in the general price level and vice versa. If this is the case, then we have the *vertical* long-run aggregate supply (AS) curve in Figure 10.7.

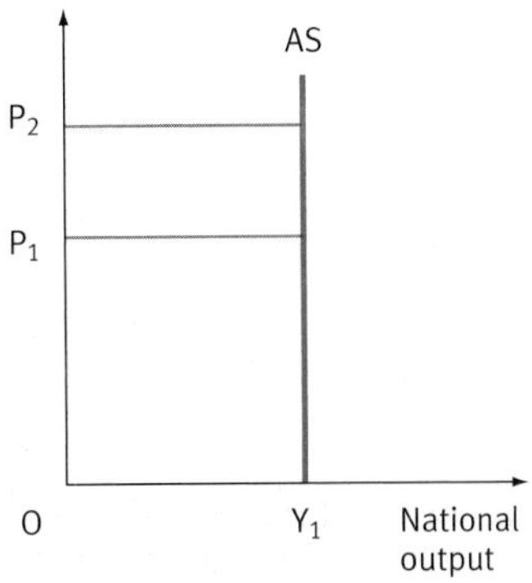

Fig 10.7 Aggregate supply (AS) schedule in the long-run time period (or short-run time period if input costs fully reflect any changes in prices)

NOTE

Flexible wage contracts and fuller information

Workers in the long run can gather full information on price level changes and can renegotiate wage contracts in line with higher or lower prices. This time, any given percentage increase in the general price level from P_1 to P_2 is matched by increases in input costs. For example, if general prices rise by 5% then wages rise by 5% so that the 'real wage' does not fall. In this situation there is no increase in the profitability of production when prices rise from P_1 to P_2, so that long-run aggregate supply remains unchanged at Y_1.

Watch out!

Of course, a short-run aggregate supply curve might be vertical if no 'money illusion' exists. Alternatively, a long-run aggregate supply curve could itself slope upwards from left to right if 'money illusion' persists into the long-run time period.

AD/AS and equilibrium national output

It will be useful at this stage to look at how AD and AS schedules can be used to find the equilibrium levels for the general price level and for national output.

We initially assume that wages and other input costs do not fully adjust to price level changes to that the aggregate supply (AS) curve slopes upwards from left to right and is not vertical.

Only where AD and AS *intersect* at a general price level of P_1 and national output Y_1 in Figure 10.8 do we have an equilibrium outcome for the economy. Any other combination of price level and national output is unsustainable, with an excess of either aggregate demand or aggregate supply.

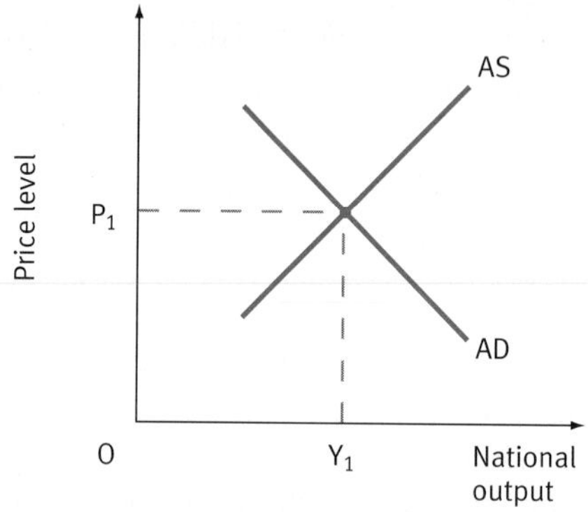

Fig 10.8 Equilibrium values for the price level and national output

For example, for price levels *above* P_1, AS exceeds AD, putting downward pressure on prices and national output. As the general price level falls, aggregate demand (AD) expands (positive 'real balance effect', via increase in real value of wealth holdings raising C and likely reductions in interest rates, raising C and I etc.) and aggregate supply (AS) contracts (profitability is squeezed as prices fall faster than the less flexible input costs for producers). Only at P_1/Y_1 do we have an equilibrium outcome.

Checkpoint 8 Can you explain why price levels *below* P_1 are not sustainable in Figure 10.8?

As we consider the various policy issues involving inflation, unemployment, economic growth, the balance of payments and exchange rates, we shall use aggregate demand and aggregate supply analysis wherever appropriate.

Inflation

Inflation is a term often applied to a situation in which there is a persistent tendency for the general level of prices to rise. The 'rate of inflation' over the past 12 months is, in effect, telling us how much extra money we would need now in order to be able to purchase the same 'basket' of goods and services as we did 12 months ago.

Measuring inflation

A number of measures have been used to calculate the rate of inflation in the UK.

- *The Retail Price Index (RPI).* This has been the main official measure in the UK, showing the change from month to month in the cost of a representative 'basket' of goods and services bought by a typical household. The rate of inflation measured using the RPI is often referred to as the *headline* rate of inflation. In January 2004 the RPI stood at 183.6 which means that average prices have risen by 83.6% between January 1987 and January 2004. As the index is an average, this figure conceals the fact that some prices have increased more rapidly (rent 155%, water 176% and cigarettes 208%), whilst other prices have fallen (audio-visual equipment by around 70%).

  Once the RPI has been constructed, the rate of inflation can then be calculated, with the most usual measure being the 12-monthly change in the RPI. For example, the RPI stood at 183.6 in January 2004. In January 2003 it stood at 179.3 and therefore the annual rate of inflation over the period to January 2004 is:

  $$\frac{183.6 - 179.3}{179.3} \times 100\% = 2.4\%$$

- *RPIX.* For policy makers in the UK, however, the RPI has been superseded by the RPIX (the RPI excluding mortgage interest payments). The RPIX is referred to as measuring 'underlying' inflation and this was (until 2003 – see below) the subject of the government's 2.5% inflation target. Excluding mortgage interest rates from the RPI eliminates a rather perverse effect, namely that raising the interest rate to moderate inflationary pressure will actually increase the RPI measure of inflation!

- *RPIY.* However, both the RPI and the RPIX are influenced by increases in indirect taxes and in the council tax. If these taxes increase, for example, a rise in excise duty on cigarettes to discourage smoking, then the RPIX measure of inflation will increase without any increase in inflationary pressure in the economy. The Bank of England publishes the RPIY (RPIX minus VAT, local authority taxes and excise duty) to eliminate this effect.

- *Consumer Price Index (CPI).* This was adopted in December 2003 as the official measure of inflation in the UK and is based on *Harmonised Index of Consumer Prices* (*HICP*), the official measure in the EU. The European Central Bank aims to keep EU inflation below 2% as measured by the HICP, and 2% is now also the target for UK inflation using the CPI.

Box 10.3 considers the RPI in more detail.

Box 10.3 **The Retail Price Index (RPI)**

The RPI measures the change from month to month in the cost of a representative 'basket' of goods and services of the type bought by a typical household.

A number of stages are involved in the calculation of the RPI. The first stage is to select the items to be included in the index and to weight these items according to their relative importance in the average family budget. Obviously, items on which a family spends a large proportion of its income are given heavier weights than those items on which the family spends relatively little. For example, in 2003 the weight given to tea in the index was 1, whereas that for electricity was 14 (out of a total 'all items weight' of 1,000). The weights used are changed annually to reflect the changes in the composition of family expenditure.

The weights used for groups of items are shown in Table 10.4. It can be seen that food has been replaced as the largest item by housing (rent, mortgage interest, rates and council tax, water charges, repairs and dwelling insurance). This is part of a longer-run trend associated with differing income elasticities of demand for the items in the 'basket'.

Table 10.4 General index of retail prices: group weights

	1987	2003
Food	167	109
Catering	46	51
Alcoholic drink	76	68
Tobacco	38	30
Housing	157	203
Fuel and light	61	29
Household goods	73	72
Household services	44	61
Clothing and footwear	74	51
Personal goods and services	40	41
Motoring expenditure	127	146
Fares and other travel costs	22	20
Leisure goods	47	48
Leisure services	30	71

Adapted from Office of National Statistics

The second stage in deriving the RPI involves collecting the price data. For most items, prices are collected on a specific day each month, usually the Tuesday nearest the middle of the month. Prices are obtained from a sample of retail outlets in some 180 different areas. Care is taken to make sure a representative range of retail outlets, small retailers, supermarkets, department stores, etc. are surveyed. In all, around 150,000 price quotations are collected each month. An average price is then calculated for each item in the index.

The final stage is to calculate the RPI from all these data. All index numbers must relate to some base period or reference date. In the case of the RPI the base period is January 1987 = 100.

CPI and RPI

It is worth noting that the CPI and the RPI are different in a number of ways.

- The RPI excludes the richest 4% of households and the poorest pensioner householders when calculating the weights to be used in the index, believing these patterns of expenditure to be 'unrepresentative'. However, the CPI includes everyone.

- The basket of goods also differs mainly in its treatment of housing and related costs. A number of items included in the RPI are excluded from the CPI, such as council tax, mortgage interest payments, house depreciation and buildings insurance.

The CPI measure of inflation for the UK has systematically been below that of both the RPI and RPIX. For example, in 2003 the CPI gave an inflation rate in the UK of only 1.4% compared to around 2.5% using RPIX.

Businesses have expressed some concern that the lower recorded figure for inflation using the CPI might encourage the UK Chancellor to raise VAT and other taxes on goods and services without breaching the 2.5% inflation target! However, when the government changed from RIPX to CPI in December 2003 it also reduced the inflation target under the new index from 2.5% to 2%.

Watch out!

If inflation is a period of rising prices, people assume that *deflation* is a period of falling prices. This is actually incorrect. Deflation is usually used to refer to an economy which is slowing down, in which output is falling and unemployment rising. Prices might or might not fall in a situation of 'deflation'. *Disinflation* is technically the correct word to use for falling prices.

Governments are anxious to curb the rate of inflation because of the 'costs' associated with a high inflation rate.

Costs of inflation

- 'Shoe leather costs' whereby individuals and businesses make more frequent trips to banks etc. since holding cash is more expensive (e.g. higher opportunity cost in terms of interest forgone).
- 'Menu costs' whereby businesses have to change price tags, cash tills, vending machines and price lists more frequently.
- 'Decision-taking costs' whereby future contracts become less certain, with businesses now requiring a higher future return (i.e. higher risk premium) to cover increased future uncertainties from inflation.
- 'Inflation illusion' whereby businesses lose customers who think that prices have risen excessively when in fact money incomes have risen even more rapidly so that real incomes have increased. By cutting back on consumer spending in the (mistaken) belief that prices have risen too rapidly, aggregate demand may fall and an economic slowdown occur.
- 'Redistribution costs' whereby businesses on fixed contracts or individuals on fixed money incomes lose out. Also, creditors lose since the real value of repayments to the lender is reduced in the future.
- 'Fiscal drag' whereby if the government fails to increase tax allowance in line with inflation, then even with tax rates unchanged more tax is paid by businesses (e.g. corporation tax) and individuals (e.g. income tax) than before. The extra withdrawals from the circular flow may then discourage economic activity.

Benefits of inflation

Of course, there are also beneficiaries from inflation.

- Businesses will find it easier to pass on cost increases (e.g. higher wages) as price increases during times of modest inflation.
- Businesses and individuals who owe money (i.e. are debtors) will gain since inflation reduces the real value of their debt.

Whilst there may be benefits from modest inflation, few would argue that there are any benefits from periods of excessive inflation. Case Study 10.1 uses the experience of Germany to give a useful insight into the costs of accelerating rates of inflation.

Case Study 10.1 German hyperinflation

When people discuss inflation and its problems they often examine inflation in its more 'moderate' forms. However, if inflation gets out of hand, then it can take on the extreme form sometimes described as 'hyperinflation'. Whilst this word does not have a specific definition, it tends to be used for extreme situations where, say, prices are rising in double-digit figures on a daily or weekly basis. The example of Germany in the early years of the 1920s is often used as an example.

To illustrate the German experience we can look at changes in the price of a postage stamp in these years.

The price of a postage stamp in Germany 1921 to 1923

	Deutschmarks
1 April 1921	0.60
1 Jan 1922	2
1 Jul	3
1 Oct	6
15 Nov	12
15 Dec	25
15 Jan 1923	50
1 Mar	100
1 July	300
1 Aug	1,000
24 Aug	20,000
1 Sep	75,000
20 Sep	250,000
1 Oct	2,000,000
10 Oct	5,000,000
20 Oct	10,000,000
1 Nov	100,000,000
5 Nov	1,000,000,000
12 Nov	10,000,000,000
20 Nov	20,000,000,000
26 Nov	80,000,000,000
1 Dec	100,000,000,000 or 0.10 new marks

Case Study 10.1 continued

Many stories come from this period in Germany to illustrate the problems of hyperinflation. A famous one tells of a man who filled up his wheelbarrow with deutschmarks to go the shops, only to be mugged en route to his destination; the robber tipped out the notes and stole the wheelbarrow. Another refers to the Berlin Symphony Orchestra which walked out halfway through an afternoon performance because they had just been paid, knowing that if they waited to the end of the performance their wages would be able to buy so much less. Yet another refers to coffee drinkers in Berlin's cafés who insisted on paying before they drank their cup of coffee, aware that one hour later they might be unable to afford it. It doesn't take very much imagination to realise that everyday life would simply break down if faced by such dramatic falls in the value of money.

Historically, annual price increases of less than 5% have not been considered too much of a problem, though lower figures than this have become the stated aim of many advanced industrialised economies. For example, the UK government has for many years instructed the Bank of England to keep inflation (RPIX) below 2.5% per annum and the European Central Bank aims to keep its official measure of inflation (HICP) below 2% per annum.

Questions

1 Why do some suggest that it is useful for us to carefully consider historical cases of hyperinflation, such as that in Germany, even though hyperinflation rarely occurs?

2 How might a government seek to bring a situation of hyperinflation under control?

Types of inflation

Various types of inflation are often discussed, in particular 'demand-pull' and 'cost-push' inflation, though in practice inflation may involve elements of both types. We can use our earlier aggregate demand and aggregate supply analysis to consider these two types of inflation.

Demand-pull inflation

This is seen as being caused mainly by an increase in the components of aggregate demand (e.g. consumption, investment, public expenditure, exports). A rise in any of these components will shift aggregate demand upwards and to the right from AD_1 to AD_2 in Figure 10.9(a). This raises the average level of prices from P_1 to P_2 and raises national output from Y_1 to Y_2. The rise in aggregate demand results in many more consumers buying products, but a rise in aggregate output to Y_2 requires a higher price to cover the extra production costs (marginal and average) incurred. With demand-pull inflation we move along the aggregate supply curve to a point where both output and price levels are higher.

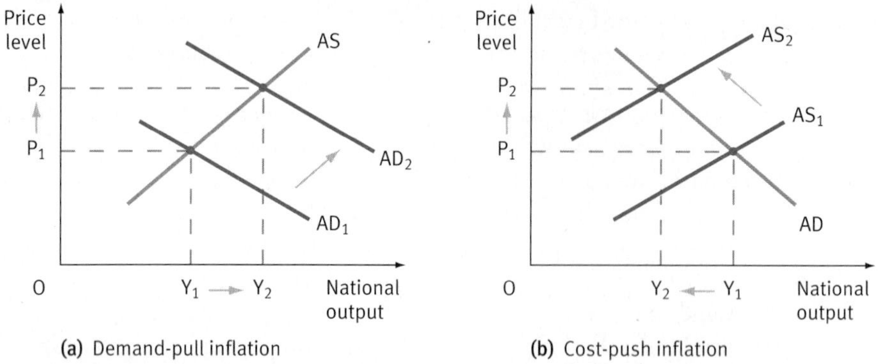

Fig 10.9 Demand-pull and cost-push inflation.

Cost-push inflation

This is seen as being caused mainly by an increase in the costs of production, which occurs independently of the level of aggregate demand. Firms then pass on these higher costs to consumers in the form of higher prices. The rise in costs reduces profit margins and results in some firms becoming insolvent so that they exit the market. As a result, the aggregate supply curve shifts upwards and to the left from AS_1 to AS_2 in Figure 10.9(b), with less output supplied at any given price. This raises the average level of prices from P_1 to P_2 but reduces national output from Y_1 to Y_2.

With cost-push inflation we move along the aggregate demand curve to a point where output is lower and price levels are higher.

Watch out!

The analysis has assumed throughout that prices adjust more rapidly than input costs, so that there is some profit incentive for higher prices to result in extra output. In other words, the AS curves slope upwards from left to right in our diagrams.

Employment and unemployment

We have already considered government policy affecting unemployment and inflation in our discussion of inflationary and deflationary gaps (Chapter 9, pp. 359–361). Here we consider various aspects of employment and unemployment in rather more detail.

Output and employment

As national output/income rises, so too will *employment* since, for a given level of technology, more labour input will be needed to produce more output. It therefore follows that a rise in national output (income) can be expected to result in a rise in employment. In 2004 employment in the UK was at an all-time high of 27.8 million people. Of course as employment rises, unemployment will usually fall.

Whilst *unemployment* in the UK reached over 3 million people in the mid-1980s, some 11% of the workforce, today the unemployment rate has fallen to around 4% of the workforce, well below the EU average of over 10% of the workforce unemployed.

Jobless growth

Nevertheless, many economies have been expressing concern in recent years at what they fear may be 'jobless growth'. In other words, a situation where a rise in national output does not seem to be associated with higher levels of employment (and therefore falling levels of unemployment), as was previously the case.

A number of possible explanations have been suggested.

1 New technologies have raised the productivity of labour significantly in many activities, so that fewer workers are required for even higher levels of output. This is often referred to as 'technological unemployment' (see p. 402).

2 Outsourcing of jobs (see p. 631) by multinational companies relocating labour intensive processes to lower wage economies. Employment may be growing worldwide but not in the high-wage, developed economies as 'footloose' multinationals reconfigure their value chains.

LINKS
We consider issues of outsourcing and multinational value chains in more detail in Chapter 15, pp. 627–635.

Measuring unemployment

There are two main methods for counting the unemployed in the UK, the first of which is now the official measure of UK unemployment.

- *Survey method*. The UK's quarterly Labour Force Survey (LFS) uses the International Labour Office (ILO) definition of unemployment: people without a job who were available to start work within the next two weeks and who had either looked for work within the four weeks prior to interview or who were waiting to start a job. The LFS samples around 61,000 households in any three-month period and interviews are taken from approximately 120,000 people aged 16 and over.
- *Claimant count*. A monthly count by the Benefits Agency of the number of people claiming unemployment-related benefits.

Many regard the survey method as the more accurate; For example, women and others who are actively seeking work but who may not qualify for benefit will not appear in the claimant count.

Types of unemployment

The various types of unemployment are outlined in Table 10.5.

Table 10.5 Types of unemployment

Term	Definition
Frictional (search) unemployment	There is always this type of unemployment as some workers will always be in the process of changing jobs
Structural unemployment	This results from longer-term changes in the demand for, and supply of, labour in specific industries as the structure of the economy changes (e.g. decline in shipbuilding and in textiles in the UK)
Regional unemployment	This results from changes in demand for the outputs of industries which tend to be located in specific regions of a country, e.g. shipbuilding in Clydeside (Scotland) and Tyneside (NE England)
Technological unemployment	Technological changes may lead to significant changes in labour and capital productivity, resulting in job losses
Real wage unemployment	This results from rigidities in the labour market which prevents the real wage from falling to a level that would 'clear' the market
Demand deficient unemployment	Where the major cause is excess supply (i.e. lack of demand) in the product market: often associated with economic recessions
Natural rate of unemployment	Defined as the rate of unemployment at which there is no excess or deficiency of demand for labour

Frictional, structural and regional unemployment are clearly defined in Table 10.5 but we might usefully consider the other types of unemployment in a little more detail.

Technological unemployment

New technologies can both create and destroy jobs. Where the new technologies involve process innovation then labour is often replaced by capital equipment in the production process and the term 'technological unemployment' is often used. For example, the US Internet banking company has introduced 'smart' technologies into every aspect of its operations, so that its $2.4bn of deposits are now managed by just 180 people, compared to the 2,000 people required to manage deposits of this size in less technologically advanced banks.

However, the new technologies may lower product prices and raise product quality, thereby increasing product demand and creating new jobs, even if these are different from the original jobs displaced. The 'employment multiplier' effect of the initial investment in new technologies (see p. 359) will further support this outcome. The *net* effect may be positive or negative for jobs.

Technological unemployment may, however, be about to enter a new phase! Rifkin (2004) reports that new technologies are increasing productivity at ever-accelerating rates in both industrial and service sectors, so much so that job destruction is outweighing job creation. He points to an astonishing 10% growth in US productivity in 2003, the steepest rise since 1950, accompanied by increasing, not falling, unemployment.

Quote

Greatly increased productivity has been at the expense of more workers being marginalized into part-time employment or given notice to quit. A shrinking workforce, however, means diminishing income, reduced consumer demand and an economy unable to grow.

Rifkin J. (2004)

Real wage unemployment

This is sometimes called 'classical unemployment' as shown in Figure 10.10.

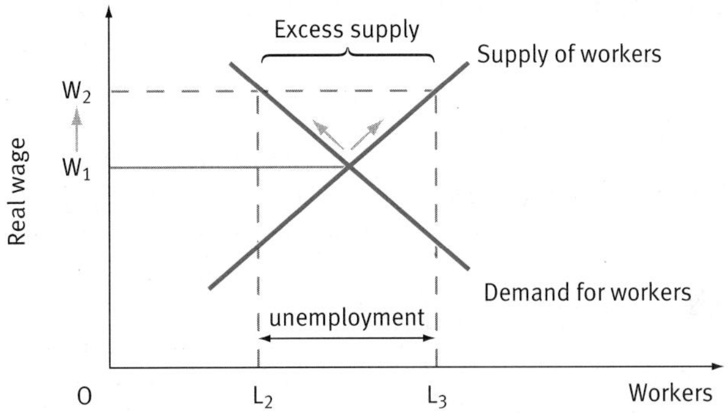

Fig 10.10 Real wage ('classical') unemployment

Demand deficient unemployment

Only at the real wage rate W_1 does the supply of labour exactly match the demand for labour (i.e. the market clears). If the real wage is too high (W_2), then more workers will offer themselves for work (L_3) but employers will only be willing to have fewer workers (L_2) at this higher real wage. The result is excess supply of workers ($L_3 - L_2$), i.e. unemployment caused by a failure of the labour market to reach the 'market clearing' real wage W_1.

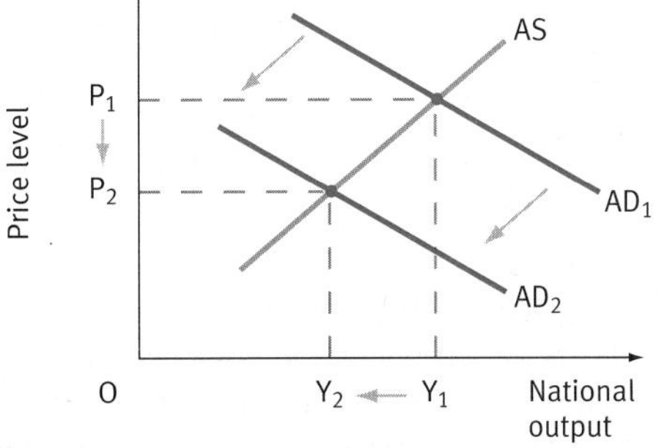

Fig 10.11 Demand-deficient unemployment

In Figure 10.11 a decrease in aggregate demand resulting from a fall in C, I, G or (X – M) will shift the aggregate demand curve downwards from AD_1 to AD_2. This will reduce the equilibrium level of national output from Y_1 to Y_2 and with it the level of employment (i.e. unemployment will result).

Natural rate of unemployment

Box 10.4 uses some rather more technical analysis to investigate the so-called 'natural rate of unemployment'.

Box 10.4 Natural rate of unemployment (NRU)

The labour market diagram shown in Figure 10.12 can be used to illustrate the idea of the 'natural rate of unemployment' (NRU), which was introduced by Milton Friedman. Here labour demand, L^D, reflects the *marginal revenue product* (MRP) of workers, i.e. the extra revenue earned from employing the last worker (see Chapter 7, p. 249). This is downward sloping, in line with the assumption of a diminishing *marginal physical product* (MPP) for workers.

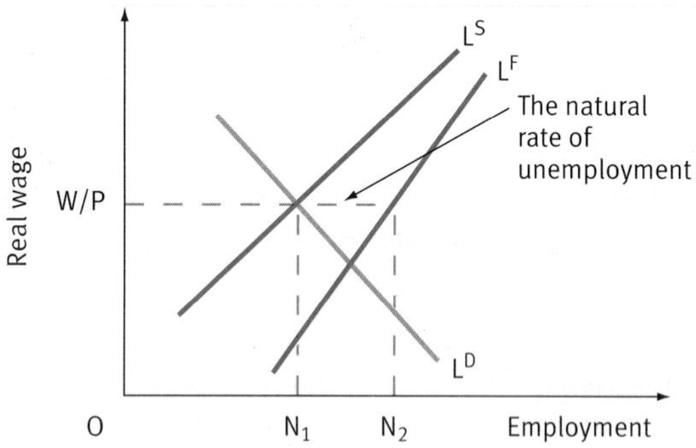

Fig 10.12 Finding the natural rate of unemployment (NRU)

- *Labour supply*, L^S, represents all those workers willing and able (i.e. they have the right skills and are in the right location) to accept jobs at a given real wage.
- *The labour force*, L^F, shows the total number of workers who consider themselves to be members of the labour force at any given real wage; of course, not all of these are willing or able to accept job offers, perhaps because they are still searching for a better offer or because they have not yet acquired the appropriate skills or are not in an appropriate location.

At the equilibrium real wage (W/P) in Figure 10.12, N_1 workers are willing and able to accept job offers whereas N_2 workers consider themselves to be members of the labour force. That part of the labour force unwilling or unable to accept job offers at the equilibrium real wage ($N_2 - N_1$) is defined as being the *natural rate of unemployment* (NRU). In terms of our earlier classification of the unemployed the NRU can be regarded as including the frictionally, structurally and regionally unemployed.

It can be seen that anything that *reduces the labour supply* (the numbers willing and able to accept a job at a given real wage) will, other things being equal, cause the NRU to increase. Possible factors might include an increase in the level or availability of unemployment benefits, thereby encouraging unemployed members of the labour force to engage in more prolonged search activity. An increase in trade union power might also reduce the numbers willing and able to accept a job at a given real wage, especially if the trade union is able to restrict the effective labour supply as part of a strategy for raising wages. A reduced labour supply might also result from increased technological change or increased global competition, both of which change the nature of the labour market skills required for employment. Higher taxes on earned income are also likely to reduce the labour supply at any given real wage.

Similarly, anything that *reduces the labour demand* will, other things equal, cause the NRU to increase. A fall in the marginal revenue product of labour, via a fall in marginal physical productivity or in the product price, might be expected to reduce labour demand. Many economists believe that the two sharp oil price increases in the 1970s had this effect, with the resulting fall in aggregate demand causing firms to cut back on capital spending, reducing the overall capital stock and hence the marginal physical productivity of labour.

Unemployment and inflation

It is often suggested that if employment rises too high (i.e. unemployment falls too low) then inflationary pressures will build up in the economy. This suggestion underpins the so-called 'Phillips curve'.

Phillips curve

The **Phillips curve** (Figure 10.13) is based on finding a 'line of best fit' for UK time series data relating unemployment to inflation over almost 100 years (1861–1957). It suggested that lower levels of unemployment will result in higher *wage inflation* as a result of higher demand for labour, which in turn will result in higher *price inflation*. The Phillips curve has often been seen as supporting a 'demand-pull' view of inflation (see p. 399). It suggests that we can only have less wage and price inflation by accepting a lower level of demand and therefore more unemployment.

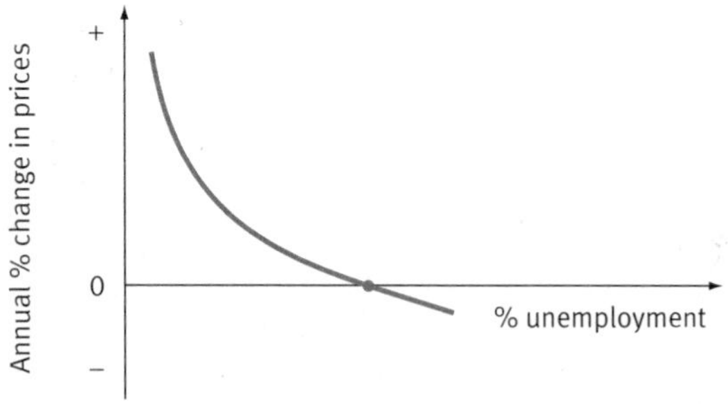

Fig 10.13 Phillips curve suggesting that higher levels of demand (lower % unemployment) results in higher rates of wage and price inflation

This simple statistical 'trade-off' between unemployment and inflation was seen to break down in the 1960s. From that time onwards, variable and often higher levels of inflation seemed to be associated with any given level of unemployment.

CHECK THE NET
www.ilo.org/public/english/employment/strat/global.htm

One of the reasons suggested for this breakdown in the Phillips curve is the growing importance of 'cost-push' inflation (see p. 400). Increases in the costs of raw materials and components or in wage rates (e.g. trade union pressures) may push costs and prices up irrespective of the pressure of demand.

Case Study 10.2 looks at unemployment from a global perspective.

Case Study 10.2 Global unemployment hits record high

Unemployment worldwide edged up to a record 185.9m in 2003 despite higher global growth, the *International Labour Organisation* says in its employment trends report in January 2004.

The unemployment increase, from 184.4m in 2002, largely reflected rising joblessness among young people, who faced an unemployment rate of 14.4% compared with 6.2% overall. The ILO estimates that the number of 'working poor' in the world – those living on less than $1 a day – remained broadly static at an estimated 550m in 2003.

Sluggish economic growth combined with Sars and job losses in travel and tourism pushed up unemployment and underemployment in the first half of 2003, the ILO says. The severe acute respiratory syndrome outbreak alone may have cost East Asian countries 2m–6m jobs.

Though the stronger economic recovery that took hold in the second half of 2003 could, if sustained, improve the global employment picture this year, the ILO warns that many countries are far from generating the number of jobs needed if they are to meet the United Nations target of halving poverty by 2015. 'The overall challenge is to absorb the 514m new entrants to world labour markets and to reduce working poverty by 2015, the report says. It urges 'pro-poor' policies centred on job creation, especially for young people, accompanied by debt reduction and measures to improve access to rich-country markets for developing country exports.

We can reduce poverty if policy makers stop treating employment as an afterthought and place decent work at the heart of macroeconomic and social policies, said Juan Somavia, ILO director-general. The Middle East and North Africa emerges as the region worst hit by open unemployment, with an overall jobless rate of 12%. One in four people aged 15–24 is without a job. Countries in the region will have to grow much faster than in the past decade to absorb the almost 4m new entrants to the labour force annually and halve unemployment and working poverty, the report says.

Sub-Saharan Africa will have to create nearly 8m jobs each year to absorb new jobseekers. 'To halve unemployment and working poverty by 2015 would require the rate of GDP growth to triple, a rather unrealistic goal for most economies,' the report notes.

Case Study 10.2 continued

Questions

1 What problems might result from a failure to tackle global unemployment?

2 How might governments and international organisations seek to reduce global unemployment?

Balance of payments

The balance of payments situation for a country will both influence the exchange rate for its currency and in turn be influenced by that exchange rate.

As well as a high level of employment (low unemployment) and low inflation, government policy will seek to contain within reasonable limits any deficit on the balance of payments and may even seek a surplus.

The UK balance of payments is often broken down into the *current account, capital account* and *financial account.*

Current account

This consists of two main sub-accounts, the 'balance on goods' (formerly 'visible trade balance') and the 'balance on services' (formerly 'invisible trade balance'). Exports are

Table 10.6 Components of UK current account 1992–2003 (£m)

	Trade in goods and services							
	Balance on goods							
Year	Total	Oil	Non oil	Balance on services	Balanace on goods & services	Investment income[1] balance	Transfer balance	Current balance
1992	−13,050	+1,610	−14,660	+5,482	−7,568	+128	−5,534	−12,974
1993	−13,066	+2,612	−15,678	+6,581	−6,485	−191	−5,243	−11,919
1994	−11,126	+3,937	−15,063	+6,379	−4,747	+3,348	−5,369	−6,768
1995	−12,023	+4,323	−16,346	+8,481	−3,542	+2,101	−7,574	−9,015
1996	−13,722	+4,810	−18,532	+9,597	−4,125	+1,204	−5,788	−8,709
1997	−12,342	+4,560	−16,902	+12,528	+186	+3,906	−5,812	−1,720
1998	−21,813	+3,042	−24,855	+12,666	−9,147	+12,558	−8,225	−4,814
1999	−27,372	+4,449	−31,182	+11,794	−15,578	+2,536	−6,687	−19,729
2000	−30,326	+6,536	−36,862	+11,838	−18,488	+9,312	−10,032	−19,208
2001	−40,620	+5,577	−46,197	+13,000	−27,620	+16,188	−6,188	−18,038
2002	−46,455	+5,487	−51,942	+15,166	−31,289	+21,119	−8,795	−18,817
2003	−47,290	+4,110	−51,400	+14,617	−32,673	+22,097	−9,854	−20,430

[1] This total includes both 'compensation to employees' and 'investment income' but in statistical terms it is nearly all investment income.

Adapted from ONS (2003) *UK Balance of Payments*; ONS (2004) *Data Releases* (various)

given a positive sign, imports a negative sign: when exports exceed imports, we speak of a 'surplus' and when imports exceed exports, a 'deficit'.

- **Balance on goods** is split into oil goods and non-oil goods.
- **Balance on services** includes shipping, insurance, finance etc.

The current account is completed by adding two further items: the 'investment income balance' (i.e. net income from interest, profits and dividends) and the 'transfer balance' (i.e. net value of government transfers to institutions such as the EU, World Bank etc.). Table 10.6 presents the components of the UK current account over the past ten years.

Case Study 10.3 looks more carefully at the balance on oil goods and some emerging concerns for the UK.

Case Study 10.3 Disappearing oil

The importance of oil to the UK balance of payments was clearly seen in Table 10.6. Unfortunately, the future may be less comforting in this respect! In September 2003 imports exceeded exports of oil for the first time since August 1991.The turnabout from a £400m surplus in August 2002 to a £63m deficit in August 2003 helped to widen the trade gap to a record £3.9bn in September alone.

The overall current account deficit with the rest of the EU, where much of the oil goes, also reached a monthly record of £2.2bn. Over the July–September 2003 period the UK has been spending 3% more than it is producing.

September 2003's oil shortfall was a blip, the Office of National Statistics claimed, as important refineries were out of use for maintenance. Crude oil production is estimated to have recovered to 2.17m barrels per day (bpd). However, the UK Offshore Operators Association predicts a bleak trend for oil production in the UK. North Sea oil output peaked at 2.9 m bpd in 1999, but is expected to be just 1.6m bpd in 2008.

At recent prices, the balance of payments would then be about £4bn a year worse off, eliminating regular monthly oil surpluses.

Before North Sea oil and gas, the UK used to run an annual trade deficit of between £2bn and £4bn on fuels. Recently, there has been a surplus of about £6bn.

Interestingly, the situation would be worse for the UK but for China! China's rapid economic growth, estimated by some at around 10% per annum, has caused a surge in demand for raw materials and energy to produce its explosive growth of output. That in turn has increased the demand for oil, which is estimated to be around 6m barrels of oil per day, up 10% on 2003.

Case Study 10.3 continued

Questions

1 How serious are these projected reductions in oil output for the UK balance of payments?

2 What other implications might this have for the UK economy?

3 What policy responses might the UK government consider?

Capital account

This records the flow of money into the country (positive sign) and out of the country (negative sign) resulting from the purchase or sale of fixed assets (e.g. land) and selected capital transfers.

Financial account

This records the flows of money into the country (positive sign) and out of the country (negative sign) resulting from investment-related or other financial activity.

- *Direct investment* usually involves physical assets of a company (e.g. plant, equipment).
- *Portfolio investment* involves paper assets (e.g. shares, bonds).
- *'Other financial flows'* may involve the movement of deposits between countries.

If the net value of the items mentioned in the three accounts so far are negative, we speak of a *balance of payments deficit;* if positive, of a *balance of payments surplus.*

Balancing item

The overall accounts are constructed so that they *must* balance (accounting identity), with this balance achieved by either drawing on reserves (if deficit) or adding to reserves (if surplus). The 'balancing item' represents these values, which are required to maintain the accounting identity.

Exchange rate

This can be quoted as the number of units of the *foreign currency* that is needed to purchase one unit of the domestic currency: e.g. £1 = €1.50. Alternatively, it can be quoted as the number of units of the *domestic currency* needed to purchase one unit of the foreign currency: e.g. €1 = £0.666.

The exchange rate is a key 'price' affecting the competitiveness of UK exporters and UK producers of import substitutes.

- *A fall* ***(depreciation)*** *in the sterling exchange rate* makes UK exports cheaper abroad (in the foreign currency) and imports into the UK dearer at home (in £ sterling).

- *A rise (**appreciation**) in the sterling exchange rate* makes UK exports dearer abroad (in the foreign currency) and imports into the UK cheaper at home (in £ sterling).

We can illustrate the latter using the £ : $ exchange rate. In recent times sterling has risen (appreciated) significantly in value against the US dollar.

Example: £1 = $1.50 (2002)
£1 = $1.85 (March 2004)

As a result, a £100 export from the UK costing $150 in the US in 2002 costs $185 in 2004. Similarly, an import from the US costing $150 would sell for £100 in the UK in 2002 but £81.08 in 2004.

The change in value of UK exports and UK imports after a change in the exchange rate will depend crucially on the **price elasticity of demand** (PED) for both exports and imports. The more elastic the demand for exports and imports, the greater the impact on the balance of payments of any change in the exchange rate, and vice versa.

Types of exchange rate

- *Nominal exchange rate.* This is the rate at which one currency is quoted against any other currency. The nominal exchange rate is therefore a *bilateral* (two country) exchange rate.
- *Effective exchange rate* (EER). This is a measure which takes into account the fact that sterling varies in value by different amounts against other currencies. It is calculated as a *weighted average* of the bilateral rates against all other currencies, and is expressed as an index number relative to the base year. The EER is therefore a *multilateral* (many country) exchange rate, expressed as an index number.
- *Real exchange rate (RER)* is designed to measure the rate at which home products exchange for products from other countries, rather than the rate at which the currencies themselves are traded. It is thus a measure of competitiveness. When we consider *multilateral* UK trade, it is defined as:

  $$RER = EER \times P(UK)/P(F)$$

  In other words, the real exchange rate for the UK (RER) is equal to the effective exchange rate (EER) multiplied by the ratio of home price, P(UK), to foreign price, P(F), of products.
  - If UK prices rise relative to foreign prices, the real exchange rate (RER) will rise, unless the sterling effective exchange rate (EER) falls sufficiently to offset this impact.
  - Similarly, if the sterling effective exchange rate (EER) rises, the real exchange rate will rise, unless UK prices fall sufficiently relative to foreign prices.

Table 10.7 outlines the nominal rate of exchange for sterling against other currencies and the overall sterling effective exchange rate (EER) against a 'basket' of other currencies.

Table 10.7 Sterling nominal exchange rates: 1990–2004

	US dollar	French franc	Japanese yen	German mark	Sterling effective exchange rate (1990 = 100)	Euro
1990	1.79	9.69	257	2.88	100.0	–
1991	1.77	9.95	238	2.93	100.7	–
1992	1.76	9.33	224	2.76	96.9	–
1993	1.50	8.50	167	2.48	88.9	–
1994	1.53	8.48	156	2.48	89.2	–
1995	1.58	7.87	148	2.26	84.8	–
1996	1.56	7.98	170	2.35	86.3	1.21
1997	1.64	9.56	198	2.84	100.6	1.45
1998	1.66	9.77	217	2.97	105.3	1.49
1999	1.62	–	240	–	103.8	1.52
2000	1.50	–	264	–	105.6	1.60
2001	1.44	–	175	–	105.8	1.61
2002	1.50	–	188	–	106.0	1.59
2003	1.69	–	189	–	102.4	1.40
2004*	1.85	–	195	–	105.7	1.44

* 1st quarter

Notice the rapid *appreciation* in the nominal exchange rate of sterling against the US dollar since 2002 (i.e. the US dollar has *depreciated* significantly against sterling). However, sterling has *depreciated* in value against the euro in the last few years.

Checkpoint 9

How are the changes in the sterling exchange rate over the last few years shown in Table 10.7 likely to affect the UK balance of payments?

LINKS

See Chapter 15 (p. 634) for an assessment of the role of exchange rates in determining international competitiveness.

The impact of exchange rate changes are considered in many chapters of this book, since they clearly have an important impact on the competitiveness of exports in foreign markets and of imports in domestic markets.

We now turn to an important issue in the UK, namely whether or not to join the single currency.

Single currency (euro)

Eleven countries formally replaced their national currencies with the euro on 1 January 1999, with Greece becoming the 12th member of this eurozone in 2001.

Advantages of a single currency

- *Lower costs of exchange:* importers no longer have to obtain foreign currency to pay exporters from the eurozone.

- *Reduced exchange rate uncertainty:* all members face fixed exchange rates within the eurozone.
- *Eliminates competitive depreciations/devaluations:* historically countries have tried to match any fall in the exchange rates of rival countries, with such 'competitive depreciations' creating uncertainty and discouraging trade.
- *Prevents speculative attacks:* speculators can sometimes force individual currencies to depreciate/devalue their currency by selling large amounts of that currency. The euro, being supported by all member countries, is much better equipped to resist such speculative attacks.

Disadvantages of a single currency

- *Loss of independent exchange rate policy:* governments can no longer seek to remedy a balance of payment deficit with a member of the eurozone by lowering their exchange rate, thereby making exports cheaper in that country and imports dearer from that country.
- *Loss of independent monetary policy:* the eurozone has a European Central Bank which determines the money supply and interest rate policy for all member countries.

Checkpoint 10

1 How is a fall in the exchange rate of sterling likely to affect the equilibrium values for price level and national output in the aggregate demand and aggregate supply analysis?

2 Now repeat your analysis for a rise in the exchange rate of sterling.

Case Study 10.4 looks at some less official mechanisms for expressing relative exchange rates.

Case Study 10.4 Exchange rates, lattes and burgers

There is a widely recognised theory that, in the long run, exchange rates will move towards levels at which a given 'basket' of goods and services will cost the same in different countries using the local currency. In other words, a global currency such as the dollar should, when converted into a local currency, buy the same goods and services wherever these are sold.

On that basis *The Economist* has for many years presented the so-called 'Big Mac' Index, showing how the price of a McDonald's burger varies in different countries, after exchanging the dollar into the currency of that country (Table 10.8). For example, the 'Big Mac' only costs the equivalent of \$1.23 in China, using the yuan/dollar exchange rate in January 2004. Yet the same 'Big Mac' costs \$2.80 in America in January 2004. This suggests that the Chinese currency, the yuan, is *undervalued* by 56% against the US dollar. In other words, if 1 yuan exchanged for 56% more US dollars *than was the case in January 2004*, then the 'Big Mac' would have had the same dollar-equivalent price in both countries.

Case Study 10.4 continued

Table 10.8 % Refers to under (–) or over (+) valuation of each national currency against the US dollar

Country/Area	McDonald's 'Big Mac' Index	Price of 'Big Mac' $
US	0%	2.80
Britain	+23%	3.45
China	–56%	1.23
Euro area	+30%	3.70
Switzerland	+82%	5.11

Whilst on the 'Big Mac' Index the Chinese currency would seem undervalued, the euro would seem *overvalued*. The average price of a 'Big Mac' in the 'euro area' in January 2004 was $3.70, using the euro : dollar exchange rate of that date. This suggests that the euro is around 30% overvalued against the dollar, given the $2.80 price of the 'Big Mac' in the US. This time, 1 euro would need to exchange against 30% less US dollars than was the case in January 2004 for the 'Big Mac' to have had the same dollar-equivalent price in both countries.

Since January 2004 a new 'Tall-Latte' Index has also been devised by *The Economist*, using exactly the same principle. By coincidence the cost of 'Tall-Latte' in the US is also around $2.80. Comparing the prices of 'Tall Lattes' in various countries against that in the US, using current exchange rates against the dollar, gives us the date shown in Table 10.9.

Table 10.9 Estimated % under (–) or over (+) valuation of each national currency against the US dollar

Country/Area	Starbuck's Tall-Latte Index	McDonald's Big Mac Index
Britain	+17%	+23%
Canada	–16%	–16%
China	–1%	–56%
Euro area	+33%	+30%
Malaysia	–25%	–53%
Mexico	–15%	–21%
Switzerland	+62%	+82%
Thailand	–31%	–46%

Adapted from *The Economist*, 17 January 2004

Questions

1 Why are 'Big Macs' and 'Tall-Lattes' each used as the basis for an index?

2 What do you notice from Table 10.9?

3 What use might Table 10.9 be to businesses, individuals and governments?

4 What criticisms might be made of such indices?

Economic growth

Economic growth is usually defined as the rate of change of national output (income). When this is negative, we often use the term *economic recession*, although strictly speaking we should only use this term when national output has fallen in value over two successive quarters. Economic growth is usually expressed in 'real' terms, i.e. after taking inflation into account.

Governments rarely announce growth targets. However, historically GDP has grown in the UK at an average rate of just over 2% per annum (in real terms) over the past 50 or so years.

In terms of the *production possibility frontier* of Chapter 1 (Figure 1.1, p. 4), economic growth can involve either:

- a move from a point inside the frontier towards a point nearer to or actually on an unchanged frontier; or
- a move from a point inside or on an existing frontier to a point previously outside the frontier, as a result of an outward shift in the frontier itself.

In the first case, recorded economic growth involves a fuller use of existing productive resources. For example, higher aggregate demand may have contributed to such economic growth, allowing a fuller use of existing productive capacity.

In the second case, recorded economic growth involves some increase in the productive capacity of the economy as a whole. Whilst higher aggregate demand may also have played a part in such growth, there would seem also to have been an improvement in the 'supply side' of the economy. It is to this issue that we now turn.

Supply-side policies

Some people have suggested that the UK experienced a supply-side 'revolution' during the 1980s and 1990s, which included a wide range of policies which sought to raise the productivity of both labour and capital.

Such 'supply side' policies have included, amongst others:

- assistance with investment;
- trade union reform;
- deregulation/privatisation;
- making more training grants available;
- increasing the number of people at universities;
- helping people to set up new firms;
- income tax cuts to increase incentives to work;
- cuts in welfare payments to encourage people to return to work;

- a government commitment to keep inflation low in order to aid investment plans;
- cutting government expenditure in order to release resources to the private sector;
- abolishing exchange controls in order to allow capital to move freely.

Any increase in labour or capital productivity resulting from these supply-side policies would then shift outwards the production possibility frontier of Chapter 1. Successful supply-side policies would also increase the aggregate supply curve in Figure 10.14, shifting it downwards and to the right from AS_1 to AS_2. The result is shown as raising the equilibrium level of national output (e.g. GDP) from Y_1 to Y_2 and reducing the average price level from P_1 to P_2.

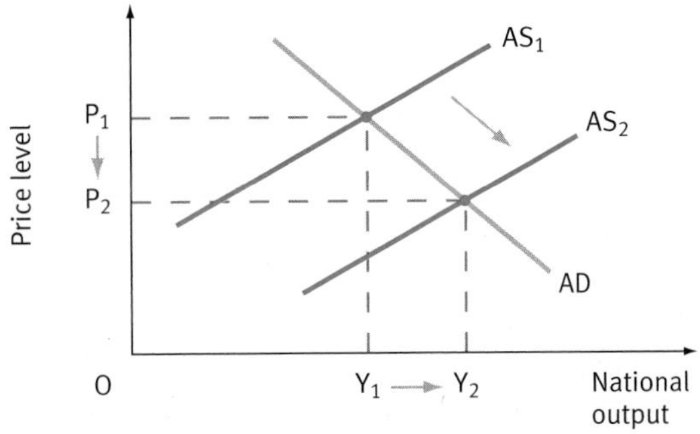

Fig 10.14 Supply-side policies

Checkpoint 11 Can you use the aggregate demand and aggregate supply schedules to show how coupling supply-side policies with increases in aggregate demand might help to achieve non-inflationary growth?

Many of these supply-side policy issues are considered elsewhere in the book, especially in Chapter 7 on labour and other factor markets.

Activity 10.2

1 In this question you'll see a description of a particular type of policy instrument used by government in an attempt to tackle unemployment. Try to match the lettered description with the numbered type of unemployment that is likely to be the focus of each policy.

Description

(a) The government increases the number of job centres and uses more advanced computers to improve the information database.

(b) A new skills training initiative is aimed at increasing the ability of those out of work to take the jobs on offer in a rapidly changing environment.

(c) To offset the downswing in the business cycle, the government announces a major increase in public expenditure.
(d) A programme to support small business start-ups is launched on Tyneside after the recent announcement of further closures in the shipbuilding industry.
(e) The government puts pressure on trade unions to make pay claims which are below the increase in productivity over the past year.

Terms

(i) Demand deficient unemployment
(ii) structural unemployment
(iii) regional unemployment
(iv) frictional unemployment
(v) real wage unemployment
(vi) technological unemployment

2 True or False

(a) A fall in the rate of inflation means that the average price level is now lower. True/False
(b) A rise in the rate of inflation means that the percentage rise in average prices is higher than previously. True/False
(c) One of the costs of inflation is that those on variable incomes do better than those on fixed incomes. True/False
(d) If a rise in raw material costs feeds through to higher prices we use the term 'cost-push' inflation. True/False
(e) The Phillips curve suggests that higher levels of unemployment lead to higher levels of inflation. True/False

3 Inflation can be measured using different indices.

RPI = Retail Price Index
RPIX = RPI excluding mortgage interest payments
RPIY = RPI excluding mortgage interest payment and indirect taxes

For each of the following situations identify which of the above measures of inflation would show the largest increase.

(a) Over the past year the cost of a basket of products purchased by a typical household rises by 5%, mortgage interest payments by 6% and indirect taxes by 7%.
(b) Over the past year the cost of a basket of products purchased by a typical household rises by 4%, mortgage interest rates by 2% and indirect taxes by 1%.
(c) Over the past year the cost of a basket of products purchased by a typical household rises by 3%, mortgage interest rates by 2% and indirect taxes by 5%.

4 In this question you'll see a description of a particular type of transaction in the balance of payments of the UK. Try to match that description with its correct term from the balance of payments accounts.

Description

(a) A UK resident purchases shares in a US firm.
(b) A UK firm exports farm machinery to Poland.
(c) A French multimillionaire purchases a fixed asset (land) in the UK.

(d) BP (UK) makes a major sale of oil to Germany.
(e) The UK pays for a major deficit with the US by running down its gold and foreign exchange reserves.
(f) A Japanese multinational purchases a car component factory in the North East of England.
(g) Virgin Atlantic receives more income from US passengers on its routes.

Terms

(i) Current account: balance on oil goods
(ii) Current account: balance on non-oil goods
(iii) Current account: balance on services
(iv) Capital account
(v) Financial account: direct investment
(vi) Financial account: portfolio investment
(vii) Financial account: reserves

Answers to Checkpoints and Activities can be found on p. 705–35.

Key Terms

Aggregate demand The total demand in the economy, usually expressed as C + I + G + (X – M).

Aggregate supply The total output in the economy. In the short run a rise in the average price level is usually assumed to exceed rises in input costs, raising profitability and providing an incentive for an expansion in aggregate supply.

Appreciation A rise in the exchange rate of one currency against another. Often used in the context of floating exchange rates.

Balance on goods Net value of trade in tangible goods (exports +, imports –). Previously known as the 'visible trade balance'.

Balance on services Net value of trade in services (exports +, imports –). Previously known as the 'invisible trade balance'.

Balanced budget When tax revenue equals public expenditure.

Budget deficit When tax revenue falls short of public expenditure.

Budget surplus When tax revenue is greater than public expenditure.

Built-in stablisers Result in a *net* increase in withdrawals in 'boom' conditions and a *net* increase in injections during recession.

Business cycle The tendency for economies to move from economic boom into economic recession and vice versa.

Capital account Records the flows of money into the country (positive sign) and out of the country (negative sign) resulting from the purchase or sale of fixed assets (e.g. land) and selected capital transfers.

Consumer Price Index (CPI) Since December 2003 this has replaced RPIX as the official measure of inflation in the UK.

Cost-push inflation Inflation seen as being caused mainly by an increase in the costs of production, which firms pass on as higher prices.

Current account Consists of two main sub-accounts, the 'balance on goods' (formerly 'visible trade balance') and the 'balance on services' (formerly 'invisible trade balance').

Depreciation A fall in the exchange rate of one currency against another. Often used in the context of floating exchange rates.

Direct investment Involves physical assets of a company (e.g. plant and equipment).

Eurozone The grouping of countries with the euro as their common currency.

Financial account Records the flows of money into the country (+) and out of the country (–) from investment-related (direct and portfolio) or other financial activity (e.g. movement of deposits between countries).

Fiscal drag The tendency for the tax-take to rise as a result of a rise in money incomes.

Frictional unemployment Due to the time it takes workers to change jobs.

'Golden rule' Over the economic cycle the government will only borrow to invest and not to fund current expenditure.

HICP (Harmonised Index of Consumer Prices) Uses a different 'basket' of goods to the RPI. Now the UK as well as the EU 'official' inflation measure.

Inflation Average level of prices in the economy rises. Different measures exist (RPI, RPIX, RPIY etc.).

Natural rate of unemployment The rate of unemployment at which there is no excess or deficiency of demand for labour.

Other financial flows Records the movement of deposits between countries. Part of the 'financial account' of the balance of payments.

Phillips curve A curve showing the relationship between (price) inflation and unemployment. The original Phillips curve plotted wage inflation against unemployment in the UK over the years 1861–1957.

Portfolio investment Involves investment paper assets (e.g. shares, bonds).

Public sector net cash requirements (PSNCR) Now used instead of the 'Public Sector Borrowing Requirement' (PSBR).

Real wage unemployment Rigidities in the labour market are seen as preventing the ratio of money wage to prices falling to a level that would 'clear' the market.

Regional unemployment The geographical location of particular industries and changes in long-term demand play a key role here.

Reserves Part of the 'financial account' of the balance of payments. Reserves may be run down in times of overall deficit, and added to in time of surplus. They help to preserve the balance of payments accounting identity (i.e. defined so that they must balance overall).

Retail Price Index (RPI) Shows the change from month to month in the cost of a representative 'basket' of goods and services bought by a typical household.

RPIX Retail Price Index (RPI) excluding mortgage interest payments.

Stagflation Where real GDP falls but the price level rises.

Structural unemployment Arises from longer-term changes in the demand for, and supply of, labour in specific industries.

Technological unemployment Leads to significant changes in labour and capital productivity, resulting in job losses.

Trade cycle *see* 'Business cycle'.

Unemployment The number of people actively looking for work who are currently out of a job.

Key Points

- Fiscal policy involves changes in government expenditure and/or taxation.
- Fiscal policy can be 'automatic', involving 'built-in stabilisers', or discretionary.
- Direct taxes tend to be more progressive than indirect taxes but a fuller comparison involves issues of macroeconomic management, economic incentives, economic welfare and administration.

- The UK government has a 'golden rule' whereby over the economic cycle the government will only borrow to invest and not to fund current expenditure.
- Monetary policy involves influencing the money supply and/or the rate of interest.
- As well as cash, there are a range of 'near money' assets of varying degrees of liquidity.
- Unemployment and inflation are important policy issues in their own right, but have been linked together in the Phillips curve.
- Various types of unemployment can be distinguished – frictional, structural, regional, technological, demand deficient, real wage and 'natural'.
- Inflation can be measured using various indices, such as RPI, RPIX, RPIY and now the Consumer Price Index (CPI).
- The balance of payments can be split into various components, including current and capital accounts, each of which can be broken down still further.
- The exchange rate has a key impact on the price of exports and imports.
- The euro has various advantages and disadvantages.

Assessment Practice

Multiple choice questions

1 **Which *two* of the following are consistent with the idea of automatic fiscal stabilisers?**

(a) The fact that the tax of unleaded petrol is lower than that on leaded petrol
(b) The fact that as people's incomes increase the amount that they pay in taxes also increases
(c) The fact that people sent to prison do not receive benefits
(d) The fact that government spending falls during 'boom' times as unemployment falls
(e) The fact that congestion charges reduce traffic in city centres

2 **Which *three* of the following types of unemployment might be involved if the coal industry in the UK collapses as a result of individuals and firms switching over to oil, gas and other sources of energy?**

(a) Frictional unemployment
(b) Demand deficient unemployment
(c) Regional unemployment
(d) Real wage unemployment
(e) Structural unemployment

3 **Which *two* of the following situations are most likely to result in 'demand pull' inflation?**

(a) Increases in the rate of savings and the rate of taxation
(b) A rise in investment of 5% with a rise of productivity of 5%

(c) A rise in the combined value of investment and government spending of 5% with no change in productivity
(d) A fall in the rate of savings and the rate of taxation for an economy already operating at full capacity
(e) A fall in the rate of savings and the rate of taxation for an economy with a considerable amount of excess capacity

4 **A fall in the sterling exchange rate against the US dollar would have which *two* of the following impacts?**

(a) UK exports to US become cheaper (in dollars).
(b) UK exports to US become dearer (in dollars).
(c) UK imports from US become cheaper (in sterling).
(d) UK imports from US become dearer (in sterling).
(e) No change in export or import prices, whether in dollars or sterling.

5 **A rise in the sterling exchange rate against the euro would have which *two* of the following impacts?**

(a) UK exports to France become cheaper (in euros).
(b) UK exports to France become dearer (in euros).
(c) UK imports from France become cheaper (in sterling).
(d) UK imports from France become dearer (in sterling).
(e) No change in export or import prices, whether in euros or sterling.

6 **Which of the following government policy measures is likely to reduce *frictional unemployment*?**

(a) Increased government spending in the regions
(b) Reductions in indirect and excise taxes
(c) Reductions in income taxes
(d) More efficient and better informed job centres
(e) Higher unemployment benefit

7 **Which *two* of the following are (other things equal) likely to cause the UK's balance on current account to deteriorate?**

(a) Rise in the sterling value of exports of financial services
(b) Fall in the sterling value of the deficit previously experienced for trade in non-oil goods
(c) Fall in the sterling value of the surplus previously experienced for trade in oil
(d) Fall in the sterling value of imports of financial services
(e) Rise in the sterling value of the deficit previously experienced for trade in non-oil goods

8 **Which *two* of the following circumstances would be most favourable (other things equal) for UK exporters to eurozone countries?**

(a) A fall in the exchange rate of sterling against the euro
(b) A rise in the exchange rate of sterling against the euro
(c) A strengthening of the euro against sterling
(d) A weakening of the euro against sterling
(e) A relatively higher rate of price inflation in the UK than the eurozone, exchange rates unchanged

9 **If the economy experiences inflation, then aggregate**

(a) demand increases more slowly than aggregate supply
(b) supply increases faster than aggregate demand
(c) demand and supply increase at about the same rate
(d) demand increases faster than aggregate supply
(e) there is sufficient information to answer the question

10 **Of the following sequences of price levels, which correctly represents a 5% inflation rate?**

(a) 100, 105, 105, 100
(b) 100, 105, 110, 115
(c) 100, 101, 102, 103
(d) 100, 105, 110.25, 115.76
(e) 100, 100, 100, 100

Data response and stimulus questions

1 **Look carefully at the data in the following table.**

Tax as a % of GNP	1981		2001		GDP growth (yearly average) 1981–2001	
	Percentage	Rank	Percentage	Rank		
Australia	33.5	14	31.5	15	3.4	3
Austria	49.6	4	45.7	3	2.4	=9
Belgium	49.6	4	45.3	5	2.0	=11
Canada	40.0	12	35.2	=13	2.8	=5
Denmark	55.6	3	49.0	2	2.1	10
Finland	39.6	13	45.4	4	2.7	6
France	47.6	7	36.4	=12	2.0	=11
Germany	42.3	9	36.4	=12	2.0	=11
Greece	31.6	16	40.8	9	1.9	=12
Ireland	41.6	10	29.2	17	5.5	1
Italy	33.4	15	41.8	8	1.9	=12
Japan	28.3	19	27.1	18	2.6	7
Luxembourg	40.0	11	42.4	7	5.2	2
Netherlands	49.4	6	39.9	10	2.4	=9
Norway	48.7	2	44.9	6	2.8	=5
Spain	27.2	20	35.2	=13	2.8	=5
Sweden	56.9	1	53.2	1	1.9	=12
Switzerland	30.8	18	34.5	14	1.4	13
United Kingdom	42.4	8	37.4	11	2.5	8
United States	31.3	17	29.6	16	3.1	4

Adapted from OECD (2002) *Revenue Statistics*; OECD (2002) *Economic Outlook*, No. 71, June

Questions

(a) How might this data influence government policy?
(b) How might this data influence the policy of a major multinational seeking new locations for its productive facilities? What other considerations might the multinational take into account?

2 The data in the following table represents the outcome of attempts by successive government to achieve the four key objectives of low unemployment, low inflation, high growth and balance of payments equilibrium.

Achieved values in the UK for a number of policy objectives

Year	Unemployment as a % of working population	Annual change in RPI (%)	Annual change in GDP (at market prices) (%)	Balance of payments (current account) (£m)
1983	10.4	5.3	3.8	+1,258
1984	10.7	4.6	2.3	−1,294
1985	10.9	5.7	3.8	−570
1986	11.2	4.0	3.8	−3,614
1987	10.3	4.2	4.5	−7,538
1988	8.3	4.9	5.1	−19,850
1989	6.4	7.8	2.1	−26,321
1990	5.8	9.4	0.0	−22,321
1991	8.1	5.9	−1.5	−10,659
1992	9.8	3.7	0.0	−12,974
1993	10.3	1.6	2.3	−11,919
1994	9.4	2.4	4.3	−6,768
1995	8.1	3.5	2.7	−9,015
1996	7.4	2.4	2.6	−8,709
1997	5.4	3.1	3.5	−1,720
1998	4.6	3.4	2.2	−4,814
1999	4.2	1.5	2.0	−19,729
2000	3.7	3.0	3.0	−19,208
2001	3.3	1.8	2.0	−18,038
2002	3.2	1.7	1.7	−18,817
2003	3.1	2.6	2.8	−20,430

Adapted from ONS (2003) *Economic Trends: Annual Supplement*; ONS (2003) *UK Balance of Payments*; ONS (2004) *Data Releases* (various)

Questions

(a) Consider any possible conclusions you might draw as regards government policy from the data in the table.
(b) How might the data achieved in the UK for these four objectives in recent years affect business confidence?

3 Look carefully at the data in the table below showing what happens to tax taken from this family as gross earnings rise.

Married couple (one earner working more than 30 hours per week) with two children under 11 (rent £52.27, council tax £16.40 per week)

	June 2002			
	(£ pw)	(£ pw)	(£ pw)	(£ pw)
Gross earnings*	125.00	150.00	200.00	250.00
Plus Child benefit	26.30	16.30	26.30	26.30
Working family tax credit	112.26	99.88	80.56	61.86
Housing benefit	5.53	0.00	00.00	00.00
Council tax benefit	2.02	0.00	00.00	00.00
Less: Income tax	0.00	0.00	9.87	20.87
National Insurance	3.60	6.10	11.10	16.10
Net income	*267.51*	*270.08*	*285.89*	*301.19*

* 30 hours per week at the minimum wage (June 2002) was £123.00

Adapted from DWP, Tax/Benefit Model Tables (June 2002)

Questions

a) **What does this table suggest?**

b) **What implications are there for government policy?**

True/False questions

1 A budget deficit is where government spending falls short of government revenue.
True/False

2 The Public Sector Net Cash Requirement (PSNCR) refers to the potential government borrowing needed to cover a budget deficit.
True/False

3 Direct taxes are usually more progressive than indirect taxes because, unlike indirect taxes, as income rises a higher proportion is usually taken by direct taxes.
True/False

4 Unemployment benefits are helpful in providing an element of 'built-in stability'.
True/False

5 Monetary policy can involve changes in either the money supply and/or the rate of interest.
True/False

6 The balance of payments accounts are sometimes called an 'identity' since, by definition, they are constructed so that they must balance.
True/False

7 A deterioration in the 'balance on goods' must result in a deterioration in the current account balance.

True/False

8 'Stagflation' occurs when real GDP falls but the price level rises.

True/False

9 A rise in the sterling exchange rate against the euro will tend to make it more difficult for UK exporters of products to the eurozone countries.

True/False

10 Critics of membership of the single currency often point to the fact that there is reduced exchange rate uncertainty for eurozone countries.

True/False

Essay questions

1 Why is unemployment regarded as a problem? What policy measures might be used to tackle this problem?

2 Do you agree that we can only have less unemployment if we are willing to accept higher inflation? Explain your answer.

3 Why do governments try to make use of 'built-in stablisers'? Are these always successful?

4 Evaluate the benefits and costs of a government pursuing a low exchange rate policy.

5 Do you agree with the suggestion that the UK should join the euro? Explain your reasoning.

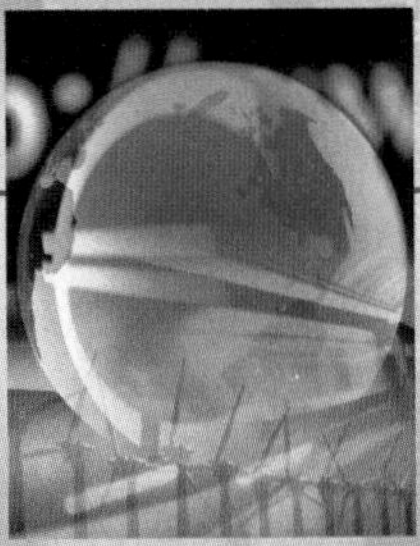

Chapter 11

Demographic and social environment

Introduction

This chapter reviews the changing demographic characteristics in the UK and, more briefly, elsewhere. An assessment is made of some of the implications for households, businesses and government of the demographic changes identified. Various methods of 'classifying' the UK and other populations are considered, with particular attention paid to socio-economic, social and cultural dimensions. Other patterns and trends related more broadly to changes in lifestyles and social attitudes are also reviewed. Again household, business and governmental implications of emerging developments are evaluated.

Further materials relevant to the issues discussed in this chapter can also be found elsewhere in the book. For example, a wide range of labour market practices, including aspects of gender, ageism and work–life balance, are covered in Chapter 7. Hofstede's work on socio-cultural dimensions is examined in Chapter 14, and ethical/environmental issues are reviewed in Chapter 12 and elsewhere in the book. Of course, the demographic and socio-cultural dimension makes an important contribution to the PEST (PESTLE) strategic perspectives of Chapter 15.

Learning objectives:

By the end of this chapter you should be able to:

- identify some key population patterns and trends in the UK and elsewhere, including ageism, falling birth and death rates, etc.
- assess the relevance of these trends to households, businesses and government
- discuss the basis for socio-economic classification in the UK and other advanced industrialised economies, paying particular attention to occupation, income and education
- examine changing socio-cultural norms and their impact on home, work and consumer behaviour
- consider the broader changes in lifestyle and social attitudes and their relevance to individuals, businesses and government.

Demographic patterns and trends

Demographics is the study of how populations change over time. Demographers analyse changes in births, deaths and the age composition of populations as well as patterns of disease and so on. In the UK, the *Government Actuary Department* (GAD) collects population statistics and attempts to produce projections of how the population will change over the next few decades.

Changes in demographic patterns affect the demand for goods and services, especially in the medium and long term. Careful analysis of these patterns and trends is therefore important for planners and decision makers in both business and government.

Population

Fifty years ago, world population was around 2.5 billion people; today it is over 6.1 billion – and growing at a rate of 1.2% per year. This may sound only a modest rate of growth but it means an extra 77 million people every year to feed, clothe, house, educate and generally care for. And of course growth is cumulative, so that by 2050 the world population is expected to be somewhere between 7.9 and 10.9 billion people.

Many Western countries witnessed a sharp increase in births during the 20 years following the Second World War. Britain has 17 million of these 'baby-boomers' born between 1945 and 1965. The effect of such 'baby boomers' has been likened to watching a large python that has swallowed a mouse, with the bulge moving slowly and inexorably down the python, not unlike the impact of this large demographic bulge moving through time.

The world population 'explosion' and the resulting strain on resources has concerned economists and policy makers for many decades, so it may strike you as odd when you learn that many European countries are urging their citizens to have *more* children! Why? The answer lies in the ever-changing structure of human populations and the effect this has upon us all.

> **DATA**
>
> The UK population was estimated to be 58.8 million in 2003, a growth of 17% over the last 50 years. However, China has the largest population at present (1.3 billion in 2004) but India will probably have overtaken it by 2050.

Population change

Populations change naturally over time. For any given time period, the change in population is given by:

Population change = Births – Deaths + Net migration

Net migration is the difference between the number of people entering the country to live (*immigration*) and the number leaving permanently (*emigration*). For the first 80 years of the twentieth century, UK net migration was actually *negative* – more people were leaving the country than entering it. An exception was during the 1950s when large numbers of Afro-Caribbean people settled in the UK and net migration was *positive*. Since the 1980s net migration in the UK has been positive and is expected to remain so.

However, what concerns many Western countries is not so much the *size* of their populations but the problems associated with their *ageing* populations. For example, the average age of the UK population was 39.1 years in 2001, but by 2026 it will probably be around 42.4 years. It is worth considering this major issue of 'ageing' in rather more detail.

Ageing population

The average age of the UK population is increasing and especially at the older (75 years and over) end of the age spectrum (Table 11.1). Of course, those over 65 years are dependent in various ways on those who are of working age.

Table 11.1 Proportions of older adults in the UK

	65–74 years	75 years and over
1961	8	4
2001	9	7
2011*	9	8
2026*	11	10

* Estimates

Adapted from National Statistics (2003) *Social Trends*, London: HMSO

Checkpoint 1 Why might we want to identify separately the proportion of adults aged 75 years and over?

The population is ageing because:

1 *More people are living longer*, resulting in a higher proportion of elderly people, because of advances in health care and a better standard of living giving improved nutrition and housing. The rise in life expectancy of the old has been accelerating over the past two decade. For example, in 1980 male life expectancy at 60 was a further 16 years; in 2004 it is a further 20 years.
2 *Fall in the birth rate* (lower proportion of young people). This is more difficult to relate to a single factor, but involves different lifestyles and cultural values.

It is expected that somewhere around the year 2014 the number of people over 65 years in the UK will actually exceed the number of children under 16. The situation is similar for the EU as a whole, where the percentage of over-65s has increased by almost 50% since 1970 (Table 11.2).

Indeed, ageing populations are occurring in countries across the world. For example, between 1950 and 2003 the median age (at which 50% of the population is below and 50% above) of the world's population rose by only 3 years, from 23.6 years in 1950 to 26.4 in 2003. However, over the next 50 years or so the UN projects that the median age will rise dramatically to 37 years by 2050, with 17 advanced industrialised economies having a median age of 50 years or above. This has major implications for international business in terms of productive location (e.g. adequate

Table 11.2 % of EU population aged 65 years and over

EU country (selected)	1970 (%)	2001 (%)
Italy	11	18
Greece	11	18
Sweden	14	17
Belgium	13	17
Germany	14	17
France	13	16
UK	13	16
Netherlands	10	14
All EU	*12*	*17*

Adapted from National Statistics (2003) *Social Trends*, London: HMSO

supply of labour of working age) as well as the range of products likely to be in global demand.

Why should this be a problem? The answer is in two parts. First, in the UK and many other countries, the state pensions that people draw upon retirement are funded by the contributions of current workers (*Pay As You Go* system). The proportion of workers to pensioners is known as the *support ratio*, sometimes simplified to 'tax-payers per pensioner'. Therefore, if there are more and more pensioners, and fewer and fewer workers to support them, it will be difficult to maintain the real value of state pensions. Currently in the UK there are four 'workers' per pensioner, giving a support ratio of 4 : 1. In 50 years' time, this is expected to fall to somewhere around 2.5 : 1, a situation often described as the 'demographic time-bomb'.

Watch out!

A more accurate definition of the *support ratio* is: the ratio of economically active people to dependents, which include those under 16 years as well as those over 65 years.

Second, we have already noted that the average age of the UK and many other populations is rising because of two key factors.

(a) *A fall in births*, which is progressively reducing the percentage of the population 'under 16 years'. For example, those under 16 years were around 23% of the UK population in 1961 but are expected to be only 17% of the UK population in 2026. It follows that the percentage of the population of child-bearing age can be expected to continue to fall over time so that, other things equal, the number of births can be expected to fall below the number of deaths and the population actually decline.

But why is this happening? We need to examine this a little more closely. Box 11.1 considers the birth rate in more detail.

Box 11.1 Birth rate

Demographers calculate that in order to maintain a steady, unchanging population, a country usually needs an average family size (*total fertility rate* or *TFR*) of 2.1 children. Table 11.3 shows that some countries fall well below this requirement, whilst others are well above it.

Definition *Total fertility rate*: the average number of children born to one woman at current fertility levels.

Table 11.3 Fertility rates of selected countries

Country	TFR
Africa	5.0
Denmark	1.74
France	1.77
Germany	1.37
Italy	1.21
North America	1.9
UK	1.7
EU average	*1.3*
World average	*2.7*

Adapted from National Statistics (2003) *Social Trends*, London: HMSO

Not one European country, other than Albania, has a fertility rate that is above replacement.

Checkpoint 2 Why do you think that it is not enough for each family to have just two children to keep a steady population?

Before leaving the population section, Box 11.2 considers the views of some early writers on the issue of population explosion.

Box 11.2 Population projections and Malthus

Thomas Malthus (1766–1834) claimed that the human population would, left unchecked, grow exponentially (in a *geometric progression*). However, food production would grow only linearly (in an *arithmetic progression*), restricted by the need to bring new, less productive land into cultivation (an earlier forerunner of the theory of diminishing returns). Population would therefore double every 25 years and food production would be unable to keep pace. Periodic famines and high infant mortality, together with occasional wars, were seen by Malthus as the most likely 'checks' to population explosion. Malthus noted that even in nineteenth-century Britain, food production was already falling short of population growth, as evidenced by the high price of bread and increasing public expenditure on relief of the poor.

A not dissimilar picture was portrayed by Dr Ehrlich in his best-selling book of 1968, *The Population Bomb*. He predicted that 'the battle to feed humanity is over. In the course of the 1970s the world will experience starvation of tragic proportions – hundreds of millions of people will starve to death'.

Both Malthus and Ehrlich failed to perceive that population growth has turned out to have an internal check: as people grow richer and healthier, they have smaller families. Indeed, the growth rate of the human population reached its peak of more than 2% a year in the early 1960s. The rate of increase has been declining ever since. It is now 1.26% and is expected to fall to 0.46% in 2050. Both the United Nations and IIASA have estimated that most of the world's population growth will be over by 2100, with the population stabilising at just below 11 billion (UN) or around 9 billion (IIASA).

Malthus and Ehrlich also failed to take account of developments in agricultural technology. These have squeezed more and more food out of each hectare of land. It is this application of technology and human ingenuity that has boosted food production, not merely in line with, but ahead of, population growth. It has also, incidentally, reduced the need to take new land into cultivation, thus reducing the pressure on biodiversity.

(b) *A fall in deaths* as medical advances and improved living standards reduce the death rate. For example, boys born in the UK in 1951 had a life expectancy of 66.4 years, which had increased to over 76 years by 2003. Girls born in the UK in 1951 had a life expectancy of 71.5 years, increasing to over 80 years by 2003. The overall result is that life expectancy has increased by 5–6 years every 25 years.

Net migration

At present, many countries still have a growing population, thanks to positive net migration. Indeed, encouraging higher rates of immigration has been put forward as a 'solution' to the problem of labour shortage and an ageing population.

Checkpoint 3 Can you suggest why others argue that relying on net migration is unlikely to solve these problems?

Projections suggest that at present net migration rates the UK population will indeed decline around the year 2040 with a peak population of around 64 million. Meanwhile, the workforce will be getting smaller as fewer and fewer young people enter the labour market. Thus firms will be short of labour – and governments short of taxpayers!

Action to defuse the 'demographic time-bomb'

Governments have been aware of the problems of an ageing population for many years. The UK government cut the link between the average wage and the state pension over 20 years ago and has stated that the retirement age for women will rise from 60 to 65 in 2008.

The following policies have been suggested as possibly helping reduce the ageing population problem.

1 Increase the size of the economically active population

- *Increase female participation rates.* This has already happened in the UK to a certain extent but critics say that the government could still do more to encourage mothers back into the workforce.
- *Increase the overall participation rate.* Estimates suggest that if all EU countries had the overall participation rate of Denmark (81.1%) this would add more than 30 million people to the EU workforce and exceed the shortfall in labour expected over the next 20 years. In particular, governments could find ways to return discouraged workers back into the labour force.
- *Increase fertility rates.* For example, in an effort to boost fertility, the Italian government is offering couples €1,000 for each child born. Italy has the lowest birth rate and fastest-ageing population in Europe. However, experts think that the monetary incentives will have only a short-term effect.
- *Encourage later retirement.* Not everyone retires on their 65th birthday. The average age of retirement of people on occupational pension schemes in the UK is about 57 years and 63 years for other workers.
- *Discourage early retirement on medical grounds.* This is somewhat controversial because it means that people who retire early owing to ill health (and claim sick pay and allowances) would have to face stiffer medical examinations to determine whether they were indeed ill.
- *Raise the retirement age.* Currently this is 60 for women in the UK and 65 for men. From 2008 women will retire at 65. At the moment there are no plans in the UK to raise the male retirement age.

2 Make the workforce more productive

We have seen in various chapters (e.g. Chapter 7) that increased productivity brings higher wages and thus increased tax revenues.

Checkpoint 4 Can you think why an increase in labour productivity will tend to raise wages and tax revenues?

3 Reduce the 'black economy'

This could be a source of considerable untapped tax revenues. Estimates of the 'black' or unofficial economy have been put as high as 12% of GDP in the UK, with a major loss of potential tax revenue (see Chapter 9, p. 326).

Case Study 11.1 looks in more detail at some of the implications for households and businesses of coping with an ageing population.

Case Study 11.1 Carry on working!

FT

In industrialised countries around the world, official projections of life expectancy are being revised upwards. In the UK in 2004 the government actually lifted its estimates of life expectancy for those now in their sixties and eighties by between 10% and 13%, even though the previous estimates were published only two years ago.

This shift, coupled with falling birth rates, means people will need to have longer working lives and to save more during them to pay for their retirement. Longer working lives will, however, require a profound cultural shift that both employers and employees have barely begun to grasp. A report from the House of Lords warned in January 2004 that if compulsory retirement ages are to go, then job assessment will have to be based on competency, not age.

This will mean challenging some long-established ideas about promotion and pay being based on seniority. Employers will have to operate transparent personnel policies, justifying who is recruited, promoted, demoted or made redundant. And 'employees will have to accept regular monitoring and assessment of their job performance', the report says.

Employees across Europe, where early retirement has become entrenched in the past 20 years, will face a significant challenge to the widespread aspiration to finish work early, says Philip Taylor of Cambridge University's *Interdisciplinary Research Centre on Ageing*. Longer working lives also imply that an individual's last job is likely not to be his or her most senior one. 'That is not something many people feel comfortable with yet,' he says. 'It is not just about how people feel about themselves and their status. It is about how your co-workers relate to you.' 'Not a lot of men will feel comfortable after working their way up to middle or junior management to have to take a job in a more junior position, as they move beyond 65 years. It is a big culture change that is required.'

This is equally true for companies, many of which will find that the shrinking supply of younger workers as birth rates fall means retaining people longer. 'Employers are going to have to scramble to find the talent they need,' says Jeff Chambers, vice-president of human resources at SAS, the privately owned US software company. The average age of SAS's 5,000 employees is now 41. Within the next five years, a quarter will become eligible for retirement. For the first time in its 27-year history, the company is having to work out how to retain older employees. 'I think a lot of employers will introduce phased retirement programmes. Major corporate employers will have to come up with a value proposition (to older employees) that offers reduced hours and more flexibility,' says Mr Chambers.

Phased retirement plans come in many forms. Toyota allows its production line workers in Japan to return to work on annual contracts after retirement at 60. One suggestion that has surfaced in the UK is that pensions should be based not on final salary but on a percentage of career-average earnings. That would not only make company pensions cheaper to provide, it would make it easier for people to work

Case Study 11.1 continued

fewer hours, or in a less senior job as they near retirement, without taking a big hit on their pension.

Longer life is also putting pressure on the age at which state pensions should be paid. Sweden has become the first country to make its state pension age *actuarially adjusted* – so that as life expectancy rises, the state pension age will rise in line. Japan is raising state pension age from 60 to 65, and the UK is doing the same for women. Elsewhere the debate is over whether current state pension ages can hold in the face of greater longevity.

But in all this, for both state and private provision, there is a silver lining. While individuals may have to work longer they will not necessarily have to work for that much longer, according to Donald Duval, president of Britain's Society of Pension Consultants. 'If people work on just an extra two or three years, there is a gain both ways,' he says. 'They are reducing the length of time their pension has to fund them, and they are paying taxes which helps with state provision, and quite small changes in state pension age can have big effects on the costs.'

Source: *Financial Times*, 16 January 2004, p. 9

Questions

1 How will working longer have implications for:
   (a) employees;
   (b) employers;
   (c) government?

2 Why might working only a few extra years make an important contribution to resolving the pension problem?

Socio-cultural patterns and trends

Most societies have some form of *hierarchy*, which ranks people according to their standing in society. Traditionally, UK society was seen to consist of three 'classes': working class, middle class and upper class, with most of the wealth and influence concentrated into the land-owning, aristocratic upper classes. However, times change and inherited wealth is not the dominant factor it once was. Surveys in 2004 suggest that 86 out of the 200 wealthiest people in England *earned* their money rather than inherited it.

When defining social class today we need to consider other factors, namely:

1 occupation;
2 income;
3 education.

Of course, these three factors are arguably interdependent. For example, educational attainment will strongly influence the occupations available to a person and thus their eventual income. Similarly, the occupations and income of parents will influence the quality of education available to their children, and in turn the occupations available to them.

Occupational classifications

Marketers define social class according to occupation, placing people into 'socio-economic groupings'. People within a particular social class associate mainly with others in that class; consequently, these social classes display similar tastes, values and purchasing patterns. Table 11.4 provides the most widely used occupational breakdown of socio-economic classes.

Table 11.4 Socio-economic classes

Category	Description
A	Higher management, professionals and administrators
B	Intermediate-level managers, professionals and administrators
C1	Junior managers, professionals and administrators. Also supervisory and clerical posts
C2	Skilled manual workers
D	Semi- and unskilled manual workers
E	State pensioners, widows, casual workers, lowest-grade workers, long-term unemployed

Example:

C2s buy more 'Fairtrade' products

A Mori poll in January 2004 is just one example of how socio-economic class is useful to marketers. It found that a higher proportion of the C2 class of skilled manual workers were prepared to pay more for 'Fairtrade' products than any other group.

The 2001 UK Census revealed that 26% of people *with a job* placed themselves in the category of managers, senior officials or professionals (A or B). Another 26% had administrative/secretarial jobs or were in the 'associate professional and technical' category, which includes nurses and technicians (C1). Thus around 52% of those in work could be classed as A, B or C1. Only 12% described themselves as skilled tradesmen or women (C2) whilst another 12% had 'elementary occupations' such as hotel porters and traffic wardens (D, E).

Studies have found that there is little mobility between socio-economic classes; children born in the 1970s have tended to take jobs similar to their parents and also marry within the same socio-economic class. Around 70% of the earnings of children of rich parents can be ascribed to 'social capital', that is, the networks and influence arriving from family connections, upbringing, background, friends, membership of clubs or societies as well as marriage. These intergenerational links are particularly strong on the land where 35% of graduate farmers have followed their fathers' occupations. Similarly, 20% of health professionals have the same job as their fathers.

Since 1987 disposable income of the top 10% of earners has tended to grow faster than that of the bottom 10% of earners. Thus the income gap between category A and categories D and E has been widening. In the early years of the millennium this gap widened more than usual owing to the high bonuses paid to senior managers and professionals, especially in the financial sector.

Case Study 11.2 looks at linkages between these socio-economic classes and catalogue purchases.

Case Study 11.2 Catalogue shopping and social class

Mail order catalogue agencies became popular in the 1950s and 1960s with the rise in disposable income after the war. In the UK, catalogues were aimed at C2 and Ds, the largest socio-economic group of the time, using agents – usually women – who sold goods to a circle of family, friends, neighbours and acquaintances. Such circles were often referred to as 'clubs' and were an integral part of some close-knit communities. Agents received commission on the amount of goods they sold whilst customers appreciated the weekly payment option at a time when credit was difficult to obtain. By the late twentieth century the industry had been reduced to five main retailers: *Littlewoods, Great Universal Stores* (GUS), *Grattan*, *Freemans* and *Empire* (later to become *Redcats*).

In 1985 GUS launched *Innovations* – often given away as a free supplement in Sunday newspapers. The Innovations mini-catalogue aimed to bring the latest in technology to its customers and became required reading for those seeking quirky and unusual gifts.

However, agency catalogue shopping is in decline. Agents now buy mainly for their own families whilst the traditional customer base finds it easy to obtain credit elsewhere. High street retailers have always been around 15 to 20% cheaper than agency catalogues and now firms such as *Tesco* and *Next* offer their own direct-order catalogue service. Added to this is the growing popularity of Internet shopping and the rise of TV shopping channels such as QVC.

The catalogue business is finding it difficult to compete. *Freemans* was bought in 1999 by German firm Otto Versand, owners of *Grattan*. In 2000 GUS bought online retailer *jungle.com* but was forced to close the loss-making Innovations in 2003. Meanwhile the *Littlewoods* group is seeking permission from the Competition Commission to buy GUS and *Kays* catalogue.

Analysts believe that if the catalogue companies are to survive they must be more flexible and more effective at individual marketing.

Case Study 11.2 continued

Questions

1. What type of market structure describes the agency catalogue industry?
2. What has happened to the traditional target market of the catalogues?
3. Why have the catalogue companies found it so difficult to survive?
4. What steps did the companies take to fight back?

Culture

Social class is not the only factor that influences people's tastes, values and economic decisions. Equally important is the *culture* to which people belong (see also Chapter 14, pp. 548–550).

Culture can be considered as the set of beliefs, values and perceptions that prevail in a society. These are passed down the generations and reinforced by the educational, legal and social institutions of that society. Some beliefs are common to most societies, for instance the importance of honesty and the value placed on human life; these are enduring and almost universal. However, other cultural norms are subject to change. In the UK the role of women has changed and with it attitudes towards marriage, divorce and the role of the family.

Ethnicity and culture

DATA

Ethnic minorities tend to be concentrated in the large urban areas with 45% of minority ethnic people living in London. This may explain why people in a recent survey estimated ethnic minorities at 22.5% of the population instead of the actual figure of 8%.

CHECK THE NET

The Commission for Racial Equality is found at www.cre.gov.uk.

Whilst culture is a feature of ethnic origin, the tabloid image of a 'rainbow Britain' is misleading. In 2001 around 4.6 million people were of minority ethnic origin – just under 8% of the total population; half of this group were Asians, mostly of Indian, Pakistani or Bangladeshi origin.

Ethnic minorities may retain their cultural identities and attitudes whilst society around them is changing. For example, the economic activity rate (*participation rate*) amongst Bangladeshi and Pakistani women remains low even though the role of women in general and participation rates have changed dramatically in the UK and other Western societies.

Gender and culture

Fifty years ago it was unusual (some thought unthinkable) for a married woman with husband and children to carry on working. (Doctors and other professionals may have been an exception, but there were very few of those.) Attitudes began to change during the recessions of the 1980s when men found it increasingly difficult to find work whereas their wives and partners found ready employment in supermarkets and the growing service industries.

In 1984 the UK participation rate for women was 67%, whereas in 2003 it had risen to 73%. However, the participation rate for men over the same period has fallen from 89% to 84%. Despite a rising participation rate, women are less likely to be

DATA

In 1982 there were 2.7 million more jobs done by men than women but by 2003 the number of jobs done by men and women was almost equal – 13.0 million by men compared to 12.7 million by women. However, we should note that these are *total jobs*, not *hours worked*.

employed in top managerial positions than men – in 2003 only 19% of the female workforce in the UK could be described as occupying senior managerial or professional posts, compared to 31% of the male workforce in the UK.

Marriage and cohabitation

As the role of women has changed in the UK, so has the importance of *marriage* as an institution. In 1971 around 65% of women and 71% of men were married whilst in 2001 this had fallen to 54% and 52% respectively. Meanwhile, *cohabitation* is on the increase. The fact that data were not collected until fairly recently perhaps reflects the attitude of society as much as the figures themselves. In 1979 some 11% of non-married women were cohabiting, but nearly a generation later this figure had almost trebled to 30% in 2001 (*Social Trends*, 2003).

The UK divorce rate doubled between 1951 and 1961 and doubled again up to 1972 following a change in the divorce laws. Divorces peaked at 180,000 in 1993 and have been falling ever since, although there was a slight increase in 2001. Despite this, the median length of marriage before divorce proceedings was 11 years in 2001, only slightly less than in 1963 when it was just over 12 years.

Falling marriage rates and increased marriage breakdowns are part of a European-wide trend (see Table 11.5).

Table 11.5 Marriage and divorce rates across Europe

	Rates per 1000 population	
2001	**Marriages**	**Divorces**
Denmark	6.6	2.7
UK	5.1	2.6
Irish Republic	5.1	0.7
Italy	4.9	0.7
Sweden	4.0	2.4
EU average	5.1	1.9

Adapted from National Statistics (2003) *Social Trends*, London: HMSO

The changing attitudes of society towards marriage and divorce are also reflected in abortion rates and numbers of births outside marriage. The abortion rate has almost doubled in the period 1971–2001 from 12% to 23%, whilst the number of teenage pregnancies in the UK has been increasing – contrary to the European trend. There were very few births outside marriage in the first 60 years of the twentieth century but this proportion began to rise in the 1960s and 1970s. By 2001 around 40% of children were born out of wedlock in the UK, but three-quarters of these were born to cohabiting parents, perhaps suggesting a more stable family unit than is often supposed.

LINKS

There is more discussion of a range of gender issues in Chapter 7, pp. 268–269.

Religion and culture

With such a change in attitudes to the sanctity of the family, one would expect that religion would no longer play such an important part in people's lives. However, 72% of the UK population in 2001 described themselves as Christian, with Islam as the second largest religion at a little under 3%.

Did you know?

In the 2001 census 390,000 people gave their religion as 'Jedi Knight' (from the Star Wars *films), thus outranking Sikhism as Britain's fourth most popular religion. Statisticians were unconvinced and placed the would-be Jedi Knights amongst the 7.7 million people who said they had no religion.*

Chapter 14 (pp. 548–550) looks at important socio-cultural dimensions involving the work of Hall and Hofstede.

Activity 11.1 looks further at some of the issues covered so far in this chapter.

Activity 11.1

1 Look carefully at Figure 11.1.

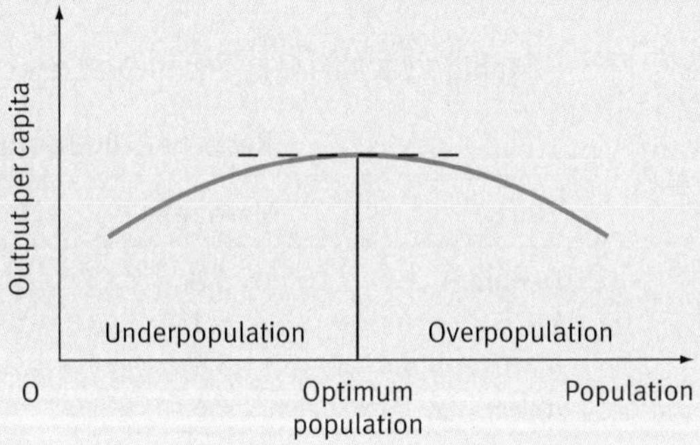

Fig 11.1

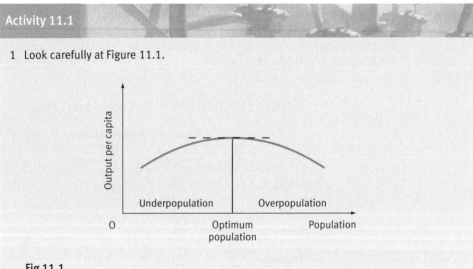

(a) What do you understand by 'optimum population' from this diagram?
(b) What problems can you identify with being over or below the 'optimum'?
(c) Can you suggest possible governmental policy approaches in each case?

2 Read the extract involving bingo and answer the questions which follow.

The game of bingo became popular in post-war Britain as a form of cheap mass entertainment. However, the popularity of television meant a decline in audiences and bingo took on a dowdy image, becoming associated with little old ladies gambling for pennies on their Saturday night out. During the 1990s, however, this decline was halted and revenues and profits began to increase. Some bingo halls now have a turnover of around £250,000 per week in an industry where players stake over £1bn per year on games.

Lately marketers have refocused their attention on their traditional market base – the working-class female – with glossy advertisements showing bingo as the 'girls' night out'. Around 70% of players are female and one-third of players are single females – a demographic group that has grown since bingo's heyday in the 1970s.

Change in the numbers of non-married women

(Percentages)	1971	2000
Single	19	26
Widowed	15	13
Divorced	1	9
Married	65	52

Adapted from National Statistics (2003) *Social Trends*, London: HMSO

Question

Consider some of the implications for bingo operators and other businesses of the data shown in the table.

Answers to Checkpoints and Activities can be found on pp. 705–35.

Lifestyles and social attitudes

Economic, political, cultural and social changes during the past 50 years have resulted in changing lifestyles in the UK. For example, rising housing costs compel young people to stay in the family home for longer, often delaying marriage. Indeed, the average age of marriage in the UK is now 30.5 years for men and 28.2 years for women, whereas 40 years ago it was 25.6 for men and 23.2 years for women.

Implications of changing lifestyles

More home improvements

Whilst most people are hoping to increase the value of their property by DIY activity, research suggests that changing demographics are also a factor. Children stay at home longer, whilst more elderly people are moving in with their offspring owing to a lack of retirement home places. Consequently, families are redesigning their homes to make them more suitable. UK householders spent 50% more on DIY projects in 2003 than a year earlier. An estimated 18.7 million people regularly visit DIY stores to stock up on materials, with the average spend per project now in the region of £2,610.

Later motherhood

Changing working patterns for women mean that motherhood is also delayed. In the UK the average first-time mother in 1971 was 24 years old; today she is likely to be well over 29 years old. Many parents now in their late 30s and 40s (often described as the 'sandwiched generation') are still raising children at a time when their own parents are increasingly in need of support.

Longer working hours

Meanwhile, people are working long hours to support a higher living standard. One-quarter of working men and 11% of working women in the UK now work more than 50 hours per week, with managers and senior officials the group most likely to work long hours. Although the most common working week for men was 40 hours in 2001, the second most common working week was over 60 hours. In fact, Britons work the longest hours in Europe.

Surveys suggest that at least one-fifth of workers are dissatisfied with their hours of work and a large proportion complain of *over-employment*; the 'over-employed' are defined as those who want to work fewer hours and are willing to take an equivalent pay cut. Such over-employment increases with age, as indicated in Table 11.6.

Table 11.6 Over-employment: full-time workers

Age	16–17	18–24	25–34	35–49	50+
%	4	5	10	14	17

Adapted from National Statistics (2003) *Social Trends*, London: HMSO

Chapter 7 (p. 266) has considered aspects of the work–life balance in more detail.

Less healthy diets and obesity

An implication of a long-hours culture and time shortages has been a less healthy diet, with more focus on fast foods. Case Study 11.3 looks at this in more detail.

Case Study 11.3 Fast goods for fast lifestyles

Working the longest hours in Europe has turned the British into 'convenience seekers' demanding consumer goods to fit their hectic lifestyles. Consumers who are too tired, or have too little time, to cook are turning more and more to convenience foods, which have seen a 68% increase in sales since 1992 (current prices) compared with a 33% growth of the food market overall.

Sales of analgesics (pain relief remedies) increased by 50% in real terms over the same period. Some analysts have interpreted this as a trend for self-medication and self-diagnosis by people too busy to consult a doctor.

Retailers are cashing in by offering 'fast fashion' for women who want to make fast purchasing decisions and update their wardrobe more often. There is a similar trend in tourism where pressures of work and longer hours force holidaymakers to take more short breaks.

Case Study 11.3 continued

UK residents took over 39 million holidays abroad in 2001, with Spain the most popular destination (26% of holidays abroad). Spending on airfares has increased by 57% over the last 10 years.

Questions Identify other likely winners and losers from the trends in this case study.

DATA

Lifestyle changes in 2004

- Just 11% of households buy oranges, down from 23% in the mid-1980s, according to the *National Food Society*. The purchase of apples has dropped by 10%.
- Fewer than 10% of all seven-year-olds walk to school today. Since the mid-1980s the percentage of children driven to school has almost doubled.
- Three out of four children do not play sport regularly, a study by *Sport England* found.
- A quarter of children watch at least four hours of television a day; 95% of products advertised on children's television are for junk food, the *International Obesity Task Force* says.

The issue of obesity has grown further in prominence in recent years. For example, a British Medical Association report in February 2004 (*Archives of Disease in Childhood*) found that the average waist measurement of 13-year-old boys and girls had risen by 4 cm ($1\frac{1}{2}$ inches) or two clothing sizes over the past 20 years. The report goes on to emphasise the well-established links between obesity and diabetes and heart disease.

Certainly food producers are paying attention to these concerns, partly to respond to consumer demands for healthier food but also to avoid future litigation. In 2001 students from George Washington University filed a lawsuit against McDonald's, accusing it of failing to disclose that its French fries were prepared with beef fat. McDonald's agreed an out-of-court settlement of $10m. However, in 2003 a lawsuit failed in seeking to blame McDonald's for obesity, with the judge ruling that the plaintiffs 'did not demonstrate that McDonald's products involve a danger that is not within the common knowledge of consumers'.

Smoking and drinking

We have seen how the role of women has changed in the UK but now it seems that women are changing their lifestyles to match those of men. Between 1940 and 1970 the number of women smokers was half that of men, today the numbers are about equal. In 1984, 25% of men but only 9% of women consumed alcohol above the official safety guidelines. By 2001 the proportion of men who drank more than deemed safe had risen to 29% but the increase in female drinking almost doubled to 17%.

Stress levels

The rise in the female participation rate means that more women than ever before are subjected to the stress of holding down a job whilst running a home. Studies have found that men and women suffer equal levels of stress even when women hold *lower* positions than men, because women were more badly affected by domestic stress than men. Women still do the majority of housework, averaging three hours per day (excluding shopping and childcare) compared with one hour forty minutes for men.

LINKS

A more detailed breakdown of male and female activities can be found in Chapter 16, p. 677.

On the other hand, men tend to have a longer working week than women, working on average an extra two hours per day.

Life expectancy

All these factors affect the health and life expectancy of the individual.

The average life expectancy of both men and women has increased over the past five years but the improvement rate for women is slowing. Experts predict that by the end of the twenty-first century men will be outliving their wives.

Case Study 11.4 reflects on some life-expectancy implications for today's households.

Case Study 11.4 Life changes everything

People with private pensions often receive a sum of cash upon retirement. This cash can be re-invested with the original insurance company to obtain a continued source of income for life, known as an annuity income. During the 1970s and 1980s – a time of double-digit interest rates – life insurance salesmen offered guaranteed fixed rate annuities of a meagre 6% or 7% as a marketing gimmick. The industry was confident that these guarantees were hardly worth the paper they were written on and thus unlikely to be taken up.

But times have changed; interest rates have plummeted and life-expectancy rates have soared – which makes these guarantees very valuable indeed. Values vary, but a 65-year-old man could expect a 30% improvement in his annuity income *if he has a guarantee*. Annuity rates in general have halved during the past decade. UK life insurance companies are so concerned that they have set aside reserves of £12bn to offset the costs of around 1 million pensioners taking up their guarantees within the next few years.

Meanwhile, the European Commission is concerned about the lack of pension provision for women. Proposed plans will end gender discrimination in the insurance premiums that men and women pay in the hope that more women will make plans for their futures. However, this is also a concern for insurance companies who use statistical differences between the sexes (such as life expectancy and driving records) to charge women higher premiums for pensions and annuities whilst charging men more for life insurance. Women also receive lower annuities than men, based on the fact that the same lump sum of cash has to last longer and thus must be spread more thinly over more years.

The European Commission argues that when factors which are not linked to sex, such as lifestyle, are removed from the calculations, the differences in life expectancy are reduced. However, insurers maintain that they already set fair prices based on genuine risk and that the Commission's plans would have a perverse effect by increasing the cost of women's life insurance by 10–16%.

Case Study 11.4 continued

Questions

1 Why have guaranteed fixed-rate annuities become such a worry for insurance companies?

2 Why do women receive lower annuities than men?

3 Do you think the European Commission has a good argument for removing discrimination from the insurance market?

Family ties

Recent newspaper headlines have raised concerns about the increasingly fragmented nature of the UK social fabric. Nearly one-third of all UK households in 2003 consisted of a single person living alone, compared with 17% in 1971. However, despite many people preferring to stay single and childless, 70% still place keeping in close touch with family as their main priority in life. Over half of all UK adults report seeing their mother at least once a week and two-fifths see their father once a week or more. More than half of all adults also see their best friend at least once a week.

As family size declines but people live longer, children of tomorrow will have fewer siblings, cousins, aunts and uncles. However, there will be more grandparents and great-grandparents to look after them whilst parents work – a situation known as the 'bean-pole effect'. Currently, around 60% of all grandparents either see their grandchildren at least once a week or communicate with them via telephone, letter, fax or e-mail. Only 2% of grandparents never see their grandchildren at all.

Teenager health issues

However, health experts are alarmed at the unhealthy lifestyles of British teenagers and give the gloomy prediction that many of them will die before their parents. The number of overweight children has doubled in the past 20 years; today one in five 15-year-olds are obese whilst one-quarter are regular smokers. Binge drinking and promiscuity are also on the increase. Doctors are particularly concerned about the rise of the sexually transmitted disease chlamydia, which may not cause symptoms in women but remain undetected for years before rendering thousands infertile. These patterns in teenage lifestyles have been termed the 'health time-bomb' of British teenagers.

It has been suggested that this so-called 'health time-bomb' will have three possible effects on UK demographics:

1 Unhealthy children grow up to become unhealthy adults. If too sick to work they could form an additional burden on the economy, becoming dependants before they even retire. This will decrease the 'support ratio'.

2 The support ratio will also decrease if children die before their parents because there will be fewer 'taxpayers per pensioner'.

3 Increased infertility will lower the fertility rate and thus lower the support ratio.

These three factors add up to an even lower *support ratio* than was suggested at the beginning of this chapter. However, if many of today's teenagers do *not* reach retirement age, then from a cold statistical standpoint the problem will perhaps not be so great! What happens in the long term depends even more upon the generation following on from today's teenagers. If the offspring of today's teenagers follow the lifestyle of their parents, then the UK population may decline even more rapidly than previously thought.

Business implications of demographic and social changes

Populations can be perceived in two broad ways, firstly as a market and secondly as a source of labour. Thus changing demographics have both market and resource implications for businesses.

1 The changing market

Although most Western populations are expected eventually to decline, that will not happen for many years to come. Businesses meanwhile would do well to focus on the changing demographic patterns that have already been discussed in this chapter. Here we identify some market-related issues linked to demographics and social attitudes, building on a number of points already discussed earlier in the chapter.

At one time, businesses and their marketing departments largely ignored 'old' people, stereotyping them as frail, inactive folk with little spending power. However, as the baby boomers approach retirement age, marketers are already recognising the lure of the 'grey pound'.

Rise of the 'grey market'

As we have seen, this is one of the fastest-growing market segments. By 2010 one-fifth of Europeans will be aged 62 or over, more than the entire population of Canada! Furthermore, thanks to modern standards of living, these people will be relatively healthy and leading what marketers like to call 'multidimensional lives'. They may have lower incomes than younger segments but most will have paid off their mortgages and, unlike their children, be relatively debt-free yet have considerable leisure time in which to 'shop around'. Marketers must beware of their methods, however; a survey of the over-55s revealed that one-third of respondents had not bought a product because of the way in which an elderly person was stereotyped in the advertising.

Watch out!

One observant data analyst for Heinz foods noticed that significant quantities of their baby foods were bought and consumed by the elderly. It seemed a brilliant marketing wheeze, therefore, to produce a similar range of sieved foods aimed at this growing marketing segment with its ill-fitting dentures and preference for small portions. Alas, the line failed miserably. Elderly consumers were too proud to admit (even to the lady at the till) that they needed strained foods, whereas they could always say that they bought baby foods for their grandchildren!

Case Study 11.5 looks more carefully at this 'grey market'.

Case Study 11.5 **'Grey market' on the rise**

An important and growing market segment involves the 'grey market'. Nearly 44% of Britain's adults are over 50 and this proportion is rising rapidly. By 2005, this so-called third generation will have swelled by more than 13% in just 10 years. In 20 years, one in two adults will be over 50.

This demographic group is not just large; it's also rich. A report by Mintel, the research company, found that the distribution of wealth within the UK is 'heavily skewed' towards the older generation. It has the largest proportion of outright homeowners, and more investment and savings products than the adult population at large. Soaring house prices and maturing life-insurance policies have added to this wealth.

As well as living longer, this group is staying healthier for longer. Older people also have plenty of time to fill, particularly with workers retiring earlier. In short, as another Mintel study found, the older generation has the desire, the money and the time to spend cash – particularly on holidays. The 14.1 million third-agers took 32.1 million holidays in 2002, up from 28.7 million in 1996.

The older generation now accounts for a substantial portion of the UK tourism market – about 22% of domestic holidays and 26% of holidays abroad. Two-thirds of all people between the ages of 45 and 64 without children at home took a holiday in 2002, according to TGI Europa research. The British are the best travellers, but third-agers also account for 40% of tourism in Germany and 17% in Ireland.

All these figures are set to rise as a result of a gradual shift in culture, as well as the simple growth of numbers. Experts said the older generations were more confident and motivated than ever, and this manifested itself in world travel. Empty nests free up both time and money for parents but can be big motivators, too – the trip of a lifetime that has been postponed is now possible, and older generations are prepared to spend lavishly.

Questions

1 Identify some of the goods and services likely to be affected by the rise in the grey market.

2 What other implications might result from this trend?

Rise of technological consumerism

It is young people who are embracing the 'digital lifestyle' of digital cameras, digital TVs, MP3 players etc., according to research presented at the 2003 International Broadcasting Convention in Amsterdam. Unlike the baby-boomer generation, the under-34s do not sit down to watch TV but treat it as a form of ambient entertainment whilst they do other things – a warning to TV advertisers perhaps. In response to this, an audio-description channel is to be launched which will describe what is happening on-screen.

The 'digital lifestyle' is consumer driven by people who do not wish to sit huddled around a TV or PC, but who want to receive e-mails, find photos, music and films easily whilst wandering around the house and garden. The answer is arguably a home network, but only 2% of UK and 30% of US broadband users have achieved this – the technology is just too complex for most people. The dream of the PC and TV converging into one product has been abandoned in favour of the consumer-led concept of the digital lifestyle. The next step is to agree international standards – never easy – before perfecting products that are easy to install and keep working without requiring a degree in IT.

Case Study 11.6 identifies some important lifestyle patterns based on the results of the 2001 census in the UK and explores some of their implications.

Case Study 11.6 Neighbourhood takes over from occupation

FT

The 2001 census confirms the impression that we increasingly segregate ourselves in various ways and are becoming more complex. Some of the more notable trends are:

- Young people attending university have resulted in the conversion of traditional working-class neighbourhoods into student territory, where bars and cheap restaurants, convenience stores, launderettes and travel agents drive out traditional hardware stores, betting shops and old-fashioned pubs. The growth of student numbers is a principal cause of regeneration in many large provincial towns such as Bristol, Leeds and Nottingham.
- Lower marriage rates, the trend towards cohabitation and easier separation have resulted in many more single people and childless partners wanting to own a small house or flat. This has resulted in 'dinky development' – cheap, typically two-bedroom flats, built on brown-field sites for people for whom easy access to city centre fun is more important than the quality of schools and the size of gardens.
- Second-generation immigrants from Asia and the Caribbean are now moving from the communities of big divided houses where their parents lived – Brixton and Willesden – into areas of older Victorian terraces such as Edmonton and Croydon, previously occupied by white clerical and manual workers.
- Indians, in contrast to other immigrant groups, have moved to more prestigious areas of inter-war semis in places such as Harrow, Hounslow, Ilford and Wolverhampton, to create a new type of neighbourhood 'Asian enterprise'.
- The continuing sale to council tenants of better quality, low-rise council estates, particularly in Scotland and the south-east of England, has reduced the differences between council housing and much of the cheaper privately owned housing built during the 1930s. Unemployment on these estates is low and car (and white van) ownership is high.

Case Study 11.6 continued

- Better-off people, who would once have retired to a coastal resort, are increasingly favouring picturesque country villages, particularly in the south and south-west of England, rendering them unaffordable to local youngsters. In 2001, Britain's countryside had a far older age profile than in 1991.
- The 2001 census marks the arrival of a category of rural neighbourhood: 'summer playgrounds'. Older, wealthier, urban Britons are releasing equity in their main home to purchase a rural get-away for weekends and summer lettings. Padstow, Salcombe and Sheringham are examples of communities dominated by affluent weekenders.

Source: *Financial Times*, 8 October 2003, p. 33

Questions

1 Identify various goods and services which might be impacted, favourably or unfavourably, by the trends identified.

2 What other implications for society and government might follow from the trends identified?

2 The changing labour force

If the demographic time-bomb is realised, then businesses may well find that they are increasingly short of labour. We have seen from Chapter 7 that a shortage of labour will force up wages, thus a shrinking workforce might well mean higher real wages for employers to pay. Firms that *cannot* pay market-clearing wages have the following options:

- Go out of business.
- Stay in business but change to a product with greater value added.
- Relocate production abroad.
- Increase productivity by:
  - increased capital investment;
  - improved training of workforce;
  - rethinking current working practices.

As we note in Chapter 14 and elsewhere, rising labour costs have already seen many firms moving production from the UK and other Western countries to cheaper sources of labour. Even the service industry has been affected by the relocation of call centres to India. For firms that choose to stay in domestic production, clearly increased capital investment and improved training are vital if they are to make the most of a dwindling labour force.

Working practices basically mean 'the way we do things'. Changes in working practices might help increase productivity. These changes can be as basic as reorganising the factory floor to make it more efficient, or providing crèches and childcare facilities in order to encourage more working mothers.

Businesses may also have to retain workers for longer. People aged over 50 are usually the first to be released when a firm wishes to 'downsize' – and the last to be taken back when economic conditions improve. The Department of Trade and Industry has calculated that since 1979, this drop in work rates of the over-50s has cost the UK economy £16bn in lost GDP and a further £3–£5bn outlay in benefits and lost taxes.

In 2006 the EU will introduce rules to outlaw age discrimination, although not all firms are happy with this. A government survey reported that 12% of UK firms were concerned about retaining older workers with deteriorating skills. On the other hand, unions point out, deteriorating skills are one result of current training policies – only 7% of workers over the age of 55 receive any form of work-related training in the UK.

LINKS

Chapters 7 and 16 develop further some of these labour force and labour market scenarios linked to demographic and social change.

Meanwhile the baby boomer generation is reaching the age when firms are most likely to dispense with their services. However, the effect of dismissing 17 million people (almost 30% of the population) before retirement remains to be seen.

Some experts think that the popular press has exaggerated the effects of the 'demographic time-bomb'. They argue that it is unfair to concentrate attention on the number of pensioners when the economy already supports many other people who are dependants – such as children, the chronically sick, the unemployed, and those in prison. In addition, many retired people do unpaid charity work as well as looking after grandchildren and sick relatives, so they are not the 'burden' that the support ratio might imply.

In any case, some economists believe that workers in 2030 could be almost twice as productive as those of today. This, coupled with the measures listed previously, would offset some of the adverse effects claimed for an ageing population.

Activity 11.2

1 The strains of modern living are encouraging more and more women to seek stress-relieving activities such as yoga, meditation, massage, shiatsu and reflexology. 'Spiritual spending' totals £670m per year in the UK whilst spa retreats and yoga holidays account for a further £20m.

Marketers recognise that 'well-being' is a major high street trend and have used yoga to sell such diverse products as insurance, beer, air freshener and weed killer. One advertising agency described yoga as a reliable medium through which advertisers can communicate with the 'Special K demographic'. (Special K is a low-fat breakfast cereal manufactured by Kellogg.)

Questions

1 Who do you think are the 'Special K demographic'?

2 Can you think of any instances of yoga being used to promote products?

2 Read the text associated with these two specific products, then answer the questions which follow.

(a) Pizza

Improved technology and changing demographics are helping Domino's Pizza capture an increasing share of the UK's £1bn pizza delivery market. They currently control one-fifth of the market, but expect to double this by 2010.

People watching The Simpsons on interactive television can order a Domino's pizza during advertising breaks, simply by pushing the red button on their remote control. At present, around 3% of Domino's pizzas are ordered this way but the firm is optimistic that online ordering has great potential. Research suggests that it is the increasingly large numbers of single and childless couples in the UK who are most likely to order online. A piping hot pizza can be delivered to the door in less time than it takes to cook a meal – a valuable asset for time-conscious people.

(b) Bisto

Smaller families and changing lifestyles mean that British families are less likely to sit down to the traditional 'meat and two veg' every evening. Instead, they tend to dine separately on something quicker and more convenient. But if you think this spells the end of Bisto, the gravy product invented nearly 100 years ago, think again. Bisto commands over 60% of the still-growing £91m UK gravy market, with Oxo (nearest branded rival) taking a mere 7%. Success is down to clever marketing and development of new products to keep ahead of the main rivals – supermarkets' own brands. Bisto's products have different 'demographics', ranging from those who like to cook a meal from scratch and prefer the powder, to pour-on sauces for cooks in a hurry.

The family is now at the heart of Bisto's advertising, with busy mothers defined as the target market. Fortunately for Bisto, there has also been a revival of interest in traditional British cooking; cottage pie and sausages and mash are becoming fashionable once more.

Questions

1 What are the changing lifestyles/attitudes involved in the discussion of these two products?
2 Can you identify other products which might also benefit from these lifestyle changes? Be specific and suggest ways in which these products can put marketing ideas into practice.
3 Can you identify other products which might be *threatened* by these lifestyle changes? Be specific and suggest any 'defensive' strategies they might adopt to prevent a collapse in future demand.

Answers to Checkpoints and Activities can be found on pp. 705–35.

Key Terms

'Baby-boomers' A term often used to refer to those born in the 'bulge' period after the Second World War.

'Black economy' The percentage of national income which is not officially declared, and which therefore does not appear in the national income statistics.

'Demographic time-bomb' A term usually linked to an ageing population, showing a fall in the support ratio involving the economically active to pensioner ratio.

'Grey market' Refers to the (often increasing) market segment involving older people (beyond a specified age).

Cohabitation Living together as partners rather than married.

Culture The set of beliefs, values and perceptions that prevail in society or are attributed to a specific grouping of people.

Gender Male and female issues.

Net migration The difference between immigration and emigration. If positive, then more people come into the country than leave it.

Over-employed Those who want to work fewer hours and are willing to take an equivalent pay cut.

Participation rate The percentage of any given group which is economically active.

Population change Given by the equation 'Births – Deaths + Net migration'.

Socio-economic class A grouping of individuals or households, usually using occupational data (Categories A–E).

Support ratio Strictly the ratio of economically active people to dependents (under 16 and over 65). Often used as a measure of ageing population, using the more specific ratio of economically active people to pensions.

Total fertility rate (TFR) The average number of children born to one woman at current fertility levels.

Key Points

- Most advanced industrialised economies are experiencing demographic change involving progressively fewer young people and greater numbers of old people.
- Population change will depend on births, deaths and net migration.
- In the UK as in many other countries, the ageing population is due in part to a decrease in birth rate and decline in death rate.
- The sustainability of pensions when there is a decline in the 'support ratio' is a pressing issue.
- Various government policy responses can help defuse this 'demographic time-bomb', including increases in the participation rates, later retirement, greater productivity and a reduction in the 'black economy'.
- Socio-economic characteristics of the population are changing, with important implications for households, businesses and governments.
- Cultural and lifestyle changes are also occurring at historically rapid rates, as in the case of marriage and divorce, later motherhood, longer working hours, less healthy lifestyles, family ties and stress levels.

Assessment Practice

Multiple choice questions

1 **The 'demographic time-bomb' is used to describe the situation where:**

(a) There is a trend towards larger families.
(b) There is a trend towards more women going out to work.
(c) Immigration is increasing.
(d) People are living longer and the birth rate is declining.
(e) People are living longer and the birth rate is increasing.

2 **'Total fertility rate' means:**

(a) The average number of pregnancies a woman may be expected to have during her lifetime, based on current trends.
(b) The average number of children a woman may be expected to have during her lifetime, based on current trends.
(c) The actual number of children a woman has had during her lifetime.
(d) The actual number of pregnancies a woman has had during her lifetime.
(e) The total number of children born into a population in a particular year.

3 **The 'support ratio' can be defined as:**

(a) the ratio of economically active people to dependants
(b) the ratio of dependants to economically active people
(c) the ratio of dependants to children
(d) the ratio of taxpayers to children
(e) the ratio of children under 16 to adults over 65.

4 **Many Western countries are experiencing an ageing population because:**

(a) people are living longer
(b) women are having more children
(c) women are having fewer children
(d) children are dying at an early age, leaving a larger proportion of older people.
(e) both (a) and (c).

5 **Which *two* problems are generally associated with an ageing population?**

(a) Shortage of labour
(b) Declining birth rate
(c) Too many old managers with out-of-date ideas
(d) Too many young managers with no experience
(e) Increasing cost of pension payments as the proportion of retired people increases

6 **Which *three* of the following policies could a government pursue in order to overcome the 'demographic time-bomb'?**

(a) Increase maternity benefits and payments for all mothers.
(b) Encourage women to stay at home whilst their partners go out to work.
(c) Award cash payment to people who take early retirement.
(d) Award cash payments to people who take late retirement.
(e) Seek ways of encouraging discouraged workers back into the labour force.

7 **Changing working patterns in the UK and many Western countries over the past 50 years, have resulted in which *one* of the following?**

(a) More women staying at home and looking after the home.
(b) More women going out to work.
(c) More men going out to work.
(d) People marrying at a younger age.
(e) People delaying marriage.

8 **The 'baby-boomers' are important consumers because:**

(a) they are few in number but are relatively wealthy
(b) they are a declining demographic group but are very influential
(c) they form a large and increasing proportion of the population
(d) individually they may not be particularly wealthy, but as a group they have considerable purchasing power
(e) they will soon be extinct as a demographic group.

9 **If the 'demographic time-bomb' is true, which *three* of the following apply?**

(a) Businesses may be forced to sack workers before they reach retirement age.
(b) Businesses may be short of labour.
(c) Businesses may have to retire workers early.
(d) Businesses may have to retain workers who are beyond the official retirement age.
(e) Businesses will have to increase productivity to compensate for a reduction in the labour force.

10 **In the future, the effect of an ageing population might result in which *three* of the following?**

(a) Increase the real wage as the labour supply dwindles.
(b) Lower the real wage as the labour supply dwindles.
(c) Compel firms to relocate due to higher domestic wages.
(d) Compel firms to rethink their training and working practices.
(e) Encourage firms to take on more workers as wages deteriorate.

Data response and stimulus questions

1 Read the following text, then answer the following questions.

Baby-boomers

From WW2 to Woodstock to Woodstoves to the World Wide Web, what a long, strange trip it's been. Born in that baby-making bonanza which took place between 1945 and 1964 and now aged 39–58, the arrival of this generation has been a most predictable of demographic events. Yet few in our leisure-and-hospitality world are repositioning themselves to meet the unprecedented opportunities presented by this age cohort.

The baby-boomers concept first emerged in the US. Most American marketing texts agree that the baby-boom ran for a 20-year period following the end of WW2 – 1945 to 1964; during these 20 years some 77 million Americans were born. Many in the UK and Europe regard the ten years from 1945 to 1954 as the boomer decade.

Let's look at a few baby-boomer facts:

- The over-50s possess 80% of the UK's wealth and 40% of its spending – worth £145bn per year.
- This is the only population group set to increase – from 20 to 27 million by 2025.

Therefore the 50-plus age group is the only expanding market segment in the UK – indeed, as it is in all of Western Europe and North America. They have more disposable income or discretionary spend than all other consumer groups combined. For many, substantial inheritance from their property-owning parents, completion on their mortgages and liberation from the costs of children as they in turn graduate to achieve empty-nester status has left them with significant capital and – for the first time – a very positive balance of income over expenditure.

In the US, Alisor McGuire of Elderflower Ltd found a complete turnaround in boomer attitudes compared with those of their parents, who were parsimonious, prudent and deferred gratification by continually saving for a rainy day. Her research exposed an outlook in the US which 'forgot saving for the future – making the most of the present is the priority'. This generation has coined a new cluster: SKINS – 'Spend the Kids' Inheritance ... Now!' For them, 'Pleasure rather than duty is the order of the day.' As one boomer put it succinctly to an interviewer: 'I've written a will and if there's anything left my kids will get it: if there isn't, tough!' Most estimates put the UK some 5–10 years behind the US.

Source: Adapted from D. McCaskey (2003) *Hospitality Review* No. 29, April

Questions

a) Consider some of the implications of this 'baby-boomer' analysis for households, businesses and governments.

b) If the UK is some '5 to 10 years behind the US', what might this imply?

2 Consider the demographic trends shown in Table 11.7. The UK would be in the 'High income' group of countries.

Table 11.7 Demographic trends in country/income groups

Country/Income group	Annual pop^n growth rate (%) 1975–2001	2001–2015	Urban pop^n (% of total) 1975	2001	2015	Pop^n under 15 (% of total) 2001	2015	Pop^n 65 years + (% of total) 2001	2015	Total fertility rate (per woman)* 1970–1975	1990–2002
Developing economies	2.6	2.4	25.9	38.9	47.6	33.1	28.1	3.1	3.4	6.6	5.4
High income economies	0.7	0.4	75.0	78.7	82.2	18.6	15.8	14.5	18.3	2.1	1.7

* Average number of children a woman would bear if age-specific fertility rates remained unchanged during her lifetime.

Adapted from *UN Human Development Report* (2003), New York: HDRO

Question

What implications might you draw from the demographic information shown in the table?

True/False questions

1 World population is increasing by about 1.2% each year.

True/False

2 Demographers think that, within 50 years, many Western countries will have more births than deaths.

True/False

3 An 'ageing population' means that more older women are having children than before.

True/False

4 On average, European women have more children than African women.

True/False

5 Insurance companies are currently benefiting from the 'ageing population'.

True/False

6 Lee is a junior manager in a large firm. His social class is likely to be category C1.

True/False

Essay questions

1 Discuss the factors which will determine the direction and magnitude of population change.
2 What are the major causes and consequences of an ageing population?
3 How can governments adapt their policies to cope with the problems caused by an ageing population?
4 Examine the impacts of the so-called 'baby boomers' on business behaviour.
5 Consider some of the major lifestyle changes in the UK in recent years. How are these relevant to individuals, firms and governments?

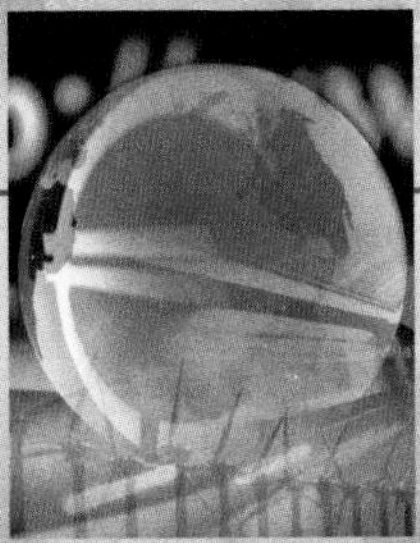

Chapter 12

Political, legal, ecological and technological environment

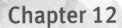

Introduction

Various acronyms (letter arrangements) are widely used to identify the features of the external environment in which the organisation finds itself. PEST is one (Political, Economic, Socio-cultural and Technological), PESTLE is another, with Legal and Ecological/Environmental added on to PEST.

The economic environment has already been considered in detail from a micro perspective in Chapters 1 to 8 and from a macro perspective in Chapters 9 and 10. The socio-cultural (and demographic) environment was the focus of Chapter 11. Here we concentrate on the political, legal, ecological and technological environments which may also play key roles in shaping the opportunities and threats faced by the organisation. Whilst the focus of this chapter is the 'external environment' in which the organisation must operate, the strengths and weaknesses inherent in the organisation (i.e. the 'internal environment') will of necessity by touched upon at times. However, a more detailed assessment of the strategic interface between internal and external environments is left to Chapter 15.

Learning objectives:

By the end of this chapter you should be able to:

- examine the various ways in which political factors influence business and organisational decision making
- assess the impacts of legal and regulatory frameworks on businesses and organisations
- evaluate the relevance of 'sustainability' and other ecological issues to decision making within businesses
- discuss the opportunities and threats from a rapidly changing technological environment.

Political environment

Most organisations operate within a *nation state* (e.g. UK) and many also operate within *supra-national bodies* which comprise collections of nation states (e.g. EU). Decisions within both types of political entity can have major impacts on the prospects for business organisations achieving the objectives they have set themselves. We review the various types of political risk and some of the techniques that might be used to counter these risks.

Types of political risk

Two broad categories of political risk are often identified, namely 'macropolitical' and 'micropolitical'.

Macropolitical risks

These potentially affect *all* firms in a country, as in the case of war, a sudden change of government, the onset of national economic recession, and so on. Such risks may even result in governments seizing the assets of the firm without compensation. However, macropolitical risks more usually take the form of the 'threat' of adverse economic circumstances in a country, for example economic recession with less aggregate demand for a broad range of products. Similarly, higher general levels of inflation or taxation might adversely affect all firms, as might security risks related to terrorism etc.

Micropolitical risks

These only affect *specific* firms, industries or types of venture. Such risks may take the form of new regulations or taxes imposed on specific types of businesses in the country.

Example: **GlaxoSmithKline targeted in the US**

An example of micropolitical risk emerged in January 2004 when GlaxoSmithKline (GSK), Europe's biggest drugs company, was hit with a $2.9bn tax bill from authorities in the US. The US tax authorities are claiming that GSK used 'transfer pricing' (see Chapter 14, p. 569) between its subsidiary companies supplying the US market to depress recorded profits (and therefore tax revenues) in the higher-taxed US market.

Case Study 12.1 looks further at micropolitical risks, this time in the context of a particular industry (here freight) rather than a particular company. It also indicates that what may at first appear to be a micropolitical risk impacting a single industry can have broader implications for the economy as a whole.

Case Study 12.1 Freight companies pay for security threat

FT

- November 2001 *Customs Trade Partnership Against Terrorism (C-TPAT)*. Carriers, customers brokers, freight forwarders or importers joining the programme must conduct a thorough self-assessment, tighten their supply-chain security and be subject to regular reassessments. While C-TPAT is a voluntary programme, companies not in it are more likely to have their cargo delayed by inspections. Companies must be C-TPAT compliant before they can join other initiatives, such as Fast (see below) or the importer Self-Assessment programme ...
- January 2002 *Container Security Initiative (CSI)*. Through the CSI, US customs officers are being deployed in foreign ports. The idea is to engage ports – and their countries' governments – that send the highest volumes of container traffic to the US to help identify and inspect high-risk containers before they reach the states.
- September 2002 *Free and Secure Trade (FAST)*. Carriers and importers that have enrolled in C-TPAT – and whose drivers are rigorously vetted and drive trucks fitted with special transponders – receive faster customs clearance through this programme. The programme also reduces the information required by US Customs and creates dedicated lanes at border crossings for Fast participants.
- November 2002 *Operation Safe Commerce (OSC)*. A public/private partnership OSC tests new procedures and technologies to enhance the security of container shipments. Tests are being carried out at three transport hubs: the Port Authority of New York and New Jersey, the Ports of Seattle and Tacoma and the Ports of Los Angeles and Long Beach.
- December 2002 *24 Hour Rule*. Carriers must file a detailed manifest electronically or by paper with US Customs 24 hours before a US-bound container is loaded on to a vessel in a foreign port. Rules for other transport modes have followed, requiring manifests to be submitted an hour before trucks arrive in the US (30 minutes for FAST trucks), two hours for rail carriers and four hours for air carriers.
- December 2003 *Bio-Terrorism*. Launched by the US Food and Drug Administration, it requires those shipping food products for consumption by humans or animals to the US to give inspectors advance notice before shipments arrive. The FDA and US Customs have agreed to share information so companies will not need to submit details twice about incoming shipments.
- July 2004 *International Ship and Port Facility Security Code*. Drawn up by the International Maritime Organisation, it contains mandatory regulations for all port facilities receiving vessels of more than 500 gross tonnes on international routes.

Source: *Financial Times*, 13 January 2004

Questions

1 What types of costs are being imposed on the freight industry by such legislation?

2 Consider the impacts of these additional costs on the freight industry and the economy as a whole.

Checkpoint 1 Can you provide other examples of micropolitical risk?

It may be useful to disaggregate the types of political risk further, as indicated for macropolitical risks in Table 12.1.

Table 12.1 Types of macropolitical risk and their impacts on firms

Type	Impact on firms
Expropriation Confiscation	Loss of sales Loss of assets Loss of future profits
Campaigns against foreign goods	Loss of sales Increased cost of public relations campaigns to improve public image
Mandatory labour benefits legislation	Increased operating costs
Kidnappings, terrorist threats and other forms of violence	Disrupted production Increased security costs Increased managerial costs Lower productivity
Civil wars	Destruction of property Lost sales Disruption of production Increased security costs Lower productivity
Inflation	Higher operating costs
Currency devaluations/depreciation	Reduced value of repatriated earnings
Currency revaluations/appreciation	Less competitive in overseas markets and in competing against imports in home market
Increased taxation	Lower after-tax profits

Checkpoint 2 Can you give any recent examples of macropolitical risk?

Responding to political risk

A common criticism of political risk analysis is that it usually takes place too late, when projects are already under way. More management time and effort is now being directed towards appraising political risk at the initiation stage of projects as companies become more aware of the importance of political risk to their future operations. For example, organisations seeking to internationalise typically investigate the following factors in countries which might become the focus of fdi activity: the system of government, foreign capital controls, industrial regulations, history of civil unrest, diplomatic tensions and so on.

Assessing political risk factors

Managers or their representatives may well visit the countries under investigation, as well as using information and data sources from libraries, the Internet, industry associations, government agencies, banks and insurers. Country-risk reports are also available from risk assessment companies and specialists in particular business activities, often consisting of a country profile and macro-level market/non-market risk assessment. However, such analyses may not include the fine detail that might be vital for particular ventures, and at best provide only an indication of the socio-political background.

Prioritising political risk factors

Once identified and assessed, such political risks can be *prioritised*, as in Figure 12.1. The 'gross risks' (expected values) associated with the various political factors or events are sometimes placed by businesses in a two-by-two diagram, giving four 'boxes'. Box A shows risks (high impact/high likelihood) requiring *immediate action*, resulting in attempts by the firm to reduce either the probability of their occurrence or the adverse impacts should they occur. Perhaps it would also be sensible to have in place contingency plans to cover some of the risks in boxes B and C, but those in D would be of lesser concern.

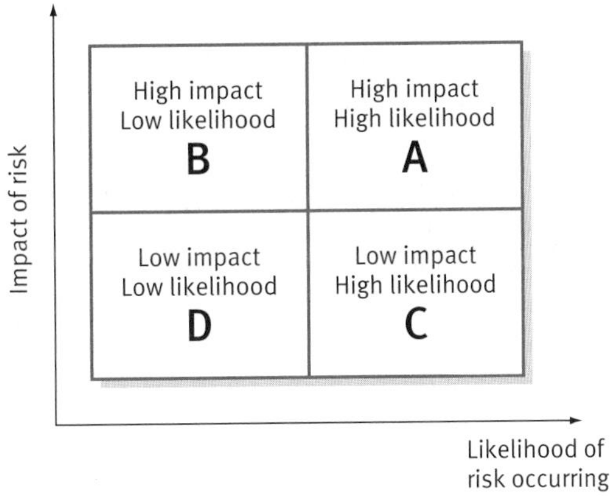

Fig 12.1 Prioritising (political) risk

Box 12.1 looks at ways in which a *quantitative value* might be placed on those political risks regarded as high priority.

Box 12.1 **Expected value and political risk**

It is not only the *probability* of a particular political risk factor occurring but the magnitude of its potential *impact* on the objectives of the company which must also be taken into account. It is worth remembering that the *expected value* of an event is the sum of the probability of each possible outcome multiplied by the value (impact) of each outcome.

$$EV = \sum_{i=1}^{n} p_i x_i$$

where p_i = probability of outcome i (as a decimal)

x_i = value of outcome i

n = number of possible outcomes

So if the firm estimated a 60% probability of a 'strike' type of labour dispute occurring so that profits are £20m and a 40% probability of a 'work to rule' occurring so that profits are £40m, the expected value (EV) should a labour dispute occur would be:

$$EV\ (£m) = (0.60 \times 20) + (0.40 \times 40)$$
$$= \underline{£28m}$$

A change in the firm's assessment of the probabilities of these events occurring or the value of their impacts should they occur would, of course, influence the expected value calculation.

Improving relative bargaining power

In an attempt to overcome political risk, some firms may seek to develop a stronger bargaining position in the country within which they are operating. For example, a firm might attempt to create a situation in which the government of the country loses more than it gains by taking action against the interests of the company. This could be the case when the firm has technical knowledge that will be lost to the country if the company moves elsewhere (with significant job losses) to avoid new regulations. Such bargaining power may be improved if the firm is as fully integrated as possible with the local economy, so that it becomes part of the country's infrastructure. Techniques here may include: developing good relations with the host government and other local political groups; producing as much of the product locally as is possible; creating joint ventures and hiring local people to manage and run the operation; carrying out extensive local research and development; developing good employee relations with the local labour force. These techniques raise the 'costs' to the host country economy of unwelcome interference in the firm's activities.

Checkpoint 3 Can you give any examples of companies seeking to reduce political risk in this way?

Restricting exposure to government influence

The firm may seek to limit, in advance, the 'costs' to the business should the host government interfere in its activities. Such techniques may include doing as little local manufacturing as possible, locating all research and development outside the country, hiring only those local personnel who are essential, manufacturing the same product in many other different countries, and so on.

Case Study 12.2 looks at the suggestion that there is increased political risk for those doing business in Russia.

Case Study 12.2 Political risk for business in Russia

There has been much criticism, both within and outside Russia, at the way in which privatisation of state assets took place in the early 1990s. In particular, a small group of businessmen (the so-called 'oligarchs') and their companies gained control of huge amounts of previously Russian state industries at what many saw as 'knock-down' prices. These men did not, however, become billionaires by violence or mafia-style tactics, but by using their political influence more effectively than others during Russia's free-for-all transition to capitalism.

One such oligarch was Mikhail Khodorkovsky who, in 1996, became chairman of Yukos, then Russia's second largest oil company (now the largest) with $170bn in oil reserves. Khodorkovsky went on to gain control of massive mineral and timber interests, and was named in 2002 by *Forbes* as Russia's richest man. Amy Chua [*World on Fire*, Heinemann, 2003] stresses that it was political influence, starting with communist linkages before 1990 and continuing with close government linkages after communism, that was the platform for the concentration of wealth in Khodorkovsky's hands.

How things can change! Political intrigue would, it now seems, be the root cause of his fall. President Putin, having been helped to power by the oligarchs, has now turned on many of them, especially those (like Khodorkovsky) who have financed and supported his political opponents. In October 2003 Mr Khodorkovsky was arrested for alleged fraud and tax evasion. Yukos claimed to have endured some 678 official enquiries from prosecutors in only two months and faced threats to remove its oil licences. Not only shares in Yukos but in the whole Russian stock market plunged (over 25% lost in three weeks) after the arrest of the Yukos chairman, as did the share price of Exxon, BP and other major international oil companies with interests in Russia. Financial assets were also withdrawn from Russia as Russian and overseas investors (individuals and governments) withdrew over $50bn in the following few months, worried that Russia was no longer a safe place to hold assets.

There is a general concern for those with an interest in Russian business that the Yukos affair is 'a sign that the state is not willing to see business as a partner but only as a subordinate', said Vladimir Ryzhkov, of the Russian Duma (Parliament). Anatoly Chubais, Chairman of the state electricity company, called on Mr Putin for clarification. 'I want business to understand the authority's position on business.'

Case Study 12.2 continued

Questions

1. What types of political risk have been increased by the Yukos situation?
2. How might this situation have adverse effects on Russian and international business?
3. How might such businesses respond to this increased political risk?

To minimise political risk the company must be fully aware of present developments in the countries in which it operates, and of likely future developments. For example, MNEs operating in Japan might usefully review the findings of a major report by the *Invest Japan Forum* in December 2002 which identified specific problems in the Japanese business practice and culture which have contributed to the so-called 'lost decade' of effectively zero growth for Japan. The report describes Japan as 'closed' and blames 'problems within the country that are structural and also issues which are rooted in mental attitude'. The main proposals of the report are outlined below. What is important to note here is that many of the proposals involve recommendations to the *Japanese government* to implement and support various changes. An MNE with Japanese interest will need to assess the political likelihood of these changes being made and any impacts which might then result. The report suggested:

- Sweeping changes to the Law on Special Measures for Industrialisation and commercial code to make cross-border M&A activity far easier.
- Changes to tax laws in line with demands from Japanese industry. Particularly looking for tax breaks for R&D activity.
- Greater transparency for financial markets. The report proposes setting up an independent oversight authority along the lines of the US Securities and Exchange Commission.
- A forced change in the mentality of bureaucrats, reminding them they are public servants and placing a new emphasis on making them 'user friendly'.
- Creating a more outward-looking attitude in Japanese industry by introducing foreign language teaching at younger levels.
- Central government to use plain speech in explaining itself.

Before leaving the idea of political risk and its impacts, we might note an *indirect* way of assessing the market's perception of the degree of political risk in a government. This involves checking the *credit rating* given to the bonds (IOUs) issued by that government. Box 12.2 considers such credit rating further, with any perception of an increased risk that a government might find it difficult to repay its loans to its creditors resulting in a downgrading of its bond rating.

Box 12.2

Assessing risk via bond ratings

Before issuing bonds in the public markets, an issuer will often seek a rating from one or more private credit ratings agencies. The selected agencies investigate the issuer's ability to pay interest on the bonds and to repay the full initial loan when the bonds 'mature' (fall due for repayment). The credit agencies look in particular at such matters as financial strength, the intended use of the funds, the political and regulatory environment in which the issuer is operating and any potential economic changes in that environment. After conducting these investigations, the agency will make its estimate of the 'default risk', i.e. the likelihood that the issuer will fail to service the bonds as required. The expense involved in making this rating is normally paid for by the issuer, although in some cases an agency will issue such ratings on its own initiative.

The well-known companies, *Moody's Investors Service* and *Standard & Poor's*, both based in New York, dominate the ratings industry. Two smaller firms, *Fitch IBCA* and *Duff & Phelps Credit Rating Co.*, also issue ratings for many types of bonds internationally. The firms' ratings of a particular issue are not always in agreement, as each uses a different methodology. Table 12.2 interprets the default ratings of the four international firms.

Table 12.2 What bond ratings mean

	Moody's	Standard & Poor's	Fitch IBCA	Duff & Phelps
Highest credit quality; issuer has strong ability to meet obligations	Aaa	AAA	AAA	AAA
Very high credit quality; low risk of default	Aa1 Aa2 Aa3	AA+ AA AA–	AA	AA+ AA AA–
High credit quality, but more vulnerable to changes in economy or business	A1 A2 A3	AA+ AA AA–	AA	AA+ AA AA–
Adequate credit quality for now, but more likely to be impaired if conditions worsen	Baa1 Baa2 Baa3	BBB+ BBB BBB–	BBB	BBB+ BBB BBB–
Below investment grade, but good chance that issuer can meet commitments	Ba1 Ba2 Ba3	BB+ BB BB–	BB	BB+ BB BB–
Significant credit risk, but issuer is presently able to meet obligations	B1 B2 B3	B+ B B–	B	B+ B B–
High default risk	Caa1 Caa2 Caa3	CCC+ CCC CCC–	CCC CC C	CCC
Issuer failed to meet scheduled interest or principal payments	C	D	DDD DD D	DD

There are also many other ratings agencies that operate in a single country, and several that specialise in a particular industry, such as banking.

A downgrading of the credit ratings of either private company or government bonds can have serious implications for the issuer. Lenders will insist on higher interest rates on any future loans to that company or government in order to cover the increased risks of making such loans.

This can be important for both individual businesses and for the macroenvironment in which they operate since higher interest rates are likely to depress aggregate demand (both consumption and investment) in the country and increase the prospects of economic recession.

Legal environment

Legal systems have a major impact on the ways in which national and international business is conducted. In this section we consider the relevance of the legal environment to business, noting that in practice it is often difficult to separate political and legal environments, with the latter heavily influenced by the former. Nor can we only concentrate on national laws. With the growth of supra-national bodies (e.g. EU) and other global institutions, laws and regulations devised outside the UK can have a major influence on UK business activity.

Types of legal system

The different types of legal system can generally be divided into the following categories: common law; statute law; code law; religious law; bureaucratic law. These categories need not be mutually exclusive: for example, common law can coexist with various types of code law, e.g. civil law.

- *Common law*. This is the foundation of the legal system in the UK and its former colonies, including the US, Canada, Australia, India, New Zealand and much of the Caribbean. Common law is essentially unwritten, has developed over long periods of time and is largely founded on the decisions reached by judges over the years on different cases. When a judge makes a particular decision, then a *legal precedent* is established.
- *Statute law*. Common law countries depend not only on case law but also on statutory law, i.e. legislation, laws passed by government. In the UK this involves Acts of Parliament which are first published as 'bills' to be debated in the House of Commons and House of Lords.
- *Code law*. This is the world's most common system. It is an explicit codification in written terms of what is and what is not permissible. Such laws can be written down in criminal, civil and/or commercial codes which are then used to determine the

outcome of all legal matters. When a legal issue is in dispute it can then be resolved by reference to the relevant code. Most continental European countries, together with their former colonies, follow this type of legal system.

- *Religious law*. Religious law is based on rules related to the faith and practice of a particular religion. A country that works in this way is called a *theocracy*. Iran is one such example. Here a group of mullahs (holy men) determine what is legal or illegal depending on their interpretation of the Koran, the holy book of Islam.
- *Bureaucratic law*. This occurs in dictatorships and communist countries when bureaucrats largely determine what the laws are, even if these are contrary to the historical laws of the land. MNEs operating in such countries have often found it difficult to manage their affairs as there tends to be a lack of consistency, predictability and appeals procedures.

Effects of laws on business

National laws affect national and international business in a variety of ways. There may be legal rules relating to specific aspects of business operations such as the ways in which financial accounts are prepared and disclosed. National laws may also affect aspects of the companies' internal organisation such as its human resource management and health and safety policies. These might include factors such as the provision of maternity and paternity leave, payment of a statutory minimum wage, physical working conditions, protection of employees against hazards at work and pollution, pension and medical provisions and childcare facilities.

Of course, the nature of these rules and regulations may, to some extent, reflect the national government's stance towards trade and industrial policies. Some governments positively encourage inward investment whilst others may create a whole web of red tape to discourage imports or inward investment.

Certainly businesses which operate internationally should be aware of national regulations in the following areas.

- *Trade restrictions*. Law and various types of regulations may be imposed to restrict trade, even to the extent of imposing sanctions or embargoes on trade with particular countries. Sanctions can take many forms, such as restricting access to high-technology goods, withdrawing preferential tariff treatment, boycotting the country's goods or denying new loans.
- *Foreign ownership restrictions*. Many governments may limit the foreign ownership of firms for economic or political reasons. This may sometimes be applied to particular industrial sectors, such as air transportation, financial services or telecommunications.
- *Environmental restrictions*. Sometimes domestic laws in a country can indirectly affect the competitiveness of international firms which operate there. For example, the extensive legislation involving the environmental packaging of goods in Germany means higher costs if products are to meet these environmental restrictions.

CHECK THE NET
The Business Bureau provides information on legal issues facing business: www.vianetworks.co.uk.

■ *Exit restrictions.* International businesses also need to take account of the costs of exiting a country, should they need to. Many countries impose legal restraints on the closing of plants in order to protect the rights of employees.

EU laws and regulations

European Union laws are adopted after passing through various EU bodies, as indicated in Figure 12.2. For example, most laws involving business issues are initiated by proposals from the *European Commission*. These proposals are then passed to the *Council of Ministers* for comment, amendment and ultimately approval. However, the *European Parliament* has the power to reject new legislation coming before it (see Box 12.3).

Figure 12.2 summarises the present process (it may change if a new EU constitution is ratified) and Box 12.3 gives more detail on the roles of the various EU bodies in the legislative process.

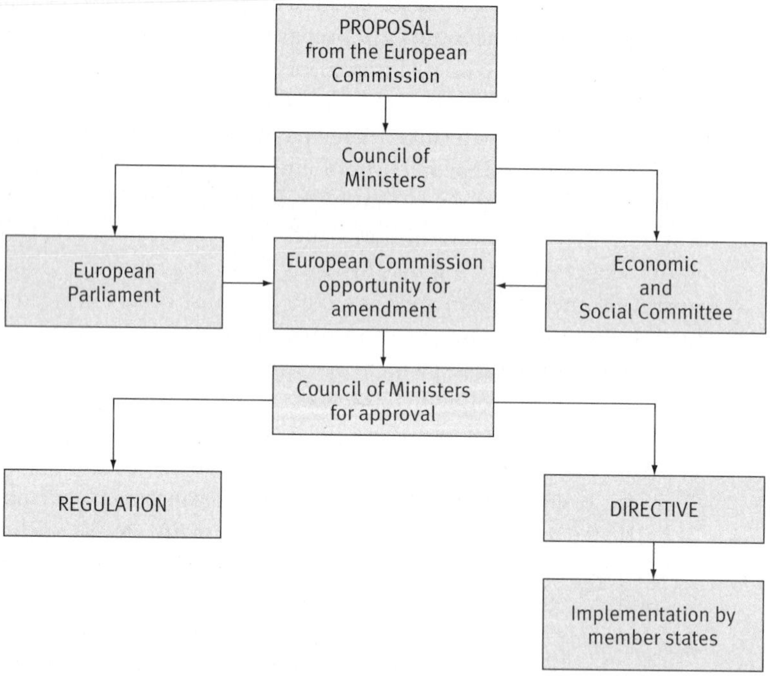

Fig 12.2 The consultation procedure for law-making in the EU

Voting takes place in the Council of Ministers on the basis of a *qualified majority*. Until enlargement of the EU in 2004, 62 out of 87 votes and at least 10 out of 15 countries must be in favour. Countries have different numbers of votes, with Germany, France, Italy and the United Kingdom each having 10 votes. However, disagreements on how voting rights should be allocated after enlargement was a major factor in the breakdown of talks on a new EU constitution in December 2003.

Within this framework European Union law takes three main forms:

- *Regulations*. These are applied directly without the need for national measures to implement them.
- *Directives*. These bind members of the EU with respect to objectives but allow individual countries to decide the form and means of implementation; most legislation with respect to banking and finance takes the form of Directives.
- *Decisions*. These are binding in all aspects according to whether they are addressed to member states, to institutions or to individuals.
- *Recommendations and opinions*. These are not binding.

In 2003 alone approximately 270 Regulations, 35 Directives and 140 Decisions were adopted.

Box 12.3 **EU institutions and EU law**

Some of the specific details involving the following institutions is currently under discussion in terms of the new EU constitution.

European Commission (EC)

Since 1995 the *European Commission* has consisted of 20 commissioners appointed by the national governments. On appointment they are expected to act independently of national interests. The five larger member states (France, Germany, the UK, Spain and Italy) have two commissioners each and the ten other member states each have one commissioner. The EC is divided into 35 separate Director-Generals (DGs), each of which deals with specific policy areas. The European Commission is often regarded as the 'pillar' of the EU in the economic policy domain, proposing most business-related legislation.

European Parliament (EP)

The *European Parliament* consists of members (MEPs) who, since 1979, have been directly elected by member states on a five-year mandate. It has the power to dismiss the European Commission, and can therefore exert considerable influence on the EC at times of crisis. For example, in 1999 the EP insisted on the EC appointing a special investigating committee to enquire into alleged irregularities, which it secured under the threat of it dismissing the Commission. Nevertheless, its main influence is on the *legislative process*, within which its procedural authority varies depending on the particular policy area.

- *Consultation procedure*. Here the EP merely gives an opinion and has no effective sanction over the central decision-making agency, the Council of Ministers (see below).
- *Budget treaties*. Here the EP has important powers, including that of rejecting the budget in its entirety.
- *Single European Act* (SEA). Here the EP must give its assent to the accession of new member states and for Association Agreements with third countries.
- *Co-decision procedure* (*Article 251*). Here the power of the EP extends to 37 separate policy areas, in each of which the EP can reject legislation coming before it. In effect, the EP is now a co-legislator with the Council of Ministers.

European Court of Justice (ECJ)

This consists of 15 judges and 9 advocates-general. The ECJ does not formulate policy but its rulings on matters referred to it in involve the interpretation and application of EC law and these play a key part in the implementation and effectiveness of policy proposals over time.

Council of Ministers

This consists of the ministers of the member states. The actual ministers involved depend on the policy areas in question; for example the Agricultural Ministers will meet when the policy area is the Common Agricultural Policy (CAP). There are some 100 meetings of the Council of Ministers each year, with the Council of Agricultural Ministers, the Council of Economics and Finance Ministers (Ecofin) and the Council of Foreign Ministers having the most frequent meetings. Meetings are chaired by the minister from the member state which holds the current 'presidency' of the Council for a six-month period. National civil servants support their ministers in these meetings.

Decisions of the Council can use *qualified majority voting* (QMV) in many areas, though *unanimous voting* is required in certain areas (e.g. tax policy). A decision by QMV requires 62 of the 87 votes, distributed according to a weighting system (e.g. France, Germany, Italy and the UK have 10 votes each, Belgium, Netherlands, Portugal and Greece 5 votes each, and so on).

European Council

This consists of the 15 heads of state, 15 foreign ministers, EC president and vice president, meeting at least twice yearly. This is responsible for political and strategic decision making.

As we note in Chapter 14, not only is the EU a major destination for UK exports (around 60% of total goods exports) and a major source of UK imports (around 54% of total goods imports), it is also the location in which many subsidiary companies of UK-owned multinationals operate. Indeed EU laws and regulations often take precedence over UK laws and regulations. For all these reasons the content of EU law is of vital importance to UK individuals and businesses.

Case Study 12.3 looks at the impact of EU law (in the form of Directives) on UK individuals and businesses in the particular context of tyre disposal.

Case Study 12.3 Directive on tyre disposal

Scrap tyres have become a major headache for the UK and other EU governments. A European Directive banned landfills on whole tyres in 2003 and shredded tyres by 2006. The option of dumping tyres in major landfill sites will be closed and new ways will have to be found to dispose of the 13 million tyres that are stockpiled or put in landfills every year in the UK. The problem is huge. The number of tyres is forecast to increase by up to 60% by 2021, as the number of vehicles rises. Every day, 100,000 tyres are taken off cars, vans, trucks, buses and bicycles in the UK. It is widely estimated that there are now more than 200 million tyres lying around. By

Case Study 12.3 continued

their very nature, tyres are difficult to dispose of since they are designed not to fall apart while you are driving along the motorway.

Although tyres remain substantially intact for decades, some of their components can break down and enter the environment. Environmental concern centres on the highly toxic additives used in their manufacture, such as zinc, chromium, lead, copper, cadmium and sulphur. The Environment Agency launched a campaign in 2002 in the UK to alert the public and industry to the need to prolong the life of existing tyres and to find new recycling methods. 'You can find landfill sites that cover an entire valley, with black as far as the eye can see,' said an Environment Agency spokesman. 'We have always viewed tyres as a resource, rather than something to be dumped.'

The best use of tyres is probably to retread them, but this is now expensive, and fewer than ever are recycled in this way. According to the Used Tyre Working Group, a joint industry and government initiative sponsored by the main tyre industry associations, just 18% of Britain's tyres are retreaded. A further 48,500 tonnes are converted into 'crumb rubber' used in carpet underlay and to make surfaces such as those on children's playgrounds.

More controversially, 18% are burnt as a 'replacement fuel' in the manufacture of cement. This is fast becoming the most popular way of disposing of them, but it is of increasing concern to environmentalists and scientists. 'Tyre burning emits ultra-fine particles that have a toxicity all of their own,' says Vyvyan Howard, senior lecturer in toxicopathology at Liverpool University. 'The toxicity is even stronger if this contains metals such as nickel and tin, which you get when you throw the whole tyre into the furnace. If the metal content of the particles goes up, then there is going to be an increasing impact on health.' The cement companies deny that they are affecting people's health.

Meanwhile, the UK sends 26% of its tyres to landfill, far less than some other EU countries. France sends almost 50%, Spain 58%, but Holland sends none. The UK is now racking its brains as to how to dispose of the 13 million tyres that accumulate each year. Many believe the onus is on the manufacturers to produce tyres that lend themselves to greater recycling.

Question

What does this case study suggest about the relevance of EU legal decisions to UK businesses and individuals? Give examples of possible impacts of this Directive involving tyres on both.

LINKS

You can find more detail on the EU in other chapters of this book, e.g. Chapter 8 (pp. 290–292), Chapter 14 (pp. 573–576).

Intellectual property rights (IPRs)

Most advanced industrialised economies are progressively becoming 'knowledge based', so that questions of *intellectual property rights* (IPRs) are becoming ever more important. The value of intellectual property can quickly be destroyed unless companies enforce their rights in this area. Intellectual property rights can take various forms, with patents, trademarks and copyrights being particularly important.

Patents

Patent law confers ownership rights on the *inventor*. To qualify as the subject matter of a patent the invention must be novel, involve an inventive step and be capable of industrial application. 'Novel' seeks to exclude granting monopoly ownership rights to something that already exists; 'inventive' seeks to establish that a step has been taken which would not be obvious to experts in the field; 'industrial application' seeks to avoid the restrictions which would result from ideas and principles being patentable, instead limiting such protection to specific applications of these ideas. Patents depend upon registration for their validity.

Trademarks

Trademarks have been defined as '... any sign capable of being represented graphically which is capable of distinguishing goods or services of one undertaking from those of other undertakings' (*UK Trade Marks Act 1994*). This is sometimes referred to as the 'product differentiation' function. Such trademarks require less intellectual activity than patents or copyright to be deemed protectable, with the focus instead being on the commercial activity associated with such trademarks. As with patents, trademarks depend on registration for their validity, which gives the holder the exclusive right to *use* the mark in the UK for 10 years, subject to further renewals in periods of 10 years. Infringement occurs where others use the trademark without permission.

To simplify global protection of trademarks the *World Intellectual Property Organisation* (WIPO) allows trademark owners to seek protection in up to 74 countries with one application. Established as far back as 1891 in Madrid, WIPO originally comprised mainly French-speaking nations but the 1996 *Madrid Protocol* made English a second working language. The US, the country with the largest trademark activity, joined WIPO in 2003 and by 2004 over 412,000 international trademarks were registered. The decision by WIPO in 2004 to make Spanish a third working language is expected to increase still further both the number of countries covered by the international trademark agreement and the number of international trademarks registered.

WIPO defines a trademark as:

- any sign that serves, in trade, to differentiate the goods and services of one person or company from those of another;
- consisting of a word, figures, label, sound, in three dimensions;
- that which identifies the products of that person or company so that it is not confused with others.

Copyrights

Copyright law prevents the copying of forms of work (e.g. an article, book, play, poem, music score etc.) rather than the ideas contained within these forms. However, sometimes the copyright can be extended to the 'structure' underpinning the form actually used (e.g. the plot of a book as well as the book itself).

Copyright (unlike patents and trademarks) applies automatically and does not require registration. For copyright to apply there must be three key conditions.

(i) *A recorded work which is 'original'*, in the sense that the work is different from that of its contemporaries.

(ii) *Of an appropriate description*, i.e. literacy, dramatic, music, artistic, sound recordings, films and broadcasts all qualify. Even business letters can receive protection as 'literacy works'.

(iii) *Being sufficiently connected to the country in question*, since copyright is essentially national in character, at least in the first instance. So in the case of the UK, the author (or work) must be connected to the UK by nationality, domicile, source of publication or some other acceptable way.

The period of copyright extends to the life of the author + 70 years. Copyright protection is not absolute: for example, limited copying of copyright material is permitted for purposes of research or fair journalistic reporting. Breaching copyright beyond any existing provision can result in an injunction to desist and/or the award of damages.

Copyright is different to the other types of IPR as it is an unregistered right (in the UK). Copyright comes into effect immediately as soon as something is put onto paper, film, the Internet etc. The UK Patent Office recommends marking your work with the copyright symbol © followed by your name and the date. This is a warning to others who may consider copying your ideas. However, in the UK this is not legally necessary.

Checkpoint 4 Can you give any recent examples involving patents, trademarks or copyright?

Table 12.3 provides some examples of the types of works protected by copyright.

Table 12.3 Examples of works protected by copyright

1	Original literary works, e.g. novels, articles in newspapers
2	Original musical works
3	Original artistic work, e.g. paintings, drawings, photographs, diagrams, logos
4	Original dramatic works; these include dance or mime
5	Published editions of works
6	Films, videos and DVDs
7	Broadcasts and cable programmes
8	Sound recordings, based on any medium.
9	Any original work displayed over the Internet

Adapted from The UK Patent Office website (see www.patent.gov.uk)

CHECK THE NET

The UK government site relating to intellectual property rights is www.patent.gov.uk.
The US Patent and Tradesmark Officer website is www.upto.gov.
The World Intellectual Property Organisation (WIPO) site is www.wipo.int.

Trade-related aspects of intellectual property rights (TRIPS)

The WTO Agreement on *Trade-Related Aspects of Intellectual Property Rights*, the so-called TRIPS Agreement, is based on a recognition that increasingly the value of goods and services entering into international trade resides in the know-how and creativity incorporated into them. The TRIPS Agreement provides for minimum international standards of protection for such know-how and creativity in the areas of copyright and related rights, trademarks, geographical indications, industrial designs, patents, layout-designs of integrated circuits and undisclosed information. It also contains provisions aimed at the effective enforcement of such intellectual property rights, and provides for multilateral dispute settlement. It gives all WTO members transitional periods so that they can meet their obligations under it. Developed-country members have had to comply with all of the provisions of the Agreement since 1 January 1996. For developing countries and certain transition economies, the general transitional period ended on 1 January 2000. For the least-developed countries, the transitional period is 11 years (i.e. until 1 January 2006).

Activity 12.1 involves materials on both the political and legal environments.

Activity 12.1

1 Which of the following scenarios would be given the highest priority in political risk assessment?

(a) High impact, low likelihood
(b) Low impact, high likelihood
(c) Low impact, low likelihood
(d) High impact, high likelihood
(e) Low expected value for the possible event

2 Which *three* of the following approaches may be adopted by an international business attempting to reduce the political risks from operating in a host country?

(a) Avoid using local labour or developing skills in local labour markets.
(b) Improve the relative bargaining power of an international business vis-à-vis the host country.
(c) Ensure that any technology the international business owns is available to the host country whether or not the business operates there.
(d) Use protective and defensive techniques to limit the 'costs' to the international business should the host country interfere in its activities.
(e) Use integrative techniques to ensure that the international business becomes part of the host country's infrastructure.

3 Which *one* of the following confers ownership rights on the inventor?

(a) Trademarks
(b) Patents
(c) Copyrights
(d) Litigation
(e) Arbitration

4 Match each of the *lettered* descriptions with the correct *numbered* term.

Descriptions

(a) Where subsequent judicial decisions are directly influenced by earlier decisions.
(b) Risks associated with events such as war which affect all the firms in a country.
(c) Describes the type of legal system which often occurs in dictatorships and communist countries.
(d) The world's most common system and explicitly states what is and is not permissible.
(e) Risks associated with the prospect of company specific taxes being imposed.
(f) Where 'fatwas' and other decrees from mullahs determine what is lawful.

Terms

(i) Micropolitical
(ii) Common law
(iii) Religious law
(iv) Bureaucratic law
(v) Macropolitical
(vi) Code law

Answers to Checkpoints and Activities can be found on pp. 705–35.

Ecological environment

We noted in Chapter 4 (pp. 149–151) that firms which actively support 'green' policies need not necessarily do so at the expense of profit. Here we look in rather more detail at the reasons why businesses may have a strong interest in taking into account the ecological environment in which they operate.

The last section pointed out *legal* reasons for complying with EU directives aimed at a more environmentally friendly tyre disposal. But what *voluntary* reasons might encourage a firm to move in the direction of environmental awareness?

Environmental awareness in a global economy

In today's global economy a number of driving forces are arguably raising environmental concerns to the forefront of *corporate* policy debate.

- *Environmentally conscious consumers*. Consumer awareness of environmental issues is creating a market for 'green products'. Patagonia, a California-based producer of recreational clothing, has developed a loyal base of high-income customers partly because its brand identity includes a commitment to conservation. A similar successful approach has been used by the Body Shop. Case Study 12.4 looks more carefully at the suggestion that consumers are growing more environmentally conscious.

  It has been suggested that three key conditions are required for success with '*environmental product differentiation*', i.e. segmenting the market so that consumers will pay higher prices for overtly 'environmentally friendly' products.

  - First, the company must have identified a distinctive market segment consisting of consumers who really are willing to pay more for environmentally friendly products.
  - Second, the branding/corporate image must clearly and credibly convey the environmental benefits related to the products.
  - Third, the company must be able to protect itself from imitations for long enough to profit from its 'investment' in the previous two conditions.

Checkpoint 5 Can you give any examples of 'environmental product differentiation'?

- *Environmentally and cost-conscious producers*. Producers are increasingly aware that adherence to high environmental standards need not be at the expense of their cost base. In other words, they can be environmentally friendly at the same time as reducing (rather than raising) their cost base.
- *Environmentally and credit-risk-conscious producers*. International businesses are increasingly aware that failure to manage environmental risk factors effectively can lead to adverse publicity, lost revenue and profit and perhaps even more seriously a reduction in their official credit rating, making it more difficult and costly (e.g. higher interest rates) to finance future investment plans.
- *Environmentally conscious governments*. Businesses have a further reason for considering the environmental impacts of their activities, namely the scrutiny of host governments. Where production of a product causes environmental damage, it is likely that this will result in the imposition of taxes or regulations by government.

Case Study 12.4 The green consumer

It is not easy to be environmentally friendly. It usually requires time, money, effort, patience, kindness or other qualities in short supply. However, opportunities are available to make a difference that may not cost the individual too much! For example, Greenpeace has joined up with npower to launch *Juice*, a new, green electricity supply that for the first time costs exactly the same as ordinary electricity supplies. Juice is building new wind power. Not only is the price of electricity from wind power competitive, but the more subscribers sign up, the more new wind power

Case Study 12.4 continued

stations will be built by npower. (Most existing green suppliers of electricity use existing old hydro-electric stations, with no promise to build more.) The first new 30-turbine wind power station is planned for a site off the North Wales coast, providing electricity for the first 50,000 subscribers. It will be four miles offshore, inaudible and virtually invisible. Until it is built, subscribers will get green supplies from existing renewable sources. Once more than 50,000 households sign up, another site will be developed, and so on. Phone 0800 316 2610 or click to www.npower.com/juice for instant connection to this new source of electricity with no cost and no sweat as they do the change-over from your present supplier.

This is the first time Greenpeace has endorsed a commercial enterprise – answering critics who accuse them of always being against things rather than for something. There is something refreshing about green campaigners lobbying for an energy supplier, as they are not being paid or taking any profits. Interestingly, npower – a big commercial player – is marketing Juice as 'clean' energy as they think the word 'green' applied to power would be viewed suspiciously by non-ideological customers. In 2003 the market for green power was still pathetically small – just 18,000 subscribers, but now there is absolutely no excuse why anyone who has ever had a green thought should not convert to Juice today.

Many regard the UK government as having been slow on promoting green energy. While German and Danish wind turbine industries soar ahead with government start-up grants, there is a real danger Britain will lose out on this major new industry. Greenpeace wants to see demand for Juice force the government's hand. With an official target of producing 10% of energy from renewable sources by 2010, so far the government has reached only 2.8%, paying out just £250m over three years to subsidise all renewables. It has been estimated that at least £1,000m a year will be needed for wind alone, to lay down cables linking distant wind sites to the national grid. Even more will be needed to get solar energy off the ground, to create a big enough market to bring down the costs of solar panels – another gigantic future industry other governments are stealing from under our noses.

One problem for wind power has been strong resistance to giving planning permission for wind farms – even far offshore. But the Greenpeace backing for npower is designed to defuse local protests. Recently planning permission was about to be granted on one offshore site when a rare hen harrier was spotted and the scheme dropped for 'environmental' reasons. However, Greenpeace points out that the hen harrier is as much at risk from global warming as the rest of us if we fail to develop renewable energy supplies. By signing up in great numbers, subscribers will demonstrate public support for wind power.

Most supermarkets stock at least some of the 70 Fairtrade brands of coffee, tea, chocolate, bananas, sugar, honey or orange juice: the Co-op, Waitrose and Sainsbury's stock the most. The Fairtrade kite mark guarantees that poor farmers in developing economies are not exploited by global corporations and that farm workers in such

Case Study 12.4 continued

countries are not oppressed by near slave conditions. Such high quality Fairtrade products now cost the same as other quality goods; 68% of people profess to support Fairtrade principles, so why is only 1% of the coffee purchased Fairtrade? True, most supermarkets tuck it away, but why not bend down to a lower shelf for good high-roast coffee, or avoid the Nescafé instant for Cafédirect. Only the poorest households have any excuse for not choosing Fairtrade now.

Why do green Ecover washing and washing-up products still command less than 1% of the market? Plant-based instead of petrochemical-based, they do far less harm to the environment and cost the same as mid-market detergents, while working just as well. It is quite easy not to buy a rug without the Rug-Mark kite, guaranteeing it has not been made by children or other exploited workers. It is easy not to buy peat bags from garden centres, or garden furniture without the Forest Stewardship Council mark, ensuring it is made from renewable forests. It would save £50–£100 a year in electricity to turn off the television and video instead of leaving them on stand-by. Recycled paper is just as fine and yet cheaper than Andrex.

You can even, in one phone call (0800 905090), move your bank account into the Co-op bank, which offers sensible ethical investment (it says no to animal testing for cosmetics, but yes to animal testing for medicines). In surveys the Co-op bank has the most contented staff and customers who can use the Internet, Link machines or any post office to pay money in or out. So why does it have just 3% of the banking market?

All these things are dead easy – just a simple shopping choice. So why not? Many more people profess to care than can be bothered to make even these minimal changes. Next time you or anyone else grumbles about what the government has or hasn't done on the green and ethical front, just ask what small things you or they have done first.

Questions

1. What argument might be used to support Greenpeace in its endorsement of a commercial enterprise?
2. What is the environmental case for encouraging consumers to buy electricity generated by wind energy?
3. Why might businesses seek to work with, rather than against, pressure groups such as Greenpeace?

Environmental sustainability

'Sustainable' and 'sustainability' are now key trigger words in the world of advertising for positive, emotive images associated with words such as 'green', 'wholesome', 'goodness', 'justice', 'environment', amongst others. They are used sophisticatedly to sell cars, nappies, holidays and even lifestyles. Sustainability sells – how has this come about and what exactly are we being encouraged to buy?

As long ago as 1987, a United Nations report entitled *Our Common Future* provided the most widely used definition of sustainable development: 'development which meets the needs of the present without compromising the ability of future generations to meet their own needs'. Of course, there have been many different views as to how this definition should affect individual, corporate and government actions, though one theme that has been constant in most views is that of 'intergenerational equity'.

CHECK THE NET

The issue of sustainability can be considered at: www.sustainability.co.uk
The National Environment Trust is at www.environet.policy.net/
Visit The Body Shop website for material on human rights and environmental issues: www.bodyshop.co.uk
Pressure group websites include
www.foe.co.uk
www.greenpeace.org.uk
www.panda.org

- *Intergenerational equity*: where the development process seeks to minimise any adverse impacts on future generations. These clearly include avoiding adverse environmental impacts such as excessive resource depletion today reducing the stock of resources available for future use, or levels of pollution emission and waste disposal today beyond the ability of the environment to absorb them, thereby imposing long-term damage on future generations.

Case Study 12.5 reviews some of the impacts of this concern on consumer and corporate behaviour. It considers the increased use of tree planting as a positive 'offset' (trees absorb carbon dioxide, CO_2) to environmental damage associated with the CO_2 emissions from the firm's other activities.

Case Study 12.5 Environmental sustainability sells

FT

This year's fashionable Christmas present is a tree-planting certificate, according to *Future Forests*, an environmental pressure group. 'Buy a living and breathing gift that helps protect the climate,' it urges. Planting trees to help mitigate climate change has never been more popular. Book a skiing holiday, hire a car or take out a mortgage and you may be offered the chance to plant trees to offset your carbon emissions. In Italy the public is being urged, in a '12 days for the planet' advertising campaign, to go 'carbon neutral' by offsetting its greenhouse emissions.

Companies are also taking the plunge. *Tetra Pak UK*, the packaging company, has just announced in 2003 its intention to go carbon-neutral by the end of that year, partly by investing in tree-planting in Uganda. *Swiss Re*, the reinsurer, also announced in 2003 that it would 'act on what we preach' by going carbon-neutral over the next 10 years. As well as cutting emissions by 15% by improving energy efficiency and reducing flights, it will invest \$2.5m (£1.4m) in offset projects through the World Bank Community Development carbon fund.

Case Study 12.5 continued

The World Bank reported in December 2003 that there had been rapid growth in demand for carbon credits 'with consumer appeal' for individuals, companies and events wanting to offset emissions. Community-based agro-forestry and other forestry deals are providing particularly attractive, with the market roughly tripled over recent years to about 500,000 tonnes of carbon dioxide in 2003, it said. Prices range from £55 to £512 a tonne.

But not everyone is enthused by the idea. 'The concept of carbon neutrality is intellectually flawed,' says Tom Delay, chief executive of the *Carbon Trust*, which helps UK businesses to cut emissions. Critics argue that carbon offsets distract attention from reducing greenhouse gas emissions. Large-scale tree planting is especially controversial.

But advocates of carbon offset schemes say they encourage greater efforts to reduce emissions. Tetra Pak UK thinks it can cut its energy use per unit of production by 24% before 2005. 'The savings we can make by saving energy and improving environmental performance will offset the cost of the offsets,' says Richard Hands, environment manager.

Most charities that organise carbon offsets schemes are aware of the controversy over using trees to soak up carbon dioxide. Half of *Future Forests'* projects are, in spite of its name, renewable energy schemes. In practice, environmental purists prefer to invest in renewable energy projects, it says. But tree planting helps get the message about carbon neutrality to a mass audience.

Some offset schemes go even further to satisfy the concerns of environmentalists. The US-based *Climate Neutral Network* insists that a large proportion of any company's efforts is devoted to reducing the carbon dioxide emissions of the US, the world's largest emitter. 'Pollution prevention has to begin at home,' says Sue Hall, its executive director. For example, *Shaklee*, a health products company, believes that in 2000 it became the world's first climate-neutral company, when it replaced the boilers in local schools in Portland, Oregon. This reduced emissions and cut the schools' energy bill by $250,000 – giving Shaklee the basis for a powerful marketing campaign.

Companies should always look for 'compelling business strategies' when they consider going carbon-neutral, says Ms Hall. For example, when *BP*, the oil company, used carbon offsets to launch a brand of 'climate cool fuel', it boosted its business five-fold with *Interface*, the carbon tile company. In the US, as in Europe, enthusiasm for climate-neutrality is gaining momentum, says Ms Hall. 'It is an idea whose time has come – and not a minute too soon.'

Source: *Financial Times*, 5 December 2003, p. 13

Questions

1 Why are firms so keen to demonstrate their commitment to environmental sustainability?

2 How do environmentalists view the debate on 'carbon neutrality'?

Hardly surprisingly, in view of the above, business is increasingly attracted to 'green marketing'.

Green marketing

An important issue in today's business environment is that a firm must be seen to be 'green' among the local community, customers, potential customers and all stakeholders in the business. Ottman (2000) suggests the following green marketing strategies in order to get this message across.

1. Adopt a thorough approach to corporate greening. This includes all functions of the business. Everything from being energy efficient to introducing environmentally friendly fuel.
2. Appoint a highly visible Chief Executive Officer (CEO) with environmental leanings and make him/her the centrepiece of your corporate social image, e.g. Anita Roddick of The Body Shop.
3. Be transparent. Allow stakeholders access to information so that they know exactly what are the level of potential health risks associated with various projects.
4. Work cooperatively with third parties, such as government agencies and environmental pressure groups.
5. Vigorously communicate your company's commitment to accountability and continuous improvement. This can include 'cause-related marketing'. For example, the UK supermarket giant Tesco works with a different charity every year.
6. Act now. Do not wait to get the green message across.

'Green marketing' has already been seen to strike a chord with consumer groups. For example, in Chapter 4 (p. 151) we noted that companies adopting a more explicitly ethical stance had outperformed other companies in terms of various stock market indices.

However, for 'green marketing' to be ultimately successful the company must actually embody the image it portrays. We see below (p. 483) that BP is seeking to rebrand itself as 'Beyond Petroleum' rather than 'British Petroleum', recognising that too close an association with fuels implicated in global warming is not to its advantage! However, despite the careful attempts to associate BP with a 'green' agenda, BP Amoco was fined £60,000 in 2002 (the highest recorded fine in the UK) for pollution from a petrol station, after leaking petrol endangered drinking water in Luton. In the rest of the world in 2002 BP registered 11 recordable injuries due to hazardous work conditions, with the Norwegian Petroleum Directorate issuing a severe reprimand to BP citing 'many violations of health, environmental and safety standards'. In a further blow, one of the UK's leading ethical investment funds, Henderson Global Investors, announced that it was selling millions of pounds of BP shares because it could no longer assure its investors of the company's commitment to worker safety and to the environment in Alaska.

Checkpoint 6

Select a company from *one* of the following industries:

1 Chemicals
2 Cosmetics
3 Furniture retailing.

Conduct your own research to find out the extent to which they are involved in green marketing. Make your own recommendations as to how your chosen firm can develop/improve its green marketing.

Technological environment

Technological change can have important effects on the decisions taken by businesses. Technological change can involve new processes of production, i.e. new ways of doing things which raise the productivity of factor inputs, as with the use of robotics in car assembly techniques which has dramatically raised output per assembly line worker. Around 80% of technological change has been *process innovation*. However, technological change can also be embodied in new products (goods or services) which were not previously available. Online banking and many new financial services are the direct result of advances in microprocessor-based technologies. Less than 20% of technological change has involved such *product innovation*.

Information and communication technologies

Many technological advances involve information and communication techniques (ICT) of one type or another. Telematics provides a useful example of new opportunities resulting from ICT developments.

Telematics

Telematics adapts ICT technologies to create vehicle management systems, thereby helping resolve many logistical problems. Tracking systems that can pinpoint a vehicle's location down to a few metres with the help of global positioning system (GPS) satellites are now commonplace, and can help suppliers monitor the progress of deliveries and increase efficiency in the supply chain. New automated monitoring systems, which are much like the black-box recorders found in aircraft, go one step further. As well as delivering a constant stream of data detailing each vehicle's speed and location, they can provide diagnostic information on engine and driving performance, which can then be transmitted wirelessly to engineers working remotely.

According to telematics providers, the benefits of these systems are not restricted to greater visibility and efficiency. They also point out that an important factor driving demand in telematics is the need to comply with new legislation. MobilAria, a subsidiary of the world's largest automotive parts maker Delphi, recently marketed its FleetOutlook system on the grounds that it would help companies comply with forthcoming regulations from the US Department of Transportation. The company claims that its system will track, record and automate everything from driver work logs to fuel tax accounts.

Again on the legislative side, the aforementioned black box from IBM and SIS got a public relations boost when the Irish government officially welcomed its introduction last month. Data collected by the boxes would help the country achieve European road safety targets, said transport minister Seamus Brennan.

UPS, the logistics group, estimates that a forthcoming upgrade to its own in-house fleet management system will cut about 100m miles a year from the routes covered by its delivery trucks, saving approximately 14m gallons of fuel. Managers can work out much more efficient routes when they know exactly how many parcels are coming through the system on a given day.

And customers benefit as well, says Ken Lacy, UPS chief information officer. 'When you have got the ability to have a total view of everything that is moving through your channels, you can imagine the reduction in inventory that you have to carry.' UPS's system currently tracks smart labels attached to about 90% of the packages it delivers every year, he adds, many of them along the same routes used by the Pony Express riders of old.

Case Study 12.6 reviews some major technological advances in the wireless Internet and the impacts this is having on a wide range of goods and services.

Case Study 12.6 The picture gets brighter

FT

Few consumer technologies hold such promise and have been so high profile as the wireless Internet. For years the hype zoomed ahead of the reality and, except for Japan, a mass market for new data services failed to take root. However 'after years of 3G promises, the pieces – the handsets, the features and applications, the bandwidth and the networks – are starting to come together to make next generation wireless a reality,' says Alex Slawsby, analyst at IDC. Business users will benefit from faster networks, but it is the huge potential of the consumer market that really sets hearts racing.

Japan still leads the world – it has 75 million wireless Internet users including 1 million using DoCoMo's 3G service – but the big difference over a few years ago is that use of data services in other countries is now growing fast. Forrester Research predicts one in four Europeans will use wireless Internet services regularly in 2005. O_2, the UK operator, forecasts that 25% of revenues will come from data by the end of 2004.

Once, data meant mainly text messages (SMS), but that is changing as consumers buy the latest multimedia handsets. 'Half our new data revenue growth is now coming from non-SMS services,' says Kent Thexton, chief marketing and data officer at O_2. O_2's latest offering is a wireless music service launched in November 2003. Consumers download chart hits via their handset to a proprietary player, where the music is stored and played. Rights management software stops them sharing the file illegally, while fancy compression software reduces download times. 'It is like iTunes for mobiles,' says Mr Thexton, comparing the service to Apple's successful Internet music service.

Case Study 12.6 continued

The music industry sees great potential in wireless as a new delivery channel. Just ask 50 Cent, a popular US rap artist. More than 500,000 people have downloaded his 'In Da Club' single to their phones, making it the top-selling ring-tone in US music history. Only 13% of US consumers will pay for ring-tones, according to Forrester Research. But those that do are the customers that operators love: trend-setting youngsters likely to spend much more on data services than their old-fashioned parents. Handset manufacturers are now keen to reach this youth market. Fans of Nelly, a hip-hop artist, can buy a phone customised with songs, video clips, ring-tones and screen pictures of Nelly. The phone, from Korean manufacturer Curitel, uses 'soft skin' technology from Wild Seed, a small software house, to personalise it.

Upstart Asian manufacturers such as Curitel are making big waves in the handset industry. They are adept not just at exploiting new technologies but also spotting consumer trends – such as the popularity of the clamshell format. European manufacturers such as Siemens and Nokia have belatedly responded with their own clamshell phones.

Nokia disagrees that innovation in handsets is inexorably shifting East. It cites its new N-Gage game-playing console, which lets youngsters download games or play them online, play MP3 files and listen to the radio. Oh, it can also make calls. Downloading games has huge potential as consumers are tiring of the standard games built into their phones. In Europe, Analysys predicts this market could grow ten-fold to be worth €3bn in 2008.

The growth of Java phones makes it easier to develop games for different handsets. Nevertheless, device compatibility remains a big issue for developers of multimedia content who must contend with varying technical specifications and user interfaces. Compatibility issues are a notorious problem for video content. Singapore's M1 launched a video clips service earlier this year. But it initially limited the service to Sony Ericsson phones to reduce compatibility problems. LogicaCMG, a provider of messaging software, has developed 'transcoding' software that makes it easier for video clips and MMS messages to be viewed on different devices.

MMS roaming is another issue the industry must address. M1 recently signed a roaming deal with China Mobile, allowing Singaporean tourists to send picture messages while holidaying in China to folk back home. Such deals are necessary because many messages today get lost owing to incompatibilities between networks. Christoph Caselitz, president for mobile applications at Siemens Mobile, believes these sorts of technical issue can be solved through standards bodies such as the Open Mobile Association (OMA).

In 2004 there will be 1.4 billion mobile phone users worldwide but in mature European and Asian countries, the mobile phone has lost its novelty value and average voice revenues are declining. Hence Vodafone's lavish advertising campaign that uses football star David Beckham to promote its Vodafone live! range of data services such as picture messaging, games and polyphonic ring-tone downloads. In the latest

Case Study 12.6 continued

advertisement Beckham, currently with Spanish club Real Madrid, uses his phone to send MMS snaps of Madrid's sunny skies back to former team mates in rainy England. This growing emphasis on softer issues such as branding and marketing shows how the wireless industry is imitating the consumer and media industries.

Another big change is the industry's closer ties with handset makers, content providers and software companies. To pump out games, music and video clips to millions of wireless devices, operators need not only fast networks but also clever software, good content deals and snazzy handsets.

A far more complex and dynamic value chain is thus evolving in which network operators, hardware suppliers, content producers and software houses are jockeying for power. Today, it is far from clear who will win the biggest slice of the pie.

Source: *Financial Times*, 26 November 2003, IT Review, p. 25

Questions

1 Identify some of the 'opportunities' created by these new technologies.
2 Identify some of the 'threats' created by these new technologies.

Activity 12.2 gives you the opportunity to review some of the materials on the ecological and technological environments.

Activity 12.2

1 Read the text below on BP seeking to create an environmentally friendly image.

Global rebranding of BP

In recent times the image of oil-based products has hardly been positive. As a fossil fuel it has been linked to CO_2 emissions and therefore to problems such as global warming and the emission of other hazardous substances. It is factors such as these which have led BP, the company which started the Middle East oil boom in the early twentieth century, to state in July 2000 that its name in future would signify 'beyond petroleum' rather than British Petroleum. Chief Executive Sir John Browne spent over £100m over the next 12 months reinforcing this image with a new logo, a makeover for its petrol station and a media advertising blitz. The new logo has been named the Helios mark after the Greek sun god and is meant to signify dynamic energy from oil to gas and solar, said Sir John.

The official reason for this rebranding from its headquarters at Britannica House is that it reflects the growing interest in cleaner, more environmentally friendly fuels such as natural gas and solar power. Since the recent takeover of Amoco, BP has certainly become a major gas producer and a world leader in the development of solar power, even though the amount of money being spent is insignificant compared to its oil exploration. However, some believe that Sir John also has ambitions outside of the energy field, and that the new logo will aptly cover a growing product portfolio such as an office cleaning company or a supermarket chain as much as a hydrocarbon group. In fact a supermarket chain is on the way because BP has plans to open up retail outlets at all its major petrol stations as part of ambitions to increase retail revenues by 10%. BP Connect stores will feature in-store e-kiosks where customers can check weather and traffic conditions, use touch screen monitors to order food, call up directions, receive sports and news coverage etc. Even solar panel energy is planned for these petrol stations.

Probably the most important reason, however, is an acceptance that the traditional image of the oil company has become a negative one in the hearts and minds of the consumer. Petrol prices are high and are meeting consumer resistance and there is also a growing demand throughout the business sector for a social and ethical dimension in all that is done.

Further, the oil companies are aware that one petrol is the same as any other, making it almost impossible to build brand loyalty, as indicated by the fact that BP was 58th in a recent survey by consultant Interbrand on globally recognised product names.

Such rebranding is good business practice, and is being done by every truly successful brand around the world, says Robert Jones, a director at consultant Wolff Olins. Brands such as Starbucks, Disney or Virgin are despised by a few but liked by millions. In a market filled with coffee bars, Starbucks stands for sociability as well as beverages. Disney stands for much more than cartoons and theme parks. It stands for fun – while Sir Richard Branson's Virgin is nothing if not youthful and irreverent. It can sell anything its founder comes up with – records, airlines, financial services, mobile phones and even energy.

Questions

1 **Why has BP undertaken such global rebranding?**

2 **Comment on the prospects for the success of this strategy.**

2 Read the text below on technological change.

British libraries experience technological change

The UK government is supporting a plan to transform Britain's public libraries by linking them into a nationwide computer network. The aim is an integrated grid linking libraries, schools and government, made possible by technological change. The cost of the project is projected at over £750m, the majority of funding coming via the UK lottery fund.

The objective for Britain's libraries is to offer free Internet access. This will allow people living in the local community to search for the extensive information available via the *Internet*. This is not intended to replace the more traditional role of the library, but to complement its current services.

Question

Can you identify some of the opportunities and threats which might result from this technological change?

3 Which *three* of the following conditions will help firms to segment the market so that consumers will pay higher prices for overtly 'environmentally friendly' products?

(a) Consumers are indifferent to environmental issues.
(b) The company must have identified a distinctive market segment consisting of consumers who really are willing to pay more for environmentally friendly products.
(c) The branding/corporate image must clearly and credibly convey the environmental benefits related to the products.
(d) The company must be able to protect itself from imitations for long enough to profit from its 'investment' in environmentally friendly products.
(e) Studies suggest a lack of consumer willingness to pay for environmental characteristics of products.

Answers to Checkpoints and Activities can be found on pp. 705–35.

Key Terms

Bureaucratic law Where those who are involved in its administration have an important influence on its interpretation.

Code law Explicit set of written rules.

Common law Unwritten, based largely on precedent.

Decisions Binding on all members of EU.

Directives EU objectives are established but the means to achieve them left in the hands of individual nations.

Expected value The probability of each outcome multiplied by the value (impact) of each outcome and summed over all outcomes.

Intellectual property rights (IPRs) Patents, trademarks and copyright protecting knowledge in its various forms.

Macropolitical risk Affects all firms and most or all activities.

Micropolitical risk Only affects specific firms or activities.

Regulations Applied in EU without the need for national measures.

Religious law Based on religious principles.

Statute law Legislation passed by governments.

Sustainability Whereby what is inherited in environmental terms is passed on, intact, to future generations.

Key Points

- 'Macropolitical' risks affect all firms in a country whereas 'micropolitical' risks are more narrowly focused.
- Political risks can be assessed and prioritised. High impact and high probability risks will be given precedence.
- Firms can seek to improve their bargaining power with governments by seeking to embed themselves in the host country and raise the 'costs' of any unwelcome interference.
- Alternatively, firms can minimise their active engagement with the host country, limiting in advance any 'costs' of interference.

- Legal systems can have important impacts on international businesses. EU Directives, for example, can cause major changes in business practices.
- Environmental 'friendliness' can be a positive strategy for businesses, in their own self-interest.
- Technological change, whether in process or product, creates both opportunities and threats.

Assessment Practice

Multiple choice questions

1 Rules and practices which cover groups of countries such as the EU.

(a) Macropolitical risk
(b) Legal precedent
(c) Micropolitical risk
(d) Intellectual property rights
(e) Supranational regulations

2 The airline industry faces higher taxes because of air-pollution.

(a) Macropolitical risk
(b) Legal precedent
(c) Micropolitical risk
(d) Intellectual property rights
(e) Supranational regulations

3 Terrorism raises worldwide security costs.

(a) Macropolitical risk
(b) Legal precedent
(c) Micropolitical risk
(d) Intellectual property rights
(e) Supranational regulations

4 Chinese authorities prosecute a local firm for breaching a US pharmaceutical company's patent.

(a) Macropolitical risk
(b) Legal precedent
(c) Micropolitical risk
(d) Intellectual property rights
(e) Supranational regulations

5 Which *three* of the following approaches may be adopted by MNEs attempting to reduce the political risks from operating in a host country?

(a) Avoid using local labour or developing skills in local labour markets.
(b) Improve the MNE's relative bargaining power vis-à-vis the host country.

(c) Ensure that any proprietary technology the MNE owns is available to the host country whether or not the MNE operates there.
(d) Use protective and defensive techniques to limit the 'costs' to the MNE should the host country interfere in its activities.
(e) Use integrative techniques to ensure that the MNE becomes part of the host country's infrastructure.

6 Which of the following sets of initials refers to a major international agreement seeking to protect 'knowledge-based' aspects of international trade?

(a) OECD
(b) WTO
(c) GATT
(d) UNESCO
(e) TRIPS

7 Which *three* of the following supranational institutions play a key role in EU policy making and are independent of the national governments?

(a) International Monetary Fund (IMF)
(b) European Parliament
(c) European Commission
(d) World Trade Organisation
(e) European Court of Justice

8 What has been described as 'any sign capable of being represented graphically which is capable of distinguishing goods or services of one undertaking from those of another and which has legal effect'?

(a) Copyright
(b) Patent
(c) Logo
(d) Trademark
(e) Litigation

9 Which *one* of the following is an important aspect of 'sustainability'?

(a) Intergenerational inequity
(b) Generational inequity
(c) Precautionary principle
(d) Litigation
(e) Intergenerational equity

10 Which of the following refers to a disputes procedure which seeks to resolve a conflict out of court?

(a) Litigation
(b) Lawsuit
(c) Plaintif
(d) Arbitration
(e) Consultation

Data response and stimulus questions

1 Look back to Figure 12.1 (p. 459).

The information below reflects four possible events in a country in which an MNE is operating. The probability of each event (p) and its predicted impact on profits (*x*) are shown.

Calculate the *expected value* of each event and suggest in which of the four boxes, A, B, C and D each of the following events should be placed.

(i) Internal conflict p (0.2), *x* (–£50m)
(ii) Rise in exchange rate p (0.7), *x* (–£15m)
(iii) Fall in real income p (0.1), *x* (–£10m)
(iv) Restrictions on investment p (0.8), *x* (–£40m)

2 Read the following case study on technological change, then answer the questions which follow

'Multi-tasking' machines to feed demand for all shapes and sizes in quick time

Behind the emergence of 'multi-tasking' machine tools is the increasing trend among manufacturers towards lean production techniques, in which parts are made in small volumes but at high speed and with more emphasis on using the same families of production equipment for different tasks. Routines of this sort have been imposed on manufacturers as they have tried increasingly to make their parts in more shapes and sizes, to feed the increasing demand by consumers for more variation in the end product, whether this is a car or a mobile phone.

A leader in multi-tasking systems is Yamazaki Mazak of Japan, one of the world's biggest machine tool makers. Tomohisa Yamazaki, president of the family-owned company, says an increasing proportion of its annual sales of some $1.1bn is being accounted for by such products, which normally sell for between $300,000 and $1m and can carry out up to 500 different types of cutting or shaping operations that previously would have required several different machines. 'By introducing these machines, our customers can make themselves more competitive, even in high-cost countries,' says Mr Yamazaki.

In the past three years, the company has used its multi-tasking machines in its own plants in Japan, replacing previous generations of inflexible automation. In the process, it has saved itself approximately $80m a year by cutting stocks of parts and reducing machining times.

While machines that combine turning and milling are by no means new, the performance of the new systems has been increased in recent years by the growing sophistication of the motors and control software machine tools depend on.

Complex operations managed by a single machine would not be possible without software that controls the drive motors used in each machining operation and enables individual cutting devices to work – sometimes for just a few seconds – on a particular shaping operation and then stop to allow another cutting system, approaching from a different angle and using a different motor, but part of the same machine, to take over.

Source: *Financial Times*, 21 October 2003, p. 17

Questions

1 What are the benefits to a firm from using 'multi-task' machines?

2 How might these new technologies influence the value chain?

True/False questions

1 Inflation is a type of micropolitical risk.

True/False

2 Greater priority in political risk assessment should be given to events which a high probability and high impact (should they occur).

True/False

3 If a multinational involves as many local people as possible within the host economy then it is likely to have more political influence with the host government.

True/False

4 Common law is the foundation of the legal system in the UK and its former colonies. It is unwritten, has developed over long periods of time and is founded on earlier decisions reached by judges.

True/False

5 Code law occurs in dictatorships and communist countries and is written down.

True/False

6 Bureaucratic law is consistent and predictable.

True/False

7 The turnover of Fairtrade products has grown by 40% in the UK in 2003, indicating a growing number of ethically conscious consumers.

True/False

8 Governments which favour the 'polluter pay' principle are less likely to raise taxes on environment.

True/False

9 If new technology halves the total cost of production but doubles output then average cost will be unaffected.

True/False

10 The majority of technology change has involved processes of production.

True/False

Essay questions

1 Select one recent example of a micropolitical risk. Evaluate the likely impacts of this on a firm you are familiar with.
2 Select one recent example of a macropolitical risk. Evaluate the likely impacts of this on a firm you are familiar with.
3 Choose any recent legal controversy and evaluate the potential impact of that controversy on a firm you are familiar with.
4 Can you explain why it might be in the self-interest of a firm to be ecologically responsible?
5 Choose any recent technological advance. Analyse the opportunities and threats which might follow from that advance.

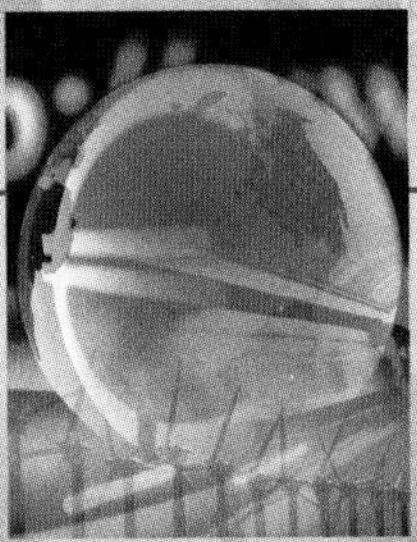

Chapter 13

Functions of management: domestic business environment

Introduction

In this chapter we review some important management functions, namely the marketing, human resource and management accounting functions of firms operating within the domestic business environment. Chapter 14 extends the discussion of these three key functional areas for management into situations in which multinational firms are operating across international borders.

Learning objectives:

By the end of this chapter you should be able to:

- review the principal activities involved in domestic marketing
- examine the key elements in the 'marketing mix', including product, price, promotion and place
- explain why it is so important to manage people efficiently
- assess the HRM function and the effectiveness of various HRM approaches within domestic companies
- understand the benefits and limitations of accounting data for management, including the use of ratio analysis and estimates of break-even output.

Chapter 14 looks in more detail at various *international* aspects of these functional areas of management as well as considering the broader international business environment.

Marketing

Marketing is an integrated activity that takes place throughout the organisation and seeks to align customer needs with the capabilities and goals of the organisation. Market analysis, market planning and management and the so-called 'marketing mix' are important activities for the marketer.

Market analysis

Market analysis can itself be broken down into at least three elements.

1. *Environmental analysis*. This may involve scanning the environment for risks and opportunities, and seeking to identify factors outside the firm's control. Once the environment has been scanned, the organisation must develop a marketing strategy or focus to give a sense of direction for marketing activity. Market segmentation, market research and market planning and management are key elements in devising such a strategy.
2. *Buyer behaviour*. Firms need to have a profile of their existing and potential customer base, and to know how and why their customers purchase. Marketing seeks to identify the buyers, their potential motivation for purchase, their educational levels, income, class, age and many other factors which might influence the decision to purchase.
3. *Market research*. This is the process by which much of the information about the firm's customers and its environment is collected. Without such market research, organisations would have to make guesses about their customers. Such research may involve using data which already exist (secondary data) or using surveys and other methods to collect entirely new data (primary data).

It may be useful to consider each of these elements in turn.

Environmental analysis

PEST, PESTLE, SWOT and other techniques of assessing the external and internal environment in which the firm operates are considered in Chapters 12 and 15 and make an important contribution to environmental analysis.

Buyer behaviour

Major decisions need to be taken as to which *market segments* to target. A market segment is a group of potential customers who have certain characteristics in common, for example being within a certain age range, income range or occupational profile (see Box 13.1). Some of these market segments may be identified as more likely to purchase that product than others. When these segments have been identified, the organisation needs to decide whether one segment or a number of segments are to be targeted. Once that strategic decision is made, then the product can be positioned to meet the particular needs or wants which characterise that segment. The task here is to ensure that the product has a particular set of characteristics which make it competitive with other products in the market.

Box 13.1 Market segmentation

Producers tend to define markets broadly, but within these markets are groups of people who have more specific requirements. Market segmentation is the process by which a total market is broken down into separate groups of customers having identifiably different product needs, using characteristics such as income, age, ethnicity and so on.

Occupational profile

There are many different methods of segmenting a market. One widely used technique is to classify people according to the occupation of the head of the household as shown in Table 13.1, since market research suggests that consumer buying behaviour changes as individuals move from one such group or 'class' to another. Interestingly, BSkyB reported in mid-2000 that the 'old' analogue TV system attracted 46% of ABC_1 users, whereas the 'new' digital TV system was attracting 52% of ABC_1 users. The suggestion here was that digital TV appealed to a more 'up-market' audience because it allows users to access home shopping and other interactive services as well as the Internet.

Table 13.1 Occupation of head of household

Group	Description	% of population
A	Higher managerial and professional	3
B	Middle management	11
C_1	Supervisory and clerical	22
C_2	Skilled manual	32
D	Semi-skilled and manual workers	23
E	Pensioners, unemployed	9

VALS framework

Originally developed by Arnold Mitchell in the US in the 1960s, this framework has been much refined and is increasingly used by national and international marketers. It focuses on psychological, demographic and lifestyle factors to segment consumer groups. The latest version of VALS segments the English-speaking population aged 18 or older into eight consumer groups.

- *Innovators* – high esteem, take charge, sophisticated, curious. Purchases reflect cultivated tastes for up-market, niche products and services.
- *Thinkers* – motivated by ideas, mature, well educated and reflective. Purchases favour durability, functionality and value.
- *Believers* – strongly traditional and respect authority. Choose familiar products and established brands.
- *Achievers* – goal-oriented lifestyles centred on family and career. Purchase premium products that demonstrates success to their peers.

- *Strivers* – trendy and fun-loving. Purchase stylish products that emulate the purchasers of higher income groups.
- *Experiencers* – unconventional, active and impulsive. Purchase fashionable products and those related to socialising and entertainment.
- *Makers* – practical, responsible and self-sufficient. Purchase basic products, reflecting value rather than luxury.
- *Survivors* – lead narrowly focused lives with few resources, seek safety and security. Purchase low-cost, well-known brands (i.e. exhibit brand loyalty) and seek out available discounted products.

Segmentation has allowed the growth of small specialist or 'niche' markets. As people have become more affluent, they have been prepared to pay the higher price for a product that meets their precise requirements. The growth of niche markets has also been important in supporting the existence of small firms. In many cases the large firm has found many of these segments to be too small to service profitably.

Example:

Shampoo and market segmentation

Shampoo was once considered one market, but new product development, branding and packaging have segmented this in many ways. Shampoo products may be seen to be segmented into medicated hair products (Head & Shoulders), two-in-one (Wash & Go), children's shampoos (L'Oreal Kids), 'balanced' shampoos (Organics, Fructis) and environmentally sensitive shampoos (The Body Shop range). Such strategies permit manufacturers such as Unilever and Procter & Gamble to place a premium price on many of their shampoo products. These forms of lifestyle segmentation are now used by many firms in preference to the social class distinctions of the previous four decades.

However, Case Study 13.1 warns against assuming that past methods of market segmentation will be valid in the future.

Case Study 13.1 The 'no brow' consumer FT

Marketers spend a lot of time trying to understand how consumers' age, income and lifestyle affect their choice of brands. Now research suggests brand owners could have a new challenge on their hands: a type of consumer who does not fit the traditional socioeconomic or demographic criteria. This consumer has been dubbed 'no-brow'.

No-brow is not a youth trend or confined to city-dwelling trendies. But it is an attitude towards brands and consumerism that prevails among those traditionally categorised as BC_1 – so-called 'middle Englanders' – who make up the UK population's largest group by disposable income. 'Until very recently it was easy for a brand-owner to reach middle England. All you needed was the right proposition, the right price and appropriate distribution,' says Pearse McDabe, planning director of

Case Study 13.1 continued

brand design consultancy Fitch: London. 'But everything's changed. Current consumer behaviour is challenging received wisdom and marketing convention.'

In an attempt to understand what is happening, Fitch undertook quantitative analysis of data from sources including Mintel, Verdict Research and TGI, and qualitative research among couples aged between 25 and 40 in Greater Manchester and Watford. The findings suggest that BC_1 consumers feel increasingly frustrated with the homogeneous nature of the mass market, and are losing their loyalty to traditional brands. As a result, they are engaged by so-called upmarket or high-brow brands but are just as willing to buy cheaper, low-brow brands. They regularly mix and match a wide variety of high- and low-status brands to satisfy their preoccupations with individualism and self-expression.

One reason for the rise of the 'no brow' is the blurring of the line between traditional definitions of 'mass market' and 'premium'. This has been driven by a number of mass market brands assuming a premium positioning, such as Tesco with the launch of its Tesco Finest range and the so-called 'democratisation' of premium, luxury brands such as Hackett, the British men's wear label, Ralph Lauren and Burberry, which are now seen by ordinary consumers as attainable.

All this leaves the brand owner struggling to define a target market and battling against declining consumer loyalty as consumers buy into a broader, more eclectic mix of high- and low-brow brands, Fitch's findings suggest, increasingly, the no-brow consumer does not want to buy something that has already been packaged. This extends beyond fashion and into interiors, food and even travel, where a growing number of people fly budget airlines but check into five-star hotels at their destination.

IKEA, Nissan and John Lewis, the department store chain, are among brands that, either deliberately or otherwise, are close to the no-brow mindset. Fitch's research shows that no-brow consumers value them for providing flexibility instead of a bespoke product or service; for providing both emotional and rational reasons to buy; and for brand values such as consistency, authenticity and integrity.

Nokia, Debenhams and Orange, meanwhile, are brands that would benefit from more closely tapping into no-brow attitudes, Mr McCabe believes: 'Those rolling out standard formats everywhere should wake up to the fact that no-brows are growing tired of that. They don't want standardisation, they want distinctiveness. But while they want distinctiveness, they don't want to be overtly conspicuous.'

Source: *Financial Times*, 27 November 2003

Questions

1 What is meant by 'no brow' consumers?

2 What relevance does this approach have to traditional market segmentation approaches?

3 Can you identify business implications of this trend?

Market research

Market research can be divided into two types:

- *desk research* which means using information which has already been gathered for another purpose (secondary data), and
- *field research*, which involves obtaining information specifically directed towards a particular marketing issue and which is usually original (primary data).

Desk research

There are numerous sources of secondary information available to the marketer.

- *National publications.* In the UK the Office for National Statistics (ONS) publishes detailed annual (sometimes monthly or quarterly) data on most types of economic and socio-economic indicator. Similar information is available in most advanced industrialised economies.
- *National trade associations and Chambers of Commerce (or equivalents).* These business agencies in the various countries can be invaluable in providing up-to-date market information.
- *Trade journals.* These often provide up-to-the-minute profiles of various aspects of industries, countries or specific market sectors.
- *Financial press.* The various FT indices and ratios (and their equivalents elsewhere) provide an invaluable source of up-to-date information on firms and industrial sectors.
- *Internet.* Finally, of course, there is the Internet, though information found here is only as good as the researcher who is using it. Remember that many of the Web pages are commercially based, and companies will not reveal any secrets that they feel might be useful to their competitors.

The major problems with secondary data are that it is available to competitors, it may be of limited value in terms of comparability between countries, and there may be large gaps in statistical coverage in certain countries. However, it is quick, easy to access, and may save valuable time as compared to field research.

Field research

Primary data may be obtained from a variety of sources. The main advantage of field research is that it is customised to the firm and is unavailable to competitors. However, it is expensive and time-consuming and may present particular problems, such as collecting data in some national cultures which have little experience of using scientifically based research methods. Survey methods that assume a high level of literacy, certain education levels, access to telephones or a willingness to respond by those surveyed may need to be reassessed in some international situations.

- *Research agencies.* In most countries there are many enterprises that are specialists in research. Companies can specify the type of data they are interested in and the agency will carry out the research on their behalf.

> **CHECK THE NET**
> The Market Research Society can be found at:
> www.bmra.org.uk
> www.marketresearch.org.uk

- *Company networks/personnel*. Original data may be obtained from company networks (e.g. suppliers who also work for rival firms). Sometimes members of a company are sent to investigate the nature of specified markets through 'shopping trips' which, whilst not rigorously scientific, can help the organisation 'get a feel' for the types of markets they may enter.

Planning and management

These various marketing activities need to be integrated throughout the organisation, and this can only be done through careful planning and managing of the whole process.

- *Planning* is the process of assessing market opportunities and matching them with the resources and capabilities of the organisation in order to achieve its objectives. However, planning is not just a one-off exercise. It needs to be integrated into the ever-shifting environment of the firm so that new issues are constantly addressed and met. Forecasts made at this stage will have a major effect on production, financial decisions, research and development and human resource planning.
- *Managing* the process can involve many aspects. For example, in order for the planning to be ongoing, the whole process needs to be monitored to ensure that customer needs are being met effectively. This may involve measuring the outcomes of marketing strategies against objectives that may have been set at the strategic stage, for example checking whether specific targets have been met for individual products. Customer surveys may also be used to audit the quality of the services delivered. Whatever the method, it is important that monitoring is built into the plan, so that major or minor adjustments can be made. Managing may also involve *organising* the marketing function, for example allocating different tasks to different individuals or different departments.

> **CHECK THE NET**
> Information on market issues including objectives, planning and management can be found at:
> www.brandrepublic.com
> www.keynote.co.uk
> www.euromonitor.com
> www.bized.ac.uk

Marketing mix

Refining the marketing strategy and making it operational invariably involves considering the 4 Ps of the so-called 'marketing mix', i.e. product, price, promotion and place. For example, marketing strategy involving the 4 Ps may involve attempts to use or modify the various stages of the 'product life cycle' (Chapter 4, p. 160), i.e. the so-called introduction, growth, maturity and decline stages. Table 13.2 outlines some possible marketing mix responses to the product life cycle.

Table 13.2 Marketing responses to the product life cycle

	Introduction	Growth	Maturity	Decline
Marketing emphasis	Create product awareness Encourage product trial	Establish high market share	Fight off competition Generate profits	Minimise marketing expenditure
Product strategy	Introduce basic products	Improve features of basic products	Design product versions for different segments	Rationalise the product range
Pricing strategy	Price skimming or price penetration	Reduce prices enough to expand the market and establish market share	Match or beat the competition	Reduce prices further
Promotional strategy	Advertising and sales promotion to end-users and dealers	Mass media advertising to establish brand image	Emphasise brand strengths to different segments	Minimal level to retain loyal customers
Distribution strategy (Place)	Build selective distribution outlets	Increase the number of outlets	Maintain intensive distribution	Rationalise outlets to minimise distribution costs

We might now consider each of the four Ps in rather more detail.

Product

This is the starting point of the marketing mix, since decisions involving price, promotion and place are usually based on the characteristics of a product which already exists.

Standardised or differentiated product

We have already noted in Chapter 2 the cost benefits from large-scale production of a *standardised product*. These 'economies of scale' can reduce average costs in non-technical areas such as promotion, distribution and administration as well as in the more technical areas of production. They can be significant when the domestic market is the main concern and still more so when we consider the still larger international market in Chapter 14.

Of course, there are also arguments in favour of a more *differentiated product*, as when consumer responses in different market segments vary significantly. For example, high income groups (Groups A, B and C_1 in Table 13.1) may attach greater importance to certain product characteristics than lower income groups (e.g. C_2, D and E) and may be willing to pay a price premium for these characteristics.

Example:

Product differentiation in disposable nappies

The disposable nappy is a well-known product, yet producers are constantly seeking ways of updating the design of disposable nappies, with higher prices often associated with the updated and redesigned version of this (mature) product. The point here is that the 'update' helps retain existing customer loyalty, helps attract new customers and may also give some latitude for price variation (increase). Procter & Gamble, the makers of Pampers Baby-Dry and Pampers Premium disposable nappies, have continuously sought to upgrade and differentiate products such as these in order to maintain the 'mature phase' for as long as possible, i.e. to use updating investments as a means of delaying the onset of the 'decline phase'.

Table 13.3 outlines some factors the firm must take into account when making the decision as to product standardisation or product differentiation.

Table 13.3 Factors supporting product standardisation or product differentiation

Factors supporting standardisation	Factors supporting product differentiation
Rapid technological change, reducing product life cycles (places a premium on rapid global penetration)	Slow technological change, lengthening product life cycles
Substantial scale economies	Few scale economies
Strong and favourable brand image	Weak and/or unfavourable brand image
Homogeneous consumer preferences (within a given group, e.g. high income, and/or between groups)	Heterogeneous consumer preferences (within a given group, e.g. high income, and/or between groups)

Branding

Establishing product characteristics which are different from those of the firm's main competitors may be important in helping the firm establish a brand image. Of course, brand image may depend not so much on *actual* product differences but on consumer *perceptions* of product differences, created and reinforced by extensive advertising.

Certainly the potential benefits of brand image may influence the product characteristics sought at the introduction stage of the product life cycle or the modifications considered during the growth or maturity stages of that life cycle. For example, a product may be modified in order to reposition it and/or extend the reach of the brand at the maturity stage of the product life cycle. Such 'brand extension strategies' often appeal to larger companies who are well aware of the value to sales and profits resulting from past investment in brands.

LINKS

Chapter 14 (p. 570) extends the list of factors in this table when 'product' is considered within the *international marketing mix*.

Example:

Brand value

Calculations of brand value involve comparing the prices of similar generic (own-brand) products with the higher price of the branded product. Data from *Interbrand* in 2003 ranked the top five global brands and their associated brand values as follows:

Coca-Cola	£43.2bn
Microsoft	£39.8bn
IBM	£31.8bn
General Electric.	£25.7bn
Intel	£19.2bn

Successful branding can help increase consumer demand (shift the demand curve to the right) and may also make demand less price elastic (see Ch. 2, p. 46).

Price

In terms of the product life cycle, different pricing strategies are often associated with different stages of the life cycle. For example, in the *introduction* and *growth* stages two pricing approaches are often used.

Penetration pricing

Here price for a new product may even be set below average cost in order to capture market share. The expectation is that prices can be raised and profit margins restored later on in the growth/maturity stages, helped by the fact that average costs may themselves be falling in those stages via the various economies of scale.

Example:

Freeview captures market share

'Freeview', the successor to ITV Digital, was the first to provide 'free' access to 25 channels for the cost of a once-for-all purchase of a £100 set-top decoder, rather than expensive and recurrent subscription charges. Over 500,000 decoders were sold in the first three months of operation in 2003.

'Price-skimming'

Here a high price is set for a new product in the *introduction/early growth* stages which 'skims off' a small but lucrative part of the market. Producers of fashion products, which have a short life and high innovative value as long as only a few people own them, often adopt a skimming strategy. Companies such as IBM, Polaroid and Bosch have operated such price-skimming systems over time. Bosch used a successful skimming policy, supported by patents, in its launch of fuel injection and antilock braking systems.

Example:

Price-skimming in soap-capsules

In 2001 both Unilever and Procter & Gamble launched liquid soap-capsules, i.e. capsules of pre-measured doses of liquid detergent which could be placed into washing machines, to save people the bother of working out how much soap to use per wash. As a 'premium priced' product, the capsules were seen by the two companies as offering good price-skimming opportunities.

Other pricing approaches

In the *mature* stage of product life cycles a wide variety of pricing strategies may suggest themselves, depending on firm objectives and market characteristics. Many of these pricing strategies have already been covered in other chapters of this book.

- *Price elasticity of demand* (Chapter 2, p. 49). If demand for the product is relatively inelastic, a price increase will raise revenue. However, if demand for the product is relatively inelastic then a price reduction will raise revenue.
- *Prestige pricing* (Chapter 2, p. 69) Where higher prices are associated with higher quality ('Veblen effect').
- *Firm objective* (Chapter 4, p. 146) The more interested the firm is in profit rather than revenue or market share objectives, the higher price the firm is likely to set.
- *Competitor pricing* (Chapter 6, p. 233) As, for example, where the firm follows the prices set by the market leader or engages in price warfare under oligopoly market structures.
- *Price discrimination* (Chapter 6, p. 234) If demand for a given product can be broken down into market segments, some being more price sensitive than others, then revenue and profits can be increased by charging a different price in each market segment.

NOTE: MORE PRICING TERMINOLOGY

Some other pricing terms and approaches include:

- *Loss leader (bait) pricing* where a limited number of products are priced at or below cost to entice customers who may then pay full price on other purchases (e.g. for selected products in supermarkets).
- *Clearance pricing* where rock-bottom prices are charged to clear stock and make resources available for alternative uses.
- *Parallel pricing* where several firms change prices in the same direction and by broadly the same amount.
- *Product line pricing* where the pricing of one item is related to that of complementary items, with a view to maximising the return on the whole product line. For example, the price of a 'core' product might be set at a low level to encourage sales and then the 'accessories' priced at high levels.

Promotion

Promotion is necessary to make consumers aware of what a firm has to offer. The major elements of promotion include advertising, sales promotion, personal selling, public relations and so on.

Advertising

General advertising. This may be used to increase consumer awareness of the product, consolidating the commitment of existing customers and attracting new customers. Where successful, advertising will help *shift* the demand curve for the product outwards, increasing market share. At the same time successful advertising may cause the demand curve to *pivot* and become steeper (i.e. less price elastic). Both outcomes may provide the firm with opportunities to raise revenue and profit.

Checkpoint 1

If general advertising causes the demand curve for the product to become less elastic (steeper), how might the firm benefit?

Comparative advertising. This appears to be increasingly common in the UK. Recent legislation means it is now legal for a firm to name a competitor in their advertising and compare service/pricing. However, any statement made should be true and not mislead the customer. An example of comparative advertising is the 2003/4 campaign conducted by easyJet versus British Airways, whereby easyJet pointed to many customer advantages of using its services compared to those of BA. This type of advertising has proved popular for potential customers of car insurance, telephone user charges, bank accounts, loans etc. because it has provided transparency and given customers the ability to compare rates, saving customers time and energy searching for the information themselves. However, if a firm continuously compares itself with a competitor, customers may begin to wonder why this is the case.

Sales promotion

This involves short-term product-focused activities, such as encouraging trial purchases with the hope that these result in repeat business. More in now spent in the UK on sales promotion than general advertising. 'Push' and 'pull' tactics are often employed.

- 'Push' tactics focus on the producer offering incentives to key players in each distributional 'channel' to promote their products (e.g. the firm may offer incentives to wholesalers so that they 'push' the firm's products to retailers etc.). Offering higher discounts to those who stock and display your product is a typical 'push' tactic. Providing point-of-sale materials such as display cabinets and refrigerated units may also prove helpful, as might good after-sales support services.
- 'Pull' tactics focus on the final consumer, the idea being to stimulate consumer demands which will then stimulate ('pull') retailers/wholesalers into stocking the firm's products. Advertising may itself be a 'pull' tactic to support sales promotion. Of course, the adverts must be socially and culturally appropriate to the contemporary market.

Example: **Goodbye to the man in black**

Cadbury has decided to kill off the 'man in black' campaign for its Milk Tray assortments after a 35-year run. Changing social relationships mean that this advert, developed in the 1960s, is proving less effective now that relationships between men and women are less courtly and health and fitness attributes are now more closely associated with male to female gift giving.

Personal selling and public relations (PR)

Personal selling is very much based on relationship building and networking. Personal selling is usually divided between soft and hard selling. 'Soft selling' is not based on pressure tactics and is usually conducted over a long period of time. 'Hard selling' is the opposite in that sales people are heavily motivated by commission and may resort to pressure tactics in order to reach sales targets. *Public relations* (PR) is less focused than personal selling, and involves developing an ambiance or context conducive to sales over an extended period of time. PR is also favoured by companies seeking to sell products facing advertising restrictions, as, for example, tobacco-related products.

Place

Distributional and logistical issues may be involved here. Producers must select an appropriate distributional channel for their product, such as producer to wholesaler/retailer, direct selling to customers (missing out intermediates), Internet selling and so on. A choice of transport system will often be involved for tangible products both for inputs and outputs.

Types of distributions channel

'Distributional channel' refers to the route the product takes from producer to the final consumer. Such channels must fulfil a number of functions, including the physical movement of the products and their presentation to the customer.

Factors influencing the choice of distributional channel include the following.

- *Customer characteristics.* Wherever possible, marketers will put the customer at the centre of this choice. What is the number and geographical location of customers, how often do they purchase, where do they expect to find the products (goods or services) in question? For example, if the majority of customers are clustered in a small number of large cities and expect to purchase the product in large retail environments in which rival or complementary products are displayed, then producer to retailer/wholesaler channels are likely to be selected.
- *Product characteristics.* For example, 'perishable' products such as fruit, vegetables and even daily newspapers must select distributional channels which minimise time-to-customer. Products with a high ratio of value to weigh/volume (i.e. 'high value density') lend themselves to direct selling. Dangerous or very valuable products will require distributional channels which can guarantee safety and security.
- *Channel characteristics.* The lowest-cost route to customers may influence channel choice, as may the channel already selected by competitors. Increasingly, companies are looking at targeting customers directly. Through bypassing intermediaries, producers gain greater control of channel management and obtain more insight into customer characteristics.

Example: **e-commerce distributional channels**

Producers may use e-commerce to sell directly (online) to retailers or to customers. The ability to sell direct online has helped to generate hundreds of new companies, such as 'Amazon.com' (books) and 'Lastminute.com (travel, entertainment). Many of these firms are able to offer highly competitive prices because by selling direct, the channel of distribution is shortened, thereby saving money which can then be passed on to the customer as lower prices.

LINKS

For more on the international marketing mix, see Chapter 14, pp. 565–571.

Activity 13.1 gives you the opportunity to self-check some of your work on marketing.

Activity 13.1

1 Choose a popular food product and examine the *marketing mix* used in recent years for that product.

2 Select a major household product (e.g. TV, washing machine, refrigerator etc.). Use all the *secondary* sources of information available to you to find out more about that product. List the sources involved.

3 Decide upon a well-known branded product. Suggest how you might go about estimating the *brand value* associated with that product.

4 For the product used in Question 3, examine the channels of distribution used in reaching the market. Can you explain why those channels are used and any other options that might exist?

Answers to Checkpoints and Activities can be found on pp. 705–35.

Human resource management

Human resource management (HRM) involves a wide range of activities that deal with the human side of an organisation. Until the early 1980s the title more commonly associated with these activities was 'personnel management', then taken to refer mainly to practical aspects such as recruitment, staff appraisal, training and job evaluation. What perhaps distinguishes HRM from personnel management is the more *strategic* emphasis now given to this role.

Quote

> HRM can be regarded as ... a strategic and coherent approach to the management of an organisation's most valued assets – the people working there who individually and collectively contribute to the achievement of its goals.
>
> *Armstrong (1999)*

HRM is widely seen as having a strategic dimension and involving the total deployment of all the human resources available to the firm, including the integration of personnel and other HRM considerations into the firm's overall corporate planning and strategy formulation procedures. It is seen as proactive, seeking to continuously discover new ways of utilising the labour force in a more productive manner with the intention of giving the business a competitive edge.

Harvard model

In an attempt to investigate HRM issues at the strategic level, a model of human resource management was developed by Beer *et al.* (1984) at Harvard University.

According to this Harvard model, HRM strategies should develop from an in-depth analysis of:

(a) the demands of the various stakeholders in a business (e.g. shareholders, the employees, the government etc., and
(b) a number of situational factors (e.g. the state of the labour market, the skills and motivation of the workforce, management styles etc.)

According to the Harvard researchers, both stakeholder expectations and situational factors need to be considered when formulating human resource strategies and the effectiveness of the outcomes should be evaluated under four headings:

1 commitment (i.e. employees' loyalty);
2 competence (i.e. employees' skills);
3 congruence (i.e. shared vision of workers and management);
4 cost efficiencies (i.e. operational efficiency).

The Harvard model suggests that human resource policies should be directed towards raising attainment levels for each of these four categories; for example, competence could be increased through the provision of extra training, adjustments to recruitment policy, different incentivisation schemes and so on.

Hendry and Pettigrew (1990) offer an adaptation of the Harvard model (Figure 13.1) that attempts to integrate HRM issues with a still broader range of external

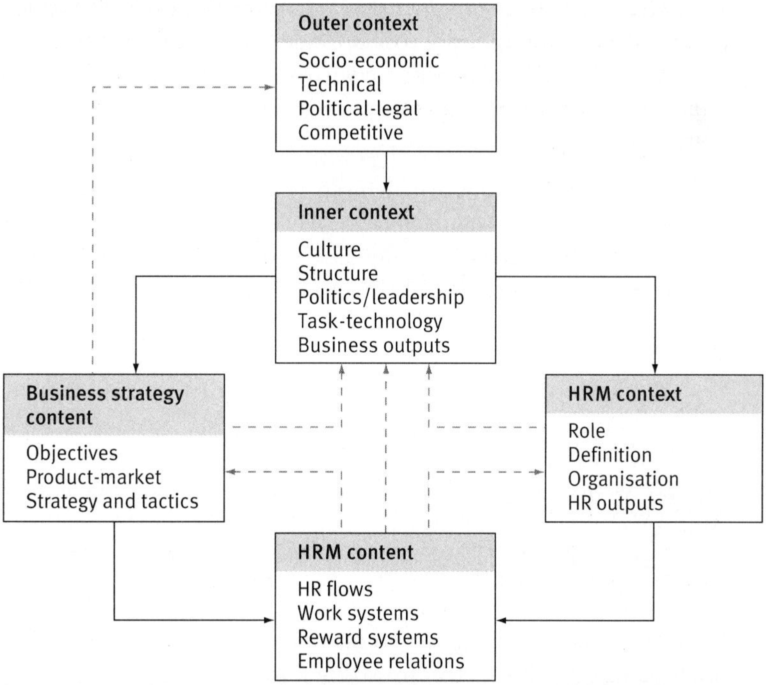

Fig 13.1 Model of strategic change and human resource management

societal influences (such as socio-economic, technical, political, legal and competitive issues) which may vary considerably in different countries. These 'outer context' issues will influence HRM strategies and practices, as will a variety of 'inner context' and business strategic issues.

Case Study 13.2 reviews the strategic nature of the HRM function using the Royal Bank of Scotland as a context for the discussion.

Case Study 13.2 HRM and the Royal Bank of Scotland

The RBS has been undergoing major changes in recent years, partly as a result of growth via merger and acquisitions (e.g. merged with the National Westminster Bank in 1999, and partly as a result of developments within the financial services sector in which it operates. The mission statement of the RBS includes: 'to provide financial services of the highest quality'; as with other organisations RBS must then develop objectives and strategies in an attempt to provide more focus and guidance for employees in seeking to achieve the company's mission. The role of the HRM department will be to support the process of sharing an understanding about what needs to be achieved, and then managing and developing people in a way which will facilitate the achievement of these objectives. For example, in common with other companies in the financial services sector, the RBS is seeking to change from a culture that rewards performance using a 'slow' incremental pay system, into one that more closely relates pay to personal performance and achievement. The HRM department is therefore introducing new performance appraisal systems and incentive schemes in an attempt to help the company achieve its long-term strategic objectives. By introducing more beneficial bonus and profit-sharing schemes, whereby pay is more closely related to individual and corporate performance, employees will arguably become more motivated to contribute to the achievement of the overall goals of the RBS.

A further internal factor that has influenced the HRM function at RBS is the merger with National Westminster Group. This merger was, of course, seen as being of potential benefit to many employees by creating new opportunities and offering enhanced career prospects in the new, larger business. It was recognised in 1999 that the merger would also place greater emphasis on the HRM function of the company and may even involve an expansion of the existing department and its operations. It was seen as necessary to review the current HRM practices of the new and enlarged business and consider revising them in order to bring them into line with the objectives of the RBS. As well as increasing the activity of the HRM department in areas such as recruitment, selection, training and development, this expansion would inevitably also require the clear communication of the RBS's culture, values and strategy across a wider and more disparate cohort of employees. It was recognised to be essential that the HRM functions of both businesses be closely integrated so that there would be a well-defined, common goal for the new, expanded business.

Due to increasing levels of competition within the financial services industry, all organisations in this sector are striving to improve productivity. It is argued that one way of achieving this improvement is to manage human resources more effectively. The

Case Study 13.2 continued

HRM department of the RBS could seek to achieve this by various means; for example, by empowering employees (i.e. allowing workers to make job-related decisions, thereby increasing staff involvement), by encouraging teamwork (in order to improve quality and efficiency) and introducing clear and consistently applied communication and assessment mechanisms (to enhance staff performance and increase awareness).

By introducing these initiatives into the workforce, it may be possible for the RBS to encourage employee involvement, thereby maximising the contribution made by employees. The direct effect of involvement in the organisation is expected to be an increase in the individual employee's commitment to the workplace or the job (one of the four important categories under the Harvard model). This commitment will hopefully be reflected in increased productivity, lower labour turnover and reduced absenteeism. For the RBS this empowerment of employees may also call for new skills on the part of both the managers and employees and it will be the role of the HRM function to try to successfully implement these changes. The HRM department will be involved in designing policies and procedures to encourage employee involvement in line with the overall strategic plan of the RBS. For example, managers may need training in the techniques of participative management if they have been used to a control management style, and employees may require confidence-building sessions and training in decision making. This departure from a control culture which focuses upon close supervision can also have an impact on organisational structures; for example, the tall hierarchies with numerous reporting levels, traditionally associated with companies like the RBS, may need to be replaced by the more modern, flatter structures which better facilitate empowerment.

A further component of the external environment that HRM specialists within the RBS need to consider involves the workforce and the changes that are occurring within it. For example, the British labour force has increased by 1.6 million people over the past decade (i.e. from 27.8 to 29.4 million), with an estimated 1.3 million of this increase being women, so that by 2006 women will represent 46% of the entire British labour force. These statistics arguably highlight the importance to the HRM department of the RBS of effectively utilising programmes for managing diversity among its workforce, whereby women and other minority employees receive support, recognition and the same opportunities as non-minority workers.

The increasing proportion of women in the workforce may be attributed in part to socio-economic influences such as the social acceptability of women in employment and the growing availability of part-time work. These factors may oblige the RBS to adopt more open approaches to recruitment and to consider the necessity of providing more extensive training. It will be the role of the HRM department to proactively implement strategies to successfully manage diversity amongst the workforce. This may involve addressing stereotypes to ensure that a job does not become 'sex-typed' (i.e. deemed appropriate only for one gender) and developing gender-neutral job titles to encourage both male and female applicants.

Case Study 13.2 continued

The HRM department of the RBS might be requested to undertake a thorough analysis of the internal environment in order for the organisation to retain its competitive edge. These internal influences may include: the company's strategy, objectives and values; the leadership styles and goals of top management; the organisational structure, size and culture; and the nature of the business.

Questions

1 Outline the strategic implications of this case study for the HRM function within an organisation.

2 Can you identify policies which might support the four outcomes identified in the Harvard model, namely commitment, competence, congruence and cost efficiencies?

HRM and line management

A *line manager* is the person with direct responsibility for employees and their work. Although the job specification of line managers is likely to focus on task completion of employees within designated functional areas (marketing, administration etc.) they will invariably acquire responsibilities for the personal development of employees, not least when involved in staff appraisal. Line managers seem increasingly to be involved in training and recruitment issues within the modern organisation.

In practice, only those at the highest levels of responsibility for the HRM function within an organisation will be involved in board-level meetings where strategic options are discussed. Nevertheless, those involved in the HRM function at *all* levels are expected to subscribe to the view that competitive advantages for an organisation can best be developed by maximising the potential of its employees.

HRM responsibilities

Despite the concern to avoid excessively task-specific responsibilities, HRM specialists are invariably deployed on certain functional activities within organisations, including the following:

- recruitment and selection
- training and development
- human resource planning
- provision of contracts

Table 13.4 Main activities of human resource/personnel specialists

Activity of human resource specialists	Types of involvement of the human resource specialist	Type of involvement of the line manager
Recruitment and selection	Design of policies and procedure for fair recruitment and selection in order to contribute to the fulfilment of the organisation's corporate strategy. Carry out interviews or monitor and give advice on interview technique or on terms and conditions of employment	Carry out interviews
Training and development	Involved in planning the training and development opportunities for the whole organisation, to meet the needs of the organisation as expressed in its strategic plan and to meet the needs of individuals. May design and organise training courses for groups and sometimes run them. May keep training records centrally and request information from line managers as part of planning exercise or to monitor success of training and development.	May also be involved in planning and provision of training and development opportunities to meet the needs of individuals and the needs of the organisation as expressed in its strategic plan, primarily for employees in his or her own department. May provide training and may also keep records of training and provide information to central personnel/HRM department
Human resource planning	Depending on the level of appointment, is likely to be involved to various degrees in contributing to the strategic plan. Collection and analysis of data, monitoring targets for the whole organisation. Providing information to managers. Conducting exit interviews and analysing reasons for leaving	Collect information on leavers and provide information on anticipated requirements for manpower for his or her department
Assessing performance of employees	Involvement in design and implementation of techniques to assess performance of employees effectively in a way that links clearly with the organisation's strategic plan. Train, inform and involve people in performance management techniques. Monitor the effectiveness of the procedures. May maintain central records about performance of individual employees	Contribute to discussion of performance management techniques. Assess performance of those in own department. Involve teams and individuals in setting and agreeing targets and monitoring performance. Monitor their success and give feedback
Payment and reward of employees	Establish appropriate payment and reward systems for all employees in order to contribute to the organisation's strategic plan. Monitor the success of these. Collect comparative data for other organisations. Deal with individual problems about pay. May be involved in negotiations about payment or rewards systems. Tell individuals of their level of pay when they join the organisation or change jobs. May deal with individual problems or complaints about pay	May be involved in and contribute views about appropriate systems of payment or reward to be used in the organisation. May be involved innegotiation to some extent over issues relating to own department. May deal with problems concerning pay, raised by employees in his or her department in the first instance
Encouraging involvement	Will have an extremely important role in creating a culture within the organisation in which employees are encouraged to be involved in decision making. Will be involved in designing policy and procedures to encourage employee involvement in line with strategic plan. Will provide training to encourage employee involvement	Will contribute to organisation's policies and will encourage involvement of employees in his or her department

Source: Adapted from Foot, M. and Hook, C. (2002) *Introducing Human Resource Management*, 3rd Ed., FT/Prentice Hall

- provision of fair treatment
- provision of equal opportunities
- assessing performance of employees
- employee counselling
- employee welfare
- payment and reward of employees
- health and safety
- disciplining individuals
- dealing with grievances
- dismissal
- redundancy
- negotiation
- encouraging involvement.

Table 13.4 selects six of these functional activities and considers the respective responsibilities of HRM specialists and line managers.

In undertaking these tasks the HRM specialist will, in effect, be seeking to put into practice well-established principles involving managing people effectively. Box 13.2 outlines some of these principles in the particular context of motivation.

Box 13.2 **Motivation theory and HRM**

The human relations approach to management relied heavily on the work of Elton Mayo, who undertook work on the link between productivity and working conditions. He found that productivity rose even when working conditions deteriorated. Mayo conducted a whole series of experiments at the Hawthorne Plant of General Electric between 1927 and 1932. His conclusions were as follows.

- *Work pacing*. The pace at which people produce is one set informally by the work group.
- *Recognition*. Acknowledgement of an employee's contribution by those in authority tends to increase output, as do other forms of social approval.
- *Social interaction*. The opportunities provided by the working situation for social interaction between fellow workers, especially if they could select for interaction those with whom they were compatible, enhanced job satisfaction and sometimes influenced output.
- *The Hawthorne effect*. Regardless of what changes were made to the way the employees were treated, productivity went up as they seemed to enjoy the novelty of the situation and the extra attention – the so-called 'Hawthorne effect'.
- *Grievances*. Employees responded well to having someone to whom to let off steam by talking through problems they were having.
- *Conforming*. The pressure from workmates in the group was far more influential on behaviour than any incentive from management.

The importance of this work was to show the effect of work groups and social context on behaviour. It also helped to generate new ideas about the nature of supervision to include better communication and better management of people. It was perhaps most important in recognising the critical nature of informal processes at work as well as the rational, scientific procedures that management prescribes, the latter being the conclusions from earlier work by F. W. Taylor.

Maslow and 'hierarchy of needs'

Maslow argued that workers have a 'hierarchy of needs' (Figure 13.2). The first three needs, physiological, safety and social needs, are identified as *lower-order* needs and are satisfied from the *context* within which the job is undertaken. Self-esteem and self-actualisation are identified as *higher-order needs* and are met through the *content* of the job.

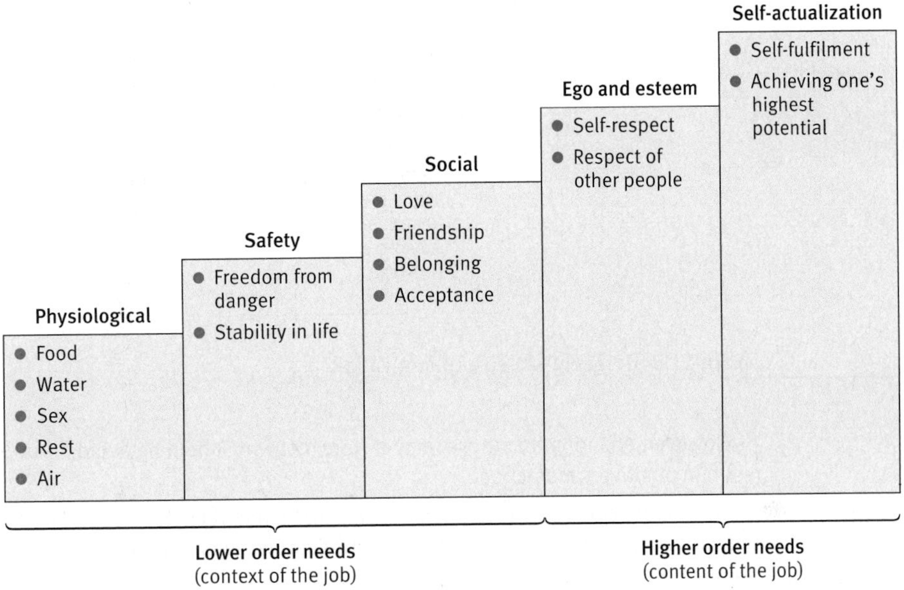

Fig 13.2 Maslow's 'hierarchy of needs'

Maslow went further. He argued that at any one time one need is dominant and acts as a motivator. However, once that need is satisfied it will no longer motivate, but be replaced by the next higher-level need.

The implications of this theory for managers including their having to try to satisfy their workers' needs both in terms of the organisational context in which work takes place and what the worker is required to do. Some examples of how this might be achieved include:

- *physiological* – pay, rest periods, holidays;
- *safety* – health and safety measures, employment security, pensions;
- *social* – formal and informal groups, social events, sports clubs;
- *self-esteem* – power, titles, status symbols, promotion.

Herzberg and the 'two factor theory'

Herzberg's 'two factor theory' was based on a survey of what made managers feel good or bad about their job. He discovered that the factors which created dissatisfaction about the job related to the context within which the job was done. He termed these factors 'hygiene factors', as indicated in Figure 13.3.

Hygiene factors (avoid dissatisfaction)

- Company policy
- Supervision
- Working conditions
- Salary
- Relationship with peers
- Personal life
- Relationship with subordinates
- Status
- Security

Motivators (create satisfaction)

- Achievement
- Recognition
- Work itself
- Responsibility
- Advancement
- Growth

Fig 13.3 Herzberg's theory of motivation

However, ensuring that these factors were met whilst helping avoid dissatisfaction did not result in positive satisfaction.

The factors contributing to positive job satisfaction related more to the content of the job. The presence of each of these factors (motivators) was capable of causing high levels of satisfaction.

The implications for the practising human resource manager were twofold. First, to ensure that the hygiene factors are met adequately to avoid dissatisfaction, but not to expect these to motivate employees. Second, to ensure that the motivators are met to create positive job satisfaction.

Checkpoint 2 Can you suggest any other ways in which motivational theory might be of practical use to the HRM specialist?

Activity 13.2 provides some self-check questions on the HRM function.

LINKS

For more on HRM in an international context see Chapter 14, pp. 555–559.

Activity 13.2

1 Examine three advertisements for jobs in personal management/human resource management. Make a list of the range of activities described in those job advertisements. Are there any differences in approach and duties shown by those advertising for human resource managers and those advertising for personnel managers?

2 Try out the websites given below and find out more about issues of concern to those involved in human resource management in the UK.
www.dti.gov.uk
The Department for Trade and Industry (many useful DTI publications, discussion documents and booklets can be found on this site).
www.open.gov.uk
The government (useful information site, especially for the text of legislation).
www.tuc.org.uk
The Trade Union Congress (this gives the TUC's views on many current HRM issues and new legislation in Britain).
www.cipd.co.uk
The Chartered Institute of Personnel and Development (the website for the professional body that represents personnel and development professionals in the UK).
www.incomesdata.co.uk
Incomes Data Services Limited (some very useful articles on a range of HRM topics, including a section on management pay and remuneration, plus lists of context for IDS publications).
www.peoplemanagement.co.uk
People Management (journal produced on behalf of the CIPD with topical articles relating to personnel management issues).

3 David works for a medium-sized company in the human resources department. His view is that: 'The human resource is the chief asset of the company. It is also the major cost, taking up over 70% of the business's costs in any one time period. It is therefore essential to gain the maximum possible return from this expenditure. People need to be motivated if they are to be made best use of. Anything which adds to the productivity of individual employees should be seen as an essential ingredient of human resource policy.'

Sarah also works for a medium-sized company in the human resources department. She agrees with John that the human resource is the key resource. She says: 'Human resources should be seen as an asset by the organisation. The organisation needs to look at how it can best meet the needs of this asset in order to help people to develop themselves to the full. By involving people in decision making, it is possible to enable them to help the organisation to develop while meeting their own development needs.'

Questions

(a) Are David and Sarah saying the same thing or can you see a difference in their approach?

(b) How might the views of these two individuals influence the sorts of activities they would undertake in human resource management?

(c) Can you give any specific examples of actions that David might take which would be different to the actions that Sarah would take?

Answers to Checkpoints and Activities can be found on pp. 705–35.

Accounting and management

Accounting has been defined as: the process of identifying, measuring and communicating economic information about an organisation or other entity, in order to permit informed judgements by users of the information. It can be divided into two types, financial accounting and management accounting.

- **Financial accounting.** This is concerned with the production of the principal accounting statements that provide stakeholders in the business (management, employees, shareholders, creditors, consumers and government) with an accurate view of the firm's financial position. It uses *historic data* and is predominantly backward looking in that it summarises what has happened in the previous accounting period. The principal output would include profit and loss accounts, balance sheets and cash flow statements.
- **Management accounting.** This generates information for internal use to aid the analysis, planning and control of the firm's activities. Management accountants are principally *forward looking*, acting as 'information providers' to senior management. This information might be in the form of financial forecasts, budgets, contribution statements and break-even charts.

NOTE

All businesses have a legal obligation to produce a set of accounts even if it is only for tax purposes. Private limited companies and PLC's must file a set of accounts each year with the Registrar of Companies, which is then available for public scrutiny. See Black, G. (2005) for more detail on the content of this section.

Together the two types of accounting provide insights for stakeholders into the success or failure of *past* decisions and operations and help management be better aware of the *future* opportunities and difficulties likely to be encountered.

Accounting concepts and conventions

Concepts

There are four fundamental concepts that underlie the production of a set of accounts.

- *Going concern* – assumes the business will continue to trade 'for the foreseeable future'.
- *Accruals or matching principle* – relates revenues and costs to the period in which they occur.
- *Prudence or conservatism* – avoids an over-optimistic view of the performance of the business; the accountant recognises revenue only when it is realised in an acceptable form but provides for all expenses and losses as soon as they are known.
- *Consistency* – maintains the same approach to asset valuation and the allocation of costs so that comparisons can be made over time.

Conventions

Many accounting conventions have been adopted over time as tried and tested general rules. Here are five key accounting conventions.

- *Objectivity* – accounts are based on measurable facts that can be verified.
- *Separate entity* – the company is recognised as a legal person in its own right, entirely separate from its managers and owners.
- *Money measurement* – all assets and liabilities are expressed in money terms.
- *Historic cost* – all valuations are based on the original cost rather than current worth. Where items fall in value through use, they are depreciated or written down in value. This gives the company an objective valuation of its assets.
- *Double entry* – all transactions involve two sides: giving and receiving. This is acknowledged in the double-entry system of bookkeeping where the source of funds is balanced by the use made of them.

Legal requirements

The *Companies Acts of 1985 and 1989* contain regulations which limited companies must follow in the preparation of their published financial information statements. The main points are:

- Public limited companies and some larger private limited companies must have their accounts independently audited and confirmed by the auditors that they represent a 'true and fair view'.
- A set of accounts must be sent to shareholders and also made available for public scrutiny at Companies House.

The concepts and conventions which shape the presentation of the accounts have become a matter of intense debate following recent corporate 'scandals'. Case Study 13.3 indicates how important it is for businesses and individuals that sensible decisions are made as to these accounting standards.

Case Study 13.3 Why accounting standards matter! FT

In Britain, many companies are issuing alarming figures showing deficits in their pension funds. The sobering financial transparency provided to UK employees may soon spread to other countries. The International Accounting Standards Board is seeking a global convergence on an agreed standard for accounting for pensions – and is modelling its proposals largely on rules recently introduced in the UK.

Sir David Tweedie, IASB chairman, wrote FRS 17, as the UK rule is known, when he was head of the UK Accounting Standards Board. In the 20 months since it came into force, some companies have blamed it for forcing the closure of their relatively generous defined benefit pension schemes. But Sir David has no regrets. 'I think it is one of the best things we have done,' he says.

Like the IASB's standard on financial instruments, the new rule on pensions is expected to put a heavy emphasis on 'fair value' accounting. As a result, it may run into opposition. Under FRS 17, the measurement of the assets in a defined benefit

Case Study 13.3 continued

pension scheme should reflect their fair or market value. FRS 17 also tells accountants how to arrive at the present value for future liabilities; it tots them up and discounts back at an interest rate equal to that on AA-rated corporate bonds.

According to WM Company, a performance measurement consultancy owned by State Street, the US bank, British pension funds lost about £100bn ($160bn) in 2002. Morgan Stanley says the gap between pension liabilities of companies in the FTSE 100 index and assets available to meet them widened to £85bn at the end of January 2003. Credit ratings agencies are responding to FRS 17 by downgrading the debt of companies such as BAE Systems, the defence group, where they have concerns about pension deficits. 'They have got the same problems in America – funds in deficit,' Sir David argues. '[But] it is not visible.'

Many UK employers, however, argue that FRS 17 is misleading: although a pension shortfall is presented as a liability, it is not one about to come due in full any time soon. Companies have used FRS 17 since mid-2001, after stock markets began falling. If stock markets start rising, the gaping holes in many pension funds will be reversed; indeed, a rise in interest rates may have a similar impact.

Sir David refutes the idea that the deficit or surplus in a pension scheme has only limited utility because it is a snapshot at the end of a company's fiscal year. He highlights how under FRS 17 companies are required to put figures in their annual reports that set out the scheme's trend position over five years.

He also challenges companies to assert that deficits are a temporary blip. 'If it is not, you are going to have to take cash – which might have gone on dividends and investments – and put it into your pension fund. People should know that.'

Sir David's successor at the UK Accounting Standards Board decided last year to delay bringing FRS 17 into full force pending the outcome of the IASB's deliberations on a new global standard on pensions. The move followed an intensive campaign against the accounting rule by employer organisations and trade unions and pressure from the UK government.

But the sting in the tail is that the international rule may turn out to be even tougher than FRS 17: the IASB voted in January to ban the practice of reflecting projected rates of returns on pension fund assets in income statements. At present, companies are allowed to reflect anticipated gains in the profit and loss statement.

Some US companies in particular use estimates viewed as recklessly optimistic. FRS 17 does allow some leeway: the IASB may be stricter.

Source: *Financial Times*, 10 March 2003. Reprinted with permission

Questions

1 Outline the case for and against the FRS17 rule on pensions in the UK.

2 Why might a similar rule under consideration by the IASB create still more problems?

The **annual report** of a public limited company (PLC) will include the following components:

- *Chairman's statement* – a general review of the past period of trading, comments on market conditions and an assessment of future prospects.
- *The Directors' Report* – a more detailed report on the company's activities and policies.
- *A profit and loss account, balance sheet* and *cash flow statement.*
- *Notes to the accounts* – further explanation of the figures in the main financial statements.
- *Auditor's report* – an inspection of the accounts on behalf of the shareholders to ensure truth and fairness.

Checkpoint 3 Can you suggest who might benefit from the annual report?

Here we consider the various accounts included within the annual report, closely following the work of Brindley, B. and Buckley, M. (2004).

Profit and loss (P&L) account

This summarises the income and expenditure of a specified period, showing whether the organisation has made a profit or loss. Careful examination can reveal how effectively the business is coping with the market and any changes in it. Examining the P&L over several years will help identify the trend for sales, costs and profitability.

The profit and loss (P&L) account is in three parts.

1. The trading account

The trading account shows whether or not the firm is making a gross profit from its core activities. It includes the revenue from sales (also referred to as turnover) minus the direct cost of production (the cost of goods sold). In order to conform to the 'matching principle' only the cost of those goods actually sold must be included. To achieve this the following formula is used:

Opening stock
\+ Purchases
– Closing stock
= Cost of goods sold

This takes account of the stock brought forward from the previous year and available for sale, and the stock left unsold at the end of the year.

The format for the trading account is:

	£m
Sales turnover	180
Less cost of goods sold	90
Gross profit	90

If cost of goods sold exceeds turnover a 'gross loss' is made.

2. The profit and loss account

The second of these three parts has the name of the whole account. It shows whether the firm makes an operating profit, when all other expenses are deducted from the gross profit, such as administration, selling costs and depreciation. This is a useful indicator of the trading performance of the business. To this figure must be added any non-operating revenue, which then gives us the *profit before interest and tax (PBIT)*. Interest payable is then deducted to give the *profit liable to tax*. Interest is dealt with as a separate item, as it reflects how the company is financed rather than how it carries on its core business.

The format for the profit and loss account is:

	£m
Gross profit	60
Less expenses	25
Operating profit	35
Add non-operating income	10
Profit before interest and tax (PBIT)	45
Less interest	4
Profit before tax	41

3. The appropriation account

The appropriation account explains how the profit after tax is used. The after-tax profit could be used to pay dividends to shareholders or to keep as retained or undistributed profits (reserves) for future use in the business. Shareholders generally expect dividends to rise in line with any improvement in the performance of the business. Management, however, may want to retain profit to help expand the business.

The format for the appropriation account is:

	£m
Profit before tax	60
Tax	22
Profit after tax	38
Dividends	14
Retained profit	24

Balance sheet

The balance sheet is a financial snapshot of the business on a particular date. It illustrates an organisation's resources in terms of what it owns (*assets*) and what it owes (*liabilities*). The balance sheet is important because it illustrates the financial health of the business. It shows whether the business can meet its short- and long-term debts and by allowing comparisons to be made with earlier balance sheets, it also reveals any changes taking place in the business.

The double entry system

Double entry bookkeeping is a system of accounting that recognises that all transactions have a dual nature, a giving and a receiving. Each event is recorded in two accounts as a *debit* in one and a *credit* in another. For example, £2,000 spent on materials will reduce cash by £2,000 but increase stock by £2,000, leaving the balance sheet in balance.

Assets and liabilities

Assets are the items that the business 'owns'. They can be classified according to how long the business expects to use them.

- *Fixed assets*: assets that are to be used for more than a year, for example machinery, vehicles and buildings.
- *Current assets*: short-term assets whose value changes frequently during the year, for example stock, debtors and cash.

Liabilities are the amounts that the business owes and can be classified as follows.

- *Current liabilities*: those debts that have to be paid within 12 months and may consist typically of creditors, overdrafts, declared dividends and tax due.
- *Long-term liabilities*: money owed by the firm that has more than a year to maturity, such as bank loans and debentures.
- *Shareholders funds*: money or resources invested by the shareholders for long-term use by the business, such as share capital and retained profit.

Use of funds

The *top half* of a vertical balance sheet displays the assets that a business owns less its current liabilities at the bottom. It is normally set out in a two-column format, so that individual items can be shown on the left, leaving the main totals to be seen clearly on the right (values in brackets are to be deducted).

Balance sheet as at 31/12/2004

	£m	£m
Fixed assets		
Land + buildings	50	
Machinery + vehicles	4	54
Current assets		
Stock	26	
Debtors	6	
Cash	4	
	36	
Less: Current liabilities	(26)	
Net current assets (working capital)		10
Assets employed		64

Source of funds

For a limited company, assets employed are matched by share capital, reserves and possibly long-term loans.

	£m	£m
Financed by:		
Shareholders' funds		
Ordinary share capital	18	
Retained profit	9	27
Long term liabilities		
Bank loan	6	
Mortgage	8	14
Capital employed		41

The balance between permanent capital provided by shareholders and borrowed funds ('gearing') is important. Too much borrowing places an interest burden on the business that legally must be met.

Working capital

Working capital is defined as current assets minus current liabilities. It is vitally important as many businesses fail not because they are unprofitable but because they lack sufficient liquid assets to pay their short-term debts. Small companies are often affected when they expand too quickly. Cash is needed immediately to pay for extra materials and labour but problems arise when the increased sales are on credit. This situation forces the business to increase overdrafts or loans. This raises the firm's costs and places it at risk from a rise in interest rates.

The cash flow statement

Even profitable businesses can fail due to their inability to find enough cash to pay their creditors, so a third statement is produced which concentrates on changes in the *liquidity* of the company during the financial period. Liquidity is the ability of a company to access enough cash and bank resources to meet liabilities as they fall due, and the statement focuses on the overall change in cash balances during the financial period. The cash flow statement usually breaks down information into cash flows from operating activities (e.g. trading), investing activities (e.g. buying and selling fixed assets) and financing activities (e.g. issue of shares, raising or repaying loans).

Ratio analysis

This involves the examination of accounting data to gain understanding of the financial performance of a company. It is useful to all stakeholders as it provides insights into the performance, financial liquidity and shareholder returns of the business over time.

The construction of several simple ratios from the information contained within the balance sheet can give a clear assessment of the company's performance by making the following comparisons:

- with its own performance in previous time periods;
- with that of other companies in the same sector; and/or
- with accepted standards of performance, i.e. with particular values ('norms') for each ratio.

For illustration we present the Tesco performance in 2003 for these various ratios.

Profitability ratios

Profitability ratios measure the relationship between profit in its various forms and sales, assets and capital employed.

- *Gross profit margin* – this ratio examines the relationship between profit (before overheads are taken into account) and sales.

  $$\text{Gross profit margin} = \frac{\text{Gross profit}}{\text{Sales}} \times 100\%$$

  Tesco's gross profit margin of 6% compares favourably with the 4% typical for food retailers.

- *ROCE (Return On Capital Employed)* – this is the most important ratio as it measures the efficiency with which the business generates profits from the capital invested in it.

  $$\text{ROCE} = \frac{\text{Operating profit}}{\text{Capital employed}} \times 100\%$$

  Tesco's ROCE ratio is a healthy 10%.

These profitability ratios provide a picture of the profitability and efficiency of the business.

Activity ratios

Activity ratios measure how well a firm manages it resources.

- *Stock turnover* – this measures how long it takes for a firm to sell and replace its stock. Each time the stock is sold it generates more profit so the aim is to turn the stock over as quickly as possible. The ratio can be expressed as a number of days or as a number of times per year.

  $$\text{Stock turnover} = \frac{\text{Stock}}{\text{Sales}} \times 365 \text{ days}$$

This ratio will vary widely according to the sector of economic activity. Tesco's stock turnover ratio is less than 4%, suggesting that their stock is sold entirely every 14 days.

- *Debtor turnover* – this measures how quickly debtors are paying their bills, i.e. the average collection period.

$$\text{Debtor turnover} = \frac{\text{Debtors}}{\text{Sales}} \times 365 \text{ days}$$

Supermarkets have hardly any debtors since goods are paid for on a cash-and-carry basis, giving a debtors turnover ratio of below 2%.

Liquidity ratios

Liquidity ratios provide a measure of risk, as they are concerned with the short-term financial health of the business. Too little working capital and the business will not be able to meet its debts. However, too much working capital represents an inefficient use of resources.

- *Current ratio*: measures how well short-term assets cover current liabilities. For most businesses a ratio between 1.5 and 2 is ideal.

$$\text{Current ratio} = \frac{\text{Current assets}}{\text{Current liabilities}}$$

$$= \frac{\text{Stocks} + \text{Debtors} + \text{Cash}}{\text{Overdraft} + \text{Creditors} + \text{Taxation} + \text{Dividends}}$$

A ratio of more than 1.5 is not necessarily a sign of strength, since it may mean excessive stocks or debtors, or an uneconomic use of liquid funds. Food retailers are unusual in that their rapid turnovers, together with the cash-and-carry nature of their business, will give relatively low 'stock' and 'debtor' items respectively. In this way 'current assets' will be small and so a very low current ratio is to be expected. Tesco's 2004 figure of around 0.4 must be viewed in this context.

- *Quick assets ratio* (*acid test ratio*). This is a more stringent test of liquidity as it only takes account of current assets that can easily be turned into liquid funds (cash and debtors).

$$\text{Quick assets ratio} = \frac{\text{Current assets} - \text{Stock}}{\text{Current liabilities}}$$

Most firms seek a value of at least 1, though again traders with a rapid turnover of cash sales will have a lower level of current assets and therefore a very low ratio – as with Tesco's 0.5.

Gearing ratio

The gearing ratio focuses on the long-term financial health of the business by showing how reliant it is on borrowings. Highly geared companies have a large interest burden that might prove difficult to sustain in an economic downturn.

$$\text{Gearing ratio} = \frac{\text{Long-term loans}}{\text{Capital employed}} \times 100\%$$

A gearing ratio of around 33% is typical, with a percentage above this reflecting a highly geared company. Tesco is highly geared at around 43%.

Shareholder ratios

Shareholder ratios reflect the returns on investments.

- *Earnings per share* (EPS): a good indicator of management's use of the investors' capital as it measures the profit performance over time.

  $$\text{EPS} = \frac{\text{Net profit after tax}}{\text{Number of ordinary shares}}$$

  Tesco had earnings of around 12 pence per share in 2003, with its share price then around 192 pence. The more highly regarded the company, the higher its P/E ratio, suggesting that the market anticipates a sustained earnings performance over a lengthy period.

- *The price/earnings ratio* (P/E ratio). This is an indicator of investor confidence as it shows the relationship between earnings and the current market price of the share.

  $$\text{P/E ratio} = \frac{\text{Share price}}{\text{Earnings per share (pence)}}$$

  Tesco's P/E ratio is around 16, higher than the average for supermarkets of around 14.

- *Dividend yield*. This is the annual dividend expressed as a percentage of the current market price for shares and shows the return that a new investor could expect. It is easy to compare this ratio to other forms of investment, such as savings accounts.

  $$\text{Dividend yield} = \frac{\text{Dividends per share}}{\text{Market price per share}} \times 100\%$$

  Tesco's dividend yield is around 3%, compared to a supermarket average of around 3.3%. However, Tesco's lower dividend yield reflects the fact that its share price has kept strong relative to supermarkets as a whole.

Shareholders want to see two trends, an increasing return on investment in the form of improved dividends and an increase in the capital value of the investment in the form of a rising share price.

Ratio analysis can provide useful information to all the firm's stakeholders, making possible comparisons with other firms in the same sector of economic activity. However, as we have noted, care must be taken in interpreting the results.

Break-even analysis is another useful source of information for management and stakeholders in general.

Break-even analysis

The idea here is to find that level of output which the firm must achieve if it is to 'break even', i.e. to cover all its costs. The usual assumption is that all relationships are straight line (linear).

Check that you are familiar with the following definitions of revenue, cost and profit. As we shall see, these definitions are widely used in break-even analysis.

- **Total revenue** = Price × Quantity sold
  i.e. $TR = P \times Q$
- **Average revenue** = Revenue per unit sold
  i.e. $AR = \frac{TR}{Q} = P$
- **Total cost** = Total fixed cost + Total variable cost
  i.e. $TC = TFC + TVC$
- **Total profit** = Total revenue − Total cost
  i.e. $TP = TR - TC$

At the break-even level of output, total revenue exactly equals total cost so that total profit is zero.

At Break-even output

$TR = TC$

i.e. $TR = TFC + TVC$

and $TP = TR - TC = 0$

Types of cost

- **Fixed costs.** These are costs that *do not* vary with output, and are sometimes called 'overheads'. Costs such as business rates, lighting, heating are often regarded as fixed costs. Fixed costs are incurred before production begins and are unchanged thereafter.
- **Variable costs.** These are costs that *do* vary with output, and are sometimes called 'running costs'. Costs such as wages, raw materials, energy are often regarded as variable costs.

Costs and linearity

The linearity (straight line) assumption underlying break-even analysis is reflected in the cost lines of Figure 13.4a.

In this example the firm has:

Total fixed costs (TFC) = £50,000
Average variable costs (AVC) = £0.50 per unit

Notice that both TFC and TVC are represented by straight lines with *constant* slopes or gradients.

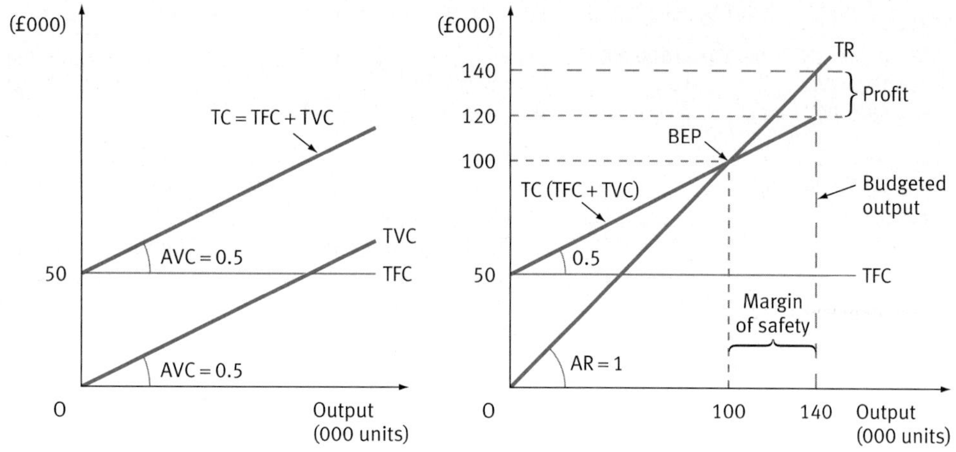

(a) Costs under the linearity assumption

(b) Revenue, costs and profit under the linearity assumption

Fig 13.4 Aspects of break-even analysis

- slope of TFC = zero
- slope of TVC = AVC = 0.50

You should be familiar with the fact that we obtain the TC line by summing vertically the TFC and TVC lines. The slope of TC will be the same as that for TVC, i.e. 0.5.

NB. Since AVC is constant at £0.5 per unit, *marginal cost* (MC) = AVC in this case. In other words, each extra (marginal) unit adds £0.5 to total cost, which is the same as the £0.5 AVC per unit.

Revenue and linearity

Figure 13.4(b) reproduces the cost lines of Figure 13.4(a), together with a total revenue (TR) line drawn on the assumption that the firm can sell each unit at a price (AR) of £1.

Of course, the TR then has a slope (= AR) of 1 and an intercept of zero (since zero output means zero revenue).

NB. Since price (AR) is constant at £1 per unit, *marginal revenue* (MR) = AR in this case. In other words, each extra (marginal) unit adds £1 to total revenue, which is the same as the £1 AR per unit.

Break-even point (BEP)

The **break-even point** (BEP) is often defined as that level of output for which all costs are covered;

i.e. where TR = TC so that TP = zero.

In Figure 13.4(b) we can see that BEP occurs at an output of 100,000 units.

CHECK

$TR = P \times Q = £1 \times 100{,}000 = £100{,}000$
$TC = TFC + TVC$
$\underline{TFC = £50{,}000}$

$TVC = AVC \times Q$
$TVC = £0.5 \times 100{,}000$
$\underline{TVC = £50{,}000}$
i.e. $\underline{TC = £50{,}000 + £50{,}000 = £100{,}000}$

$TP = TR - TC$
i.e. $TP = £100{,}000 - £100{,}000$
$\underline{TP = £0}$

Clearly we can solve for BEP either:

(a) using graphical analysis;
(b) using simple algebra.

Even if we use graphical analysis, simple algebra can be a useful check on our solution.

The following expressions will help our calculations of BEP.

Contribution per unit. This tells the firm what each unit of output is contributing (over and above the variable costs of its production) to the fixed costs already incurred.

$$\text{Contribution per unit (C/U)} = \text{Price (AR)} - \text{AVC}$$

We can now express the break-even point (BEP) as:

$$\text{BEP} = \frac{\text{Total fixed costs}}{\text{Contribution per unit}}$$

In our example:

$$\text{C/U} = £1 - £0.5$$
$$\text{C/U} = £0.5$$
$$\text{BEP} = \frac{\text{TFC}}{\text{C/U}} = \frac{£50{,}000}{£0.5} = 100{,}000 \text{ units}$$

In other words, the firm must produce 100,000 units if it is to earn sufficient revenue over and above its variable costs to cover the £50,000 of fixed costs already incurred.

Budgeted output

Budgeted output is the level of output the firm intends (budgets) to produce. One would normally expect the budgeted output to be *greater than* the BEP.

Suppose the budgeted output in Figure 13.4(b) is 140,000 units. At this budgeted output:

$$\text{TR} = \text{P} \times \text{Q} = £1 \times 140{,}000 = £140{,}000$$
$$\text{TC} = \text{TFC} + \text{TVC}$$
$$= £50{,}000 + (140{,}000 \times £0.5)$$
$$= £50{,}000 + £70{,}000 = £120{,}000$$
$$\text{TP} = \text{TR} - \text{TC}$$
$$\text{TP} = £140{,}000 - £120{,}000$$
$$\underline{\text{TP} = £20{,}000 \text{ at budgeted output}}$$

In other words, at a budgeted output of 140,000 units, the firm can expect to earn a total profit (TP) of £20,000, as can be seen in Figure 13.4(b).

Margin of safety

The firm will usually seek to operate with some margin of safety, here defined as the difference between budgeted (intended) output and the break-even output.

$$\text{Margin of safety} = \text{Budgeted output} - \text{Break-even output}$$

In Figure 13.4(b)

$$\text{Margin of safety} = 140{,}000 - 100{,}000$$

$$\underline{\text{Margin of safety} = 40{,}000 \text{ units}}$$

The margin of safety is often expressed as a *percentage of the budgeted output.*

$$\text{Margin of safety (\%)} = \frac{\text{Budgeted output} - \text{BEP}}{\text{Budgeted output}} \times 100$$

$$\text{i.e. Margin of safety} = \frac{40{,}000}{140{,}000} \times 100$$

$$\underline{\text{Margin of safety} = 28.6\%}$$

This tells us that the output of the firm can fall by as much as 28.6% *below* its budgeted output and still break even or better.

In other words, the margin of safety is a useful measure of *risk*. The larger the margin of safety, the lower the risk of indebtedness should unexpected events cause the firm to fall short of the budgeted output.

Activity 13.3 gives you an opportunity to check some of these aspects of accounting and management.

Activity 13.3

1 If the current assets exceed the current liabilities, we can definitely say that:

(a) the business has made a profit;
(b) fixed assets are greater than current assets;
(c) the current ratio is over 1 : 1;
(d) the acid test ratio is over 1 : 1.

2 A limited company has a very low gearing level. Which of the following statements best describes that company?

(a) It has few borrowings.
(b) It is a very risky company.
(c) It has high borrowings.
(d) It has very high fixed assets.

3 If a company's shares are stated to have a P/E ratio of 15 times, which of the following statements is certain about that company?

(a) The share price is fifteen times the dividend per share.
(b) The dividend is fifteen times the profits per share after tax.
(c) The dividend is fifteen times the profits per share before tax.
(d) The share price is fifteen times the earnings per share.

4 A company's sales total £600,000, its debtors £40,000 and its creditors £60,000. Which one of the following is correct?

(a) Debtors collection period is 36.5 days and its creditor payment period is 24.3 days.
(b) Debtors collection period is 24.3 days and its creditor payment period is 36.5 days.
(c) Debtors collection period is 73 days and its creditor payment period is 36.5 days.
(d) Debtors collection period is 46.6 days and its creditor payment period is 73 days.

5 Which of the following most accurately describes a profit and loss account?

(a) All income less all expenses
(b) All cash received less all cash paid
(c) All assets less all liabilities
(d) All income less all cash paid

6 A company sells a product which has a variable cost of £3 a unit. Fixed costs are £10,000. It has been estimated that if the price is set at £5 a unit, the sales volume will be 10,000 units; whereas if the price is reduced to £4 a unit, the sales volume will rise to 15,000.

(a) Draw a break-even chart covering each of the possible sales prices, and state the budgeted profits, the break-even points and the margins of safety.
(b) Compare the two possible situations. Consider the assumptions and limitations of your analysis.

Answers to Checkpoints and Activities can be found on pp. 705–35.

Key Terms

Break-even point That output at which all costs are covered.

Desk research: The collection of secondary data.

Gearing ratio Reflects the financial risk to which the company is subject. It is the ratio of external borrowing to total capital employed.

'Hierarchy of needs' Maslow's theory of motivation suggesting 'lower' and 'higher' order needs.

Liquidity ratios Give an indication of the availability of cash or readily marketable assets to meet current (short-term) liabilities. Include current ratio and quick assets (acid test) ratio.

Margin of safety The difference between budgeted (intended) output and the break-even point. Serves as an indicator of risk.

Market segmentation Groups of consumers with similar characteristics. Occupational classifications (A, B, C_1, C_2, D and E) are widely used.

Marketing mix The marketing tools that an organisation can use to influence demand (product, price, promotion and place).

Operating ratios Can be used to assess the efficiency with which various aspects of the operations of the business are managed. Include stock turnover ratio, debtors' turnover ratio and creditors turnover ratio.

Penetration pricing Low price to secure market share.

Prestige pricing High price associated with high quality.

Price discrimination Charging different prices for an identical product to different markets.

Price skimming High price to 'cream off' those committed to purchasing the product.

Primary data New data collected for a specific project.

Product life cycle A model for describing the common patterns of sales growth and decline over the lifetime of a product.

Product-line pricing Prices are set for each item with the whole of the product line in mind.

Profitability ratios Include profit margin and return on assets ratios (also known as the return on capital employed ROCE).

Pull strategy Promotional activity that aims to stimulate demand in customers to 'pull' goods through the distributional system.

Push strategy Promotional activity that targets distribution intermediaries in order to 'push' goods through the system.

Secondary data Data which already exists in published form.

Key Points

- The 'marketing mix' involves price, product, promotion and place.
- Field and desk research, using primary and secondary data, are key elements in market research.
- Segmentation of markets into groups with similar characteristics helps marketers better understand buyer behaviour.
- HRM specialists have an important strategic role within the business as well as personnel-related responsibilities.
- HRM specialists can more effectively influence productivity and job satisfaction within an organisation by being aware of the various theories of motivation.
- All limited companies in the UK have to publish financial information.
- All PLC's have to appoint an independent auditor to report to the shareholders on the truth and fairness of the financial statements.
- The majority of the financial information contained within the annual report is required by either legislation (the Companies Act), Stock Exchange regulations or accounting standards.
- Important financial statements include the balance sheet, the profit and loss account and the cash flow statement which provide still further information via various accounting ratios.
- Break-even analysis gives the firm and investors some idea of the level of risk associated with the firm's operations.

Assessment Practice

Multiple choice questions

1 **Which of the following is the most usual indicator of social class to the marketer?**

(a) Household size
(b) Car ownership
(c) Occupation
(d) Personality

2 **Which of the following refers to primary data?**

(a) Tables of data published by the government
(b) Tables of data available on the Internet
(c) Tables of data provided by a multinational enterprise
(d) Data resulting from your own questionnaire

3 **'Price skimming' refers to which of the following?**

(a) Setting a low price to gain market share
(b) Setting a high price to maximise revenue
(c) Following the price leadership of another company
(d) Being engaged in 'price warfare'

4 **Effective advertising may result in which of the following?**

(a) A steeper, less elastic demand curve
(b) A flatter, more elastic demand curve
(c) A unit elastic demand curve
(d) A perfectly elastic demand curve

5 **Which of the following statements best sums up the role of the human resource manager in personnel activities?**

(a) The human resource manager is the sole person who should be involved in all personnel activities.
(b) Both the human resource manager and line manager are likely to be involved in differing ways in a range of personnel activities.
(c) The line manager always acts alone in all organisations in dealing with human resource management activities.
(d) The human resource manager is only concerned with personnel activities at a tactical level.

6 **Which of the following statements would be true of the human resource management approach to managing people at work?**

(a) It tackles issues in a piecemeal way.
(b) It relies on traditional forms of communication.
(c) There is not much involvement of the workforce in decision making.
(d) It is strategic.

7 **Which one of the following is one of Herzberg's hygiene factors?**

(a) A reasonable salary
(b) An opportunity to take responsibility in one's place of work
(c) Developing a sense of achievement in the working environment
(d) Recognition in the workplace

8 **How are Herzberg's theory and Maslow's hierarchy of needs model most alike?**

(a) Both theories highlight satisfaction and motivation at work.
(b) The theories were developed at the same time, using similar source data.
(c) The role of hygiene factors in supporting organisational motivation was emphasised in both theories.
(d) Herzberg's theory relates to the higher levels of Maslow's hierarchy.

9 **A high 'gearing ratio' suggests which of the following?**

(a) The company is extremely profitable.
(b) The company potentially has a low interest burden in the long run.
(c) The company potentially has a high interest burden in the long run.
(d) The company is highly liquid.

10 **A good 'margin of safety' occurs when:**

(a) break-even point equals budgeted output
(b) budgeted output falls short of break-even point
(c) budgeted output is well above break-even point
(d) intended output is reduced below break-even point.

Data response and stimulus questions

1 **It was reported by the Office of Fair Trading in 2000 that the production costs of beer and lager were similar but that the price of lager was considerably higher than beer. Nevertheless, over the previous decade, despite the higher price, lager had increased its share of the market from 51% to 61% at beer's expense.**

Question

Can you explain these findings to a marketer who seems to be puzzled at this information?

2 **Read the case and then answer the questions which follow.**

Management and motivation in the Benefits Agency

The Benefits Agency is responsible for delivering a range of UK state benefits to the public. Most Agency staff work in a network of local offices that are organised into district management units. The 159 districts are organised into 13 area units. Each area director is accountable to the Agency's top management team.

The Benefits Agency used to form part of the Department of Social Security (DSS), the largest organisation in the UK Civil Service. Traditionally, the Civil Service provided a secure place to work. Staff usually joined straight from school and were expected to follow precisely defined rules in order to ensure equality of treatment to all citizens. The work was routine, and the Service valued conformist behaviour; innovation was discouraged. The career path was predictable, jobs were secure, and a pension was guaranteed on retirement. The management structure was hierarchical; any unusual problem was referred up to the next level for decision.

In the early 1990s government policy brought radical change; the Benefits Agency would become a separate organisation within the Civil Service. It would conduct the same functions on behalf of government but would be managed differently.

A chief executive was appointed in 1991 on a three-year contract (which in itself sent out signals about the previous jobs for life culture). He defined a new vision: 'To provide the right money to the right person at the right time and the right place.' To deliver this more customer-centred service he gave district managers more control over their budget, thereby reducing control by senior managers at HQ. Management in some areas ignored the new freedoms and continued to manage in the old, hierarchical way.

One of the areas interpreted the freedom as giving authority to make very wide changes. The management board of this area defined their vision as: 'To be the leading provider of Social Security services in the UK.' District managers in this area were encouraged to give more decision-making power to staff dealing with the public, and staff were encouraged to be innovative in their approach. A critical factor in achieving this vision was to have the right number of skilled and motivated staff.

Behaviour that had been valued was now a barrier to promotion. Staff who had hoped to gain promotion by playing the rules now found they had little chance. Some became disillusioned but continued to deliver – at a reduced level of productivity. Some could not adapt and left. Others applied their efforts to a new goal – that of resisting change.

Another group enthusiastically embraced the new culture where innovation, creativity and risk taking were valued. Districts introduced the 'one-stop' approach, so that one member of staff (rather than several) could deal with all the benefits that a person claimed. This led to the creation of multi-function teams, and to big changes in the way staff worked. Staff responded enthusiastically to these changes, even though pay awards were still strictly controlled and promotion opportunities had become fewer.

The mid-1990s brought further changes. A new chief executive was appointed in 1995. In line with the government's policy of controlling public expenditure, the Agency's budget was reduced drastically in 1996. At the same time the National Audit Office, the body responsible for auditing public organisations, criticised the inaccuracy of benefit payments and the scope the system offered for fraud.

The new chief executive amended the Agency's vision to 'pay the right money to the right person at the right time every time'. The top management team became uneasy about the increased freedom of the area directors. Examples of a return to the older structure began to appear, such as the introduction of centrally controlled checking teams and increases in the number of mandatory management checks. Staff in the region reacted with dismay, and management again had the problem of how to create a skilled and motivated staff.

In 1998 another chief executive was appointed. The move towards tighter central control continued but lessons had been learnt. The Agency's senior management recognised that many improvements in service delivery had come from ideas generated by committed individuals with flair and imagination. There was no desire to lose this by going back to the strong command and control approach – but there had to be a balance between innovation and accountability. The Agency continued to encourage motivation but introduced a process to evaluate each idea against business objectives.

On 16 March 2000 the prime minister announced far-reaching reforms to the way the government provides services to people looking for work and claiming benefits. A new Agency, Jobcentre Plus, would be created to combine the Employment Service and those parts of the Benefits Agency dealing with people of working age. This agency will deliver a single, work-focused, integrated service to employers and benefit claimants – helping people into work and helping employers fill their vacancies.

Although the agency is new, the people working in it will transfer from the existing agencies. This means bringing together management and staff of two separate agencies. People who have been used to different cultures, values, personnel policies, pay and promotion structures and management styles will now be working together to create the new organisation. The need to establish common values has been identified by the chief executive of the new agency.

> Both the Benefits Agency and the Employment Service have such values which they have introduced successfully over recent years. But Jobcentre Plus is a new organisation, with different objectives, and we need to build a new set of values to reflect its priorities and interests, and the aspirations of its staff and partners.

This is probably the biggest change that staff in both agencies have encountered. The problem for managers in trying to motivate staff in this changing climate is immense. Staff are uncertain of the future – will the nature of the work change, will new skills be required, will there be job losses, will the staff from one agency be more valued than the other, are all the previous values worth nothing?

Source: Case study adapted from: Boddy, D. (2002) *Management: An Introduction*. Harlow: Pearson Education.

Questions

1 What attracted staff to work in the Benefits Agency before these changes when it used to form part of the DSS?

2 How are they likely to have reacted to the changes introduced in 1991?

3 What rewards did management of the Benefits Agency use when it was operating as part of the Department of Social Security?

4 How were these different after the change in approach?

5 How did staff react to the changes?

6 Why might staff feel demotivated when told about the creation of the new agency, Jobcentre Plus?

7 Make recommendations to the managers in terms of motivating staff within this changing climate.

8 Are any theories of motivation relevant to this situation?

3 Price earnings ratio

Read the text below, then answer the question which follows.

When comparing the performance of national or international businesses, the price/earnings ratio of the company is often compared against that of its rivals in the sector of economic activity in question and that for all shares in the Financial Times top 100 companies. Here we consider the case of Tesco PLC.

Price/earnings ratio: Tesco 15.6, Sector 14.23, All-Share 19.36

$$\text{P/E ratio} = \frac{\text{Share price}}{\text{Earnings per share}}$$

where earnings per share is profit after tax divided by the number of ordinary shares.

The price/earnings (P/E) ratio is the most important single measure of how the market views the company and is the most common means of comparing the market values of different shares. The P/E ratio tells us the number of times the market price exceeds the last reported earnings. The more highly regarded the company, the higher its P/E ratio, with the market anticipating a sustained earnings performance over a lengthy period. The P/E ratio will depend in part upon the company's past record, but also upon that of the industrial sector of which it is a part, and upon the overall level of the stock market. A P/E ratio of 17–20 was regarded as typical in 2003.

The sector figure of 14.23 for food retailers is itself much lower than average (19.36), and Tesco's own P/E ratio of 15.6 probably indicates market sentiment regarding Tesco's dominant place within the sector whilst recognising the intense competition from other retailers such as J. Sainsbury and Asda. Changes in future expectations will affect both share price and the P/E ratio, of which the share price is the numerator.

Question

What underlying factors might result in a rise in the Tesco price/earnings ratio?

True/False questions

1 Secondary data is derived from original sources by your own investigations.
True/False

2 We segment markets when they have different characteristics which lead to different types of consumer behaviour.
True/False

3 Penetration pricing is most often used in the introduction stage of the product life cycle.
True/False

4 Price is more likely to be reduced if demand is relatively price elastic (i.e. price responsive).
True/False

5 Elton Mayo showed in his experiments on productivity that informal processes at work, including work group interaction, were just as important as work procedures in raising motivation and productivity.
True/False

6 Herzberg's 'hygiene factors' tell us how to create positive job satisfaction.

True/False

7 Maslow tells us that one need will tend to be dominant at any one time but that once it is satisfied it will no longer motivate, and other higher-order needs will need to be met.

True/False

8 Liquidity ratios provide a useful measure of risk in that they are concerned with the short-term financial health of the business.

True/False

9 Total profit is zero at the break-even point.

True/False

10 Assets are the amounts that the business holds.

True/False

Essay questions

1 How might the firm's pricing strategies be influenced by the product life cycle?
2 Consider the case for product differentiation and additional branding activity.
3 How might a knowledge of motivation theory help the HRM specialist in practice?
4 Do you agree with the suggestion that the increasing use of line managers means that we no longer require HRM specialists?
5 Do accounting standards matter? Explain your reasoning.

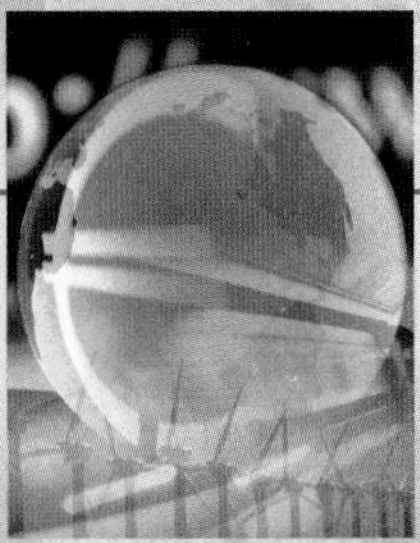

Chapter 14

International business environment

Introduction

How do businesses seek to internationalise their operations and why do so many businesses fail when entering a new international market? Even though many firms opt for an alliance with a foreign partner when entering an international market, many such alliances still fail. Reasons for such high failure rates can largely be attributed to a lack of understanding of the international business environment and the factors that affect how an international company operates.

This chapter takes forward the discussions in Chapter 13, paying particular attention to the *international* business environment, along with how functional areas of management such as marketing and HRM may need to adapt to an international setting. It reviews the increasingly important contribution of the multinational enterprise (MNE) to international business activity and takes an in-depth look at the three major trading regions vital to international business, namely the European Union, North America and the Pacific Rim. Within this so-called 'triad' particular attention is paid to the rapidly developing Chinese economy. Many economists predict that China will eventually become the world's largest economic market, although the country remains an extremely complex international environment, with relatively few foreign companies operating in China experiencing short-term success. Reasons for this will be considered, as well as possible success factors identified. After assessing the role of the World Trade Organisation and other major international institutions in supporting international business, the chapter concludes by reviewing the case of those who advocate free trade in international business and those who advocate protectionism.

Although this and other chapters incorporate a 'globalised' perspective, a more detailed consideration of the characteristics associated with globalisation is undertaken in Chapter 15 (pp. 625–637).

Learning objectives:

By the end of this chapter you should be able to:

- explain the problems companies face when entering a new international market

- understand how marketing, HRM and other management functions must be adjusted to the international business environment if overseas business activities are to be successful
- review the characteristics of the multinational enterprise, its relevance to international business and its approaches to international HRM and international marketing
- examine the importance to international business of the so-called 'triad' consisting of the EU, North America and Pacific Rim regions
- show an understanding of why China is considered a future economic world leader
- identify the arguments involved in the free trade versus protectionism debate and be aware of the role of the key international institutions in promoting international trade and investment.

The internationalisation process

In today's highly competitive markets, many companies see internationalisation as a natural progression from producing solely for the domestic market. There are a number of reasons why firms internationalise. It may be that the domestic market is saturated, or that production (and sales) needs to expand beyond the domestic market in order to achieve lower average costs, or that overseas governments offer attractive incentives for the firm to invest abroad. Figure 14.1 indicates some of the reasons for internationalisation.

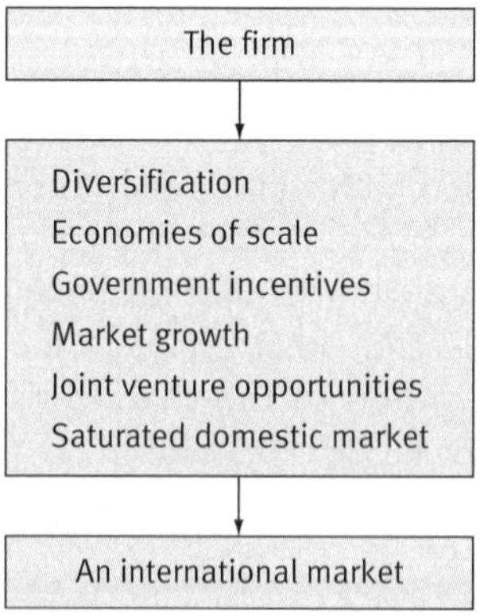

Fig 14.1 Reasons firms internationalise

The difficult question many companies face is not whether to internationalise, but *how* to internationalise. The options regarding the choice of method for internationalisation are reviewed in Table 14.1.

Table 14.1 Stages in the internationalisation process

Stage	Description
Stage 1: Domestic marketing	The firm is only involved in the domestic market and does not export at all
Stage 2: Pre-export	The firm searches for information with a possible view to exporting
Stage 3: Indirect or direct exporting	The firm starts exporting on a small basis, to geographically adjacent and culturally similar countries. Likely mode of entry involves indirect (using an agency) exporting or direct exporting
Stage 4: Active involvement	There is a systematic effort to increase sales through exporting to multiple countries. Likely mode of entry involves joint ventures, licensing or franchising
Stage 5: Committed involvement	The firms depends heavily on foreign markets. Likely mode of entry involves foreign direct investment (fdi)

- After moving beyond domestic marketing, the next stage towards internationalisation is often rather limited, involving a search for information with a possible view to exporting.
- After this 'pre-export' stage the firm may start exporting via an independent agent. Such 'indirect exporting' often involves the agent (e.g. export house, confirming house or buying house) taking responsibility for the physical distribution of products and even for setting up the sales and distribution channels in the foreign market.
- As the firm gains more experience and makes a more long-term commitment to exporting, it may seek to control the export process itself, distributing and selling its own products to the foreign market, i.e. by 'direct' exporting.
- More active involvement might include establishing joint ventures or engaging in licensing or franchising arrangements overseas, especially when more than one country is involved.
- Finally, the firm may reach a point where it sees it as appropriate to commit itself still further by establishing production facilities in one or more foreign country, i.e. becoming a multinational enterprise (MNE).

The internationalisation process very often begins with a firm becoming involved with an international market it readily understands. The level of understanding attributed to an international market can be based on language, a familiarity with the social and lifestyle patterns of behaviour (culture), knowledge of the economy and of the legal and institutional frameworks within the country. The importance of having a network of contacts can also influence the internationalisation process. For example, a firm that already has established suppliers in Taiwan may use this long-term relationship to support possible market entry into that country. The suppliers can advise on market entry procedures, government contacts and the nature of the market. Having a network of close relationships within a country can be the difference between entering or passing over a particular international market.

Example:

UK firms prefer Dublin

Many UK companies prefer entering the Republic of Ireland as an early stage in the internationalisation process. Dublin, in particular, is a thriving business centre that shares many similarities with British cities. Close geographical proximity and language and cultural affinity make it an attractive proposition for UK firms making that first step towards internationalisation.

Methods of internationalisation

We touched on some of these methods in the context of firm growth in Chapter 5. However, the focus here is on their role in the internationalisation process. The various market entry options open to firms considering internationalization are now considered. We note that each carries a varying degree of risk, as indicated in Figure 14.2. Indirect exporting carries the least risk, in that it requires little commitment and resources, while foreign direct investment implies a long-term commitment and can be hugely expensive. However, rewards to firms are often directly related to the degree of risk, with the lowest returns from indirect exporting and the highest returns from fdi.

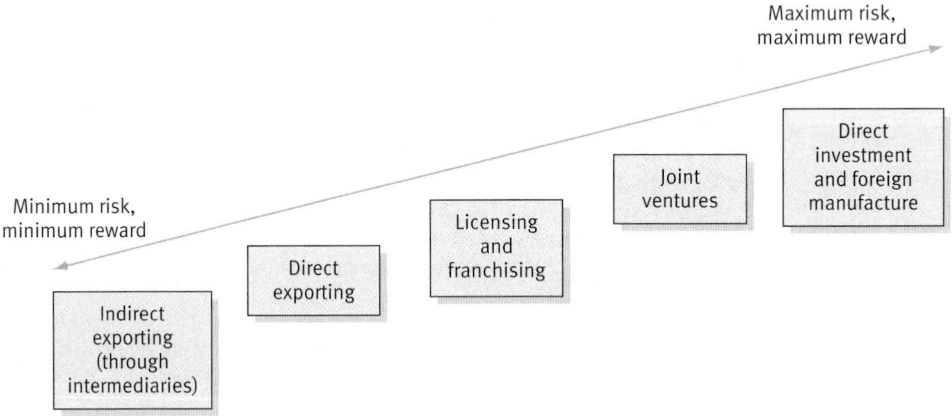

Fig 14.2 Internationalisation methods

Indirect exporting

Indirect exporting happens when a firm does not itself undertake any special international activity but rather operates through intermediaries. Under this approach the exporting function is outsourced to other parties which may prepare the export documentation, take responsibility for the physical distribution of goods and even set up the sales and distribution channels in the foreign market. The role of the intermediary may be played by export houses, confirming houses and buying houses.

- *Export house* buys products from a domestic firm and sells them abroad on its own account.
- *Confirming house* acts for foreign buyers and is paid on a commission basis. Brings sellers and buyers into direct contact (unlike export house) and guaranteed payment will be made to exporter by end user.
- *Buying house* performs similar functions to those of the confirming house but is more active in seeking out sellers to match the buyer's particular needs.

Direct exporting

Direct exporting would typically involve a firm in distributing and selling its own products to the foreign market. This would generally mean a longer-term commitment to a particular foreign market, with the firm choosing local agents and distributors specific to that market. In-house expertise would need to be developed to keep up these contacts, to conduct market research, prepare the necessary documentation and establish local pricing policies. The advantages of such an approach are that it:

- allows the exporter to closely monitor developments and competition in the host market;
- promotes interaction between producer and end-user;
- involves long-term commitments, such as providing after-sales services to encourage repeat purchases.

Franchising

McDonald's and Burger King are perhaps the two best-known examples of international franchises. However, franchising is a very popular method of market entry and is not limited to the fast food industry. Examples include cleaning (Chem-Dry), clothing (Benetton) and childcare (Tiny Tots).

In international franchising, a supplier (*franchiser*) permits a dealer (*franchisee*) the right to market its products and services in that country in exchange for a financial commitment. This commitment usually involves a fee upfront and royalties based on product sales.

- *Advantages for the franchisee* are that they are buying into an existing brand and should receive full support from the franchiser in terms of marketing, training and starting up. When customers walk into a McDonald's restaurant; they know exactly what to expect. This is one advantage of global branding.
- *Disadvantages for the franchisee* include restrictions on what they can and can't do. For example, McDonald's have very strict regulations concerning marketing, pricing, training etc. A franchisee cannot simply change the staff uniform, alter

prices or vary opening hours as the company operates a standardised approach to doing business.

- *Advantages for the franchiser* are that overseas expansion can be much less expensive and that any local adaptations can (with agreement) be made by those well acquainted with cultural issues in that country.
- *Disadvantages for the franchiser* include possible conflict with the franchisee for not following regulations and agreements as well as a threat that the franchisee may opt to 'go it alone' in the future and thus become a direct competitor.

Licensing

This allows one company (the *licensee*) to use the property of some other company (*the licensor*). Very often this relates to intellectual property, e.g. trademarks, patents and copyright (see Chapter 12, p. 470). For example, a medium-sized UK stationery company may decide it wishes to produce a range of stationery based on Walt Disney characters. In order to do this, the company would need to approach Disney and discuss the possibility of gaining a licence to sell Disney branded goods in the UK. The licensee (in this case the UK stationery company) pays a fee to Disney in exchange for the rights to use their brand name/logo.

An advantage of licensing to licensors is that they do not have to make a substantial investment in order to gain a presence in overseas markets and they need not acquire the local knowledge which may be so important for success in such markets. Licensing is also an effective way of increasing levels of brand awareness. However, a licensor can be damaged if a licensee produces products of an inferior standard. Licensing is very common in the film and music industry. Products include calendars, videos, books, posters and clothing.

Joint venture

Narrowly defined, a joint venture occurs when two or more firms pool a portion of their resources within a common legal organisation. A joint venture is popular for firms entering an international market at a large cultural distance (p. 548) from the home market. For example, many Western firms opt for a joint venture when entering China and Taiwan, simply because of major cultural differences, including language, social relationships, style of management and political environment. A joint venture takes place because both firms believe that their partner has something to offer. In the case of a Western firm entering Taiwan, the Western firm is getting access to new markets, a partner with local language and cultural knowledge and an already established network of contacts. It is likely that the Taiwanese firm is in turn expecting to gain access to new technology, to marketing expertise and above all to extra finance from their Western partner. Nevertheless, international joint ventures tend to experience high failure rates.

Two particular types of international joint venture are considered below.

- *Equity joint venture* (EJV). This remains a popular method of market entry for foreign companies with the equity stake by the foreign partner usually not lower than 25% of voting shares. The equity joint venture requires investment from all of the parties who jointly operate it, share the risks of it in accordance with their different proportions of investment, and are jointly held responsible for the profits and losses of it. For companies looking to access a large share of the Chinese market, the establishment of multiple equity joint ventures provides a means for obtaining the connections necessary for doing business in China.

- *Co-operative joint venture* (CJV). This differs from an equity joint venture in that it usually has a profit sharing mechanism rather than equity ownership by each company. Reasons for choosing a cooperative joint venture may include less need to formally value capital contributions, greater flexibility in relation to profit sharing and fewer restrictions on management structure.

Of course, there is a risk that the extent to which each partner relies on the other's skills can change over time, sometimes to such an extent that there may no longer be a need for the international joint venture to continue. Studies have found that, at the time many international joint ventures were formed, each partner admitted that they could not have carried out the task without their partner's help, but that within a short space of time the partners learned so much from each other that they no longer felt the need for shared management. However, international joint ventures can also lead to increased trust and commitment. In Chinese culture, personal trust develops over time and involves 'getting to know' a partner. Past experience between partners is extremely important because it can help develop close long-term relationships built on trust and commitment, which can then lead on to even closer collaboration in the future.

LINKS
Examples and discussions of strategic joint ventures are presented in Chapter 15 (pp. 638–641).

Foreign direct investment (fdi)

Foreign direct investment (fdi) is a high-risk strategy whereby a firm sets up its own facilities in an international market. Some of the problems of joint ventures (especially those involving decision making and culture clashes) can be avoided by wholly owning the foreign subsidiaries. This can be achieved through acquisition of an existing firm or through establishing an entirely new foreign operation ('greenfield' investment).

Acquisition of an existing foreign company has a number of advantages compared to 'greenfield' investment; for example, it allows a more rapid market entry, so that there is a quicker return on capital and a ready access to knowledge of the local market. Because of its rapidity such acquisition can pre-empt a rival's entry into the same market. Further, many of the problems associated with setting up a 'greenfield' site in a foreign country (such as cultural, legal and management issues) can be avoided. By involving a change in ownership, acquisition also avoids costly competitive reactions from the acquired firm.

LINKS
Strategic aspects of mergers and acquisitions policies are considered in more detail on pp. 627–641.

Case Study 14.1 reviews some of the issues involved in the internationalisation process using the example of Portugal.

Case Study 14.1 Internationalisation of Portuguese firms

An important recent development has been the strong surge in Portuguese investment abroad. During the 1990s and the early years of the new millennium Portugal's outward foreign direct investment multiplied at an impressive rate. By 2003 Portugal was among the leading 15 countries that invest overseas, with most of the fdi taking the form of cross-border acquisitions or partnerships. Internationalisation efforts have followed a distinct pattern in terms of their economic geography. Typically the first moves were made into the neighbouring economy, Spain. An example of this 'toe in the water' stage was the acquisition by Cimpor, the leading Portuguese cement maker, of Corporación Noroeste, a Spanish cement maker based in Galicia. The next move was for Portuguese firms as diverse as Cenoura, Petrogal, Transportes Luis Simões and Caixa Geral de Depósitos to penetrate the wider Spanish market. A survey conducted among Portuguese companies found that the priority markets for internationalisation were Spain (69.9%), the former Portuguese African colonies or PALOPs (47.3%), the rest of the EU (38.7%) and Brazil (35.5%).

A clear pattern and trajectory is discernible in Portugal's internationalisation efforts. Typically the first moves, as indicated above, are made into the neighbouring economy. As a result of these rapidly expanding two-way flows, an EU regional bloc based in the Iberian peninsula came into existence during the 1990s as a buoyant new trading area. Using Spain as a springboard, the next natural step was into North Africa and the countries that were formerly Portugal's African colonies (PALOPs). The latter were attractive because they were undertaking privatisation programmes, while Brazil became a focal point for economic relations with Mercosur. The most recent stage has involved investments in the more advanced EU economies. In some cases, a presence has also been established in Eastern Europe, notably Poland, Hungary and Russia.

The Portuguese expansion strategy is driven by the need to stay competitive in order to survive by 'growing' the size of domestic firms via international involvement. The problem of scale is important. Given the country's dimensions, large nationally based groups are inevitably thin on the ground. World-ranking tables, for instance, placed Portugal's largest bank, CGD, in 146th place. In such circumstances, there exists an ever-present danger that Portuguese firms will fall prey to foreign, perhaps Spanish, transnationals.

Questions

1. What does the Portuguese experience suggest about the internationalisation process?
2. What policies might be used to encourage further internationalisation by Portuguese firms?

Portugal is increasingly being challenged by Eastern Europe as an attractive location for MNE investment in motor vehicles and many other manufacturing activities. Mike Havard, managing director of *CM Insight*, in his report in October 2003 predicted that former Eastern bloc countries, especially the Czech Republic and Hungary, will attract a higher proportion of EU-based inward investment. These countries are geographically well situated, have good language skills (English and other north European languages, including Russian) relevant to growing EU markets, and will be inside the EU itself by 2004. Wage rates per unit output are estimated at some 50% lower in the Czech Republic than in Portugal for many manufacturing activities.

Activity 14.1 gives you the opportunity to further investigate the internationalisation process.

Activity 14.1

Case Study: Havering Promotional Products (HPP)

Established in the late 1960s, HPP specialises in the manufacture and supply of business and advertising gifts. Based in the London Borough of Havering, the company employs a total of 100 people. Products include pens, desk accessories, mugs and key rings, which are printed with the client's name and are designed as give-aways to customers.

The business and promotional gifts market has become increasingly competitive recently. This is due to low barriers of entry, an increase in the number of competitors and the domestic market reaching a maturity stage.

Having experienced 15 years of sales and profit growth, HPP's management was concerned to find that the sales performance in 1999 was static, and that in 2000 it declined. This was disappointing, as part of the firm's long-term corporate strategy is to increase year-on-year profits by several percent, thus achieving economies of scale. As 100% of HPP's business was within the UK, the firm finally took the decision to look at international markets. With no previous experience of operating in an international environment, the responsibility for handling this was given to David Sanchez, Assistant Marketing Manager, who was one of the few within the company with any language ability.

A market research agency was appointed to find out why the firm's brand image and performance were so disappointing in the UK and to analyse possible international markets the firm could enter. The research findings suggested the following:

1 Although the firm is well known in the industry, it is seen as old fashioned, and has been quoted as the 'Marks & Spencer' of the promotional gifts market.
2 The firm does not come across as having a particular strong brand identity.
3 The promotional gifts market in the UK is almost stagnant.
4 Prices of HPP are perceived to be higher than the industry norms. Many people quoted the biggest firms in the market – 'Gifts for All' and 'STW Promotional Gifts' – as being considerably cheaper for similar products.
5 HPP is seen as having a strong London base with only a limited ability to service clients outside this area.
6 There appear to be international market opportunities in Eastern Europe and China within the promotional gifts industry. This is largely due to the increasing amount of foreign direct investment from overseas into these countries.

When respondents were asked how likely it was that they would do business with HPP over the next 12 months, the mean (average) pattern of responses suggested that this would be 'fairly unlikely'. The conclusion also highlighted that a small number of respondents even believed the company to have gone out of business within the preceding six months!

The board of directors all agreed that the report should be taken seriously and recommended that a marketing consultant be employed to make recommendations on future strategy.

Questions

1 Explain why HPP should internationalise. Use case examples of other companies wherever possible.
2 Discuss the range of international market entry methods that are available to HPP.
3 Think of an example of a successful joint venture in an international market. Investigate the background to the joint venture, and then analyse the benefits both parties to the venture have derived, as well as any possible areas of conflict.

Answers to Checkpoints and Activities can be found on pp. 705–35.

International business environment

There are a number of elements of the international business environment that can also influence the internationalisation process. These are outlined in Figure 14.3.

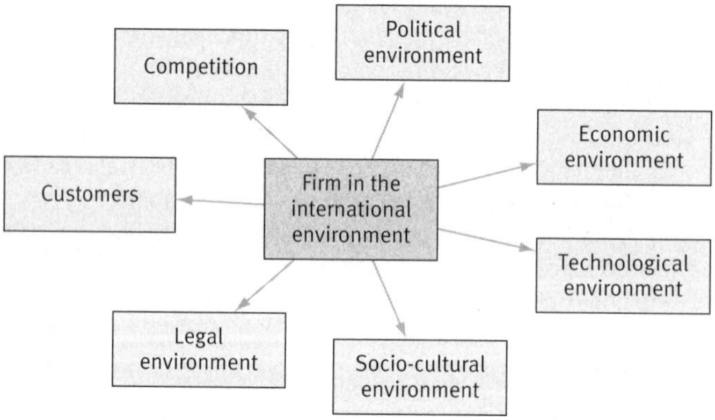

Fig 14.3 International environment

We have already considered many of these elements in Chapter 12, though mainly from a *domestic* point of view. However, a company operating in an international market is likely to experience these environmental issues from a different perspective as compared to its domestic market. Here we briefly highlight some of the key external environmental questions which firms need to consider when entering international markets.

Questions for firms entering international markets

The following are just some of the question which a firm seeking to enter a particular overseas market might ask.

Economic environment

- What is the current rate of unemployment?
- Are there enough suitably qualified potential employees living in the area?
- How will inflation affect pricing?
- What is the current level of interest rates?
- Can the economic climate be described as stable?

Political/legal environment

- What is the legislation concerning working hours?
- How important is the contract?
- Is the country's legal system fully developed?
- Is there any new legislation pending that will have a serious impact on how we run our business?

Socio-cultural environment

- What are local tastes towards our product?
- Will the name be accepted locally?
- Does our product go against any religious values?
- Do we need to make changes in order to appeal to different sub-cultures?

Technological environment

- What is the figure for Internet access per head of the population?
- Is broadband capability available to subscribers?
- What percentage of the population has the necessary buying power to buy certain technological products?
- Does the culture embrace advancement in technology?

Competition

- What is the nature of the current market? For example, is it highly fragmented or oligopolistic?
- Who are our main competitors (both local firms and multinational)?
- How will they react to our entering the market?
- How can we compete against existing competitors in the marketplace?

Customers

- Are customer needs overseas likely to be different to those in our domestic market?
- How will we segment the market?
- Who is our main target audience?
- How will our product be positioned in the marketplace?
- Where are our customers likely to be located?
- What routes (channels) will we use in trying to reach our customers?

It may be useful, when considering the internationalisation process, to look in a little more detail at some of these questions.

Cultural and ethical issues

Whilst there are many definitions of 'culture', most agree that it refers to ways in which people structure, share and transmit values and information within a particular society. According to Hall (1960), cultures differ widely in the extent to which unspoken, unformulated and inexplicit rules govern how information is handled and how people interact and relate to each other. In 'high context' cultures, much of human behaviour is covert or implicit, whereas in 'low context' cultures much is overt or explicit. For Hall, the high context cultures include countries or regions such as Japan, China, the Middle East, South America and the southern European countries. Most Western countries (including the US) are regarded as low context cultures.

High and low context cultures

High-context cultures:

- Much information transmitted by the physical context (i.e. non-verbal means, e.g. body language) or internalised within people.
- Strong bonds and high involvement between people (more group oriented than individualistic).
- Greater distinctions between insiders and outsiders.
- Cultural patterns long lived and slow to change.
- Punctuality and schedules have low priority.

Low-context cultures:

- Much information transmitted by explicit, coded messages (less via non-verbal means, e.g. body language).
- Fragile bonds and low involvement between people (more individualistic than group oriented).

- Fewer distinctions made between insiders and outsiders.
- Change easy and rapid.
- Punctuality and schedules important.

China is particularly high context in cultural terms, for example it is regarded as impolite to deny anything. Hence instead of saying 'no', other phrases are used to describe an inconvenience which imply that the answer is no. Whilst Chinese often use high context patterns, Westerners are more inclined to use low context patterns. German culture is traditionally associated with being low context, for example being very 'frank' in their spoken communication.

Being aware of such cultural aspects is vitally important to international business. In 2003/2004 a well-used TV advert for HSBC stresses its credentials for international business by its awareness of cultural differences worldwide. It shows an Englishman eating platefuls of unappetising snake fish dishes in Hong Kong in an attempt to please Chinese businessmen, unaware that a clean plate implies that the host has provided insufficient food for the guest. Both parties are bemused – the Englishman longing to receive no more food, the Chinese businessman longing for the Englishman to leave some food to indicate sufficiency and thereby acknowledge the host's generosity. HSBC trumpets its global banking reach as making it well positioned to advise potential business partners on cultural differences as an aid to international deal making.

CHECK THE NET
For aspects of Asian culture check:
www.apmforum.com
http://english.china.com
www.japanecho.com

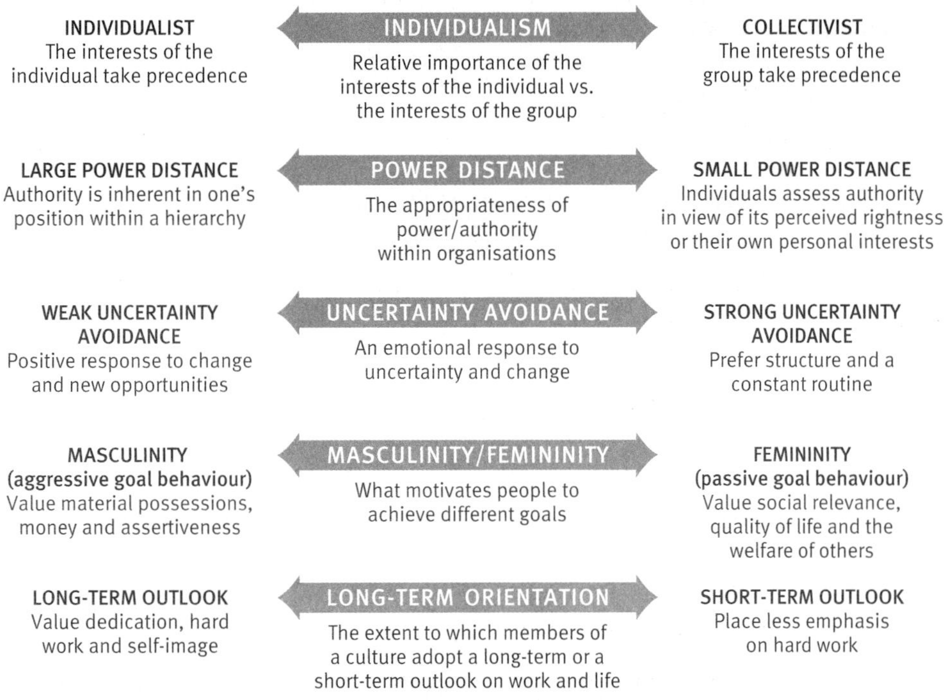

Fig 14.4 Hofstede's five dimensions of culture
Source: Adapted from Griffin and Pustay (1996)

Hofstede's cultural dimensions

Hofstede (1980) has researched the nature and extent of cultural differences and identified different 'dimensions of culture' (Figure 14.4).

Hofstede has shown that certain management practices can be compatible, and others incompatible, with the culture of a society, as expressed via these different 'dimensions'. He further suggested that cultural incompatibility undermines the successful transfer of managerial practices from developed countries to developing countries.

Ethical issues

We have already touched on the importance of ethical issues in Chapter 4. No longer can international companies run their overseas businesses however they want. Key ethical issues such as employing child labour and gift-giving can, if breached, result in great damage to a firm. Since the world is now so interconnected, customers are better informed about such practices, and often express concerns about firms that do not appear to be employing ethical standards.

Ethics refers to what is acceptable in a particular society. However, ethical issues are often complex since the international business environment is made up of different cultural values and it is these values that determine what is regarded as ethical or unethical. For example, in some societies gift-giving and using relationships to generate results is perfectly acceptable, though in many of the world's developed countries such practices are regarded as unethical.

Example:

Tesco introduces ethical advisers

Tesco, the UK's leading supermarket chain, has in the past received negative publicity as a result of a TV documentary about the conditions for workers growing foodstuffs, such as mange tout in Africa, exported to the supermarket chain. It has therefore established its own code of conduct and set up a 70-strong team of ethical advisers to help monitor the goods it sells in its stores. The advisers check foodstuffs and other products the chain sells so that its new code of conduct, designed to ensure that its Third World suppliers do not exploit child or forced labour, is adhered to.

Microenvironment

Figure 14.5 identifies some of the more local influences on the firm's attempt to internationalise, which are sometimes described as being part of the firm's *micro-environment.*

Directors

When entering an international market, it is important that the board of directors is fully behind the strategy. Entering a new market is a high-risk strategy that can only work if the entire company's management is fully behind the project. For example,

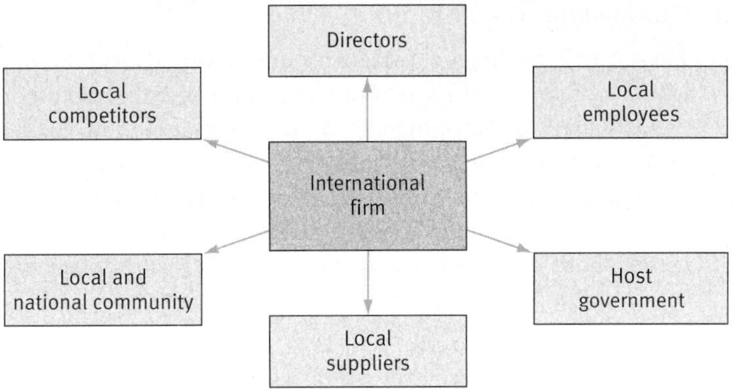

Fig 14.5 Microenvironment

entering a complex market such as China can take many years before a Western firm begins to generate profit. This can test the patience of many a director!

Local employees

If entering an international market involves setting up production facilities, it is important that a firm considers the number of potential employees living locally who will be able and willing to work for the company. If there is a severe lack of appropriately skilled staff, then arrangements need to be made to develop training programmes in order to overcome these.

Local suppliers

These provide the firm with the intermediate inputs (e.g. components, raw materials etc.) which allow the production of the final products for customers. It is important to identify suitable suppliers in the overseas economy, as choosing unreliable partners can damage a channel of distribution, ultimately affecting a firm's competitiveness in an international market. If a firm is planning on selling existing products to new markets, it is likely that it will review the ability of existing suppliers to meet the demand from new market entry. However, if the strategy is one of diversification (new product, new market), then new supplier(s) will need to be found. The relationship between a firm and its supplier is very much built on trust and adaptation. In Japanese business markets it is not unusual for a firm to continue to use the same suppliers for decades.

Local and host national community

Setting up production facilities in a new international market requires strong support from the local and host national community. This is true not only in terms of people willing to work for the company, but also in community support for the firm through demonstrating a willingness to buy its products. Toyota has a large manufacturing plant in Derbyshire, UK, and makes every effort to show its commitment to the community by employing local staff and working with the local community by supporting local projects. It has also reoriented its supply chain to include more local and UK component suppliers.

Local competitors

These can be a direct threat to an international firm. Sometimes it can be difficult to win customers from local companies quite simply because local people may work for them so that they have high levels of customer loyalty. In order to gain customers from local competitors international firms may need to use sales promotion activities (e.g. introductory special offers) or product differentiation strategies (e.g. highlighting important differences between their products and local products). The intention behind both approaches is to persuade local consumers that this new product adds value as compared to existing products.

Host government

International firms need to be aware of the impact of government at both national and local levels on their operations. At the national level, central government may offer tax and other incentives to firms to encourage market entry. However, central government can also hinder international market entry by increasing import tariffs for certain foreign products. At the national and local level, governments and authorities may aim to protect local firms by developing a range of restrictions and 'red tape' (bureaucracy) for foreign investors.

Multinational enterprise (MNE)

Put simply, a multinational enterprise (sometimes called a transnational) is a company that has headquarters in one country but operations in other countries. It is not always obvious that a firm is a multinational. The growth in alliances, joint ventures and mergers and acquisitions means that consumers tend to recognise the brand, rather than know who the parent company is. Who, for example, now owns Jaguar or Land Rover? The answer in this case is Ford.

Checkpoint 1 Can you think of brands for three different types of product and identify the multinational company which owns those brands in each case?

Dunning (1993) defines the multinational as a firm 'that engages in foreign direct investment and owns or controls value-adding activities in more than one country'. Typically the multinational would not just own value-adding activities, but might buy resources and create goods and/or services in a variety of countries. Whilst the central strategic planning takes place at headquarters, considerable latitude will usually be given to affiliates (subsidiaries) to enable them to operate in harmony with their local environments.

LINKS

Chapter 15 (pp. 627–631) looks in more detail at the strategies for global production adopted by MNEs.

Ranking multinationals

Healey (2004) points out that from a statistical point of view, there are two main methods of ranking the world's top multinationals: first, ranking them according to the amount of foreign assets they control and second, ranking them in terms of a 'transnationality index'.

- *Foreign assets.* Table 14.2 ranks the top ten multinationals according to the *value of foreign assets* they control and we can see that four of the top ten are from the US, three from the UK two from France and one from Germany. They are primarily based in the petroleum, electronics/computing and motor vehicle sectors.

Table 14.2 World's top ten multinationals ranked by foreign assets (and transnationality index) 2001

Ranking					
Foreign assets	**Transnationality index**	**Company**	**Country**	**Industry**	**Transnationality index (%)**
1	13	Vodafone	UK	Telecommunications	83
2	83	General Electric	US	Electrical and electronics	39
3	15	BP	UK	Petroleum	81
4	36	Vivendi Universal	France	Diversified	66
5	82	Deutsche Telekom AG	Germany	Telecommunications	40
6	39	Exxon/Mobil	US	Petroleum	65
7	85	Ford Motor Company	US	Automotive	39
8	87	General Motors.	US	Automotive	30
9	48	Royal Dutch/Shell	UK	Petroleum	59
10	21	Total FinaElf	France	Petroleum	75

Source: Adapted from *World Investment Report* UNCTAD (2003) pp. 187.

- *Transnationality index.* However, Table 14.2 also provides each company's transnationality index and its transnationality ranking. The *transnationality index* takes a more comprehensive view of a company's global activity and is calculated as the average of the following three ratios:
  - foreign assets/total assets;
  - foreign sales/total sales;
  - foreign employment/total employment.

For example, we can see that the second largest multinational company is General Electric in terms of the foreign assets it owns. However, its transnationality index of 39% means that it is only ranked 83rd in terms of this criterion. The reason for this is that even though it has large investments overseas in absolute value, in *percentage* terms most of its assets, sales and employment are still located in the US. This is in contrast with Exxon Corporation where 65% of its overall activity in terms of the three ratios is based abroad, and Vodafone where this figure rises as high as 83%.

If we wanted to find the companies which operate mostly outside their home country, we would have to look at the ten top multinationals in terms of the transnationality index only. These are shown in Table 14.3 and here we see the dominance of EU companies in sectors such as machinery construction, food/beverages, pharmaceuticals/chemicals, electrics/electronics, media and business services. The companies with the highest transnationality index are often from the smaller countries in terms of population as a more restricted domestic market creates incentives to operate abroad if they are to maximise their growth in terms of revenue or profits.

Table 14.3 World's top ten multinationals ranked by the transnationality index (and foreign assets), 2001

Ranking: Transnationality index	Ranking: Foreign assets	Company	Country	Industry	Transnationality index (%)
1	61	NTL Incorporated	US	Telecommunications	99.9
2	55	Thomson Corporation	Canada	Printing and publishing	97.7
3	24	ABB	Switzerland	Machinery and equipment	95.6
4	71	Holcim AG	Switzerland	Non-metallic mineral products	92.9
5	39	Roche Group	Switzerland	Pharmaceuticals	91.8
6	36	Lafarge SA	France	Construction materials	89.7
7	28	Philips Electronics	Netherlands	Electrical and electronic equipment	88.4
8	84	WPP Group PLC	UK	Business services	87.4
9	87	Pearson PLC	UK	Media	86.2
10	47	Diageo PLC	UK	Food and beverages	85.8

Source: Adapted from *World Investment Report* UNCTAD (2003), p. 187.

Technical definitions of multinationals, however, fail to convey the true scope and diversity of global business, which covers everything from the thousands of medium-sized firms which have overseas operations to the truly gigantic multinationals like IBM, General Motors and Ford. Some multinationals are *vertically integrated*, with different stages of the same productive process taking place in different countries (e.g. British Petroleum). Others are *horizontally integrated*, performing the same basic production operations in each of the countries in which they operate (e.g. Marks & Spencer). Many multinationals are household names, marketing global brands (e.g. Rothmans International, IBM, British Airways). Others are holding companies for a portfolio of international companies (e.g. Diageo) or specialise in capital goods that have little name-recognition in the high street (e.g. BTR, Hawker Siddley, GKN).

How important are the multinationals?

In 2003 the United Nations Division on Transnational Corporations and Investment estimated that there are almost 65,000 multinationals, collectively controlling a total of over 850,000 foreign affiliates (subsidiaries) and employing over 35m people worldwide. Table 14.4 provides an overview of multinational activity. It shows that in 2002 the sales of multinationals' foreign affiliates (subsidiaries) exceeded the total global export of goods and services, and amounted to 55% of world gross domestic product (GDP). It also shows that foreign direct investment has grown much faster than the rate of growth of exports for much of that period.

Table 14.4 Multinational activity in a global context

		Average annual growth rates (%)		
	2002 ($bn)	1986–90	1991–5	1996–2002
fdi outflows	647	25.7	16.5	27.8
fdi outward stock	6,866	18.0	10.6	14.2
Sales of foreign affiliates of MNEs	17,685	16.0	10.1	9.8
World gross domestic product	32,227	10.8	5.6	1.4
World gross fixed capital formation	6,422	13.4	4.2	0.9
Total exports of goods and services	7,838	15.6	5.4	2.9

Adapted from *World Investment Report* UNCTAD (2003), Table 1.1 and previous reports.

Although not shown in Table 14.4, the gross output of the world's largest 100 MNEs alone was $4.8 trillion (i.e. $4,800bn) in 2002, accounting for around 14% of world GDP and providing employment for over 13m persons, i.e. around 13% of world employment. Ranked by either turnover or GDP, half of the world's largest economic 'units' are multinationals, rather than countries. Only 14 nation states have a GDP that exceeds the turnover of Exxon, Ford or General Motors.

Historically, the bulk of multinational activity has been concentrated in the developed world. Indeed, as recently as the mid-1980s, half of all multinational production took place in only five countries – the United States, Canada, the UK, Germany and the Netherlands. This pattern is now changing rapidly. The rapid industrialisation and economic growth in the newly industrialising nations of the world has led to a sharp increase in multinational investment in Asia and (to a lesser extent) Latin America. Some of these countries, notably the 'four tigers' (Taiwan, South Korea, Hong Kong and Singapore), now have per capita GDP levels which exceed those of most European nations and their indigenous companies are now beginning to establish production facilities in the 'old world', although the 1997 'Asian crisis' slowed down this process.

NOTE

The so-called 'triad' of North America, the European Union and the Pacific Rim economies of East and South East Asia account for approximately 80% of the world's exports and 84% of world manufacturing output and almost all multinational activity. We consider these three key regions for international business separately at the end of the chapter.

International human resource management (IHRM)

When conducting international business, firms will also need to integrate the domestic HRM approaches considered in Chapter 13 (p. 504) into their international operations. How they do this will depend on the approach they adopt as regards HRM policies.

Approaches to IHRM

Four approaches have been identified to describe the ways in which MNEs might conduct their international HRM policies.

- *The ethnocentric approach.* In the ethnocentric approach, all key position in the host country subsidiary are filled by nationals of the parent company. This approach offers the most direct control by the parent company over the host country subsidiary, and is often adopted when there is felt to be a need to maintain good communications between the headquarters of the MNE and the subsidiary. This ethnocentric approach is often followed in the early stages of internationalisation when the MNE is seeking to establish a new business or product in another country.
- *The polycentric approach.* Here, host country nationals are recruited to manage the subsidiaries in their own country. This allows the MNE to take a lower profile in sensitive economic and political situations and helps to avoid intercultural management problems.
- *The geocentric approach.* This approach utilises the best people for all the key jobs throughout the organisation, whatever their nationality or whatever the geographical location of the post to be filled. In this way an international executive team can be developed.
- *The regiocentric approach.* Here the MNE divides its operations into geographic regions and moves staff *within* particular regions, e.g. Europe, America, Asia rather than between regions.

Choices between these different approaches will depend on the culture, philosophy and the local conditions in which the firm operates. Some international companies may adopt an ethnocentric approach in some countries and a polycentric approach in others. However, a key element in this choice will involve the question as to how an international firm can manage a dispersed and diverse workforce responsively and effectively, retaining a measure of overall cohesion whilst being sensitive to local conditions.

Checkpoint 2 Choose a company that follows an ethnocentric approach. Analyse the appropriateness of this method, making suggestions as to why you agree or disagree with their chosen management orientation.

Case Study 14.2 looks further at IHRM issues using Hofstede's cultural dimensions (p. 549) to inform the running of overseas subsidiaries.

Case Study 14.2 IHRM and cultural characteristics

Whilst the global nature of multinational activity may call for increased consistency, the variety of cultural environments in which the MNE operates may call for differentiation. Workplace values and behaviours are widely regarded as being influenced by national as well as corporate cultural characteristics. As Laurent (1986) claims, '*if we accept the view that human resource management (HRM) approaches are cultural artefacts reflecting the basic assumptions and values of the national culture in which organisations are embedded, international HRM becomes one of the most challenging corporate tasks in multinational organisations*'.

Greece is clustered in the 'Mediterranean culture' sector of managerial models, with native managers assumed to be less individualistic and more comfortable with highly bureaucratic organisational structures in order to achieve their objectives. In Hofstede's terms Greece is characterised by large power distance and strong uncertainty avoidance (see Figure 14.4, p. 549). Since the early 1960s, Greece has been the host country for many foreign firms, initially in manufacturing and more recently in services.

It is broadly accepted that management practices which reinforce national cultural values are more likely to yield better outcomes in terms of performance, with a mismatch between work unit management practices and national culture likely to reduce performance (Newman and Nollen, 1996). The suggestion here is that multinational firms, which have established their affiliates in Greece, will be more efficient if their management practices are better adapted to the national culture of Greece. Theory suggests that this adaptation will be better achieved where the national culture of the home country of the MNE is close to that of Greece. In other words, MNEs from collectivist, large power distance and strong uncertainty avoidance countries will be at a *small cultural distance* from Greece and will better integrate into the organisational culture of the Greek affiliate. The following hypothesis is therefore suggested by Kessapidou and Varsakelis (2000).

Hypothesis: MNEs from home countries at a *large cultural distance* from Greece will prefer to employ local managers and permit more decentralised IHRM practices.

This hypothesis would then predict that MNEs from home countries with national cultural characteristics of the individualist, small power distance and weak uncertainty avoidance variety (i.e. the opposites to Greece) will prefer to employ local managers and permit more decentralised IHRM practices.

In their analysis of the operations of 485 foreign affiliates in Greece over the years 1994–96, Kessapidou and Varsakelis found considerable evidence to support this hypothesis. MNEs from home countries at a large cultural distance from Greece (e.g. UK, Netherlands, US with cultural distance factors 4.27, 4.03 and 3.47 respectively) were much more likely to employ local managers and adopt a decentralised approach to IHRM than countries at a small cultural distance from Greece (e.g. Italy, France and Spain with cultural distance factors 1.46, 0.99 and 0.58 respectively).

Source: Adapted from Kessapidou, S. and Varsakelis, N. (2000).

Question What relevance does this case study have for IHRM aspects of multinational firm activity?

Organisational culture and IHRM

The issue of organisational 'culture' is touched on in a recent book, *Who says elephants can't dance* by Louis Gerstner, the managing director of IBM, who places particular emphasis on organisational culture in IHRM issues and ultimately in business success. Faced with huge losses in the early 1990s, Gerstner embarked on a challenging strategy to change IBM from a (*multidomestic*) company selling IBM products only via national subsidiaries (e.g. IBM France) to a *global company* selling solutions to problems and packaging the most appropriate products and services (even if some are non-IBM) to meet the individual needs of customers. To meet this need for 'culture change' at IBM a whole raft of IHRM practices were established. For example, IBM established incentive systems for its employees whereby their bonuses depended less on selling IBM products and more on meeting goals within the customer service sphere. Again, education and training packages were designed to give IBM sales personnel expertise across a wide range of computer functions so that they would be able to devise multi-functional solutions incorporating hardware and software elements.

Developing cross-cultural awareness

Taking the issue of national cultural attributes in IHRM issues further can be important for the organisation, as suggested in a recent report by *ER Consultants* at Cambridge. Cross-cultural awareness at an individual level may be developed through formal systems such as induction training and team building or informally in a discussion over lunch or through a mentoring relationship. Running training sessions on cross-cultural differences for delegates from different countries can also be effective. Some of the key issues include the openness of communication, style of management and, above all, how to motivate people in different parts of the world so that they felt part of the same organisation.

At an organisational level there are a number of cultural factors which are integral to the structures of organisations that can effect the perception of information and communication. These can be mapped on a number of different dimensions, but perhaps the most well known and important are the dimensions developed by Geert Hofstede. As already noted (p. 549) one of the dimensions he identified was that between Individualism and Collectivism, which refers to the extent to which people prefer to take care of themselves and their immediate families, remaining emotionally independent from groups and organisations. For example, he placed the US, Australia and England towards the 'Individualist' end of the spectrum but Columbia, Venezuela and Equador towards the 'Collectivist' end of the spectrum.

Within a highly individualistic country, autonomy is more important than in highly collectivist countries where security is more important. In individualist countries, specific friendships are more important than being part of an 'in group'. The different dimensions have a number of practical implications in areas ranging from understanding the structure of organisations and how to get things to happen through to implementing processes that will be effective across different cultures, e.g. competency frameworks, surveys etc.

It can be useful to be aware of cross-cultural behaviour patterns. How do you say to someone at work that:

CHECK THE NET

For culturally specific resources check www.itp.berkeley.edu/-thorne/HumanResources.html The human resource network has a number of brief guides on HRM issues: www.hnetwork.co.uk Many human resources issues are covered at www.lpd.co.uk A wide range of motivational theorists are considered at: www.westrek.hypermart.net

- Their lack of eye contact is making you suspicious of them (English perception of Asian behaviour).
- They should say hello to each individual person in the office, not everyone at once because it is rude (French perception of English behaviour).
- A weak handshake is a sign of a weak character (American perception of English behaviour).
- You can actually mean no (Japanese understanding of language).

The essence of good cross-cultural communication is to ensure that such differences are not viewed as negative behaviours. It is only by raising awareness of these differences explicitly that we can begin to tackle such misunderstandings.

International marketing

This is concerned with marketing arising in the course of managing the firm's international operations and takes further the marketing strategies already discussed in a more domestic context in Chapter 13 (p. 492). Challenges in international marketing include: unstable governments, difficulty in combating intellectual property right infringements, corruption, foreign exchange problems, tariffs and trade barriers and understanding cultural differences.

Many brand names do not travel well. There are many examples of companies that have adopted a standardised approach to their branding, but have not researched the implications of translation when launching a brand into another country. For example, Coca-Cola when they first launched in China realised the name translated as 'bite the wax tadpole'. Fortunately, Esteé Lauder was quick to notice their proposed export of Country Mist makeup to Germany could experience problems. This is because 'mist' in Germany is slang for 'manure'. Subsequently the product became Country Moist in Germany.

Very often brand names are changed in order to follow a standardisation strategy. For example, in the UK the following products have changed names to fall in line with the same product in other countries: Starburst (formerly Opal Fruits), Cif (formerly Jif) and Snickers (formerly Marathon). Mars (the manufacturers of Snickers and Starburst) decided the sweets should be called the same name in the UK as they are in the rest of the world. Reasons for having one universal brand name can be attributed to cost savings by producing a single global advertising and marketing campaign for all countries. Also, with increased travel, consumers are able to recognise a brand abroad. Usually companies adopt expensive advertising campaigns advising of the name change. This needs to be done in a positive way to ensure the brand image maintains its current position in the mind of the consumer.

Steps in international marketing:

We now consider each of the following steps in international marketing.

1 Examine the international environment.
2 Should we go international?
3 Which markets to enter?
4 How to enter?
5 Type of marketing programme?

Examine the international environment

Before entering a new marketplace extensive research needs to be carried out on the international environmental issues facing the company. For example, the number of competitors, state of the economy, is there a market for our product or services? What do potential customers think about us? A firm may produce a short list of potential international markets. The factors for selecting an international market are many, but ultimately depend on the potential demand from consumers and the extent of the competition.

The approach to market research in a national (UK) setting has already been considered in Chapter 13 (p. 496). Key factors in undertaking international market research include:

1 Understand the macro-environment (e.g. GNP, demographic changes, inflation, exchange rates etc.).
2 Understand the micro-environment (e.g. firm sizes, productivities, cost structures, competitor reactions, consumer behaviour, distribution channels available etc.).
3 Understand cultural differences.
4 Determine who is going to undertake the research.

CHECK THE NET
Material on global marketing and segmentation strategies can be obtained from:
www.marketing.week.co.uk
www.globalweb.co.uk

Should we go international?

If the firm does decide to go international it may be because of any one or more of the following factors.

- *Increasing the size of the market.* Developing new markets abroad may permit the firm to fully exploit scale economies, particularly important when these are substantial for that product. In some cases the minimum efficient size for a firm's production may be greater than the total sales potential of the domestic market. In this case the firm's average costs can only be reduced to their lowest level by finding extra sales in overseas markets.
- *Extending the product life cycle.* Finding new markets abroad may help extend the maturity stage of the product life cycle. This can be particularly important when domestic markets have reached 'saturation point' for a product.

- *Supporting international specialisation.* In an attempt to reduce overall production costs, separate elements of an overall product may be produced in large scale in different geographical locations worldwide. For example, labour-intensive components will often be produced in low-cost labour locations, whereas capital-intensive components are more likely to be produced in high technology locations. The final product, once assembled, must by definition be marketed internationally to achieve the huge sales volumes which are a prerequisite for international specialisation.
- *Helping reduce investment pay-back periods.* Finding overseas markets helps achieve high-volume sales early in the product life cycle, thereby reducing the pay-back period needed to return the initial capital outlay and making many investment projects more attractive. This may help to compensate for modern trends towards shorter product life cycles which are tending to inhibit investment expenditure.
- *Reducing stock-holding costs.* Overseas markets may provide new sales outlets for surplus stocks (inventories), thereby reducing warehousing and other stock-holding costs.

Which markets to enter and what market entry method to adopt?

A decision must eventually be made as to which market(s) to enter. A company will hope the extensive research will indicate in which overseas market they are most likely to achieve their objectives through internationalisation. We have already noted the attraction of entering countries at close geographical and cultural proximity to the country in which the firm has begun operations.

As already discussed earlier (pp. 538–546) the type of market entry method selected will depend in part on the risk–reward perception that the firm has of the different methods of internationalisation. It also depends on the stage the firm has already reached in the internationalisation process (Table 14.1, p. 539). Many firms often prefer to adopt an exporting method as the lowest-risk entry strategy, but also because it may be appropriate when first entering a complex market. The relative merits of the more committed international market entry methods such as licensing, franchising, joint ventures and foreign direct investment must obviously be assessed here.

Type of marketing programme?

A firm may need to rethink its marketing strategy when entering an international market. The product may be positioned differently in the international market, requiring a different approach to promotional activity. For example, the Belgian beer Stella Artois is positioned as a premium-priced lager in the UK, while in Belgium it is marketed as a cheaper alcoholic beverage. There may be stricter legislation in the international market concerning advertising. In fact, the firm will need to revisit any marketing approach it has adopted in the domestic market and consider an appropriate *international marketing mix*. After reviewing the international marketing situation facing IKEA, we return to the possible components of the international marketing mix in the next section.

Case Study 14.3 provides a useful example of international marketing issues using IKEA.

Case Study 14.3 'IKEA – flat pack success!'

IKEA continues to be a global phenomenon. Ingvar Kamprad founded IKEA in 1943. Today, Inter IKEA systems B.V. is now the owner and franchiser of the IKEA concept. All IKEA stores operate on a franchise basis. IKEA of Sweden AB is responsible for the IKEA product range; making sure all IKEA products are endorsed 'Design and Quality, IKEA of Sweden'. The IKEA Group is owned by a charitable foundation in the Netherlands.

IKEA introduced its first store in the UK in 1987. Competition comes from MFI, Texas, B&Q and small and medium-sized mail-order firms. IKEA's competitors vary from country to country, although no other furniture company in the UK operates with the same global success. The recent opening of a new IKEA in Beijing, China, highlights this global expansion.

The company now has over 158 stores in 29 countries around the world and employs over 35,000 people. This growth includes the UK, which has created thousands of new jobs. The company has seen annual turnover increase to over 11 billion euros ($8.4bn). Europe generates the largest sales per region at 79.2%, followed by North America 16%, Asia 3.0%, Australia and Middle East both around 1% (see Figure 14.6). International activity is an important part of the firm's business. IKEA generates over 75% of its turnover from international business. However, the firm does as little as possible to tailor its ranges to local tastes, preferring to opt for a standardisation approach. IKEA in Beijing, China, has the same concept, branding, and many product ranges as IKEA Lakeside (UK). To many customers, part of IKEA's appeal is its Swedishness.

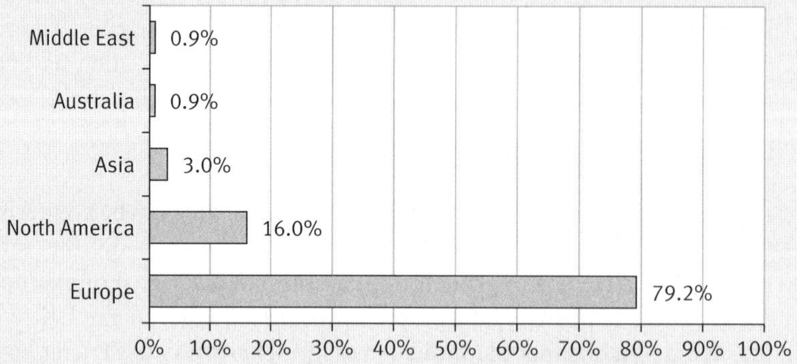

Fig 14.6 IKEA sales by region

IKEA is renowned for its innovative Swedish-designed furniture. The profile of its 12,000-product range is well-designed, high quality at low prices. The firm's mission is 'we shall offer a wide range of well-designed, functional home furnishing products at prices so low that as many people as possible will be able to afford them'. IKEA provides a comfortable environment for its customers, with mock room settings so

Case Study 14.3 continued

that they can see products in context. These include books in bookcases, lamps on tables and fake fruit in fruit bowls! Many IKEA stores offer a home decoration service if customers wish to furnish an entire room or home, and a kitchen planning service. Using computer simulations, specially trained kitchen planners can help plan and choose a person's ideal kitchen. The company provides free pencils and tape measures for making notes and checking dimensions. Amenities include a restaurant, Swedish food shop, children's play area and hotdog stall. Customers are able to self-select the products they want from pallets in the company's warehouse, and then take these to the checkout for payment.

A strong selling point to many people is the fact most of the products are flat packed, making it easier for the buyer to transport. By providing products in this format, IKEA is able to reduce its costs in relation to manufacturing and distribution. The company provides home delivery for larger items, although this is not included in the product price. Items are easy to assemble, and the tools required for assembly are sold with the furniture. IKEA produces a catalogue of its product range, which is available in store free of charge.

The company is mainly a business-to-consumer (B2C) organisation and therefore offers no trade discount for organisational purchasers. In order to portray a customer-orientated approach, all employees wear staff uniform, and certain stores in the UK are now open until 10 pm weekdays to meet consumer demand for late-night shopping. This is promoted locally with outdoor advertising, whilst TV advertising continues to promote brand awareness. Stores are large, warehouse-style complexes located out of town. An example in the UK is the store based at Lakeside Retail Park in Essex.

The company has ongoing Environmental Action Plans, the last one covered the financial years 2000–2003, and concentrates on environmental improvements within five areas: products and materials, forestry, environmental work at suppliers, goods transport and environmental work at the stores. A Waste Management Manual for the IKEA Group is established. It means that all stores must, as a minimum requirement, sort the five most common fractions of their waste. This ensures that 75% of a store's waste is reused, recycled or used for energy production. In order to avoid contributing to the devastation of intact natural forests in need of protection, trees from these forests are not used for the manufacture of its solid wood products. Each store has its own environmental coordinator whose job includes organising and carrying out environmental training for the store's co-workers. The aim of this training is to give people an insight into, an understanding of, and information about the environment in general and environmental work within the IKEA Group. Also included in the Environmental Action Plans is making the stores' energy consumption as efficient as possible. Methods used are energy-efficient lighting, tests with alternative energy systems such as solar power, geothermal energy and energy from underground aquifers. Up to 90% of the waste from IKEA stores worldwide goes to specialist companies for recycling, which is currently being introduced as a comprehensive waste-sorting programme.

Case Study 14.3 continued

IKEA works closely with both suppliers and packaging manufacturers to develop sensible packaging that offers effective, environmentally friendly solutions. The aim is to use a single material to make recycling easier. Most IKEA packaging consists of what is probably the most environmentally friendly material of them all, corrugated cardboard with a high content of recycled material. By measuring and monitoring the environmental impact of its transport activities, IKEA hopes to be able to improve the systems it uses to assess the environmental work of the freight companies it works with. This will encourage distributors to continue with their own environmental improvement initiatives, at the same time as it makes it easier for IKEA to select the right freight company.

Currently approximately 2,150 IKEA suppliers in 56 countries manufacture the products that are marketed and sold in the IKEA catalogues and via the IKEA stores. A large proportion of IKEA products come from suppliers in countries where environmental work is, on the whole, well developed, but the firm also purchases products from countries where environmental work is less developed.

IKEA currently employs the advertising agency St Luke's for its UK advertising campaigns. Until 1995 IKEA was promoted through tactical campaigns in the UK, which focused on price and range. St Luke's won the highly competitive pitch for this project on the premise that further growth for IKEA in the UK could not be achieved without tackling the British preference for traditional furniture. By breaking this taboo area for advertisers, with the 'Chuck out the Chint' campaign, the agency fuelled a cultural shift in favour of more modern tastes. The chintz campaign generated an unusual amount of media attention in the months following its launch. Shortly after this campaign came an even more irreverent and tongue-in-cheek series of ads, highlighting the correlation between people's taste in furniture and their habits or lifestyles. Based on genuine market research, the furniture findings campaign went out on posters and TV nationally and stimulated a media debate about contemporary tastes in the UK.

More recently IKEA's advertising has become even more provocative with a series of tactical campaigns for sales and office furniture, which have created considerable (but expected) public response. They have, nevertheless, supported a year-on-year sales growth of over 30% in all stores.

Like all multinational firms, IKEA does not always receive positive promotion. A recent television programme in Sweden says the furniture firm is continuing to exploit child labour. The documentary reported that children working in factories in the Philippines and Vietnam were under the minimum age set in international agreements. A spokesperson for IKEA defended the company, saying the contract with its supplier in the Philippines had been suspended, when under-age children were found to be making wicker baskets. She emphasised that IKEA was committed to preventing under-age child labour, but said the problem was complicated, since local suppliers employed children. They were not directly employed by IKEA.

* *Source*: Adapted from www.ikea.com + various sources

Case Study 14.3 continued

Questions

1 Conduct an environmental analysis of the company.
2 Discuss a suitable market entry method for IKEA entering South Korea.
3 Select one of IKEA's main competitors and discuss what steps they can take in order to try to compete with IKEA.

International marketing mix

In order for a firm to compete successfully in an international market we have noted that it will need to consider the extent to which the *domestic marketing mix* needs to be adapted. We now consider each of the four 'Ps' in turn from a more international perspective.

Promotion

International marketing communications (IMC) is a broad term often used in this context and consists of advertising, personal selling, direct marketing, trade shows, public relations and sales promotion. Certainly advertising tends to be the favoured method for international marketers in consumer marketing, whilst personal selling is widely used by international business-to-business marketers as the main form of communication. However, the promotional elements selected will depend on the international target market.

- *What is the technological infrastructure of the country?* This will influence the prospects for reaching the final consumer. For example, in most industrialised countries over 90% of households own a TV, but this is often only a minority in the developing countries. If using direct selling by telesales, what proportion of the target market in that country possesses a telephone? If planning a poster campaign, what are the panel sizes available in different countries? Panel sizes are different, for example, in France and the UK, which can be important given the high costs of preparing and printing panels of varying sizes.
- *What appeals culturally in the advertisement?* English advertisements quite frequently use humour, French ones use erotic imagery, while in Germany the advertisements tend to be very factual. Great attention therefore needs to be paid to style and content in terms of the cultural impact of the campaign. If using direct selling, what type of sales force will be acceptable? For example, should we use local salespeople, an expatriate sales force or nationals from third countries?

Example:

Culture, humour and advertising strategy

Many pan-European advertising campaigns have failed to deliver because of lack of research into how cultural differences may impact the viewer's response to the advertising. For example, an advert for slimming pills showing an overweight person on the left, pointing to slimming pills in the middle, pointing to a slim person on the right is appropriate if the advert runs in a country where the population reads from left to right. However, if the advert were to go out in Japan (where the population read from right to left), this would translate as: eat slimming pills to gain weight!

It is worth remembering that different cultures have different types of humour. Something that may appear humorous to a UK audience may not necessarily have the same affect in Germany. Also, special attention needs to be paid to the use of celebrities in advertising. First, for the purpose of a pan-European campaign, the celebrity should be known throughout Europe. Second, they should carry a positive reputation, encouraging people to buy the product. Third, ideally there should be a certain amount of synergy between the celebrity and the product, e.g. David Beckham advertising Adidas sports wear. David Beckham is certainly well known throughout Europe, but will he be as favourable in Greece as he is in other parts of Europe? (Beckham helped put paid to Greece's hopes of reaching the 2002 World Cup finals.)

Checkpoint 3

Find your own example of a product that has not travelled well when entering a new market. Discuss what steps the firm could have taken in order to overcome the problem of cultural differences.

- *What are the regulations on advertising in this particular country?* The UK, Belgium, the Netherlands and Denmark ban TV commercials for tobacco products but allow press adverts. In the UK any advertisement for tobacco products must carry a health warning. Sweden bans the advertising of 'junk food' to children whereas the UK does not, despite the Food Commission in the UK reporting in late 2003 that during 39 hours of TV viewing for children, there were some 18 adverts per hour, almost half of which involved food items high in sugar, salt and saturated fat. Are there any legal restrictions on the use of direct marketing (such as the use of information stored on computer databases)? Are there any legal restrictions on sales promotions? (Some countries do not allow certain types of free offers to be made; for example, money-off coupons are not allowed in Norway.) Are there any restrictions on comparative advertising?

Example:

Comparative advertising in the Thai shampoo market

Unilever and Procter & Gamble are taking their global battle against dandruff to the Thai courts. The global giants, responsible for the majority of leading brands found in supermarkets, have been questioning the effectiveness of each other's product in a country where direct comparative advertising is rarely used. Unilever sought an emergency court injunction to stop P&G broadcasting a

Head & Shoulders advertisement that the Anglo-Dutch company says 'intends to attack' Clinic Clear, the leading brand in Thailand's Bt2bn (US$49m) anti-dandruff shampoo market. Unilever also wants Bt471m from P&G for damage to Clinic Clear's reputation. P&G countered with a lawsuit this week demanding Bt750m in damages for a subsequent Unilever advertisement that claimed Clinic Clear is 'three times more effective' than Head & Shoulders. Orapin Milindasuta, managing director of P&G Thailand, said in a statement that she was 'appalled by the directness and viciousness' of Unilever's offensive against Head & Shoulders. But Chutharat Thanapaisarnkit, managing director of Ogilvy Public Relations, said Unilever had no choice but to 'protect the brand' after P&G's 'aggressive' campaign. 'We claim an eye for an eye,' Ms Chutharat said.

- *What are the different media habits of the country?* For example, the current circulation figures per 1,000 of population of women's weekly magazines is around 29 in Germany, compared to 15 for the UK and 5 for Spain. Similar figures for TV guides are 37 for Germany, 10 for the UK and 7 for Spain.
- *What type of packaging do we use to retain the brand image yet meet country requirements* (e.g. ecological requirements demanded in Germany)? Do we need special types of labels? How much information needs to be presented about the content of the product?

We can see from these questions that international promotion is not an easy proposition. It requires an intimate knowledge of the market in each country. Indeed it is quite likely that relationship marketing and personal selling are more important in collectivist societies such as Japan and China, since there is greater emphasis on networking and long-term relationships. Public relations (PR), on the other hand, can help to overcome advertising difficulties. PR is a favoured form of promotion for tobacco companies in many countries, in order to overcome the tight restrictions regarding the advertising of cigarettes. Personal selling may be used to help overcome direct marketing problems; for example, it may be difficult to gather effective data for direct marketing in some countries as government legislation restricts access to such data.

Price

The price element of the marketing mix was covered in Chapter 13, p. 500. However, these pricing strategies may need to be adapted to the international market. For example, the Belgium lager Stella Artois is positioned as a low-price value brand in Belgium, but a high-price premium brand in the UK.

Price in any marketing context is governed by competition, production costs and company objectives. International pricing decisions will reflect these aspects and will also need to take into account market differences between countries, exchange rates, difficulties of invoicing and collecting payment across borders, the effects of tariffs and purchase taxes on competitiveness, governmental regulations of the host country and the long-term strategic plan of the company in the different markets in which it operates.

Listed below are some of the major issues faced by those setting prices in different countries.

- **Market differences.** Clearly, some overseas markets are more attractive for a particular product than others in terms of population size, standard of living (e.g. real GNP per head), age profile, purchasing patterns etc.
  - *High income markets.* Clearly, international markets with a higher real income per head have a greater 'willingness to pay' and therefore the firm may seek a higher price in such markets.
  - *Low competition markets.* Some international markets have fewer local competitors providing substitute products. The firm may seek a higher price in such markets.
  - *Separated international markets with different price elasticities.* Of particular interest in terms of international price setting is the possibility and profitability of setting different prices in different geographical markets. When the same product is priced higher in one (international) market than another, this is termed *price discrimination.*
  - For this to be *possible*, there must be barriers preventing resale in another country at the higher price (transport costs, tariff barriers etc.).
- **Longer channels of distribution.** Costs of transporting products and associated insurance are just two factors that help to contribute to the final price of a product. In reality, the longer the channel of distribution, the higher the price likely to be charged for a traded product. Imported products tend to be more expensive than locally made products partly because they pass through a larger number of intermediaries. Many firms are now looking at shortening the channel of distribution by using the Internet to target customers, with any savings made passed on to the customer as a lower price.
- **High proportion of target audience in country.** The target audience has a direct impact on pricing. If the country has a high proportion of the target audience in its population, then the firm may be able to charge a higher price.
- **Exchange rates.** When exchange rates fluctuate this can change the potential profitability of international contracts. For example, marketers must be alert as to any potential movements in the exchange rate between the date of quotation/invoicing and the date of payment so that the profit margin is not eroded. Price may have to be adjusted to cover adverse exchange rate movements. To reduce the impact of such problems currencies may be purchased on futures markets, or products may be priced in 'harder', more stable currencies. Of course when both parties have a single currency, such as the euro, these problems will be avoided.
- **Cross-border payments.** In contracts for internationally traded products it is important to specify exactly what a price covers. For example, does it cover cost, insurance and freight?
- **Tariffs and other taxes.** Increases in *tariffs* (purchase taxes) on overseas sales can force a firm to raise the quoted price of its exports in order to retain its profit margin. Whether it will be able to pass these taxes on to the consumer as a higher

price will, of course, depend on the price elasticity of demand for the product. The *less* price elastic the demand, the more of any tax increase can be passed on to the overseas consumer (see Chapter 2 p. 57). Tariffs and taxes can have other impacts on trade issues. In an attempt to avoid such tariffs (and sometimes to overcome currency problems) there has been a growth in *countertrade*, namely the barter of goods and services between countries. Some 5% of all international trade has been estimated as being of this type. Further, any increases (or differences between countries) in *profit-related taxes* (e.g. corporation tax) can result in MNEs adopting a policy of 'transfer pricing' (see p. 596). Here firms sell products on to subsidiaries within another country at prices which bear little relation to the true costs incurred at that stage of the overall production process.

- **Government regulations.** As well as taxes, overseas governments may influence the firm's price-setting policies by regulations, perhaps setting maximum or minimum prices of products or minimum quality standards for particular products.
- **Strategic objectives.** Overseas price setting may, of course, be influenced by the strategic objectives of the firm. For example, where market share or revenue maximisation is a primary objective then prices will tend to be lower (e.g. penetration pricing) than they might be under, say, a profit-maximising objective.

Product

A key issue in marketing is the extent to which a standard or differentiated product should be provided.

Standardised or differentiated?

There are good business reasons for trying to make a *standard product* acceptable to as many customers as possible – for example, it can help reduce average costs in design, production, promotion and distribution. Theodore Levitt of the Harvard Business School contends that tastes and preferences in many cultures are becoming more homogeneous due to the increased frequency of world travel and improved worldwide telecommunications. He claims that when marketers appreciate the fact that consumers share basic interests they can market the same product worldwide and achieve economies of scale. A global marketing strategy is one that maintains a single marketing plan across all countries and yields global name-recognition. Coca-Cola and McDonald's are examples of companies that use a global approach to market their products in different countries.

As sports enthusiasts will be aware, the 'Beckham brand' is of huge value in marketing terms and has itself become the focus of repositioning and brand extension strategies. For example, in July 2003 plans were announced to turn the entire Beckham family from a primarily UK brand into a global brand. The Beckhams have formed a 'joint venture' with Simon Fuller, creator of Pop Idol, who will create opportunities for the Beckham brand extending from product endorsement to television shows, mobile phone video clips to fashion boutiques, with the ultimate aim of establishing the couple in Hollywood. 'The Beckham brand is about aspiration and family values, the couple who came from nothing to achieve their dreams,' said Mr Fuller.

Even when arguments for standardisation are strong, those who follow this path may still make subtle variations – for example, McDonald's uses chilli sauce in Mexico instead of ketchup, whilst in India it serves the 'Maharaja Mac' which features two mutton patties. The motto 'Think global, and act local' symbolises a patterned standardisation strategy which involves developing global product-related marketing strategies while allowing for a degree of adaptation to local market conditions. Some product types would appear more suitable for standardisation than others. Office and industrial equipment, toys, computer games, sporting goods, soft drinks are usually standardised across national borders.

On the other hand, arguments can also be advanced in favour of *product differentiation*. Where international market segments differ from one another, even when some group characteristics are held in common, then a more differentiated product strategy may be advisable. For example, if high income households in Spain display different wants and needs from high income households in Germany, then products may have to be adapted in an attempt to sell to both groups of consumers simultaneously. Where products are highly culturally conditioned (as with many types of food, some types of drink, clothing etc.), differentiated products and marketing strategies are commonplace.

As most companies are looking for some standardisation, they will often use a *modular product design* that allows the company to adapt to local needs whilst still achieving economies of scale. Car makers are beginning to adopt this form of production, with a basic body shape forming the shell around which different features are built (e.g. windscreen designs, sun roofs etc).

LINKS

In the international context we can add two further items to Table 13.3 (p. 499) supporting product standardisation:
International product standards
Short cultural distance to overseas market and two supporting product differentiation:
Local product standards
Large cultural distance to overseas market.

Place

Again, at the international level new aspects need to be considered as regards 'place', e.g. the distributional channel selected. Four main types of channel are commonly identified.

- *Direct system*: no intermediaries involved, with orders sent directly from a factory or warehouse in the home country to the overseas purchaser.
- *Transit system*: exports sent to a transit (or 'satellite') warehouse/depot in another country. This then acts as a 'break bulk' point, with some items despatched in bulk over long distances and others in smaller units to more local destinations.
- *Classical system*: here each foreign country has its own separate warehouse/depot. Exports are sent to these and then distributed within that national market. Such warehouses/depots both 'break bulk' and perform a stockholding function, with nationals of that country being served by locally held inventories.
- *Multicountry system*: as for the classical system, except that the separate warehouses/depots may serve several adjoining countries rather than one country only.

Choice of distributional channel

In practice, a few key factors will determine the choice of distributional channel:

- *foreign customer base*: the direct system is more likely to be used where a small number of large overseas purchasers are involved;
- *export volumes*: the use of 'break-bulk' or stockholding warehouses/depots will only be economically viable when export volumes exceed certain 'threshold' levels;
- *value density of product*: those products with a high ratio of value to weight/volume (i.e. high value density) are more suited to direct systems since they can more easily absorb the higher associated transport costs;
- *order lead times*: where direct systems are inappropriate (e.g. low value density) yet customers required rapid and reliable delivery, stock may have to be held locally (i.e. classical or multi-country systems).

Recent evidence suggests a rise in *direct, transit* and *multicountry systems*. The rise of e-commerce is increasing direct systems use with international and personalised delivery via parcel networks (e.g. 'just for you', J4U delivery). Transit and multi-country systems have also been increasing, with many MNEs consolidating warehousing in a few large 'pan-European' distribution centres. Sony, Rank Xerox, Philips, Kellogg's, Nike and IBM have moved in this direction and away from the classical system previously adopted. Some of these choices of distribution channels may be influenced by opportunities for 'economies of scope'.

Activity 14.2

1 Here you'll see a description of a particular situation. Try to match the *lettered* description with its correct *numbered* term.

Descriptions

(a) Benefits include the use of a tried-and-tested business idea.
(b) A firm (the rider) with a compatible product pays another firm (the carrier) to use its distribution.
(c) When a firm distributes and sells its own products to an overseas market.
(d) When each partner brings a specific competency to a joint venture.
(e) When a firm uses a 'confirming house' to bring it into contact with foreign buyers.

Terms

(i) Direct exporting
(ii) Indirect exporting
(iii) 'Piggy backing'
(iv) Franchising
(v) Specialised joint venture
(vi) Shared value-added joint venture

2 Read the following text and answer the questions which follow.

Japanese companies struggle in Mexico

Panasonic, the Japanese consumer electronics manufacturer, has erected a series of assembly plants in Tijuana, Mexico that employ nearly 3,000 people and turn out between 10,000 and 11,000 television sets every day. However, the recent removal of attractive tariff exemptions that had previously led to Panasonic locating its factories in Mexico will cost the company over £2m each year. Nevertheless Japanese companies intend to stay in Mexico. Its low wage costs – less than half those of cities only 30 minutes drive away in California – yet broadly comparable productivity figures make it an attractive location for manufacturing.

Question

1 What are the implications of situations like this for multinational firm activities?
2 What impacts might you expect in the advanced industrialised economies?

3 Which *two* of the following might explain the progressive decrease in share of textiles in UK output and employment?

(a) Low wage competition from countries with an even lower level of productivity per person employed in the textile industries
(b) Improvements in UK design inputs into textile products
(c) Low wage competition from countries with an equivalent level of productivity per person employed in the textile industries
(d) The progressive decline in the primary sector in the UK
(e) The relatively low income elasticity of demand for textile products over prolonged periods in which real incomes have increased substantially

4 You are managing director of a US multinational manufacturing microwave ovens. You must choose between four otherwise equally appropriate geographical locations for setting up a new factory to assemble these microwave ovens, for which 50% of all components are imported and 90% of all finished products are exported.

Rank the attractiveness of these four countries for industrial location in terms of their macroeconomic environments (1 – most attractive) on the basis of the following data. All figures refer to average annual percentage changes recorded over the past five years.

UK	
Manufacturing productivity	+2%
Wage costs	+3%
Exchange rate	+4%
Manufacturing employment	−3%

Netherlands	
Manufacturing productivity	+5%
Wage costs	+3%
Exchange rate	−2%
Manufacturing employment	+1%

France	
Manufacturing productivity	+4%
Wage costs	+4%
Exchange rate	−2%
Manufacturing employment	−2%

Denmark

Manufacturing productivity	+5%
Wage costs	+2%
Exchange rate	−4%
Manufacturing employment	+2%

Answers to Checkpoints and Activities can be found on pp. 705–35.

It may be useful, in the context of reviewing the international business environment, to examine in rather more detail the three members of the so-called 'triad', namely the EU, North America and the Pacific Rim countries (especially China).

European Union (EU)

The European Union is part of the so-called 'triad' of the global economy. It accounts for some 35% of world exports by value and contributes around 28% of world manufacturing output by value. It is clearly important that international business be aware of the market opportunities (and threats) created by the EU. This is certainly true for UK-based MNEs, since around 60% of UK goods are exported to the EU countries and around 54% of UK goods are imported from the EU countries. After enlargement of the EU in 2004, these figures are likely to rise still higher.

Origins of the EU

The European Union has been in existence in various forms for over 40 years, arguably beginning with the formation of the European Economic Community (EEC) on 1 January 1958 after the signing of the Treaty of Rome. This sought to establish a 'common market' by eliminating all restrictions on the free movements of goods, capital and persons between member countries. By dismantling tariff barriers on industrial trade between members and by imposing a common tariff against non-members, the EEC was to become a protected free-trade area or 'customs union'. The formation of a customs union was to be the first step in the creation of an 'economic union' with national economic policies harmonised across the member countries.

The original 'Six' became 'Nine' in 1973 with the accession of the UK, Eire and Denmark, and 'Ten' in 1981 with the entry of Greece. The accession of Spain and Portugal on 1 January 1986 increased the number of member countries to 12. In January 1995 the 12 became 15, as Austria, Finland and Sweden joined. The population of the EU encompassed over 382m people in 2003 with a GDP exceeding ECU 9 trillion. The enlargement of the EU to 25 countries in 2004 means that a further 75m people will be added, together with another 30m in 2007 when Bulgaria and Romania join.

LINKS

The institutions involved in EU decision making are reviewed in Chapter 12 (pp. 466–469).

Single European Act (SEA)

The *Single European Act* came into force in July 1987. The objective was not simply to create an internal market by removing frontier controls but to remove all barriers to the movement of goods, people and capital. Achieving a single European market has meant, among other things, work on standards, procurement, qualifications, banking, capital movements and exchange regulations, tax 'approximation', communication standards and transport.

Maastricht Treaty

The Treaty on European Union which was signed at Maastricht on 7 February 1992 represents one of the most fundamental changes to have occurred in the EU since its foundation. Although, legally speaking, merely an extension and amendment to the Treaty of Rome, Maastricht represents a major step for the member states. For the first time, many of the political and social imperatives of the Community have been explicitly agreed and delineated. Maastricht takes the EU beyond a 'merely' economic institution and takes it towards the full potential, economic and social union foreseen by many of its founders. Some of its major objectives are as follows:

1 to create economic and social progress through an 'area without internal frontiers' and through economic and monetary union (EMU);
2 to develop a common foreign, security and defence policy which 'might lead to common defence';
3 to introduce a 'citizenship of the Union'.

Characteristics of the EU

Country-specific data

Table 14.5 presents some of the important characteristics of the 15 member countries. It shows how diverse they are in terms of population, industrial structure, standard of living, unemployment level and inflation rate. In terms of population the UK is the third largest member, with a smaller proportion engaged in agriculture than in other EU countries and the third largest in services. In overall wealth, however, the UK drops down the rankings. It has the second largest GDP in absolute terms, but comes sixth in terms of GDP per capita, some 15% above the EU average.

EU enlargement

In October 2002, the EU Commission approved the most ambitious expansion plans in its history when ten countries were told that they had met the 'Copenhagen criteria' for membership. The criteria include such aspects as institutional stability, democracy, functioning market economies, and adherence to the aims of political, economic and monetary union. These ten countries were deemed to be ready to join in the EU in 2004, while a further two – Bulgaria and Romania – would be due for membership in 2007. Table 14.6 provides some economic data on these countries, together with their dates of accession.

Table 14.5 The EU 15 in the year 2002: some comparative statistics

	Economically active population						Share of EU				
Member country	Population (million)	Agriculture (%)	Industry (%)	Services (%)	GDP € (bn)	GDP per capita € (000)s	GDP (%)	Population (%)	Index of GDP per capita	Unemployment (%)	Inflation (%)
Austria	8.2	7.2	33.2	59.6	216.4	26.4	2.4	2.2	111.2	4.3	1.4
Belgium	10.3	2.5	6.1	71.4	261.4	25.4	2.9	2.7	106.0	6.8	1.8
Denmark	5.4	4.0	27.0	69.0	186.6	34.5	2.0	1.4	145.5	4.2	2.3
Finland	5.2	7.1	27.6	65.3	139.5	26.8	1.5	1.4	112.4	9.1	2.0
France	61.2	4.6	25.9	69.5	1,504.0	24.6	16.5	15.8	103.0	8.8	1.6
Germany	82.4	3.3	37.5	59.2	2,107.0	25.6	23.2	21.8	107.2	8.1	1.3
Greece	11.0	20.4	23.2	56.4	139.9	12.7	1.5	2.8	53.5	9.9	3.1
Ireland	3.9	10.7	27.2	61.1	124.8	32.0	1.4	1.0	133.3	4.4	4.7
Italy	58.0	7.0	32.1	60.9	1,252.0	21.6	13.7	15.3	90.5	8.9	2.7
Luxembourg	0.4	2.8	30.7	66.5	21.7	54.3	0.2	0.1	228.1	2.2	1.9
The Netherlands	16.2	3.9	22.4	73.7	446.3	27.5	4.9	4.2	116.0	3.1	3.4
Portugal	10.3	12.2	31.4	56.4	129.7	12.5	1.4	2.6	52.7	4.6	3.5
Spain	40.5	8.7	29.7	61.6	689.8	17.0	7.6	10.5	71.3	11.4	3.6
Sweden	8.9	2.9	26.1	71.0	246.9	27.7	2.7	2.4	116.0	4.9	2.0
UK	60.2	2.0	26.4	71.0	1,645.0	27.3	18.1	15.8	114.8	4.0	0.9
Total EU	382.1	3.9	28.2	67.9	9,111.0	23.8	100.0	100.0	100.0	7.6	1.9

Notes: 'Total EU' percentages for agriculture, industry and services are weighted averages.

Adapted from European Commission (2003) European Economy, No. 3

Table 14.6 EU enlargement 2004–7

	Pop. (m)	GDP per capita (% of EU average)	General government budget (% of GDP)	Unemployment rate (%)	Inflation (%)
Bulgaria (2007)	7.9	28	1.7	19.9	7.4
Cyprus (2004)	0.8	80	−3.0	4.0	2.0
Czech Rep. (2004)	10.2	57	−5.5	8.0	4.5
Estonia (2004)	1.4	42	−0.4	12.4	5.6
Hungary (2004)	10.2	51	−4.1	5.7	9.1
Latvia (2004)	2.4	33	−1.6	13.1	2.5
Lithuania (2004)	3.5	38	−1.9	16.5	1.3
Malta (2004)	0.4	55	−7.0	6.5	2.5
Poland (2004)	38.6	40	−3.9	18.4	5.3
Romania (2007)	22.4	25	−3.4	6.6	34.5
Slovakia (2004)	5.4	48	−5.6	19.4	10.8
Slovenia (2004)	2.0	69	−2.5	5.7	8.6

Adapted from European Commission (2002) *Towards the Enlarged Union*

Establishing the EU 25 will not be easy since even the optimists believe it will take a decade to fully absorb the ten new nations, whose per capita income is less than 40% of the EU 15 average. Demands for larger subsidies for farming from the new entrants will become an inevitable problem; e.g. in Poland, 25% of the population gain some income from farming. Others argue that most of the gains will go to countries such as Germany, Austria and Italy which are physically closer to the new entrants.

North America

North America is also one of the 'triad' of regions seen as underpinning the global economy. The US accounts for some 19% of world exports by value and contributes about 27% of world manufacturing output by value. The US alone is expected to contribute 1% (almost one-third) of the projected global growth rate of just over 3% in 2004. When we consider North America (US and Canada) and the North American Free Trade Association (US, Canada and Mexico), those contributions to the global economy grow still larger.

Although the United States is less dependent in trade terms on the global economy than many believe, its influence is felt everywhere. The US has a population of 287,400,000, which is smaller than the EU's single market, but has a huge land area (9,158,960 square kilometres) which is very resource rich with plentiful supplies of water, timber, coal, iron ore, petrol, gas, copper, bauxite, lead, silver, zinc, mercury and phosphates, amongst others.

North American Free Trade Association (NAFTA)

NAFTA is a free trade association formed between the United States, Canada and Mexico on 1 January 1994. The main purpose of the agreement was to reduce tariffs and increase international competitiveness, as indicated by the goals of the NAFTA agreement:

1. To strengthen bonds of friendship and cooperation
2. As a catalyst to international cooperation
3. To create, expand and secure future markets
4. To establish fair rules of trade
5. To ensure a predictable framework for business planning
6. To enhance firms' competitiveness in foreign markets
7. To foster creativity and innovation
8. To create new employment opportunities
9. To promote development
10. To strengthen environmental regulations.

NAFTA has been particularly successful for Mexico which is now the second largest trading partner of the US. The impact of the US on the international business environment is impossible to capture in terms of a few summary statistics. Its political, military, economic and socio-cultural influence is felt throughout the globe. One example of such pervasive influence we might usefully consider involves the US currency.

US and the dollar

The US dollar has dominated international currency markets for more than 50 years. Although currencies such as the euro are increasing in importance, the bilateral exchange rate that most countries pay particular attention to is between their own currency and the US dollar. For example, even though we noted above that the UK now has the majority of its trade with the EU, the £ : $ exchange rate is still hugely important. Investment bank Morgan Stanley calculated in late 2003 that an 8% fall in the dollar against sterling removes £1.2bn from UK dividend payments. This is via the decline in profits of UK firms as exports to the US become more expensive and imports dearer. In fact the dollar fell by over 20% against the £ between mid-2003 and mid-2004, and by almost 30% against the euro over the same period. The eurozone countries are therefore even more disadvantaged in their trade with the US, and as their economies stagnate this has a further damaging effect on UK exports to the EU.

Nor do the impacts of the falling dollar stop there! China has pegged its own currency, the Renminbi, against the dollar, so that it too is falling against the £ and euro, giving the already competitive Chinese exports to the UK and EU a still further boost.

US and bilateral trade treaties

One of the concerns of those supporting global free trade has been the growing importance of *bilateral* trade treaties, especially those agreed between the US and individual countries. As we note below, these treaties give preferential access to US producers rather than equal treatment to all producers, as intended by multilateral bodies such as the World Trade Organisation (WTO).

LINKS

The WTO multilateral principles are examined on pp. 582–583.

Case Study 14.4 looks at the implications of these bilateral trade treaties, especially those involving the US, in more detail. What is again indicated is how extensive is the reach of the US into global economic and political developments.

Case Study 14.4 Bilateral trade treaties are a sham

FT

Pascal Lamy, the European commissioner for trade, recently wrote that 'half the world's economists' were opposed to the epidemic of bilateral free trade agreements (FTAs). That was a splendid example of British understatement from a Frenchman. The fact of the matter is that nearly all scholars of international economics today are fiercely sceptical, even hostile, to such agreements. By contrast, politicians

Case Study 14.4 continued

everywhere have succumbed to a mania that originated in Europe but is now eagerly promoted by Robert Zoellick, the US trade representative, with Asia – the last holdout – now joining in. We are witnessing possibly the biggest divide between economists and politicians in the postwar period. Unfortunately, the economists are right. The politicians' lemming-like rush into bilateral agreements poses a deadly threat to the multilateral trading system. There are three reasons.

First, bilateral trade deals are undermining an essential principle of the World Trade Organisation: that the lowest tariff applicable to one member must be extended to all members (the most favoured nation status rule). Whilst it is true that the architects of the WTO/General Agreement on Tariffs and Trade exempted free trade areas from the 'most favoured nation' (MFN) rule, they surely did not foresee that a proliferation of agreements would fragment the trading system. By the end of last year, 250 FTAs had been notified to the WTO. If those currently under negotiation are concluded, that number will approach 300. The result is a 'spaghetti bowl' of rules, arbitrary definitions of which product comes from where and a multiplicity of tariffs depending on source.

Second, if the Europeans started this fad, the Americans are now pursuing it with zeal, exploiting their hegemonic power and the lure of preferential access to a multi-billion dollar market. Unlike Brussels, Washington has adopted bilateral FTAs to advance the agendas of domestic lobbies, agendas that are not related to trade. The US is using one-on-one agreements with small countries as models for other multilateral trade agreements, hawking them around the world as the ideal way to further trade liberalisation.

Third, America's tactic is weakening the power of poor countries in multilateral trade negotiations. Bilateral deals fragment the coalitions of developing countries, as each abandons its legitimate objections to the inclusion of extraneous issues in trade treaties. Having abandoned these objections in a bilateral deal with the US, how can those countries pursue them in WTO negotiations?

The process of trade liberalisation is becoming a sham, the ultimate objective being the capture, reshaping and distortion of the WTO in the image of American lobbying interests. The protection of intellectual property provides a good example of US tactics. Washington has used both inducements and punishments to secure its interests. During negotiations over the North America Free Trade Agreement, Mexico was told that the price of a deal was acceptance of intellectual property protection provisions.

It was a price Mexico was prepared to pay. But the US has also demanded that other countries accept similar provisions or face retaliatory tariffs. Subsequently, during the Uruguay round of trade liberalisation, the US was able to insert the trade-related intellectual property regime (Trips) into the WTO, even though no fully argued case had ever been made that Trips, which is about royalty collection and not trade, should be included.

Case Study 14.4 continued

Mexico also had to accept provisions on environmental and labour standards annexed to the NAFTA treaty. But such standards were put right at the centre of the free trade agreement with Jordan, drafted in the last days of the Clinton administration. And with the Bush administration currently negotiating an agreement with Central America, Democrats are under pressure from the labour and environmental lobbies to demand not just the enforcement of local standards but higher standards altogether.

In the free trade agreements with Chile and Singapore, the US Treasury insisted on inserting a ban on the use of capital controls, even though the International Monetary Fund has finally come round to the view that they might, on occasion, be justified. Chile and Singapore finally gave in, agreeing to a dispute settlement and compensation mechanism should such controls ever be used. Washington has thereby created another precedent.

Thanks to the myopic and self-serving policies of the world's only superpower, bilateral free trade agreements are damaging the global trading system. They are undermining the most favoured nation rule ensuring equal treatment in the WTO. Bilateral deals have become a vehicle for introducing extraneous issues into the WTO for the benefit of narrow US domestic interests. They are thereby distorting the role of the WTO.

Source: *Financial Times*, 14 July 2003. Reprinted with permission

Questions

1 Why are *developed economies* generally supportive of bilateral trade treaties?

2 Why are *developing economies* and their supporters often opposed to the use of bilateral trade treaties?

3 Carefully consider how this case study could be used by both critics of the WTO and by supporters of the WTO.

East and South East Asia

Here we consider the 'Pacific rim' countries of East and South East Asia, which also form part of the 'triad' of the global economy (together with Europe and North America). East and South East Asia account for some 26% of world exports by value and contribute around 29% of world manufacturing output by value. However, we shall concentrate on the rapid rise of the Chinese economy within this broader region.

The Chinese economy

China is fast becoming an economic giant, not only in Asia, but also on the world stage. Between 1978 and 1997, China's GDP registered an average annual growth rate of 9.8%, with the per capita GDP growth rate at 8.4% per annum. Between 1998 and 2004 the Chinese economy has been estimated to be growing at around 8% per annum. If it maintains this growth rate, many economists believe it will become the world's largest economy by the year 2020 in terms of absolute value of GDP, though not in terms of GDP per head. For the last two centuries one country has emerged as the dominant economic power. The nineteenth century belonged to the UK, the twentieth century to the US and it looks like the twenty-first century will belong to China.

Table 14.7 presents some selected information on the contribution of China, US, EU and others to the growth in world business activity over the time periods indicated. Some balance of payments and asset-holding data is also presented for China.

Table 14.7 Contributions to World Business Activity

- *Global GDP growth: % shares 1995–2002*
  China 25%, Rest of SE Asia 20%, US 14%, EU 5%
- *Real annual GDP growth: % shares 1995–2002*
  China 8%, Rest of SE Asia 4.5%, US 3.2%, EU 2.3%
- *Annual import growth: % shares 1995–2002*
  China 12.2%, US 6.2%, EU 3%
- *China balance of payments situation 2003*
  - with US: Chinese annual surplus of $144bn
  - with rest of world: Chinese annual deficit of $126bn
- *Chinese holding of US securities (bills, bonds, shares)*
  $500bn in 2003, and rising at an annual rate of $150bn a year

In 2004, China itself is expected to contribute almost 1% to global GDP growth, almost one-third of the total. Various authors have attributed China's rapid economic development to the transformation from a centrally planned economy towards a market system and the opening of the economy through the 'Open Door Policy'. Since the open door policy was installed during the late 1970s, China has become a highly attractive market for foreign companies. There has also been significant growth in foreign trade.

CHECK THE NET
www.cbbc.org provides information on doing business in China.

Since China is undergoing massive reform, it can be difficult for a foreign firm to keep track of the constantly changing political and legal factors. China has been described as a planned economy characterised by a weak capital market structure, institutional instability and poorly specified property rights. The latter is a major issue for foreign firms entering China. Developing a global brand involves huge investment. Poor enforcement of intellectual property rights (IPR) not only results in companies losing sales to cheaper imitations, but also it can damage the product's brand equity and image. Case Study 14.5 looks at a recent example involving intellectual property rights in China.

Case Study 14.5 Durex in China

SSL PLC is a major producer of health-related products and is responsible for the famous condom brand 'Durex'. Since its registration as a condom brand in 1929, the name has become well known in many countries. Durex has a 22% global market share, has become a premium seller in over 40 countries, and is number two in 23 countries. In recent years the company has taken steps to conquer the Chinese market by establishing a 50/50-equity joint venture (EJV) with a Chinese privately owned company. Set up in 1998, the EJV is based in the Chinese coastal city of Qingdao, Shandong Province.

The condom market in China is very competitive. Durex's main competitors in China are essentially the other foreign brands. However, one of the company's local competitors is a brand called Jissbon, which in the short term has resulted in being a real issue for Durex. The world-famous condom producer filed a lawsuit against Jissbon on 24 June 2002. Durex is accusing Jissbon of stealing information from Durex's website and printing it word-for-word to describe its own product.

On its website, Jissbon described itself as 'a British-based world famous condom producer with a 70-year history and 20% of the global market share whose products are sold in more than 140 countries'. The description is very similar to that of Durex.

Durex claims the design of Jissbon's website and even the details it provides are copied from Durex. As a result, Durex accused Jissbon of making claims that Durex can genuinely make about its own brand. In response to Durex's accusations, Jissbon admitted that some of the information on its website is false but stressed that the website is not for business purposes but intended to change people's ideas of condoms and safe sex.

Durex asked for a formal apology and compensation of 5 million yuan (US$602,410) from Jissbon, saying that Jissbon has caused great loss to Durex's valuable image.

The case was finally settled in December 2002. Jissbon had to give Durex 100,000 yuan, alter their website and make a public apology in the national press.

Source: Wilson, J. (2003)

Questions

1. What steps can companies take in an attempt to prevent IPR infringement?
2. Discuss the impact IPR infringement has on the consumer.

Fake products and trademark violations are rife in China. However, since China's accession to the WTO the Chinese government has cracked down hard on IPR infringement. The following extract from *Beijing Today* (Beijing newspaper) on 23 August 2002 is evidence of stricter controls:

> A Chinese motorcycle maker has been fined about $110,000 for pirating trademarks belonging to Japan's Yamaha conglomerate, a lawyer for Yamaha

> said on Thursday. The ruling by the Tianjin People's High Court earlier this month, also requires the Tianjin Gangtian Group to apologise to Yamaha and remove the trademark name from their products.

The sentence in the Yamaha case is one of the highest of any pirating cases in China. The fine probably reflects a very small percentage of lost sales to Yamaha as a result of IPR infringement.

A vital aspect of doing business in China is that permission to conduct business is controlled by the government. The host government controls and restricts a foreign company's activities by encouraging and offering support or by discouraging and banning its activities; this depends on the potential benefits the foreign company is likely to deliver. As China is a developing country, a sudden change in policy could seriously affect a firm's business environment.

In the year 2008, all eyes of the world will be focused on Beijing, as China becomes host to the Olympic Games for the first time. The Chinese government is investing millions of dollars in reducing the pollution and developing the infrastructure required for staging such an event. Beijingers are actively encouraged by the government to learn English in preparation for the influx of foreign visitors that will descend on the city. This is an ideal opportunity for the country to continue to share its culture with the outside world. Although the Chinese government is investing billions of dollars into cleaning up the natural environment, especially in Beijing (in time for the Olympics), parts of China continue to suffer from environmental abuse. China already contains several of the world's most polluted cities. A primary cause of this pollution is the country's heavy reliance on coal as its main source of energy.

The long-term rewards that can be gained for foreign firms seeking market development in China are obvious. Joining the WTO and the Olympic Games provide real investment opportunities. However, the complexity of the market, particularly the cultural and legal factors, cannot be ignored.

International institutions and international business

International business can benefit by being aware of the institutional context in which international trade and investment takes place. In this section we review the roles of some of the important international institutions involved with trade and investment.

The WTO and GATT

General Agreement on Tariffs and Trade (GATT)

The General Agreement on Tariffs and Trade was signed in 1947 by 23 industrialised nations that included the UK, the US, Canada, France and the Benelux countries. The objectives of GATT were to reduce tariffs and other barriers to trade in the belief that freer trade would raise living standards in all participating countries. Since 1947 there have been eight 'rounds' of trade negotiations, with the average tariff in the industrialised nations falling from 40% in 1947 to below 5% in 1995 when the GATT was replaced by the World Trade Organisation (WTO). Supporters of the role of GATT point to facts such as the volume of world trade rising by 1,500% and world output by 600% over the years of its existence.

The World Trade Organisation (WTO)

The World Trade Organisation replaced GATT in 1995 and now has 147 members, with the People's Republic of China, Chinese Taipei and Cambodia being the latest to join. The WTO's members in total account for more than 90% of the value of world trade. The objectives of the WTO are essentially the same as GATT's, namely to reduce tariffs and other barriers to trade and to eliminate discrimination in trade, and by doing so contribute to rising living standards and a fuller use of world resources.

WTO principles

Both the GATT and its successor, the WTO, have sought to implement a number of principles:

- *Non-discrimination.* The benefits of any trading advantage agreed between two nations (i.e. in bilateral negotiations) must be extended to all nations (i.e. become multilateral). This is sometimes referred to as the 'most favoured nation' clause.
- *Progressive reduction in tariff and non-tariff barriers.* Certain exceptions, however, are permitted in specific circumstances. For example, Article 18 allows for the protection of 'infant industries' by the newly industrialising countries, whereas Article 19 permits any country to abstain from a general tariff cut in situations where rising imports might seriously damage domestic production. Similarly, Articles 21–5 allow protection to continue where 'strategic interests' are involved, such as national security.
- *Solving trade disputes through consultation rather than retaliation.* Again, certain exceptions are permitted. For example, Article 6 permits retaliatory sanctions to be applied if 'dumping' can be proven, i.e. the sale of products at artificially low prices (e.g. below cost). Countries in dispute are expected to negotiate bilaterally, but if these negotiations break down a WTO-appointed working party or panel can investigate the issue and make recommendations. Should any one of the parties refuse to accept this outcome, the WTO can impose fines and/or sanction certain types of retaliation by the aggrieved party.

CHECK THE NET

Visit the WTO website (www.wto.org) to find a wealth of information on international trade. Free online registration provides regular WTO news sent direct to your e-mail.

International Monetary Fund (IMF)

The IMF plays a key role in providing foreign currencies and other sources of world liquidity to support the growth of international trade and payments. It also provides specific packages of financial support for economies in times of need. This latter role involves a variety of 'stabilisation programmes', which provide essential funding but only on condition that the countries receiving funds agree to implement specific programmes of change agreed with the IMF.

The main components of typical IMF stabilisation programmes include some or all of the following:

- *fiscal contraction* – a reduction in the public sector deficit through cuts in public expenditure and/or rises in taxation;
- *monetary contraction* – restrictions on credit to the public sector and increases in interest rates;
- *liberalisation of the economy* via reduction or elimination of controls, and privatisation of public-sector assets;
- *incomes policy* – wage restraint and removal of subsidies and reduction of transfer payments.

However, some have criticised these IMF stabilisation programmes. For example, by deflating demand, the IMF has imposed large adjustment costs on borrowing countries through losses of output and employment, further impoverishing the poor and even destabilising governments.

World Bank

The World Bank is, in effect, a grouping of three international institutions, namely the International Bank for Reconstruction and Development (IBRD), the International Development Association (IDA) and the International Finance Corporation (IFC).

International Bank for Reconstruction and Development (IBRD)

The origins of the World Bank lie in the formation of the IBRD in 1946. The IBRD sought to help countries raise the finance needed to reconstruct their war-damaged economies. This often took the form of guaranteeing loans that could then be obtained at lower interest rates than might otherwise have been possible.

International Development Association (IDA)

In 1958 a second international institution was created to operate alongside the IBRD, namely the International Development Association. The main objective of the IDA was to provide development finance for low-income nations which had insufficient resources to pay interest on the IBRD loans.

International Finance Corporation (IFC)

The International Finance Corporation was established in 1959. Unlike the previous two bodies, the IFC concentrates on lending to *private* borrowers involved in development projects. Initially much of this lending was for specific infrastructure projects such as dams, power facilities, transport links etc. More recently, the focus of lending has shifted towards improving the efficiency and accountability of the administrative and institutional structures in the recipient countries.

UN international institutions

Here we consider a number of institutions that operate under the auspices of the United Nations. The UN itself was established by charter in 1945 and consists of 185 member states. Its mission statement is to establish a world order based on peace, prosperity and freedom, and its most visible decision-making body is the UN General Assembly, in which all members participate.

United Nations Conference on Trade, Aid and Development (UNCTAD)

The conference first met in 1964 and has met subsequently at three- or four-year intervals. All members of the UN are members of the conference which has a permanent executive and secretariat. UNCTAD seeks to give particular support to the LDCs in their various trade disputes with the more developed economies. An important contribution of UNCTAD has been to support the introduction of the 'Generalised System of Preferences' (GSP) in 1971 which has helped give some of the exports of LDCs preferential access to the markets of the advanced industrialised economies.

United Nations Industrial Development Organisation (UNIDO)

This was established in 1966 to provide technical assistance for developing countries seeking to industrialise. It helps countries to undertake industrial surveys, formulate industrial development strategies, conduct project appraisals and implement productivity and marketing strategies.

Organisation for Economic Cooperation and Development (OECD)

The OECD was established in 1961 as a grouping of the advanced industrialised economies. Its main objectives were to encourage high levels of economic growth and employment amongst its member states, together with a stable financial system. It also seeks to contribute to the economic development in non-member states (including LDCs) and to expand world trade on a multilateral basis.

Group of Seven/Eight/Ten

This refers to the seven major industrial countries within the OECD that meet at fairly regular intervals to consider global economic issues, especially those of a macroeconomic nature. The seven countries involved are Canada, France, Germany, Italy, Japan, the UK and the US (the Russian Federation has been added to this number on an informal basis in recent times when the G7 became G8). The so-called Group of Ten (G10) countries are the G7 countries plus Belgium, the Netherlands and Sweden.

In recent times many of these international institutions and arrangements have become the focus of criticism and their meetings have often been the occasion for large-scale protest.

Free trade and government protectionism

In this section we briefly review the arguments advanced in favour of both free trade and protectionism, before looking more carefully at the actual techniques used by governments in seeking to protect their key sectors of economic activity.

Arguments in favour of free trade

The main argument advanced by 'free traders' is that countries are better off by *specialising and trading* than being self-sufficient. In terms of the production possibility curve of Chapter 1 (p. 4) we are considering the claim that by engaging in trade, countries can achieve a situation outside that curve. If they remained self-sufficient and engaged in no trade they would only achieve resource allocations on or inside the production possibility curve.

Two particularly important theories have encouraged such specialisation and trade.

Absolute advantage

As long ago as 1776, Adam Smith in his *Wealth of Nations* had suggested that countries could benefit from specialising in products in which they had an *absolute advantage* over other countries, trading any surpluses with those countries. By 'absolute advantage' Smith meant the ability to produce those products at lower resource cost (e.g. fewer labour and capital inputs) than the other countries.

This was an essentially limited view as to the benefits of international business. For example, in a simple two-country, two-product model, each country would have to demonstrate that it was *absolutely more efficient* than the other in one of these products if specialisation and trade were to be mutually beneficial.

Comparative advantage

David Ricardo sought, in 1817, to broaden the basis on which trade was seen to be beneficial by developing his theory of *comparative advantage*. Again we can illustrate by using a simple two-country, two-product model. In this approach, even where a country has an absolute advantage (less resource cost) over the other country in *both* products, it can still gain by specialisation and trade in that product in which its *absolute advantage is greatest*, i.e. in which it has a *comparative advantage*. Similarly, the other country which has an absolute disadvantage (higher resource cost) in both products can still gain by specialisation and trade in that product in which its *absolute disadvantage is least*, i.e. in which it also has a *comparative advantage*.

Box 14.1 outlines the original analysis used by David Ricardo in championing free trade.

Box 14.1 Comparative advantage

Ricardo used the following example, shown in Table 14.8, to demonstrate his theory.

Table 14.8 Before specialisation and before trade

Labour hours required to produce

Country	1 gallon wine	1 yard cloth
Portugal	80	90
England	120	100

- Portugal has an *absolute advantage* in both wine and cloth over England, since fewer resources (labour hours) are needed to produce each product.
- England has an *absolute disadvantage* in both products.
- Portugal's absolute advantage compared to England is greater in wine (80 : 120) than in cloth (90 : 100). We say that Portugal has a *comparative advantage* in wine.
- England's absolute disadvantage compared to Portugal is less in cloth (100 : 90) than in wine (120 : 80). We say that England has a *comparative advantage* in cloth.

Provided the terms of trade (i.e. rate of exchange between wine and cloth) are appropriate we can show that *both* countries can gain by specialising according to comparative advantages and trading with one another.

Table 14.9 assumes that Portugal uses all its 170 hours of labour on wine production and England uses all its 220 hours of labour on cloth production (assuming constant returns to labour). No trade has yet taken place.

Table 14.9 After specialisation and before trade

Country	Resource	Output of wine	Output of cloth
Portugal	170 hours labour	$2\frac{1}{8}$ gallons	—
England	220 hours labour	—	$2\frac{1}{5}$ yards

We now assume *terms of trade* in which 1 gallon of wine exchanges for 1 yard of cloth. Table 14.10 shows the possible consumption situation for each country, after specialisation and after trade.

Table 14.10 After specialisation and after trade

Country	Consumption of wine	Consumption of cloth
Portugal	$1\frac{1}{8}$ gallons	1 yard
England	1 gallon	$1\frac{1}{5}$ yards

We can now compare the *self-sufficiency* situation for each country in Table 14.8 with the situation after specialisation according to comparative advantage and after trade in Table 14.10. Clearly each country is better off, consuming more of one product and no less of the other.

- Portugal has an extra $\frac{1}{8}$ gallon of wine, and no less cloth.
- England has an extra $\frac{1}{5}$ yard of cloth, and no less wine.

Conclusion: Specialisation and trade is preferred to self-sufficiency in Ricardo's theory.

The suggestion that free trade is beneficial to all who participate is one of the strongest arguments used in its favour. By specialising in products in which countries have comparative advantages and trading their surpluses, supporters of free trade argue that world resource allocation is improved to the benefit of all.

Welfare gains from trade

Before turning to criticisms of this viewpoint, we can express the case for free trade using more up-to-date techniques than those of Ricardo in 1817. Here we make use of concepts already introduced earlier in the book, namely that 'economic welfare' can be regarded as the sum of *consumer surplus* (Chapter 2, p. 72) and *producer surplus* (Chapter 3, p. 120).

Figure 14.7 is used to explain this approach. It shows that free trade could, in theory, bring welfare benefits to an economy previously protected.

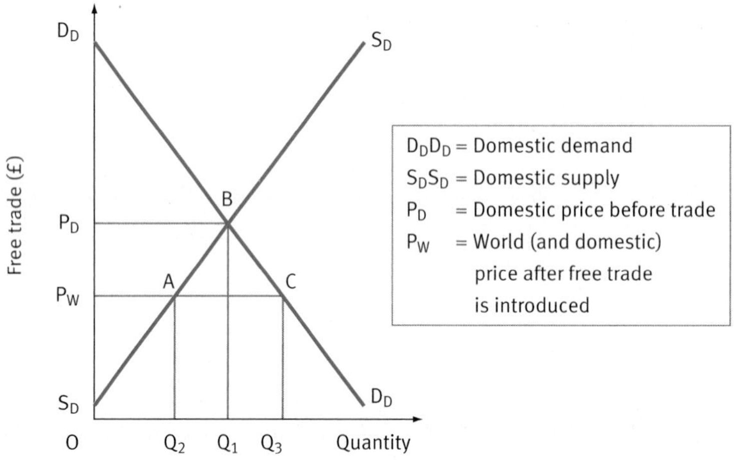

Fig 14.7 Gains from free trade versus no trade

Suppose the industry is initially *completely protected*. The domestic price P_D will then be determined solely by the intersection of the domestic supply ($S_D - S_D$) and domestic demand ($D_D - D_D$) curves. Suppose that the government now decides to remove these trade barriers and to allow foreign competition. For simplicity, we assume a perfectly elastic 'world' supply curve $P_W - C$, giving a total supply curve (domestic and world) of SDAC. Domestic price will then be forced down to the world level, P_W, with domestic demand being OQ_3 at this price. To meet this domestic demand, OQ_2 will be supplied from domestic sources, with Q_2Q_3 supplied from the rest of the world (i.e. imported).

- The *consumer surplus*, which is the difference between what consumers are prepared to pay and what they have to pay, has risen from D_DBP_D to D_DCP_W.
- The *producer surplus*, which is the difference between the price the producer receives and the minimum necessary to induce production, has fallen from P_DBS_D to P_WAS_D.
- The gain in consumer surplus outweighs the loss in producer surplus by the area ABC, which could then be regarded as the *net gain* in economic welfare as a result of free trade replacing protectionism.

Arguments in favour of protectionism

Not everyone would agree with the suggestion that free trade is necessarily in the best interests of individual countries. A number of arguments have been used to justify the use of tariffs and other means of protection against imported products:

- to prevent dumping (i.e. sale of products at artificially low prices, even below average cost);
- to protect infant industries (i.e. new industries which need support in their early stages in order to grow strong enough to compete with overseas companies);
- to protect strategically important industries (e.g. defence, those which underpin other industries);
- to maintain employment (e.g. protecting major labour intensive industries at risk from overseas competition).

In the next section we consider some of the *policy mechanisms* that governments might use when seeking to protect their domestic industries.

Methods of protection

Those involved in international business face a number of methods by which individual countries or regional trading blocs seek to restrict the level of imports into the home market.

Tariff

A *tariff* is, in effect, a tax levied on imported goods, usually with the intention of raising the price of imports and thereby discouraging their purchase. Additionally, it is a source of revenue for the government. Tariffs can be of two types: *lump sum* (or *specific*) with the tariff a fixed amount per unit; *ad valorem* (or *percentage*) with the tariff a variable amount per unit. There is a general presumption that tariff barriers will discourage trade and reduce economic welfare.

Non-tariff barriers

In recent years there has also been a considerable increase in trade that is subject to *non-tariff* barriers. The main types of non-tariff barrier in use include the following.

- *Quotas*. A quota is a limit applied to the number of units (or the monetary value) of an imported good that may be sold in a country in a given period.
- *Voluntary export restraints (VERs)*. These are arrangements by which an individual exporter or group of exporters agrees with an importing country to limit the quantity of a specific product to be sold to a particular market over a given period of time. VERs are, in effect, quotas.
- *Subsidies*. The forms of protection we have described so far have all been designed to restrict the volume of imports directly. An alternative policy is to provide a subsidy to domestic producers so as to improve their competitiveness in both the home and world markets.
- *Safety and technological standards*. These are often imposed in the knowledge that certain imported goods will be unable to meet the specified requirements.
- *Time-consuming formalities*. During the 1990s the EU alleged that 'excessive invoicing requirements' required by US importing authorities had hampered exports from member countries to the US.
- *Public sector contracts*. Governments often give preference to domestic firms in the issuing of public contracts.
- *Labour standards*. This bears some resemblance to the point made above concerning safety and technological standards but is rather more controversial. Does the enforcement of minimum labour standards represent a source of support for the poorest workers in the developing world or is it simply a hidden form of protection?

CHECK THE NET

As well as the WTO website (see p. 583), other sources of information on international trade and payments, international institutions and exchange rates include:
www.imf.org
www.oecd.org
www.worldbank.org
www.un.org
www.dti.gov.uk
www.europa.eu.int
www.eubusiness.com

Activity 14.3

1 In a two-product, two-country model, which of the following corresponds to Ricardo's theory of 'comparative advantage'?

(a) Each country specialising in that product in which it is absolutely most efficient
(b) Each country specialising in that product in which it is absolutely least efficient
(c) Each country specialising in that product in which it is relatively most efficient (or relatively least inefficient)
(d) Each country specialising in that product in which the terms of trade are most favourable
(e) Each country specialising in that product in which the terms of trade are least favourable

2 Which of the following is often said to be a benefit of specialisation and trade?

(a) Reaching a consumption bundle inside the country's production possibility frontier
(b) Reaching a consumption bundle on the country's production possibility frontier
(c) Reaching a consumption bundle inside the country's terms of trade
(d) Reaching a consumption bundle outside the country's terms of trade
(e) Reaching a consumption bundle outside the country's production possibility frontier

3 Which *three* of the following are often used to support a policy of protectionism?

(a) Mature industry argument
(b) Infant industry argument
(c) Protecting strategically important industries
(d) Encouraging 'dumping'
(e) Preventing 'dumping'

4 True/False

(a) A country has a comparative advantage (in a two-product model) in that product in which it has a lower opportunity cost than the other country.
True/False
(b) The international product life cycle (IPLC) is usually applied to a variety of knowledge intensive products.
True/False
(c) Inter-industry trade refers to situations where a country exports certain terms from a given product range while at the same time importing other items from the same product range.
True/False
(d) A fall in the sterling exchange rate will make UK exports cheaper abroad and imports into the UK dearer at home.
True/False

5 Where member countries reduce or abolish restrictions on trade between each other while maintaining their individual protectionist measures against non-members.

(a) Common market
(b) Economic union
(c) Free trade area
(d) Customs union
(e) Common Agricultural Policy (CAP)

6 Where, as well as liberalising trade amongst members, a common external tariff is established to protect the group from imports from any non-members.

(a) Common market
(b) Economic union
(c) Free trade area
(d) Customs union
(e) Common Agricultural Policy (CAP)

7 Where the customs union is extended to include the free movement of factors of production as well as products within the designated area.

(a) Common market
(b) Economic union
(c) Free trade area
(d) Customs union
(e) Common Agricultural Policy (CAP)

8 Where buffer stock purchases have often been used to achieve the target price for various products.

(a) Common market
(b) Economic union
(c) Free trade area
(d) Customs union
(e) Common Agricultural Policy (CAP)

9 Where national economic policies are also harmonised within the common market.

(a) Common market
(b) Economic union
(c) Free trade area
(d) Customs union
(e) Common Agricultural Policy (CAP)

Answers to Checkpoint and Activities can be found on pp. 705–35.

Key Terms

'First-generation franchising' Where the franchisor has limited involvement with the franchisee.

Foreign direct investment (fdi) Investment across borders involving plant, machinery and other capital items.

Greenfield investment Investment involving the setting up of new buildings and plant.

Internalisation A reason for operating as a multinational by owning production or service facilities overseas. Higher transaction costs of *indirect* involvement (e.g. franchise) make ownership preferable; i.e. ownership internalises the transaction costs.

Location-specific advantages Advantages of specific location to the multinational's operations.

Multinational enterprise A company that owns or controls production or service facilities in more than one country.

Ownership-specific advantages Competitive advantages over other firms in overseas markets related to assets owned by the MNE.

'Piggybacking' Where different companies share resources in order to access foreign markets more effectively.

Portfolio investment Investment involving financial assets (e.g. stocks, shares, etc.).

'Second-generation franchising' Where the franchisor has extensive involvement with the franchisee.

'Shared value-added joint venture' Where partners contribute to the same function in the joint venture.

'Specialised joint venture' Where each partner brings a specific and different competence to the joint venture.

Transnational *see* 'Multinational enterprise'.

Transnationality index A measure of a firm's multinational involvement which uses the average of three different ratios: namely, foreign assets to total assets, foreign sales to total sales and foreign employment to total employment.

Key Points

- Forms of internationalisation may involve direct/indirect exports, licensing/franchising and alliances/joint ventures and foreign direct investment (fdi).
- A 'multinational' is a company that owns or controls production or service facilities in more than one country.
- The 'transnationality index' is a useful measure of the degree of multinational involvement of a firm.
- Multinationals account for around 30% of GDP in the UK and almost half of manufacturing employment.
- Successful multinational activity from the home base usually depends on the possession of 'ownership-specific' advantages over firms in the host country, together with 'location-specific' advantages which favour overseas production.
- Cost-oriented multinationals mainly focus on reducing costs of production via overseas production (often via vertical integration); market-oriented multinationals mainly focus on easier sales access to overseas markets via overseas production (often via horizontal integration).

Assessment Practice

The following questions will help to determine your level of understanding of some of the issues raised in this chapter.

Multiple choice questions

1 **Which *two* of the following are most likely to be associated with a cost-oriented multinational?**

(a) Establishing assembly operations in close geographical proximity to major international markets
(b) Using backward vertical integration to secure components from lower-priced overseas locations
(c) Using conglomerate mergers on an international scale to reduce risks
(d) A healthcare company establishing overseas affiliates in high income countries with ageing demographic profiles
(e) Global rationalisation of production operations to gain maximum economies of scale

2 **Which *two* of the following are most likely to be associated with a market-oriented multinational?**

(a) Establishing assembly operations in close geographical proximity to major international markets
(b) Using backward vertical integration to secure components from lower-priced overseas locations
(c) Using conglomerate mergers on an international scale to reduce risks
(d) A healthcare company establishing overseas affiliates in high income countries with ageing demographic profiles
(e) Global rationalisation of production operations to gain maximum economies of scale

3 **Which *two* of the following might be regarded as location-specific advantages for multinational involvement?**

(a) Setting up an overseas production operation because of the uncertainty of franchising operations to 'local' firms already in the market
(b) A high-tech electronics company moving into university science parks overseas
(c) Exploiting a well-established global brand image to dominate overseas markets
(d) Seeking to extend the product life cycle by moving into overseas markets which are still in the 'growth' phase for that product
(e) Undercutting the prices of 'local' producers in overseas markets by exploiting the global economies of scale available to the multinational

4 **Which *two* of the following might be regarded as ownership-specific advantages for multinational involvement?**

(a) Setting up an overseas production operation because of the uncertainty of franchising operations to 'local' firms already in the market
(b) A high-tech electronics company moving into university science parks overseas
(c) Exploiting a well-established global brand image to dominate overseas markets
(d) Seeking to extend the product life cycle by moving into overseas markets which are still in the 'growth' phase for that product
(e) Undercutting the prices of 'local' producers in overseas markets by exploiting the global economies of scale available to the multinational

5 **Which *one* of the following provides an example of 'internalisation' as a reason for multinational activity?**

(a) Setting up an overseas production operation because of the uncertainty of franchising operations to 'local' firms already in the market
(b) A high-tech electronics company moving into university science parks overseas
(c) Exploiting a well-established global brand image to dominate overseas markets
(d) Seeking to extend the product life cycle by moving into overseas markets which are still in the 'growth' phase for that product
(e) Undercutting the prices of 'local' producers in overseas markets by exploiting the global economies of scale available to the multinational

6 Which *three* of the following ratios are used in constructing the transnationality index?

(a) Foreign employment to total employment
(b) Foreign managers to total managers
(c) Foreign sales to total sales
(d) Foreign costs to total costs
(e) Foreign assets to total assets

7 A firm that adopts a polycentric approach to doing business is regarded as:

(a) employing over 250 staff
(b) forming a strategic alliance with a supplier
(c) being culturally sensitive
(d) employing the latest technology.

8 The US is regarded as:

(a) a low-context culture
(b) a high-context culture
(c) a medium-context culture
(d) a homogeneous culture.

9 Which of the following is NOT a way in which a company may internationalise its business activity?

(a) Direct exporting
(b) Indirect exporting
(c) Using joint ventures with overseas firms
(d) Establishing a subsidiary in a different geographical region of the home country
(e) Franchising operations in overseas countries

10 Japan is regarded as:

(a) a low context culture
(b) a high context culture
(c) a medium-context culture
(d) a homogenous culture

Data response and stimulus questions

1

Scores obtained by Hofstede on four cultural dimensions

Country	Individualism	Power distance	Uncertainty avoidance	Masculinity
Canada	80	39	48	52
France	71	68	86	43
Germany	67	35	65	66
Great Britain	89	35	35	66
Mexico	30	81	82	69
Netherlands	80	38	53	14
USA	91	40	46	62

Questions

(a) Using the data, suggest why a multinational operating in Mexico might act differently to a multinational operating in Great Britain.

(b) Comment on any other implications of these scores for international business activities.

2 The following price comparisons for identical products were observed in February 2004 between New York (NY) and London using the £/$ exchange rate at that date.

- **Fender stratocaster (guitar)**
  £438 NY: £645 London
- **Apple iPod**
  £158 NY: £249 London
- **Levi 50s**
  £26 NY: £45 London
- **Rolex yacht master gold watch**
  £10,372 NY: £12,390 London
- **Pair of Jimmy Choo stilettos**
  £392 NY: £360 London
- **Nike airwave trainers**
  £42 NY: £70 London

(a) How have movements in the £/$ exchange rate contributed to these differences? (Note on average the US prices were 20% higher only 12 months previously.)

(b) What implications might follow from such price differentials?

3 Look carefully at the table opposite, which shows two scenarios for an MNE whose production is vertically integrated, with operations in two countries. Basic manufacture takes place in country A and final assembly and sale in country B. In country A the corporate tax rate is 25%, while in country B it is 50%.

In Scenario 1, the 'transfer price' (i.e. the internal price used by the company to calculate profits in different countries) is set at the market price of $50m in country A for the intermediate products which are now to be 'shipped' to country B for incorporation into the final product. The operation in country B incurs additional costs of $40m, after which the final product is sold in country B for $100m; thus the subsidiary will declare a profit of £10m and incur a tax liability of $5m. The company as a whole will face a total tax liability of $7.5m in countries A and B taken together.

Question

Can you explain what is happening in Scenario 2?

$m	Scenario 1		Scenario 2	
	Country A	Country B	Country A	Country B
Costs	40	90	40	100
Sales	50	100	60	100
Profit	10	10	20	0
Tax liability	2.5	5	5	0
Total tax	7.5		5	

True/False questions

1 When a firm sells overseas by using intermediaries such as an export house, we refer to this as direct exporting.

True/False

2 A confirming house buys products from a domestic firm and sells them abroad on its own account.

True/False

3 Economies of scale enable multinationals to produce in large volume at low unit costs and are therefore a type of ownership-specific advantage.

True/False

4 The offer of free factory space, zero business rates and other subsidies to induce foreign firms to set up production in a country is an example of ownership-specific advantages.

True/False

5 A multinational engaging in exploration in one country, component production in another and assembly in a third might be called a vertically integrated multinational.

True/False

6 A multinational engaged in the assembly function in three separate countries might be called a vertically integrated multinational.

True/False

7 When one firm pays another firm to gain access to its distribution network in another country, we call this 'piggybacking'.

True/False

8 'First-generation franchising' refers to situations where the franchisee receives extensive guidance and instructions from the franchisor.

True/False

9 Patents, trademarks and copyrights are often referred to as 'intellectual property rights'.

True/False

10 In a 'shared value-added' joint venture, each partner brings a specific competency; e.g. one might research, the other might manufacture.

True/False

Essay questions

1 Based on a company of your choice, identify what you believe to be an appropriate international market for that company to enter. Your answer should include an environmental analysis and an explanation of market entry method.
2 Suggest ways in which global brands and global advertising campaigns might benefit a company. Provide suitable case examples.
3 Explain potential cultural factors a US firm needs to be aware of before entering the Asian market.
4 Given important environmental issues in recent years, consumers are becoming increasingly concerned about food products. In response to this, how might manufacturers of health food products adapt their international marketing techniques?
5 Discuss possible market entry methods for a large UK firm considering entering Japan.

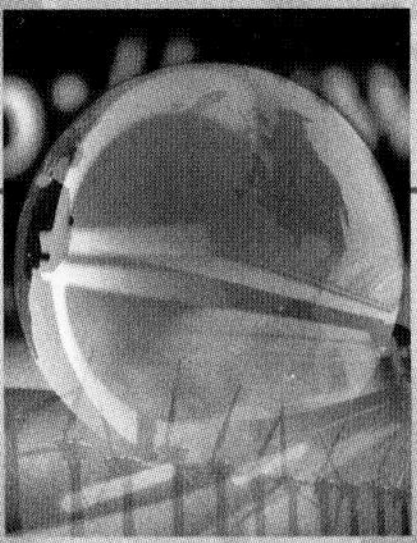

Chapter 15

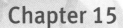

Strategies in a globalised business environment

Introduction

Throughout this book we have already touched on many aspects of strategic business analysis. As early as Chapter 2 we noted the importance of the linkage between price elasticity of demand and revenue to the firm's pricing strategy. In Chapter 3 we reviewed the pricing strategies required in both short-run and long-run time periods for the firm to remain in a particular industry and in Chapter 13 examined the role of price in the marketing mix. Similar strategic implications for price and output policy have been mentioned in most or all chapters of the book. Chapter 14 reviewed a wide range of strategic issues involved in the internationalisation process. However, in this chapter we focus more on the *frameworks* within which the business can refine and develop broad strategic initiatives before examining how businesses seek to implement these strategies in a globalised environment.

Learning objectives:

By the end of this chapter you should be able to:

- identify the main stages in developing and operating a strategy, whether at corporate, business unit or functional levels
- examine the more 'conventional' strategic approaches by *businesses* within essentially stable sectors of the economy; these include Porter's 'Five Forces' and 'generic' strategies, Ansoff's matrix, SWOT and PEST analyses, Boston matrix, amongst others
- examine strategic approaches involving *national* business activity, such as Porter's 'Diamond' and Vernon's 'International product life cycle'
- outline some of the key patterns and trends attributed to globalisation and assess their implications for multinational enterprises (MNEs) which must continually re-evaluate the nature and geographical location of the activities which comprise their value chains

- review the newer approaches to strategy within globalised economies, where previously stable sectors of economic activity are undergoing rapid change, and the contribution of joint ventures and alliances to strategic initiatives
- review further strategies involving reconfiguring value chains in order to remain competitive within the global economy.

Strategic frameworks for corporate activity

As previously mentioned, aspects of the strategic approaches covered here may have been touched on elsewhere. However, in this chapter we adopt a more 'holistic' approach, bringing entire strategic frameworks to bear on particular business problems.

Many definitions have been applied to business strategy which, while differing in detail, broadly agree that it involves devising the guiding rules or principles which influence the direction and scope of the organisation's activities over the long term. Johnson and Scholes describe strategy as:

Quote

> The direction and scope of an organisation over the long term which achieves advantages for the organisation through its configuration of resources within a changing environment to meet the needs of markets and to fulfil shareholder expectations
>
> *(Johnson and Scholes, 2003).*

In this definition, as in many others, there is clearly a focus on:

- long-term direction;
- internal resource allocation;
- external environmental factors.

Levels of strategy

For larger organisations strategy may be developed at three different levels.

- **Corporate (enterprise) level.** Here the strategy involves the *organisation as a whole*, its objectives and mission statement, the sectors of economic activity with which it wishes to be involved, the geographical location of its activities, the mechanisms (e.g. mergers, alliances, joint ventures) by which it might grow, the activities for which highest priority might be given in allocating scarce resources.
- **Business level.** Here the strategy involves a *particular part of the organisation*, such as a particular division or subsidiary, a particular market or industry sector. At the business level the focus is on issues of competitive strategy, such as how the business intends to compete effectively within that particular market or industry.

- **Functional (operational) level.** Here the strategy involves the approach to be adopted within *functional areas* such as marketing, production, finance, human resource management and distribution.

Strategic management

Achieving a consistent approach across these three levels may require careful management, especially for larger, more complex organisations. *Strategic management* is a term widely used to describe this process.

Quote

> The term strategic management refers to the managerial process of forming a strategic vision, setting objectives, crafting a strategy, implementing and executing the strategy, and then over time initiating whatever corrective adjustments in the vision, objectives, strategy and execution are deemed appropriate.
>
> *(Thompson and Strickland, 1999)*

Figure 15.1 provides a visual summary of the five tasks implied by this definition.

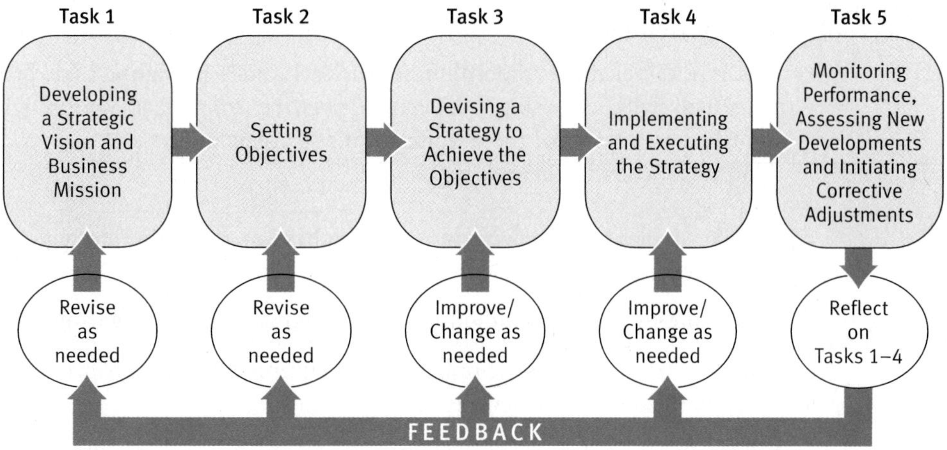

Fig 15.1 The five tests of strategic management
Source: Adapted from Thompson and Strickland (1999)

Informing and shaping the five tasks of Figure 15.1 are three key elements (or processes), namely:

- strategic analysis;
- strategic choice;
- strategic implementation and evaluation.

We might usefully look at each of these in rather more detail.

Strategic analysis

This is a key element underpinning Tasks 1, 2 and 3 above. Strategic analysis is concerned with providing information for decision makers to help them better understand the present and future context in which the organisation must operate. Careful analysis of both the *internal* and *external* environments of the organisation will help inform decision makers as to their prospects for meeting previous stated objectives as well as help them set realistic future objectives.

Strategic analysis will seek to respond to questions such as:

- What are the strengths and weaknesses within the organisation itself?
- How is the external environment currently affecting the organisation and what changes, if any, are likely to occur in that environment?
- What opportunities exist or might arise for using the strengths identified?
- What threats exist or might arise from the weaknesses identified?

Responding to questions such as these provides a *context* in which a strategic vision can be developed or refined (Task 1), objectives set or adjusted (Task 2) and a strategy devised to meet those objectives (Task 3).

Strategic choice

This is a key element underpinning Tasks 3 and 4 in Figure 15.1. Strategic choice is concerned with choosing between *alternative courses of action* which have been identified as a result of the organisation's strategic analysis.

Strategic choice will seek to:

- make explicit the policy options which stem from the strategic analysis already undertaken;
- evaluate the benefits and costs to the organisation of the various policy options;
- help in selecting of those policy options deemed most appropriate for advancing the organisation's stated objectives;
- help in integrating the policy options selected to form a coherent strategy, guiding the organisation's decision making at the appropriate level (corporate, business or functional).

Box 15.1 reviews Porter's suggestion of three broad themes which might guide the integration of different policy options to form a coherent whole. Box 15.1 also reviews Ansoff's suggestion that the integration of policies (strategies) can be given coherence by assessing their impacts on markets and on products.

Box 15.1 **Strategic options**

Porter's generic strategies

Writing in 1980 in his pioneering book on *Competitive Strategy*, Porter described three generic strategies open to firms. These are overall cost leadership, differentiation and focus.

- *Overall cost leadership strategy* requires the business to achieve lower costs than other competitors in the industry while maintaining product quality. This strategy requires aggressive investment in efficient plant and machinery, tight cost controls and cost minimisation in functional areas. An organisation must understand the critical activities in the business's value chain that are the sources for cost advantage and endeavour to excel in one or more of them.
- *Differentiation strategy* is based on creating 'something unique, unmatched by its competitors' which is 'valued by its buyers beyond offering simply a lower price' (Porter, 1985). This entails achieving industry-wide recognition that the business produces different and superior products compared to competitors, which might result from using superior technology or providing superior customer service.
- *Focus strategy* involves selecting 'a particular buyer group, segment of the product line, or geographic market' as the basis for competition rather than the whole industry. This strategy is 'built around serving a particular target very well' in order to achieve better results. Within the targeted segment the business may attempt to compete on a low cost or differentiation basis.

Figure 15.2(a) illustrates Porter's generic strategies.

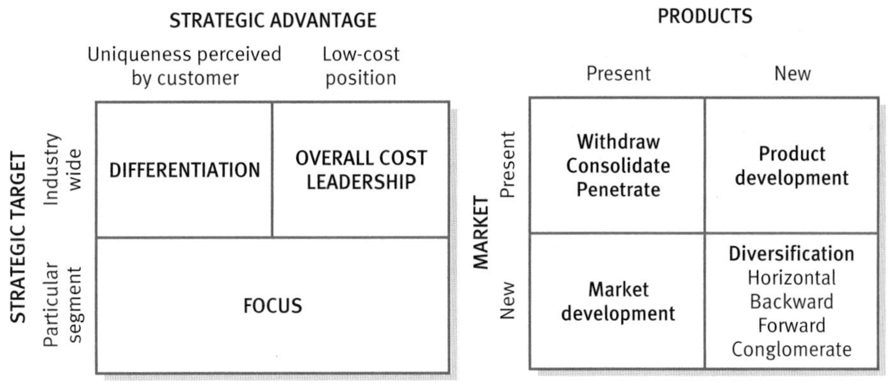

(a) Porter's Generic Strategies

(b) Ansoff's Product-Market Strategies

Fig 15.2 Porter's generic strategies and Ansoff's product-market strategies.

Ansoff's product-market strategies

Igor Ansoff (1968) used the implications of policies for markets and for products to define strategic options. He presented the various strategic options in the form of a matrix (Figure 15.2b).

- *Market penetration strategy* refers to gaining a larger share of the market by exploiting the firm's existing products. Unless the particular market is growing, this will involve taking business away from competitors, perhaps using one or more of the 4 Ps (see Chapter 13, p. 497 and Chapter 14, p. 565) in a national or international context respectively.
- *Market development strategy* involves taking present products into new markets, and thus focusing activities on market opportunities and competitor situations.
- *Product development strategy* is where new products are introduced into existing markets, with the focus moving towards developing, launching and supporting additions to the product range.
- *Diversification strategy* involves the company branching out into both new products and new markets. This strategy can be further subdivided into horizontal, vertical and conglomerate diversification.

As we shall see, techniques such as SWOT, PEST and scenario planning, amongst others, can be most useful in helping the business select between different policy options and integrating those selected to form a coherent strategy.

Strategic implementation and evaluation

This is a key element underpinning Tasks 4 and 5 in Figure 15.1. Once the firm has chosen one or more strategies at whatever level (corporate, business or operational), it must seek to put those strategies into effect and continuously monitor and review their impacts.

- *Strategy implementation* is concerned with the processes to be used in carrying out the strategic decisions already made. Strategy implementation will usually involve:
  - deciding on the overall total of resources available;
  - deciding on the precise allocation of that total;
  - confirming lines of responsibility and accountability for using these resources.

  In other words, strategy implementation will usually involve questions of resource allocation and of organisational structure and design.
- *Strategy evaluation* is concerned with monitory performance, assessing new developments and initiating any corrective adjustments involving Tasks 1–4 (Figure 15.1) as may be deemed necessary.

Adopting managerial best practice

A key element for successful strategic management is an awareness of the strengths and weaknesses of new approaches to management and a readiness to modify, where appropriate, existing organisational structures to incorporate managerial 'best practice'.

For example, a major study in the UK examined the contribution of cross-border management approaches to productivity differences in manufacturing and reported its findings in October 2003. The results of this *Productivity report* (Proudfoot Consulting) October 2003 suggested that manufacturing plants/factories in the UK are only being used to 60% of their capacity. It noted that if productivity could be raised from 60% to 85% capacity, then UK GDP would rise by 10% (£90bn). It concluded that the main source of low manufacturing productivity in the UK involves management-related problems.

Sources of 'lost' productivity:

- insufficient management planning and control (37%);
- inadequate supervision (25%);
- poor worker morale (14%);
- inappropriately qualified workforce (11%);
- IT-related problems (9%);
- ineffective communication (4%).

Conclusions of report:

- Too many managers lack the skills necessary to deliver a culture of high productivity ... don't spend enough time dealing with the barriers we have identified that prevent people working most effectively.
- Managers are too preoccupied with day-to-day matters to make strategic moves to boost productivity.
- Managers are poor at measuring their own performance and benchmarking it against their peers.
- Managers are poor at tackling low workforce morale and matching qualification levels to skill needs.

Clearly an effective strategic management approach will take into account the findings of such studies and re-evaluate existing practices in the light of emerging evidence.

SWOT and PESTLE analyses

As we have already noted, these techniques may be particularly useful, both in conducting a strategic analysis and in making a strategic choice.

During the 1970s Kenneth Andrews proposed a framework for strategy formulation based on the premise that the final strategy adopted by a company should seek a '*fit*' between its internal capabilities (strengths and weaknesses) and the external situation (opportunities and threats). This is commonly known as *SWOT analysis* (Figure 15.3a) and involves undertaking the following.

1 An *internal analysis* which should identify those things that the organisation does particularly well (*strengths*) and those features that inhibit its ability to fulfil its purposes (*weaknesses*). The features to be assessed may include the organisational structure itself together with various functional activities such as personnel, marketing, finance and logistics.

2 An *external analysis* which should highlight the general environmental influences that the organisation must cope with, such as the political, economic, social and technological factors (PEST) already considered in Chapters 9–12. Indeed, we noted in Chapter 12 that PEST is often expanded to PESTLE, bringing the additional legal and ecological external factors into consideration (Figure 15.3b). This analysis of the external environment will lead to the identification of a number of *opportunities* and *threats*.

Strategic alternatives then arise from matching current strengths to environmental opportunities at an acceptable level of risk.

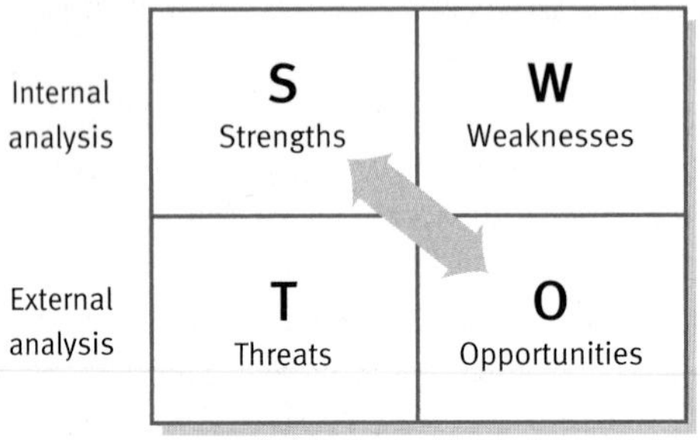

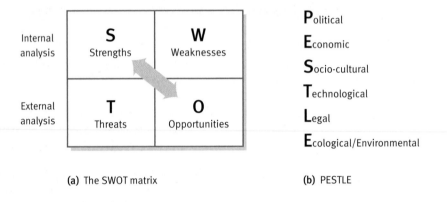

(a) The SWOT matrix

Political
Economic
Socio-cultural
Technological
Legal
Ecological/Environmental

(b) PESTLE

Fig 15.3 SWOT and PESTLE approaches.

It may be useful at this stage to apply this broad-based approach to a particular business situation, namely to that of Starbucks. You might usefully read Case Study 15.1 and respond to the questions asked. We will then conduct a SWOT and PESTLE analysis of Starbucks' situation looking forward from 2004.

Case Study 15.1 Starbucks' strategic development

Starbucks was born in 1971 with the collaboration of three academics, Jerry Baldwin, Zev Siegal and Gordon Bowker. It is thought that the name Starbucks originated from the Moby Dick character Starbuck, who was the coffee-loving first mate aboard Ahab's ship. Initially the company was set up with the sole purpose of selling coffee beans to the public along with coffee machines. In 1981 Howard Shultz, a manager of Swedish Kitchen Style equipment, went to see Starbucks as they were placing large orders for one of his company's drip coffee machines. On arrival at the Pikes Place store in Seattle he was immediately taken by the smell of coffee and impressed by the service and the knowledge base of the staff. Baldwin told Shultz that Starbucks staff not only saw their role as selling the product but also educating their customers. At this time the company had no official mission statement or vision, but even so it was obvious to Shultz that Starbucks stood for top quality, fresh

Case Study 15.1 continued

roasted whole bean coffee and quality service by a staff who were strongly committed to educating their customers to appreciate the qualities of fine coffees.

Howard Shultz saw immense potential in Starbucks and set about joining this company, not an easy task when the three friends had experienced almost ten years of successful growth! Eventually in September 1982 Shultz secured a position as Head of Marketing with responsibility for Starbucks' four Seattle stores.

Shultz visited Italy shortly after joining to conduct market research at the International Housewares Show and encountered what was then a new concept to him, namely espresso bars. These were more than places for locals to drink coffee, rather they acted as community centres where people spent time together in premises run mainly by charismatic individuals known as 'baristas' serving a variety of coffees including 'caffe latte'. Shultz recognised a concept which he believed would have huge appeal to an American audience.

Shultz saw opportunities for Starbucks to build on its tradition of quality and good service and extend its product range beyond the supply of coffee beans and equipment to become a chain of innovative coffee houses. This strategic vision was, however, at odds with that of Baldwin, Siegel and Bowker who were largely content with retaining the status quo of a small successful company.

Realising that his vision could not be realised within the constraints of the company, in 1985 Schultz opened his own coffee house, Il Giornale, and used its success to found a chain of coffee houses under that name. Baldwin and Bowker supported the new venture, Baldwin as an investor and Bowker as a consultant, and Starbucks coffee beans were used in all Il Giornale coffee houses. Within two years Shultz had earned sufficient profits to acquire Starbucks itself and in March 1987 he bought out the whole Starbucks enterprise, including the name.

Arguably, it was from this point onwards that Starbucks began to move towards the business we know so well today. Shultz retained the original staff, demonstrating his commitment to them and his recognition of their vital role in communicating with customers. He quickly introduced healthcare plans for full- and part-time workers, a potentially expensive strategy which paid off by reducing further an already low staff turnover. In any case, most employees were young and often at college or university, so that medical expenses were containable. Shultz implemented other human resource strategies, including various methods to ensure that all employees had the opportunity to express their views as to operational matters within the company.

In its 1999 annual report, Starbucks states:

> The company's retail goal is to become the leading retailer and brand of coffee in each of its target markets by selling the finest quality coffee and related products and by providing superior customer service, thereby building a high degree of customer loyalty. Starbucks strategy for expanding its retail business is to increase

Case Study 15.1 continued

> its market share in existing markets and to open stores in new markets where the opportunity exists to become a leading speciality coffee retailer.

In 2003 Starbucks' website was even more specific in terms of expressing its objectives:

> We seek to establish Starbucks as the premier purveyor of the finest coffee in the world while maintaining our uncompromising principles while we grow.
>
> The following six guiding principles will help us measure the appropriateness of our decisions:
>
> ■ Provide a great work environment and treat each other with respect and dignity

Starbucks Coffee
Where/what
Partners
New channels (exclusive supply arrangements)
Airlines
United, Canadian
Airports
Host International
Bookstores
Barnes & Noble
Cruise lines
Holland America
Department stores
Nordstrom
Hotels
ITT Sheraton, Weston Hotels
Supermarkets
Kraft Foods
New markets (through licences with retailers)
Japan
Sazaby (joint venture)
Malaysia
Berjaya Coffee (licensee)
Philippines
Restaurant Brands (licensee)
Singapore
Rustan Coffee (licensee)
South Korea
Bonvest Holdings (licensee)
Taiwan
ESCO (licensee)
Thailand
President Group (joint venture)
Coffee Partners (licensee)
New products
Ice cream
Dreyer's
Bottled Frappuccino
PepsiCo
Coffee-enhanced dark beer
Red Hook Brewery
Online catalogue
America Online
Key success factors
Starbucks invests very little capital in international expansion (<5% of revenue)
Local partners bear all business risk
Licensing allows stricter control over all operations than does franchising –e.g. parent-company consultants visit each store once a month
Local partners contribute regulatory and cultural expertise – e.g. on product adaptations

Fig 15.4 Starbuck's 'capital-light' growth strategies

Case Study 15.1 continued

- Embrace diversity as an essential component in the way we do business
- Apply the highest standards of excellence to the purchasing, roasting and fresh delivery of our coffee
- Develop enthusiastically satisfied customers all of the time
- Contribute positively to our communities and our environment
- Recognise that profitability is essential to our future success

Starbucks.com, 2003

Figure 15.4 above shows how Starbucks has tended to use a variety of joint ventures and licensing arrangements with local partners to move into new markets, both home and overseas, as well as to increase penetration within these markets. Its 'capital light' market entry strategy is clearly towards the minimum risk/minimum reward end of the spectrum of strategies shown in Figure 14.2 (p. 540).

Finally, Box 15.2 gives a snapshot of Starbucks' activities over the timeline 2002–2003.

Box 15.2 Starbucks timeline 2002–3

2002
- Signs memorandum of understanding with Fairtrade Labelling Organisations International (FLO) enabling Starbucks to enter into licensing agreements with national Fairtrade organisations to sell Fairtrade certified coffee in the countries where Starbucks does business
- Publishes its first Corporate Social Responsibility Annual Report
- Introduces Starbucks Barista Quattro thermal coffeemaker, a 4-cup version of its popular Barista Aroma and Saeco Italia, a fully automated home espresso machine
- Celebrates 10-year anniversary of Starbucks IPO
- Introduces Starbucks DoubleShot to the ready-to-drink coffee category
- Signs licensing agreement with TransFair Canada to bring Fair trade Certified coffee to more than 270 retail locations in Canada
- The Starbucks Foundation awards more than 500 grants to literacy, schools and community-based organisations across North America (totalling $5.9m since 1997)

Case Study 15.1 continued

- Reinforces its dedication to coffee origin countries and the farmers who produce Starbucks coffee through an expanded line of Commitment to Origins Coffee
- Extends the Frappuccino line to include non-coffee options, Chai, Vanilla and Coconut Crème, Frappuccino ice-blended beverages.
- Expands its high speed wireless Internet service branded T-Mobile HotSpot to more than 2,000 Starbucks stores
- Tazo and Mercy Corps establish Collaboration for Hope and Advancement in India (Chai), a project to build strong communities in the tea-growing district of Darjeeling where Tazo purchases some of the finest teas available in the world
- Organises more than 35,000 volunteer hours in the month of September and contributes more than $275,000 through the Starbucks Make Your Mark programme to charitable organisations across North America
- Starbucks Coffee International opens in Omar, Indonesia, Germany, Spain, Puerto Rico, Mexico, Greece and southern China

Current location total = *5,886*

2003

- The Starbucks Foundation awards more than 650 grants to literacy, schools and community-based organisations across North America (totalling $6.5m since 1997)
- Begins three-year $225,000 commitment to America SCORES, a national non-profit, youth development organisation that uses the sport of soccer and literacy to inspire teamwork among at risk children in urban public schools
- Introduces Shade Grown Mexico and Fair Trade Certified coffees to the coffee selection available to Hyatt hotel and resort's guests
- Develops innovative, next-generation Starbucks Card combining credit and stored value technologies
- Begins relationship with Bank One and Visa to develop the next evolution of the Starbucks Card

Current location total = *6,294*

Source: www.starbucks.com

Case Study 15.1 continued

Questions

1 Look back to Figure 15.1 (p. 601). From the case study and your own knowledge of Starbucks, can you identify aspects of any of the five tasks in the strategic management of Starbucks:

(a) in the period 1971–March 1987

(b) in the period March 1987 to the present time?

2 Look back to Figure 15.2 (p. 603). Can you identify aspects of any of these strategic approaches being adopted by Starbucks in the period since March 1987?

SWOT and PESTLE applied to Starbucks

It will be a useful exercise to apply the SWOT and PESTLE analyses of Figure 15.3 (p. 606) to the present-day Starbucks as it looks towards the future. Whilst the following analysis is illustrative only, it draws wherever possible on established facts and events and possible future scenarios for Starbucks.

In Table 15.1 we identify some strengths and weaknesses from our analysis of the internal environment of Starbucks. However, the boxes for opportunities and threats are left blank for the moment. The PESTLE analysis is conducted *before* these are filled since this will give a useful overview of the *external* environment in which Starbucks is now operating, and is likely to be operating in the near future. After conducting the PESTLE analysis we will be in a better position to match Starbucks' competitive advantages/disadvantages (strengths/weaknesses) to the changing external environment. Only then can we be in a position to identify opportunities and threats and to fill in the final two boxes of Table 15.1.

Table 15.1 SWOT analysis for Starbucks: strengths and weaknesses only

S	W
– Strong brand image for quality products and relaxed ambience – High staff motivation and commitment – Reputation for social responsibility (both internally – e.g. treatment of own staff – and externally – e.g. links with Fair Trade organisation) – 'Capital light' and extensive global coverage of stores – 'Local' responsiveness of products and services via use of locally licensed partners	– Associated by some with the alleged excesses of global capitalism – Despite some product differentiation via localisation, still largely homogenous in terms of product and ambience – Higher staff costs per head than rivals
T	O

Table 15.2 uses a PESTLE approach to assess likely changes in the external environment for Starbucks from 2004 onwards.

Table 15.2 PESTLE analysis for Starbucks

Political	– Threat of terrorism, especially in major cities where most Starbucks are located, may significantly reduce the customer base – Pressures for tax-raising schemes by governments on coffee drinking. For example, the so-called 'sin tax' in Seattle in 2003 proposed taxing every cup of coffee drunk to raise money for day care for poor children. Whilst this was defeated in a public referendum, governments are looking more closely at raising revenue by taxing 'luxury' goods and services associated with higher income lifestyles – Some developing countries are investigating reviving the International Coffee Agreement which, until its abandonment in 1989, kept coffee prices much higher by setting quotas for production levels in coffee-growing areas
Economic	– More buoyant than expected global growth from 2004 onwards is likely to raise real incomes per head in many key markets – Some key competitors have withdrawn from the market, e.g. Coffee Republic announced in 2003 that it was moving from the pure coffee bar model to a more food-focused formula involving US-style sandwich delicatessens (Republic Deli)
Social	– Increasing average age via demographic change in many countries is reducing the market base (young age groups visit Starbucks more frequently than older age groups) – Anti-obesity drive is focusing on more spartan lifestyles and lower calorific intakes of both food and drink – 'Idea' stores are being introduced in UK libraries and museums (and in other countries) selling coffee and other products to create an ambience quite unlike that traditionally associated with such institutions
Technological	– New technologies are increasing the output per acres of coffee growers and the increased supply is reducing world coffee prices
Legal	– Legalisation is under way in the UK to lengthen pub opening hours, potentially attracting some customers away from coffee drinking in Starbucks – A smoking ban in public places may become UK law in the near future, reducing the current competitive advantage Starbucks has as a 'non-smoking' environment amongst coffee and beverage establishments
Environmental	– There is evidence of an increased public interest in and awareness of issues of corporate social responsibility (see Chapter 4, pp. 149–151)

We can now return to complete our SWOT analysis for Starbucks, as indicated in Table 15.3.

Table 15.3 SWOT analysis for Starbucks

S	W
– Strong brand image for quality products and relaxed ambience – High staff motivation and commitment – Reputation for social responsibility (both internally – e.g. treatment of own staff – and externally – e.g. links with Fair Trade organisation) – 'Capital light' and extensive global coverage of stores – 'Local' responsiveness of products and services via use of locally licensed partners	– Associated by some with the alleged excesses of global capitalism – Despite some product differentiation via localisation, still largely homogenous in terms of product and ambience – Higher staff costs per head than rivals
T	**O**
– Decreased demand in city centre Starbuck locations via terrorism – Higher real price of coffee if either 'sin taxes' are levied or coffee producer cartel is reinstated – Association with US and global capitalism makes it a target for protests and damages brand image – Association with unhealthy lifestyles and obesity – New ready-to-drink (RTD) coffee substitutes for home use – Rival coffee/tea providing companies are making still greater (and well publicised) commitments than Starbucks to Fairtrade suppliers	– Higher real incomes are increasing demand for Starbucks products given that they have a high income elasticity of demand ('luxury' category) – New coffee bar locations available in city centres as Coffee Republic sells unwanted outlets – Higher output of coffee growers is reducing price of coffee – Gain in 'public esteem' via Fair Trade coffee sales, annual Social Responsibilities reports, etc. strengthens brand image

Devising a strategy

Given that we have conducted a *strategic analysis* (see p. 602) via SWOT and PESTLE, we must now move towards *strategic choice* (p. 602) by devising a strategy for Starbucks. Of course the strategy will, as we noted earlier (p. 600), depend on the *level* concerned.

Corporate (enterprise) level

Corporate objectives have been laid down by Starbucks in its 'six guiding principles' outlined above (p. 608). However, these are rather general and may be made more specific by the Starbucks board. For example, the sixth guiding principle 'Recognise that profitability is essential to our future success', might be operationalised as a corporate target in the following ways:

- Achieve x% annual profit growth as an average over the period 2004–7.
- Achieve y% annual revenue growth as an average over the period 2004–7.
- Achieve z% market share of the coffee bar market by 2007, and so on.

The board might then seek to give general direction as to the set of policies which it expects to employ to achieve these corporate objectives.

Here, for illustration, we will seek to describe some possible broad-based '*corporate strategies*' using the terminology of Porter's generic strategies and Ansoff's product-market strategies already encountered (Figure 15.2, p. 603).

For example, in terms of Porter's generic strategies, Starbucks might select:

- *differentiation strategy* whereby further attention is given to developing its existing image of superior high quality products in the coffee bar genre, perhaps by developing new product lines or using new technologies to make existing product lines still more attractive.

Since these generic strategies need not be mutually exclusive, Starbucks might at the same time select:

- *focus strategy* whereby, say, it targets attracting a higher proportion of the 'grey market' of older customers who, at present, form a very small proportion of its existing customer base.

In terms of Ansoff's product-market strategies Starbucks might select:

- *market penetration strategy* whereby it seeks to attract customers from rival coffee shops, perhaps using special offers, extensive advertising or other comparative marketing policies.

Again, it might at the same time select:

- *market development strategy* whereby it seeks to take its existing products into new markets, as in seeing the 'grey consumer' as already mentioned. This might also involve new geographical markets, perhaps seeking new outlets in the ten accession countries to the EU in 2004.

Of course, these are merely illustrative ideas at the corporate level of strategy. You might be able to suggest other alternatives based on the earlier materials.

Business level

Business (or competitive) strategy will involve more policy detail as to how Starbucks intends to compete within a *particular* market or industry. For illustrative purposes we now consider the *UK market*.

The SWOT and PESTLE analysis will need to be revisited and more carefully honed to the internal and external environment facing Starbucks UK. The ensuing business strategy might include the following policy components.

Achieving, say, 2004–7 profit, revenue and market share targets along the lines outlined above (p. 613) but this time refined to the particular situation of the UK market by:

- purchasing 30 of the 50 outlets released by Coffee Republic in the UK in 2003, following its withdrawal from the pure coffee bar market;

- raising prices of drinks and food in Starbucks by 5% per year over the period (higher than the predicted rate of inflation of 2.5% per year), given that studies suggest a relatively price inelastic demand and rising UK real incomes;
- responding to a major survey showing high degree of sensitivity of Starbuck's customers to 'social responsibility' by increasing use of Fairtrade products from 10% to 20% (with extensive publicity of this policy);
- using more effective just-in-time delivery systems to distribute drink and food supplies to Starbucks shops, reducing storage costs and 'waste' from time expiry of products;
- developing a major promotional campaign in the national UK media (press, TV, radio, cinemas, Internet);
- providing additional in-store attractions in the UK to attract new target customers (e.g. more newspapers, quality journals for 'grey' market);
- introducing 'loyalty cards' to encourage repeat purchases.

Functional level

The *functional strategy* will be honed to a particular functional area of the organisation. This functional level may involve the whole organisation or be confined to a particular geographical area. Here, for illustrative purposes, we shall use *HRM* in the geographical context of the UK.

The ensuing functional strategy might include the following policy components. Achieving 2004–7 targets specified for the HRM department of Starbucks UK (x% fall in staff turnover, y% increase in female employees and z% increase in employees from ethnic minorities) by:

- increasing the flexible working conditions available to Starbucks' employees beyond the minimum levels established by the April 2003 UK Act;
- raising hourly wage rates by 2% more than UK inflation in each year;
- extra advertising of job vacancies in media sources widely used by women and ethnic minorities in the UK.

Porter's Five Forces analysis

Porter argued that 'the essence of strategy formulation is coping with competition' and that in addition to undertaking a PEST analysis, it is also necessary to undertake a structural analysis of the industry to gauge the strengths and weaknesses of the opposition and also determine the competitive structure of a given market. The key elements in Porter's Five Forces analysis (Figure 15.5) can be identified as the threat of (i) *potential entrants* and (ii) *substitutes*, as well as the power of (iii) *suppliers* and (iv) *buyers*, together with an exploration of (v) *the degree of competitive rivalry*.

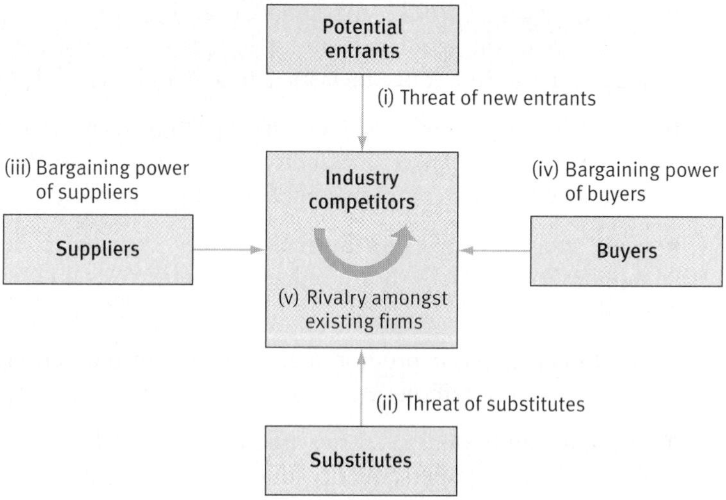

Fig 15.5 Porter's 'five forces' analysis
Source: Reprinted with the permission of The Free Press, a Division of Simon & Schuster Adult Publishing Group, from COMPETITIVE ADVANTAGE: Creating and Sustaining Superior Performance, by Michael E. Porter. Copyright @ 1985, 1998 by Michael E. Porter. All rights reserved.

(i) Threat of potential entrants

The threat of new entrants into an industry depends on the barriers that exist in the market and the expected reaction of existing competitors to the entrant. Porter identified six possible sources of barriers to entry, namely economies of scale, differentiation of the product, capital requirements of entry, cost advantages, access to distribution channels and legislative intervention.

(ii) Threat of substitute products

The threat of substitute products can alter the competitive environment within which the firm operates. A new process or product may render an existing product useless. For an individual firm the main issue is the extent to which there is a danger that substitutes may encroach on its activities. The firm may be able to minimise the risks from substitutes by a policy of product differentiation or by achieving a low-cost position in the industry.

(iii) Bargaining power of suppliers

Suppliers have the ability to squeeze industry profits by raising prices or reducing the quality of their products. Porter states that a supplier is powerful if few suppliers exist in a particular market, there are no substitute products available, the industry is not an important customer of the supplier, or the supplier's product is an important input to the buyer's business. Japanese firms have shown the importance of establishing a strong relationship with suppliers so that they 'become an extension of the firm itself'.

(iv) Bargaining power of buyers

In general, the greater the bargaining power of buyers, the greater is their ability to depress industry profitability. Porter identified a number of determinants of bargaining power, including the concentration and size of buyers, the importance of purchases to the buyer in cost terms, the costs of switching between suppliers, and the degree of standardisation of products. Buyers should be treated as rivals but should have a 'friendly relationship based on performance and integrity'.

(v) Rivalry amongst existing firms

Finally, the extent of rivalry between firms can influence the competitive environment within which the firm operates. Rivalry is influenced by the above forces but also depends on the concentration of firms in the marketplace and their relative market shares, the rate of industry growth, the degree of product differentiation, and the height of exit barriers. Porter refers to the tactics used by firms to seek an advantage over their competitors as 'jockeying for position'. This usually takes the form of policies towards pricing, promotion, product innovation and service level.

According to Porter, strategy formulation requires that each of the above forces be carefully analysed in order to successfully:

(i) *position the company* so that its capabilities provide the best defence against the competitive forces;
(ii) *influence the balance* of the forces through strategic moves, thereby improving the company's position;
(iii) *anticipate changes* in the factors underlying the forces and respond to them.

Competitive advantage

The strategic focus of Porter and his contemporaries often involves companies being seen as seeking to identify and exploit *competitive advantages* within stable industrial structures. Such competitive advantages were often expressed in terms of the additional 'added value' the more successful firms in an industry were able to generate vis-à-vis the most marginal firm in that industry.

Quote

> Where no explicit comparator is stated, the relevant benchmark is the marginal firm in the industry. The weakest firm which still finds it worthwhile to serve the market provides the baseline against which the competitive advantage of all other firms can be set.
>
> *(Kay, J. 1993)*

These competitive advantages could be attributed to a host of potential factors:

- *architecture* (a more effective set of contractual relationships with suppliers/customers);
- *incumbency advantages* (reputation, branding, scale economies etc.);
- *access to strategic assets* (raw materials, wavebands, scarce labour inputs etc.);
- *innovation* (product or process, protected by patents, licences etc.);
- *operational efficiencies* (quality circles, just-in-time techniques, re-engineering etc.).

Checkpoint 1 Use the earlier Case Study 15.1 on Starbucks and your own investigations into Starbucks to conduct a five-forces analysis. What further strategic issues does this raise?

LINKS

You could usefully re-read the earlier Case Study 14.4 on IKEA (p. 562). Although that case study was more concerned with marketing aspects, it also provides strategic insights additional to those presented in Case Study 15.2.

Case Study 15.2 looks at the Swedish furniture group IKEA. It provides a further opportunity for you to use SWOT, PESTLE and 'Five Forces' analysis in devising strategies for IKEA at each of the three levels, corporate, business and functional.

Case Study 15.2 IKEA and growth strategies

FT

It is business as usual at IKEA's Helsingborg office in southern Sweden, where wall signs highlight the company's latest cost-saving initiative: Kill-a-watt. Staff are urged to turn off lights, taps and computers when they are not being used. In fact it is a competition: whichever IKEA store or office round the world saves most electricity between November and January will win a prize.

IKEA's spartan corporate culture stems from Ingvar Kamprad, its founder, who famously drives an old Volvo and buys his fruit and vegetables at afternoon markets when prices are cheaper. IKEA staff always travel economy class and take buses rather than taxis. But cost-cutting is more necessary than usual now. The Swedish home furnishings group has just had its toughest year in 2003 for a decade and Anders Dahlvig, chief executive of IKEA group, is not just blaming weak economic conditions internationally. 'The truth is that this year we have not stretched ourselves to the limit. We are less than fully satisfied with what we have achieved,' he says.

IKEA's sales rose 3% to €11.3bn (£7.9bn) in the year to 31 August 2003 – but that was after including the impact of 11 new stores. Like-for-like sales growth was zero. The privately owned group never comments on its profits but it is a reasonable guess that they were affected.

Mr Dahlvig, 46, says the stronger euro had an impact, as sales at constant currencies were 6% higher. He also blames the economic downturn in central Europe, where the group makes about half its sales. But there were also other issues. There was a greater than expected impact from cannibalisation: the impact that new stores have on the sales of existing stores in countries where IKEA is already present. For example, last year IKEA opened a fourth store in Toronto and second stores in Washington and San Francisco.

In a year-end report, Mr Dahlvig also highlighted three other areas where IKEA needed to do better: range, service and product availability. 'Customers should never come to our stores only to find that the product they want is temporarily out of stock. The lines of customers at the check-outs ... should never be so long that they deter people from visiting the store,' he wrote. IKEA has faced a constant barrage of criticism for the quality of service in its UK stores but Mr Dahlvig insists that the complaints are specific to that market.

Case Study 15.2 continued

In any case, the early parts of the 2003/4 financial year show a better sales trend. Sales have been running 10% higher than a year ago, excluding currency effects. But Mr Dahlvig is cautious: 'My personal feeling is that the economies are not picking up right now. We are not counting for any help from the economy for the next 12 to 18 months. If things pick up it will be a positive.'

Notwithstanding difficult market conditions, IKEA's relentless expansion goes on. It had 165 stores in 22 countries at the end of August, excluding 21 franchisees. It will open 16 new stores this financial year and, further ahead, is planning a big expansion in Asia, which will include its first store in Japan in 2005. 'In a five-to-ten year time frame, China and Japan could be our main growth engine,' he says. The group already has two Chinese stores and is looking at further sites in Beijing and Shenzen.

Russia, where there are two stores, is also becoming more important. In 2004 the group will open its first store outside Moscow and St Petersburg, at Kazan. 'This will give us a good indication of the potential for expansion in the Russian provinces,' Mr Dahlvig says.

He admits that competition is hotting up. He says the group is increasingly being challenged by hypermarkets and DIY retailers – companies such as Wal-Mart and B&Q. In addition, supermarkets such as Tesco of the UK are expanding outside their core areas, while dedicated home furnishing groups such as Conforama of France are developing a regional presence. 'It's understandable. At some point these companies become saturated in food or clothing and they need to expand in other segments if they want to grow,' he says. IKEA is responding with its store expansion programme and with more aggressive pricing. 'We have reduced our prices by 15 to 20% on average over the last five years,' Mr Dahlvig says.

In any case, he is confident that the IKEA concept is hard to imitate. 'Many competitors could try to copy one or two of these things. The difficulty is when you try to create the totality of what we have. You might be able to copy our low prices, but you need our volumes and global sourcing presence. You have to be able to copy our Scandinavian design, which is not easy without a Scandinavian heritage. You have to be able to copy our distribution concept with the flat pack. And you have to be able to copy our interior competence – the way we set out our stores and catalogues.'

And what about the long-term challenges facing the group? Mr Dahlvig admits that as the group grows bigger it will become harder for it to remain 'quick, lean and simple'. Being big has advantages – in purchasing, for example – but it can also lead to bureaucracy and slow reactions to consumer change.

Something else is looming. In most countries, IKEA still has plenty of room for growth, with market shares in the 5–10% range. But in some countries the company is now so big that it may be nearing saturation point in terms of its appeal. For example, in Germany, the group's largest market, the group has 31 stores. In Sweden, where it has 13 stores, it has 20% of the home furnishings market. 'The more stores

Case Study 15.2 continued

we build and the more we increase our market share, the more we have to find ways to appeal to a broader public. Scandinavian design and style is a niche and it is not to everyone's taste. But we don't want to be just another supplier of traditional furniture. Scandinavian design is what makes us unique. We have to find a balance.'

A weekend trip to an IKEA store is hell, if you believe some sections of the UK media. Long queues and poor product availability in the UK are in danger of overshadowing the company's reputation for low prices and Scandinavian design, critics say. Anders Dahlvig admits that the 'UK experience is not what we would like it to be'. But he says the UK is a special case and there is one overriding reason for the problems. 'Retailing laws in the UK have made it impossible for us to expand because of the restrictions on building out of town. If we had the same situation as in Germany, France and the US, we would have more stores and bigger stores in the UK and the situation would be different.'

IKEA's Brent Park store in north London has acquired a particularly bad reputation – although Mr Dahlvig refuses to describe it as the worst store in the group. He insists that IKEA is doing everything it can to improve things: staying open longer, adding check-outs and encouraging shoppers to come on weekday evenings rather than at weekends. But, he adds, 'More stores or extended stores is the only really good way to satisfy fully the capacity problem that we have. The other things just put plaster on the wound.'

A new store has just opened in Cardiff, Wales and two stores are being expanded – at Croydon and Thurrock. The last new store to open in England, where the planning problems are particularly acute, was in Bristol in 1999. None is under construction.

Mr Dahlvig says the UK does not appear to be under-performing when it comes to sales. But he adds, 'If a lot of people are disappointed, I am sure they are avoiding our stores at weekends. Those are sales that we would otherwise have.'

Source: *Financial Times*, 24 November 2003, p. 12

Questions

Again you could remind yourself of extra detail on IKEA by re-reading Case Study 14.4 (p. 562) before answering the following questions.

1 Use as many of Porter's 'five forces' as you can in analysing the situation facing IKEA.
2 What growth strategies might you recommend at a corporate (enterprise) level for IKEA?
3 What strategies might you recommend at the business level for IKEA, where the business unit in question is IKEA UK?

Portfolio analysis

The Boston Consulting Group's portfolio matrix provides a useful framework for examining the balance of the portfolio of products in a multi-product firm. It can therefore be helpful in guiding the strategic direction of that organisation.

The organisation's portfolio of products is subjected to a detailed analysis according to market share, growth rate and cash flow. The four alternative categories of company (or product) that emerge from the model are given the labels of Stars, Cash Cows, Dogs and Problem Children (or Question Marks), as can be seen in Figure 15.6.

- *Stars* have high market share, high growth, but limited cash flow due to the substantial amount of investment required to maintain growth. Successful Stars go on to become Cash Cows.
- *Cash Cows* have a high market share but slow growth. They tend to generate a very positive cash flow that can be used to develop other products.
- *Dogs* have a low share of a slow-growth market. They may be profitable, but only at the expense of cash reinvestment, and thus generate little for other products.
- *Problem Children* have a low share of a fast-growing market and need more cash than they can generate themselves in order to keep up with the market.

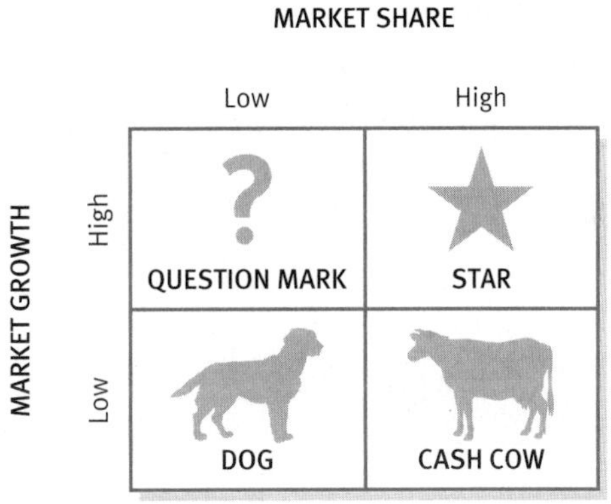

Fig 15.6 The Boston Matrix

However, there have been several criticisms aimed at the Boston portfolio, namely that it is prone to oversimplification and that it takes no account of other key variables such as product differentiation and market structure.

National strategic perspectives

In the *national* context, Porter has also examined competitive advantages as a basis for strategic initiatives. Porter identifies six key variables as potentially giving a country a competitive advantage over other countries:

1. *demand conditions*: the extent and characteristics of domestic demand;
2. *factor conditions*: transport infrastructure, national resources, human capital endowments etc.;
3. *firm strategies: structures and rivalries*: the organisation and management of companies and the degree of competition in the market structures in which they operate;
4. *related and supporting industries*: quality and extent of supply industries, supporting business services etc.;
5. *government policies*: nature of the regulatory environment, extent of state intervention in industry and the regions, state support for education and vocational training etc.;
6. *chance*.

Porter's diamond

The first four of these variables form a *diamond* shape, as shown in Figure 15.7, when mapped as the most important determinants of national competitive advantage.

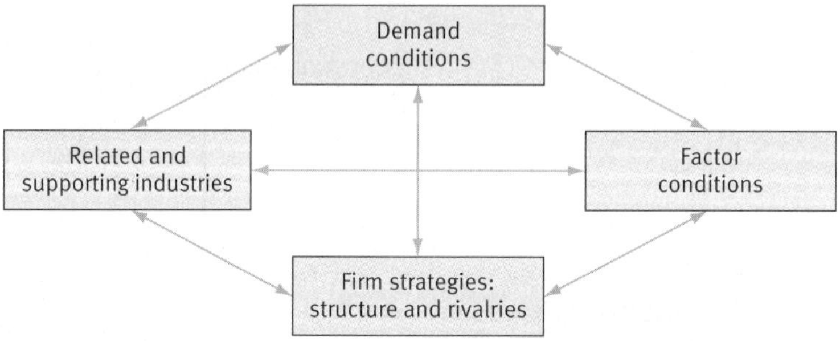

Fig 15.7 Porter's diamond: the determinants of competitive advantage
Source: Adapted from M. Porter (1998) *The Competitive Advantage of Nations*, Palgrave, p. 72

In Porter's view, the four determinants are interdependent. For example, favourable 'demand conditions' will only contribute to national competitive advantage when combined with appropriate 'factor conditions', 'related and supporting industries' and 'firm strategies: structures and rivalries' so that companies are *able* and *willing* to take advantage of the favourable demand conditions. To sustain national competitive advantages in modern, high technology industries and economies, Porter argues that all four determinants in the 'diamond' must be favourable. However, in less technology-intensive industries and economies, one or two of the four determinants being favourable may be sufficient for a national competitive advantage: e.g. natural resource dependent industries may only need favourable 'factor conditions' (presence of an important natural resource) and appropriate infrastructure to extract and transport that resource.

The last two determinants 'government policies' and 'chance' outlined above (p. 622) can interact with the four key determinants of the diamond to open up new opportunities for national competitive advantage. For example, government policies in the field of education and training may help create R&D and other knowledge-intensive competitive advantage for a nation. Similarly, 'chance' events can play a part, as in the case of Russia supporting a greater US presence in Uzbekistan during the war in Afghanistan in 2001/2, thereby creating new opportunities for US oil companies to exploit the huge oil resources in that country.

Example:

Britain is attractive to business

A KPMG survey in February 2004 found that Britain was the third cheapest advanced industrialised country in the world in which to do business – better even than the US and outperformed only by Canada and Australia. The survey compared the after-tax cost of starting and operating 12 types of business over a ten-year period, with the UK particularly competitive in the aerospace, automotive, telecommunications and pharmaceutical sectors. Britain had the second lowest effective income tax rates amongst the advanced economies, the fourth lowest relative labour costs, including wages and salaries, and other employer payments for labour. The report noted, however, that 'cost is not the sole factor for business attraction ... talent and skills base together with academic support are also major contributors ... to attracting inward foreign direct investment'.

Checkpoint 2

Can you identify some possible impacts of 9/11 in terms of national competitive advantage?

International product life cycle (IPLC)

The suggestion here (e.g. Vernon and Wells, 1991) is that the pattern of products traded between countries will be influenced by the stage of production reached by a nation in the international life cycle of a variety of knowledge-intensive products. The *new product stage* (invention/development) will typically occur in the (advanced industrialised) innovating country but then the balance between production and consumption (and therefore between export and import) may shift *geographically* as different stages of the product life cycle are reached. In Figure 15.8 we can see a stylised IPLC for a knowledge-intensive product over three stages of the product life cycle (new product, mature product, standardised product) and for three broad geographical regions (innovating country, other advanced countries, less developed countries – LDCs).

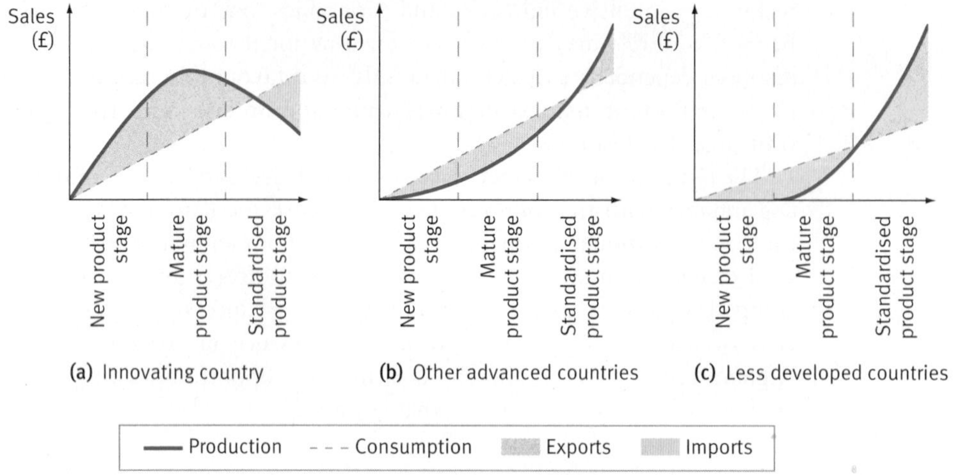

Fig 15.8 The international product life cycle (IPLC) for knowledge-intensive products

- *New product stage*. Here production is concentrated in the *innovating country*, as is market demand. A typical scenario for this stage would be where the (initially) relatively low output is sold at premium prices to a price-inelastic domestic market segment (with few, if any, exports). There may be a small amount of production via subsidiaries in 'other advanced countries' but little or none in the LDCs.
- *Mature product stage*. Both production and consumption typically continue to rise in the *innovating country*, with scale economies beginning to reduce costs and price to a new, more price-sensitive mass market segment. Exports to other countries become a higher proportion of total sales. Output of the generic product also rises in the 'other advanced countries', via the output of subsidiaries or of competitors in these countries which have the knowledge-intensive capability of developing close substitutes. These countries typically import a high proportion of their sales from the innovating country, as do the LDCs.
- *Standardised product stage*. At this stage the technology becomes more widely diffused and is often largely 'embodied' in both capital equipment and process control. Low-cost locations become a more feasible source of quality supply in this stage, often via multinational technology transfer. The LDCs may even become net exporters to the innovating country and to the other advanced countries.

Globalisation and strategic options for MNEs

The multinational enterprise (MNE) was considered in some detail in Chapter 14 (pp. 552–555). Here we first review the key characteristics of globalisation and then focus on the ways in which the *value chain* for MNEs within a globalised environment is continually being appraised as to the *geographical location* of various elements. We also consider the strategic issues of whether or not parts of the value chain currently in-house might be *outsourced* by the MNE.

Globalisation

There is much debate as to what exactly is meant by 'globalisation'. Those who believe that globalisation is something really new tend to point to three key elements.

- *Shrinking space*. The lives of all individuals are increasingly interconnected by events worldwide. This is not only a matter of fact but one which people increasingly perceive to be the case, recognising that their jobs, income levels, health and living environment depend on factors outside national and local boundaries.
- *Shrinking time*. With the rapid developments in communication and information technologies, events occurring in one place have almost instantaneous (real-time) impacts worldwide. A fall in share prices in Wall Street can have almost immediate consequences for share prices in London, Frankfurt or Tokyo.
- *Disappearing borders*. The nation state and its associated borders seem increasingly irrelevant as 'barriers' to international events and influences. Decisions taken by regional trading blocs (e.g. EU, NAFTA) and supra-national bodies (e.g. IMF, World Trade Organisation) increasingly override national policy making in economic and business affairs as well as in other areas such as law enforcement and human rights.

Others argue that 'globalisation' is a meaningless term, since world trade and investment as a proportion of world GDP is little different today from what it was over a hundred years ago and that international borders were as open at that time as they are today, with a similar proportion of the world's population migrating between countries.

Globalisation certainly has many dimensions (see Box 15.3) which cannot be captured in their entirety using statistical data. However, we have already noted the significant and sustained growth in the 'transnationality index' for MNEs (p. 553), indicating a greater global involvement. If we look at just three further specific indicators, namely international communications, international travel and international currency transactions, again there would seem to be changes occurring at a pace quite unlike that previously experienced.

- *International communications*. There have been dramatic rises in various modes of international communication. For example, the time spent on international telephone calls has risen from 33 billion minutes in 1990 to over 90 billion minutes by 2003. Internet usage is also rising exponentially, with the 2003 'Human Development Report' noting that the number of Internet hosts per 1,000 people rose from a mere 1.7 million in 1990 to 17.8 million in 2001, with cellular mobile phone subscribers per 1,000 people worldwide also rising from only 2 in 1990 to 153 in 2001. Various studies have found a strong and positive correlation between the extent of the telephone network and Internet usage. From this perspective it is important to note that the number of telephone mainlines per 1,000 people has more than quadrupled in many *developing countries* over this period, from 21 per 1,000 people in 1990 to over 87 per 1,000 people in 2001.

- *International travel.* The number of international tourists more than doubled from 260 million travellers a year in 1980 to over 600 million travellers a year in 2003. The growth of tourism is closely correlated with the growth of world GDP and is an important source of income and employment for many developed and developing countries alike. However, increases in the perceived and actual risks associated with travel and tourism since 11 September 2001 and its aftermath have been linked to a drop in worldwide tourism of 2.2% from its peak in 2001.
- *International currency transactions.* The daily turnover in foreign exchange markets has dramatically increased from \$15bn in the mid-1970s to over \$1,800bn in 2003. This has contributed to greater exchange rate volatility, on occasions putting severe pressure on national economies and currencies.

Box 15.3 broadens the discussion on globalisation to embrace a broad set of characteristics which in total represent something quite different from what has gone before.

Box 15.3 Globalisation

New markets

- Growing global markets in services – banking, insurance, transport.
- New financial markets – deregulated, globally linked, working around the clock, with action at a distance in real time, with new instruments such as derivatives.
- Deregulation of antitrust laws and growth of mergers and acquisitions.
- Global consumer markets with global brands.

New actors

- Multinational corporations integrating their production and marketing, dominating world production.
- The World Trade Organisation – the first multilateral organisation with authority to force national governments to comply with trade rules.
- A growing international network of non-governmental organisations (NGOs).
- Regional blocs proliferating and gaining importance – European Union, Association of South-East Asian Nations, Mercosur, North American Free Trade Association, Southern African Development Community, among many others.
- More policy coordination groups – G7, G8, OECD, IMF, World Bank.

New rules and norms

- Market economic policies spreading around the world, with greater privatisation and liberalisation than in earlier decades.
- Widespread adoption of democracy as the choice of political regime.
- Human rights conventions and instruments building up in both coverage and number of signatories – and growing awareness among people around the world.
- Consensus goals and action agenda for development.

- Conventions and agreements on the global environment – biodiversity, ozone layer, disposal of hazardous wastes, desertification, climate change.
- Multilateral agreements in trade, taking on such new agendas as environmental and social conditions.
- New multilateral agreements – for services, intellectual property, communications – more binding on national governments than any previous agreements.
- The (proposed) Multilateral Agreement on Investment.

New (faster and cheaper) tools of communication

- Internet and electronic communications linking many people simultaneously.
- Faster and cheaper transport by air, rail, sea and road.
- Computer-aided design and manufacture.

International business and the value chain

We noted in Chapter 14 that international business is dominated by MNEs which, within the globalised economy, are increasingly transnational in operation, including horizontally and vertically integrated activities more widely dispersed on a geographical basis. This brings into focus the *value chain* in Figure 15.9, which breaks down the full collection of activities which companies perform into 'primary' and 'secondary' activities.

- *Primary activities* are those required to create the product (good or service, including inbound raw materials, components and other inputs), sell the product and distribute it to the marketplace.
- *Secondary activities* include a variety of functions such as human resource management, technological development, management information systems, finance for procurement etc. These secondary activities are required to support the primary activities.

It is useful to remember that an effective international business strategy must encompass *all* parts of the value chain configuration, wherever their geographical location. Here we concentrate on international strategic approaches which might help the firm maximise the sum of these individual activities. International strategies which yield *global synergies* for the firm over its entire value chain are likely to be of particular interest, where synergies refer to the so-called '2 + 2 > 4 effect' whereby the whole becomes greater than the sum of the individual parts.

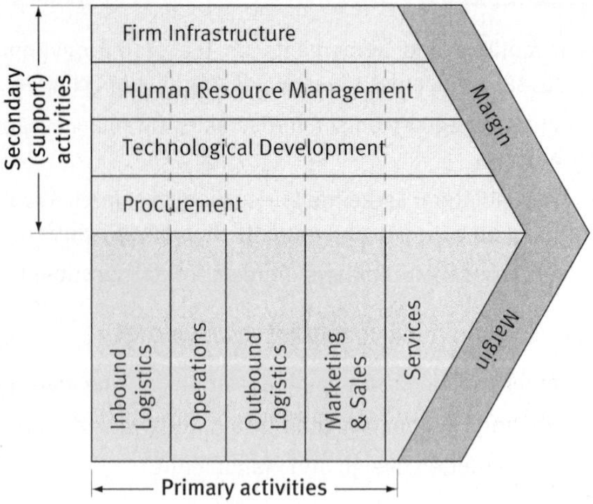

Fig 15.9 Value chain

International business strategies

The enormous variety of operations embraced by the term 'multinational' has led some writers to distinguish between four key strategies when competing in the international business environment: a global strategy, a transnational strategy, a multi-domestic strategy and an international strategy. The appropriateness of the particular strategy selected will depend to a considerable extent on the pressures faced by the international business in terms of both cost and local responsiveness, as indicated in Figure 15.10. These will become clearer as we discuss the nature of these various strategies and their associated advantages and disadvantages.

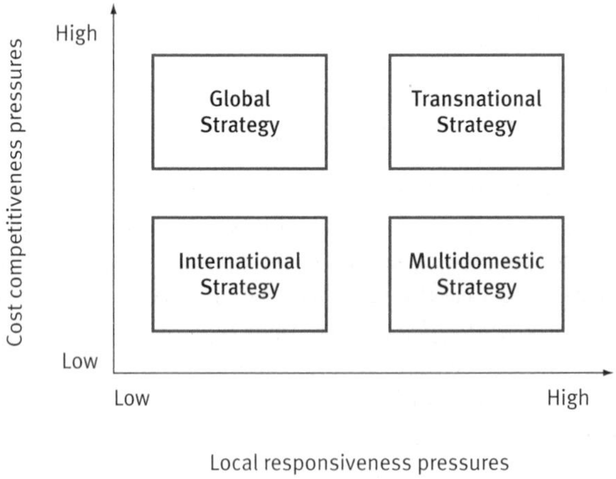

Fig 15.10 Four international strategies

Global strategy

This is particularly appropriate when the firm faces high pressures in terms of cost competitiveness but low pressures in terms of being responsive to local market conditions. Firms adopting a *global strategy* focus on being cost competitive by securing the various economies of scale, scope and experience outlined in Chapter 3 (pp. 100–108). Production, marketing and R&D activities tend to be concentrated in a few (and in extreme cases a single) favourable geographical locations rather than being widely dispersed. The emphasis of the global firm is on a homogenous, standardised product to maximise these various technical and non-technical economies. Of course, such a low-cost strategy is only possible where few pressures exist to localise either production or marketing. If localisation pressures were high, then shorter production runs of a locally differentiated product would invariably raise both technical (production) and non-technical (function/support services) costs.

The global strategy is best suited to industrial products for which there are high pressures for cost reductions but relatively low pressures for the product to be differentiated to meet local market requirements. The semiconductor industry is widely regarded as suitable for this strategy, with global standards placing a premium on firms such as Intel, Motorola and Texas Instruments producing standardised products at minimum cost. A global strategy does not suit many consumer goods markets where product differentiation is a key to local/cultural acceptability.

Transnational strategy

This is particularly appropriate when the firm faces pressures in terms of both cost competitiveness and responsiveness to local conditions. Of course, such local responsiveness may involve more than the 'local' market acceptability of a differentiated product. It might, for example, also reflect entry barriers which effectively protect the local market from the import of a standardised product, however locally acceptable to consumers.

Firms adopting the *transnational strategy* cannot depend on cost reductions via scale economies from producing a standardised product in a few selected geographical locations. Rather they must seek cost reductions by exploiting *location economies* appropriate to a particular element of the value chain; for example, locating labour-intensive component production in countries where relative labour costs are low. Another cost reduction mechanism open to a transnational strategy might involve benefiting from *experience economies* related to cumulative production across a larger number of geographical locations. *Global learning* may be a further mechanism yielding cost reductions, as when foreign subsidiaries themselves add value to any core competencies transferred from the parent company. The foreign subsidiaries may go on to develop the expertise to become the primary centres for further, initially unforeseen, value added activities, thereby increasing global efficiency. Foreign subsidiaries may then be able to use this 'global learning' to transfer their own (newly acquired) core competencies to other foreign subsidiaries or back to the parent company itself.

These cost reduction outcomes via a transnational strategy must, of course, remain consistent with the high pressure towards local responsiveness. For example, local responsiveness may require product differentiation and non-standardised marketing and HRM approaches appropriate to local socio-cultural sensitivities.

Implementing a transnational strategy is likely to require a high degree of complex organisational coordination across geographically dispersed primary and secondary activities within the global value chain. There is also likely to be an element of conflict between cost reductions via the various mechanisms outlined above and cost increases resulting from an increased local responsiveness which inhibits scale economies of both a technical and non-technical nature. How then can the international business implement a transnational strategy?

There are of course many variants, but a widely used method for implementing this strategy involves the idea of 'modularity' in both design and production. This approach is currently being widely used in the car industry as part of a transnational strategy, whereby production activities are progressively broken down into a number of large but separate elements that can be carried out independently in different international locations, chosen according to the optimum mix of factor imports (cost and quality) for each element. Final assembly, characterised by local responsiveness in terms of product differentiation involving design and other features, often takes place at, or near to, the intended market.

Ford is following this approach, making many different models but using the same 'platform' – the basic chassis and other standardised internal parts. Design and technological breakthroughs of this kind permit even the transnational strategy to benefit from scale economies, as in the production of the basic platform. However, Ford plans to product ten different vehicles from this common platform, with differentiated features reflecting the need to respond to localised consumer preferences.

LINKS

The idea of relative unit labour costs (RULCs) will play a part in the firm's decision as to whether and where to relocate any part of its value chain (see Box 15.4, p. 634) as part of a transnational strategy.

Multidomestic strategy

This is particularly appropriate when the firm faces low pressures in terms of cost competitiveness but high pressures in terms of local responsiveness. The *multidomestic* strategy tends to involve establishing relatively independent subsidiaries, each providing a full range of value chain activities (primary and secondary) within each national market. The subsidiary is broadly free to customise its products, focus its marketing and select and recruit its personnel, all in keeping with the local culture and the expressed preferences of its customers in each local market.

Such a strategy is more likely to occur when economies of scale in production and marketing are low, and when there are high coordination costs between parent and subsidiary. A disadvantage of such local 'independence' may also be an inability to realise potential experience economies. A further disadvantage may manifest itself in the autonomous actions of subsidiaries, sometimes paying little regard to broader-based corporate objectives. A classic example in this respect is the decision by the US subsidiary of Philips NV in the late 1970s to purchase the Matsushita VHS-format video-cassette recorders (VCRs) and put its own label on them, when the parent company was seeking to establish its own V2000 VCRs as the industry standard.

International strategy

This is particularly appropriate when the firm faces low pressures as regards both cost competitiveness and local responsiveness. The *international strategy* places the main focus on establishing the 'core architecture' (e.g. product development and R&D)

underpinning the value chain at the home base of the MNE and seeking to translate this more or less intact to the national markets overseas. Some localised production and marketing activities may be permitted, but these will be limited in scope. McDonald's, IBM, Microsoft, Wal-Mart, Kellogg's and Procter & Gamble are often cited as companies pursuing an international strategy in which head office keeps a tight rein over product strategy and marketing initiatives.

Over time, some additional local customisation of product and marketing has tended to accompany the international strategy, not least because of some well-publicised failures from an overly strict adherence to the 'core architecture' at head offices. For example, IKEA, the Swedish furniture retailer, transferred its retailing formula developed in Sweden into other nations. Whilst such transfer has proved successful in the UK and elsewhere, it most certainly failed in the US, with product ranges proving inappropriate to both the larger American physiques (e.g. beds, sofas too small), the American preferences for larger storage spaces (drawers, bedroom chests and other containers too confined), and European-sized curtains proving incompatible with the sizes of American windows. After entering the US market in 1985, IKEA had realised by the early 1990s that it would need to customise its product range to the American market if it was going to succeed there, which it has duly done to considerable success.

Such celebrated failures, together with a growing awareness of the benefits of at least a limited amount of local responsiveness, have somewhat diluted the international strategy, though it still remains one in which a centralised core architecture persists. It is most appropriate to situations where the parent firm possesses core competencies which are unmatched by indigenous competitors in foreign markets and where the key characteristics of the product are broadly welcomed by consumers in those markets.

Outsourcing

A key strategic decision for many MNEs is whether or not to outsource elements of the value chain which are currently 'in house'. A major attraction of outsourcing is the potential for reducing costs, as we noted in the case of Dyson moving production of its bagless vacuum cleaner from Wiltshire, UK to Malaysia (Case Study 1.2, p. 16).

Case Study 15.3 looks more carefully at the strategic implications of outsourcing.

Case Study 15.3 Outsourcing: opportunity or threat! FT

When Ross Perot warned of a 'giant sucking sound as jobs go south' during the 1992 presidential campaign he was voicing a widespread fear in the US that the North American Free Trade Area would destroy American jobs. But his words could have come from the lips of those in the UK today who fear the damaging effects of the movement of jobs from Britain to the Indian subcontinent and South East Asia.

Mr Perot was wrong, many US business groups now claim, since NAFTA created many more jobs in the US than it lost to Mexico, its poorer neighbour. And there is

Case Study 15.3 continued

growing evidence that the opponents of offshore outsourcing and offshoring, where companies send operations abroad but retain ownership control, will find their dire predictions of a UK jobs exodus are equally overblown.

First, the benefits of offshore outsourcing and offshoring have been shown to be far greater for the country that is moving work abroad than the cost of doing so. A report by the McKinsey Global Institute in August found that for every dollar a US company invests abroad, it creates $1.45–$1.46 of which $1.14 returns to the US.

Many UK manufacturers which started moving work offshore long before the current spate of service industry cases claim that going to south-east Asia enabled them to keep their headquarters in Britain. Some companies have even begun pulling work back from the other side of the world. Trumeter, which has made measurement equipment in the north-west since 1937, has outsourced its manufacturing functions to south-east Asia for many years. Another 40 jobs are set to go from the company's headquarters in Radcliffe, on the edge of Manchester, as processes move to Malaysia. However, Trumeter is also about to bring back to Radcliffe an assembly line operation that employs 67 people in Thailand by automating much of the process. Peter Weidenbaum, executive chairman, says the move will create six to nine jobs in Radcliffe, where 100 people are employed, but will save him a third of the cost of the labour intensive Thai operation. 'We have got to concentrate on industries that are not labour-intensive because as soon as we start to compete on labour we are up against the lower-cost suppliers in the Far East,' Mr Weidenbaum says.

Anne-Marie Forsyth, chief executive of the Call Centre Association, the UK trade body, says it remains unproven whether companies can relocate 'customer facing' services overseas. 'The service part of outsourcing is still very much on trial,' she says. She points out that while there are 800,000 people working in call centres in the UK, in India there are only 6,000–8,000 'UK facing' call centre jobs as opposed to back-office or processing jobs that have been moved offshore. 'It's very much a test,' she says. 'The question is at what stage are we going to see businesses have the confidence to put front-end customer contact in places like India? That's going to be the driver. Some of the players who've tried it have already taken their services back.'

Phil Taylor of the University of Stirling and Peter Bain of Strathclyde University argue in a report that while some Scottish call centre jobs, mostly in financial services, would be affected over the next two years, there were strong factors that could keep call centre operators in the UK. 'Powerful forces are driving outsourcing but equally there are countervailing factors inhibiting the migration of services overseas,' they argue. Moreover, they add that Scotland's call centre industry continues to grow and could sustain further growth. Call centres employ 56,000 people in Scotland, or 2.3% of the workforce, and the sector added 10,000 new jobs between 2000 and 2003, according to the study.

The number of call centres in Scotland also grew during the period of the research, from 220 to 290, and 92 of those approached by the authors said they expected to add more jobs by 2006.

Case Study 15.3 continued

Nigel Roxburgh, secretary of the National Association of Outsourcers, says that offshore business is a trend that will not go away. However, he notes that it will drive up wages in countries that import jobs, such as India, as it has already done in countries such as Hong Kong, which were the offshore outsourcing centres of the previous generation. This will make the relative merits of going offshore less attractive for UK business. Not that this should make UK businesses and government complacent, Mr Roxburgh says. 'The NAO is sympathetic to the people who are being made redundant,' he says. 'It believes that there should be government action to ensure that people are not discomfited by the change. But in the long term, offshore outsourcing should be better for everyone.'

Financial companies have been at the forefront of the growing, some say worrying, trend among UK companies towards shifting operations from the UK to Asia and in particular to India. Aviva's decision to treble its staff in India to 3,700 comes just weeks after HSBC said it would move 4,000 jobs from the UK to Asia. Others, including Lloyds TSB, Prudential and Abbey National have done the same, while American Express did so back in 1994. Substantial cost savings are the main attraction. Aviva estimates it can run operations in India 40% cheaper than in the UK.

'The differential in labour costs is crucial,' said Guy Douteil, partner at Custman Wakefield, which advises companies on real estate strategies. 'India is also a highly educated country; it turns out 2m graduates a year and they speak English.'

And while there are still weaknesses in the country's infrastructure, Mr Douteil said the cost savings are so substantial that funds can be diverted to plug deficiencies in transport and telecommunications. It is not just India that is an attractive outsourcing – or offshoring – destination. HSBC is transferring staff to China and Malaysia, while eastern Europe is also popular, with Accenture recently expanding its back-office operations in the Czech Republic and the Slovakian Republic.

The trend has drawn sharp criticism from trade unions. Amicus reiterated its warning that the UK could lose 200,000 jobs in financial services alone by 2008. The Communications Workers' Union estimates 50,000 jobs have already been lost from the UK to cheaper labour markets. 'This is a drip, drip process,' said Ian Gibson, MP for Norwich South. 'The people of Norwich are extremely worried about the future of the business in the town.'

Source: *Financial Times*, 3 December 2003

Questions

1 What are the costs and benefits of outsourcing
   (a) to advanced industrialised economies;
   (b) to developing economies?

2 How might the new trend towards outsourcing 'back-office' jobs affect corporate strategies?

This whole issue of outsourcing can be more clearly understood in the context of 'relative unit labour costs' (RULCs). It is this measurement that is the most widely accepted indicator of international competitiveness and that will ultimately determine whether and where any particular part of a firm's value chain will be outsourced.

Box 15.4 Relative unit labour costs (RULCs)

Labour costs per unit of output (unit labour costs) depend on both the wage and non-wage (e.g. employer National Insurance contributions in the UK) costs of workers and the output per worker (labour productivity). For example, if the total (wage and non-wage) costs per worker double, but productivity more than doubles, then labour costs per unit will actually fall.

However, the exchange rate must also be taken into account when considering international competitiveness, and this also is included in the definition of RULC below. For example, for any given value for labour costs per unit, if the exchange rate of that country's currency falls against a competitor, then its exports become more competitive (cheaper) abroad and imports less competitive (dearer) at home.

The calculation of RULC is therefore as follows.

$$\text{RULC} = \frac{\text{Relative labour costs}}{\text{Relative labour productivity}} \times \text{Relative exchange rate}$$

This formula emphasises that (compared to some other country) lower RULC for, say, the UK could be achieved by reducing the UK's relative labour costs, or by raising the UK's relative labour productivity, or by lowering the UK's relative exchange rate, or by some combination of all three.

More information of international labour costs and productivity is given in 'Data Response' Question 1 of 'Assessment Practice' (p. 648).

The strategic decision as to where to locate any particular element of the value chain must include all three elements. Certainly information such as that for India, shown in Table 15.4, will merit consideration by MNEs adopting a transnational strategy.

Table 15.4 India's low cost advantage

	Per capita income US$	Salary of educated person as multiple of per capita income	Salary of educated person US$	Salary of educated person, purchasing power parity US$
IT Professional				
US	34,280	2.2	75,000	75,000
UK	25,120	3.8	96,000	93,120
India	460	55.4	26,000	159,380
Graduate				
US	34,280	1.2	45,000	45,000
UK	25,120	1.9	48,000	46,560
India	460	14.1	6,500	39,845

Source: Adapted from National Association of Software and Service Companies, India

However, such information must be considered in the context of exchange rate changes, as indicated in the RULC formula. Indeed, exchange rate changes may themselves influence the international business strategies adopted by companies.

Example:

Falling dollar and business strategies

Overseas MNEs seeking to compete effectively in the US are facing, whatever strategies they employ, still further problems in 2004/5 with the low value of the dollar. For example, the dollar fell in value against the pound sterling by around 12% in 2003. Investment bank Morgan Stanley calculates that a 10% fall in the dollar against the pound will disadvantage UK trade with the US by over £1.4bn per year, with US exports to UK cheaper in sterling and UK exports to the US dearer in dollars. For UK-based MNEs operating in the US with a 'transnational strategy', whereby elements of the value chain are located outside the US with, say, manufacture or assembly of the finished item inside the US, this has major disadvantages. The prices of components imported into the US are rising, increasing their cost base. A 'global strategy' faces similar problems, where the finished item is produced *outside* the US and then imported for US consumers to buy. In some respects the low dollar is encouraging a 'multidomestic strategy' for non-US MNEs whereby the entire value chain, or at least the major part of it, is located in largely independent subsidiaries inside the USA. Exports from the US subsidiaries to the rest of the world benefit from the low dollar, whilst expensive imports of components etc. are minimised under such a strategy.

Checkpoint 3

What other factors need to be taken into account other than that shown in Table 15.4 to gain a better idea of international competitiveness between the UK, US and India?

New dimensions of strategic choice

C. Prahalad, an authority on globalisation, has suggested that the changes this is bringing to the competitive landscape are changing the basis for strategic choice. He suggests that industrial and service sectors are no longer the stable entities they once were:

- Rapid technology changes and the convergence of technologies (e.g. computer and telecommunications) are constantly redefining industrial 'boundaries' so that the 'old' industrial structures become barely recognisable.
- Privatisation and deregulation have become global trends within industrial sectors (e.g. telecommunications, power, water, healthcare, financial services) and even within nations themselves (e.g. transition economies, China).
- Internet-related technologies are beginning to have major impacts on business-to-business and business-to-customer relationships.
- Pressure groups based around environmental and ecological sensitivities are progressively well organised and influential.

- New forms of institutional arrangements and liaisons are exerting greater influences on organisational structures than hitherto (e.g. strategic alliances, franchising).

In a progressively less stable environment there will arguably be a shift in perspective away from the previous strategic focus of Porter and his contemporaries in which companies are seen as seeking to identify and exploit *competitive advantages* within stable industrial structures. Instead, in the 'discontinuous competitive landscapes' which characterise today's global economy, Prahalad (1999) suggests four key 'transformations' which must now take place in strategic thinking.

1 *Recognising changes in strategic space*. Deregulation and privatisation of previously government controlled industries, access to new market opportunities in large developing countries (e.g. China, India, Brazil) and in the transitional economies of Central and Eastern Europe, together with the rapidly changing technological environment, are creating entirely new strategic opportunities. Take the case of the large energy utilities. They must now decide on the extent of integration (power generation, power transmission within industrial and/or consumer sectors), the geographical reach of their operations (domestic/overseas), the extent of diversification (other types of energy, non-energy fields) and so on. Powergen in the UK is a good example of a traditional utility with its historical base in electricity generation which, in a decade or so, has transformed itself into a global provider of electricity services (generation and transmission), water, gas and other infrastructure services. Clearly the strategic 'space' available to companies is ever expanding, creating entirely new possibilities in the modern global economy.
2 *Recognising globalisation impacts*. As we discuss in more detail below, globalisation of business activity is itself opening up new strategic opportunities and threats. Arguably the distinction between local and global business will itself become increasingly irrelevant. The local businesses must devise their own strategic response to the impact of globalised players. Nirula, the Indian fast food chain, raising standards of hygiene and restaurant ambience in response to competition from McDonald's, is one type of local response, and McDonald's providing more lamb and vegetarian produce in its Indian stores is another. Mass customisation and quick response strategies require global businesses to be increasingly responsive to local consumers. Additionally, globalisation opens up new strategic initiatives in terms of geographical locations, modes of transnational collaboration, financial accountability and logistical provision.
3 *Recognising the importance of timely responses*. Even annual planning cycles are arguably becoming progressively obsolete as the speed of corporate response becomes a still more critical success factor, both to seize opportunities and to repel threats.
4 *Recognising the enhanced importance of innovation*. Although innovation has long been recognised as a critical success factor, its role is still further enhanced in an environment dominated by the 'discontinuities' previously mentioned. Successful companies must still innovate in terms of new products and processes but now such innovation must also be directed towards providing the company with faster and more reliable information on customers as part of mass customisation, quick response and personalised product business philosophies.

These factors are arguably changing the context for business strategy from positioning the company within a clear-cut industrial structure, to stretching and shaping that structure by its own strategic initiatives. It may no longer be sensible or efficient to devise strategic blueprints over a protracted planning time-frame and then seek to apply the blueprints mechanically, given that events and circumstances are changing so rapidly. The *direction* of broad strategic thrust can be determined as a route map, but tactical and operational adjustments must be continually appraised and modified along the way.

Nor can the traditional strategy hierarchies continue unchallenged – i.e. top management creating strategy and middle management implementing it. Those who are closest to the product and market are becoming increasingly important as well-informed sources for identifying opportunities to exploit or threats to repel. Arguably the roles of middle and lower management in the strategic process are being considerably enhanced by the 'discontinuities' previously observed. Top managers are finding themselves progressively removed from competitive reality in an era of discontinuous change. Their role is rather to set a broad course, to ensure that effective and responsive middle and lower management are in place to exercise delegated strategic responsibilities, and to provide an appropriate infrastructure for strategic delivery. For example, a key role of top managers in various media-related activities may be to secure access to an appropriate broad-band wavelength by successfully competing in the UK or German auctions. Such access is likely to be a prerequisite for competitive involvement in a whole raft of Internet-related products for home and business consumption via mobile telephony.

Figure 15.11 provides a useful summary of the traditional and emerging views of international business strategy.

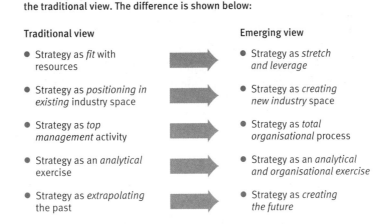

The emerging view of strategy contrasts dramatically with the traditional view. The difference is shown below:

Traditional view		Emerging view
• Strategy as *fit* with resources	→	• Strategy as *stretch and leverage*
• Strategy as *positioning in existing* industry space	→	• Strategy as *creating new industry* space
• Strategy as *top management* activity	→	• Strategy as *total organisational* process
• Strategy as an *analytical* exercise	→	• Strategy as an *analytical and organisational exercise*
• Strategy as *extrapolating* the past	→	• Strategy as *creating the future*

Fig 15.11 New views of strategy in a global economy

Strategic joint ventures and alliances

In a global economy in which rapid technological change is a fact of life, even the larger companies often find it beneficial to undertake strategic joint ventures or alliances with other companies. Sometimes these arrangements might even take place with rivals, as for example Ford and Honda undertaking a joint venture involving expensive R&D in advanced engine development, but competing aggressively against each other's vehicles which contain the same engine specifications.

Strategic joint ventures or alliances between companies are more likely when both companies see the benefit of coming together but when a more formal merger or acquisition is ruled out. For example, when two companies merging would give them too high a share of the market for regulatory bodies to allow the merger to go ahead, then a joint-venture or alliance may be an acceptable alternative.

Joint ventures

Joint ventures (unlike alliances) involve creating a new identity in which both the initiating partners take active roles in formulating strategy and making decisions. Joint ventures can help:

- share and lower the costs of high-risk, technology-intensive development projects;
- gain economies of scale and scope in value-adding activities that can only be justified on a global basis;
- secure access to a partner's technology, its accumulated learning, proprietary processes or protected market position;
- create a basis for more effective future competition in the industry involved.

Joint ventures are particularly common in high-technology industries where hugely expensive R&D is often required to remain at the cutting edge of high technology. Joint ventures usually take one of two forms, namely specialised or shared value-added.

Specialised joint ventures

Here each partner brings a specific competency; for example, one might produce and the other market. Such ventures are likely to be organised around *different functions*. One specialised joint venture has involved JVC (Japan) and Thomson (France). JVC contributed the specialised skills involved in the manufacturing technologies needed to produce optical and compact discs, computers and semiconductors, while Thomson contributed the specific marketing skills needed to compete in fragmented markets such as Europe.

The major benefits of *specialised joint ventures* include an opportunity to share risks, to learn about a partner's skills and proprietary processes and to gain access to new distribution channels. However, they carry risks as well, perhaps the greatest being that one partner's exposure of its particular competences may result in the other partner gaining a competitive advantage which it might subsequently use to become a direct competitor. This happened to GE when it entered into a specialised joint venture with Samsung to produce microwave ovens. Samsung now competes with GE across the whole range of household appliances.

Shared value-added joint ventures

Here both partners contribute to the *same function* or value-added activity. For example, Fuji-Xerox is an example of a shared value-added joint venture with the design, production and marketing functions all shared.

Shared value-added joint ventures pose a slightly different set of risks: partners can more easily lose their competitive advantage since the close working relationships involve the same function. If the venture is not working, it may be more difficult to exit since coordination costs tend to be much higher than they are in specialised joint ventures, with the more extensive administrative networks having usually been established.

Critical success factors for any type of joint venture or indeed alliance might include the following.

- *Take time to assess the partners.* Extended courtship is often required if a joint venture of either type is to be successful; Corning Incorporated of the US formed its joint venture with CIBA-GEIGY only after two years of courtship. Being too hurried can destroy a venture, as AT&T and Olivetti of Italy discovered when they formed a joint venture to produce personal computers which failed because of an incompatibility in management styles and corporate cultures as well as in objectives.
- *Understand that collaboration is a distinct form of competition.* Competitors as partners must remember that joint ventures are sometimes designed as ways of 'de-skilling' the opposition. Partners must learn from each other's strength whilst preserving their own sources of competitive advantage. Many firms enter into joint ventures in the mistaken belief that the other partner is the student rather than the teacher.
- *Learn from partners whilst limiting unintended information flows.* Companies must carefully design joint ventures so that they do not become 'windows' through which one partner can learn about the other's competencies.
- *Establish specific rules and requirements for joint venture performance at the outset.* For example, Motorola's transfer of microprocessor technology to Toshiba is explicitly dependent on how much market share Motorola gets in Japan.
- *Give managers sufficient autonomy.* Decentralisation of decision making should give managers sufficient autonomy to run the joint venture successfully. Two of the most successful global value-adding joint ventures are those between Fuji-Xerox and Nippon-Otis which are also amongst those giving management the greatest autonomy.

It has been found that extensive training and team building is crucial if these joint ventures are to succeed. There are three ways in which effective HRM may be critical:

- developing and training managers in negotiation and conflict resolution;
- acculturation (i.e. cultural awareness) in working with a foreign partner;
- harmonisation of management styles.

Case study 15.4 investigates a strategic joint venture between Nestlé and Coca-Cola in the beverages sector.

Case Study 15.4 Coca-Cola and Nestlé combine

FT

One of the biggest marketing successes of the past decade has been the coffee shop chain. But the next move for coffee – and for its less hyped cousin, tea – could be to the fridge. Coca-Cola and Nestlé, two of the biggest names in the beverages and food sector, have spotted an opportunity in the so-called *ready to drink* (RTD) sector and have together devised a plan to dominate a fragmented global market by reinventing coffee and tea.

One would have thought Coca-Cola already sold enough cold, flavoured, brown liquid. But this is different; the plan is to capture what could be a massive consumer trend by creating branded offers around the existing concepts of iced tea and coffee. The potential for growth is huge. According to Mintel's January 2002 Adult Soft Drinks report: 'The category value of the global RTD market grew at a compound annual rate of over 6% from 1997 to 2002 (second only to bottled water) and is forecast to grow at close to 10% per annum in the next five years.'

Coca-Cola and Nestlé's Zurich-based 50–50 joint venture, *Beverage Partners Worldwide* (BPW), wants to explore the RTD opportunities in every market and come up with a brand extension or repositioning of an existing product, or a brand-new offering. Hence the testing in Greece this summer of Black Ice, a spicy Mocha coffee-style RTD; hence trials in Belgium and Switzerland of microwave ovens in Coca-Cola vending machines, allowing the same can of coffee to be sold hot or cold; hence recent rebranding of Nestea in Europe and Asia.

BPW is headed by Hans Savonije, a Dutchman who was previously with Coca-Cola for four years and with Unilever for 17 years before that. Of BPW's 46 marketing, product developing and finance people, 17 are from Coke and 10 from Nestlé. In the two and a half years since its launch, the venture has extended its operations to 55 markets, 17 of them in the past 18 months. In 2002–03 the rapidly expanding group introduced half a dozen new products and aims to achieve 25% growth a year.

Mr Savonije declines to reveal how much the parent companies are investing in BPW but says it has an annual wholesale value between \$1.2bn and \$1.4bn (£690m and £800m). BPW comes up with a new RTD suggestion and develops it. Once it is cleared by both parents, it is up to BPW to get it on the shelves.

Case Study 15.4 continued

Nestlé brings the food science and research and development know-how: Coca-Cola has the distribution and field marketing expertise. 'We use existing resources of both companies and make them sweat a bit more,' says Mr Savonije. BPW has also been getting help from WPP-owned brand agency Added Value on product innovation and both Added Value and its sister design agency, Enterprise IG, have worked on Black Ice.

The market is still immature except for Asian countries, particularly Japan. Unilever's Lipton Ice is the only big rival. More than 90% of BPW's business is still Nescafé and Nestea. Mr Savonije sees tea-flavoured drinks in particular as immensely versatile. 'You can position different ranges of tea drinks from being close to Coke, which is very sweet, to water which is pure and boring.'

And this is the trick because unlike Coke itself, whose flavour appeals worldwide, tea is much more of a local taste. In Egypt BPW has brought out El Rayek, a very sweet tea drink. There is ongoing work for the Argentine and Brazilian markets on an iced *mate*, the bitter, hay-like tea drunk incessantly through a straw in those countries. And while Nestlé Ice Rush with menthol flopped with consumers in North America, it has proved popular in Hong Kong and Taiwan.

Mr Savonije is convinced of the category's staying power. 'It won't be a fad,' he says. 'The whole trend in society is towards more balance in life. It's a snowball and it won't stop.' Perhaps there is even potential to usurp Coke, the biggest soft drink brand in the world. David Nichols, managing director at Added Value, points out that the Swiss and Belgians now drink more iced tea than Coke, adding 'It's eminently possible that tea etc. could take over from Coke, but it's a long way off.'

But with Coca-Cola's efforts to transform itself into a leading drinks company in all sectors, and Nestlé hoping to become a total food company, BPW is hardly seen as a threat, says Mr Savonije: 'It fits into their strategy.'

Source: *Financial Times*, 11 December 2003

Questions

1 How would you describe this joint venture?
2 What strategic benefits might result to either partner in this joint venture?

We now complete our analysis of corporate strategy by reviewing a number of different approaches to remaining competitive within a globalised environment. These involve strategies for retaining current value chain configurations as well as adapting them.

Case materials: corporate strategic responses to global forces

There now follows four case study examples touching on different strategic approaches to global forces. Read them carefully and then answer the questions which are presented at the end of the case studies (p. 644).

1 Safeway and Coca-Cola dream up a merchandising cocktail

Safeway has more stores of less than 20,000 sq ft than any of its competitors, meaning it has to work harder at product selection and merchandising. Last year, Richard Hayhoe, a category operations manager for Safeway, realised the chain was missing a trick by expecting consumers to find the soft drinks aisle when smarter merchandising could present appropriate sizes and styles of bottles or cans at other points in the store where they would draw attention.

Mr Hayhoe worked with Coca-Cola on planning a new approach. Chiller cabinets for cans and 500 ml bottles were placed beside check-outs and racks of larger bottles beside ready meals. Coca-Cola also started attaching merchandising material to the cardboard palettes of drinks, so they could be unloaded straight from the truck on to the shop floor, often in front of the entrance. The supermarket and manufacturer jointly funded development and Safeway paid for the creation of new gondolas and refrigerators. Mr Hayhoe says he has no doubt that what the store called the 'reinvigoration project' has had a significant impact on sales, although this is difficult to prove given this year's hot summer.

The collaboration between store and manufacturer has continued to yield results. Before Vanilla Coke was launched this summer Safeway took advantage of its links with the drinks manufacturer to plan the launch in detail. Safeway was able to get the drink into its stores three days before other supermarkets, raising its market share, while Coca-Cola benefited from an early commitment on orders from Safeway and the chance to send sampling teams into its stores.

Source: *Financial Times*, 13 November 2003, p. 17

2 From milk churn to washing machine: a history of innovation

Innovation is a vital activity at Miele. The company puts about 12% of its annual sales into research and development, a figure more reminiscent of semiconductor businesses than of companies making kitchen appliances. The accent on new ideas was central to the company – which owns 681 worldwide patents – from its inception.

The founders of the business, Carl Miele and Reinhard Zinkann, started by making machines for separating cream from milk, which were sold to farmers in the agricultural region of northern Germany where Miele has always been based. The pair branched out in 1900, a year after the company started, into butter churns – large containers fitted with hand-propelled paddles to make the milk curdle.

Miele's first washing machines followed in 1901. It was a simple matter for the company's technicians to take the butter churns, fill them with soapy water rather than milk and replace the paddle with a mechanical agitator to wash clothes. Electric power was added later; the company made its first vacuum cleaner in 1927 and its first dishwasher in 1929.

Markus Miele, the company's current joint managing director and the great grandson of the first Mr Miele, says the company tries continually to improve its products. A few years ago, it rethought the design for the large metal drums that contain the wash load in modern front-loading washing machines. 'The drums had 4,000 holes (for letting water in and out) and our engineers thought for years that it was impossible to reduce them in number without interfering with the water passage. But after a lengthy series of tests we showed you could reduce the figure to 700 without impeding performance. The change made the systems simpler to make and more resilient (by increasing their stiffness).'

What does Mr Miele think of James Dyson, the UK domestic appliance entrepreneur who – through his company, Dyson Appliances – has blazed a trail in Europe by introducing the first bagless vacuum cleaner? 'Mr Dyson has done an impressive job in marketing, which has helped us because he has helped to make the public keener on buying high-cost appliances. But it's not correct to say he devised (bagless cleaners) before anyone else. We thought of this idea some years before but we never marketed the products because having vacuum cleaners without bags causes problems for the consumer in terms of disposing of the dirt. We think it's better to use bags, which is why we have not gone down this route.'

Source: *Financial Times*, 14 November 2003, p. 13

3 Five steps to keep Beaconsfield Footwear marching on

Stewart Houlgrave has taken a number of steps to make sure Beaconsfield Footwear does not suffer the fate of most members of the now defunct Lancashire Footwear Manufacturers Association, which was put out of business by the mass-produced shoe imports now accounting for more than 90% of all shoes sold in the UK.

1. Trying to end reliance on low-margin volume products and build relationships with final customers through the launch of the Hotter shoe brand, emphasising 'comfort' rather than price or fashion. A typical Hotter customer is 45-plus and female and takes a lot of holidays.
2. Building up a mail-order business to remove dependence on high street chains, where buying decisions hinge solely on price.
3. Retaining a UK manufacturing base, allowing more flexible response to end-consumer demand and on-the-spot control of the fit and quality of Hotter shoes – a critical element in establishing a brand image as a 'comfort shoe'. Hotter has outsourced the most labour-intensive part of shoe production to India.
4. Emphasising the 'British made' label. Design, resourcing of materials and 'lasting' of the shoe are all done in the UK and the shoes are delivered by Royal Mail.
5. Maintaining customer contact via a 60-seat call centre located in the new factory. There is no question of outsourcing Hotter's number one customer service tool. 'When you call us you speak to real people, not buttons,' says Mr Houlgrave.

Source: *Financial Times*, 25 November 2003, p. 13

4 Hardy casts around for a route to recovery

World-famous fishing tackle manufacturer House of Hardy faces the challenge of safeguarding an obsession with quality and maintaining a strong and well-established brand name, while fighting fierce competition from Asian and US companies.

Its management team is taking the following steps:

- Thinking the unthinkable in the 'make/buy analysis' – the question of what it makes itself and what it buys in. 'Made in England' will be retained for Hardy tackle, but the company is conducting trials on importing some components.
- Embracing a dual-brand strategy. The Greys ranges are mid-market products, while the Hardy ranges are pitched to the top end. Production of Greys rods have shifted over the past couple of years to South Korea and China, where costs can be 50% lower: Greys reels are made in the UK and South Korea.
- Focusing on core strengths. Hardy has abandoned peripheral businesses such as making clothes and bags and has appointed a US distributor for its tackle.
- Fighting complacency borne of Hardy's long heritage. The company is analysing competitors' offerings and reviewing its pricing structure.
- Emphasising design. New products must have the visual 'wow factor' as well as the outstanding performance Hardy already offered.
- Grasping painful nettles. Cutting 30% of its employees – many of them with long service – was grim, but the management insists that it had no option but to cut costs at the Alnwick, Northumberland, base.
- Embracing lean manufacturing. A forthcoming review will look at manufacturing processes and study how products can be designed to achieve greater manufacturing efficiency.
- Expanding the youth market. About 3.5m people in the UK go fishing, half of them doing so regularly, but social change means young people may be less likely to fish with their dads and granddads. House of Hardy is supporting initiatives to get more youngsters out fishing.

Source: *Financial Times*, 2 December 2003, p. 17

Questions

1 Making specific reference to individual case material, suggest strategies being proposed by firms who are seeking to avoid outsourcing and yet remain competitive when located in relatively high wage economies.

2 Making specific reference to individual case material, suggest opportunities that present themselves to reconfigure existing value chains in order to remain competitive in a globalised environment.

Key Terms

Boston Matrix A device by which products can be rated according to sales growth and market share. Developed by the Boston Consulting Group in the US and involving categories such as 'problem children', 'stars', 'cash cows' and 'dogs'.

Cost-plus pricing Where a conventional profit mark-up is added to a cost-base to give the price.

Focus strategy Where the company identifies a segment in the market and tailors its strategy to serve that market, excluding all other segments.

Generic strategies Porter identified three such strategies; namely, cost leadership (emphasis on cost reduction), differentiation strategy (emphasis on superior product characteristics) and a focus on strategy in which the company identifies a segment in the market and tailors its strategy to serve that market, excluding all other segments.

Global strategy Emphasises large-scale production of a standardised product securing economies of scale, scope and experience.

International strategy 'Core' architecture located in home base with limited aspects of the value chain only located overseas.

Multidomestic strategy Emphasises responsiveness to the different conditions in each national market by establishing relatively independent subsidiaries with a full range of value chain activities.

PEST An analysis involving the political, economic, social and technological environment in which the firm operates.

PESTLE Political, economic, social, technological, legal and environmental.

Porter's diamond Highlights four interdependent determinants of national competitive advantages, namely demand conditions, factor conditions, related and supporting industries and firm strategies, structures and rivalries.

Porter's Five Forces An analysis involving an assessment of the threat of (1) potential entrants and (2) substitutes, as well as the power of (3) suppliers and (4) buyers, together with an exploration of (5) the degree of competitive rivalry.

Prestige pricing Where price is set in the context of quality being associated with price (e.g. Veblen effect, Chapter 2, p. 69).

Product line pricing Where the pricing of one item in a set of related products on a 'product line' is influenced by factors more closely related to the whole 'product line' than the individual product itself.

Strategy Guiding 'rules' or principles influencing the direction and scope of the organisation's activities in the long term.

SWOT An analysis of the strengths, weaknesses, opportunities and threats facing the company from both internal and external sources.

Transnational strategy Emphasises establishing each element in the value chain in the most appropriate geographical setting.

Key Points

- Corporate strategy is defined as involving the direction and scope of an organisation over the long term.
- 'Competitive advantage' refers to the strengths of the more successful firms in an industry vis-à-vis the most marginal firm in that industry.
- SWOT (Strength, Weakness, Opportunities, Threats) analysis emphasises both external and internal environmental factors.

- PEST (Political, Economic, Social and Technological) analysis focuses on the external environment in which the firm operates, to which law and ecology are sometimes added to make PESTLE. It may be used in support of SWOT analysis.
- The stage reached in the product life cycle both nationally and internationally can have important implications for price and non-price strategies undertaken by the firm.
- The Boston matrix uses categories such as 'Question Marks', 'Stars', 'Cash Cows' and 'Dogs' to support a balanced portfolio approach by multi-product firms.
- The Ansoff matrix uses 'new' and 'present' categories of product and market to identify strategic direction.
- Porter's 'Five Forces' analysis can be used to help the firm 'position' itself in terms of the appropriate strategic responses to those forces, whilst Porter's 'diamond' emphasises national rather than firm competitiveness.
- Porter's 'generic' strategies involve broad directions of strategy such as overall cost leadership, product differentiation and focus strategies.
- In a global context MNEs must continually reconfigure their value chains to reflect both cost-competitive opportunities and pressures towards local responsiveness.
- MNEs may adopt global, multidomestic, transnational and national strategies.
- 'Relative unit labour costs' (RULCs) are a key index of international competitiveness and play an important role in strategic choice.

Assessment Practice

Multiple choice questions

1 Under which of the following circumstances is the firm most likely to consider a price cutting strategy?

(a) Perfectly inelastic demand
(b) Relatively inelastic demand
(c) Unit elastic demand
(d) Relatively elastic demand
(e) Other firms raising their prices

2 Brand extension strategies are often used to delay the onset of the:

(a) introduction phase of the product life cycle
(b) growth phase of the product life cycle
(c) maturity phase of the product life cycle
(d) decline phase of the product life cycle
(e) 'Cash Cow' phase of the Boston Matrix.

3 **The Boston matrix essentially supports:**

(a) product specialisation
(b) process specialisation
(c) an unbalanced portfolio of products
(d) a concentration on question marks
(e) a balanced portfolio of products.

4 **In Porter's 'Five Forces' analysis, if a few large producers in the industry form a price-fixing agreement, we would say that the:**

(a) threat of potential entrants increases
(b) threat of substitutes is significant
(c) power of buyers increases
(d) degree of competitive rivalry in the industry is huge
(e) degree of competitive rivalry in the industry is low.

5 **In Porter's 'Five Forces' analysis, if there are now fewer public houses 'tied' to particular brewers, we would say that the:**

(a) threat of potential entrants increases
(b) threat of substitutes is significant
(c) power of buyers increases
(d) degree of competitive rivalry in the industry has risen
(e) degree of competitive rivalry in the industry has fallen.

6 **Which *one* of the following international strategies involves an MNE in responding to high cost pressures and high local responsiveness pressures in a way which often involves a more geographical dispersed value chain.**

(a) Multidomestic
(b) Transnational
(c) Global
(d) International

7 **Which *one* of the following international strategies involves an MNE in responding to high cost pressures and low local responsiveness pressures so that core competencies remain centralised and a standardised product is sold worldwide.**

(a) Multidomestic
(b) Transnational
(c) Global
(d) International

8 Outsourcing a labour-intensive process in the value chain to a firm in another country is more likely if:

(a) relative labour costs are high and relative labour productivity is low in the overseas country
(b) relative labour costs are low and relative labour productivity is high in the overseas country
(c) relative labour costs and relative labour productivity are identical in both domestic and overseas country
(d) the quality of the product produced by firms in the overseas country is low
(e) contracts are frequently challenged and overruled in the overseas country.

9 Which *two* of the following refer to using a low-price strategy?

(a) Price skimming
(b) Penetration pricing
(c) Parallel pricing
(d) Cartel pricing
(e) Loss-leader pricing

10 Which of the following refers to a situation where a product generates high profits which can then be invested in developing new products?

(a) Question marks
(b) Cash cows
(c) Dogs
(d) Stars
(e) Growth stage

Data response and stimulus questions

1 Look carefully at the following data on the pattern of international labour costs.

Labour costs and labour productivity, 2002

Country	Total labour costs ($ per hour)	Total labour costs ($ per hour Index: UK = 100)	Labour productivity (Index UK = 100)
Mexico	2.3	14.3	40.3
Korea	8.1	50.3	43.5
France	15.9	98.8	135.5
UK	16.1	100.0	100.0
Japan	19.6	121.8	92.0
US	20.3	126.1	125.9
Germany	22.9	142.2	127.4

Question

What strategic implications might follow for international businesses from data such as this?

2 Look carefully at the data in the table below, showing price differentials for 10 identical products across Europe. The data is adapted from a major survey by Dresdner Kleinwort Wasserstein (DKW), the investment bank.

How prices across Europe compare

	London (€)	Stockholm (€)	Frankfurt (€)	Paris (€)	Rome (€)	Madrid (€)	Amsterdam (€)
Coke	1.92	1.58	1.90	1.17	1.31	1.33	1.45
Nestle Gold Blend	6.51	6.58	8.19	6.67	4.38	4.94	5.90
Kellogg's Cornflakes	1.84	2.12	1.84	2.06	1.90	1.66	2.38
Pringles	2.15	2.30	1.49	1.54	1.83	1.65	1.68
Mars Bar	0.54	0.76	0.51	0.60	0.45	0.53	0.48
CDs	21.79	19.40	17.07	18.85	20.61	19.10	21.79
DVDs	28.61	39.46	25.74	29.78	27.53	26.79	31.12
Adidas shoes	93.45	79.61	82.38	95.00	84.35	84.72	74.98
Levi jeans	70.09	82.33	78.93	76.04	69.00	70.50	89.95
McDonald's Big Mac	3.27	3.19	2.65	2.95	2.50	2.45	2.60

Question

As international marketing manager responsible for one or more of these products, explain why you might have supported price differentials of the type indicated across these European markets.

3 Case study: International strategies

Read the text below, then answer the questions which follow.

In the 1990s the share prices of global brand-owners such as Coca-Cola, McDonald's and Walt Disney soared as investors savoured the companies' growth prospects. Another sign of the times was the trend for companies to brand or rebrand themselves with global-sounding names seemingly plucked from Esperanto, such as Diageo, Novartis and Invensys.

Then, something unexpected happened: a reaction set in. People around the world started demanding more local sovereignty and more protection for their cultural identities. Most worryingly for global brand-owners, consumers in newly opened markets started expressing a desire for local products – which, as local manufacturers adopted Western business methods, were simultaneously showing a big improvement in quality.

By the end of the 1990s, most global brand-owners were switching chief executives as their share prices plummeted in response to slowing growth rates. In March 2000 in a signed article in the *Financial Times*, Douglas Daft, Coca-Cola's new chief executive, offered a startling analysis of what had gone wrong. Coca-Cola, Mr Daft wrote, had traditionally been a 'multi-local' company but as globalisation had gathered pace, it had centralised its decision

making and standardised its practices. 'We were operating as a big, slow, insulated, sometimes even insensitive "global" company and we were doing it in a new era when nimbleness, speed, transparency and local sensitivity had become absolutely essential to success,' he wrote. But Coca-Cola had learnt its lesson, Mr Daft said. It was that 'the next big evolutionary step of "going global" now has to be "going local". In other words, we have to rediscover our own multi-local heritage.' Astonishingly, it was almost the opposite of what Prof. Levitt had advocated. Yet now it is the almost universally accepted wisdom. The one-size-fits-all approach is out; 'think local, act local' is in. Coca-Cola owns not one brand but more than 200, mostly local; McDonald's varies its menu to suit local tastes; MTV has different programming to suit different countries and regions.

Whilst homogenisation has affected some product categories – mainly in the technology sector, where there are no cultural barriers to overcome – the paradox of globalisation is that it has led not to a convergence of tastes but to a vast increase in the number of choices available to consumers. People can now buy products from all over the world: global, regional and local.

Another paradox is that technology is aiding the fragmentation. 'Prof. Levitt was assuming that the only way to get scale was through standardisation. It was essentially the Henry Ford argument,' says Lowell Bryan, a McKinsey director and former student of Prof. Levitt. 'But technology has changed the economics of production. Now, you can have both economies of scale and also deliver very discrete, specialised products.'

Question

(a) How does the case study suggest international business strategies have changed over time?
(b) What have been the reasons for such change?

True/False questions

1 In Ansoff's matrix, a diversification strategy may involve new products and new markets.
True/False

2 The threat of potential entrants may cause existing (incumbent) firms to keep prices low, even if the current market situation would permit higher prices.
True/False

3 Cash Cows can help generate the profit needed to finance investment in the question marks which may become the Stars and Cash Cows of the future.
True/False

4 A 'price war' is more likely to break out where price elasticity of demand is highly inelastic.
True/False

5 In the decline stage of the product life cycle it may be worth cutting price to attract many new customers.
True/False

6 A multidomestic strategy is a response to high local responsiveness pressures and involves relatively independent subsidiaries being established in other countries with most of the value chain elements present in those subsidiaries. Cost pressures will often be low in this case.

True/False

7 Corporate strategy refers to devising strategies at the level of a particular business unit within the enterprise.

True/False

8 In the Boston matrix, 'Question Marks' tend to have relatively high growth rates for sales revenue but relatively low market share.

True/False

9 Focus strategy is one of Porter's three 'generic strategies' and refers to strategies targeted to particular segments of market activity.

True/False

10 The threat of substitutes is not one of the 'five forces' identified by Porter.

True/False

Essay questions

1 How might a firm use the ideas of corporate strategy to improve its situation? Use actual examples to illustrate your answer wherever appropriate.
2 Under what circumstances would a multinational enterprise adopt (a) a global strategy and (b) a multidomestic strategy?
3 Examine the case for an increased use of outsourcing by a multinational enterprise located in the UK.
4 To what extent would you agree that Porter's 'five forces analysis' covers all we need to know about corporate strategy?
5 Identify and evaluate the major methods that a business might consider using in order to assess its competitive position.

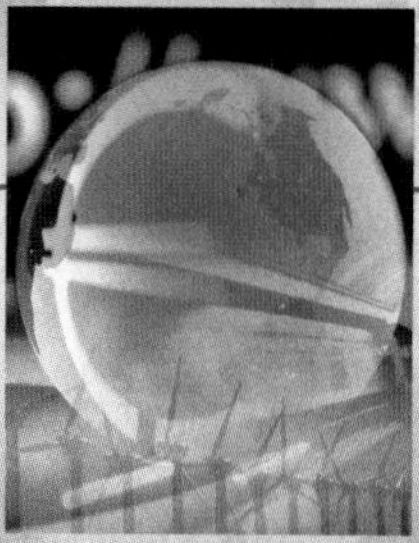

Chapter 16

Leisure, hospitality and sports sectors

Introduction

The chapter begins by examining the rise of the service or tertiary sector in the UK economy over the past 50 years or so. We note that this experience is common across all the advanced industrialised economies. Some of the implications of this growth of services and decline of industry are considered, especially the issue of 'de-industrialisation'.

From financial services, to transport services, to education and the National Health Service, to mention just a few, the tertiary sector is too wide to be captured in any meaningful way in one chapter. Instead we concentrate on some of the key characteristics which underpin *all* service sector provision. We then explore in rather more detail the particular sectors of leisure, hospitality and sports.

Learning objectives:

By the end of this chapter, you should be able to:

- define the major sectors of economic activity and identify changes in the relative importance of these sectors over time
- explain why the tertiary sector has increased its share of economic activity and consider some of the consequences associated with the relative decline in industrial activity (de-industrialisation)
- examine the key characteristics which underpin service sector provision, including issues involving the nature of services (e.g. 'perishability'), their demand and cost structures, and their susceptibility to external environmental factors
- identify and assess the implications of structural shifts within the service sector, from provision initially within highly fragmented market structures to provision within increasingly consolidated market structures
- evaluate the contribution of the 'progression of economic value' model to service sector provision and the increasing tendency for service sector activities to be 'outsourced'

- use examples involving case-study materials from the leisure, hospitality and sports sectors to illustrate these and other service sector principles patterns and trends.

Changing economic structure

Why have so many jobs been lost in manufacturing businesses in recent years and can this process be reversed? In any case, does such **de-industrialisation** really matter, given that service sector businesses are growing so rapidly? We begin by considering the changes taking place in the structure of the UK economy, before comparing such changes with those in other advanced industrialised economies, and considering both their causes and consequences.

Economic sector

An economy may be analysed in terms of its component parts, often called 'sectors'. Sectors may be widely drawn to include groups of services (e.g. financial services) or narrowly drawn to identify parts of service activities (e.g. private medical insurance), depending on our purpose. Structural change is often discussed in terms of the even more widely drawn 'primary', 'secondary' and 'tertiary' (service) sectors.

It will be useful at the outset to define these, and other conventional sector headings.

(a) **The primary sector.** This includes activities directly related to natural resources, e.g. farming, forestry, fishing, mining and oil extraction.

(b) **The secondary sector.** This covers goods production in the economy, including the processing of materials produced by the primary sector. *Manufacturing* is the main element in this sector, which also includes construction and the public utility industries of gas, water and electricity.

(c) **The tertiary sector.** This includes all the private sector services, e.g. distribution, insurance, banking and finance, and all the (mainly) public sector services, such as health, education and defence.

Some even speak of a *quaternary sector*, seen as including information creating, handling and processing activities. The term 'post-industrial society' is also sometimes used to refer to the increasing importance of knowledge and information-related activities in modern advanced economies.

Structural change

Structural change means change in the *relative size* of these sectors, whether in terms of contribution to national output (income) or to total employment.

Through time we should *expect* the structure of an economy to change as a result of changing patterns and trends.

- *Changing patterns of demand.* The pattern of demand for a country's products will change with variations in incomes or tastes, and this will in turn affect both output and employment. Suppose there is a period of economic growth so that real incomes rise, then the demand for goods and services with high and positive **income elasticities** (see Chapter 2. p. 64) will tend to increase relative to those with low or even negative income elasticities.

Example:

Income elasticities of demand

Between 1983 and 2003 real household expenditure on financial services rose by as much as 168% and expenditure on healthcare services increased by a similar amount over that period. On the other hand, household expenditure on food products grew by only 19.7% whilst expenditure on 'alcohol, drink and tobacco' actually fell by 11.7%. Such changes have clear implications for the pattern of output and employment.

- *Demographic changes.* An ageing population is changing both demand patterns and production possibilities. The number of people aged 65 and over in the UK has increased by 53% since 1961, rising from around 6 million to over 9.5 million in 2004. Older people require more healthcare services but fewer educational services, for example. A higher proportion of retired people not only influences patterns of demand but also reduces the labour force available to the economy.
- *Technical factors.* New products and new processes of production result from technical progress. The Internet is creating economic activities involving goods and services which could not have been predicted only a few years ago.
- *Competition factors.* Higher productivity of labour or capital or a lower exchange rate may make some of the country's goods and services more competitive than those of its rivals, and vice versa.
- *Location factors.* Multinational corporations have the ability to locate activities in particular countries worldwide, and that includes service sector activities which are increasingly subject to such outsourcing.

De-industrialisation

This term is often used to describe the declining share of the *secondary sector* in total output or employment. Sometimes it is used in the more specific context of a decline in the share of *manufacturing* in total output or employment. On either definition it is clear that de-industrialisation has taken place in the UK, as can be seen from Table 16.1.

Table 16.1 Percentage shares of GDP at factor cost

	1964	1969	1973	1979	1990	2001
Primary	*5.8*	*4.3*	*4.2*	*6.7*	*3.9*	*3.9*
Agriculture, forestry and fishing	1.9	1.8	2.9	2.2	1.8	1.0
Mining and quarrying including oil and gas extraction	3.9	2.5	2.5	4.5	2.1	2.9
Secondary	*40.8*	*42.0*	*40.9*	*36.7*	*31.5*	*24.8*
Mineral oil processing	0.5	0.5	0.4	0.6	0.6	1.0
Manufacturing	29.5	30.7	30.0	27.3	21.9	16.6
Construction	8.4	8.4	7.3	6.2	6.9	5.4
Electricity, gas and water supply	2.4	2.4	2.8	2.6	2.1	1.8
Tertiary	*53.8*	*53.0*	*54.9*	*56.5*	*64.4*	*71.3*
Distribution, hotels, catering, repairs	14.0	13.3	13.1	12.7	13.5	15.6
Transport and storage	4.4	4.4	4.7	4.8	4.9	5.2
Post and telecommunication	1.6	1.9	2.3	2.5	2.7	2.8
Financial intermediation, real estate, renting and business activities	8.3	8.6	10.7	11.0	16.7	18.3
Ownership of dwellings	5.4	4.4	5.1	5.8	5.9	6.4
Public administration, national defence and social security	7.6	7.0	6.1	6.1	6.3	4.8
Education, health and social work	6.9	7.1	7.7	8.1	8.9	13.0
Other services	5.6	5.2	5.1	5.7	5.5	5.2

Adapted from ONS (2002) United Kingdom National Accounts and previous issues

The primary sector's share of output has fallen from 5.8% in 1964 to 3.9% in 2001. The upward shift in the 1970s represented the arrival of North Sea oil production, since when the downward trend has continued.

The secondary sector's share of output fell from a peak of 42.0% in 1969 to only 31.5% in 1990 and the recession then further reduced this to 24.8% by 2001. By 1990 *manufacturing* produced only 21.9% of UK output, which fell further to 1.6% by 2001.

The tertiary sector's share of output has grown throughout the period since 1969, necessarily so as the shares of the primary and secondary sectors have fallen. The financial sector more than doubled its share of output between 1964 and 2001 to become the largest sub-sector within the tertiary sector in terms of output share.

With the exception of the growth of the North Sea oil sector, these changes in economic structure have occurred throughout the advanced industrial countries (see Table 16.2). The fall in the share of manufacturing in GDP in the UK is also typical of the other advanced industrialised economies, as is the growth in services for such economies.

Table 16.2 Advanced industrialised economies, distribution of GDP: percentages

	1960	1980	1985	2001
Agriculture	6.0	3.1	2.6	1.7
Industry	41.0	36.5	34.2	28.6
(manufacturing)	(30.4)	(24.7)	(23.2)	(20.1)
Services	53.0	60.4	63.2	69.7

Adapted from OECD (2002) *OECD in Figures* and previous issues

Causes of de-industrialisation

Various causes have been suggested to account for the decline in secondary sector output and particularly manufacturing.

- *Maturity argument.* In older, more 'mature' economies workers from primary and secondary sectors are needed to support the expansion of the tertiary (service) sector.
- *Crowding out.* The relatively high levels of government expenditure on public sector services (e.g. health, education) in the UK has resulted in higher taxes and interest rates, thereby discouraging ('crowding out') private sector output and employment.
- *Low productivity.* Low productivity levels in UK industry make it difficult to compete effectively on price in home and overseas markets.
- *High wages.* The relatively high wages in UK industry make it difficult to compete effectively on price in home and overseas markets.
- *High exchange rate.* The relatively high pound over many years has made UK exports more expensive and imports cheaper. North Sea oil and gas have made sterling more attractive to hold ('petro currency'), keeping its 'price' (the exchange rate) relatively high.

LINKS
Relatively low labour productivity, relatively high wages and a high exchange rate all contribute to increasing 'relative unit labour costs' (see Chapter 15, p. 634) and therefore making UK industry less competitive, contributing to de-industrialisation.

Others have pointed to low levels of skill and poor management as also contributing to the loss of industrial output and employment.

Consequences of de-industrialisation

Does the loss of industrial output and employment matter? After all, the tertiary (service) sector has managed to create as many jobs as have been lost in industry! A number of arguments have made as to why de-industrialisation *does* matter!

- *Backward linkages.* These are generally stronger for manufacturing-type activities than for services. For example, the car producer must buy engine components, metal products and textiles from other manufacturers (unless vertically integrated) and will also purchase the services of designers, vehicle transporters, accountants, lawyers, bankers etc. As a result, each £1 spent on industrial output has a more significant impact on the rest of the economy than the same £1 spent on services.

- *Innovation potential.* The majority of innovations (e.g. as indicated by new patents) occur in the manufacturing sector.
- *Growth prospects.* Recorded productivity growth tends to be highest in manufacturing, because of the greater scope in these activities for increased productivity via capital investment and technical progress.
- *Balance of payments.* Most traded products are industrial: for example, a 2.5% rise in UK service sector exports is needed merely to offset a 1% fall in manufacturing exports.

The particular nature of services

Here we look at some of the distinctive properties of services in general before turning to a more detailed investigation of the leisure, hospitality and sports sectors.

Perishability

When we think of perishability, we tend to think of goods such as food, with limp lettuce, sour milk, rotting fruit and vegetables past their sell-by date. However, *all* services are arguably 'perishable' in the sense that they cannot be stored. Most services are usually consumed *at the same time* as they are purchased, as in the case of education, transport, hotel, sports and theatre services, amongst others. That seat unoccupied on today's flight to Los Angeles, that hotel bedroom unoccupied tonight, that un-let squash court this morning, those six theatre tickets which failed to sell last night; all these service opportunities have 'perished' as they cannot now be sold; the opportunity has been lost. No revenue has been gained and the available resource has been under-utilised. What a waste!

This perishable nature of services often leads to price discrimination, as for example cheap price offers to 'shift' spare capacity. Who has not travelled off-peak on a train? Maybe some of you may have flown at 'stand-by' rates. After all, for the service provider, it may be better to collect 50% or even 10% of the published fare rather than have no fare at all and thus a perished opportunity to sell.

Experiential characteristics

Although not unique to services, arguably they are more frequently involved in meeting a growing demand for 'consumer experiences'. The 'progression of economic value' model is shown in Figure 16.1, with *experience* as the next step in a staged process beyond conventional services. An experience occurs:

Quote

> ... when a company intentionally uses services as the stage and goods as the props to engage customers in a way that creates a memorable event.
>
> *(Pine and Gilmore, 1998)*

The quality and nature of the experience provided is so evidently at the crux of business success in the hospitality sector, as in a wide range of services/experience sectors,

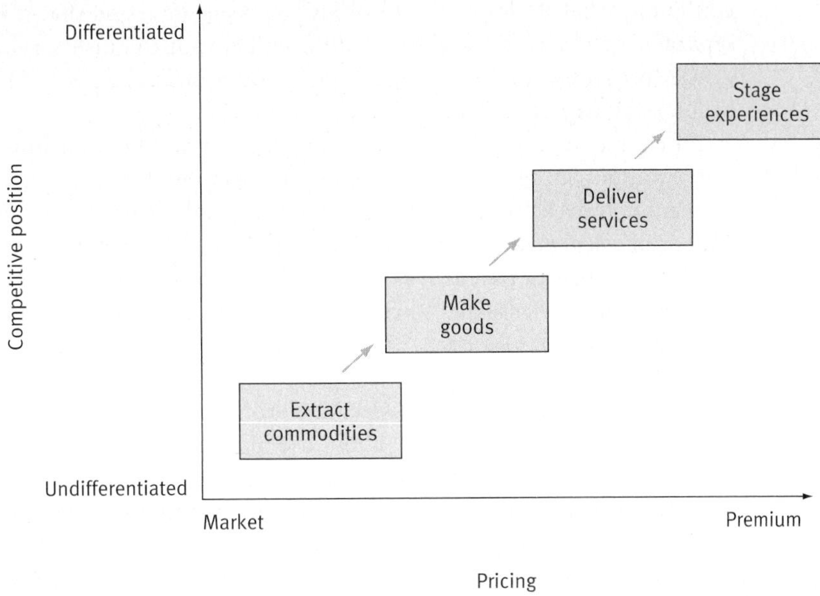

Fig 16.1 The progression of economic value

including education and health care. A truly memorable experience may be one to recommend and, where appropriate, revisit. It may be highly differentiated and customised and be able to charge a premium price to those seeking that experience.

Whilst Pine and Gilmore saw companies as creating value by stage-managing experiences for customers (e.g. Disney theme parks), a more recent contribution by two prominent thinkers on value creation, Prahalad and Ramaswamy (2004), goes even further. They see customers as co-creators of value with producers, as for example participating in product development (drug trials, testing 'beta' versions of software) and forming virtual communities (Napster online music file-sharing service, Lego Mindstorms range of DIY robots, Harley Davidson's community of enthusiasts around motorcycles, John Deere farm equipment, etc.). In these ways products and services become the foundation on which broader experiences are built.

Quote

> the burgeoning complexity of offerings ... confounds and frustrates most time-starved consumers. Product variety has not necessarily resulted in better consumer experiences ...
>
> *(Prahalad and Ramaswamy, 2004)*

In their view the future belongs to companies that 'co-create value' in partnership with customers, involving shared experiences.

Intangibility

The term 'tangible' is often applied to physical products which can be touched and handled. The term 'intangible' is more usually applied to services and refers broadly to non-physical characteristics such as atmosphere, ambience, context, interpersonal communication, attitude and so on. It has been suggested that it is 'intangibility' that separates products from services and even helps distinguish services from experience, in the 'progression of economic value' shown in Figure 16.1. In this view, a service becomes an experience through its performance.

Of course, intangibility may develop around and be built upon tangible elements. For example, a restaurant's reputation must incorporate good food as well as ambience. Indeed, because services are intangible, customers often rely on tangible cues or physical evidence. This includes all those aspects of the service provision which can be seen, heard, touched, tasted, smelt, felt or sensed. Zeithami and Bitner (2000) use the term 'servicescape' to refer to the interface between tangibles and intangibles in the provision of services.

> ... many aspects of the physical environment serve as explicit and implicit signals that communicate about the place to its users. ... Quality of materials used in construction, floor coverings, items displayed can all create symbolic meaning and create an overall aesthetic impression ... it is without doubt that the servicescape provided can have a profound effect on both customers and employees.

Heterogeneity

Services, especially those which focus on the experiential components, are difficult to standardise, i.e. make homogeneous. No two performances can ever quite be the same! However, through deconstructing the overall service provision into its component parts and seeking to perfect the delivery of each part, at least some reliability may be built into the service provision. Provided at least the majority of these component parts of the service are provided to a good standard, the occasional underperformance in one or two parts may restrict the variation in service delivery to within tolerable limits.

Low marginal costs

The marginal cost of sales, i.e. that extra variable cost which results from one more customer, is generally low for services; e.g. what is the cost of an extra individual taking a spare seat on a plane or a train? How much extra did it cost to let out that squash court between 9 am and 10 am? Perhaps some extra energy costs if the court is individually lighted and heated and the extra cost of hot water for the players' shower after the game. To let a vacant hotel room tonight may only bring the additional cost of laundry and disposables, which has been estimated as between £5 and £30, dependent on hotel rating (0 to 5 stars).

By contrast, fixed (or semi-variable) costs of sale are often relatively high for services; staffing, business rates, rent, energy or other such costs can be a significant hurdle even before the first sale is made.

CHECK THE NET

You can visit the websites of *Lastminute.com* and *Expedia.co.uk* and note the range of products and services on offer, often at highly discounted prices.

Increased consolidation

Most service sector industries are going through a period of consolidation, often not just nationally but internationally. Consider food retailing where Tesco and Sainsbury are not only seeking to increase their market share in the UK but are also developing international profiles. The world's largest company, Wal-Mart, has taken significant market share in many countries, including 16% of the UK market through its purchase of Asda. The tendency towards further *consolidation* in these sectors projects a future of increasingly influential large groups (including consortia) on the one hand and large numbers of small independent or unaffiliated providers on the other. The middle-ground previously occupied by medium-sized, often regional groups of service providers may disappear as they are no longer in a financially tenable position. Without the economies of scale to be gained by the larger consolidated groups of service providers, and the better yields or profitability from their global distribution and inventory management systems, many believe that these medium-sized groups cannot successfully compete.

Necessities rather than luxuries

There has been enormous societal changes in Western economies since the 1960s (see also Chapter 11). We have witnessed greater employment for women and a resulting growth in dual-career families, together with a steady shift from an industry-based economy to today's post-industrial economy where the service sector dominates. Many services which were seen as luxuries in the early 1960s are now regarded as providing standard household consumables; e.g. regular eating out, health club membership and overseas holidays are all seen as commonplace today, but only the very rich could previously afford them.

Technological change

Technological change has historically been largely considered in the context of goods production. Now it is impacting services in a wide variety of product and process applications. Take, for example, the growth of 'global distribution systems'. There were almost certainly rooms at a variety of inns available or vacant in Bethlehem on the night when Jesus was born; the real problem was how could the innkeepers let Mary and Joseph know of this availability? Before the arrival of today's 'global distribution systems', supply and demand have always had difficulty in informing each other. Today airlines, hotels, theatres, to name a few, now have online availability displays which can take instant reservations and payment. Technology has also spawned the setting up of a number of agencies which act as clearance houses (previously called bucket shops) for available services.

Case Study 16.1 looks at some impacts in the airline sector of the new GDS technology.

Case Study 16.1 GDS and airlines

FT

Travel agents face a day of reckoning in 2004 as airlines become ever more desperate to cut costs. Only those agile enough to adapt to the sweeping changes will survive.

More and more airlines are reducing or eliminating the agents' commission, while the incentive payments agents receive for bookings from the global computer reservations systems are under threat. Add competition from the Internet, plus a new

Case Study 16.1 continued

tendency for customers to book direct with tour operators, and change looks likely even for agents who rely on package holidays for most of their income.

Travel retailers are being forced to change from their role as agents of suppliers to agents of their customers. Some, especially those managing travel for corporate clients, have already adjusted by charging their customers for services such as analysing staff travel patterns. But such is the pace of change that most agents, whether handling business or leisure travel, will have to charge customers for some bookings.

Lufthansa will stop commissions for German agents completely on 1 September, having already reduced it for agents in some other countries. In Germany, the airline will market net fares to which it will add €30 to domestic and short-haul tickets and €45 to long-haul flights, representing the cost of handling bookings made direct with the airline.

Agents will be free to add their own mark-up to cover costs and profit but matching Lufthansa's €45 for a long-haul flight would not come close to the 9% of most long-haul premium fares they currently receive from Lufthansa. Agents will be under pressure to retain the loyalty of corporate clients by ensuring they get the best negotiated or spot fares.

Gerd Rieke, spokesman for Germany's Association of Business Travel Management, says some small independent travel agents will have a hard time. 'I would not be surprised if the big chains grew and many of those smaller agents were drawn under the umbrella of franchise organisations.'

Airlines have also focused on the cost of selling seats via the global distribution system operators whose airline ticket reservations and distribution terminals are used in travel agents' offices. First, the airlines lured customers from agents with cheaper fares available only via the airlines' websites. Now some have reached agreements with GDS operators so that agents can book the cheaper fares via their GDS screens but receive lower fees. British Airways has such a deal with Sabre and Galileo.

Meanwhile, UK agents hooked up to the other two GDSs, Amadeus and World-span, will pay £3 extra for every flight booked. Galileo will also charge agents 50p per BA flight. Although Galileo still makes incentive payments to agents for reservations with other airlines, it does not expect that to last. Sabre will not charge agents but says incentive payments – 'our largest single expense line' – are under review.

But the news for agents is not all bad. If the BA deal is pursued by other airlines, agents will have more low fares to sell. If they can compare such fares with offers from no-frills carriers, or if the deal persuades more of those carriers to sell via the GDSs, they will save customers valuable time that would help justify charging them.

Ian Reynolds, Association of British Travel Agents' CEO, notes: 'There are still excellent opportunities for agents who can genuinely add value to customers' travel plans and provide a service that a customer can see is worth paying for.'

Source: *Financial Times*, 21 January 2004, p. 12

Case Study 16.1 continued

Questions

1 Why are travel agents under threat?
2 How are they trying to adjust to their new situation?
3 Who might be the winners and losers from the new GDS technology?

Activity 16.1 gives you the chance to check your progress on the content so far.

Activity 16.1

1 Visit www.stelios.com and select one of the ever-increasing range of Easy brands – easyJet, easyCars, easyCinema, easyDorm, easyCruise or easyBus. See if you can find examples of any of the ideas discussed so far for the service sector.

2 Visit the Guardian Unlimited/Business site and enter Tesco or Starbucks or David Lloyd to see if you can find any evidence of consolidating markets in Retail, in the Coffee Shop market, in the Leisure and Fitness Club market. Also visit the websites of these companies.

3 Which *two* of the following are likely to result in the tertiary sector taking a higher proportion of total output and employment?

(a) A low income elasticity of demand for services with rapid economic growth
(b) A high income elasticity of demand for services with rapid economic growth
(c) A shift of consumer tastes in favour of manufactured goods
(d) A shift of consumer tastes in favour of services
(e) A shift of consumer tastes in favour of renewable energy sources

4 Which *three* of the following suggest that the recorded tertiary sector growth cannot be regarded as a perfect substitute for the recorded manufacturing sector decline?

(a) Weaker backward linkages in manufacturing than services.
(b) Stronger backward linkages in manufacturing than services.
(c) Most innovation and productivity growth occurs in manufacturing.
(d) Least innovation and productivity growth occurs in manufacturing.
(e) For every £1 less spent on manufacturing exports there must be £2.50 more spent on service exports if the balance of payments is not to deteriorate.

5 Which *two* of the following might explain the progressive increase in share of 'health care services' in UK output and employment?

(a) Low income elasticity of demand for healthcare services in an expanding economy
(b) High income elasticity of demand for healthcare services in an expanding economy
(c) Low price elasticity of demand for healthcare services
(d) An ageing population in the UK
(e) The shift from branded to generic drugs in healthcare treatments

6 In this question you need to match the *lettered* description with its correct *numbered* term.

Description

(a) De-industrialisation is blamed on the UK possessing North Sea oil.
(b) To compensate for a 1% fall in manufacturing exports, the exports of services must expand by 2.5%.
(c) The high value of government spending on health and education means higher taxes and higher interest rates for the private (market) sector.
(d) As the advanced industrialised economies have moved towards tertiary sector activities, labour has been drawn from the primary and secondary sectors.
(e) Each £1 spent on manufacturing output creates more income and employment than each £1 spent on service output.
(f) De-industrialisation has been faster in the UK than in the US because output per person employed in industry has grown less rapidly in the UK than in the US.

Terms

(i) Economic maturity
(ii) Crowding out
(iii) Sterling as a 'petro-currency'
(iv) Backward linkages
(v) Labour productivity
(vi) Innovation
(vii) Balance of payments

Answers to Checkpoints and Activities can be found on pp. 705–35.

In practice, it is often difficult to separate service sectors. For example 'leisure' arguably includes many of the activities we might incorporate within the 'hospitality' and 'sports' sectors. Whilst recognising such overlaps, we first focus on 'leisure', before paying more detailed attention to the 'hospitality' and 'sports' sectors.

Leisure sector

There has been a sustained international growth in leisure activities over many years. For example, in 1880 some 80% of the time left over after necessities such as sleeping and eating were attended to was used for earning a living. Today that percentage has fallen to below 40% over the average lifetime of an individual in the advanced industrialised economies and is projected to continue falling to around 25% over the next decade. This dramatic increase in leisure time availability in the higher income advanced industrialised economies clearly has major implications for consumption patterns and therefore for the deployment of productive resources.

The UK is widely recognised as having the longest working hours in the European Union, which must clearly reduce the time available for 'leisure', however defined. Of course, 'leisure' can be defined in various ways. One definition might regard all the daily time available, other than that used for employment and study, as 'leisure time'. Other definitions might take a more limited view and other daily activities from the 'leisure' definition, such as 'household and family care', 'childcare' and even sleeping.

Table 16.3 shows that what we exclude from the leisure definition makes a considerable difference to the amount of 'leisure time' considered available. The data in Table 16.3 is based on *The UK 2000 Time Use Survey* which asked adults aged 16 and over in the UK to keep a detailed diary of how they spent their time.

Table 16.3 Time spent (hours per day) on various activities, by sex, in the UK, 2000–01

	Hours per day	
Activity	**Males**	**Female**
Employment/Study	4.2	2.5
Sleeping	8.2	8.2
Housework	1.7	3.0
Childcare	0.1	0.6
TV and video	2.6	2.2
Travel	1.6	1.6
Eating	1.7	1.7
Social life	0.8	0.8
Shopping	0.3	0.7
Sports and other activities	0.3	0.2
Entertainment and culture	0.1	0.1
Other	2.3	2.4
Total	24 hrs	24 hrs

Adapted from National Statistics (2003), *Social Trends* and National Statisics (2000), *The UK* 2000 *Time Use Survey*, London: HMSO

Although there are many similarities between men and women, some differences are also apparent. Women still do the majority of the household chores, despite their increased participation in the labour market. Women spent around 3 hours a day on average on housework (excluding shopping and childcare) compared to the 1 hour 40 minutes spent by men. Women also spent more time than men looking after children. However, men worked or studied on average for almost 2 hours a day more than women.

Here we will broadly consider leisure as including all time not required for:

- employment/study;
- household and family care;
- childcare.

Watch out! **Some might also include 'sleeping' as necessary for revitalising the body and therefore not a discretionary leisure activity.**

Businesses, households and leisure activities

A greater concern with work–life balance has already been noted in Chapters 7 and 11. It is clearly important for businesses to identify and predict the products (goods and services) that will be positively and negatively affected by any resulting increase in leisure time available. However, at the same time it is important to recognise that the current *absence* of leisure time implied by Britain's position at the top of the hours-worked league in Europe has already exerted an influence on the patterns of household expenditure.

The Mintel *British Lifestyles Report* (2003) provides useful data from a survey which questioned 2005 adults. Mintel argues that British spending patterns reflect both adjustments to the existing longer working hours culture – and a desire to improve the future balance between work and home. Over the past five years, a lack of time has meant that many consumers prefer a quick trip to the chemist over consulting a doctor, and more but shorter holidays rather than the traditional two- or three-week break. Holidays are increasingly valued by workers as 'necessary as opposed to discretionary'. Fast food (take-aways) has become increasingly popular in the past five years, but convenience foods (pre-packaged) now constitute the meal of choice for most working families. The convenience food industry has grown 43% over the past 10 years and is predicted to grow by a further 32% in the period 2002–07.

Example:

In the US, 60 cents in every $1 spent on food is consumed in restaurants and take-aways. In the UK at present, only 30p in every £1 is spent in this way and most analysts predict that over the next five years, our food spend will mimic the US pattern, with over 60% of food spending 'catered' rather than retailed. The major food retailers are very aware of this potential 'loss of stomach share' (their term) and are developing a range of new take-away products.

Keeping in touch with family was the most important lifestyle priority, according to 70% of consumers, which in part accounts for the continued growth in communication-related products, such as mobile telephones, Internet and broadband, over recent years.

Table 16.4 provides a useful breakdown of the *predicted* growth-areas for consumer spending in Britain's increasingly more leisure-oriented society over the five-year period 2002–07.

The number of people in their 60s will surpass the number of under-fives for the first time over the next five years – and the survey highlights the likely product 'winners' from an ageing population, with financial services among them. It suggests we will see a 50% growth in life assurance, a 47% growth in accident and health insurance, and a 37% growth in personal pensions over the next five years.

Other predicted rapid growth areas include health and fitness (59%), cinema going (43%) and overseas travel (41%). We have already noted that convenience food (32%) and fast foods (30%) are expected to grow strongly, as are domestic and garden help (16%) and cleaning and laundry services (16%), many of these linked to the rise in working mothers. Just under half of UK women now work, as well as taking care of their home and family.

Table 16.4 Predicted % growth areas for consumer spending in Britain, 2002–07

Product/activity	% growth 2002–07
Health and Fitness	59
Life Assurance	50
Accident and Health Insurance	47
Cinema	43
Overseas Travel	41
Personal Pensions	37
Convenience Foods	32
Fast Foods	30
Medicines	20
Domestic and Garden Services	16
Cleaning and Laundry Services	16

Adapted from Mintel *British Lifestyles Report* (2003)

The average Briton in 2002 was buying 35% more goods or services than in 1992, with the estimated average household income now around £36,000. However, the average debt owed by each household nearly matches household income at £33,000. As a nation, we are now in debt to the tune of £8,000bn – more than double the figure 10 years ago.

Whilst we have paid some attention to the impacts of ageism on service demand, one demographic group is of particular interest to providers of leisure services, namely the so-called 'baby-boomers'.

Baby-boomers

There is no doubt that the major purchaser of leisure services over the next two or three decades will be the baby-boomer. Born between 1945 and 1964, the arrival of this generation has been one of the most predictable of demographic events. In the 20 years after the Second World War, some 77 million Americans were born, whilst in the UK, 17 million were born.

Let's look at some 'baby-boomer' facts.

- The 50-plus age group possess 80% of the UK's wealth and contribute around 40% of its consumer spending, worth £145bn per year. They are at the top of their earning power, are inheriting from home-owning parents and are often achieving good retirement lump-sums and pensions. Many, with their mortgages now finished, have both significant capital and a very positive balance of income over expenditure.
- The 50-plus age group is set to increase from 20 million to 27 million in the UK by 2025.
- The 50-plus age group has all the necessary ingredients for being the focus of expanding leisure businesses: they have time, money and an inclination to spend. They have been described as *children in time, sandwiched between the austerity of*

their parents and the consumerism of their children. This is in a sense a 'forever'-young group likely to reject the conventional life-stage cycle brought on by the ageing process.

The 50-plus age group has been shown by research in the US, and more recently in the UK, to have undergone a complete turnaround in attitudes as compared to those of their parents, who were generally frugal and who deferred gratification by continually saving for a rainy day. The boomers' outlook has been summarised as 'forget saving for the future – make the most of the present'.

Paul Slattery of Kleinwort Benson captured the baby-boomer impact in the following words. *The priority since WW2 had been to acquire goods such as houses, cars, brown and white goods. However, as boomers' needs were fully met, the emerging priority has exposed massive growth potential in demand for leisure activities. These include eating and drinking in restaurants and bars, holiday-taking, staying in hotels and pleasure centres, playing and watching sport, participation in arts, culture and gambling.*

There is also much evidence of this generation's drive to 'keep young and beautiful'. The Mintel report of March 2003 showed that consumers spent £12.8bn on health and beauty products, almost a 15% increase on 2000. You might wish to investigate the increase in UK plastic surgery where men and women in their 40s and 50s are currently seen as the highest growth market, mostly liposuctions and tummy tucks.

Allegra Strategies in June 2002 found that most of the growth in health and fitness clubs, from 4,822 in 2002 to 5,081 by 2004, was entirely attributable to the growing cohorts of increasingly affluent baby-boomers. The latest and most desired addition to these clubs was spa facilities, a boomer essential.

The youth market is shrinking, elders or seniors are being replaced by boomers, a market with very different needs and wants. Those businesses which respond to boomer needs will arguably prosper, although it will be essential that they provide the kind of *experience* demanded by these very exacting and most experienced buyers.

Case Study 16.2 gives more detail on these baby-boomers.

Case Study 16.2 Rock and Rollers just keep on rocking

FT

Forget the images of Stannah stairlifts, with a smiling old woman drifting up carpeted stairs, today's generation of older people are definitely more hip than hip replacement, writes Lisa Urquhart.

Recent reports show the 50-pluses have more money, live longer, and, increasingly, are taking the view they should spend their hard-earned cash instead of giving it to the chancellor.

Datamonitor reports that 70% of Britain's richest people – those with more than £200,000 in liquid assets – are 55 and above. It also found that average disposable income for European 50- to 64-year-olds in 2002 was £13,990, the highest for all demographic segments.

Case Study 16.2 continued

Already a consumer force to be reckoned with, the Future Foundation is predicting that by 2020 silver spenders aged 50–64 will account for 34% of leisure spending. This is eclipsed only by those in the 30–49 age bracket and dwarfs the 8% spend by 16–30-year-olds.

But it is not just about having more money. Older people, according to Saga, are choosing to spend on exotic holidays, instead of cruises and gardening.

One indication of the change in leisure habits is that the De Vere Village Hotel near Leeds will next year resume its weekend 50–80 clubbing breaks during the summer months – the cold weather perhaps being a deterrent to the scantily clad grey panthers out on the prowl.

Source: *Financial Times*, 27 November 2003, p. 23

Question What business implications are implied by this case study?

Whilst our focus is on the broad leisure sector, we should take into account some recent problems encountered by that sector in the UK and elsewhere.

Economic environment and selected leisure activities

Hospitality and tourism. At the beginning of the new millennium, the UK hospitality and tourism sector had enjoyed a decade of unprecedented growth from an increasingly affluent society when, without warning, a series of factors seriously disrupted this booming hospitality demand and the sector entered one of the most difficult trading environments it has ever experienced. Causes of this reversal of fortune for the UK hospitality and tourism sectors included the following.

1. *US downturn*. Problems were encountered at the end of the Clinton era in the late 1990s with the cyclical downturn in the US economy. As US visitors are a major driver of UK hotel demand, this downturn resulted in reduced visitor numbers and expenditure in the UK.
2. *Foot and mouth*. In 2000 the UK experienced a huge outbreak of foot and mouth disease, accompanied by the worldwide distribution of pictures of animals being craned into burning pits. As well as putting off incoming tourists, internal visitors were deterred from many parts of the UK by 'quarantines' on access to infected areas.
3. *Terrorism*. Just as the foot and mouth problem was receding, there followed the terrorist atrocity of 11 September 2001 in New York, following which demand for travel and accommodation nose-dived worldwide. Table 16.5 provides some further detail as to the impacts of 9/11.

Table 16.5 Impacts of 9/11 on the airline and tourism sectors over the following 12 months

Airlines	Tourism
■ Two national flag carriers, Swissair and Belgium's Sabena, failed. ■ In America US Airways filed for Chapter XI protection from bankruptcy and United Airlines announced serious financial trouble. ■ The world's airlines made a total loss of \$12bn (£7.7bn) on international flights over the 12 month period. ■ Insurance premiums have soared, costing the UK airline industry an extra \$250m and the global airline industry \$3bn. ■ Passenger numbers fell by 4% in 2001 and a further 3% in 2002. ■ Around 200,000 jobs were cut by airlines, 10,000 in the UK. ■ Transatlantic passenger traffic dropped by 25% over the period. ■ Hundreds of planes were mothballed in the Mojave desert, Arizona.	■ Worldwide income from tourism dropped by 2.2% to \$462bn in 2002. ■ Tourists accounted for only 10% of sales in West End stores, down from 20% before 11 September. ■ Between September and December 2001, tourist arrivals fell by 9.2% worldwide. ■ The hardest-hit areas were the Middle East (down by 11%) and South Asia (down by 24%). ■ Tourists visiting New York spent \$1bn less in 2002. ■ Delta airlines estimated a loss of \$600m due to passenger delays from increased airport security discouraging 'day tripper' flights in the US.

Sources: Various

4 *SARS (Severe Acute Respiratory Syndrome)*. This pneumonia-like virus killed 774 people around the world and infected more than 8,000, created panic, devastated economies and crippled the travel and tourism industry for months in 2003.

Probably one of the most poignant and bitter summaries of this period was made by Guy Hands, whose company Namura lost the £213m it invested in its £2.3bn leveraged acquisition of Le Meridien Hotels which, with 137 hotels, was a well-known global brand, when he said: 'All we now need is a plague of frogs'.

Not only hotels and travel operators lost out in this most difficult trading environment. London's theatres, museums, galleries and restaurants all reported a marked downturn in their volume of trade; some were forced into receivership. All sorts of retailers lost out, e.g. Harrods, Aspreys, Fortnum & Mason are all highly dependent on tourism, and in particular on the American dollar. Total visitors to the UK fell from 25.7 million in 1998 to 24.2 million in 2002 and the amount spent by these visitors dropped from £12.6bn to £11.7bn respectively. Although US visitors are still the UK's largest source, they dropped from a peak of 4.1 million people in 2000 to 3.6 million by 2002.

Terrorism and security will continue to be major issues; consider the media blitz surrounding sky marshals and flight cancellations attributed to potential terrorist activity in 2004. Another event similar to 9/11 would destabilise the world travel markets, slashing demand from tourism and hospitality. SARS is still prevalent in

China; can it be contained and eradicated or are there yet more global epidemics in the offing? Avian (chicken) flu became another global concern in 2004. However, past experience has shown that there is often a 'bounce-back effect' whereby deferred demand is taken up in succeeding years.

Cinema going. Table 16.4 (p. 667) noted that cinema visits are predicted to continue growing by a further 43% over the 2002–07 time period. Case Study 16.3 reviews the most comprehensive survey of cinema going in the UK, published in June 2003.

Case Study 16.3 Cinema going in the UK

The survey of the *UK Film Council* (2003) recorded 176 million visits to the cinema in 2002/3, a 70% increase over the past decade. Spending by cinema-goers reached £755m in 2002/3, a 13% increase on the previous year. More than one in four people in the UK now go at least once a week. However, they are invariably watching films made by the big US studios. For example, the overall top 20 list contained 13 US productions and a further 5 US co-productions.

The report provides many useful insights. Men preferred action, science fiction and horror films, whilst women voted for relationship dramas, romantic comedies and films with family appeal. Comedies were the most popular genre, providing 26% of the box office returns. Fantasy films, dominated by *The Lord of the Rings* and *Harry Potter*, was the second most popular genre (with 14% of turnover), followed by action movies (13% of turnover).

The report shows that the average cinemagoer is likely to be young and well off. Cinema going is unevenly distributed across age, class and region. Almost 70% of the audience is aged under 35 and Londoners buy a quarter of all cinema tickets. The AB social group accounts for 21% of the population and 28% of ticket sales by value. Figures on the representation of people from ethnic minorities in the film industry are regarded as imprecise, but suggest that the proportion is below the 6.1% level in the national workforce. While 10.9% of employees work in cinema management, the largest single employee group, 22%, is made up of cleaners.

In the era of the DVD, cinemas must recognise that Hollywood studios and their distributors depend less and less on box office takings. Today the video and DVD market is around four times the size of the box office market. Further, in the case of blockbuster films, the studios often earn far more from merchandising revenues than from box office takings. In other words, a box office flop can still be an eventual success for the studios, whereas the cinemas depend on films being successful immediately.

Questions

1 What implications might this report have for cinema-related businesses in the UK?

2 Can you identify some of the new problems facing cinema owners?

Branding in the leisure sector

The quality and nature of the experience staged is so evidently at the heart of business success in a broad range of leisure activities. Increasingly, stagers of experiences are taking a formulaic approach, e.g. T.G.I. Fridays, Disney, Centre Parks. To these companies, their *brand* is a value creator; to the customer it should represent a promise of fulfilment of function and performance over time. Progressively, we are faced with more and more choice, especially in the ways we might spend our discretionary income. With greater consumer choice comes greater indecision. As a result, brands have got to work harder than ever before to influence consumer decision making.

At a simple level, brands could be defined as: *a recognised name, term, symbol, smell, taste, sound, marque or design which identifies the specific product, service and or experience attributes of one seller and differentiates them from those of a competitor*. A successful brand is a trusted brand. All writers on branding conclude that successful brands have unique points of differentiation from the competition as well as values that their customer segment really wants.

A strong brand is all-pervasive and brand-owners and all connected with its delivery and staging must live the brand ethos. If, for instance, we are in the business of staging enjoyable and memorable experiences, that is our strength and our brand will decay every time the experience is not up to scratch or expectation. It is possible and often essential to disaggregate all the components involved in staging an experience, in particular when concerned with providing consistent quality in delivery. Some

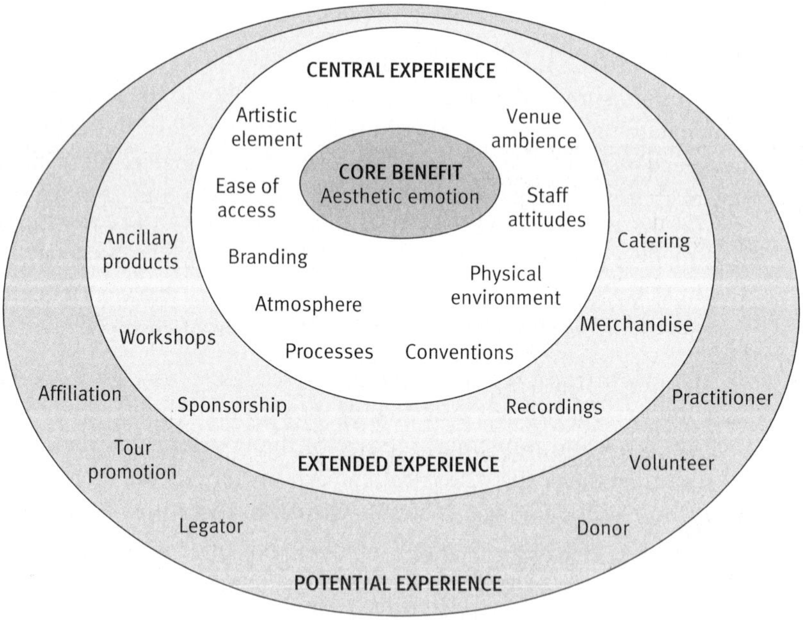

Fig 16.2 A holistic experience: components involved in delivering a performance at the Royal Opera House

Source: Adapted from Elizabeth Hill, Catherine O'Sullivan and Terry O'Sullivan (1995), reprinted from *Creative Arts Marketing*, Hill, E., O'Sullivan, T., pp. 106–107, Butterworth Heinemann, Oxford 1995, with permission from Elsevier.

of these components are outlined in the model designed by Hill, O'Sullivan and O'Sullivan (1995), where they have embraced every aspect of the delivery of a Royal Opera House, Covent Garden performance (Figure 16.2). For other aspects of leisure, this model could be applied to a weekend break, a night at the Ministry of Sound or Fabric or to a wedding breakfast or a bar mitzvah.

To be consistently successful, the service-centred leisure activities must progressively develop their delivery and staging techniques to ensure that the promises made and the publicity generated are met in terms of the experience enjoyed, or they will go out of business.

Hospitality sector

Hospitality is itself a broad sector covering a wide range of activities, including hotels, guesthouses, public houses and restaurants of all shapes and sizes. Clearly the tendencies we have already noted for households to increase their expenditure on time-saving activities such as eating out and on holidays and travel provide new opportunities for this broad sector.

Much of the following discussion focuses on hotels but the principles are broadly applicable within the hospitality sector.

Hotel-related businesses

Occupancy

Occupancy, an hotelier's preoccupation, is normally measured over the period of one week. A 200-roomed hotel would achieve 100% *occupancy* if all 1,400 available rooms were let in one week. This is very difficult to achieve as most hotels experience low demand for rooms on Sunday nights and often run at half empty or less. On the other hand, there are many occasions when all available rooms are booked months in advance and, as capacity is fixed, demand has to be turned down or referred to other hotels, preferably in the same group.

To further frustrate hoteliers, late cancellation and non-arrivals or 'no shows' create problems as it is often difficult to re-let at short notice. To overcome the 'non-arrival' wasted resource problem, many hoteliers and other service operators adopt 'over-booking' policies, although in recent years the ability to secure services via pre-payment using a credit card has much reduced this difficulty. Records are kept of this 'referred demand' since it can be used to support financial feasibility studies aimed at justifying the extension of capacity by building more rooms.

Low variable and marginal costs

We have already noted (p. 660) that variable and marginal costs tend to be low for services in general, and this is certainly true of the hotel and hospitality sector. The relationships between fixed and variable costs in providing the service and the selling price charged for the service are important in calculating the *break-even* level of output.

Formula

$$\text{Break-even} = \frac{\text{Total fixed costs}}{\text{Contribution per unit}}$$

where 'contribution per unit' is what each unit of sale contributes towards the fixed costs already incurred.

$$\text{i.e. Break-even} = \frac{\text{Total fixed costs}}{\text{Selling price} - \text{Average variable cost}}$$

An example from the hotel sector should help to clarify this point.

Example: A 100-room hotel sells rooms at a net price of £55 (exc. VAT, food etc.). The cost of letting is £5 per room let and the total fixed cost attributable to a day's trading is £2,000. We wish to determine how many rooms need to be let to break even.

In our example:

$$\text{Break-even} = \frac{£2{,}000}{£55 - £5} = \frac{£2{,}000}{£50}$$

i.e. break-even = 40 rooms let or 40% occupancy

Many hotels break even at around 30–40% occupancy at the published room rate (known as *rack rate*). However, room rates often have to be adjusted downwards, e.g. to attract block bookings of tourist groups which are highly price sensitive or to stimulate demand when little or none is forecast. Suppose a travel agent will only book a £55 hotel room at 50% of rack rate = £27.50, leaving a contribution of £22.50. Then in our example 80 rooms or 80% occupancy would have to be achieved to break even. It is easy to see how the pricing tread-mill can operate!

You can sometimes find hotels listed in the national press which are letting their rooms at a zero selling price, with the proviso that the guests take breakfast and dinner from which some profit can be made. Such hotels are said to be 'marginal', moving from profit to loss throughout the week and season (many close in the off-season). In such cases owners and their families often live on site, taking outside work.

At the other end of the scale, the major global brands of hotels mostly enjoy high occupancy at high *average achieved room rate* (AARR) and earn high profits because of the high marginal rate of profitability on each room beyond 'break-even point'. These profits can be ploughed back into maintaining the brand quality, improving its global marketing and fulfilling the needs of all of its stakeholders.

Stelios Haji-Ioannou, founder of easyJet, the low-cost airline, is currently (2004) developing *easyHotels* where he is reducing the cost of sale of a hotel room for his *easyDorm* brand, by creating small cubicles with disposable bedding available at extremely low prices.

Yield revenue management

Yield revenue management uses information about customer purchasing behaviour and product or service sales patterns to develop pricing recommendations and inventory controls that produce greater revenues (and sometimes lower costs) and deliver products that are better matched to specific customer needs. It is the bringing together of information-systems technology, market segmentation analysis, statistics on probability, organisational design, business experience and sector knowledge into an integrated revenue generating strategy. This is a technique widely used in the hospitality sector and in other service activities such as airlines, cruise ships, sporting events and rock concerts.

Formula

$$\text{Yield} = \frac{\text{Revenue realised}}{\text{Revenue potential}}$$

Yield management techniques are becoming increasingly complex and sophisticated and the wide range of variables to be incorporated lends itself to the use of computerised systems. These in turn have given a major advantage to the larger brands as this data can form the basis of *customer relationship marketing* (CRM) programmes which can develop into customer loyalty devices.

Hubbard formula

There is a long-standing rule of thumb for the hotel industry known as the *Hubbard formula*. This simply states that every £1,000 invested in building a room should represent £1 on the net room rate.

- *Top range hotels.* A 40–50-room extension to the Savoy Hotel, for which there is planning permission, would cost £350,000–£450,000 per room. Rooms would therefore need to sell at £350–£450 + VAT.
- *Medium range hotels.* A typical Post House-type operation would cost less, perhaps £100,000–£150,000 per room to build. Typical rooms sell at £100–£150 + VAT.
- *Budget hotels.* Budget hotels of the type springing up along the roadsides, in the suburbs and in major city centres (over 1,000 hotels in the past 10 years) cost, depending on location, £30,000/£50,000/£70,000 per room to build. These can readily achieve high occupancies at room rates of £40–80 + VAT, often more than meeting the Hubbard formula and therefore seen as attractive earners by the major operators who are investing in their rapid growth.

Ownership arrangements

The nature of the *ownership arrangement* for many hotel chains will determine how strictly they apply the Hubbard or similar formulae to room pricing. For example, Holiday Inns may operate over 2,500 hotels worldwide but actually only own, in the sense of freehold, fewer than 50 hotels. Many of the other Holiday Inns are operated under a management contract on behalf of banks, pension funds and others. These institutions may have an interest in long-term capital accrual and therefore be less concerned with the short-term profitability of room-letting activities.

Experience issues

We have already noted the increasing importance of 'experiences' in the provision of services. This is certainly also the case for the hospitality sector and for hotel-related businesses within it. When the 'experience' that is provided and continues to be provided meets the promise made and the expectations generated, trust is developed. This is a prerequisite to building a long-term relationship, leading in turn to consumer loyalty and extending the possibility of achieving the potential 'lifetime' value from that customer.

Example: In January 2001, Whitbread's Travel Inn budget hotel brand, the UK's largest with over 300 hotels, launched their guarantee on national television: 'Everything That You Need for a Good Night's Sleep or Your Money Back'. To provide this guarantee was by no means easy; after much research and intensive training, all staff were fully ready to fulfil this promise and all were empowered to grant the refund if required. Staff turnover dropped by 30% and new staff were attracted by the guarantee. Travel Inn knew that this strategy would serve to positively differentiate their brand in a highly consolidated and competitive market. Problems that cause the guarantee to be invoked are shared throughout the company and solutions adopted in all outlets. It could be as simple as an agreement with refuse collectors, draymen and other site visitors never to arrive before 9.30 am. In other cases, solutions (e.g. to noise problems) may mean triple or quadruple glazing in all outlets.

Sports sector

Again a precise definition of this sector is extremely difficult. It is certainly a broad sector, including a wide range of sporting activities and the associated services, experiences and goods associated with undertaking these activities.

Types of sporting activity

Table 16.6 outlines participation in selected sports in the UK, based on adults aged 16 and over reporting participation in that sporting activity during the four weeks prior to the survey.

Being involved in sporting activities, either alone or as a member of a team or club, is a popular way of spending leisure time. Around a fifth of men and a quarter of women had walked/hiked during the four weeks prior to completing the UK *Time Use Survey* in 2000. Keep fit and swimming were the next most frequent sporting activities

Table 16.6 Participation in selected sports: by sex, 2000–1

Sports activity	Men (%)	Women (%)
Walking/hiking	19	23
Snooker	15	4
Swimming	13	17
Cycling	12	7
Football	10	1
Golf	9	1
Weights	8	4
Keep fit	8	18
Running/athletics	7	3
Racket sports	6	4
Darts	4	2
Bowls	2	2

Family Expenditure Survey (2003) adapted from *The UK 2000 Time Use Survey*

for women, with snooker, swimming and cycling the most frequent for men. Football and golf were also popular for men. However, nearly half of those surveyed did not participate in any sporting activity in the month prior to interview.

Much attention is being placed today on greater involvement in sporting activities, especially at school, as part of a healthier lifestyle and in particular to counter the growing problem of obesity. However, it is not just *active* sporting involvement that contributes to the UK economy, but also *passive* sporting involvement.

Passive sporting involvement

A full accounting of the contribution of the sports sector to the UK economy would need to capture expenditure on attendance at a wide range of sporting venues, the purchases made there, the role of sports in helping to sell a host of electrical and electronic products (e.g. those based on televised sports), its contribution to fashion and lifestyle in publishing and other media activities, and so on. Clearly it is impossible to fully document the direct and indirect 'value added' that can be attributed to the sports sector, let alone any aesthetic and social benefits, such as the 'feel good' factor following successful sporting endeavours (e.g. England winning the World Rugby Union Cup in 2003). Here we select a few examples to illustrate the important and pervasive impact of sporting activities on economic and social well-being.

Case Study 16.4 shows how important passive sporting involvement is in the marketing sportswear.

Case Study 16.4 Basketball and shoes

FT

Sportswear manufacturers rely on endorsement deals with top stars to promote new products and maintain visibility of their brands. In sports such as soccer and rugby, Adidas-Salomon has scored some notable coups. The group has had a long marketing relationship with David Beckham, arguably the most famous sportsman on the planet, and recently used him in a television advertisement with Jonny Wilkinson, the English rugby player.

With Beckham regularly appearing on the front pages of newspapers and Wilkinson appearing for England in the Rugby World Cup, the pair have the potential to generate significant benefits for Adidas.

However, while Adidas can boast a strong position in soccer and rugby, it risks losing ground in the US, where the sports barely register. The US is the largest athletic shoe market in the world and basketball endorsements are what drive sales. This summer Nike, Adidas's main rival, signed the hottest prospect in the sport from under its nose.

Together with Reebok, Adidas was in the running to sign a sponsorship deal with Lebron James. But the player, who made his NBA debut for the Cleveland Cavaliers in 2003, opted to go with Nike after a carefully orchestrated wooing campaign.

The rejection of Adidas could yet have repercussions for the German group. As Nike showed with its sponsorship of Michael Jordan in the 1980s, the right basketball star can lead to huge increases in sales. Indeed, Jordan helped to transform Nike from a little-known athlete shoemaker into a global sports brand.

With Reebok diversifying into sponsorship of hip hop stars such as 50 Cent, the time may be right for Adidas to consider a subtle change of strategy if it is to avoid losing market share.

Source: *Financial Times*, 10 November 2003, p. 10

Questions

1 Why is sporting activity so important to Adidas and Nike?

2 What might the 'subtle change of strategy' involve for Adidas?

Activity 16.2 gives you the opportunity to reflect on issues raised in the leisure, hospitality and sports sectors.

Activity 16.2

1 As baby-boomers are of such significance in today's UK economy:

(a) Visit Google.com and enter baby-boomer. From the thousands of sites that deal with this subject, select a few and build your own portfolio of boomer facts.

(b) Identify and analyse the importance of boomers to the leisure and other service businesses in your area.
(c) Discuss boomer attitudes with your parents or other relatives who fall into the boomer age groups.

2 Compare and contrast two recent commercially provided experiences. In particular, identify those factors that enhance the experience and those that detract from it. Advise the providers as to how their experience could be improved.

3 Determine the various ways in which a service may be booked. Consider the advantages and disadvantages of each from the viewpoints of both the supplier and the buyer.

4 Visit the website of any of the major UK hotel operators. Go to their Annual Results sections and print out their explanations of the turndown profitability attributed to lower occupancy and lower average achieved room rates (AARRs). Simply enter Whitbread, Holiday Inn, Hilton, Le Meridien, Accord Hotels or Starwood Hotels. You could also try the British Tourism Authority site to check latest 'incoming' tourism figures.

Answers to Checkpoints and Activities can be found on pp. 705–35.

Key Terms

'Baby-boomers' The population bulge resulting from higher birth rates in the years following the Second World War (over-50s).

Break-even The output required to generate sufficient revenue to cover all costs.

Consolidation The growth in size of providers, often via mergers and acquisitions.

De-industrialisation The absolute and relative decline of industrial activity in a country. Often seen as indicated by a fall in the secondary sector's share (especially the manufacturing part of that sector) in total output and/or total employment.

Experience Part of the 'progression of economic value' model; seen as the next stage beyond general services.

Heterogeneity Applied to the problem facing services in ensuring a consistent standard of performance.

Hubbard formula A 'rule of thumb' whereby every £1,000 invested in building a room should represent £1 on the net room rate.

Intangibility Refers to the non-physical characteristics of services such as atmosphere, ambience, context, interpersonal communication, attitude etc.

Occupancy The percentage of rooms let in a given time period.

Perishability Often applied to services since they cannot be stored.

Primary sector Includes activities directly related to natural resources, e.g. farming, mining and oil extraction.

Progression of economic value model A staged process which leads eventually to 'experiences' as the highest value-creating activity.

Quaternary sector Includes information creating, handling and processing activities.

Rack rate The published room rate.

Secondary sector Includes activities related to the production or process of goods in the economy, e.g. manufacturing. Also includes construction and the public utility industries of gas, water and electricity.

Tertiary sector Includes all the private sector services (e.g. distribution, insurance, banking and finance) and all the public sector services (e.g. health, education, public administration).

Yield revenue management An integrated revenue-generating strategy.

Yield Revenue realised divided by revenue potential.

Key Points

- The UK and other advanced industrialised economies have seen a rapid growth in the tertiary (service) sector and decline in the primary and secondary sectors (de-industralisation).
- Services have distinctive properties, including perishability, experiential characteristics, intangibility, heterogeneity and low marginal costs.
- Changing demographics and lifestyles are influencing demand patterns for services as well as goods.
- The 'baby-boomers' (over-50s) are a key market segment for service providers.
- Leisure activities have high income elasticities of demand, although adverse environmental factors (e.g. terrorism) can dampen the general increase in demand as real incomes increase.

Assessment Practice

Multiple choice questions

1 **Within the service sector, who is the UK's largest employer?**

(a) The teaching profession
(b) The Inland Revenue
(c) The National Health Service
(d) The Armed Forces

2 **Which of the following is likely to result in de-industrialisation?**

(a) High labour productivity and low wages in manufacturing
(b) Low labour productivity and high wages in manufacturing
(c) A high income elasticity of demand for manufactured goods and a rapidly growing economy
(d) A low and falling exchange rate

3 **A household's income that remains after the basic necessities are purchased is called?**

(a) Disposable income
(b) Discretionary income
(c) Non-discretionary income
(d) In-disposable income

4 **When taking an hotel reservation, certain details are more essential than others. From the following, which contains the essentials?**

(a) Customer name, address, telephone number and e-mail address
(b) Customer name, address, reason for booking, arrival and departure dates
(c) Travel agent details, customer name, room type required
(d) Dates of arrival and departure and room type required

5 **Yield revenue management, when applied to services, requires which of the following conditions to apply?**

(a) Knowledge of booking patterns and variable lead times
(b) Knowledge and in part predictability of demand patterns
(c) Knowledge of the effect on demand of price variation
(d) All of the above

6 **From a franchisor's perspective, what are the two main advantages of this business format?**

(a) Rapid growth in market coverage and penetration
(b) Spreading the risks and costs of capital investment, stock and operating costs
(c) Achieving diseconomies of scale in purchasing and marketing
(d) Benefiting from the entrepreneurial drive of franchisees

7 **From a franchisee's perspective, what are the three main advantages of this business format?**

(a) Participation in a system with an established name and reputation, often on a national or international scale
(b) Significant support in set-up, training, systems etc.
(c) National advertising and PR profile, unachievable by an independent
(d) Greater operating independence for the business

8 **Which of the following options is the prime motivator for international travel?**

(a) Business or corporate travel
(b) Visiting friends and relatives – VFR
(c) Tourism
(d) Religion

9 **Which of the following is *not* a benefit achievable from consolidation?**

(a) The emergence of market leaders with the power to shape events
(b) The emergence of the well-informed customer or pro-sumer
(c) A higher market profile and an array of brands at different market levels
(d) Economies of scale and experience

10 **The 'baby-boomer' is the largest and fastest-growing market segment in all Western economies and for the next two or three decades will be a major purchaser of services.**

Which of the following is *not* associated with this cohort?

(a) They are often called GLAMS or The Greying Leisured Affluent Majority.
(b) The over-50s possess over 80% of the UK's wealth.
(c) They mainly take a prudent approach, saving for a rainy day/deferred gratification.
(d) In the US some are classified as SKINS – Spend the Kids' Inheritance ... Now.

Data response and stimulus questions

1 Sport is uniquely powerful. Nothing captivates world attention, unites nations and transcends language and cultural barriers in the same way as the world's largest sporting events. At certain times the Olympics or a World Cup Rugby of Football has become a universal point of contact for everyone. Their incredible reach and influence make such events not only the sporting pinnacle for competitors, but also provide businesses with a global marketing showcase and governments with powerful political opportunities.

Deloitte & Touche, Travel Tourism and Leisure Report, Issue 2, June 2003

The Olympic Games has the most kudos of all. Your task is to consider the pros and cons of the London Olympic Bid for 2012. Estimates put the costs of bid making at £13m and if won, the cost of staging it at around £2.4bn of public money. You'll find much information on the government website and much analysis on the various media sites.

Deloitte and Touche considered the outcomes of the previous three Olympic Games where results were available to them: 1992 Barcelona, 1996 Atlanta and 2000 Sydney; in summary, they found:

- *Barcelona*. This made a loss of $1.4bn but Barcelona and Spain have gained much lasting benefit from the boost given to tourism and a range of infrastructure benefits and seafront development.
- *Atlanta*. Here the games were deemed entirely commercial, arguably drifting away from the Olympic spirit; they were highly profitable, requiring no government funding – often referred to as the Coca-Cola Olympics.
- *Sydney*. The Australian authorities spent $3.8bn and earned $3.0bn in direct revenue. However, Australia has seen a 10% growth in tourism, which is continuing to rise post-games as many of the negatives of 'long-haul' travel are dispelled. The cultural impact in terms of global marketing and self image significantly outweighed the financial investment, in the view of the Deloitte and Touche.

So, you should consider aspects other than direct revenue and cost streams in your analysis.

NOTE

Case Study 9.5 (p. 356) may give some useful ideas that you might develop.

2 Look carefully at the following text on Lastminute.com which continues to play an important role in the leisure, sports and hospitality sectors. Then answer the questions which follow.

'Last Minute.Com'

Lastminute.com (www.lastminute.com) is a business that relies totally on the Internet. The objective of the company is to use the reach of the Web to put offers from service providers in front of consumers. It gives service providers an outlet to sell items such as airline tickets, hotel rooms and theatre tickets for any date in question, right up to the last minute (hence the name). The later the consumer leaves the purchasing, the more likely they are to get a bargain.

The co-founders of lastminute.com are Brent Hoberman and Martha Lane Fox. The company launched in 1998 with a modest £600,000 of funding to cover start-up costs. An additional

£6.5m worth of funding was secured in June 1999, from an investor group led by Global Retail partners and also including Intel Corporation, T-Venture, Amadeus Capital partners and Harvey Goldsmith.

In March 2000, lastminute.com launched onto the UK stock market. The company was valued at over £570m, with its share price at £3.80. The company grew quickly, from just a handful of staff at launch, to 100 in the UK, with another 30 staffing offices in Paris and Munich.

Lastminute.com aimed to build on this initial success by establishing relationships with new business partners and providing a quick, efficient service for its customers. Given the large number of Internet-based firms that have gone out of business, Lastminute.com has done well to survive in a turbulent environment in which the competitiveness of the e-commerce market, combined with fears of the levels of security of shopping online, contributed to the sharp decline in lastminute.com's share price. At one stage the share price fell to 80p, £3 lower than its original launch value. However, the company has recovered strongly from this position, with its share price rising above £3 in 2003/4.

Lastminute.com started out with offers mainly centred on the travel, entertainment and gift industries, with a heavy emphasis on items such as theatre tickets, flights and hotel reservations. The firm's suppliers include 30 airlines, over 500 hotels, 75 holiday providers, 400 entertainment suppliers, 60 restaurants and 120 gift providers. Partner companies include British Midlands and Amazon UK. The company has now diversified into other areas such as cleaning and laundry services, taxis, hairdressers and other services, in the hope of building on the number of registered users. If the company is to achieve its aim of developing lastminute.com into the ultimate one-stop-shopping experience, it will need to continue to forge relationships with new business partners and satisfy its existing registered users in order to halt a further decline in numbers.

Indeed, in March 2003 it acquired Holiday Autos, a car rental broker, and in January 2004 First Option, a hotel-booking agency that owns kiosks in railway stations across London. The latter was the first acquisition involving a physical rather than virtual presence. In March 2004 it also acquired Online Travel Corp, with its impressive client list which includes Thomas Cook, Lunn Poly, *The Times*, Tiscali and Freeserve.

Source: adapted from www.lastminute.com and various sources

Questions

You are an independent marketing consultant called in by lastminute.com to produce a report including the following:

(a) review the firm's current position in the market;
(b) suggest suitable types of promotion lastminute.com could use in order to further strengthen its position;
(c) recommend other possible business partners for lastminute.com.

Essay questions

1. What features distinguish services from other products?
2. Consider the factors involved in de-industrialisation. Does de-industrialisation matter?
3. What do you understand by the 'progression of economic value' model? What distinguishes 'experiences' from other stages in the model and what particular problems are implied in providing those experiences?
4. Evaluate the relevance of 'baby boomers' to the leisure sector.
5. Choose any one firm in the sports *or* hospitality sector. Now undertake a SWOT analysis to review its position.

Appendices

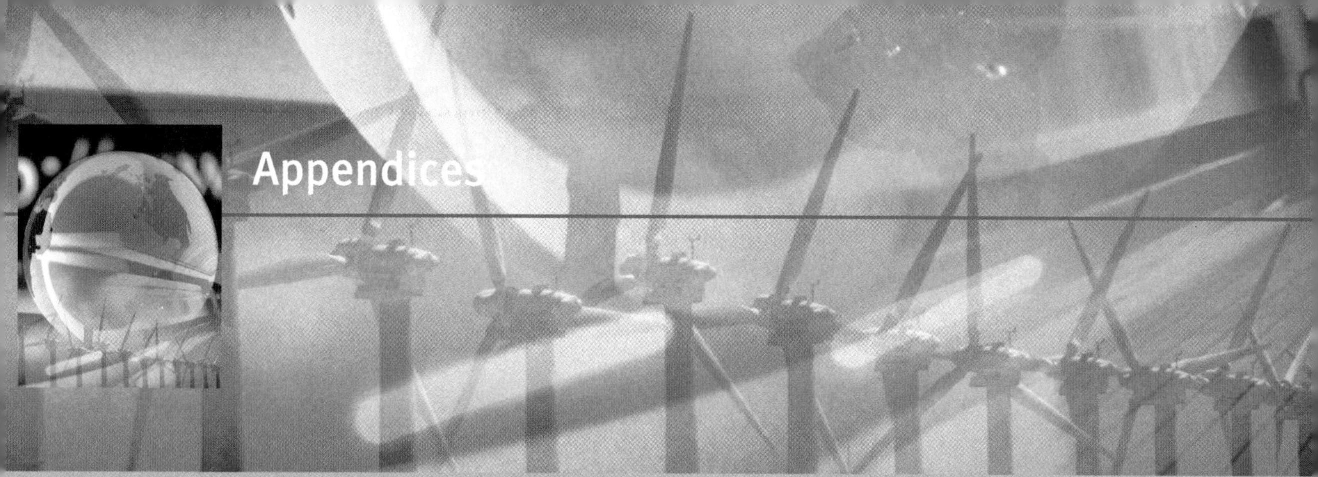

Appendix 1

Indifference curves, budget lines and the 'law of demand'

Indifference curves are lines representing different combinations (bundles) of products that yield a constant level of utility or satisfaction to the consumer. The consumer is therefore *indifferent* as between the various consumption possibilities denoted by the line.

Figure A1.1(a) can be used to illustrate the properties of an indifference curve.

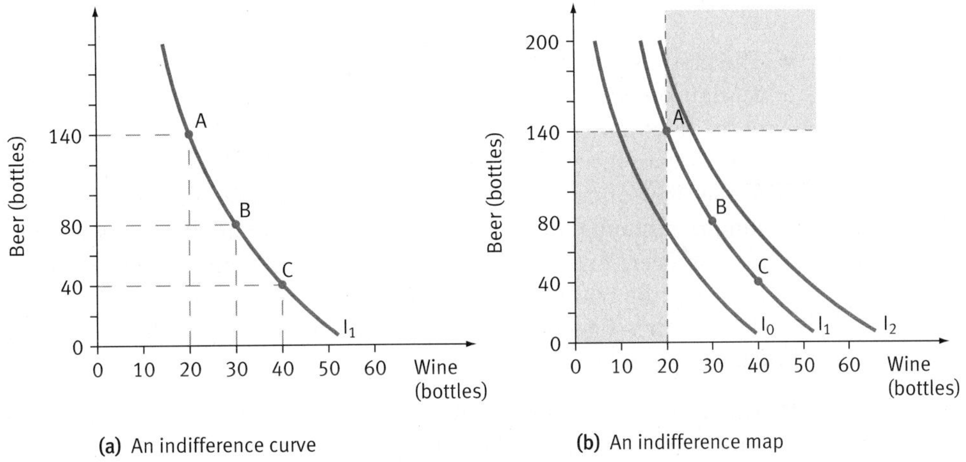

Fig A1.1 Indifference curves and maps.

In addition to diminishing marginal utility, suppose our consumer is indifferent between three different combinations of bottles of wine and beer, namely A (20 wine, 140 beer), B (30 wine, 80 beer) and C (40 wine, 40 beer). In other words, these three combinations of wine and beer yield the same level of utility to the consumer as in fact do all the combinations of wine and beer on the curve I_1. We call this curve connecting all the combinations (bundles) of products that yield a constant level of utility, an indifference curve.

Indifference maps

As we can see from Figure A1.1(b), indifference maps show *all* the indifference curves that rank the preferences of our consumer as between the two products. Indifference maps are drawn on the basis of three key assumptions.

1 *Non-satiation*. The consumer is not totally satisfied (satiated) with the amounts of the products already obtained, but prefers to have more of either. In other words, 'a good is a good', with any extra units of either product (good or service) adding some positive amount to total utility.

2 *Transitivity*. Consumers are consistent in their ranking of various consumption bundles.

3 *Diminishing marginal rate of substitution between products*. This assumption is related to our earlier idea of 'diminishing marginal utility'. However, this time it refers to the fact that as more of any one product (X) is consumed, the consumer will be willing to sacrifice progressively less of some other product (Y) for utility to remain unchanged.

Let us now examine the relevance of these assumptions to our indifference map.

- The first assumption of non-satiation implies that more of one product and no less of some other product is a preferred position, so that indifference curves above and to the right must represent higher levels of utility/satisfaction. In Figure A1.1(b) the indifference curve I_2 includes consumption bundles in the shaded box above and to the right of consumption bundle A on indifference curve I_1. These shaded consumption bundles all include having more beer and no less wine, or more wine and no less beer, or more beer and more wine than A, and are therefore preferred consumption bundles to A. It follows that all the consumption bundles on I_2 that go through this shaded area must correspond to a higher level of satisfaction than the consumption bundles on I_1.
- The second assumption, that consumers are *consistent* in their preference orderings, implies that it is impossible for separate indifference curves to intersect one another. For example, suppose we have the following consumer ranking of three bundles of products A, B and C.

  $A > B$
  $B > C$

  Then, via consistent consumer behaviour we can say that

  $A > C$

  If this assumption holds true, then indifference curves could not intersect. However, if consumer preferences are *not* consistent, then indifference curves can intersect, as they do in Figure A1.2.

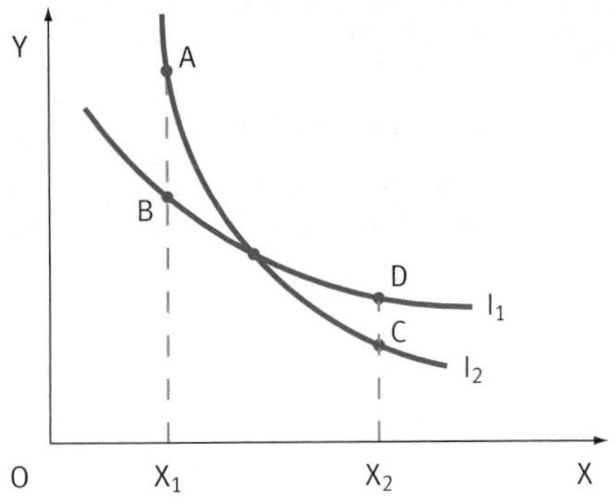

Fig A1.2 Indifference curves intersect if preferences not consistent

In Figure A1.2

A > B (more of Y, same X)
A = C (on same indifference curve)
B = D (on same difference curve)
C > D (via consistency assumption)

But D > C (more of Y, same X)!

Clearly, when indifference curves intersect this indicates that consumers are not exercising consistency in their ranking of different bundles of product.

- The third assumption of diminishing marginal rate of substitution between the products implies that we draw indifference curves convex to (bowed towards) the origin. In other words, the more of one product you are consuming, the progressively less of the other product you are willing to give up in order to consume an extra unit of that product. This means that slope of an indifference curve diminishes as we move from left to right along its entire length.

Deriving the demand curve: indifference analysis

We can use indifference curve analysis to predict the downward sloping demand curve, just as we used marginal utility analysis previously (see Box 2.4, p. 74). However, before doing this we must become familiar with the idea of the budget line of the consumer.

Budget line

In much of the analysis involving indifference curves we assume that consumers wish to maximise utility subject to a number of constraints, such as the level of household income and the prices of the products bought. These particular constraints can be represented by the **budget line** showing the various combinations of two products, X and Y, which can be purchased if the whole household income is spent on these products.

- The *slope* of the budget line will depend upon the relative prices of the two products.
- The *position* of the budget line will depend on the level of household income.

Figure A1.3 usefully illustrates these points.

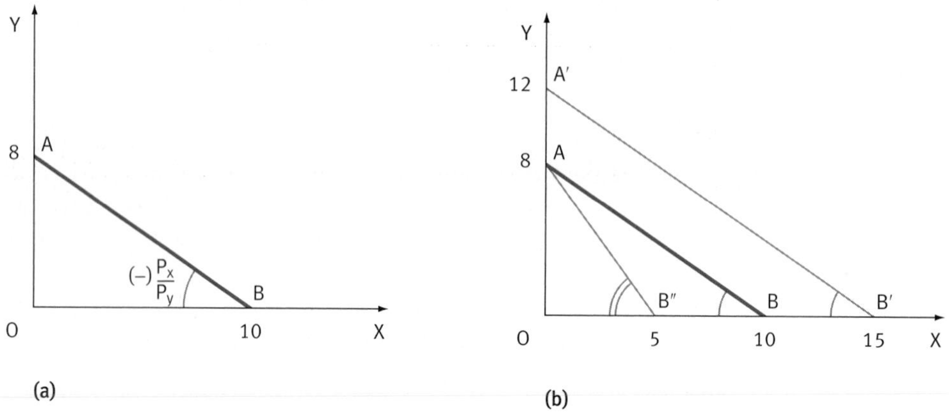

Fig A1.3 The budget line. Slope depends on relative prices; position depends on household income

Let us suppose the following:

Household income $= £200$
Price of product X (P_x) $= £20$
Price of product Y (P_y) $= £25$

In Figure A1.3(a), if all the income is spent on X, then we are at point B (10X, 0Y); if all the income is spent on Y then we are at point A (0X, 8Y). The line AB is therefore the budget line and represents the various combinations of X and Y that could be purchased if the *whole* household income was spent on these products.

The *slope* of this budget line depends on the relative price ratio:

$$\text{Slope} = (-)\frac{8}{10} = (-)\frac{20}{25} \quad \textit{i.e.}\ (-)\frac{P_x}{P_y}$$

The *position* of this budget line depends on the level of household income.

We can use Figure A1.3(b) to make this last point clear.

(a) A′B′ shows what happens to the budget line AB if there is a 50% increase in household income from £200 to £300. Notice that a rise in household income leads to a *parallel* outward shift in the budget line. The new and old budget lines have the same slope because the price ratio is unchanged.

(b) AB″ shows what happens to the budget line AB if the household income remains at the original £200 but the price of product X (P_x) rises from £20 to £40 with the price of the product Y (P_y) unchanged at £25. Notice that a change in the relative price ratio means that the slope of the new budget line is different from that of the old budget line. In this case the slope is steeper since only five units of X can now be purchased from an income of £200 if its price rises from £20 to £40, whilst it is still possible to purchase eight units of Y at its unchanged price of £25. Notice that a rise in the price of product X leads to the budget line pivoting inwards around point A.

Consumer equilibrium

We assume that the consumer seeks the maximum utility (highest indifference curve) subject to the constraints imposed on him/her. These constraints involve the level of household income (*position* of budget line) and the relative prices of the products (*slope* of budget line).

Figure A1.4 brings together our work on indifference curves and budget lines to identify the particular consumption bundle that corresponds to maximum consumer utility subject to these constraints.

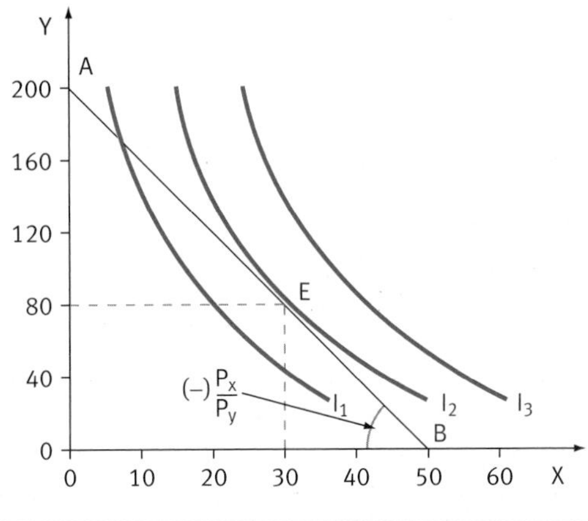

Fig A1.4 Consumer equilibrium. Reaching the highest indifference curve attainable, at point E

Given the position of the budget line AB in Figure A1.4 and its slope (–) P_x/P_y, the highest indifference curve the consumer can reach is I_2 at point E. By consuming 30 units of X and 80 units of Y the consumer has maximised utility subject to the constraints he faces. I_3 is, of course, an indifference curve yielding still higher satisfaction, but is unattainable under present circumstances.

Notice that this consumption bundle of 30X and 80Y, which corresponds to 'consumer equilibrium', represents a situation of *tangency* between the budget line and the highest attainable indifference curve. In other words, consumer utility is maximised when the slope of an indifference curve is exactly equal to the slope of the budget line (i.e. the price ratio).

Price–consumption line

Figure A1.5 uses this idea of 'consumer equilibrium' to derive the so-called **price-consumption line**, showing tangency points between budget lines with different prices of product X (P_x) and the highest attainable indifference curves.

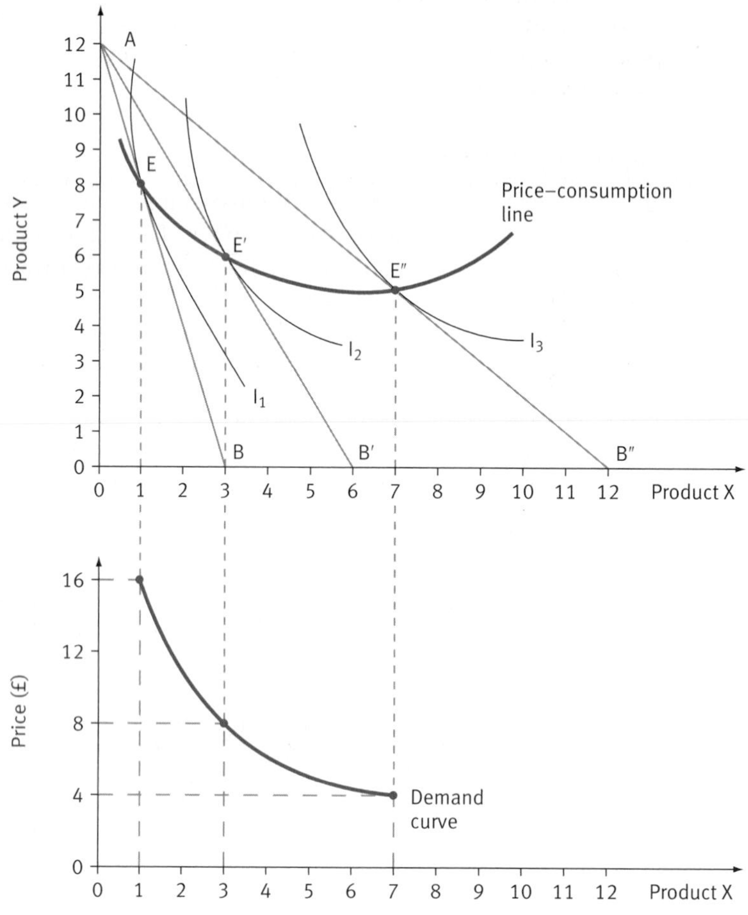

Fig A1.5 The price–consumption line and the individual demand curve

Suppose our household has a weekly income of £48, with the initial price of X (P_x) at £16 and price of Y (P_y) at £4. This gives us the initial budget line AB and the equilibrium point at E for maximum utility of I_1. At P_x = £16, one unit of good X is demanded. Suppose now that P_x falls first to £8 and then to £4, other things equal (i.e. household income and P_y). We can represent this by pivoting the budget line to AB′ (P_x = £8) and AB″ (P_x = £4) respectively. This gives us new equilibrium points of E′ and E″ where the consumer reaches the highest attainable indifference curves of I_2 and I_3 respectively.

From this, we can derive the individual demand curve in the bottom part of Figure A1.5. So at P_x = £16 we have one unit of X demanded, at P_x = £8 we have three units of X demanded and at P_x = £4 we have seven units of X demanded.

As we shall see, the demand curve for normal commodities will always have a negative slope, denoting the law of demand, namely that the quantity demanded rises (expands) as price falls.

Example: Sales of CD albums in Britain would seem to follow the 'law of demand'. These soared to a record high in 2003, despite claims that Internet piracy is killing the music business. Almost 121 million albums were bought in 2003, an increase of 7.6% on the previous year. The increase was attributed to cut-price CDs being sold at supermarkets and through legitimate Internet sites.

Box A1.1 investigates the conditions which are necessary for this law of demand to hold true.

Box A1.1 The 'law of demand'

A reduction in the price of X has, in our analysis, resulted in an overall rise in the quantity demanded of good X, as for instance in the move from E to E′ along the price–consumption line in Figure A1.5 and along the corresponding demand curve. However, this rise in the quantity demanded is the *total price effect* which may be split into two separate parts, the *substitution effect* and the *income effect*. We now examine each part in turn.

- **Substitution effect.** This refers to the extra purchase of product X now that it is, after the price fall, relatively cheaper than other substitutes in consumption.
- **Income effect.** This refers to the rise in real income (purchasing power) now that the price of one product is lower within the bundle of products purchased by the consumer. This extra real income can potentially be used to buy more of all products, including X.

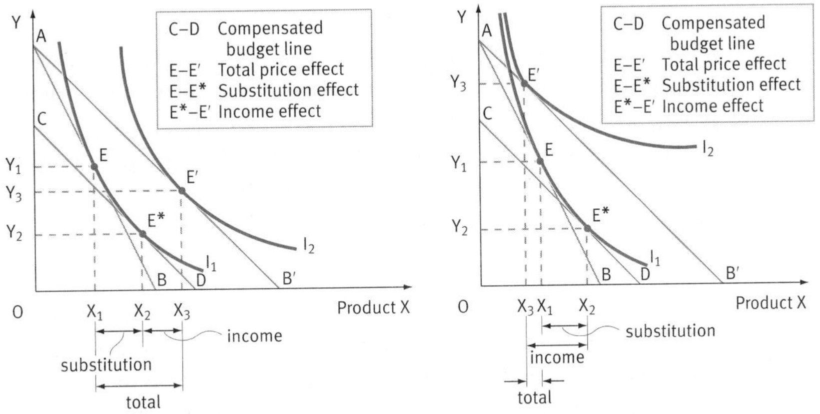

(a) Law of demand supported – i.e. downward sloping demand curve

(b) Law of demand violated – i.e. upward sloping demand curve

Fig A1.6 Income and substitution effects.

For analytical purposes it is helpful to deal separately with each effect and we do this by making use of the **compensated budget line**. In Figure A1.6 above the fall in P_x has caused the budget line to pivot from AB to AB′, representing the new price ratio between X and Y.

The **total price effect** is shown in the movement from E to E′, i.e. the rise in quantity demanded of X from X_1 to X_3. To derive the **compensated budget line** we reduce the consumer's real income, but retain the new price ratio after the fall in P_x so that the consumer is still only able to achieve the same level of utility as before. We show this by shifting the budget line AB′ inwards and parallel to itself (thereby retaining the new price ratio) until it is a tangent to the original indifference curve I_1. This occurs with the budget line CD at point E*.

We can now say that the movement from E to E* is the pure **substitution effect**, i.e. the extra amount $(X_2 - X_1)$ of X purchased solely as a result of X being cheaper relative to Y, the income effect having been compensated, i.e. eliminated.

If we now allow the income effect to be restored, the budget line returns to AB′, moving outwards and parallel to CD. We can now say that the movement from E* to E′ is the **income effect**. In this case the income effect is positive $(X_3 - X_2 > 0)$, with still more of X being purchased as a result of a rise in the consumer's real income.

We can therefore state that:

Total price effect ≡ Substitution effect + Income effect

The income effect can be positive, zero or negative, depending on the type of product in question. For *normal* products, the income effect will be positive; for inferior products, the income effect may be negative over certain ranges of income. Inferior products are cheap, but poor quality, substitutes for other products. As real incomes rise beyond a certain level, consumers will tend to replace such inferior products with more expensive but better quality alternatives.

We can now explore the situation which will result in the law of demand operating in the conventional manner, i.e. more of X being demanded at a lower price.

- Clearly, when *both* substitution and income effects are positive, as in Figure A1.6(a), the total price effect will be positive and the law of demand holds.
- However, if the product is inferior, then the total price effect may include a positive substitution effect but a negative income effect, and the overall outcome will be in doubt.
- Where the product is so inferior that the income effect is sufficiently negative to more than outweigh the positive substitution effect, the total price effect will be negative. In this case a fall in P_x will result in a fall in the demand for X and the law of demand will be violated, with the demand curve sloping upwards from left to right.

Just such an occurrence is shown in Figure A1.6(a). The negative income effect $(X_2 - X_3)$ more than outweighs the positive substitution effect $(X_1 - X_2)$. The fall in price of X causes demand to contract from X_1 to X_3.

Inferior products and Giffen products

- **Inferior products.** These are cheap but poor quality substitutes for other products. As real incomes rise above a certain 'threshold', consumers tend to substitute the more expensive but better quality alternatives for them. In other words, inferior products have negative income elasticities of demand over certain ranges of income. However, not all inferior products are Giffen products.

- **Giffen products.** These are named after the nineteenth-century economist, Sir Robert Giffen, who claimed to identify an upward sloping demand curve for certain inferior products. Of course, we should now be in a position to explain exactly when an inferior product will become a Giffen product. Remembering our identity:

  Total price effect ≡ Substitution effect + Income effect

  the total price effect will be negative when the positive substitution effect is more than outweighed by the negative income effect. This has already been illustrated in Figure A1.6(b) so that this inferior product is also a Giffen product. For an inferior product where the degree of inferiority is rather small, however, the negative income effect may be outweighed by the positive substitution effect, so that the law of demand will still hold. In other words, a fall in P_x will still result in a rise (expansion) in the quantity of X demanded and this inferior product is not a Giffen product.

Table A1.1 summarises the various possibilities.

Table A1.1 Inferior and Giffen products

Type of product	Substitution effect	Income effect	Total effect
Normal	Positive	Positive	Positive
Inferior (but not Giffen)	Positive	Negative	Positive
Giffen	Positive	Negative	Negative

Imperfect information and loss of consumer welfare

We noted above that the consumer will maximise utility (satisfaction) when there is tangency between the budget line and the highest attainable indifference curve. The *slope* of that budget line is given by the price ratio of the two products involved, X and Y. But what if one consumer has information that a product can be bought cheaply, and another consumer does not! Here we examine the implications of such imperfect information ('information asymmetry') on consumer welfare.

Figure A1.7 usefully summarises this situation. For simplicity, we assume that both consumer A and consumer B have exactly the same level of income. However, suppose consumer A is *less aware* (perhaps via less search activity) of the availability of a cheaper source of product Y than is consumer B, so that he faces a higher price for Y and therefore a *lower* product price ratio (P_X/P_Y) than does consumer B. This implies a flatter budget line (AM) for consumer A as compared to B. This is because when they spend their identical income on product Y, consumer B, who goes to the lower priced source, is able to obtain more Y than consumer A. This is *not* the case for product X, where each is equally aware of the lowest prices available.

Clearly, from Figure A1.7 we can see that in maximising utility by equating their

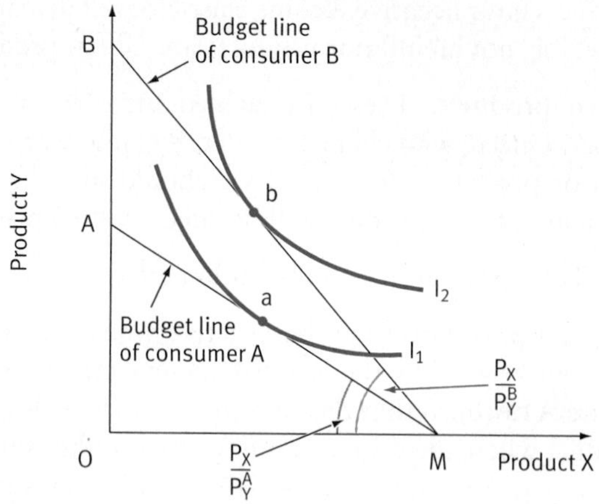

Fig A1.7 Consumer A pays more for product Y (P_Y^A) than does consumer B (P_Y^B)

respective budget lines with the highest attainable indifference curves, consumers A and B are in a different situation from each other. Consumer B, who is aware of the cheaper price available for product Y, is able to reach a higher level of utility (I_2) than consumer A (I_1).

Appendix 2

Isoquants, isocosts and production

Isoquants

Iso means constant and isoquant means constant quantity. The 1X isoquant refers to the different combinations of factors of production able to produce one unit of a product in a technically efficient manner. Let us examine isoquants a little further, using an example. In producing a given amount of a particular type of knitted garment, the firm may be able to choose between different processes of production, i.e. different combinations of capital and labour technically available to the producer. In the table the firm might be able to produce one sweater (i.e. one unit of product X) using any one of the processes outlined, where K represents units of capital and L units of labour.

Alternative processes for producing one sweater (1X) are shown in the table below:

Process	K	L
a	18	2
b	12	3
c	9	4
d	6	6
e	4	9
f	3	12
g	2	18

If we plot the points from the table, then connect them together we get the curve shown in Figure A2.1.

This curve is the 1X **isoquant**, i.e. it shows all the processes that can produce one sweater (1X) in a *technically efficient* manner.

Isoquant lines above and to the right of 1X (e.g. 2X isoquant) correspond to more of both factor inputs, so will represent higher levels of output of product X.

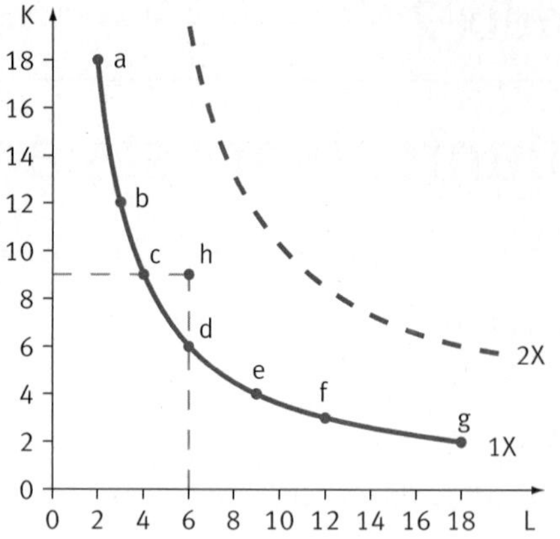

Fig A2.1 The 1X isoquant; i.e. the various processes technically able to produce 1 unit of X

Isocost lines

Just as isoquants are lines of constant quantity, so isocosts are lines of constant costs. They are similar to the budget lines of consumer behaviour except that this time they tell us the different quantities of the factors of production that producers can purchase for a given expenditure (instead of the different quantities of products that consumers can purchase for a given expenditure).

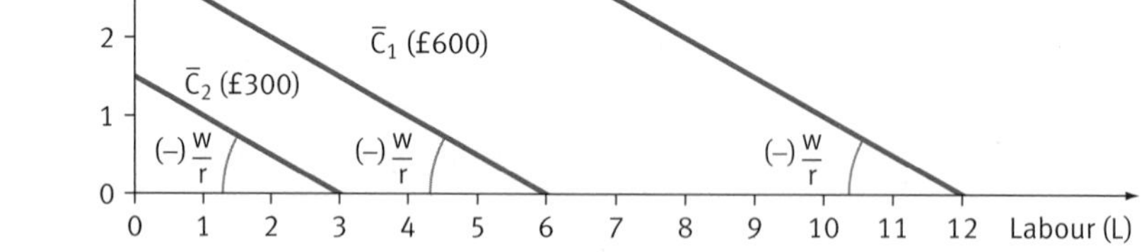

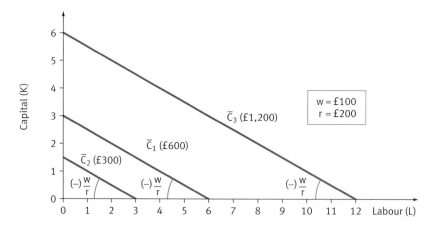

Fig A2.2 Isocost lines

The isocost line $\overline{C}_1$ in Figure A2.2 shows the various combinations of capital and labour that can be purchased for an expenditure of £600, where the price of capital (r) is £200 per unit and the price of labour (w) is £100 per unit.

- The *position* of the isocost line is determined by the value of the total expenditure of the firm on factor inputs. If expenditure halved to £300 with factor prices unchanged, the isocost line would shift inwards to $\overline{C}_2$ and if expenditure doubled to £1,200 the isocost line would shift outwards to $\overline{C}_3$. Notice that these are parallel shifts since the factor price ratio is unchanged.
- The *slope* of the isocost line is given by the factor price ratio.

$$\frac{\text{Price of labour}}{\text{Price of capital}} = (-)\frac{w}{r} = \frac{100}{200} = \frac{1}{2}$$

Strictly this factor price ratio is negative, but we usually ignore the sign, as indicated by the use of brackets around the sign.

Economic efficiency

From all the technically efficient processes of production shown as available on the isoquant, a profit-maximising producer is likely to select that process which is most **economically efficient** (or 'productively efficient'), i.e. the least-cost process.

From all the technically efficient processes of production defined by the isoquant, this economically or least-cost-efficient process will occur where there is a *tangency* between isoquant and isocost. In other words, for any given output, the profit-maximising firm will select that process which is on an isocost line nearest the origin. This will indicate which, of all the technically efficient processes indicated by the isoquant, is the least-cost process (given the current factor price ratio).

If 1X is the desired level of output, the lowest cost of producing 1X at the current factor price ratio (w/r) is $\overline{C}_1$. This 'least cost' process will involve using capital to labour in the ratio K_1/L_1.

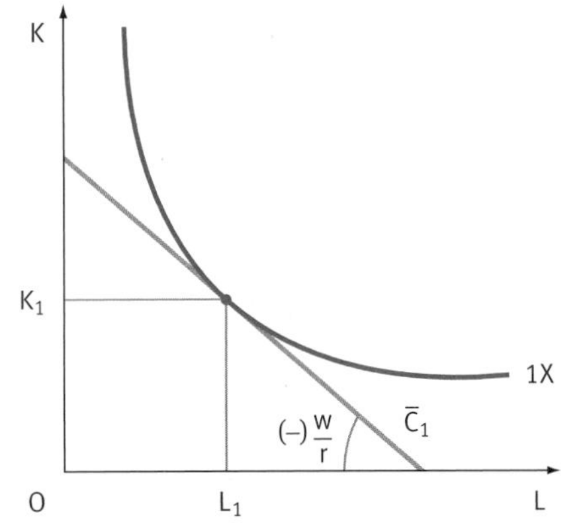

Fig A2.3 The least-cost process for producing 1 unit of product X

Changing the process of production

Suppose the price of capital now falls from r_1 to r_2 in Figure A2.4, with the isocost line now becoming steeper (since $w_1/r_2 > w_1/r_1$).

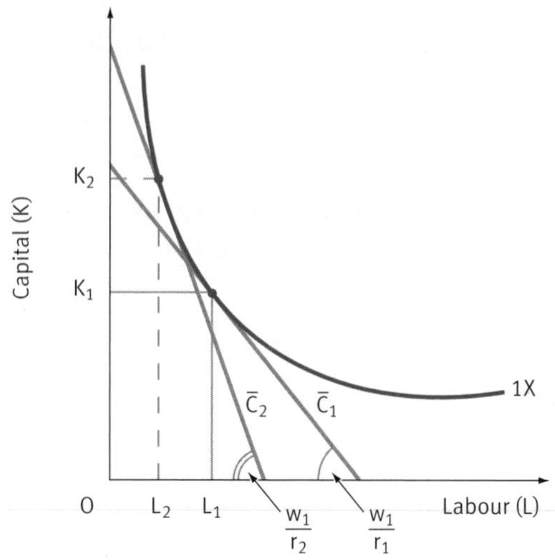

Fig A2.4 Factor substitution under changing factor–price ratio

The new minimum cost of producing 1X is $\bar{C}_2$ (i.e. tangency between the 1X isoquant and the nearest isocost line to the origin with the new slope w_1/r_2), giving a capital/labour ratio K_2/L_2. Not surprisingly, standard theory has predicted an increased use of the cheaper capital input (K_2 instead of K_1) and a decreased use of the now relatively more expensive labour input (L_2 instead of L_1).

References

Ansoff, H. I. (1968) *Corporate Strategy*, Penguin

Armstrong, D. (1999) *A Handbook of Human Resource Management*, 7th edn, Kogan Page

Bacon, R. and Eltis, W. (1978) *Britain's Economic Problem: too few producers*, 2nd edn, Macmillan

Bank of England (2002) Quarterly Report on Small Business Statistics, Business Finance Division, October

Barkema, H. G. and Gomez-Meija, L. R. (1998) Managerial compensation and firm performance, *Academy of Management Journal*, 41, 2

Baumol, W. J. (1959) *Business Behaviour, Value and Growth*, Macmillan

Bebchuk, L. (2004) in 'Special Report on Mergers and Acquisitions', *Economist*, 21 February 2004

Berle, A. A. and Means, G. C. (1934) *The Modern Corporation and Private Property,* Macmillan, New York

Black, G. (2005) *Introduction to Accounting* 2nd edn, FT/Prentice Hall.

Brindley, B. and Buckley, M. (2004) *Business Studies: A-Level Study Guide*, Pearson Education.

Buckingham, L. and Atkinson, D. (1999), 'Whisper it ... takeovers don't pay', *Guardian*, 30 November

Capron, L. (1999) 'Horizontal acquisitions: the benefits and risk to long-term performance', *Mastering Strategy*, p. 202, Financial Times/Prentice Hall

Conyon, M. and Gregg, P. (1994) Pay at the top: a study of the sensitivity of top director remuneration to company specific shocks, *National Institute Economic Review*, August

Conyon, M. and Leech, D. (1994) Executive compensation, corporate performance and ownership structure, *Oxford Bulletin of Economics and Statistics*, 56, 229–47

Conyon, M. and Nicolitsas, D. (1998) Does the market for top executives work? CEO pay and turnover in small UK companies, *Small Business Economics*, 11, 2

Cosh, A. and Hughes, A. (eds) (1996) *The Changing State of British Enterprise: Growth, Innovation and Competitive Advantage in Small and Medium Sized Firms 1986–95*, ESRC Centre for Business Research, University of Cambridge

Cyert, R. M and March, J. G. (1963) *A Behavioural Theory of the Firm*, Prentice Hall, New York

Dunning, J. (1993) *Multinational Enterprise and the Global Economy*, Addison Wesley

Economist, The (2004) 'Special Report on Mergers and Acquisitions', pp. 79–82, 21 February

European Commission (2002) Observatory of European SMEs 2002/No. 2

Ezzamel, M. and Watson, R. (1998) Market compensation earnings and the bidding up of executive cash compensation: evidence from the United Kingdom, *Academy of Management Journal*, 41, 2

Foot, H. and Hook, C. (2002) *Introducing Human Resource Management* 3rd edn, FT/Prentice Hall

Fuller, E. (2004) 'Mergers and acquisitions in the growth of the firm' in *Applied Economics* (10th edn), Griffiths, A. and Wall, S. (eds), Financial Times Prentice Hall

Gregg, P., Machin, S. and Szymanski, S. (1993) The disappearing relationship between directors' pay and corporate performance, *British Journal of Industrial Relations*, 31, pp. 1–9

Griffin, R. W. and Pustay, M. W. (1996) *International Business: A Managerial Perspective*, Addison-Wesley

Griffiths, A. (2000) Corporate Objectives, Risk Taking and the Market: the Case of Cadbury Schweppes, *British Economy Survey*, 29(2), Spring

Healey, N. (2004) 'The multinational corporation' and 'The Transition Economies' in *Applied Economics* (10th edn), Griffiths, A. and Wall, S. (eds), Financial Times Prentice Hall

Hendry, J. and Pettigrew, A. (1990) Human Resource Management: An Agenda for the 1990s, *International Journal of Human Resource Management*, 1, 1

Hill, E., O'Sullivan, C. and O'Sullivan, T. (1995) *Creative Arts Marketing*, Butterworth Heinemann, pp. 106–7

Hornby, W. (1994) *The theory of the firm revisited: a Scottish perspective*, Aberdeen Business School

Jensen, M. C. and Murphy, K. J. (1990) Performance pay and top management incentives, *Journal of Political Economy*, 98

Jobber, D. and Hooley, G. (1987) Pricing behaviour in UK manufacturing and service industries, *Managerial and Decision Economics*, 8, pp. 167–77,

Johnson, G. and Scholes, K. (2002) *Exploring Corporate Strategy*, 6th edn Financial Times Prentice Hall

Kessapidou, S. and Varsakelis, N. (2000) 'National culture, choice of management and business performance: the case of foreign firms in Greece', in *Dimensions of International Competitiveness: Issues and Policies*, Lloyd-Reason, L. and Wall, S. (eds.) Edward Elgar

Keynes, J. M. (1936) *The General Theory of Employment, Interest and Money*, Macmillan

Laurent, A. (1986) 'The cross-cultural puzzle of international human resource management', *Human Resource Management*, 25

Leech, D. and Leahy, J. (1991) Ownership structure, control type classification and the performance of large British companies, *Economic Journal*, 101

Marris, R. (1964) *The Economic Theory of Managerial Capitalism*, Macmillan

Moeller, S., Schlingemann, F. and Stulz, R. (2004) Wealth destruction on a massive scale? A study of acquiring-firm returns in the merger wave of the late 1990s, *Journal of Finance*, forthcoming

Naylor, R. and McKnight, A. (2002) in Bunting, C. 'Money back guaranteed?' *Times Educational Supplement*, 8 November

Newman, K. and Nollen, S. (1996) in *Dimensions of International Competitiveness: Issues and Policies*, Lloyd-Reason, L. and Wall, S. (eds.), Edward Elgar

Nyman, S. and Silberston, A. (1978) The ownership and control of industry, *Oxford Economic Papers*, 30, 1, March

Ottman, J. (2000), *In Business*, 22, 6.

Pine, J. and Gilmore, J. (1998) Welcome to the Experience Economy, *Harvard Business Review*, July

Prahalad, C. K. (1999) 'Changes in the competitive battlefield', *Financial Times*, 4 October. In *Mastering Strategy* (2000) Financial Times Prentice Hall

Prahalad, C. K. and Ramaswanny, V. (2004) *Co-creating unique value with customers,* Harvard Business School Press

Rifkin, J. and Heilbroner, R. L. (2004) *The End of Work: the decline of the global labour market and the dawn of the post-market era*, rev. edn, J. P. Tarcher

Shipley, D. D. (1981) Primary objectives in British manufacturing industry, *Journal of Industrial Economics*, 29, 4 June

Shipley, D. D. and Bourdon, E. (1990) Distributor pricing in very competitive markets, *Industrial Marketing Management*, 19

Simon, H. A. (1959) Theories of decision making in economics, *American Economic Review* 69, 3 June

Small Business Service (2002) SME – statistics for the UK

Smith, A. (1776) *An Enquiry into the Nature and Causes of the Wealth of Nations*,

Smith, D. (2003) 'Industry closes the gap on growth', *The Sunday Times*, 5 October

Smith, D. (2004) 'Strangled', *Sunday Times*, 7 March

Storey, D. (1982) *Entrepreneurship and the New Firm*, Croom Helm.

Storey, D. (1994) *Understanding the Small Business Sector*, Routledge, London

Storey, D., Keasey, K., Watson, R. and Wynarczyk, P. (1987) *The Performance of Small Firms*, Croom Helm

Storey, D., Watson, R. and Whynarczyk, P. (1995) The remuneration of non-owner managers in UK unquoted and unlisted securities market enterprises, *Small Business Economics*, 7

Thompson, A. and Strickland, A. (1999) *Strategic Management*, 11th edn, McGraw-Hill

TUC (2000) Small Business – Myths and Reality, March

Vernon, R. and Wells, L. T. (1991) *The Manager in the International Economy*. Prentice-Hall, Upper Saddle River, NJ

Walker, I. (2002) in Bunting, C. 'Money back guaranteed?' *Times Educational Supplement*, 8 November

Williamson, O. E. (1963) Managerial discretion and business behaviour, *American Economic Review*, 53, December

Wilson, J. (2003) 'Inter-partner relationships and performance in UK – Chinese joint ventures: an interaction approach' PhD thesis, University of Middlesex

Zeithami, V. and Bitner, M. (2000) *Services Marketing*, 2nd edn, McGraw-Hill

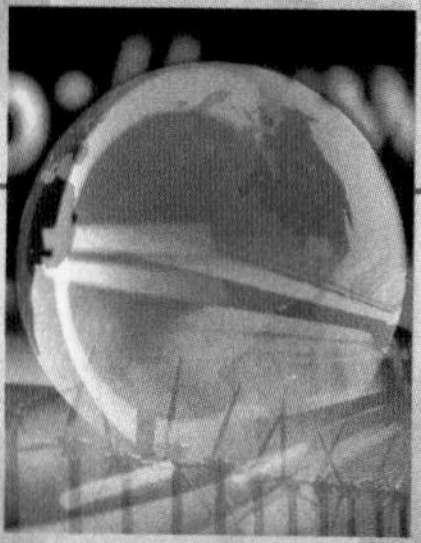

List of contributors

Alan Griffiths, BA, MSc is Reader in Economics at Ashcroft International Business School, Anglia Polytechnic University, having previously been Tutor in Economics at the University College of Wales, Aberystwyth. He has acted as a visiting fellow of the Japan Foundation at Sophia University, Tokyo and as Research Officer at the Research Institute for the National Economy at Yokohama University. He is author of a wide range of books and articles.

Stuart Wall, BA, MSc is Professor of Business and Economic Education at Ashcroft International Business School, Anglia Polytechnic University, and has been a visiting lecturer, supervisor and examiner at Cambridge University. He has acted as a consultant to the OECD Directorate for Science, Technology and Industry, and as a member of a number of degree awarding bodies in Business and Economics in the UK. He is author of a wide range of books and articles.

George Carrol, BA, MA lectures in a range of business and economic modules in the Ashcroft International Business School, Anglia Polytechnic University, including microeconomics, business analysis and management decision making. He has considerable experience in industry and is author of a number of articles and texts. Responsible for Chapter 6.

Rita Carrol, BA, MA lectures in a range of business and economic modules in the Ashcroft International Business School, Anglia Polytechnic University. She specialises in the economics of social problems, international business and business economics amongst other modules. Responsible for Chapter 11.

David McCaskey, MBA lectures in marketing and management at the Colchester Institute. He has extensive experience in managing within service sector industries and publishes regularly in a number of management related journals. A wide range of his published papers can be accessed at www.wivenhoe.gov.uk/People/mccaskey.htm Responsible for Chapter 16.

Margaret O'Quigley, BA, MSc lectures in economics at the Ashcroft International Business School, Anglia Polytechnic University, with special reference to macroeconomic modules such as monetary economics and international economics. Research interests include financial bubbles and football finance. Responsible for Chapters 9 and 10.

Jonathan Wilson, MA, lectures in international marketing at the Ashcroft International Business School, Anglia Polytechnic University. His research interests include UK/Chinese business-to-business relationships and he has presented papers at various international conferences including that of the Chinese Economic Association. He has also published in the Asia Pacific Journal of Marketing and Logistics. Responsible for Chapter 14.

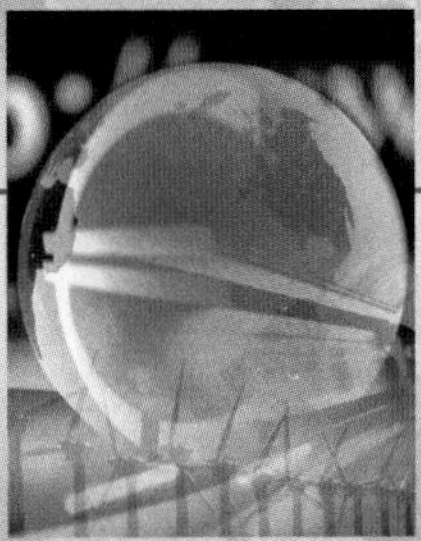

Answers to Checkpoints and Activities

Chapter 1

Checkpoints

1 Fall in price of substitute in consumption; rise in price of complement in consumption; fall in income; change of tastes against oranges; fall in advertising expenditure on oranges (and/or increase in advertising expenditure on substitutes in consumption); etc.

2 Rise in price of substitutes in production; fall in price of complement in production; rise in costs of production; change of tastes of producer against wheat; tax increase on wheat; subsidy reduction on wheat; unfavourable weather conditions; etc.

3 Less orthodox ways might include letting special groups which can be authenticated (e.g. pensioners; consumers in developing countries; etc.) purchase the excess supply at discounted prices. The aim is to avoid excess supply depressing price in the market as a whole.

Activities

Activity 1.1

(a) If the recording studio chooses to operate at point R′ on the production possibility curve then it can produce a combination of A_2 albums per year and S′ singles per year.

(b) By moving from R to R′ the studio has had to forgo $A_1 - A_2$ albums. If more singles are produced, then resources will have to be shifted away from producing albums. This means that the opportunity cost of producing more singles is the number of albums that have had to be forgone, i.e. $A_1 - A_2$ albums.

(c) A movement from N to R does not involve an opportunity cost in terms of albums forgone to the studio. This is because at N the studio is not using all its resources fully. If it used all its resources it would be able to produce at R on the production possibility curve. In other words, it could produce the same amount of albums as before (A_1) *and* more singles (S_1). The number of albums has not decreased so there is no opportunity cost in terms of albums in the movement from N to R.

(d) The possibilities are that the studio could produce more albums and the same singles (M to R), more singles and the same albums (M to R′) or more of both (anywhere north-east of M). The optimum set of combinations of singles and albums would be between R and R′ on the production possibility curve since all the resources would then be fully employed.

Activity 1.2

1 (a) True
(b) True
(c) False (decrease)
(d) False (contraction)

2 I
D
I
I
D
I
D
D

3 (a) True
(b) True
(c) False (fits together with)
(d) True
(e) False (rival with)

Activity 1.3

1 (i) (c) A to E
(ii) (d) A to D
(iii) (a) A to B
(iv) (b) C to D

2 (ii) and (iv) both increase the supply of the petrol, the complement in production (jointly supplied product) with oil.

3 (ii) and (iv) both decrease the supply of petrol.

4 (a) (v)
(b) (iii)
(c) (ii)
(d) (iv)
(e) (i)

Activity 1.4

1 (a) False (P_1)
(b) False (excess supply)
(c) True
(d) False (fall)

(e) True (move along D)
(f) False (contract)
(g) True
(h) True

2 (a) Rise: Rise (via increase in demand)
(b) Fall: Fall (via decrease in demand)
(c) Fall: Rise (via increase in supply)
(d) Rise: Fall (via decrease in supply)

3 When the demand for Microsoft XBox increases from D to D_1 then, under normal circumstances, the demand for Sony PlayStation 2 will decrease from D to D_1 because they are in competition with each other, i.e. it is a competitive demand situation. This means that when the demand for XBox increases it will take customers away from PlayStation 2, causing the demand for PlayStation 2 to decrease.

4 As the demand for wool increases from D to D_1, the price of wool rises and the quantity of wool supplied expands from Q to Q_1. To supply more wool requires more sheep so that more mutton is (eventually) supplied at any given price of mutton, i.e. wool and mutton are jointly supplied. As a result of the increase in supply of mutton, the price of mutton falls and the quantity rises.

5 As the demand for cars increases from D to D_1 then at any given price of tyres, more tyres are now demanded. In other words, the demand for tyres will also increase from D to D_1 as cars and tyres are complements in consumption.

Activity 1.5

1 US, UK, France, Poland, China, Cuba
Cuba is a highly regulated economy with little in the way of a free market, and is therefore the closest to a pure command economy. The US is at the opposite end of the spectrum, with private enterprise dominating its economy. The UK is the closest to the US in terms of free market activity, with France having relatively more state support and regulation than the UK. China is closest to Cuba, though substantial parts of its economy have been opened to free enterprise in recent years. This has been still more true of the economy of Poland.

2 (a)

Product A	**Product B**
1 Demand decreases	4 Demand increases
2 Price falls	5 Price rises
3 Decreases	6 Increases

(b) As demand for product A decreases as a result of a change in tastes in favour of product B, the price of product A will fall. This is a signal to the producer that profits from A will fall. A fall in profits will lead the producer to produce less A and more B. Why is this? As tastes shift towards B, demand for this product will increase and its price will rise in the market. This induces greater profits for product B and encourages the producer to produce more B and less A. Changes in consumer tastes have resulted in changes in relative prices and profits, providing signals to the producer to switch resources between the two substitutes in production.

(c) The free movement of resources from producing A to producing B in this market economy might not be appropriate and the government might intervene, for many reasons. For example, suppose the consumption of product B was bad for health. The government might want to introduce (or raise) a tax to make the price of B more expensive in an attempt to cut down consumption, e.g. cigarettes.

Chapter 2

Checkpoints

1 The scales used for the axes in (b) may be different from those in (d). For example, if the scales for the vertical axes were the same but for the horizontal axis the scale was 1 cm = 1,000 units for (b) but 1 cm = 10 units for (d), then (b) might actually be the more elastic demand curve.

2 – Price increase along a unit elastic demand, no change in total revenue.
– Price increase along a relatively elastic demand, total revenue will decrease.
– Price increase along a relatively inelastic demand curve, total revenue will increase.

3 (a) marginal utility is positive but falling
(b) marginal utility is zero
(c) marginal utility is negative

4 Total utility is now a maximum with 2 units of A and 7 of B so that 12/2 = 12/2 for the respective marginal utility/price ratios. The fall in price of B means 4 extra units demanded (and 1 less of A)

Activities

Activity 2.1

1 (a)

Quantity (units)	AR(£)	TR(£)	MR(£)
1	100	100	100
2	95	190	90
3	90	270	80
4	85	340	70
5	80	400	60
6	75	450	50
7	70	490	40
8	65	520	30

(b) From the diagram we can see that as AR (price) falls, quantity demanded expands so that the demand curve slopes downwards from left to right. The MR curve also slopes down from left to right but is below the AR curve throughout the length of AR. Both AR and MR curves are linear in this example (i.e. straight lines).

2 (a) (ii)
  (b) (iv)
  (c) (iii)
  (d) (v)
  (e) (i)

3 (a) True
  (b) False (raise total revenue)
  (c) True
  (d) True

4 (a) (i) and (iv)
  (b) (iii)
  (c) (i) and (iv)
  (d) (i)
  (e) (ii)

Activity 2.2

1 (b) and (c)

2 (a) and (c)

3 (a) (ii)
  (b) (v)
  (c) (i)
  (d) (iii)
  (e) (iv)

4 (c)

5 (b) Football boots (complement)

6 (d) Beer (substitute)

Activity 2.3

1 (c) and (d)

2 (a)

3 (c) and (e)

Chapter 3

Checkpoints

1 Some costs will not vary with the number of students or number of lectures undertaken, e.g. costs related to the building or infrastructure of the university. Energy costs, wage bill (lecturers, support staff), cost of teaching materials, etc. may vary with the number of students/lecturers.

2 Many possibilities here. Silicon Glen (computer industries in Clydeside), Silicon Fen (computer industries in Cambridge) and many other examples are possible.

3 New entrants into a sector of economic activity might seek to merge with or take over these (often small) firms which have learned over time how to reduce costs.

Activities

Activity 3.1

1

No. of workers (L)	Total product (TP)	Average product (AP)	Marginal product (MP)
1	40	40	40
2	140	70	100
3	255	85	115
4	400	100	145
5	600	120	200
6	720	120	120
7	770	110	50
8	800	100	30
9	810	90	10
10	750	75	−60

(a) (i) Diminishing marginal returns sets in after the employment of five workers.
(ii) Diminishing average returns sets in after the employment of six workers.

(b) Your diagram should show the marginal product curve *above* the average product curve until six workers (when they are the same). After six workers the marginal product curve is *below* the average product curve. Your diagram should look something like that in the top part of Figure 3.3.

2 (a) In the top diagram, both average product (AP) and marginal product (MP) curves rise to a peak and then fall. When the MP curve is above the AP curve, then AP will continue to rise even when MP is falling. When they both intersect, the AP curve will be at a maximum. As soon as MP is below AP then AP must fall.

(b) In the bottom diagram, both average variable cost (AVC) and marginal cost (MC) curves are U-shaped. When the MC curve is below the AVC curve then it pulls down the AVC curve. The minimum point on the AVC curve is where both AVC and MC curves intersect. For further increases in output the MC curve is above the AVC curve and therefore it pulls up the AVC curve.

(c) The two diagrams are linked because costs are a reflection of productivity. In other words, an increase in MP (i.e. increase in productivity of the last person) will lead to a fall in the marginal costs of production (MC). On the other hand, a decrease in MP (i.e. decrease in productivity of the last person) will lead to a rise in the marginal costs of production. The same principles hold for the AP and AVC curves, i.e. when AP rises/falls, the AVC curve falls/rises. The link between the two diagrams is that improving/worsening productivity will result in decreasing/increasing costs. This linkage also means that when MP and AP are at maximum values, MC and AVC respectively are at minimum values.

3

Output	TFC	TVC	TC	AFC	AVC	ATC	MC
0	50	0	50	–	–		
1	50	40	90	50	40	50	40
2	50	75	125	25	37.5	62.5	35
3	50	108	158	16.7	36	52.7	33
4	50	138	188	12.5	34.5	47	30
5	50	170	220	10.0	34	44	35
6	50	205	255	8.3	34.2	42.5	35
7	50	243	293	7.1	34.7	41.8	38
8	50	286	336	6.3	35.8	42.1	43
9	50	335	385	5.6	37.2	42.8	49
10	50	390	440	5.0	39	44	55

From the diagram (which should be similar to Figure 3.2(b), p. 96) we can see that the average fixed costs (AFC) falls continuously as output increases because the fixed costs are spread over more and more output. Both the AVC and the ATC curves are U-shaped, with the AVC being below the ATC. The difference between the two curves represents the average fixed costs (AFC). Notice that the marginal cost curve (MC) falls and then rises – it also intersects both AVC and ATC at their lowest points. This is because the MC curve determines whether AVC and ATC rise or fall. For example, if MC is below AVC, then AVC will fall; but when MC is above AVC, AVC will rise. Similarly, if MC is below/above ATC, then ATC will fall/rise.

4 (b) and (c)

5 (b) and (c)

Activity 3.2

1 The first table shows that costs of production per car (i.e. average production costs) decreases as production of cars increases. The optimum number of cars that should be produced in this car plant in order to achieve lowest average production costs is 2m per year. This table is looking at technical scale economies. Note that a car company producing only 100,000 cars per year is at a 34% cost *disadvantage* compared to one producing 2m cars per year.

The second table shows that the optimum number of cars that should be produced to minimise the various non-production costs under five categories of activities (which are related to the car industry) that are quite different. It shows that if the car plant produces 2m cars per year then this output is also sufficient to meet (or more than meet) the optimum output in the sales, advertising and risk activities. However, the 2m cars per year is not large enough to meet the optimum outputs for Finance and Research and Development. This means that at 2m cars per year, the cost of Finance per car and the R&D costs per car will not be at their lowest (optimum). These non-technical (enterprise) economies are different from the technical (production) economies.

2 (a) (ii)
(b) (i)
(c) (iii)
(d) (i)
(e) (iv)
(f) (v)

3 (a) (iv)
(b) (iii)
(c) (vi)
(d) (i)
(e) (ii)
(f) (vii)
(g) (v)

4 (a) and (c)

5 (a)

6 (e)

7 (e)

8 (b)

9 (a) False (just sufficient)
(b) False (diseconomies of scale)
(c) False (economies of experience)
(d) True
(e) True

Activity 3.3

1 (a) (iv)
(b) (iii)
(c) (v)
(d) (ii)

2 (a) False (relatively elastic)
(b) True
(c) True
(d) False (+0.75)

3 (b)

4 (b)

5 (c)

Chapter 4

Checkpoints

1 Marginal revenue and marginal cost curves would have intersected at Q_p, the output where total profit is a maximum.

2 Consumer tastes shifting progressively towards more ethical/environmental aspects may increase demand for companies/products more closely aligned to these values. Stricter government regulations in these areas may favour companies/products which already meet these standards (those failing to comply may be excluded from major markets).

3 There may still be a small number of highly committed purchasers with extremely inelastic demand characteristics. Charging these purchasers a high price may well result in increased revenue.

Activities

Activity 4.1

1 Many local possibilities here.

2 This table provides a breakdown of the number of different types of business organisations by sector. First, it can be seen that the service sector contains the largest number of VAT-based enterprises in total, accounting for some 71% of all such enterprises. It also has the largest number of enterprises in all business categories. This is not surprising, because the service sector in the UK accounts for around 70% of total UK output. Second, sole proprietors are well represented in agriculture and construction, with many single owners of small farms in agriculture and many self-employed carpenters, bricklayers, plumbers etc. in construction. Partnerships are also well represented in agriculture and services, construction and production sectors. Third, when we investigate the larger firms we see that in the production sector, some 62% of enterprises are companies or public corporations as the larger size helps them to attain economies of scale and compete in an increasingly dynamic environment. The service sector also has around a third of its enterprises in the large-scale category, e.g. in communications and finance. Note also the high percentage of general government and non-profit-making enterprises in the service industry. This should not be surprising since it covers many local government-run offices and charity organisations across the country.

Activity 4.2

1 (a) Q_2 with total profit Q_2X
  (b) Q_3 with total revenue Q_3X
  (c) Total revenue equals total costs, so that profit levels are zero (break-even outputs).
  (d) Q_3 with the minimum profit constraint of (1) since total revenue is a maximum at point C and more than the minimum profits are being earned. But the output level would to Q_2' if the minimum profit constraint rises from (1) to (2) and total revenue would fall below C.

2 Arguably only 15.9% of firms are 'true profit maximisers' since only 15.9% of firms answered with *both* 1(a) and 2(d), which you would expect from a true profit maximiser. Profit is clearly the most important single objective, with 85% of firms regarding it as either 'very important' or 'of overriding importance'.

3 (b) and (c)

4 (a) and (d)

5 (b) and (d)

6 (a) and (e)

7 (b) and (d)

8 (b) and (c)

9 (b) and (d)

Chapter 5

Checkpoints

1 Accounting, solicitors and various legal practices, hairdressing and personal services, agriculture etc.

2 Organic growth is more likely to reflect the firm's existing core competencies, to be incremental rather than high value/high risk, to avoid cultural 'shocks' via mergers/acquisitions etc. Disadvantages may be that it may take longer than mergers to achieve any desired results and may be delayed by a lack of internal core competencies or lack of internal finance etc.

3 Many possibilities here. Check the student website which accompanies this text where current examples are given.

4 Many possibilities here. Check the student website which accompanies this text where current examples are given.

Activities

Activity 5.1

1 (a) The table shows many interesting aspects of UK business. First, the growing importance of self-employment (sole proprietor and partnerships) in that 68% of businesses do not employ any workers. However, this type of business only employs around 11% of the total employees and 7% of total turnover. If we look at the whole SME sector, i.e. those firms employing fewer than 250 employees, then the picture changes in that the whole SME sector accounts for 99.8% of all businesses, employs 47.6% of all employees and accounts for 51.1% of total turnover. The SME sector therefore accounts for about half the

turnover and half the employment in the UK, often acting as stepping stones on the way to becoming larger businesses.

(b) The UK has a very small number of particularly large firms. For example, while only 0.2% of all businesses are defined as large (employing more than 250 employees), they account for as much as 52.4% of all employees and 48.9% of total turnover. These large firms are to be found mostly in manufacturing and services where intense competition and the importance of economies of scale have led to the growth of large-scale businesses.

2 (b)

3 (d)

4 (e)

5 (d) (larger firms are more likely to experience a separation between ownership and control)

Activity 5.2

1 (a) (v)
(b) (iv)
(c) (vii)
(d) (i)
(e) (vi)
(f) (iii)
(g) (ii)

2 (a) (ii)
(b) (v)
(c) (i)
(d) (iii)
(e) (iv)

3 (a) False (backward)
(b) False (forward)
(c) False (horizontal)
(d) True
(e) True
(f) True
(g) False
(h) False

Chapter 6

Checkpoints

1 Many possibilities here, but examples are unlikely to include highly branded oligopolistic product markets where entry barriers are considerable.

2 Again many possibilities, but this time extensively branded products will be good examples of entry barriers, as will substantial economies of scale (technical and non-technical), tariffs, legal requirements, geographical distance etc.

3 Railways and water industries are often mentioned, as are gas and electricity supply.

4 (1) Monopolists will benefit directly from their own advertising which, if successful, will increase demand for their output. Perfectly competitive firms already have infinite demand at the going market price and can only benefit via advertising on behalf of the industry as a whole (which may raise the market price).
(2) If economies of scale (technical and non-technical) shift the marginal cost curve further downwards than MC′ in Figure 6.10, then the profit-maximising output is higher and price lower than in perfect competition. The 'classical case' against monopoly would no longer hold true.

5 Thirty years if Bob confesses and five years if Bob doesn't confess.

6 Thirty years if Alf confesses and five years if Alf doesn't confess.

7 If A adopts a maxi-min decision rule, then it selects 'price cut' strategy as this is the best of the worst possible outcomes (60% of market share). If B adopts a mini-max decision rule, then it selects 'Extra advertising' since this is the worst of the best possible outcomes (45%, i.e. 100% – 55% of market share).

8 (1) No, since there is no single policy option that is best for Beta regardless of how Alpha reacts.
(2) Beta is likely to select a low price since (£m) 140 is better than 100 for Beta.

Activities

Activity 6.1

1 (a) P_1/Q_1
(b) P_3/Q_3
(c) Q_2
(d) b (where MR is zero, suggesting that total revenue is unchanged for price changes around P_2).
(e) Within the total area of 'deadweight loss' of adc, aec of consumer surplus is lost and ecd producer surplus is lost. However, you could have mentioned that area P_3aeP_1 was also lost from consumer surplus but was exactly matched as a gain in producer surplus – so this area has a zero *net* effect on economic welfare and does not appear in 'deadweight loss'.
(f) P_2/Q_2 (total revenue is a maximum where marginal revenue is zero).

2 Letters, in vertical order: (d), (f), (b), (e), (a), (c)

3 (a) and (e)

4 (b) and (c)

5 (a) and (d)

6 (b) and (d)

Activity 6.2

1

Perfect competition	Monopolist competition
(b) (d) (e) (g) (i)	(a) (c) (f) (h) (j)

2 (e)

3 (a)

4 (a)

Activity 6.3

1 (a) (iii)
(b) (vii)
(c) (ii)
(d) (v)
(e) (iv)
(f) (i)
(g) (vi)

2 (c)

3 (d)

4 (d)

Chapter 7

Checkpoints

1 More elastic demand for the product; becomes easier to substitute labour with capital or with another type of labour; becomes less easy to pass on wage increases to consumers as higher prices; etc.

2 An increase in DD (e.g. rise in MRP_L via rise in marginal physical productivity or rise in price of product produced) and/or decrease in SS (e.g. less labour supplied to the market).
Depends on the reasons – if entirely an increase in DD, employment rises; if entirely decrease in SS, employment falls; otherwise indeterminate employment outcome.

3 There is a higher proportion of women part-time workers, so over the year their annual earnings are significantly less than for men.

4 Perhaps ensuring that interviews for jobs have an equal number of male and female applicants etc.

5 Labour supply shortages may occur, increasing the demand for older workers who may bring higher productivity to some jobs via greater experience. Payouts on company pension schemes will also be deferred.

Activities

Activity 7.1

1 (a) The table provides information about the marginal revenue product (MRP), which is, in effect, the demand curve for labour in a perfectly competitive market. Your MRP_L diagram should show the MRP_L rising and then falling; the effective demand curve is that part of the MRP_L which is falling.

(b) (i) At a wage rate of £250, the number of workers employed will be 8.

(ii) At a wage of £80, the number of workers employed will be 11.

These solutions are arrived at by equating MRP_L (where it is downward sloping) with MC_L in each situation, where wage = MC_L in a competitive labour market.

(c) The demand curve for labour could become more elastic if it became easier to substitute one type of worker by another type of worker (e.g. more occupational or geographical mobility of labour) or by capital equipment. A given % rise in wages for this occupation would then result in a bigger % fall in the quantity of that type of labour demanded. Also, since demand for a factor is derived from demand for the product it makes, anything which makes the demand for the product more elastic will make the (derived) demand for the factor more elastic.

(d) (i) If the price of the product produced by labour rose from £5 to £8 then the marginal revenue product (MRP_L) curve would be greater because $MRP_L = MPP_L \times$ Price. The demand curve for labour would therefore shift to the right and there would be an increase in demand for labour at each wage rate.

(ii) The answers to the questions in part (b) will not necessarily remain the same because although the given wage rates are the same, the MRP_L values will be different and hence the equilibrium position in the labour market. In fact, with product price of £8 and wage of £250, nine people will be employed (one more than before). If the wage is only £80 then 11 people will be employed (same as before).

Activity 7.2

1 (a)

Wage rate (AC_L) (£)	Number of workers supplied (per day)	Total cost of labour (£)	Marginal cost of labour (MC_L)
50	1	50	50
60	2	120	70
70	3	210	90
80	4	320	110
90	5	450	130
100	6	600	150
110	7	770	170
120	8	960	190

(b) This plots the first column of the table on the vertical axis and the second column on the horizontal axis. It should look like S_L in Figure 7.3(b) (p. 259).

(c) This plots the fourth column of the table on the vertical axis and the second column on the horizontal axis. The MC_L curve should lie above the $S_L = AC_L$ curve, as in Figure 7.3(b) (p. 256).

(d) From the figure we can see that the AC_L and MC_L curves are upward sloping, with the MC_L curve lying above the AC_L. In other words, the marginal cost of hiring workers increases as more workers are employed and is above the average cost (wage) as employers bid the wage rate up against themselves.

(e) Under monopsony, the equilibrium level of wages and employment will be achieved where MC_L is equal to MRP_L. The monopsonist will employ fewer workers than in a competitive market and also pay them less than the competitive wage (again see Figure 7.3(b) (p. 256).

2 (a) Your sketch diagram should look like Figure 7.3(a) (p. 256), showing the union forcing the employer off his/her MRP_L curve (point A). In other words, by raising wages to W_3 in Figure 7.3(a), the union is able to keep employment constant at L_1 (point A).

(b) The union will be able to achieve increases in both wages and employment if it has sufficient bargaining power. For example, if the union is strong and controls the total supply of labour into the industry then it can, to some extent, dictate the bargaining outcome. Also, if the demand for the product which labour is making is inelastic, then managers might be prepared to pay a higher wage *and* keep the same number of workers if they can shift this increase in costs onto the price of their product.

Chapter 8

Checkpoints

1 For each unit of output up to OQ_2, each unit adds more to social benefit than to social cost, thereby raising total social surplus. For each unit of output beyond OQ_2, each unit adds less to social benefit than to social cost, thereby reducing total social surplus. Social surplus can only be maximised at output OQ_2.

2 Your diagram could look like that in Figure 8.1 (p. 279) but this time the MSC and MPC labels could be reversed, so that MSC is now below MPC. Social surplus would now be maximised at the higher output (OQ_1), and to give the private producer the profit incentive to produce OQ_1 a *subsidy* (opposite of tax) will be needed to shift the new MPC vertically downwards to match the lower MSC curve. Now MPC (=MSC) would equal MSB at output OQ_1.

Alternatively, your diagram could this time have MSB above MR (MPB), rather than equal to MR (MPB) as in Figure 8.1.

3 As just mentioned, this time MSB should be drawn above MR (MPB) to indicate the presence of a merit good. The higher output now needed for social surplus to be a maximum could be achieved by subsidising the merit good.

Activities

Activity 8.1

1 (a) (ii)
(b) (v)
(c) (iv)
(d) (vi)
(e) (i)
(f) (iii)

2 (a) P
(b) P
(c) P
(d) M
(e) M
(f) P
(g) M

3 (b) and (c)

4 (a) and (d)

5 (b)

Chapter 9

Checkpoints

1 (1) Withdrawals are savings, imports and taxes. As national income rises, so does that of individuals and businesses, giving more scope to save out of higher incomes (for business this saving will be undistributed profit). Also, as national income rises there will be more spending on imports and more money will be taken by the government in the form of taxes (both via income taxes and expenditure taxes).

(2) The idea here is that some consumer spending still occurs at zero national income and this is financed from past savings (i.e. negative savings or *dissaving*).

2 Injections are investment, government spending and exports. In fact as national income rises and consumers spend more, businesses will be more optimistic about the future and are likely to invest more. Government spending may be able to increase, since tax revenues will have risen. Exports might also be encouraged – since the stronger domestic economy may allow domestic firms to produce more output, perhaps growing to reach the minimum efficient size (where average total cost is a minimum) for their sector and therefore being better able to compete on foreign markets.

3 (1) aps = total savings divided by total national income
apt = total tax revenue divided by total national income
apm = total spending on imports divided by total national income

(2) aps = 1.5/20 = 0.075
apt = 4/20 = 0.2
apm = 6/20 = 0.3

(3) (a) mps > aps
(b) mpt = apt
(c) mpm = apm

4 Any vertical straight line from the horizontal axis to the 45° line creates a right-angled triangle with two (base) angles equal at 45°. This is an isosceles triangle and therefore the two sides are equal, i.e. Y and E.

5 (1) At Y_1 injections now fall short of withdrawals. National income (Y) must fall, and as Y falls so too does withdrawals (W). National income continues to fall until W falls sufficiently to match the new and lower level of injections at V_2. This occurs at Y_2, the new equilibrium value.

(2) (a) Your diagram should look like that in the top part of Figure 9.9 (p. 349), with the E (C + J) schedule intersecting the 45° line at a higher level of national income, following the increase in injections.
(b) The opposite will now occur, with a lower level of national income in the new equilibrium.

6 (1) The decrease in withdrawals from W_1 to W_2 means that withdrawals now fall short of injections at Y_1. National income now rises and withdrawals also rise along the new schedule W_2. National income continues to rise until withdrawals and injections are again equal at V_1, with national income Y_2 the new equilibrium value.

(2) On the 45° diagram a change in withdrawals would be captured by a change in the consumption function (C). For example, a rise in W will mean that there is an equivalent fall in C at any given level of national income Y ($Y \equiv C + W$). This will shift the aggregate expenditure (E) schedule downwards, since $E = C + J$.

7 It could shift J vertically downwards to go through point B, i.e. reduce injections J, perhaps by cutting G. Alternatively, it could increase taxes (T) and shift the withdrawals schedule upwards to go through point A. Or it could shift both J and W curves in these same directions (but not by as much) so that they intersect at Y_F.

8 It could shift J vertically upwards to go through point C (e.g. increase G) or shift W vertically downwards to go through point D (e.g. reduce T), or some of both so that J and W intersect at Y_F.

Activities

Activity 9.1

1 (a) (iv)
(b) (i)
(c) (vii)
(d) (ii)
(e) (v)
(f) (iii)

2 (a) (iii)
(b) (i)
(c) (viii)
(d) (vi)
(e) (ii)
(f) (vii)

3 (a) (v)
(b) (ii)
(c) (iii)
(d) (iv)
(e) (i)

4 (a)

National income (Y)	Tendency to change in national income
0	0
1,000	Increase
2,000	Increase
3,000	Increase
4,000	Increase
5,000	Increase
6,000	No change
7,000	Decrease
8,000	Decrease

(b)

National income (Y)	Withdrawals (W)	Injections (J)
0	−1,000	2,000
1,000	−500	2,000
2,000	0	2,000
3,000	500	2,000
4,000	1,000	2,000
5,000	1,500	2,000
6,000	2,000	2,000
7,000	2,500	2,000
8,000	3,000	2,000

(c) Your diagram should look like that in Figure 9.4 (p. 338) but with W intersecting J at a value of Y of 6,000. J will be a horizontal line at 2000 and W will intersect the vertical axis at −1000 and will intersect the horizontal axis when Y = 2000.

(d) Savings (S) = −1,000 + 0.2Y
Taxes (T) = 0.2Y
Imports (M) = 0.1Y
Withdrawals (W) = −1,000 + 0.5Y

(e)

National income (Y)	Consumption (C)	Injections (J)	Aggregate expenditure (E)
0	1,000	2,000	3,000
1,000	1,500	2,000	3,500
2,000	2,000	2,000	4,000
3,000	2,500	2,000	4,500
4,000	3,000	2,000	5,000
5,000	3,500	2,000	5,500
6,000	4,000	2,000	6,000
7,000	4,500	2,000	6,500
8,000	5,000	2,000	7,000

(f) Your diagram should look like that in Figure 9.9 (p. 349). The E = C + J + J schedule should intersect the 45° line at Y = 6,000. The E schedule intersects the vertical axis at a value of 3,000.

(g) The equilibrium level of national income is where the 45° line intersects the aggregate expenditure line, i.e. at the 6,000 level of national income. It can be seen from the various tables created in this exercise that the equilibrium level of national income is 6,000 whether the W = J approach or the Y = E approach to equilibrium is taken. This confirms the nature of the relationships between the variables discussed in the chapter.

Chapter 10

Checkpoints

1 See discussion of business cycle on p. 000.

2 (1) (a) Reduces national income equilibrium via extra withdrawals/reduced consumption expenditure.
(b) As for (a) except that the impacts will be mainly on those purchasing particular products which now are more expensive.
(2) By raising the marginal propensity to tax (mpt), the national income multiplier would be reduced in value.

3 (1) Increases national income equilibrium via raising injections (J) or raising aggregate expenditure ($E = C + J$).
(2) Higher national income is unlikely to mean extra output (economic growth) and employment. However, it may bring about an inflationary gap situation, stimulating price increase (see p. 360). The balance of payments may come under strain as extra spending goes on imports.

4 Extra benefits for those unemployed; higher taxes for those with higher incomes (individuals and companies); etc.

5 Too much or too little change in injections or withdrawals may take place – overshooting or undershooting the planned change in national income.

6 (a) Extra money available may stimulate higher consumer spending and perhaps less saving (fall in W). Rise in national income.
(b) As above, this time shifting $E = C + J$ upwards. Rise in national income.

7 Businesses which are more highly geared, depending more on borrowings (e.g. from financial institutions, issues of company bonds/debentures) than on their own funds or funds raised from share issues, will be more at risk from interest rate rises.

8 For example for price levels *below* P_1, AD exceeds AS putting upward pressure on prices and National Output. As the general price level rises, aggregate demand (AD) contracts (e.g. negative 'real balance effect' reducing C via reductions in the real value of wealth holdings) and aggregate supply (AS) expands (profitability is increased as prices rise faster than the less flexible input costs for producers). Only at P_1/Y_1 do we have an equilibrium outcome.

9 Since 2001 the sterling exchange rate has been rising against the (weaker) dollar, making UK exports to US dearer in dollars and imports from the US cheaper in sterling. The same is occurring for the UK against other currencies linked to the dollar (e.g. Chinese Renminbi). This is likely to cause the UK balance of payments to deteriorate against these countries. On the other hand the sterling exchange rate has been falling against the Euro, making UK exports to the Eurozone cheaper in Euros and imports from the Eurozone dearer in sterling. This will help the UK's balance of payments with the Eurozone, which is actually more important for UK trade than the US.

10 (1) A fall in the exchange rate will make exports cheaper abroad, which is likely to increase exports (X) in the aggregate demand schedule. It may also increase investment (I) in the export sector of the UK. Consumers in the UK may also switch to domestically produced products which are now cheaper than the more expensive imports from abroad, thereby raising consumer expenditure (C) and reducing imports (M). All these factors will tend to shift the aggregate demand (AD) curve to the right, raising the price level and national output, as in Figure 10.9(a) on p. 400. However the rise in import prices may also cause the aggregate supply (AS) curve to shift upwards and to the left due to cost-push pressures, as in Figure 10.9(a) on p. 400.

(2) Reverse the arguments in the answer above as the higher exchange rate will this time make exports dearer abroad and imports cheaper at home.

11 You could show a shift in AD upwards and to the right matched by a shift in AS downwards and to the right. You could shows them intersecting at the same price level as before the shifts, but at a higher level of National Output.

Activities

Activity 10.1

1

Objective	Fiscal policy	Monetary policy
Increase in economic growth	(a) (d) (e) (f) (h) (j)	(b) (l) (m)
Reduce inflationary pressures	(h) (j)	(c) (k) (n)
Reduce balance of payments deficit	(g) (i)	(c) (k) (n)
Reduce unemployment	(a) (d) (e) (f) (h) (j)	(b) (l) (m)

2 When trying to increase the growth rate of the economy, a decrease in interest rates could help to stimulate investment and consumption expenditure. However, if the economy is near full capacity this could create inflationary tendencies in the economy. An increase in tax allowances would provide more income to spend, but it could also lead to less tax revenue for the government which could increase the government's budget deficit and cause it to reduce future government spending. A reduction in the top rate of tax could act as an incentive to work and result in more growth; however, it could also lead to a more unequal distribution of income as people in the higher tax brackets benefit at the expense of other wage earners.

3 The table shows the effect of indirect taxes on different income groups. It is clear that indirect taxes (e.g. VAT) are regressive, i.e. affect those on lower incomes more than those on higher incomes. Since all people who buy products or services have to pay the tax irrespective of their income, indirect taxes will take a higher proportion of the income of the poorest groups. For example, the bottom 20% of income earners pay 34.7% of their disposable income in the form of indirect taxes, while the top 20% of income earners pay only 13.1% of their income in indirect taxes.

Activity 10.2

1 (a) (iv) (b) (vi) (c) (i) (d) (iii) (e) (v)

2 (a) False; prices are rising less quickly
(b) True
(c) True
(d) True
(e) False; lower levels of wage and price inflation

3 (a) RPI
(b) RPIY
(c) RPIX

4 (a) (vi)
(b) (ii)
(c) (iv)
(d) (i)
(e) (vii)
(f) (v)
(g) (iii)

Chapter 11

Checkpoints

1 Health expenditure per person increases substantially with age so that governments need to be aware of likely calls on the public purse. The supply of particular health treatments is also different for those aged 75 years and over, etc.

2 There is not an exact balance between boys and girls and not all children live long enough to themselves have children, especially in developing countries.

3 The skill mix involved in net migration may not be perfectly suited to the requirements of the economy and nor may the age profile. There may also be cultural and language barriers which may take time and resources to overcome.

4 Higher labour productivity is usually associated with higher wages. Higher wages (income) are in turn associated with higher expenditure and more tax payments (on both income and spending).

Activities

Activity 11.1

1 (a) The optimum population is where the output per capita of the economy is at its maximum.
(b) If the economy's output per head is decreasing then the overall efficiency of the economy is decreasing because an increase in population *above* the optimum puts pressure on resources and leads to inefficiencies. If the figure for output per capita is based on total population rather than working population then it could reflect an ageing of the population, e.g. the growth in number of retired

people who do not always contribute output to the economy. If the output per capita is *below* the optimum then there is room for economic improvement in that all the resources are not being used to the full. There may be resources available that could, with the proper amount of labour, increase the productivity of the economy.

(c) In an 'overpopulation' situation with falling output per head, the government could try to introduce policies to quicken the pace of technological change and investment levels in order to reverse the falling of labour productivity. In an 'underpopulation' situation the government could try to increase the domestic population by giving more child-related allowances or could open its borders to immigrants.

2 The table shows a significant growth in the percentage of non-married women – especially single and divorced women – and consequently a fall in the proportion of married women. It seems to indicate that the drive to greater marketing of bingo towards the non-married females is sound strategy. The proportion of single women is increasing and since they comprise some 30% of all bingo attendees, the demographic change shown in this table would seem to be good news for bingo operators. This change might stimulate them to extend their business and invest in new capacity. The growth in the proportion of single women could also stimulate other parts of the service sector, e.g. the spread of 'singles clubs'. It could also stimulate the growth of the holiday package industry for single people. It might stimulate the online ordering of convenience food if the single women have demanding careers and do not want to cook when they come home, and the growth in the percentage of single and divorced women could stimulate the development of dating agencies. In general, the growth of non-married women with more disposable income could have repercussions on many sectors, including the fashion and clothes industries.

Activity 11.2

1 (1) If you have ever seen the Special K promotions you will notice that they almost always feature young, slim women in affluent surroundings. So the 'demographic' could be interpreted as youngish, affluent women of social class C1 and above.

(2) This depends upon where you live and how much notice you take of advertisements! A recent advert for Gap jeans featured Madonna in a yoga pose.

2 (1) Changing lifestyles and attitudes are clearly to be seen in these two texts. First, the growth of single or childless couples. Second, the greater commitment of people to working long hours and the drive to be successful have led to a greater number of people who are looking for time-saving services, e.g. fast foods. Finally, 'traditional' meal times with all the family eating together have decreased.

(2) House/flat builders and rental properties have seen demand rise dramatically as the number of household units has increased (more separated families etc.). A whole range of time-saving products and services have grown rapidly – how they can be further supported via marketing initiatives will depend on your choice of products.

(3) Butchers, fishmongers, and many other local product and service providers are threatened by one-stop convenience superstores (often out of town) where a wide range of shopping needs can be fulfilled at one visit by those seeking to save time.

Chapter 12

Checkpoints

1 Many possibilities linked to firm exposure here.

2 As above, but this time all firms are at risk, e.g. collapse of exchange rate, economic recession, growth of terrorism in reducing aggregate expenditure etc.

3 Microsoft has involved itself in R&D in the UK, e.g. major investments in Cambridge and (via the Bill Gates Foundation) in many charitable causes (e.g. Aids, Malaria). Many other possible examples.

4 Many possible examples. Much debate on attempts to patent the human genome in recent times.

5 Premium prices are being successfully charged for a wide range of products which advertise themselves as being produced by environmentally sensitive procedures, e.g. wood, rugs, washing powders etc.

6 The response here depends on your own selection and research.

Activities

Activity 12.1

1 (d)

2 (b) (d) and (e)

3 (b)

4 (a) (ii)
(b) (v)
(c) (iv)
(d) (vi)
(e) (i)
(f) (iii)

Activity 12.2

1 (1) BP has become involved in global rebranding because of the changing environment. For example, the image of oil as a major source of pollutants has been highlighted by environmental groups, so that it is widely seen as being detrimental to both individual human health and to society-wide conditions such as

global warming. In addition, there has been adverse publicity for oil companies in terms of their association with the unacceptable exploitation of local people when oil exploration takes place and with sensitive issues such as drilling in conservation areas and opposing global conventions such as Kyoto.

(2) The global rebranding of BP involves the company in changing its image and diversifying its operations. The company does have many valuable sites (petrol stations) which they can use as platforms for selling all types of goods, from food to insurance. Also, the increasing importance given by BP to the search for non-oil-based energy fits neatly into the general trend towards environmentally friendly products and services. BP has a significant amount of business expertise and vast resources which it can use to diversify into many different areas of activity.

2 Linking UK libraries into a large network while also introducing free Internet access to libraries will create many opportunities. The general public will be able to search for information over the net and it would also open the opportunity for older people who have insufficient resources to pay for Internet access. The ability to search extensively will provide people with better information of what is available and make the market more 'perfect' in nature. The main threats involved in offering free Internet access in libraries is that the Internet may become a substitute for books so that the use of books may decrease. This, in turn, will affect sales of books and result in fewer incentives to write books in general. Likewise, overemphasis on the Internet may mean that in-depth analysis of subject matter which books so often provide may give way to 'bite sized' information on the Internet which does not treat the subject comprehensively.

3 (b), (c) and (d)

Chapter 13

Checkpoints

1 It can raise price and raise total revenue, since consumers are less focused on price when purchasing that product.

2 Many arrangements and practices involving groups and interactions in the workplace can be guided by the principles of Mayo, Maslow and Herzberg. Even functional areas such as recruitment and promotional policy are impacted, for example giving higher priority to those with good interpersonal skills given the importance of the social interactions highlighted by motivational theorists.

3 Many stakeholders may potentially benefit. The information in the profit and loss account, balance sheet and cash flow statements will help investors and analysts decide whether to continue investing in the company, withdraw or even deepen such investments. Employees can also gain some insights into corporate prospects, especially important where pension entitlements are company related.

Activities

Activity 13.1

All responses depend on the products you have selected for each question.

Activity 13.2

1, 2 Again, all responses depend on your individual selections.

3 (a) There are both similarities and differences. David is placing more emphasis on the factor input aspect of the human resource and its contribution to corporate objectives ('hard' HRM). Sarah is perhaps adopting a more employee centred approach, giving more emphasis to the 'fulfilment of potential' aspects of the human resource ('soft' HRM).

(b) David is less likely than Sarah to see the objectives of the human resources as being necessarily aligned with those of the employer. Incentive structures, both rewards and penalties, and more employer – directed activities in line with the corporate strategy are likely to feature in David's HRM approach. Sarah is more likely to develop activities seen by employees themselves as beneficial, being more ready to assume that their desire for self-improvement is already well established and closely aligned to the interests of the employer.

(c) There are many possibilities here. In the context of training, David would tend to focus on prescriptive training courses which seek to develop specific employee competencies seen as being directly relevant to achieving corporate objectives. Sarah on the other hand would probably support more 'reflective' employee centred training courses whereby employees seek to identify and develop personal attributes and competencies that they themselves see as relevant, with less concern for 'external' corporate priorities.

Activity 13.3

1 (c)

2 (a)

3 (d)

4 (b)

5 (a)

6 (a) Your break-even charts should capture the following and look something like Figure 13.4(b) on p. 525.

- Price = £5

Budgeted profit (at 10,000 units) = TR – TC

TR = £5 × 10,000 = £50,000

TC = TFC + TVC = £10,000 + (£3 × 10,000)

i.e. Budgeted profit = £50,000 – £40,000 = £10,000

Contribution per unit (C/U) = Price – AVC

= £5 – £3

C/U = £2

$$\text{BEP} = \frac{\text{Total fixed cost}}{\text{Contribution per unit}}$$

$$\text{BEP} = \frac{£10{,}000}{£2}$$

BEP = 5000 units

Margin of safety = Budgeted output – BEP

= 10,000 – 5,000

<u>Margin of safety = 5000 units</u>

As a percentage:

$$\text{Margin of safety} = \frac{\text{Budgeted output} - \text{BEP}}{\text{Budgeted output}} \times 100$$

$$= \frac{10{,}000 - 5{,}000}{10{,}000} \times 100$$

<u>Margin of safety = 50%</u>

In summary, for £5 price scenario

Budgeted profit = £10,000

BEP = 5,000 units

Margin of safety (%) = 50%

- **Price = £4**

Budgeted profit (at 15,000 units) = TR – TC

TR = £4 × 15,000 = £60,000

TC = TFC + TVC = £10,000 + (£3 × 15,000)

= £55,000

Budgeted profit = £60,000 – £55,000

<u>Budgeted profit = £5,000</u>

Contribution per unit (C/U) = Price – AVC

= £4 – £3

C/U = £1

$$\text{BEP} = \frac{\text{TFC}}{\text{C/U}}$$

$$\text{BEP} = \frac{\pounds 10{,}000}{\pounds 1}$$

<u>BEP = 10,000 units</u>

Margin of safety = Budgeted output – BEP

= 15,000 – 10,000

<u>Margin of safety = 5,000 units</u>

As a percentage:

$$\text{Margin of safety} = \frac{\text{Budgeted output} - \text{BEP}}{\text{Budgeted output}} \times 100$$

$$= \frac{15{,}000 - 10{,}000}{15{,}000} \times 100$$

<u>Margin of safety = $33\frac{1}{3}$%</u>

In summary for £4 price scenario

Budgeted profit = £5,000

BEP = 10,000 units

Margin of safety = $33\frac{1}{3}$%

(b) The £5 price scenario would appear to be the most attractive for the firm. Setting a price of £5 would give it a higher budgeted profit, a lower break-even point and a higher margin of safety, than would setting a price of £4. The £5 price would seem to be both more profitable and less risky for the firm than the £4 price. As well as an *extra* £5,000 in expected profit, the firm need produce and sell 5,000 *fewer* units in order to break even. The margin of safety reinforces this aspect of reduced risk, in that at a price of £5 it can experience a fall in its sales of up to 50% below its budgeted (expected) output before losses are actually incurred. In contrast, at a £4 price the firm can only see sales fall $33\frac{1}{3}$% below expectation before losses are actually incurred.

Of course all this break-even analysis is based on the linearity assumption. This may *not* actually be valid in practice. For example, the assumption that variable cost per unit (AVC) is constant at all levels of output may be unrealistic. If various economies of scale occur, then AVC might *fall* as output increases, raising contribution per unit (Price – AVC) at the £4 price scenario with its higher budgeted output. In this case the TVC and TC curves would cease to be straight line (linear).

Further, the TR curves may not be linear in practice! In order to sell more output it may be that the firm may have to *reduce price*. It may therefore make little sense to draw a TR curve as a straight line with a constant slope representing a given and unchanged price as output varies.

For these and other reasons the break-even analysis may be too simple. Nevertheless, the linearity assumption may have some validity for *relatively small changes in output*, which is often the most likely result of policy changes by a firm.

Chapter 14

Checkpoints

1 Many possibilities depending on your choice.

2 Again, depends on your choice. Some US-based multinationals have started out following this approach, but many are becoming more sensitive to local concerns, e.g. Coca Cola, McDonald's etc. Where cultural distance (e.g. Hofstede) is significant, there may be good reasons to use local nationals in key positions.

3 Depends on your choice.

Activities

Activity 14.1

1 HPP should internationalise for many reasons. First, it has concentrated on the home market too much. If it could expand overseas, it would be able to reap economies of scale to a much greater extent. Second, the promotional gifts market

in the UK is stagnant so that if it wishes to be more dynamic and to grow, it must find other markets outside the UK. Third, as the incomes of countries such as Eastern Europe and China rise as a result of more rapid growth than in the past, the demand for gifts sold by the company will grow, since this type of product is relatively income elastic.

2 HPP could enter the foreign markets by franchising the sales of gifts to a foreign country. It could also form a joint venture with a similar company abroad. This company could act as the distribution arm of HPP while benefiting from a new range of gift products from HPP to complement its own range of products. It may also be possible for HPP to take over the foreign company and 'internalise' its operations. In other words, HPP could use its skills in product design etc. in other countries without worrying that the partner company might break the agreement etc.

3 An interesting example of a joint venture was that between the two giant pharmaceutical companies, Astra and Merck Inc. of the UK, in 1994. The background for the joint venture was a licensing agreement between the two companies which began in 1984, whereby Merck had exclusive rights to most Astra products in the US and Astra could benefit from Merck's marketing muscle in the US. In 1994 a free-standing joint venture was formed between the two companies called Astra-Merck Inc., which focused exclusively on marketing, sales and drug development. This joint venture was popular for a time because it brought together expertise in the development of new drugs (Astra) with marketing strength (Merck). The joint venture lasted until 1998 when Astra wanted to look for another long-term partner with a merger in mind. Astra wanted to merge with the UK company Zeneca because they both had a complementary range of products and they both had similar management philosophies and were strong on R&D. The merger did take place in December 1998 but Astra had to pay Merck compensation for the break-up of their existing joint venture.

Activity 14.2

1 (a) (iv)
  (b) (iii)
  (c) (i)
  (d) (v)
  (e) (ii)

2 (1) This example shows the nature of the *risks* which multinationals experience when they operate outside their own home environment. For example, the change in government policy which removed tariff protection led to a significant increase in Panasonic's costs. However, the decision as to whether to stay in Mexico also depended on other powerful benefits. The lower labour costs, relatively high labour productivity plus the massive high income market of California on its doorstep (i.e. low transport costs) were strong reasons for the company to remain in Mexico.

(2) An advanced industrial country such as the US would be affected by the decision to locate the Panasonic plant in Mexico in many ways. For example, it could lead to unemployment in competing electronics industries in the US. It could also bring down wages in US electronics industries as they fight to compete with low wage countries. On the other hand, it could lead US companies to go 'upmarket' by making more expensive electronic equipment so that they would not be in direct competition with Panasonic.

3 (c) and (e)

4 Attractiveness for multinational:
(1) Denmark
(2) Netherlands
(3) France
(4) UK

Activity 14.3

1 (c)

2 (e)

3 (b), (c) and (e)

4 (a) True
(b) True
(c) False; intra industry trade
(d) True

5 (c)

6 (d)

7 (a)

8 (e)

9 (b)

Chapter 15

Checkpoints

1 Many possibilities here, with earlier analysis refocused into a five-forces structure involving potential entrants, substitutes, buyers, suppliers and industry competitors for Starbucks.

2 From a national perspective 9/11 has caused lower growth rates in global and national GDP so that most countries 'demand conditions' will be less favourable, with possible adverse consequences for 'factor conditions' and 'related and supporting industries'. Of course nations with competitive advantages in sectors such as defence and security industries may be relatively better placed than others after 9/11.

3 As well as the relative labour costs between these countries, we need to know more about the relative productivities of these different types of labour in each country. We also need to know more about changes in the relative exchange rates between the currencies of these countries. In other words we need to know more about all the items in relative unit labour costs (RULCs) between these countries (see p. 634) if we are to gain a better understanding of international competitiveness between the countries.

Chapter 16

Activities

Activity 16.1

Questions 1 and 2 depend on your own investigation.

3 (b) and (d)

4 (b), (c) and (e)

5 (b) and (d)

6 (a) (iii)
(b) (vii)
(c) (ii)
(d) (i)
(e) (iv)
(f) (v)

Activity 16.2

These questions involve action research with outcomes depending on your own approach to the suggestions.

Index